ditor: Bradley J. Potthoff
roduction Editor: Mary Harlan
esign Coordinator: Julia Zonneveld Van Hook
ext Designer: John Edeen
Cover Designer: Susan Unger
Cover photo: Blair Seitz/Picturesque
Production Manager: Patricia A. Tonneman
Illustrations: The Clarinda Company
Director of Marketing: Kevin Flanagan
Advertising/Marketing Coordinator: Julie Shough

This book was set in Galliard by The Clarinda Company and was printed and bound by Courier/Kendallville, Inc. The cover was printed by Phoenix Color Corp.

Printed in the United States of America

10 9 8 7 6 5 4 3

ISBN: 0-13-494592-1

Prtice-Hall International (UK) Limited, *London*
Prtice-Hall of Australia Pty. Limited, *Sydney*
Pice-Hall of Canada, Inc., *Toronto*
Pice-Hall of Hispanoamericana, S. A., *Mexico*
Pice-Hall of India Private Limited, *New Delhi*
Pce-Hall of Japan, Inc., *Tokyo*
S & Schuster Asia Pte. Ltd., *Singapore*
E Prentice-Hall do Brasil, Ltda., *Rio de Janeiro*

**Library of Congress Cataloging-in-Publication**
Kadolph, Sara J.
Textiles / Sara J. Kadolph, Anna L. Langford.
p. cm.
Rev. ed. of: Textiles / Sara J. Kadolph, et al. 7th ed. ©1993.
Includes bibliographical references and index.
ISBN 0-13-494592-1
1. Textile industry. 2. Textile fibers. 3. Textile fabrics.
I. Langford, Anna. II. Title. III. Title: Textiles.
TS1446.K33 1998
677—dc21
97-6187
CIP

Eighth Edition

# TEXTILES

SARA J. KADOLPH
Iowa State University

ANNA L. LANGFORD

Merrill,
an imprint of Prentice Hall
*Upper Saddle River, New Jersey* *Columbus, Ohio*

# PREFACE

## Philosophy of This Book

*Textiles* provides students with a basic knowledge of textiles so that they understand how textiles are produced and how appropriate performance characteristics are incorporated into materials and products. With this knowledge, they have the information they need to make informed decisions regarding textile materials and products and to communicate effectively with buyers, suppliers, customers, and others. A solid understanding of textile components (fibers, yarns, fabrics, and finishes), the interrelationships among these components, and their impact on product performance is necessary to fulfill day-to-day responsibilities in many careers in the textile, apparel, and furnishings industry.

Serviceability of textiles and textile products is the fundamental principle emphasized throughout the book. I emphasize the contributions of each component as it is incorporated in or combined with other components in a textile product. I stress the need to understand interrelationships among the components. I include basic information regarding how each component is processed or handled because it helps in understanding product performance and cost. Production of textiles is a complex process dealing with a wide variety of materials and techniques. To understand textiles, students need a basic understanding of the choices and technology involved.

This book will help students:

- use textile terminology correctly.
- know laws and labeling requirements regulating textile distribution.
- understand the impact of production processes and selection of components on product performance, cost, and consumer satisfaction.
- understand the forces that drive developments in the industry.
- identify fiber type, yarn type, or fabrication method.
- predict fabric or product performance based on a knowledge of fibers, yarns, fabrication methods, and finishes in conjunction with informative labeling.
- select textile components or products based on specified end uses and target market expectations for performance and serviceability.
- select appropriate care procedures for textile products.
- develop an interest in and appreciation of textiles for further study.

Understanding textiles cannot be achieved only through studying a book such as this; it also requires working with fabrics. Kits are available from several sources. In addition, many workbooks for student use in labs have been designed to help them learn this information.

## Organization of This Book

Each section of the book focuses on a basic component or aspect of fabrics and textile products or on general issues important to the use of, production of, or satisfaction with textile products. These sections are complete and can be used in any order desired. The four center sections follow the normal sequence used in the production of textiles: fiber, yarn, fabrication, and finishing.

The first section of the book introduces the study of textiles. Chapter 2 is new and approaches product development from a textile perspective. Section 2 focuses on fibers, their production, serviceability, effect on product performance, and use. Section 3 focuses on yarn production, yarn types, and the relationship of yarn type to product performance and serviceability. The information related to yarn type and product characteristics is expanded because it is being provided at many levels in product development. Section 4 examines fabrication methods. These chapters are organized by basic fabrication method, standard or classic fabric names and types, and the relationships between fabrication and product performance. Section 5 deals with finishes, which are grouped by type or effect. Dyeing and printing are also included, as well as problems that consumers and producers experience with dyed or printed fabrics. A number of new finishes have been added to this section. The final section deals with other issues related to textiles. One chapter focuses on care of textile products and has been expanded to incorporate environmental issues and multiprocess wet cleaning. Another chapter investigates legal and environmental issues. The discussion on environmental issues now illustrates current environmental efforts and explores some options regarding recycling of textiles. The final chapter discusses career opportunities requiring knowledge of textiles.

## Features of the Text

Instructors and students have always liked this text's summary and reference tables and charts, the presentation of information in a clear and consistent fashion, the emphasis on serviceability, and the numerous illustrations, graphics, and photographs. I tried to strengthen these things in this revision. I developed several new summary tables to condense information and facilitate comparisons of related materials or processes. I revised, reorganized, or updated other tables where necessary or where students or colleagues suggested improvements. I have updated or replaced approximately 30 percent of the photos and illustrations.

Although the basic content and flavor of *Textiles* remain intact, the changes help students recognize and focus on the most important material. Objectives and key terms for each chapter are revised so that students will be able to identify and understand the major concepts. After reading and studying each chapter, students should be able to define each term in the key terms list and indicate how the term relates to other terms and to the chapter content. Study questions provide students with an opportunity to test their level of understanding, focus on key concepts or applications, and integrate the information. I provide an expanded list of readings for students who would like to investigate topics beyond the scope of the text. Many of these readings are technical in nature. There are a few articles on textiles in the popular press, but these often include little substantive information. Hence, the most valuable articles and books tend to be those written from a technical perspective.

## Major Changes and Additions

My emphasis in this revision has been on updating and adding material where new processes or concerns have developed in the professional workplace, in the textile industry, or among consumers. I added explanations, expanded discussions, and clarified concepts in areas where my students had indicated the need or where colleagues expressed or suggested improvements. I revised terminology to incorporate a stronger industry perspective so that professionals can understand and communicate with other professionals. I added a pronunciation guide to the glossary so that professionals will pronounce and use terms correctly. I expanded the index to facilitate the book's use as a resource by professionals who need to locate information quickly regarding a specific term, process, or product. I omitted some obsolete processes such as those involved in yarn texturing and some photos and diagrams of marginal usefulness.

I address technological advances and contemporary industry and societal concerns that have arisen or have increased in importance since the last edition. I added a discussion of environmental impact to each major component since this is an important issue to both the industry and consumers. The book continues to focus on the three major end uses of textiles: apparel, furnishings, and industrial products.

I have limited some of the discussion related to processes at the request of reviewers. I added some information regarding how textile components are evaluated within the industry and incorporated a brief discussion of color theory in the coloration chapter to identify selected factors in color matching and shade sorting.

The discussion of dyeing and printing now provides more information on the basic processes of adding color to fabric and includes new techniques. The discussion of finishing now includes more aesthetic finishes, especially those designed to add a softer or stressed look to goods and products. Multiprocess wet cleaning as an alternate to dry cleaning has been added to the chapter on care. In addition, with the change to ultradetergent formulations, changes in detergents in the past few years are described. More information on microfibers and other fiber developments is also included.

The chapter on career opportunities now provides some information on starting salaries and includes some vignettes based on conversations with practicing professionals. This chapter is intended to help students understand how they will be using their knowledge of textiles and textile products when they work as professionals. I hope that it helps students gain a better understanding of these careers and how professionals interact with each other. Although this chapter may not be assigned in a beginning textile course, I hope that students will be encouraged to use the chapter as a means of exploring career possibilities on their own and use it when considering career options other than those that are most readily visible to them.

## Ancillaries and Supplements

This text assumes that the student requires basic information regarding textiles in order to perform professional responsibilities adequately and communicate with other professionals in an intelligent and informed manner. Hence, I incorporated several changes to make the book more useful both as a text and as a part of a professional's reference library. Key terms are defined in both the text and the glossary. The glossary has been expanded to include more than basic or classic fabric names as well as a pronunciation guide. Fiber modifications, finishes, and terminology related to performance have been incorporated. The index has been expanded to help students locate information while enrolled in the class, when in other classes that build on or use basic textile information, and when it is needed on the job. Appendix A lists fiber names in several languages that are commonly encountered because the textile industry is truly an international one. Appendix C lists selected trade names for fibers, yarns, fabrics, finishes, and cleaning procedures.

The instructor's manual includes an updated outline of the material for each chapter, a revised list of suggested activities, a bank of test questions in various formats, and transparency masters for use in class.

A Basic Textiles Swatch Kit is available for use in conjunction with this edition of *Textiles.* The swatch kit consists of 120 fabric swatches, mounting sheets, a master list with fabric name/description/fiber content, and a 3-ring binder. It is available through Textile Fabric Consultants, Inc., P.O. Box 111431, Nashville, TN 37222/615-459-7510.

## ACKNOWLEDGMENTS

I used the comments and contributions of many students and colleagues in preparing this revision. I find students' comments help me the most in evaluating the approach, wording, and style of presentation, and thus I appreciate hearing from any student or faculty member about the book. Both positive and negative comments are incredibly helpful and invaluable in revising the book. I would especially like to thank Anne Wilcock of the University of Guelph, Canada, for her help with the care chapter and Carolyn Kundel and Sandra Chisholm of Iowa State University for their suggestions and perspectives. A special thanks to Chuck Greiner of Front Porch Photography Studio, Huxley, Iowa, for his help with the photography; Rita Ostdiek of JCPenney, Inc., for her assistance with some of the photographs of professionals in action; and Colette Ergenbright of Maytag Appliances for her help with some of the care photographs. And finally, thanks to Fuff who was there every hour I worked on the book at home!

This eighth edition reflects changes in the industry and includes a great deal of new information. For their many suggestions in this regard and their help in maintaining the focus of this edition, I thank my reviewers, who helped me immeasurably:

- Diane Bower, Monterey Peninsula College
- Rita Christoffersen, University of Wisconsin, Stout
- Kathleen M. Delaney, Interior Designers Institute, Newport Beach, CA
- Mary J. Thompson, Brigham Young University

Revising this book is always an exciting challenge. I enjoy the opportunity to explore the textiles literature in more depth than my university responsibilities usually allow. I enjoy sharing the exciting area of textiles with so many others. I hope that this book hooks you on textiles as the third edition of this book did for me when I was a sophomore student just beginning to learn about textiles.

*Sara J. Kadolph*

# Contents

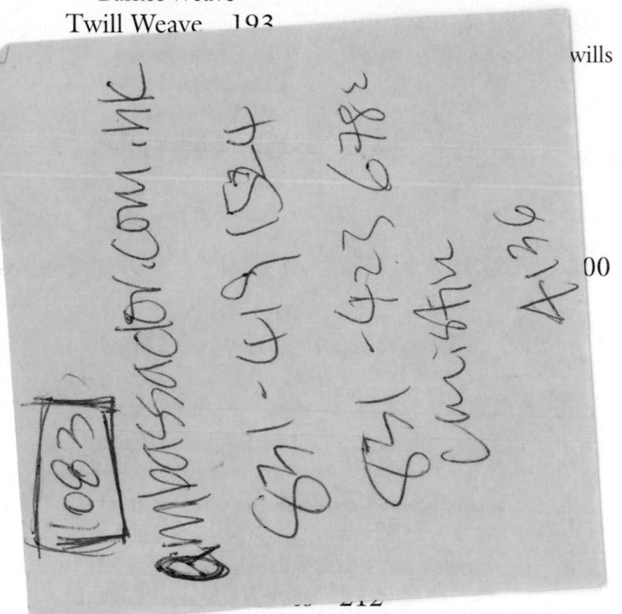



## *Chapter 14* KNITTING AND KNIT FABRICS 216



## *Chapter 15* OTHER FABRICATION METHODS 243

# *Section Five* FINISHING 271

## *Chapter 16* FINISHING: AN OVERVIEW 273



## *Chapter 17* AESTHETIC FINISHES 285



## *Chapter 18* SPECIAL-PURPOSE FINISHES 300

## Section One

# Introduction to Textiles

Chapter 1

**Introduction**

Chapter 2

**Product Development from a Textile Perspective**

Chapter 1

# INTRODUCTION

OBJECTIVES

- To become aware of the diversity of textile products.
- To understand the importance of developing a professional knowledge of textiles.
- To recognize the contributions textiles make to contemporary lifestyles as apparel, furnishings, and industrial products.

This section is divided into two chapters. The first chapter introduces the study of textiles by defining terms, identifying examples of textile products, surveying the diversity of textiles and describing the importance of the industry to the U.S. economy. The second chapter discusses the relationships among textiles, product development, and use of and satisfaction with textile products.

This text was written to aid students in learning and understanding what to expect in fabric performance and why fabrics perform as they do. Textiles are always changing as fashion and as people's needs change. New developments in production processes change textiles, as do government standards for safety and environmental quality and changes in international trade. These changes are discussed, but the bulk of the text is devoted to basic information about textile products, with an emphasis on fibers, yarns, fabric construction, and finishes. These interdependent elements contribute to the beauty, durability, care, and comfort of fabrics.

Much of the terminology used in the text may be new to students and many facts must be memorized. To understand textiles and apply that knowledge one must first learn the basics. Historical development, basic concepts, and new innovations are discussed. Production processes are explained briefly to help the student develop a better understanding of, and appreciation for, the textile industry.

An ideal starting place to gain an understanding of textiles is by defining several basic terms. (See Figure 1–1.)

**Fiber** Any substance, natural or manufactured, with a high length-to-width ratio and with suitable characteristics for being processed into fabric; the smallest component, hairlike in nature, that can be separated from a fabric.

**Yarn** An assemblage of fibers, twisted or laid together so as to form a continuous strand that can be made into a textile fabric.

**Fabric** A planar substance constructed from solutions, fibers, yarns, fabrics, or any combination of these.

**Finish** Any process used to add color and augment performance of gray goods (unfinished fabric).

**Gray goods** (**grey** or **greige goods**) Any fabric that has not been finished.

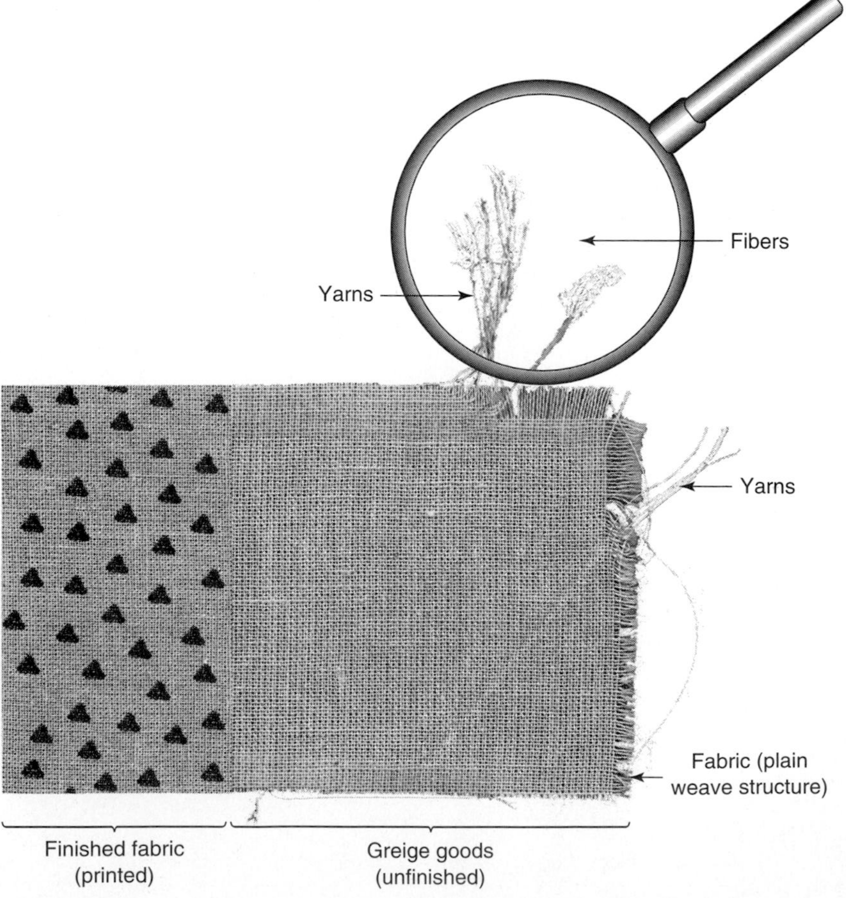


**FIGURE 1–1** ❖ The components of a fabric: fiber, yarn, structure, and finish.

**Textile** A term originally applied only to woven fabrics, now generally applied to fibers, yarns, fabrics, or products made of fibers, yarns, or fabrics.

Food, shelter, and clothing are basic human needs. Most clothing is made from textiles, and shelters are made more comfortable and attractive with textiles. Textiles are used in the production or processing of many items used in day-to-day living, such as food and manufactured goods.

We are surrounded by textiles from birth to death. We walk on and wear textile products; we sit on fabric-covered chairs and sofas; we sleep on and under fabrics; textiles dry us or keep us dry; they keep us warm and protect us from the sun, fire, and infection. Clothing and furnishing textiles that vary in color, design, texture, and cost are aesthetically pleasing. Table 1–1 lists example of textiles used in industrial products that contribute to work and pleasure. Industrial textiles contribute to our current standard of living. For example, the automotive industry uses textiles to make tire cords, upholstery, carpeting, head liners, window runners, seat belts, shoulder harnesses, fan belts, gaskets, and seals, and as reinforcement fibers in molded plastic parts.

Astronauts traveled to the moon in 20-layer, $100,000 space suits with nylon water-cooled underwear. Life is prolonged by replacing wornout body parts with textiles such as polyester arteries and velour heart valves. Bullet-resistant vests protect police, hunters, and soldiers, and shoulder and seat belts make automobile travel safer. Three-dimensional, inflatable structures protect us from desert heat and Arctic cold.

Industrial textiles surround us. We brush our teeth, hair, and clothes with bristles made of synthetic or natural fibers. Buildings are warmer with glass fiber insulation and polyethylene film barriers against wind and moisture. Roads last longer with synthetic fiberweb underlays that minimize shifting of the road base. Soil is

**TABLE 1–1** ❖ Examples of industrial textiles.

| PERSONAL HYGIENE | TRANSPORTATION | ENVIRONMENT | MEDICAL |
|---|---|---|---|
| Tooth & hair brushes<br>Medicated pads<br>Makeup brushes<br>Nail buffers<br>Incontinence pads<br>Feminine hygiene products<br>Cotton balls<br>Dental floss | Tire cords<br>Road bed underlays<br>Bicycle helmets<br>Interiors for planes, buses, cars, trucks<br>Seat belts & air bags<br>Brake linings<br>Gaskets & seals<br>Convertible tops | Erosion barriers<br>Weed control fabrics<br>Pond liners<br>Snow & silt fences<br>Drainage screens<br>Shore protectors<br>Oil spill control barriers<br>Air & water filters | Support wraps<br>Casts<br>Surgical masks<br>Sutures<br>Arteries<br>Examination gowns<br>Bandages<br>Dialysis filters<br>Gloves |
| **FOOD** | **ANIMAL CARE** | **AGRICULTURE** | **PROTECTIVE GEAR** |
| Bags & sacks<br>Bakery filters<br>Coffee filters<br>Packaging materials<br>Tea bags | Leashes<br>Blankets<br>Saddles<br>Stall liners<br>Restraints<br>Pet bed liners | Bags & sacks<br>Ropes<br>Hoses & belts<br>Bale coverings<br>Tractor interiors<br>Plant covers<br>Tree wraps | Bullet-resistant vests<br>Heat/fire–resistant suits<br>Impact-resistant helmets<br>Chemical-resistant gloves<br>Abrasion-resistant gloves<br>Suits for handling hazardous materials |
| **SPORTS & RECREATION** | **MANUFACTURED GOODS** | **MISCELLANEOUS PRODUCTS** | **BUILDING MATERIALS** |
| Helmet liners<br>Protective pads<br>Balls<br>String for rackets<br>Tents<br>Backpacks<br>Life jackets<br>Rafts & boat hulls<br>Sails<br>Fishing line & nets<br>Artificial playing surfaces | Hoses<br>Belts<br>Loading dock covers<br>Tarpaulins<br>Paint rollers<br>Wipes<br>Carpet backing<br>Mailing envelopes<br>Duct tape backing<br>Conveyor belts<br>Silk-screening mesh | Artificial flowers/plants<br>Banners & flags<br>Book bindings<br>Candle wicks<br>Casket linings<br>Communication lines<br>Felt-tip pens<br>Lampshades<br>Mops<br>Sandbags<br>Personal computer boards | Building insulation<br>Covers for wiring<br>Drop cloths<br>Pool liners & covers<br>Wall coverings<br>Venetian blinds<br>Window screens<br>Gaskets & seals<br>Duct tape<br>Awnings |

conserved with fiber erosion control barriers. Computer disks are protected with an olefin fiberweb. Wiring is insulated with fiberglass woven braids. Athletic performance is enhanced with carbon reinforcement fibers in golf clubs and tennis rackets. Body parts are protected with support wraps of woven or knit fabrics. Fruits and vegetables are packaged in net bags. Outdoor activities take place under tents and awnings to protect us from sun and rain. Manufactured goods are transported on conveyor belts made of textiles coated with thin plastic film. At the gas station, gas is pumped through a fibrous filter and a fabric-supported hose. It is hard to imagine how different our lives would be if all industrial textiles were to disappear.

In the United States, the textile industry is tremendous. It includes the natural and manufactured fiber producers, spinners, weavers, knitters, throwsters, yarn converters, tufters, fiberweb producers, finishers, equipment producers, and many others. More people are employed in the textile industry than in any other manufacturing industry, over 1.4 million. Textile products valued at over $74 billion in 1994 are produced by computerized systems. The textile industry has developed from an art-and-craft industry perpetuated by guilds in the early centuries, through the Industrial Revolution in the 18th and 19th centuries, when the emphasis was on mechanization and mass production, to the 20th century, with its emphasis on science, technology, and cost efficiency.

In this century, manufactured fibers were developed and modified textured yarns were created. New fabrications were created, production of knits increased, and many finishes and sophisticated textile production and marketing systems were developed. Manufactured fibers and soil-resistant and durable press finishes have helped keep textiles looking neat and clean.

New developments in textiles have created some problems, particularly in the selection of apparel and furnishing textiles. Many items look alike but their performance and care may differ significantly. Knitted fabrics look like woven fabrics, vinyl and polyurethane films look like leather, acrylic and polyester fabrics look like wool. Traditional cotton fabrics may be polyester or polyester/cotton blends.

To make textile selection easier for consumers, the textile industry has set standards and established quality-control programs for many textile products. Federal laws protect and inform consumers of fiber content and care requirements.

Emphasis on energy conservation, environmental quality, noise abatement, health, and safety affects the textile industry as well as other industries. The efforts of the textile industry to meet standards set by the federal government affect the consumer by raising prices for merchandise, by limiting the choices available, and by improving product and environmental quality.

Textile fabrics can be beautiful, durable, comfortable, and easy care. Knowing the components used in textile products and how these components were made will provide a better basis for their selection and an understanding of their limitations. A knowledge of textiles and their production will result in a more appropriate and better product for a particular use and a more satisfied user.

## Key Terms

Fiber
Yarn
Fabric
Finish
Gray, grey, or greige goods
Textile

## Questions

1. Define the key terms, explain the differences among them, and describe how these terms relate to textiles.
2. How do textiles influence contemporary lifestyles?
3. Describe textiles used in normal daily activities. Be sure to consider furnishing, industrial, and apparel products. How do these products help make these activities possible?
4. Select a fabric and dismantle it so that you have a fiber and a yarn. What are the differences and similarities between these components?

## Suggested Readings

Examine several of these trade publications to see what items are included and how detailed the discussion is: *America's Textiles International, Industrial Products Review, Interiors, Interior Design, Textile Chemist and Colorist, Textile Horizons, Textile Month, Textile Progress, Textile Research Journal,* and *Textile World.*

Adanur, Sabit (1995). *Wellington Sears Handbook of Industrial Textiles.* Lancaster, PA: Technomic Publishing Co.

*Chapter 2*

# Product Development from a Textile Perspective

OBJECTIVES

- To understand how textiles influence and affect product development.
- To explore the serviceability components of textiles and textile products.
- To relate product serviceability to target market needs and expectations.
- To explore the information sources that are used in product development.

How are textiles selected for specific products? Why are some textiles used for some product types, but not others? Who makes these choices and why? **Product development** refers to the design and engineering of a product so that it has the desired serviceability characteristics, appeals to the target market, can be made within an acceptable time frame for a reasonable cost, and can be sold at a profit. Product development can refer to selecting furnishings for a room, selecting materials to incorporate into an apparel or furnishing product, developing completely new styles, or modifying current company or competitors' styles. Product development is a process that involves many people with specialized knowledge, ranging from understanding product characteristics that will appeal to a specific target market to knowing how to produce the item so that it meets consumer needs.

The range of activities of product development includes basic research that leads to a new fiber like lyocell, applied research to minimize generation of environmentally harmful by-products in dyeing and finishing fabrics, developing new designs for office furnishings that reflect changing working habits, making design modifications to help a basic item like blue jeans remain fashionable, or creating fabric designs and colorways for window treatments for commercial or contract applications. When selecting the materials or fabrics to be used in a product or selecting products that will be used together, the individual must deal with many dimensions and components of textiles.

Let's consider denim to illustrate the variables that are considered in selecting or developing a fabric. Denim is a basic fabric used for jeans, skirts, shorts, jackets, hats, bags, upholstery, wall coverings, and bed sheets. Denim can differ in fiber content from 100 percent cotton to blends of cotton and polyester to wool. Denim can be made from new unused fiber, recycled cotton denim scraps, or polyester beverage bottles that have been recycled into fibers. The yarns in denim can be made in many sizes by several processes. Each yarn type and size behaves differently. Denim can be made in many weights from very heavy to relatively light. It can be finished to look crisp and new or faded and stressed. Denim can be dyed or printed in a variety of colors or patterns including the traditional indigo blue. All these factors mean that many decisions are made during product development that determine the look and performance of the fabric that will be used in the product.

Product development decisions occur throughout the textile industry to determine what is on the market. When a designer, merchandiser, producer, or engineer selects one fabric or fiber or yarn type rather than another, they help shape the image the final product will convey, how it will perform, how it will look, and what it will cost. They have determined factors such as fabric weight, stiffness, hand, texture, yarn structure and process, fiber content and modifications, coloration method, and finishes.

Sometimes, design firms negotiate with fabric producers so that some part of the fabric, for example, the color, is exclusive to that firm. Some retailers or manufacturers are large enough and control such a significant portion of the market that fabric producers are willing to modify their processes to meet the design firm's preferences. Some fabric firms, especially in the furnishings market, work with designers to produce custom fabrics or custom colors. However, many firms do not have that power in the marketplace and must work with what is available.

Fabric producers present their fabrics to designers in a variety of different formats so that designers can see the way the fabric looks and drapes, examine the texture and hand of the fabric, and see how related fabrics work together. (See Figure 2–1.) Fabrics of the same structure may be available in a range of colors; some colors may

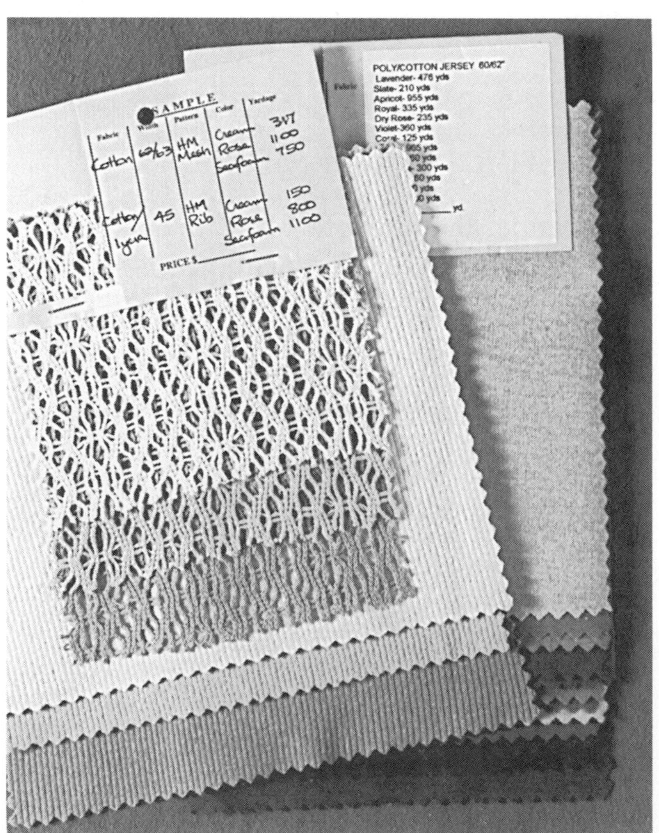


**FIGURE 2–1** ❖ Fabric presentation swatches showing range of colors and different fabrications within a color range.

be available in several different fabrications. Information provided to the designer at this point may be limited to the fabric's style number, width, fiber content, and weight, or it also may include yarn size, yarn spinning method, weave type, and finishes. Adherence to standards related to fire safety codes for interior furnishings also may be available for some furnishing fabrics.

Because fabric cost is an important factor in determining product cost, the wholesale market price of fabric is important. Figure 2–2 shows one way to present this information to the industry for several basic unfinished fabrics. Fabric information in these charts includes fabric width, number of yarns per square inch, fabric weight, current price, and price for several later delivery times.

Dye cards are used by dye manufacturers to demonstrate the colors that selected dyes produce on specific fibers. These cards help dyehouses create the colors designers specify for their designs. (See Figure 2–3.) The cards may include information regarding how a dye responds to washing, exposure to light, or other factors that cause dyes to bleed, shift hue, or fade. Many fabrics are dyed with a mixture of dyes because dyehouses only carry or stock a limited number of dyes. Dyers mix the dyes as needed to match the colors specified by buyers and designers.

❖

## Serviceability and the Consumer

**Serviceability** describes the measure of a textile product's ability to meet consumers' needs. The emphasis is on understanding the target market and relating target market needs to product serviceability. The serviceability concepts that are used in organizing the material are simple and straightforward: **aesthetics, durability, comfort and safety, appearance retention, care, environmental impact,** and **cost.** (See Table 2–1.)

These serviceability concepts provide a framework for combining textile knowledge with consumers' expectations to develop an understanding of textiles. Whenever consumers discuss textile products, they often touch on these concepts although their terms may not precisely match some of the more technical terms used in this book. Consumers evaluate their purchases and determine their satisfaction with products based on these concepts. We will use these concepts throughout the book to relate textile characteristics and performance to consumer expectations.

Cost is a very important factor to many consumers, but cost will not be discussed in much depth in this text because many outside factors, such as how a product is promoted and sold, greatly influence final product cost. Fabric cost is one component of the cost of a product. Table 2–2 gives approximate percentages for the costs of producing and finishing a basic woven fabric. Keep in mind that the costs of fabric and other materials in a product reflect only a small percentage of the final market cost of that product.

In assessing target market expectations, a firm needs to know who its consumers are, where they shop, how they live their lives, and how all these things influence what consumers look for in textile products. Some firms have specialized market research divisions that help identify consumer expectations. However, any firm that hopes to be successful must develop an understanding of its target market.

Let's use sleeping bags at the retail level as an example to illustrate differences in products, target markets, and their expectations. Sleeping bag A is sold at a specialty store that carries products for outdoor enthusiasts. This bag is a mummy-shaped bag with an outer cover of water-repellent ripstop nylon taffeta, a filling of high-volume goose down, and an inner lining of polyester modified to enhance warmth and comfort characteristics. Bag A is very lightweight and can be compressed and packed in a relatively small space. It is expensive and would require special care because of the down filling. This bag is designed to be used outdoors; the user may not have the additional protection of a tent or other structure. Sleeping bag B is a more traditional sleeping bag sold in a discount store. The outer layer of fabric is a cotton/polyester blend printcloth with a printed pattern that would appeal to a young child, the fiberfill is polyester, and the inner layer is cotton/polyester flannel. Bag B will not be as warm nor as expensive as bag A. It is designed to be used indoors by a child. It is easy care and can be machine washed and dried. Sleeping bag C is sold through a mail-order catalog and is also a traditional shape. It incorporates a specially modified polyester fiberfill for warmth without weight, a solid dark green polyester/cotton poplin outer cover, and a plaid yarn-dyed cotton flannel for the inner layer. Bag C is more expensive than bag B and is easy care. Bag C would appeal to an adult who is interested in a warm, comfortable sleeping bag to be used in a tent or other structure and who does not have a lot of time to shop. All three sleeping bags differ in their materials, their serviceability and performance, and in the way they are marketed to their specific target market.

❖

## Performance

**Performance** describes the manner in which a textile, textile component, or textile product responds when

## COTTON GRAY GOODS

| | | | Spot 3d Qtr | 4th Qtr | 1st Qtr |
|---|---|---|---|---|---|
| | | | **ALL-COTTON PRINT CLOTHS** | | |
| *63 | 68×68 | 2.61 | 84–85 | 84 | — |
| *50 | 68×68 | 3.30 | 64 | 64 | — |
| 50 | 68×68 | 3.30 | 74 | 74 | — |
| | | | **BLENDED PRINT CLOTHS** | | |
| | | | Polyester/Cotton | | |
| 100 | 78×54 | 1.95 | 1.04–1.00 | 1.04 | — |
| 64 | 78×54 | 2.99 | 72×72½ | 72 | — |
| 64 | 96×56 | 2.62 | 80-81 | 80 | — |
| *63 | 96×56 | 2.62 | 77 | 77 | 77 |
| 51 | 90×54 | 3.40 | 63 | 63 | — |
| 51 | 73×52 | 4.00 | 54 | 54 | — |
| 48 | 78×54 | 4.00 | 54–53 | 54–53 | — |
| *48 | 78×54 | 4.00 | 49 | 48 | — |
| 48 | 96×56 | 3.50 | 64–63 | 64–63 | — |
| | | | Textured Fill | | |
| 100 | 78×44 | 2.06 | 95–96 | 95 | — |
| 64 | 78×50 | 2.98 | 69 | 69 | — |
| 64 | 78×44 | 3.20 | 66 | 66–68 | — |
| 48 | 78×44 | 4.23 | 48 | 48 | — |
| | | | **65/35 BLENDS** | | |
| | | | Voile | | |
| *47 | 60×56 | | 72 | — | — |
| | | | Batiste | | |
| *47 | 88×64 | | 63 | — | — |
| | | | **SHEETINGS** | | |
| 59 | 68×72 | 1.85 | 1.25 | 1.25 | — |
| *59 | 68×72 | 1.85 | 1.05 | — | — |
| 64 | 60×60 | 1.95 | — | — | — |
| *63 | 60×60 | 1.95 | 86–87 | — | — |
| *59 | 48×44 | 1.70 | 1.26 | — | — |
| | | | **POLYESTER/RAYON TWILLS** | | |
| 64 | 78×58 | 2.28 | 1.15 | — | — |
| | | | **OSNABURGS** | | |
| 60 | 40×26 | 1.60 | 1.36 | 1.36 | — |
| 59 | 32×26 | 2.35 | 96 | 96 | — |
| | | | **S. F. APPAREL DUCK** | | |
| *47 | 84×28 | 1.87 | — | — | — |
| | | | **SAILCLOTH** | | |
| *52 | 96×36 | 1.58 | — | — | — |
| 52 | 93×36 | 1.58 | — | — | — |
| 64 | 100×36 | 1.40 | 1.36 | — | — |
| | | | **DRILLS** | | |
| *59 | 68×40 | 1.85 | 95 | — | — |
| *59 | 68×40 | 2.25 | 85 | 85 | — |

**EXPLANATION**

First column represents the width of cloth, second column the count per square inch, third column the weight in yards per pound. The fourth column is the spot price (immediate delivery), fifth and sixth columns usually give the succeeding quarters for which delivery is quoted. (*Imported fabrics).

## COTTON

**COTTON**
**NEW YORK FUTURES MARKET**

| | Close | Change |
|---|---|---|
| October | 71.97 | dn .68 |
| December | 72.57 | dn .56 |
| March | 74.01 | dn .45 |

## WOOL

**AUSTRALIAN WOOL PRICES***

*There were no wool sales last week. Sales will resume July 30.

## MAN-MADE FIBERS

**CELLULOSIC FIBERS**

| | |
|---|---|
| Rayon Staple | 1.12–1.15 |
| High Wet Modulus Rayon | 1.45 |
| 150-Denier Acetate | 2.05–2.10 |

**NON-CELLULOSIC FIBERS**

| | |
|---|---|
| Poly Blend-Staple Branded | 74–76 |
| 150-Denier Polyester Feeder | 96–99 |
| 40-Denier Nylon Dull/Pirns | 2.60–2.64 |
| 3-Denier Acrylic Staple Branded | (net) 90–1.20 |

## COTTON YARNS

**COMBED YARNS**

| Count | Singles | Plies |
|---|---|---|
| 16s | 1.96–2.08 | 2.38–2.46 |
| 18s | 1.99–2.09 | 2.44–2.50 |
| 20s | 2.02–2.11 | 2.50–2.58 |
| 24s | 2.09–2.15 | 2.65–2.75 |
| 30s | 2.15–2.21 | 2.80–2.90 |
| 36s | 2.39–2.47 | 3.00–3.25 |

Prices include California cottons

**POLY/COMBED COTTON 50/50s**

| | |
|---|---|
| 18 singles | 1.90–1.93 |
| 30 singles | 2.08–2.11 |
| 36 singles | 2.25–2.37 |

**CARDED YARNS**

| Count | Singles | Plies |
|---|---|---|
| 10s | 1.69–1.72 | 1.85–2.05 |
| 16s | 1.75–1.78 | 2.00–2.15 |
| 20s | 1.81–1.88 | 2.15–2.30 |
| 24s | 1.91–1.92 | 2.46–2.47 |
| 30s | 2.00–2.01 | 2.55–2.56 |
| 30s poly/blend | 2.05–2.16 | |

**OPEN-END YARNS**

| | |
|---|---|
| All-cotton 10s | 1.28–1.32 |
| All-cotton 18s | 1.40–1.45 |
| All-cotton 26s | 1.55–1.65 |
| All-cotton 30s | 1.68–1.75 |
| Poly/cotton 10s | 1.27–1.30 |
| Poly/cotton 18s | 1.39–1.42 |
| Poly/cotton 26s | 1.55–1.59 |
| Poly/cotton 30s | 1.65–1.69 |

## MAN-MADE GRAY GOODS

| | | Spot | 1st Qtr | 2nd Qtr |
|---|---|---|---|---|
| | | **FILAMENT FABRICS** | | |
| | | Acetate Taffeta | | |
| 45½ | 92×56 | ×80 | 73 | — |
| | | Acetate Linings | | |
| 45½ | 120×68 | 1.20 | 73 | 1.20 |
| | | Rayon Linings | | |
| *45½ | 136×80 | — | — | — |
| | | **SPUN YARN GOODS** | | |
| | | Rayon Challis | | |
| 60 | 68×52 | 2.37/yd | 1.48–1.50 | 1.48 |
| | | **NYLON GRAY GOODS** | | |
| 60 | 96×68 taffeta | — | 76–77 | — |
| 60 | 96×86 taffeta | 1.02½ | 1.02–1.02½ | — |

The above price tables are based on mill sales of average quality fabrics or yarns. In the event of inactive numbers, prices are for the last reported sales. The symbol '×' before a price indicates secondhand sales.

FIGURE 2–2 ❖ Market prices for fabrics, from DNR. (COURTESY OF DNR, FAIRCHILD PUBLICATIONS.)

| SS PROPERTIES | | |
|---|---|---|
| ACID AND ALKALINE PERSPIRATION | SUBLIMATION (325 F — 30 SEC.) | WASH TEST NO. 3 |
| 5 | 5 | SC 5 ST 5 |
| 5 | 3 | SC 5 ST 5 |
| 5 | 5 | SC 5 ST 5 |
| 5 | 5 | SC 5 ST 5 |
| 5 | 5 | SC 5 ST 5 |
| 5 | 4-5 | SC 5 ST 5 |
| 5 | 4-5 | SC 4-5 ST 5 |
| 5 | 4-5 | SC 5 ST 5 |
| 5 | 5 | SC 4-5 ST 5 |
| 5 | 5 | SC 5 ST 5 |
| 5 | 5 | SC 5 ST 5 |
| 4-5 | 4-5 | SC 4-5 ST 5 |
| 4-5 | 4-5 | SC 4 ST 5 |
| 5 | 4-5 | SC 5 ST 5 |
| 5 | 4-5 | SC 5 ST 5 |
| 4-5 | 4-5 | SC 4-5 ST 4-5 |
| 4-5 | 3 | SC 5 ST 4-5 |
| 4-5 | 5 | SC 4 ST 5 |
| 5 | 5 | SC 5 ST 5 |
| 5 | 4-5 | SC 4 ST 5 |

| NO. | ORCOZINE | COLOR SAMPLE ON ORLON 75 | NO. | ORCOZINE | COLOR SAMPLE ON ORLON 75 |
|---|---|---|---|---|---|
| 1 | YELLOW L B.Y. 13 | | 2 | YELL. 7GLL 200% B.Y. 21 | |
| 3 | YELLOW R SUPRA B.Y. 11 | | 4 | YELLOW 6DL B.Y. 29 | |
| 5 | GOLDEN YELL GL B.Y. 28 | | 6 | ORANGE G 200% B.O. 21 | |
| 7 | CHRYSOIDINE Y EX. CONC. B.O. 2 | | 8 | ORANGE RS B.O. 1 | |
| 9 | BRILL. RED 4GB 200% B.R. 14 | | 10 | RED GTL B.R. 18 | |
| 11 | BRILL. RED 5G — | | 12 | RED GRL B.R. 46 | |
| 13 | BRILL. RED FBB B.R. 49 | | 14 | RED B B.R. 22 | |
| 15 | BRILL. RED BN B.R. 15 | | 16 | FUCHSINE SB B.V. 14 | |
| 17 | RHODINE BL 200% B.V. 16 | | 18 | BLUE RGL — | |
| 19 | BLUE NF — | | 20 | ROYAL BLUE S — | |

**FIGURE 2–3** ❖ Dye card showing colors and colorfastness ratings.

something is done to it or when it is exposed to some element in the environment that might adversely affect the textile. For example, we can assess how much fading or loss of strength occurs when a textile is exposed to a known amount of artificial light for a stated time period. We can assess how much force or weight is required for a textile to tear. We can assess whether a fabric will bleed when washed and how much a fabric will shrink when machine washed and machine dried using a regular cycle with hot water.

Each component of a textile product influences the overall performance of the product relative to each serviceability concept. In other words, textile product performance cannot be determined solely on a single component such as fiber content or fabric structure. Although these two characteristics of a product are important and can have a significant impact on performance, product performance can be enhanced or negated by other factors such as yarn type, finish, product fit, construction, or product design.

Fabric performance may be assessed by the fabric producer, by the firm buying the fabric, or by an outside firm that specializes in assessing fabric performance. Unfortunately, some firms do not assess fabric performance and that can lead to problems with products that fail to meet performance expectations or that fail in con-

**TABLE 2–1** ❖ Serviceability concepts.

| | |
|---|---|
| **Aesthetics** | Attractiveness or appearance of a textile product. Is the item attractive and appropriate in appearance for its end use? How does it look? Does it make the right statement for the target market and end use? |
| **Durability** | How the product withstands use; the length of time the product is considered suitable for the use for which it was purchased. Will this item continue to be usable for as long as expected? Will the consumer be satisfied with how well it wears, how strong it is, and how long it remains attractive? |
| **Comfort and Safety** | The way textiles affect heat, air, and moisture transfer and the way the body interacts with a textile product. Its ability to protect the body from harm. Is this item comfortable for its end use in terms of absorbency, temperature regulation, hand, etc.? Will its comfort change with use or age? Is it safe to use or wear? |
| **Appearance Retention** | How the product maintains its original appearance during use and care. Will the item retain its new look with use and after care? Will it resist wrinkling, shrinkage, abrasion, soiling, stretching, pilling, sagging, or other changes with use? |
| **Care** | Treatment required to maintain a textile product's original appearance. Does the item include a recommended care procedure? Is the care procedure appropriate to maintain the product's new or nearly new look? Are these recommendations appropriate considering its end use, cost, and product type? |
| **Environmental Impact** | Effect on the environment of the production, use, care, and disposal of textiles and textile products. How has the production of this item affected the environment? How will its recommended care affect the environment? Can this product, its components, or its packaging materials be recycled? Does the product or its packaging contain any recycled materials? |
| **Cost** | Influenced by many factors, including price of materials. How much does this product cost? How much will it cost to care for this product during its lifetime? Is the cost reasonable considering the product's inherent attributes? |

**TABLE 2–2** ❖ Approximate percentage costs for a woven fabric.

| | |
|---|---|
| Raw fibers | 23% |
| Yarn spinning | 18% |
| Weaving | 33% |
| Finishing | 26% |

*Source:* Ford, J. E. (1991). "Nonwovens." *Textiles,* no. 4, p. 17.

sumers' hands. For example, items that incorporate two or more fabrics may exhibit problems with color bleeding if the designer is not aware that one of the fabrics is likely to bleed when laundered. If one of the fabrics *does* bleed in laundering, then all products that combine both fabrics into a single product incorporate this inherent flaw. Thus, all these products are likely to result in consumer dissatisfaction with the product, complaints, and returns. By failing to assess how the two fabrics interact, the designer has created an unsatisfactory product and an expensive failure for the company.

In some product and performance categories, such as the flammability of furnishings in public use areas and the flammability of children's sleepwear, performance testing is required by law. Products that do not meet minimum safety standards are not acceptable to the market.

Fabric performance often is assessed following standard industry procedures so that performance values for fabrics can be compared. In these procedures, one or more small pieces of fabric are tested for performance in a specific area, such as snagging or fading. (See Figure 2–4.) Assessing fabric performance helps in selecting a fabric appropriate for the target market and the firm.

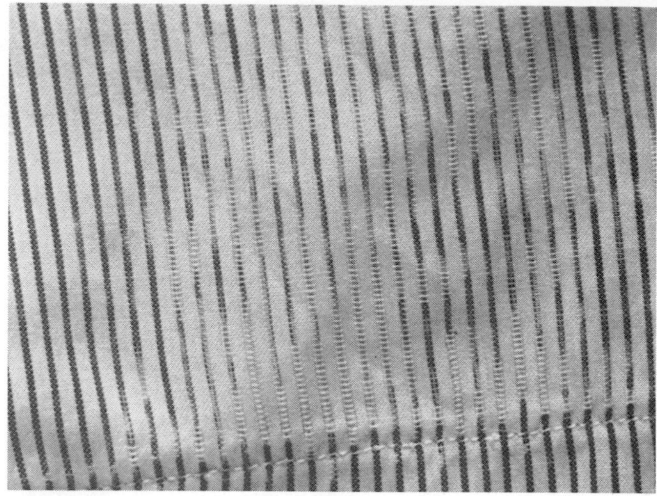

**FIGURE 2–5** ❖ Portion of shirt demonstrating color loss, probably due to an accident of unknown type during production.

Some firms have developed specifications or written descriptions describing minimum performance measures for fabrics used in their products. Their performance specifications are based on understanding their target market's expectations. These specifications help the firm assure that the fabrics they buy and products they produce meet their target market's expectations for performance. Although performance testing eliminates many problems, it is not an absolute guarantee that all products will be perfect, since some problems may be related to accidents or spills that involve a tiny portion of a fabric. (See Figure 2–5.)

**FIGURE 2–4** ❖ Samples from performance testing: snagging (left) and resistance to sunlight (right), with faded portion on right side.

**FIGURE 2–6** ❖ Appearance evaluation of shirt collars based on company standards. (COURTESY OF JC PENNEY CO., INC.)

Product **quality** is becoming a significant component in performance assessment and in competition in the global marketplace. Product quality is difficult to define because it means many different things to consumers and producers. Quality generally refers to the sum total of product characteristics, including appearance, appropriateness for the end use, performance and interactions of materials in the product, consistency among identical products, and freedom from defects in construction or materials (see Figure 2–6). Throughout this book, measures and dimensions of fabric quality will be addressed. Keep in mind that *fabric* quality is not the same thing as *product* quality. Fabric quality addresses the fabric used to produce the product. Other factors also influence product quality, but these other factors are beyond the scope of this book.

It must be stressed that neither this book nor any course or combination of courses in textiles will provide the "best" single answer for any specific end use. This book will not answer the question, "What is the best combination of fiber and yarn type, fabrication method, and finish for (fill in the name of a product)?" That answer will be based on understanding a specific target market and end use, current fashion, lifestyle, budget, access to the market, and so on. This book, however, will provide a wealth of information to use in developing and selecting products to meet a wide variety of target market needs.

## KEY TERMS

Product development
Serviceability
Aesthetics
Durability
Comfort
Safety
Appearance retention
Care
Environmental impact
Cost
Performance
Quality

## QUESTIONS

1. Define product development and describe how it determines what is on the market.
2. Identify consumer expectations for each serviceability concept for these products and target markets:
   - carpet in a fast-food restaurant in an upscale shopping mall
   - shirt/blouse for a retail management trainee for casual Fridays
   - housecoat/robe for a resident in a physical rehabilitation center

upholstery for a chair in a waiting room in a medical clinic
adhesive bandage for a heel blister for a college student

3. Explain the relationship between product performance and product development.

## Suggested Readings

Bemowski, Karen (1993, February). "Quality, American Style." *Quality Progress,* pp. 65–68.

Glock, Ruth E., and Kunz, Grace I. (1995). *Apparel Manufacturing: Sewn Product Analysis,* 2nd ed. New York: Prentice-Hall.

Nielson, Karla J., and Taylor, David A. (1994). *Interiors: An Introduction.* Madison, WI: WCB Brown & Benchmark Publishers.

Textiles Institute (1987). *Textiles: Product Design and Marketing.* Manchester, England: The Textiles Institute.

Thomas, Marita (1993, November). "Homefurnishings Market Gears Up for Business." *Textile World,* pp. 46–50.

Winchester, S. C. (1994). "Total Quality Management in Textiles." *Journal of the Textile Institute, 85,* pp. 445–459.

# Section Two

# FIBERS

Chapter 3

# TEXTILE FIBERS AND THEIR PROPERTIES

## OBJECTIVES

- To understand terms describing textile fibers and their properties.
- To use terminology correctly.
- To understand the relationships between fiber structure and fiber properties or characteristics.
- To match fiber performance to end use requirements.
- To identify common fibers based on results of fiber identification procedures.

It is important to understand fibers and their performance because fibers are the basic unit of most fabrics. Fibers contribute to the aesthetic appearance of fabrics; they influence durability, comfort, appearance retention, care, environmental impact, and cost. Successful textile fibers must be readily available, constantly in supply, and cost effective. They must have sufficient strength, pliability, length, and cohesiveness to be processed into yarns, fabrics, and products.

Textile fibers have been used to make cloth for several thousand years. Until 1885, when the first manufactured fiber was produced commercially, fibers were produced by plants and animals. The fibers most commonly used were wool, flax, cotton, and silk. These four natural fibers continue to be used and valued today, although their economic importance relative to all fibers has decreased. **Natural fibers** are those fibers that are in fiber form as they grow or develop and come from animal, plant, or mineral sources. **Manufactured fibers** or **man-made fibers** are made from chemical compounds produced in manufacturing facilities.

Textile processes—spinning, weaving, knitting, dyeing, and finishing of fabrics—were developed for the natural fibers. These traditional processes have been modified for manufactured fibers. New processes have been developed specifically for manufactured fibers and sometimes modified for natural fibers.

For example, silk has always been a highly prized fiber because of its smoothness, luster, and softness; it has always been expensive and comparatively scarce. It was logical to try to duplicate silk. Rayon (called artificial silk until 1925) was the first manufactured fiber. Rayon was produced in filament length until the early 1930s when a textile worker discovered that broken waste rayon filaments could be used as staple fiber. Acetate and nylon also were introduced as filaments to be used in silklike fabrics.

Many manufactured fibers were developed in the first half of the 20th century. Since then tremendous advances have been made in the manufactured fiber industry, primarily modifications of parent fibers to provide the best combination of properties for specific end uses. The manufactured fibers most commonly used in contemporary apparel and furnishing fabrics include polyester, nylon, olefin, acrylic, rayon, and acetate. Fibers for special and industrial applications include spandex, aramid, PBI, and sulfar. From time to time, new fibers, like lyocell, or new fiber modifications are introduced.

# Fiber Properties

Fiber properties contribute to the properties of a fabric. For example, strong fibers contribute to the durability of fabrics; absorbent fibers are used for skin-contact apparel and for towels and diapers; fire-resistant fibers are used for children's sleepwear and firefighters' clothing.

To analyze and predict a fabric's performance, start with the fiber. Knowledge of the fiber's properties will help to anticipate the fiber's contribution to the performance of a fabric and the product made from it. Fiber properties are determined by the nature of their physical structure, chemical composition, and molecular arrangement.

Some contributions of fibers are desirable and some are not. Here are some characteristics of a low-absorbency fiber:

- Static build-up
- Quick drying
- Difficult for dyer to color
- Poor skin-comfort—clammy
- Prevents evaporation of perspiration
- Dimensionally stable to water
- Good wrinkle recovery when laundered
- Waterborne stains do not penetrate
- Resin finishes are not absorbed
- Cool and slick hand

It is important to note that product characteristics also result from other components beyond the fiber itself. Fibers are used to produce yarns. The type of yarn and its structure influence hand and performance. For example, yarns made from short fibers tend to be comfortable, but they pill. The process used to produce the fabric influences the product's appearance and texture, performance during use and care, and cost. Finishes alter the fabric's hand, appearance, and performance. These three components (yarn, fabric type, and finish) will be discussed in detail in the chapters in Sections 3, 4, and 5.

Because cotton is a common consumer fiber, it is often used as a standard in the industry. It might be helpful to note how cotton's performance compares to that of other fibers when examining or studying Tables 3–3 through 3–16.

Fiber properties are determined using specialized equipment and following specified procedures called standard test methods. Assessment of specific fiber properties is important in selecting the right fiber for the end use.

## Physical Structure

The physical structure, or morphology, can be identified by observing the fiber using a microscope. In the text, photomicrographs at magnifications of 250–1,000 × will be used to clarify details of the fiber's physical structure.

**LENGTH** Fibers are sold by the fiber producer as staple, filament, or filament tow. **Staple fibers** are short fibers measured in inches or centimeters. They range in length from 2 to 46 cm (¾ of an inch to 18 inches), as illustrated in Figure 3–1. All the natural fibers except silk are available only in staple form. **Filaments** are long, continuous fiber strands of indefinite length, measured in yards or meters. They may be either monofilament (one fiber) or multifilament (a number of filaments). Filaments may be smooth or bulked (crimped in some way), as shown in Figure 3–2. Smooth filaments are used to produce silklike fabrics; bulked filaments are used in more cottonlike or wool-like fabrics. **Filament tow** is produced as a loose rope of several thousand fibers, crimped or textured, and cut to staple length.

**SIZE** Fiber size plays a big part in determining the performance and hand of a fabric (how it feels). Large fibers give crispness, roughness, body, and stiffness. Large fibers also resist crushing—a property that is important in products like carpets. Fine fibers give softness and pliability. Fabrics made with fine fibers drape more easily.

Natural fibers are subject to growth irregularities and are not uniform in size or development. In natural fibers, fineness is a major factor in determining quality. Fine fibers are of better quality. Fineness is measured in micrometers (a micrometer is 1/1,000 millimeter or 1/25,400 inch). The diameter range (in micrometers) is listed below for selected natural fibers.

| | |
|---|---|
| Cotton | 16–20 |
| Flax | 12–16 |
| Wool | 10–50 |
| Silk | 11–12 |

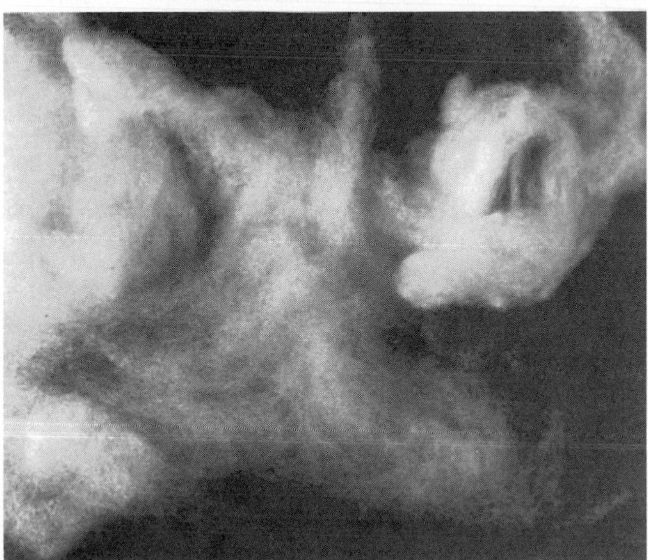

**FIGURE 3–1** ❖ Manufactured staple fiber.

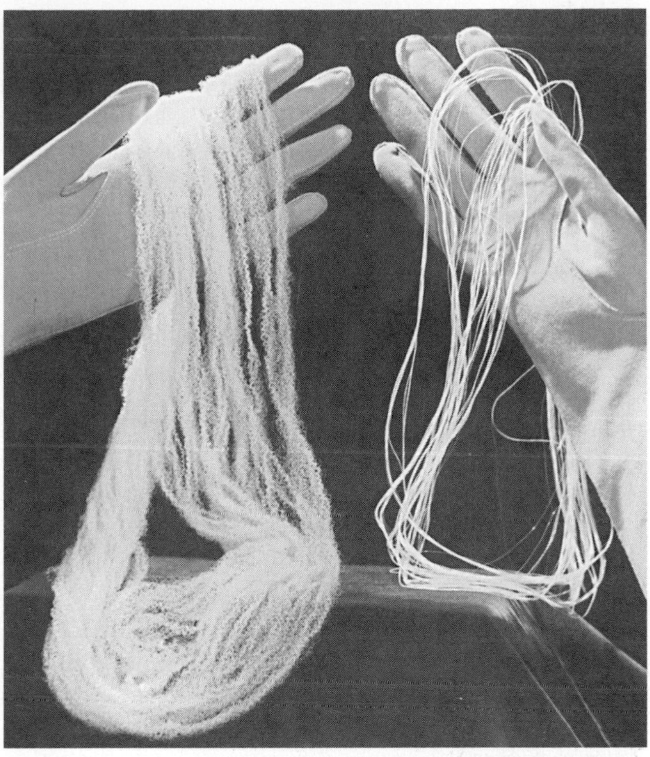

**FIGURE 3–2** ❖ Manufactured filaments: textured-bulk yarn (left); smooth-filament yarn (right).

In manufactured fibers, diameter is controlled by the size of the spinneret holes, by stretching or drawing during or after spinning, or by controlling the rate of extrusion of the spinning solution through the spinneret. Manufactured fibers can be made uniform in diameter or can be thick-and-thin at regular intervals throughout their length. The fineness of manufactured fibers is measured in denier. **Denier** is the weight in grams of 9,000 meters of fiber or yarn. When the term *denier* is used to describe a fiber, the number refers to the fineness or coarseness of the fiber. Small numbers describe fine fibers; large numbers describe large or coarse fibers. **Tex** is the weight in grams of 1,000 meters of fiber or yarn. Staple fiber is sold by denier and fiber length; filament fiber is sold by the denier of the yarn or tow. Yarn denier can be divided by the number of filaments to give denier per filament or dpf. For example:

$$\frac{\text{40 denier yarn}}{\text{20 filaments}} = \text{2 denier per filament}$$

One to 3 denier corresponds to fine cotton, cashmere, or wool; 5 to 8 denier is similar to average cotton, wool, or alpaca; 15 denier corresponds to carpet wool size. Apparel fibers range from less than 1 to 7 denier. Carpet fibers may range in denier from 15 to 24. Industrial fibers exhibit the broadest range, from 5 to several thousand, depending on the end use. For example, fibers used for weed trimmers and tow ropes are much larger than those used for absorbent layers in diapers.

Fibers of the same denier are not necessarily suitable for all end uses. Apparel fibers do not make serviceable carpets, and carpet fibers do not make serviceable clothing. Apparel fibers are too soft and pliable, and carpets made of apparel fibers do not have good crush resistance. Industrial fibers frequently are produced in various deniers, depending on the end use.

**CROSS-SECTIONAL SHAPE** Shape is important in luster, bulk, body, texture, and hand. Figure 3–3 shows typical cross-sectional shapes. These shapes may be round, dog-bone, triangular, lobal, bean-shaped, flat, or strawlike.

The natural fibers derive their shape from (1) the way the cellulose is built up during plant growth, (2) the shape of the hair follicle and the formation of protein substances in animals, or (3) the shape of the orifice through which the silk fiber is extruded.

The shape of manufactured fibers is controlled by the shape of the spinneret opening and the spinning method. The size, shape, luster, length, and other properties of manufactured fibers can be varied by changes in the production process.

**SURFACE CONTOUR** *Surface contour* describes the outer surface of the fiber along its length. Surface contour may be smooth, serrated, striated, or rough. It is important to the luster, hand, texture, and apparent soiling of the fabric. Figure 3–3 also shows surface contours of selected fibers.

**CRIMP** Crimp may be found in textile materials as fiber crimp or fabric crimp. **Fiber crimp** refers to the waves, bends, twists, coils, or curls along the length of the fiber. Fiber crimp increases cohesiveness, resiliency, resistance to abrasion, stretch, bulk, and warmth. Crimp increases absorbency and skin-contact comfort but reduces luster. Inherent crimp occurs in wool. Inherent crimp also exists in an undeveloped state in bicomponent manufactured fibers where it is developed in the fabric or the completed garment (such as a sweater) with heat or moisture.

**Fabric crimp** refers to the bends caused by distortion of yarns in a fabric. When a yarn is unraveled from a fabric, fabric crimp can easily be seen in the yarn. It also may be visible in fibers removed from the yarn.

**FIBER PARTS** The natural fibers, except for silk, have three distinct parts: an outer covering called a *cuticle* or skin; an inner area; and a central core that may be hollow.

The manufactured fibers are not as complex in structure as the natural fibers. They usually consist of a skin and a core.

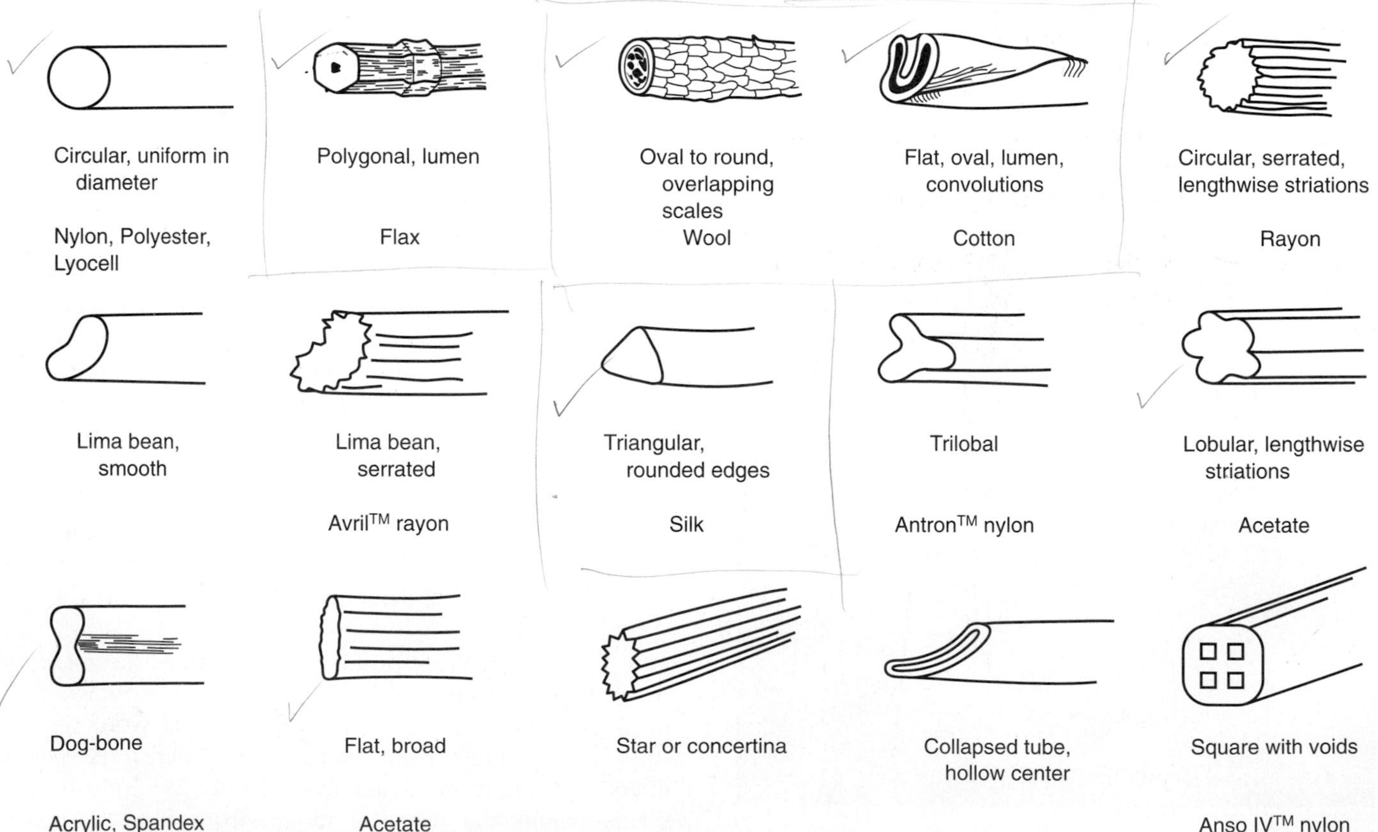


**FIGURE 3–3** ❖ Cross-sectional shapes and fiber contours.

## Chemical Composition and Molecular Arrangement

Fibers are classified into groups by their chemical composition. Fibers with similar chemical compositions are placed in the same **generic group.** Fibers in one generic group have different properties from fibers in another group.

Fibers are composed of millions of molecular chains. **Polymerization** is the process of joining small molecules—monomers—together to form a long chain or a **polymer.** The length of the chains, which varies just as the length of fibers varies, depends on the number of molecules connected in a chain; it is described as **degree of polymerization.** Long chains indicate a high degree of polymerization and a high degree of fiber strength. Molecular chains are too small to be seen, even with the assistance of a microscope.

Molecular chains may be described by weight. Molecular weight is a factor in properties such as fiber strength and extensibility. A fiber with longer chains or higher molecular weight has a higher strength and is more difficult to pull apart than a fiber with shorter chains of equal molecular weight.

Molecular chains have different configurations within fibers. When molecular chains are arranged in a random or disorganized way within the fiber, they are *amorphous.* When the molecular chains are parallel to each other or arranged in an organized fashion, they are *crystalline.* Molecular chains that are parallel to each other and to the lengthwise axis of the fiber are oriented. When most molecular chains are oriented, they have a high degree of **orientation** or are highly oriented. Fibers that are highly oriented are also highly crystalline. However, highly crystalline fibers are not necessarily highly oriented (see Figure 3–4). Fibers vary in their proportion of oriented, crystalline, and amorphous regions.

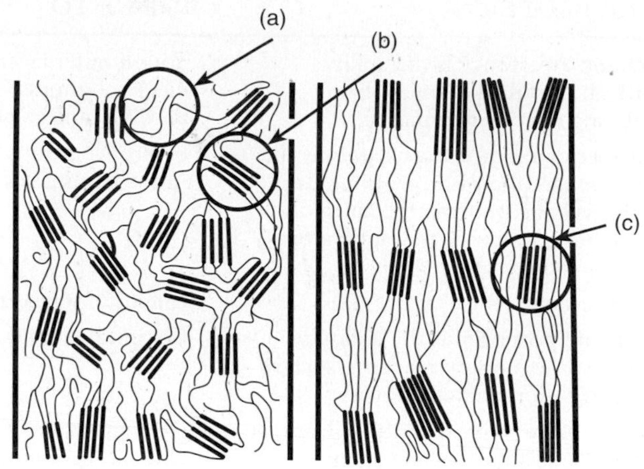


**FIGURE 3–4** ❖ Polymers: (a) amorphous area; (b) crystalline, but not oriented, area; (c) oriented and crystalline area.

The polymers in manufactured fibers are in a random, unoriented state when extruded from the spinneret. **Stretching,** or **drawing,** increases their crystallinity and orients them, reduces their diameter, and packs their molecules together (Figure 3–5). Fiber properties related to the degree of crystallinity and orientation include strength, elongation, moisture absorption, abrasion resistance, and dyeability.

Fibers that are amorphous are relatively weak and easily elongated. Amorphous fibers also have good moisture absorbency and dyeability, good flexibility, and poor elasticity. Examples of amorphous fibers include wool and rayon.

Oriented and crystalline fibers are strong and stiff. They are difficult to elongate, but have good elasticity. They don't stretch easily, but they recover quickly if they have been stretched. They tend to be nonabsorbent and difficult to dye. Highly oriented and crystalline fibers include polyester, nylon, and aramid.

Molecular chains are held to one another by intermolecular forces called **hydrogen bonds** and **van der Waals forces.** The forces are similar to the attraction of a magnet for a piece of iron. The closer the chains are to each other, the stronger the bonds are. Hydrogen bonding is the attraction of positive hydrogen atoms of one chain for negative oxygen or nitrogen atoms of an adjacent chain. Van der Waals forces are similar but weaker bonds. It is in the crystalline area that hydrogen bonding and van der Waals forces occur. These intermolecular forces help make crystalline polymers stronger than amorphous polymers.

❖

## SERVICEABILITY

Textile serviceability includes the concepts of aesthetics, durability, comfort, appearance retention, care, environmental impact, and cost that were introduced in Chapter 2. Each concept will be discussed in terms of properties that affect it (Table 3–1). For example, the

**FIGURE 3–5** ❖ Before and after drawing the fiber.

TABLE 3–1 ❖ Fiber properties.

| FIBER PROPERTY | IS DUE TO | CONTRIBUTES TO FABRIC PROPERTY |
|---|---|---|
| **Abrasion resistance** is the ability of a fiber to resist damage from rubbing or direct contact. | Tough outer layer, scales, or skin<br>Fiber toughness<br>Flexible molecular chains | Durability<br>Abrasion resistance<br>Resistance to splitting or pilling |
| **Absorbency or moisture regain** is the percentage of moisture a bone-dry fiber will absorb from the air under standard conditions of temperature and moisture. | Hydroxyl groups<br>Amorphous areas | Comfort, warmth, water repellency, absorbency, static buildup<br>Dyeability, soiling<br>Shrinkage<br>Wrinkle resistance |
| **Aging resistance** | Chemical structure | Storing of fabrics |
| **Allergenic potential** is the ability to cause some physical reaction, such as skin irritation or watery eyes. | Chemical composition, additives | Comfort |
| **Chemical reactivity** describes the effect of acids, alkali, oxidizing agents, solvents, or other chemicals. | Polar groups of molecules<br>Chemical composition | Care required in cleaning—bleaching, ability to take acid or alkali finishes |
| **Cohesiveness** is the ability of fibers to cling together during spinning. | Crimp or twists, surface contour | Resistance to raveling<br>Resistance to yarn slippage |
| **Compressibility** is resistance to crushing. | Molecular structure, fiber size, and stiffness | Crush and wrinkle resistance |
| **Cover** is the ability to occupy space for concealment or protection. | Crimp, curl, or twist<br>Cross-sectional shape | Warmth in fabric<br>Cost—less fiber needed |
| **Creep** is delayed recovery from elongation. Recovers gradually from strain. | Lack of side chains, cross links, strong bonds; poor orientation | Streak dyeing and shiners in fabric |
| **Density**—see **Specific gravity** | | |
| **Dimensional stability** is the ability to retain a given size and shape through use and care. | Physical structure, chemical structure, coatings | Shrinkage, growth, care, appearance, durability |
| **Drape** is the manner in which a fabric falls or hangs over a three-dimensional form. | Fiber size and stiffness | Appearance |
| **Dyeability** is the fiber's receptivity to coloration by dyes; dye affinity. | Amorphous areas and dye sites, chemical structure | Aesthetics and colorfastness |
| **Elastic recovery** is the degree to which fibers will recover from strain. | Chemical and molecular structure; side chains, cross linkages, strong bonds | Processability of fabrics<br>Resiliency<br>Delayed elasticity or creep |
| **Elasticity** is the ability of a strained material to recover its original size and shape immediately after removal of stress. | Chemical and molecular structure; side chains, cross linkages, strong bonds | Fit and appearance; resiliency |
| **Electrical conductivity** is the ability to transfer electrical charges. | Chemical structure: polar groups | Poor conductivity causes fabric to cling or produce static shocks |
| **Elongation** is the ability to be stretched, extended, or lengthened.Varies at different temperatures and when wet or dry. | Fiber crimp<br>Molecular structure: molecular crimp orientation | Increases tear strength<br>Reduces brittleness<br>Provides "give" |
| **Feltability** refers to the ability of fibers to mat together. | Scale structure of wool | Fabrics can be made directly from fibers<br>Special care required when fabric is wet |
| **Flammability** describes how a fabric reacts to ignition. | Chemical composition | Fabric's ability to ignite and burn |
| **Flexibility** is the ability to bend repeatedly without breaking. | Flexible molecular chain | Stiffness, drape, comfort |
| **Hand** is the way a fiber feels: tactile sensation; silky, harsh, soft, crisp, dry. | Cross-sectional shape, surface properties, crimp, diameter, length | Hand of fabric |
| **Heat conductivity** is the ability to transfer heat through a fabric. | Crimp, chemical composition<br>Cross-sectional shape | Comfort: cooling effect |

TABLE 3–1 ❖ *(continued)*

| FIBER PROPERTY | IS DUE TO | CONTRIBUTES TO FABRIC PROPERTY |
|---|---|---|
| **Heat retention** is the ability to retain heat or insulate. | Crimp, chemical composition<br>Cross-sectional shape | Comfort: warming effect, insulating |
| **Heat sensitivity** is the ability to soften, melt, or shrink when subjected to heat. | Chemical and molecular structure<br>Fewer intermolecular forces and cross links | Determines safe cleaning and pressing temperatures |
| **Hydrophilic, hygroscopic**—see **Absorbency** | | |
| **Loft,** or compressional resiliency, is the ability to spring back to original thickness after being compressed. | Fiber crimp<br>Stiffness | Springiness, good cover<br>Resistance to flattening |
| **Luster** is the light reflected from a surface. More subdued than shine; light rays are broken up. | Smoothness<br>Fiber length<br>Flat or lobal shape<br>Additives | Luster<br>Matte Shiny |
| **Mildew resistance** | Low absorption | Storage |
| **Modulus** is the resistance to stress/strain to which a fiber is exposed. | Molecular arrangement, chemical composition | Tenacity, elongation, and elasticity |
| **Moth resistance** | Molecule has no sulfur | Storage |
| **Oleophilic** describes fibers with a strong affinity or attraction for oil. | Chemical composition | Soiling; care; appearance |
| **Pilling** is the balling up of fiber ends on the surface of fabrics. | Fiber strength<br>High molecular weight | Pilling<br>Unsightly appearance |
| **Resiliency** is the ability to return to original shape after bending, twisting, compressing, or a combination of deformations. | Molecular structure: side chains, cross linkages, strong bonds | Wrinkle recovery, crease retention, appearance, care |
| **Specific gravity and density** are measures of the weight of a fiber. Density is the weight in grams per cubic centimeter. Specific gravity is the ratio of the mass of the fiber to an equal volume of water at 4°C. | Molecular weight and structure | Warmth without weight<br>Loftiness—full and light<br>Buoyancy to fabric |
| **Stiffness or rigidity** is the opposite of flexibility. It is the resistance to bending or creasing. | Chemical and molecular structure | Body of fabric<br>Resistance to insertion of yarn twist |
| **Strength** is the ability to resist stress and is expressed as **tensile strength** (pounds per square inch) or as **tenacity** (grams per denier). Breaking tenacity is the number of grams of force to break a fiber. | Molecular structure: orientation, crystallinity, degree of polymerization | Durability, tear strength, sagging, pilling<br>Sheerest fabrics possible with strong fine fibers |
| **Sunlight resistance** is the ability to withstand degradation from direct sunlight. | Chemical composition<br>Additives | Durability of fabric exposed to sunlight |
| **Texture** is the nature of the fiber or fabric surface. | Physical structure | Luster, appearance |
| **Translucence** is the ability of a fiber, yarn, or fabric to allow light to pass through the structure. | Physical and chemical structure | Appearance |
| **Wicking** is the ability of a fiber to transfer moisture along its surface. | Chemical and physical composition of outer surface | Makes fabrics comfortable |

aesthetic properties of luster, drape, texture, and hand, as they relate to apparel and furnishing fabrics, will be defined and discussed.

Learning the definitions of the properties is important in gaining a more in-depth understanding of textile fiber performance. The tables in this chapter will assist you in making comparisons among fibers. Relating this to past experience with fabrics made of that fiber will contribute to a better understanding of fiber performance and serviceability.

## Aesthetic Properties

A textile product should be appropriate in appearance for its end use. Aesthetic properties relate to the way the senses, such as touch and sight, assist in the perception of the textile. In evaluating the aesthetics of a textile product, the consumer usually determines whether the appearance is appropriate for the end use.

**Luster** results from the way light is reflected by a fabric's surface. Shiny or bright fabrics reflect a great amount of light. Lustrous fabrics reflect a fair amount of light and are used in formal apparel and furnishings. Matte, or dull, fabrics reflect little light and are used most frequently for less formal looks in apparel and furnishings. Silk fabrics are usually lustrous. Cotton and wool fabrics are usually matte. The luster of manufactured fibers can be varied during manufacturing. Fibers with high luster are referred to as bright fibers. Low-luster fibers are dull fibers. Medium-luster fibers are semibright or semidull. Yarn structure, finish, and fabric structure may change the luster of any fiber.

**Drape** is the way a fabric falls over a three-dimensional form like a body or table. Fabric may be soft and free-flowing like chiffon, or it may fall in graceful folds like chintz, or it may be stiff and heavy like satin. Fibers influence drape to a degree, but yarns and fabric structure may be more important in determining drape.

**Texture** describes the nature of the fabric surface. It is identified by both visual and tactile senses. Fabrics may have a smooth or rough texture. Natural fibers tend to give a fabric more texture than manufactured fibers because of their inherent variations. Yarns, finishes, and fabric structure greatly affect the texture of a fabric.

**Hand** is the way a fabric feels to the skin. Fabrics may feel warm or cool, bulky or thin, slick or soft. Many other adjectives may be used. Hand may be evaluated by feeling a fabric between the fingers and thumb. Both objective and subjective means of evaluating fabric hand are used to determine its suitability for an end use.

## Durability Properties

A durable textile product should last an adequate period of time for its end use. Durability properties can be tested in the laboratory, but lab results do not always accurately predict performance during actual use.

**Abrasion resistance** is the ability of a fabric to withstand the rubbing it gets in use (Table 3–2). Abrasion can occur when the fabric is fairly flat, as when the knees of jeans scrape along a cement sidewalk. Edge abrasion can occur when the fabric is folded, as when the bottom of a drapery fabric rubs against a carpet. Flex abrasion can occur when the fabric is moving and bending, as in shoelaces that wear out where they are laced through the shoe. **Flexibility,** the ability to bend repeatedly without breaking, is a very important property related to abrasion resistance.

**Tenacity,** or tensile strength, is the ability of a fabric to withstand a pulling force (Table 3–3). (Breaking tenacity for a fiber is the force, in grams per denier or tex, required to break the fiber. The tenacity of a wet fiber may differ from the tenacity of that same fiber when it is dry. Although the fabric strength depends, to a large degree, on fiber strength, yarn and fabric structure may be varied to yield stronger or weaker fabrics made from the same fibers. Strength may also be measured by how much force it takes to rip the fabric (tearing strength) or to rupture the fabric (bursting strength).

**Elongation** refers to the degree to which a fiber may be stretched without breaking, measured as percent elongation at break (Table 3–4). Elongation should be considered in relation to elasticity.

**TABLE 3–2** ❖ Abrasion resistance.

| FIBER | RATING |
|---|---|
| Aramid | Excellent |
| Nylon | |
| Olefin | to |
| Polyester | |
| Saran | Good |
| Spandex | |
| Flax | |
| Acrylics | |
| PBI | to |
| Sulfar | |
| Cotton | |
| Silk | |
| Wool* | Moderate |
| Rayon | |
| Vinyon | to |
| Acetate | |
| Glass | Poor |

* Varies with coarseness of fiber.

**TABLE 3–3** ❖ Fiber tenacity (grams/denier).

| FIBER* | DRY | WET |
|---|---|---|
| Rubber | 0.34 | same |
| Spandex | 0.7–1.0 | same |
| Vinyon | 0.7–1.0 | same |
| Fluorocarbon | 0.9–4.0 | same |
| Rayon (viscose) | 1.0–2.5 | 0.5–1.4 |
| Acetate | 1.2–1.4 | 1.0–1.3 |
| Saran | 1.4–2.4 | same |
| Wool | 1.5 | 1.0 |
| Novoloid | 1.5–2.5 | 1.3–2.3 |
| Modacrylic | 1.7–2.6 | 1.5–2.4 |
| Acrylic | 2.0–3.0 | 1.8–2.7 |
| Polyester | 2.4–7.0 | same |
| Rayon (HWM) | 2.5–5.0 | 3.0 |
| PBI | 2.6–3.0 | 2.1–2.5 |
| Nylon 6,6 | 2.9–7.2 | 2.5–6.1 |
| Sulfar | 3.0–3.5 | same |
| Cotton | 3.5–4.0 | 4.5–5.0 |
| Olefin | 3.5–4.5 | same |
| Flax | 3.5–5.0 | 6.5 |
| Nylon 6 | 3.5–7.2 | same |
| Vinal | 3.5–6.5 | 2.6–4.9 |
| Silk | 4.5 | 2.8–4.0 |
| Lyocell | 4.8–5.0 | 4.2–4.6 |
| Aramid (Nomex) | 4.0–5.3 | 3.0–4.1 |
| Glass (multifilament) | 9.6 | 6.7 |

* For fibers that are available in several lengths and modifications, the values are for staple fibers with unmodified cross sections.

## Comfort Properties

A textile product should be comfortable as it is worn or used. This is primarily a matter of personal preference and individual perception of comfort under different climatic conditions and degrees of physical activity. Comfort is complex and dependent on characteristics such as absorbency, heat retention, density, and elongation.

**Absorbency** is the ability of a fiber to take up moisture from the body or from the environment. It is measured as moisture regain where the moisture in the material is expressed as a percentage of the weight of the moisture-free material (Table 3–5). Absorbency is also related to static buildup. **Hydrophilic** fibers absorb moisture readily. **Hydrophobic** fibers have little or no absorbency. **Hygroscopic** fibers absorb moisture without feeling wet.

**Heat or thermal retention** is the ability of a fabric to hold heat (Table 3–6). People want to be comfortable regardless of weather conditions. A low level of thermal retention is favored in hot weather and a high level in cold weather. Thus, most people use textiles differently in summer and winter. Yarn and fabric structure and layering of fabrics affect this property.

**TABLE 3–4** ❖ Fiber elongation (percent elongation at break).

| FIBER* | STANDARD** | WET |
|---|---|---|
| Flax | 2.0 | 2.2 |
| Cotton | 3–7 | 9.5 |
| Glass | 3.1 | 2.2 |
| Rayon, regular | 8–14 | 16–20 |
| Rayon, HWM | 9–18 | 20 |
| Polyester | 12–55 | same |
| Vinyon | 12–125 | same |
| Lyocell | 14–16 | 16–18 |
| Vinal | 15–30 | 11–23 |
| Saran | 15–35 | same |
| Nylon 6,6 | 16–75 | 18–78 |
| Silk | 20 | 30 |
| Aramid (Nomex) | 22–32 | 20–30 |
| Wool | 25 | 35 |
| Acetate | 25–45 | 35–50 |
| PBI | 25–30 | 26–32 |
| Modacrylic | 30–60 | same |
| Nylon 6 | 30–90 | 42–100 |
| Sulfar | 35–45 | same |
| Acrylic | 35–45 | 41–50 |
| Olefin | 70–100 | same |
| Spandex | 400–700 | same |
| Rubber | 500 | same |

* A minimum of 10% elongation is desirable for ease in textile processing. For fibers that are available in several lengths and modifications, the values are for staple fibers with unmodified cross sections.

** Standard conditions: 65% relative humidity; 70°F or 21°C.

**TABLE 3–5** ❖ Fiber absorbency.

| FIBER | MOISTURE REGAIN* |
|---|---|
| Glass | 0.0 |
| Olefin | 0.01–0.1 |
| Saran | 0.1 |
| Vinyon | 0.1 |
| Polyester | 0.4 |
| Sulfar | 0.6 |
| Acrylic | 1.0–1.5 |
| Spandex | 1.3 |
| Modacrylic | 2.5 |
| Nylon 6 | 2.8–5.0 |
| Nylon 6,6 | 4.0–4.5 |
| Vinal | 5.0 |
| Acetate | 6.3–6.5 |
| Aramid (Nomex) | 6.5 |
| Cotton | 7–11 |
| Silk | 11 |
| Lyocell | 11.5 |
| Rayon | 11.5–12.5 |
| Flax | 12 |
| Wool | 13–18 |
| PBI | 15 |

* Moisture regain is expressed as a percentage of the moisture-free weight at 70°F or 21°C and 65% relative humidity.

TABLE 3–6 ❖ Thermal retention.

| FIBER | RATING |
|---|---|
| Wool | Excellent |
| Acrylic/Modacrylic | |
| Polyester | |
| Olefin | Good |
| Nylon | |
| Aramid | |
| Silk | |
| Spandex | Moderate |
| Flax | |
| Cotton | |
| Lyocell | |
| Rayon | |
| Acetate | Poor |

**Heat sensitivity** describes a fiber's reaction when it is exposed to heat (Table 3–7). Some fibers soften and melt; others are heat resistant. These thermal properties determine safe pressing temperatures.

**Density** or specific gravity is a measure of fiber weight per unit volume (Table 3–8). Lower-density fibers can be made into thick fabrics that are more comfortable than higher-density fibers made into heavy, thick fabrics.

## Appearance-Retention Properties

A textile product should retain its original appearance during use, care, and storage.

**Resiliency** is the ability of a fabric to return to its original shape after bending, twisting, or crushing (Table 3–9). An easy test is to crunch a fabric in your hand and watch how it responds when you open your hand. A resilient fabric springs back. It is wrinkle resistant if it does not wrinkle easily. It has good wrinkle recovery if it returns to its original look after having been wrinkled. A fabric that wrinkles easily stays crumpled in your hand. When it is flattened out, wrinkles and creases are apparent.

**Dimensional stability** is defined as the ability of a fabric to retain a given size and shape through use and care. Dimensional stability is a desirable characteristic that includes the properties of shrinkage resistance and elastic recovery.

TABLE 3–7 ❖ Thermal properties.

| | MELTING POINT | | SOFTENING/ STICKING POINT | | SAFE PRESSING TEMPERATURE* | |
|---|---|---|---|---|---|---|
| FIBER | °F | °C | °F | °C | °F | °C |
| **Natural Fibers** | | | | | | |
| Cotton | Does not melt | | | | 425 | 218 |
| Flax | Does not melt | | | | 450 | 232 |
| Silk | Does not melt | | | | 300 | 149 |
| Wool | Does not melt | | | | 300 | 149 |
| **Manufactured Fibers** | | | | | | |
| Acetate | 500 | 230 | 350–375 | 184 | 350 | 177 |
| Acrylic | | | 430–450 | 204–254 | 300 | 149–176 |
| Aramid | Does not melt; carbonizes above 700°F (Nomex) or 900° F (Kevlar) | | | | Do not press | |
| Glass | 2,720 | | 1,560 | 1,778 | Do not press | |
| Lyocell | Does not melt | | | | | |
| Modacrylic | Does not melt | | | | 200–250 | 93–121 |
| Nylon 6 | 419–430 | | 340 | 171 | 300 | 149 |
| Nylon 6,6 | 480–500 | | 445 | 229 | 350 | 177 |
| Olefin | 320–350 | | 285–330 | 127 | 150 | 66 |
| PBI | Does not melt | | Decomposes at 860°F | | | |
| Polyester PET | 482 | | 440–445 | 238 | 325 | 163 |
| Polyester PCDT | 478–490 | | 470 | 254 | 350 | 177 |
| Rayon | Does not melt | | | | 375 | 191 |
| Saran | 350 | 177 | 240 | 115 | Do not press | |
| Spandex | 446 | 230 | 420 | 175 | 300 | 149 |

* Lowest setting on irons: 185–225°F.

**TABLE 3–8** ❖ Specific gravity.*

| FIBER | SPECIFIC GRAVITY (g/cc) |
|---|---|
| Fluorocarbon | 0.8–2.2 |
| Olefin | 0.90–0.91 |
| Nylon | 1.13–1.14 |
| Acrylic | 1.17 |
| Spandex | 1.2 |
| Novoloid | 1.25 |
| Silk | 1.25 |
| Vinal | 1.26 |
| Acetate | 1.32 |
| Wool | 1.32 |
| Vinyon | 1.33–1.43 |
| Polyester | 1.34–1.38 |
| Modacrylic | 1.35 |
| Sulfar | 1.37 |
| Aramid | 1.38–1.44 |
| PBI | 1.43 |
| Rayon | 1.48 |
| Cotton | 1.52 |
| Flax | 1.52 |
| Lyocell | 1.56 |
| Saran | 1.70 |
| Glass | 2.48–2.69 |

* Ratio of weight of a given volume of fiber to an equal volume of water.

**Shrinkage resistance** is the ability of a fabric to retain a given size after care. It is related to the fabric's reaction to moisture or heat. A fabric that shrinks is smaller after care. The item may no longer be attractive or suitable for its original end use. Residual shrinkage refers to additional shrinkage that may occur after the first care cycle.

**Elasticity** or **elastic recovery** is the ability of a fabric to return to its original dimension or shape after elongation (Table 3–10). It is measured as the percentage of return to original length. Since recovery varies with the amount of elongation as well as with the length of time the fabric is stretched, the measurement identifies the percent elongation, or stretch, and the recovery. Fabrics with poor elastic recovery tend to stretch out of shape. Fabrics with good elastic recovery maintain their shape.

**TABLE 3–9** ❖ Resiliency.

| FIBER | RATING |
|---|---|
| Nylon | Excellent |
| Wool | |
| Olefin | Good |
| Acrylic/Modacrylic | |
| Polyester | |
| Silk | Moderate |
| Lyocell | |
| Flax | Poor |
| Cotton | |
| Rayon | |
| Acetate | |

**TABLE 3–10** ❖ Elastic recovery.

| FIBER | % RECOVERY AT 3% STRETCH* |
|---|---|
| Acetate | 48–65 (at 4%) |
| Flax | 65 |
| Cotton | 75 |
| Polyester | 81 |
| Nylon 6,6 | 82–89 |
| Silk | 90 |
| Acrylic | 92 |
| Rayon | 95 (at 2%) |
| Olefin | 96 (at 5%) |
| Nylon 6 | 98–100 |
| Spandex | 99 (at 50%) |
| Wool | 99 |
| Modacrylic | 99.5 (at 2%) |

* Unless otherwise noted.

## Resistance to Chemicals

Fibers differ in their reaction to chemicals. Some fibers are quite resistant to most chemicals. Other fibers are resistant to one group of chemicals but easily harmed by other groups of chemicals. Resistance to chemicals determines appropriateness of care procedures and end uses for fibers. Tables 3–11 and 3–12 summarize fiber reactions to acids and alkalis. Acids are compounds that yield hydrogen ions to alkalis in chemical reactions. Alkalis (bases) are compounds that remove hydrogen ions from acids and combine with the acid in a chemical reaction.

## Resistance to Light

Exposure to light (both natural sunlight and artificial light) may damage fibers. The energy in light, especially in the ultraviolet region of the spectrum, causes irreversible damage to the chemical structure of the fiber. This damage may appear as a yellowing or color change, a slight weakening of the fabric or, eventually, the complete disintegration of the fabric (Table 3–13).

## Environmental Impact

Environmental impact refers to the way the production, use, care, and disposal of a fiber or textile product affects the environment. Many consumers assume that natural fibers have less of an environmental impact than manufactured or synthetic fibers. However, the natural fibers' impact on soil conservation, use of agricultural chemicals, disposal of animal waste, water demands, and

**TABLE 3–11** ❖ Effect of acids.*

| FIBER | EFFECT |
|---|---|
| **Natural Fibers** | |
| Cotton | Harmed |
| Flax | Harmed |
| Silk | Harmed by strong mineral acids, resistant to organic acids |
| Wool | Resistant |
| **Manufactured Fibers** | |
| Acetate | Unaffected by weak acids |
| Acrylic | Resistant to most acids |
| Aramid | Resistant to most acids |
| Glass | Resistant |
| Lyocell | Harmed |
| Modacrylic | Resistant to most acids |
| Nylon | Harmed, especially nylon 6 |
| Olefin | Resistant |
| PBI | Resistant |
| Polyester | Resistant |
| Rayon | Harmed |
| Spandex | Resistant |
| Sulfar | Resistant |

* Examples of acids: organic (acetic, formic); mineral (sulfuric, hydrochloric).

**TABLE 3–12** ❖ Effect of alkalis/bases.*

| FIBER | EFFECT |
|---|---|
| **Natural Fibers** | |
| Cotton | Resistant |
| Flax | Resistant |
| Silk | Harmed |
| Wool | Harmed |
| **Manufactured Fibers** | |
| Acetate | Little effect |
| Acrylic | Resistant to weak alkalis |
| Aramid | Resistant |
| Glass | Resistant |
| Lyocell | Resistant |
| Modacrylic | Resistant |
| Nylon | Resistant |
| Olefin | Highly resistant |
| PBI | Resistant to most alkalis |
| Polyester | Degraded by strong alkalis |
| Rayon | Resistant to weak alkalis |
| Spandex | Resistant |
| Sulfar | Resistant |

* Examples of alkalis: weak (ammonium hydroxide); strong (sodium hydroxide).

**TABLE 3–13** ❖ Light resistance.

| FIBER | RATING |
|---|---|
| Glass | Excellent |
| Acrylic | |
| Modacrylic | to |
| Polyester | |
| Sulfar | Good |
| Lyocell | |
| Flax | |
| Cotton | to |
| Rayon | |
| PBI | |
| Triacetate | Moderate |
| Acetate | |
| Olefin | to |
| Nylon | |
| Wool | |
| Silk | Poor |

cleaning and processing create environmental problems. Since very few textile products are disposed of in a manner that allows for biodegradation, natural fibers do not have even that advantage in modern society. The environmental impact of each of the major consumer fibers will be discussed in the appropriate chapter.

## Care Properties

Any treatments that are required to maintain the new look of a textile product during use, cleaning, or storage are referred to as care. Improper care procedures can result in items that are unattractive, not as durable as expected, and uncomfortable. The way fibers react to water, chemicals, and heat in pressing and drying will be discussed in each fiber chapter. Special storage requirements also will be discussed.

## Cost

Cost is affected by how a fiber is produced, the number and type of modifications present, and how the fiber is marketed. Cost will be addressed in general terms for each fiber. Actual costs for fibers are related to supply of and demand for the fiber as well as costs of raw materials used to grow or produce each fiber.

## Fiber Property Charts

The fibers within each generic family have individual differences. These differences are not reflected in the tables in this chapter, except in a few specific instances. The numerical values are averages, or medians, and are intended as a general characterization of each generic group. (The values were compiled from "Man-Made Fiber Chart," *Textile World,* August 1992, and "Textile Fibers and Their Properties," AATCC Council on Technology, 1977.)

❖

# Fiber Identification

The procedure for identification of the fiber content of a fabric depends on the nature of the sample, the experience of the analyst, and the facilities available. Because laws require the fiber content of apparel and furnishing textiles to be indicated on the label, the consumer may only need to look for identification labels. If a professional wishes to confirm or check the information on the label, burning and some simple solubility tests may be used. These procedures differ in their effectiveness in identifying fibers. Microscopic appearance is most useful for the natural fibers. Solubility and sophisticated spectroscopic procedures are most effective for manufactured fibers.

## Visual Inspection

Visual inspection of a fabric for appearance and hand is always the first step in fiber identification. It is no longer possible to make an identification of the fiber content by appearance and hand alone because manufactured fibers can resemble natural fibers or other manufactured fibers. However, observation of certain characteristics is helpful. These characteristics are apparent to the unaided eye and are visual clues used to narrow the number of possibilities.

1. Length of fiber. Untwist the yarn to determine fiber length. Any fiber can be made in staple length, but not all fibers can be filament. For example, cotton and wool are always staple and never filament.
2. Luster or lack of luster. Manufactured fiber luster may range from harsh and shiny to dull and matte.
3. Body, texture, hand—soft-to-hard, rough-to-smooth, warm-to-cool, or stiff-to-flexible. These aspects relate to fiber size, surface contour, stiffness, and cross-sectional shape.

## Burning Test

The burning test can be used to identify the general chemical composition of a fiber, such as cellulose, protein, mineral, or manufactured polymers, and thus identify the group to which the fiber belongs (Table 3–14). Blends cannot be identified by the burning test. If visual inspection is used along with the burning test, fiber identification can be carried further. For example, if the sample is cellulose and also filament, it is probably rayon; but if it is staple, a positive identification for a specific cellulosic fiber cannot be made.

Be sure to work in a safe, well-ventilated area. Remove paper and other flammable materials from the area. The following are general directions for the burning test:

1. Ravel out and test several yarns from each direction of the fabric to see if they have the same fiber content. Differences in luster, twist, and color indicate that there might be two or more generic fibers in the fabric.
2. Hold the yarn horizontally, as shown in Figure 3–6. When working with long pieces of yarn, it is helpful to roll them into a flat ball or clump, as shown in the figure. Use tweezers to protect your fingers. Feed the yarns slowly into the edge of the flame and observe what happens. Repeat this step several times to check your results.

## Microscopy

A knowledge of fiber structure, obtained by seeing the fibers through the microscope and observing some of the differences among fibers in each group, is helpful in understanding fibers and fabric behavior.

**Figure 3–6** ❖ Fiber identification by the burning test.

**TABLE 3–14** ❖ Identification by burning.

| FIBERS | WHEN APPROACHING FLAME | WHEN IN FLAME | AFTER REMOVAL FROM FLAME | ASH | ODOR |
|---|---|---|---|---|---|
| Cellulose<br>Cotton<br>Flax<br>Lyocell<br>Rayon | Does not fuse or shrink from flame | Burns | Continues to burn, afterglow | Gray, feathery, smooth edge | Burning paper |
| Protein<br>Silk<br>Wool | Curls away from flame | Burns slowly | May be self-extinguishing | Crushable black ash | Burning hair |
| Acetate | Fuses away from flame | Burns with melting | Continues to burn and melt | Brittle black, hard bead | Acrid |
| Acrylic | Fuses away from flame | Burns with melting | Continues to burn and melt | Brittle black, hard bead | Chemical odor |
| Glass | No reaction | Does not burn | No reaction | Fiber remains | None |
| Modacrylic | Fuses away from flame | Burns very slowly with melting | Self-extinguishing, white smoke | Brittle black, hard bead | Chemical odor |
| Nylon | Fuses and shrinks away from flame | Burns slowly with melting; white smoke | May be self-extinguishing | Hard gray or tan bead | Celerylike |
| Olefin | Fuses and shrinks away from flame | Burns with melting | May be self-extinguishing | Hard tan bead | Chemical odor |
| Polyester | Fuses and shrinks away from flame | Burns slowly with melting; black smoke | May be self-extinguishing | Hard black bead | Sweetish odor |
| Saran | Fuses and shrinks away from flame | Burns very slowly with melting | Self-extinguishing | Hard black bead | Chemical odor |
| Spandex | Fuses but does not shrink from flame | Burns with melting | Continues to burn with melting | Soft black ash | Chemical odor |

Identification of the natural fibers is best done by using this procedure. The manufactured fibers are more difficult to identify because many of them look alike and their appearance may be changed by variations in the manufacturing process. Positive identification of the manufactured fibers by microscopy is not possible.

A cross section of the fiber will provide additional information. Longitudinal and cross-sectional photomicrographs of individual fibers are included in the fiber chapters. These may be used for reference when identifying unknown fibers.

The following are directions for using the microscope:

1. Clean the lens, slide, and cover glass.
2. Place a drop of distilled water or glycerine on the slide.
3. Untwist a yarn and place several fibers from the yarn on the slide. Cover with the cover glass and tap to remove air bubbles.
4. Place the slide on the stage of the microscope. Focus with low power first. If the fibers have not been well separated, it will be difficult to focus on a single fiber. Center the fiber or fibers in the viewing field. Then move to a lens with greater magnification. As magnification increases, the size of the viewing field decreases. Thus, if fibers are not in the center of the field when a higher magnification is selected, they may disappear from the viewing field.
5. If a fabric contains two or more fiber types, examine each fiber and both warp and filling yarns.

## Solubility Tests

Solubility tests are used to identify the manufactured fibers by generic class and to confirm identification of natural fibers. Two simple tests, the alkali test for wool and the acetone test for acetate, are described in Chapters 5 and 7, respectively.

**TABLE 3–15** ❖ Solubility tests (in order of increasing strength).

| SOLVENT | FIBER SOLUBILITY |
|---|---|
| 1. Acetic acid, 100%, 20°C | Acetate |
| 2. Acetone, 100%, 20°C | Acetate, modacrylic, vinyon |
| 3. Hydrochloric acid, 20% concentration, 1.096 density, 20°C | Nylon 6; nylon 6,6; vinal |
| 4. Sodium hypochlorite solution, 5%, 20°C | Silk and wool (silk dissolves in 70% sulfuric acid at 38°C), azlon |
| 5. Xylene (meta), 100%, 139°C | Olefin and saran (saran in 1.4 dioxane at 101°C; olefin is not soluble), vinyon |
| 6. Dimethyl formamide, 100%, 90°C | Spandex, modacrylic, acrylic, acetate, vinyon |
| 7. Sulfuric acid, 70% concentration, 38°C | Cotton, flax, rayon, nylon, acetate, silk |
| 8. Cresol (meta), 100%, 139°C | Polyester, nylon, acetate |

Table 3–15 lists solvents from weakest to strongest. Place the specimen in the liquid in the order listed. Although many solvents will dissolve some fibers, following this order will help in identifying the specific fiber in question. Stir the specimen for 5 minutes and note the effect. Fiber, yarns, or small pieces of fabric may be used. Remember that the liquids are hazardous—handle them with care! Use chemical laboratory exhaust hoods, gloves, aprons, and goggles.

## KEY TERMS

Manufactured fiber
Natural fiber
Staple fiber
Filament fiber
Filament tow
Denier
Tex
Fiber crimp
Fabric crimp
Generic group
Polymerization
Polymer
Degree of polymerization
Orientation
Stretching
Drawing
Hydrogen bonds
Van der Waals forces
Luster
Drape
Texture
Hand
Abrasion resistance
Flexibility
Tenacity
Elongation
Electrical conductivity
Absorbency
Hydrophilic
Hydrophobic
Hygroscopic
Heat conductivity
Heat retention
Heat sensitivity
Density
Resiliency
Dimensional stability
Shrinkage resistance
Elasticity
Elastic recovery

## QUESTIONS

1. Define each of the key terms as well as the terms listed in Table 3–1.
2. Differentiate between the following pairs of related terms:
   elongation and elasticity
   absorbency and dyeability
   loft and resiliency
   heat conductivity and heat sensitivity
3. How would performance change when a fiber's shape is changed from round to trilobal?
4. What differences in performance might you expect from fibers used to produce a T-shirt, carpet in a movie theater, and an outdoor banner?
5. Describe polymerization and the possible arrangements of molecules within fibers.
6. What would be an efficient procedure to identify the fiber content of an unknown fabric?

## SUGGESTED READINGS

AATCC Council on Technology (1977). *Textile Fibers and Their Properties.* Research Triangle Park, NC: American Association of Textile Chemists and Colorists.

American Fiber Manufacturers Association (1988). *Manufactured Fiber Fact Book.* Washington, DC: American Fiber Manufacturers Association.

American Society for Testing and Materials (1995). *Annual Book of ASTM Standards, Vol. 7.* Philadelphia: ASTM.

"Man-Made Fiber Chart" (August, 1992). *Textile World.*

Tortora, P. G., and Merkel, R. S. (1996). *Fairchild's Dictionary of Textiles,* 7th ed. New York: Fairchild Publications.

*Chapter 4*

# Natural Cellulosic Fibers

## OBJECTIVES

- To identify cellulosic fibers.
- To understand characteristics common to all cellulosic fibers and the differences among those most commonly used.
- To know the basic steps in processing these fibers.
- To integrate the properties of natural cellulosic fibers with market needs.

All plants contain fibrous bundles that give strength and pliability to the stems, leaves, and roots. Natural cellulosic fibers are obtained from plants whose fibers can be readily and economically separated from the rest of the plant. These fibers can be classified according to the portion of the plant from which they are removed (see Table 4–1).

Cotton is an example of a **seed fiber,** a fiber that grows within a pod or boll from developing seeds. Flax is an example of a **bast fiber,** a fiber that is obtained from the stem of the plant. Sisal is an example of a **leaf fiber,** a fiber removed from the veins or ribs of a leaf.

These fibers are cellulosic but differ in percentage of cellulose present and in physical structure. The arrangement of the molecular chains in fibers, although similar, varies in orientation and length, so that performance characteristics related to these aspects differ. Fabrics made from these fibers differ in appearance and hand but react to chemicals in essentially the same way and require similar care. Properties common to all cellulosic fibers are summarized in Table 4–2.

This chapter discusses natural cellulosic fibers. Several of these fibers have limited use in the United States; nevertheless, a discussion of these fibers has a place in an introductory textiles course because some of these fibers are imported into the United States and others may be encountered during travel or in certain careers. Although these fibers are not of great importance to the U.S. economy, they may be significant to the economy of the countries where they are produced. In addition, while many of the fibers have limited use as apparel, they are extremely important in the furnishings industry. There are, of course, many other natural cellulosic fibers that will not be discussed because of their extremely limited use.

❖

# Seed Fibers

Seed fibers are those from the seed pod of the plant. By far the most important seed fiber is cotton. This section discusses cotton and some minor seed fibers.

The first step in the production of seed fibers is to separate the fiber from the seed. (The seed of some seed fibers is used in producing oil and feed for animals.) After the seed and fiber have been separated, the fibers may be carded into a parallel arrangement for production of yarns or used for fiberfill.

**Table 4–1** ❖ Natural cellulosic fibers.

| SEED FIBERS | BAST FIBERS | LEAF FIBERS |
|---|---|---|
| Cotton | Flax | Piña |
| Kapok | Ramie | Abaca |
| Coir | Hemp | Sisal |
| | Jute | Henequen |
| | Kenaf | |

## Cotton

**Cotton** is the most important apparel fiber. In 1994, cotton met 46.1 percent of total world fiber demand and 56 percent of the worldwide demand for apparel fiber. It is grown in more than 80 countries where it is an important cash crop. Cotton has a combination of properties—pleasing appearance, comfort, easy care, moderate cost, and durability—that make it ideal for warm-weather clothing, active sportswear, work clothes, upholstery, draperies, area rugs, towels, and bedding. Even though other fibers have encroached on the markets that cotton once dominated, the cotton look is maintained. Cotton is an important part of many blended fabrics.

Cotton cloth was used by the people of ancient China, Egypt, India, Mexico, and Peru. In the Americas, naturally colored cotton was grown and used extensively. The cotton spinning and weaving industry began in India.

Cotton was grown in the southern U.S. colonies as soon as they were established. Throughout the 1600s and 1700s, cotton fibers were separated from the cotton seeds by hand. This was a very time-consuming and tedious job; a worker could separate only one pound of cotton fiber from the seeds in a day.

With the invention of the saw tooth cotton gin by Eli Whitney in 1793, things changed. The gin could process 50 pounds of cotton in a day; thus more cotton could be prepared for spinning. Within the next 20 years, a series of spinning and weaving inventions in England mechanized fabric production. The Southern states were able to meet Britain's greatly increased demand for raw cotton. By 1859, U.S. production was 4.5 million bales of cotton—two-thirds of world production. Cotton was the leading U.S. export.

The picture again changed dramatically during the Civil War. U.S. cotton production decreased to 200,000 bales in 1864, and Britain looked to other countries to fill its needs. After the war, Western states began producing cotton.

During the time of rapidly expanding cotton production in the Southern states, the New England states were building factories to manufacture yarn and fabric. Most spinning and weaving of U.S. fabrics took place in the New England states.

After the Civil War, the Southern states began building spinning and weaving mills. Between World War I and World War II, most of the New England mills

**TABLE 4–2** ❖ Properties common to all cellulosic fibers.

| PROPERTIES | IMPORTANCE TO CONSUMER |
|---|---|
| Good absorbency | Comfortable for summer wear and furnishings<br>Good for towels, diapers, handkerchiefs, and active sportswear, if sufficiently pliable |
| Good conductor of heat | Sheer fabrics cool for summer wear |
| Ability to withstand high temperature | Fabrics can be boiled or autoclaved to make them relatively germ free; no special precautions in pressing |
| Low resiliency | Fabrics wrinkle badly unless finished for recovery |
| Lacks loft; packs well into compact yarns | Tight, high-count fabrics can be made<br>Make wind-resistant fabrics |
| Good conductor of electricity | Do not build up static |
| Heavy fibers (density of ± 1.5) | Fabrics are heavier than comparable fabrics of other fibers |
| Harmed by mineral acids, minimal damage by organic acids | Acid stains should be removed immediately |
| Attacked by mildew | Store clean items under dry conditions |
| Resistant to moths, but not resistant to crickets and silverfish | Store clean items under dry conditions |
| Flammable | Ignite quickly, burn freely with an afterglow and gray, feathery ash; loosely constructed garments should not be worn near an open flame; furnishings should meet required codes |
| Moderate resistance to sunlight | Draperies should be lined |

moved south. Factors important in this move included proximity to the supply of cotton, cheaper power, less expensive nonunion labor, and special relocation incentives from state and local governments. By 1950, 80 percent of the mills were in the South. Yet in the 1980s, many mills closed because of increased costs and competition from imports.

## Production of Cotton

Cotton grows in any part of the world where the growing season is long and the climate is temperate to hot with adequate rainfall or irrigation. Cellulose will not form if the temperature is below 70°F. In the United States, cotton is grown from southern Virginia west to central California and south of that line.

Major producers of cotton are the U.S. (22.9 percent), China (20.0 percent), India (11.4 percent), Eastern Europe (9.9 percent), Pakistan (9.7 percent), Turkey (4.0 percent), Brazil (3.4 percent), and Egypt (1.2 percent). Worldwide production of cotton was over 88 million bales in 1995. Mechanization and weed control have reduced the number of hours required to produce a bale of cotton and increased productivity.

Factors affecting the U.S. production of cotton include the value of the dollar compared with other currencies, imports of cotton apparel and fabrics, changes in government incentives for growing cotton, weather conditions, and comparable changes in other countries.

Cotton grows on bushes 3–6 feet high. The blossom appears, falls off, and the *boll* or seed pod begins its growth. Inside the boll are 7–8 seeds from which the fibers grow. When the boll is ripe, it splits open and the fluffy white fibers spread out (Figure 4–1). Each cotton seed may have as many as 20,000 fibers growing from its surface.

Cotton is picked by machine or by hand (Figure 4–2). Machine-picked cotton contains many immature fibers—an inescapable result of stripping a cotton plant. After picking, the cotton is taken to a **gin** to remove the fibers from the seed. Figure 4–3 shows a saw gin, in which the whirling saws pick up the fiber and carry it to a knifelike comb, which blocks the seeds and permits the fiber to be carried through. The fibers, called **lint,** are pressed into bales weighing 480 pounds, ready for sale to a spinning mill.

After ginning, the seeds are covered with very short fibers—⅛ inch in length—called **linters.** The linters are removed from the seeds and are used to a limited extent as raw material in producing rayon and acetate. Linters also are converted into cellophane, photographic film, fingernail polish, and methylcellulose used in makeup and chewing gum. The seeds are crushed to obtain cottonseed oil and meal.

Recent advances in plant breeding have produced cottons that are insect, herbicide, and stress tolerant. Cotton breeders have focused their efforts on improving the fiber properties of the creamy white Upland and long-staple fibers related to product performance. Over the last fifteen years, cotton breeders have improved the strength of cotton by 19 percent so that fibers can be processed at higher speeds and fabrics are more durable. In addition, fiber length has been increased by 5 percent so that yarns are finer and more uniform. Current efforts in plant breeding continue to

**FIGURE 4–1** ❖ Opened cotton boll. (COURTESY OF NATIONAL COTTON COUNCIL OF AMERICA.)

focus on producing cotton varieties with better insect, disease, and herbicide resistance and with enhanced properties for better processing ease and consumer performance. In addition, efforts continue to focus on producing **naturally colored cotton** fibers of high yield and good performance characteristics in a wider range of colors.

## Physical Structure of Cotton

Raw cotton is usually creamy white in color, but small quantities of naturally colored cotton are produced. The fiber is a single cell, which grows out of the seed as a hollow cylindrical tube over one thousand times as long as it is thick.

**LENGTH** Staple length is very important because it affects how the fiber is handled during spinning and relates to fiber fineness and fiber tensile strength. Longer cotton fibers are finer and make stronger yarns.

Cotton fibers range in length from $\frac{1}{2}$ inch to 2 inches, depending on the variety. Three groups of cotton are commercially important:

1. Upland cottons, which are $\frac{7}{8}$–1$\frac{1}{4}$ inches in length, were developed from cottons native to Mexico and Central America. This cotton from *Gossypium hirsutum* is the predominant type of cotton produced in the U.S. Approximately 97 percent of the U.S. crop is one of the Upland varieties.
2. Long-staple cottons, which are 1$\frac{5}{6}$–1$\frac{1}{2}$ inches in length, were developed from Egyptian and South American cottons. Varieties include American **Pima,** **Egyptian,** American Egyptian, and **Sea Island** cottons. Cotton from *Gossypium barbadense* is grown in the southwestern U.S. and is about 3 percent of the crop.

**FIGURE 4–2** ❖ Cotton field with harvester. (COURTESY OF NATIONAL COTTON COUNCIL OF AMERICA.)

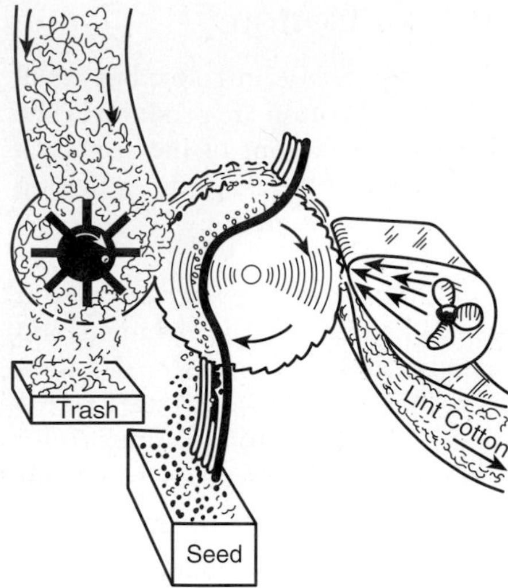


**FIGURE 4–3** ❖ Cotton gin.

3. Short-staple cottons, *Gossypium arboreum* and *Gossypium herbaceum,* are less than ¾ inch in length and are produced primarily in India and eastern Asia.

Long-staple fibers are of higher quality because they can be made into softer, smoother, stronger, and more lustrous fabrics. Because they command a higher price and less is produced than of the medium- and short-staple lengths, they are sometimes identified on a label or tag as Pima, Supima, Egyptian, or Sea Island. Or they may be referred to as long-staple or extra-long-staple (ELS) cotton.

**DISTINCTIVE PARTS** The cotton fiber is made up of a cuticle, primary wall, secondary wall, and lumen

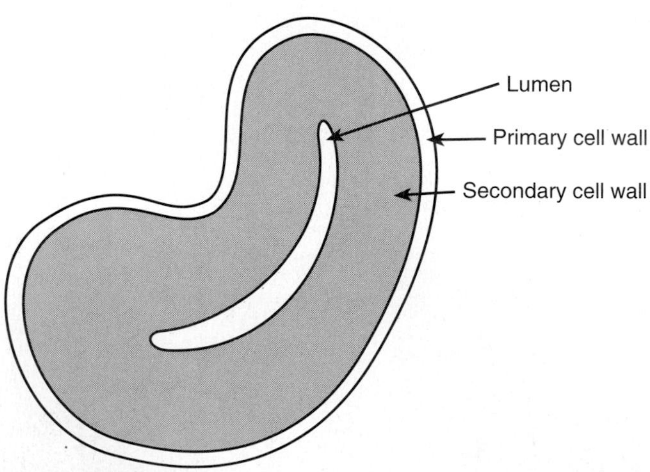


**FIGURE 4–4** ❖ Cross section of mature cotton fiber.

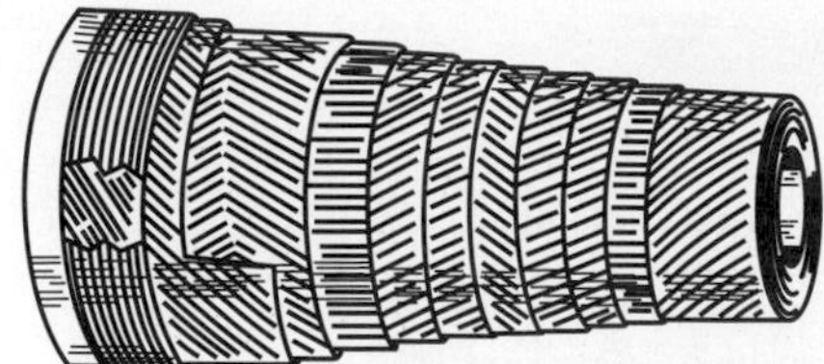

**FIGURE 4–5** ❖ Layers of cellulose (schematic).

(Figure 4–4). The fiber grows to almost full length as a hollow tube before the secondary wall begins to form.

The **cuticle** is a waxlike film covering the primary, or outer, wall. The *secondary wall* is made up of layers of cellulose (Figure 4–5).

The layers deposited at night differ in density from those deposited during the day; this causes *growth rings,* which can be seen in the cross section. The cellulose layers are composed of *fibrils*—bundles of cellulose chains—arranged spirally. At some points the fibrils reverse direction. These *reverse spirals* (Figure 4–6) are important in the development of convolutions that contribute to elastic recovery and elongation of the fiber. They are also 15–30 percent weaker than the rest of the secondary cell wall.

Cellulose is deposited daily for 20–30 days until, in the mature fiber, the fiber tube is almost filled. The **lumen** is the central canal, through which nourishment travels during fiber development. When the fiber matures, dried nutrients in the lumen may result in dark areas visible under the microscope.

**CONVOLUTIONS** **Convolutions** are ribbonlike twists that characterize cotton (Figure 4–7). When the fibers mature, the boll opens, the fibers dry out, and the central canal collapses. Reverse spirals in the secondary wall cause the fibers to twist. The twist forms a natural crimp that enables the fibers to cohere to one another.

**FIGURE 4–6** ❖ Reverse spirals in cotton fiber.

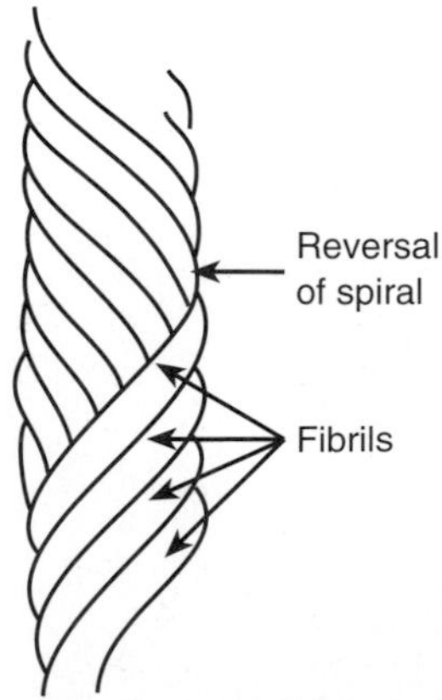

Despite its short length, cotton is one of the most spinnable fibers. The convolutions can be a disadvantage, since dirt collects in the twists, requiring vigorous washing to remove. Long-staple cotton has about 300 convolutions per inch; short-staple cotton has less than 200.

**FINENESS** Cotton fibers vary from 16 to 20 micrometers in diameter. The cross-sectional shape varies with the maturity of the fiber. Immature fibers tend to be U-shaped with a thin cell wall. Mature fibers are more nearly circular, with a thick cell wall and a very small central canal. Every cotton boll contains some immature fibers. The proportion of immature to mature fibers can cause problems in spinning and dyeing processes. Notice in Figure 4–7 the variation in size and shape of the fibers.

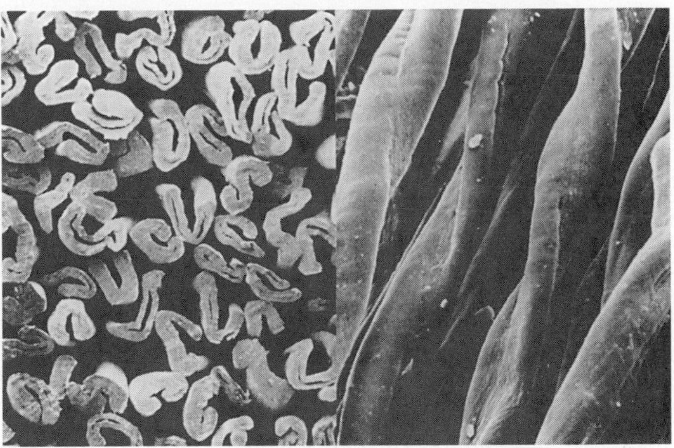

**FIGURE 4–7** ❖ Photomicrographs of cotton: cross-sectional view (left); longitudinal view (right). (COURTESY OF THE BRITISH TEXTILE TECHNOLOGY GROUP.)

**COLOR** Cotton is available in a range of colors. Naturally creamy white is highly desirable because it can be dyed or printed to meet fashion and consumer needs. These fibers may yellow or become more beige as they age. If it rains just before harvest, these fibers become grayer.

Naturally colored cotton fibers have been cultivated for thousands of years. As commercial production replaced hand processes, these fibers declined in importance. By the early twentieth century, they had become difficult to find. However, with the current interest in minimizing environmental impact, interest in naturally colored cottons has resurfaced. Naturally colored cottons produce less fiber per acre, but sell for about twice the price of creamy white cotton. Naturally brown, rust, red, beige, and green cottons have been on the market for several years. These colors deepen with age and care, which is contrary to the aging process of most colored fabrics. (See Figure 4–8.) Colored cottons are shorter and have less uniform properties than the white cottons, primarily because only recently have plant breeders been concentrating on improving their yield, color range, and properties related to product and spinning performance.

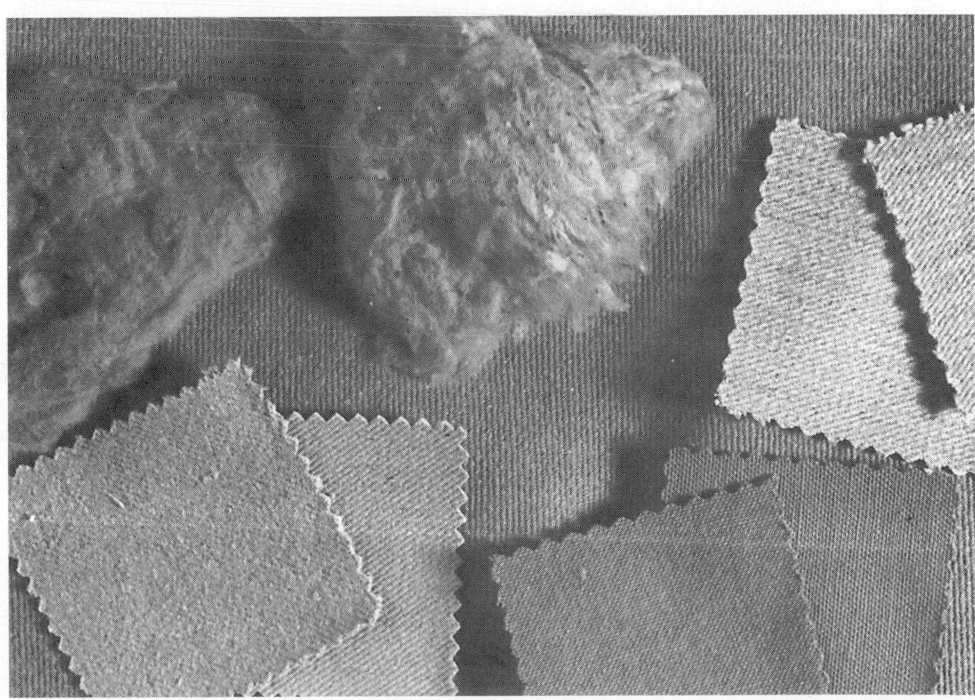

**FIGURE 4–8** ❖ Naturally colored cotton fibers and fabrics. Fabrics (top swatches of pairs) become darker with laundering.

**FIGURE 4–9** ❖ Cotton classed as 1 5/32 inch contains fibers that range in length from 1 5/8 inch to less than 1/8 inch. (COURTESY OF UNITED STATES DEPARTMENT OF AGRICULTURE.)

Naturally colored cottons are produced in Russia, India, South and Central America, and the U.S., mostly in Arizona and Texas. Plant breeders hope to add blue, lavender, and yellow to the current market colors.

Picking and ginning affect the appearance of cotton fibers. Carefully picked cotton is cleaner. Well-ginned cotton tends to be more uniform in appearance and more uniform in color. Poorly ginned cotton has brown flecks in it called *trash,* such as bits of leaf, stem, or dirt. These brown flecks decrease the quality of the fiber. Fabrics made from such fibers include utility cloth and may be fashionable when a "natural" look is popular.

## Classification of Cotton

Grading and classing of cotton is done by hand and by machine, with machine HVI (high-volume instrument) systems becoming increasingly important. Inspection of staple length and color compare the cotton from the bale with standards prepared by the United States Department of Agriculture.

Cotton classification describes the quality of cotton in terms of grade, staple fiber length, character, and fiber strength. Fiber length classifications for cotton include very short-staple cotton (less than .25 inch); short-staple cotton (.25 to .94 inch); medium-staple cotton (.94 to 1.13 inches); ordinary long-staple cotton (1.13 to 1.38 inches); and extra-long-staple cotton (greater than 1.38 inches). *Staple length* is based on the length of a representative bundle of fibers from a bale of cotton. There are 19 staple lengths ranging from less than 13/16 inch to 1 3/8 inches and beyond. A good cotton classer must be consistently able to tell differences in length of 1/32 of an inch. Actually, a sample classified as 1 5/32 inch will have fibers ranging in length from 1/8 inch to 1 5/8 inches as shown in Figure 4–9.

Grade refers to the color of the fiber and the absence of dirt, leaf matter, seed particles, motes or dead fibers, and tangles of fiber. Mote fibers will not absorb dyes; they lower fiber quality and cause defects in fabrics. The best quality grade is lustrous, silky, white, and clean. There are 39 grades of cotton. The predominant grade of cotton produced in the United States is strict low-middling cotton. *Strict* in this case means "better than."

This grading system is used primarily for the creamy white fibers that continue to dominate the market. Color is described in terms that range from white to light-spotted, spotted, tinged, and yellow. Color also is described in terms of lightness to darkness: plus, light gray, and gray. This factor of appearance is a combination of grayness and the amount of leaf present in white cotton grades.

Character refers to other fiber aspects including maturity, smoothness and uniformity of fibers within the bale, fiber fineness, strength, and convolutions. Micronaire values that reflect both fineness and maturity are sometimes assessed. Character refers to the amount of processing necessary to produce a good white fabric for commercial use. Because of yearly variations in growing conditions and variations in geographic locations, yarn and fabric producers carefully select and blend cotton so that cotton fabrics and products are as uniform as possible.

Cotton is a commodity crop. It is sold by grade and staple length. Strict low-middling cotton is used in mass-produced cotton goods and in cotton/synthetic blends. Better grades of cotton and longer-staple cotton are used in better quality shirtings and sheets. Extra-long-staple American Egyptian cotton usually is identified by the terms *Pima* and *Supima* because of its higher quality and price. Pima is used in sweaters, blouses and shirts, underwear, sheeting, and towels.

## Chemical Composition and Molecular Arrangement of Cotton

Cotton, when picked, is about 94 percent cellulose; in finished fabrics it is 99 percent cellulose. Like all cellulose fibers, cotton contains carbon, hydrogen, and oxygen with reactive hydroxyl (OH) groups. The basic unit of the cellulose molecule is *glucose*. Cotton may have as many as 10,000 glucose units per molecule. The molecular chains are arranged in spiral form.

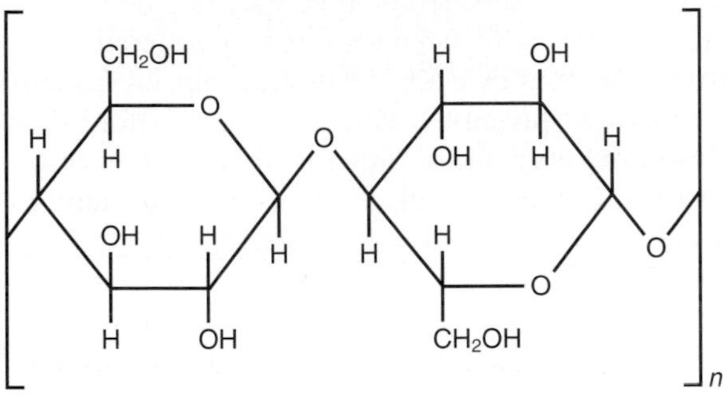

## Chemical Nature of Cellulose

The chemical reactivity of cellulose is related to the hydroxyl groups (OH groups) of the glucose unit. These groups react readily with moisture, dyes, and many finishes. Chemicals such as chlorine bleaches break the molecular chain of the cellulose by attacking the oxygen atom between the two ring units or within the ring, rupturing the chain or ring.

The cellulose molecule is a long, linear chain of glucose units. The length of the chain is a factor in fiber strength.

Cotton can be altered by using chemical treatments or finishes. Mercerization (treating yarns or fabrics with sodium hydroxide, NaOH) causes a permanent physical change. The fiber swells and the cross section becomes rounder. Mercerization increases absorbency and improves the dyeability of cotton yarns and fabrics. Liquid ammonia is used as an alternative to several preparation finishes, especially mercerization. Fabrics treated with ammonia have good luster and dyeability. These fabrics are not as stiff and harsh when treated to be wrinkle resistant compared to mercerized wrinkle-resistant fabrics.

## Properties of Cotton

Cotton is a comfortable fiber. Appropriate for year-round use, it is the fiber most preferred for many furnishings and for warm-weather clothing, especially where the climate is hot and humid. Reviewing the fiber property tables in Chapter 3 will help when comparing cotton's performance to that of other fibers.

**AESTHETIC** Cotton fabrics certainly have consumer acceptance. Cotton fabrics have a matte appearance. Their low luster is the standard that has been retained with cotton/polyester blends in apparel and furnishing fabrics.

Long-staple cotton fibers contribute luster to fabrics. Mercerized and ammonia-treated cotton fabrics have a soft, pleasant luster as a result of the chemical finishes; cotton sateen's luster is due to a combination of weave structure and finishes.

Drape, luster, texture, and hand are affected by choice of yarn size and type, fabric structure, and finish. Cotton fabrics range from soft, sheer batiste, to crisp, sheer voile, to fine chintz, and to sturdy denim and corduroy.

**DURABILITY** Cotton is a medium-strength fiber having a dry breaking tenacity of 3.5–4.0 g/d (grams per denier). It is stronger when wet: wet breaking tenacity is 4.5–5.0 g/d. Long-staple cotton produces stronger yarns because there are more contact points between the fibers when they are twisted together. Because of its higher wet strength, cotton can stand rough handling during laundering and in use.

Abrasion resistance is good. Obviously, heavy fabrics will be more abrasion resistant than thinner fabrics. The elongation of cotton is low, 3 percent, and it has low elasticity.

**COMFORT** Cotton makes very comfortable skin-contact fabrics because of its high absorbency, soft hand, and good heat and electrical conductivity (static buildup is not a problem). It has no surface characteristics that might be irritating to the skin, an important factor to those with tender skin. Cotton has a moisture regain of 7–11 percent. When cotton becomes wet, the fibers swell and become somewhat plastic. This property makes it possible to give a smooth, flat finish to cotton fabrics in pressing or finishing and makes high-count woven fabrics water repellent. However, as cotton fabrics absorb more moisture in damp conditions, they feel wet or clammy and may be too absorbent to be comfortable.

Still, cotton is a good fiber to use in hot and humid weather. The fibers absorb moisture and feel good against the skin in high humidity. The fiber ends in the spun yarn hold the fabric slightly off the skin for greater comfort. Moisture passes freely through the fabric, thus aiding evaporation and cooling.

**APPEARANCE RETENTION** Overall appearance retention is moderate. Cotton has very low resiliency. The hydrogen bonds holding the molecular chains together are weak, and when fabrics are bent or crushed, particularly in the presence of moisture, the chains move freely to new positions. When pressure is removed, there are no forces within the fibers to pull the chains back to their original positions, so the fabrics stay wrinkled. Creases can be pressed in and wrinkles can be removed, but wrinkling during use remains a problem.

Unless cotton fibers are given a durable-press finish or blended with polyester and given a durable-press finish, they wrinkle easily during both use and care.

All-cotton fabrics shrink unless they have been given a durable-press finish or a shrinkage-resistant finish. Untreated cottons shrink less when washed in cool water and drip dried; they shrink more when washed in hot water and dried in a hot dryer. When they are used again, they tend to recover some of their original dimensions—think of cotton denim jeans or fitted cotton sheets.

All-cotton fabrics that have been given a wrinkle-resistant or durable-press finish or that have been treated for shrinkage generally should not shrink noticeably. However, a little more care may be needed with handwoven cotton fabrics or those of lower quality, short-staple fibers, unless specific information about shrinkage is available on the label.

Elastic recovery is moderate. Cotton recovers 75 percent from 2–5 percent stretch. In other words, cotton tends to stay stretched out in areas of stress, such as in the elbow or knee areas of garments.

**CARE** Cotton can be washed with strong detergents and requires no special care during washing and drying. White cottons can be washed in hot water. Many dyed cottons retain their color better if washed in warm, not hot, water. If items are not heavily soiled, cold water cleans them adequately. Cotton releases all types of soil readily, but for some furnishing and apparel uses soil-resistant finishes are desirable. Chlorine bleach should be considered a spot-removal method and should not be used routinely, because excessive bleaching weakens cellulosic fibers.

Less wrinkling occurs in the dryer if the cotton items are removed when they are dry and not left in the dryer longer than necessary. Cotton fabrics respond best to steam pressing or ironing while damp. Fabrics made of cotton and a heat-sensitive fiber need to be ironed at a lower temperature to avoid melting the heat-sensitive fiber. Cotton is not thermoplastic; it can be ironed safely at high temperatures. However, cotton burns readily.

Cotton draperies should be dry cleaned. Cotton upholstery may be steam cleaned with caution. If shrinkage occurs, the fabric may split or rupture where it is attached to the frame.

Cottons should be stored clean and dry. In damp or humid conditions, mildew can form. Mildew first appears as little black dots, but it can actually eat through the fabric, causing holes if enough time elapses. If the clothing merely smells of mildew, it can be laundered or bleached and it will be fine. But if the mildew has progressed to visible spots, they may not be removable. More extensive damage cannot be corrected.

Cotton is harmed by acids. Fruit and fruit juice stains should be treated promptly with cold water before they set and become even more difficult to remove. Cotton is not greatly harmed by alkalis. Cotton is resistant to organic solvents so that it can be safely dry cleaned.

Cotton oxidizes in sunlight, which causes white and pastel cottons to yellow and all cotton to degrade. Some dyes are especially sensitive to sunlight and when used in window treatment fabrics the dyed areas disintegrate.

Table 4–3 summarizes cotton's performance in apparel and furnishing fabrics.

## Environmental Impact of Cotton

Since cotton is a natural fiber, many consumers interested in selecting products that minimize negative environmental impact believe it is a good choice. Although cotton can be considered a renewable resource, it cannot be produced without some environmental impact.

**TABLE 4–3** ❖ Summary of the performance of cotton in apparel and furnishing fabrics.

| | |
|---|---|
| **Aesthetic** | **Attractive** |
| Luster | Matte, pleasant |
| Drape | Soft to stiff |
| Texture | Pleasant |
| Hand | Smooth to rough |
| **Durability** | **Good** |
| Abrasion resistance | Good |
| Tenacity | Good |
| Elongation | Poor |
| **Comfort** | **Excellent** |
| Absorbency | Excellent |
| Thermal retention | Poor |
| **Appearance retention** | **Moderate** |
| Resiliency | Poor |
| Dimensional stability | Moderate |
| Elastic recovery | Moderate |
| **Recommended care** | Machine wash and dry (apparel)<br>Steam or dry clean with caution (furnishings) |

Current mainstream farming methods make extensive use of agricultural chemicals to fertilize the soil, fight insects and disease, control plant growth, and strip the leaves for harvest. Excess rain can create problems with runoff contaminated with these chemicals, many of which are toxic to other plants, insects, animals, and people. Additional problems with cotton relate to the intensive use of water, energy, and chemicals to clean the fiber, produce cotton fabrics, and finish and dye them.

Cotton is a water-intensive crop requiring at least 20 inches of rain per year. Cotton may be produced on land with inadequate rainfall that is supplemented by irrigation. In addition, tilling the soil contributes to potential problems with water and wind erosion of the soil. In many areas of the world cotton may be the only cash crop in the region, creating potential disastrous situations if the crop fails or prices fall.

Soil and natural waxes must be removed from the raw fiber before it is processed into yarn. In order to add color in dyeing and printing, cotton is bleached in a chemical and water solution and rinsed. Dyes, pigments, and finishing chemicals add to the appeal of cotton products from a consumer's perspective. All these steps make extensive use of water, other chemicals, and heat. The industry has made significant advances in recycling, reducing waste, and cleaning up waste water, but the net environmental effect of these processes continues to be a concern.

In an effort to provide consumers and producers with more information at point of purchase, several terms may be used to describe cotton grown under more environmentally friendly conditions. **Organic cotton** is produced following state fiber certification standards on land where organic farming practices have been used for at least three years. No synthetic commercial pesticides or fertilizers are used in organic farming. **Transition cotton** is produced on land where organic farming is practiced, but the three-year minimum has not been met. **Green cotton** describes cotton fabric that has been washed with mild natural-based soap, but it has not been bleached or treated with other chemicals, except possibly natural dyes. The term **conventional cotton** describes all other cotton.

Some retailers and manufacturers have made a commitment to use only organic cotton in their products. (See Figure 4–10.) Organic and transition cotton are approximately twice as expensive as conventional cotton. The additional costs are related to the lower yield per acre of these fibers, requirements for processing in facilities that are free of hazardous chemicals like formaldehyde, and the smaller quantities of fibers that are processed and sold. Unfortunately, many consumers are not willing to pay the additional cost for products that have no apparent differences and that demonstrate no obvious benefit to them.

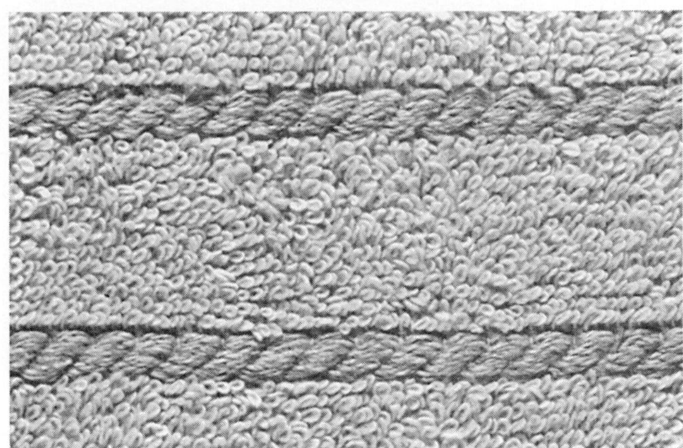

**FIGURE 4–10** ❖ Organic cotton and linen washcloth. Fibers were grown without the aid of commercial fertilizers, herbicides, or insecticides. No bleaches or dyes were used in producing the fabric.

## Identification of Cotton

Microscopic identification of cotton is relatively easy. Convolutions are generally clearly visible along the fiber. Burn tests will verify cellulose, but a more precise identification is not possible with this procedure. Fiber length may be of assistance in determining content, but remember that long fibers can be broken or cut to resemble shorter fibers in length. Cotton is soluble in strong mineral acids.

## Uses of Cotton

Cotton is the single most important apparel fiber in the United States. As a part of the total fiber market, cotton accounted for the following percentages of fiber used in these categories in 1994:

58 percent of apparel
63 percent of furnishings
10 percent of industrial uses

Focusing on cotton alone, of the 5.95 billion pounds of cotton consumed in the United States in 1994,

63 percent was used in apparel
29 percent was used for furnishings
8 percent was used for industrial products or was exported

The greatest amount of cotton is used for apparel. All-cotton fabrics are used where comfort is of primary importance and appearance retention is not as important, or where a more casual fabric is acceptable. Cotton blended with polyester in wrinkle-resistant fabrics is easy to find on the market, both in ready-to-wear apparel and in over-the-counter fabrics. Most blends retain the pleasant appearance of cotton, have the same or increased durability, are less comfortable in conditions of extreme heat and humidity or high physical activity, and have better appearance retention during wear in comparison with 100 percent cotton fabrics. However, removal of oily soil is a greater problem with blends.

Cotton is a very important furnishing fabric because of its versatility, natural comfort, and ease of finishing and dyeing. Towels are mostly cotton—softness, absorbency, wide range of colors, and washability are important in this end use. Durability is increased in the base fabric, as well as in the selvages and hems by sometimes blending polyester with the cotton. However, the loops of terry towels are cotton so that maximum absorbency is retained.

Sheets and pillowcases of all cotton or cotton/polyester blends are available in percale, flannelette, and muslin. Blend levels and counts vary a great deal. Spring- and fall-weight blankets made of cotton are also on the market. Cotton bedspreads are available in a variety of weights and fabric types.

Draperies, curtains, upholstery fabrics, slipcovers, rugs, and wall coverings are made of cotton. Cotton upholstery fabrics are attractive and durable, comfortable, and easy to spot clean. They retain their appearance well. Resiliency is not a problem with heavyweight fabrics that are stretched over the furniture frame. Cotton is susceptible to abrasion, waterborne stains, and shrinkage if cleaning is too vigorous or incorrect. Small area rugs of cotton can be machine washed.

Medical, surgical, and sanitary supplies are frequently made of cotton. Since cotton can be autoclaved (heated to a high temperature to sanitize it), it is very important in hospitals. Absorbency, washability, and low static buildup are also important properties in these uses.

Industrial uses include abrasives, book bindings, luggage and handbags, shoes and slippers, tobacco cloth, and woven wiping cloths.

Cotton Incorporated is the organization that promotes the use of cotton by consumers. It also promotes the use of all-cotton and Natural Blend® fabrics with at least 60 percent cotton (see Figure 4–11).

**FIGURE 4–11** ❖ Cotton® seal (top) for 100 percent cotton fabrics and apparel, and Natural Blend® seal (bottom) for fabrics and apparel made of at least 60 percent cotton. (COURTESY OF COTTON INCORPORATED.)

## Coir

**Coir** is obtained from the fibrous mass between the outer shell and the husk of the coconut. It is sometimes sold as coco fiber. The fibers are removed by soaking the husk in saline water. Sri Lanka is the major producer of coir fiber. Coir is a very stiff fiber that is naturally cinnamon-brown. It can be bleached and dyed. It has good abrasion, water, and weather resistance. Coir is an important fiber for indoor and outdoor mats, rugs, and floor tiles. With its stiff, wiry texture and coarse size, coir provides strong visual interest and produces fabrics whose weave, pattern, or design is clearly visible. These floor textiles are extremely durable and blend with furnishings of many styles.

## Kapok

**Kapok** is obtained from the seed of the Java kapok or silk cotton tree. The fiber is lightweight and soft. Kapok is hollow and very buoyant, but it quickly breaks down. The fiber is difficult to spin into yarns, so it is used primarily as fiberfill in some imported items from Java, South America, and India.

❖

# BAST FIBERS

Bast fibers come from the stem of the plant. Hand labor may be used to process bast fibers, and production has flourished in countries where labor is cheap. Since the fiber extends into the root, harvesting is done by pulling up the plant or cutting it close to the ground to keep fiber length as long as possible. After harvesting, the seeds are removed by pulling the plant through a machine in a process called **rippling.**

Bast fibers lie in bundles in the stem of plant just under the outer covering or bark. They are sealed together by a substance composed of pectins, waxes, and gums. To loosen the fibers so that they can be removed from the stalk, the pectin must be decomposed by a process called **retting** (bacterial rotting). There are some individual fiber differences in the process, but the major steps are the same. Retting can be done in the fields (dew retting); in ponds or pools (pool retting); in tanks (tank retting), where the temperature and bacterial count can be carefully controlled; or with chemicals such as sodium hydroxide. Chemical retting is a much faster process than any other method. However, extra care must be taken or irreversible damage can occur to the fiber. Retting can create problems with water quality if retting water is released directly into streams or lakes.

After the stems have been rinsed and dried, the woody portion is removed by breaking the outer covering, a process called **scutching,** in which the stalks are passed between fluted metal rollers. Most of the fibers are separated from one another, and the short and irregular fibers are removed by **hackling,** or combing. This final step removes any remaining woody portion and arranges the fibers in a parallel fashion. As an example, Figure 4–12 shows flax at different stages of processing.

The processes of spinning, weaving, and finishing cause further separation of the fibers. With most bast fibers, length and fineness dimensions are not clearly definable. The **primary fibers** are bound together in fiber bundles and never completely separate into individual fibers. These fiber bundles, as they are commonly used, are made up of many primary fibers. It is this characteristic of fiber bundles that give bast fiber fabrics their characteristic thick-and-thin yarns.

**FIGURE 4–12** ❖ Flax fiber at different stages of processing.

## Flax

**Flax** is one of the oldest textile fibers. The term **linen** refers to fabric made from flax. Fragments of linen fabric were found in prehistoric lake dwellings in Switzerland; linen mummy cloths more than 3,000 years old were found in Egyptian tombs. The linen industry flourished in Europe until the 18th century. With the invention of power spinning, cotton replaced flax as the most important and widely used fiber.

Today flax is a prestige fiber as a result of its limited production and relatively high cost. The term *linen,* however, is often misused in referring to fabrics that look like linen—fabrics that have thick-and-thin yarns and are fairly heavy or crisp. The term *Irish linen* always refers to fabrics made from flax. (The former use of flax in sheets, tablecloths, and towels has given us the term *linens* to describe textiles used for the bed and table.)

The unique and desirable characteristics of flax are its body, strength, durability, low pilling and linting tendencies, pleasant hand, and thick-and-thin fiber bundles, which give texture to fabrics. The main limitations of flax are low resiliency and lack of elasticity.

Most flax is produced in western Europe in Belgium, France, Italy, Ireland, the United Kingdom, Austria, Germany, the Netherlands, and Switzerland. Flax is also produced in Russia, the Commonwealth of Independent States, and New Zealand.

## Structure of Flax

The primary fiber of flax averages 5.0–21.5 inches in length and 12–16 micrometers in diameter. Flax fibers can be identified microscopically by crosswise marking called **nodes** or *joints* (Figure 4–13). The markings on flax have been attributed to cracks or breaks during harvesting or to irregularity in growth. The fibers may appear slightly swollen at the nodes and resemble some-

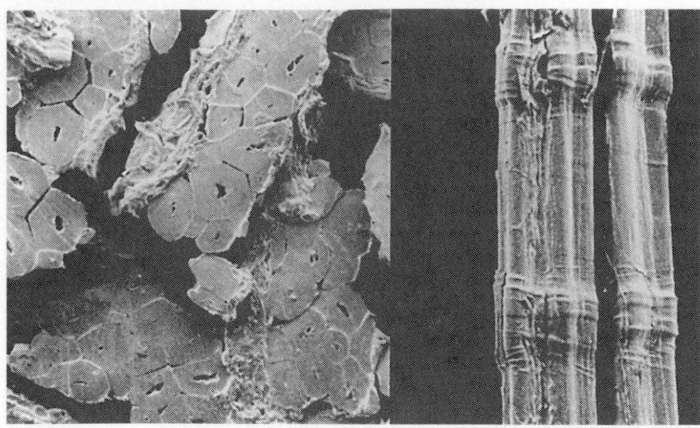

**FIGURE 4–13** ❖ Photomicrographs of flax: cross-sectional view (left); longitudinal view (right). (COURTESY OF THE BRITISH TEXTILE TECHNOLOGY GROUP.)

what the joints in a stalk of corn or bamboo. The fibers have a small, central canal similar to the lumen in cotton. The cross section (Figure 4–13) is many-sided or polygonal with rounded edges.

Flax fibers are grayish in color when dew retted and yellowish in color when water retted. Flax has a more highly oriented molecular structure than cotton and is, therefore, stronger than the cotton fiber.

Flax is similar to cotton in its chemical composition (56–65 percent pure cellulose). Compared to cotton, flax has a higher degree of polymerization (the cellulose polymer is longer) and a greater degree of orientation and crystallinity.

Short flax fibers are called **tow;** the long, combed, better quality fibers are called **line.** Line fibers are ready for wet spinning into yarn. The short tow fibers must be carded to prepare them for dry spinning into yarns that are used in less expensive fabrics.

## Properties of Flax

Reviewing the fiber property tables in Chapter 3 will help when comparing the performance of flax to that of other fibers.

**AESTHETIC** Flax has a high, natural luster that is broken up by the fiber bundles, which give an irregular appearance to yarns made from flax. This irregular appearance is part of the charm of linen fabrics. The luster of flax can be increased by flattening yarns with pressure during finishing.

Because flax has a higher degree of orientation and crystallinity and the fiber diameter is larger than in cotton, the resulting fabrics are stiffer in drape and harsher in hand. Finishes that wash and airblow the fabric produce softer and more drapeable fabrics.

**DURABILITY** Flax is strong for a natural fiber. It has a breaking tenacity of 3.5–5.0 g/d when dry and 6.5 g/d when wet. Before synthetic fibers were invented, linen thread was used to sew shoes. Flax has very low elongation of approximately 7 percent. Elasticity is poor, with a 65 percent recovery at an elongation of only 2 percent. Flax also is a stiff fiber. With poor elongation, elasticity, and stiffness, repeated foldings in the same place will cause the fabric to break. Flax has good abrasion resistance for a natural fiber because of its high orientation and crystallinity.

**COMFORT** Flax has a high moisture regain of 12 percent and it is a good conductor of electricity. Hence, static is no problem. Flax is also a good conductor of heat, so it makes an excellent fabric for warm-weather wear. Flax has a high specific gravity of 1.52, which is the same as cotton.

**CARE** Flax is resistant to alkalis, organic solvents, and high temperatures. Linen fabrics can be dry cleaned or washed without special care and bleached with chlorine bleaches. For upholstery and wall coverings, steam cleaning with caution to avoid shrinkage is often recommended. Linen fabrics have very low resiliency and require frequent pressing. They are more resistant to sunlight than cotton.

Crease-resistant finishes can be used on linen, but the resins may decrease strength and abrasion resistance. The wrinkling characteristics of flax are responsible for the strong high-fashion image of linen fabrics. Linen fabrics must be stored dry; otherwise mildew will become a problem.

Table 4–4 summarizes flax's performance when used in apparel or furnishing fabrics.

## Environmental Impact of Flax

Flax has less of an environmental impact compared to cotton. Production of flax makes use of fewer agricultural chemicals, and irrigation is seldom required. The practice of pulling the plants during harvest in order to get longer fibers does create problems with soil erosion. Removing the fiber from the stem requires significant amounts of water, which may be recycled. Depending on the type of retting used, recycling and disposal of chemicals and contaminated water are other areas of concern.

## Identification Tests

Flax burns readily in a manner very similar to cotton. An easy way to differentiate between these two cellulosic fibers is to study their fiber length. Cotton is seldom

**TABLE 4–4** ❖ Summary of the performance of flax in apparel and furnishing fabrics.

| | |
|---|---|
| **Aesthetic** | **Excellent** |
| Luster | High |
| Texture | Thick and thin |
| Hand | Stiff |
| **Durability** | **Good** |
| Abrasion resistance | Good |
| Tenacity | Good |
| Elongation | Poor |
| **Comfort** | **High** |
| Absorbency | High |
| Thermal retention | Good |
| **Appearance retention** | **Poor** |
| Resiliency | Poor |
| Dimensional stability | Moderate |
| Elastic recovery | Poor |
| **Recommended care** | Dry clean or machine wash (apparel)<br>Steam or dry clean (furnishings) |

more than 2.5 inches in length; flax is almost always longer than that. Flax is also soluble in strong acids.

## Uses of Linen

The Masters of Linen, an organization that promotes the use of linen, has developed a trademark to identify linen (see Figure 4–14). Of the fiber produced, 22 percent is used in household linens (bed, table, and bath items), 16 percent in other furnishing items for both home and commercial use, 50 percent in apparel, and 12 percent in industrial products. Furnishing items include wallpaper and wall coverings, some as wide as 120 inches. Linen fabrics are ideal for this end use because the irregular texture adds interest, hides nail holes or wall damage, and muffles noise. The wider fabrics minimize seams in the wall coverings. Linen fabrics are also used in upholstery and window treatment fabrics because of their durability, interesting and soil-hiding textures, and versatility in fabrication and design.

Apparel items of linen are usually designed for warm weather use, high fashion aspects, or professional wear. Industrial products include luggage, bags, purses, and sewing thread.

## Ramie

**Ramie** is also known as rhea, grasscloth, China grass, and Army/Navy cloth. It has been used for several thousand years in China. The ramie plant is a tall perennial shrub from the nettle family that requires a hot, humid climate. Ramie is fast-growing and can be harvested as frequently as every 60 days. Thus, several crops can be harvested each year. Because it is a perennial, it is cut, not pulled. It has been grown in the Everglades and Gulf Coast regions of the United States, but it is not currently produced in those areas.

**FIGURE 4–14** ❖ Linen symbol of quality. (COURTESY OF MASTERS OF LINEN/USA.)

Ramie fibers must be separated from the plant stalk by **decortication.** In this process, the bark and woody portion of the plant stem are separated from the ramie fiber. Because this process required a lot of hand labor, ramie did not become commercially important until less labor-intensive and relatively inexpensive ways of decorticating ramie were developed. Because ramie is a relatively inexpensive fiber that blends well with many other fibers, many items of ramie or ramie blends have appeared in the United States. Ramie is produced in China, the Philippines, and Brazil.

## Properties of Ramie

Ramie is a white, long, fine fiber with a silklike luster. In both absorbency and density, it is similar to flax. Even its microscopic appearance is similar to that of flax (see Figure 4–15).

It is one of the strongest natural fibers known; its strength increases when it is wet. Ramie is resistant to insects, rotting, mildew, and shrinkage. Its absorbency is good, but it does not dye as well as cotton.

Ramie is stiff and brittle, owing to the high crystallinity of its molecular structure. Like flax, it will break if folded repeatedly in the same spot. Consequently it lacks resiliency and is low in elasticity and elongation potential. Ramie can be treated to be wrinkle resistant.

**USES** Ramie is used in a wide variety of imported apparel items including sweaters, shirts, blouses, and suitings. It is often blended with other natural fibers. Ramie is important in furnishings, often in blends with

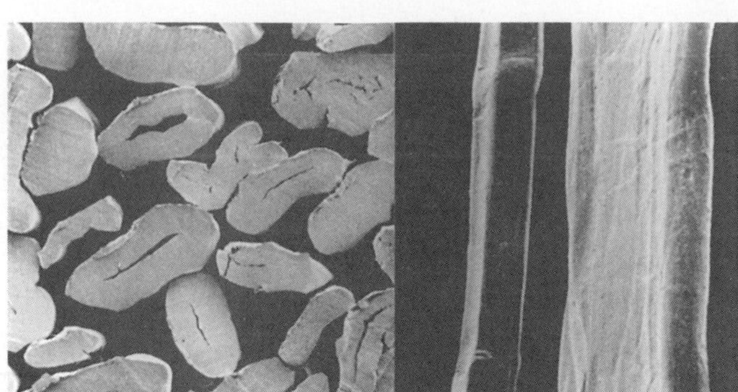

**FIGURE 4–15** ❖ Photomicrographs of ramie: cross-sectional view (left); longitudinal view (right). (COURTESY OF THE BRITISH TEXTILE TECHNOLOGY GROUP.)

**TABLE 4–5** ❖ Summary of the performance of ramie in apparel and furnishing fabrics.

| | |
|---|---|
| **Aesthetic** | **Good** |
| Luster | Matte |
| Texture | Thick and thin |
| Hand | Stiff |
| **Durability** | **Moderate** |
| Abrasion resistance | Moderate |
| Tenacity | Good |
| Elongation | Moderate |
| **Comfort** | **Good** |
| Absorbency | High |
| Thermal retention | Moderate |
| **Appearance retention** | **Poor** |
| Resiliency | Poor |
| Dimensional stability | Poor |
| Elastic recovery | Poor |
| **Recommended care** | Dry-clean or machine wash |

linen or other fibers, for window treatments, pillows, and table linens. It is used in ropes, twines, nets, banknotes, cigarette paper, and geotextiles for erosion control ground-cover fabrics.

A geotextile of ramie and polypropylene is used to reinforce steep slopes and provide a base for vegetation to minimize slumping of the ground during heavy rains. The ramie rots over time, but the polypropylene remains to add reinforcement around the plants' roots.

Table 4–5 summarizes ramie's performance in apparel and furnishing fabrics.

## Hemp

The history of **hemp** is as old as that of flax. Hemp resembles flax in macroscopic and microscopic appearance; some varieties of hemp are very difficult to distinguish from flax. Although most hemp is coarser and stiffer than flax, processing can minimize these differences. Hemp fibers can be very long: 3–15 feet. Depending on the processing used to remove the fiber from the plant stem, it may be naturally creamy white, brown, gray, almost black, or green. It can be machine washed and dried.

The high strength of hemp makes it particularly suitable for twine, cordage, and thread. Hemp is resistant to rotting when exposed to water. Although hemp had been an important industrial fiber for centuries, its importance began to decline in the late 1940s because of competition from synthetic fibers and regulations controlling the production of drugs—hemp *(Cannabis sativa)* is a close relative of marijuana. New varieties of hemp grown for fiber have extremely low levels of the compound tetrahydrocannabinol (THC) and are of no value as a source of the drug.

In recent years, hemp has begun to be used for apparel and some furnishings. Hemp is environmentally friendly and does not require use of pesticides during its production. Most hemp fiber is imported from China and Hungary, but it is also grown in Italy, France, Chile, the former Soviet Union, and Yugoslavia. Commercial production of hemp is not allowed in many countries, including the U.S. and the United Kingdom. Hemp is found in products including hats, shirts, shoes, backpacks, T-shirts, and jeans. Hemp also is used as a paper fiber and as litter or bedding for animals.

## Jute

**Jute** was used as a fiber in Biblical times and probably was the fiber used in sackcloth. Jute is one of the cheapest textile fibers. It is grown throughout Asia, chiefly in India and Bangladesh. The primary fibers in the fiber bundle are short and brittle, making jute one of the weakest of the cellulosic fibers.

Jute is creamy white to brown in color. It is soft, lustrous, and pliable when first removed from the stalk. But it quickly turns brown, weak, and brittle as the lignin ages. Jute has poor elasticity and elongation.

Jute is used to produce sugar and coffee bagging, carpet backing, rope, cordage, and twine. Olefin is a strong competitor in these end uses. Because jute is losing its market, other uses for it are being developed by jute-producing countries; for example, as a reinforcing fiber in resins to create preformed low-cost housing.

Burlap, a fabric usually made from jute, is used for window treatments, area rugs, and wall coverings. Jute has low sunlight resistance and poor colorfastness, although some direct, vat, and acid dyes produce fast colors. It is brittle and subject to splitting and snagging. It also deteriorates quickly when exposed to water. Jute is occasionally used in casual clothing like walking shorts.

### Kenaf

**Kenaf** is a soft bast fiber from the kenaf plant. The fiber is light yellow to gray, long in length, and harder and more lustrous than jute. Like jute, it is used for twine, cordage, and other industrial purposes. Kenaf is produced in Central Asia, India, Africa, and some Central American countries. Kenaf is being investigated by U.S. researchers as a source of paper fiber.

## Leaf Fibers

Leaf fibers are those fibers obtained from the leaf of the plant. Most leaf fibers are long and fairly stiff. In processing, the leaf is cut from the plant and fiber is split or pulled from the leaf. Most leaf fibers have limited dye affinity and may be used in their natural color. Most leaf fibers are of more importance in furnishings than apparel.

### Piña

**Piña** is obtained from the leaves of the pineapple plant. The fiber is soft, lustrous, and white or ivory. Piña is highly susceptible to acids and enzymes, so any acid stains should be rinsed out immediately and enzymatic presoaks should be avoided. Hand washing is recommended for piña. The fiber is used to produce lightweight sheer fabrics that are fairly stiff. These fabrics are often embroidered and used for formal wear in the Philippines. Piña is also used to make mats, bags, table linens, and other clothing (see Figure 4–16). Current research is aimed at producing a commercially competitive piña fiber that can be blended with other fibers.

### Abaca

**Abaca** is obtained from a member of the banana tree family. Abaca fibers are coarse and very long; some may reach a length of 15 feet. Abaca is off-white to brown in color. The fiber is strong, durable, and flexible. It is used for ropes, cordage, floor mats, table linens, and clothing. It is produced in Central America and the Philippines. Abaca is sometimes referred to as Manila hemp even though it is not a true hemp (see Figure 4–17).

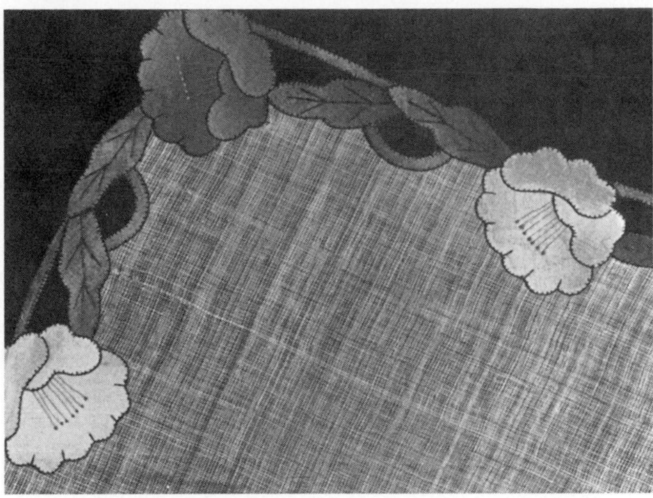

**FIGURE 4–16** ❖ Piña place mat.

### Sisal and Henequen

**Sisal** and **henequen** are closely related plants. They are grown in Africa, Central America, and the West Indies. Both fibers are smooth, straight, and yellow. They are used for better grades of rope, twine, and brush bristles. However, since both fibers are degraded by salt water, they are not used in maritime ropes.

Sisal is also important in furnishings for upholstery, carpet, and custom rugs that can be hand painted to give an individual look. Sisal provides a complementary texture and background for many furnishing styles. Sisal may be used by itself or in blends with wool and acrylic for a softer hand. The dry extraction cleaning method (see Chapter 20) is recommended. Sisal is used in wall coverings, especially in heavy-duty commercial applications, because of its durability and ease of application to a variety of surfaces.

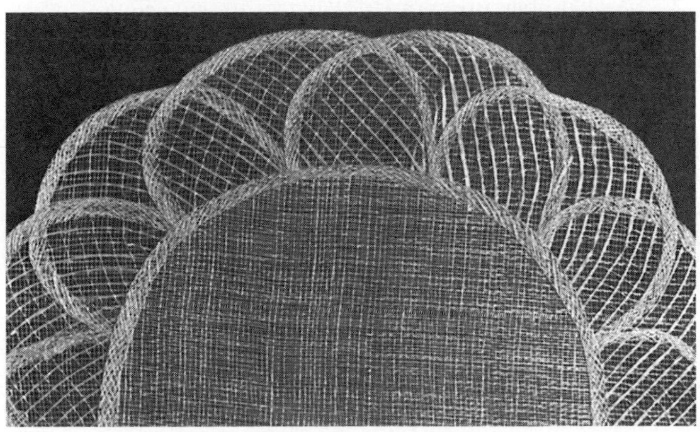

**FIGURE 4–17** ❖ Abaca place mat.

## Other Cellulosic Materials

Other cellulosic materials are important in furnishings. Rush (stems of a marsh plant), seagrass, and maize or cornhusks are used in area rugs because of their resistance to dry heat. Rush and palm fiber seats are often used on wooden frame chairs for a natural look. Yarns made from paper (wood pulp) add interest and texture in wall coverings for interiors. Wooden slats and grasses are found in window treatments. Grasses are especially appealing for wall coverings; the variable weights, thicknesses, and textures add a natural look to interiors. They can be applied to any type of wall surface, treated to be flame retardant, and colored to match the decor.

## Key Terms

Seed fiber
Bast fiber
Leaf fiber
Cotton
Gin
Lint
Linters
Naturally colored cotton
Pima cotton
Egyptian cotton
Sea Island cotton
Cuticle
Lumen
Convolutions
Organic cotton
Transition cotton
Green cotton
Conventional cotton
Kapok
Coir
Rippling
Retting
Scutching
Hackling
Primary fiber bundle
Flax
Linen
Nodes
Tow
Line
Ramie
Decortication
Hemp
Jute
Kenaf
Piña
Abaca
Sisal
Henequen

## Questions

1. Explain the properties that are common to all cellulosics.
2. To what fiber aspects are differences among cellulosic fibers attributed?
3. Compare the performance characteristics of ramie and cotton. Why are blends of these two fibers currently available?
4. Identify a cellulosic fiber that would be an appropriate choice for each of the following end uses sand explain why that fiber was selected.
   sheets for double bed for master bedroom
   tablecloth for an expensive French restaurant
   area rug for a designer's showroom
   woman's sweater for summer wear
   socks for active four-year-old child
   corduroy slacks for high school student
5. Explain the difference among naturally colored cotton, organic cotton, green cotton, transition cotton, and conventional cotton.

## Suggested Readings

Burnett, Phillip (1995, February). "Cotton Naturally." *Textile Horizons,* pp. 36–38.
"Cotton Properties." (1994, Spring). *Textiles Magazine,* p. 16.
Dookery, Alfred (1993, February). "Specialty Cottons Add Diversity." *America's Textiles International,* pp. 34–36.
Goodwin, Jill (1994, Autumn). "Hemp: A Fibre for the Future?" *Textiles Magazine,* pp. 15–16.
Grayson, Martin, ed. (1984). *Encyclopedia of Textiles, Fibers, and Nonwoven Fabrics.* New York: John Wiley & Sons.
McEvoy, Gabrielle (1994–1995, December/January). "Linen: One of the World's Oldest Fibers Is Ideal for the '90s." *Canadian Textile Journal,* pp. 20–21.
Ramaswamy, Gita (1995–1996, Winter). "Kenaf for Textiles: Revival of an Old Fiber." *Shuttle, Spindle, & Dyepot, 27*(1), pp. 28–29.
Schuster, Angela M. H., and Walker, H. Brooks (1995, July/August). "Colorful Cotton!" *Archaeology, 48*(4), pp. 40–45.
Thompson, Jon (1994, June). "Cotton, King of Fibers." *National Geographic, 185*(6), pp. 60–87.

Chapter 5

# Natural Protein Fibers

## OBJECTIVES

- To know the characteristics common to protein fibers and recognize the differences among them.
- To understand the processing of the natural protein fibers.
- To integrate the properties of natural protein fibers with market needs.
- To identify natural protein fibers.

Natural protein fibers are of animal origin: wool and specialty wools are the hair and fur of animals and silk is the secretion of the silkworm. The natural protein fibers are prestige fibers today. Silk, vicuña, cashmere, and camel's hair have always been in this category. Wool is still the most widely used protein fiber, but it is no longer as readily nor as inexpensively available as it was.

Protein fibers are composed of various amino acids that have been formed in nature into polypeptide chains with high molecular weight, containing carbon (C), hydrogen (H), oxygen (O), and nitrogen (N). Wool also contains sulfur. Protein fibers are amphoteric, having both acidic and basic reactive groups. The protein of wool is keratin, whereas that of silk is fibroin.

The following is a simple formula for an amino acid, where R refers to a simple organic functional group:

$$NH_2-\underset{\displaystyle\ }{\overset{\displaystyle R\ |}{CH}}-C(=O)-OH$$

**amino group (basic)**

**carboxyl group (acidic)**

Protein fibers have some properties in common because of the similarity of their chemical composition. These properties are important because they indicate the care required for the fabrics. All animal fibers absorb moisture without surface wetting; they are **hygroscopic.** This phenomenon is a factor in understanding why items made from protein fibers are so comfortable to use. Hygroscopic fibers minimize sudden temperature changes at the skin. In the winter, when people go from a dry indoor atmosphere into the damp outdoor air, the wool fibers absorb moisture and generate heat, protecting the wearers from the cold.

Silk and wool differ in some properties because their physical and molecular structures are different. Table 5–1 lists the properties common to protein fibers.

**TABLE 5–1** ❖ Properties common to all protein fibers.

| PROPERTIES | IMPORTANCE TO CONSUMER |
|---|---|
| Resiliency | Resist wrinkling. Wrinkles hang out between uses. Fabrics tend to hold their shape during use. |
| Hygroscopic | Comfortable in cool, damp climate. Moisture prevents brittleness in carpets. |
| Weaker when wet | Handle carefully when wet. Wool loses about 40 percent of its strength and silk loses about 15 percent. |
| Specific gravity | Fabrics feel lighter than cellulosics of the same thickness. |
| Harmed by alkali | Use neutral or slightly alkaline soap or detergent. Perspiration weakens the fiber. |
| Harmed by oxidizing agents | Chlorine bleaches damage fiber so should not be used. Sunlight causes white fabrics to yellow. |
| Harmed by dry heat | Wool becomes harsh and brittle and scorches easily with dry heat. Use steam! White silk and wool turn yellow. |
| Flame resistance | Do not burn readily; are self-extinguishing; have odor of burning hair; form a black, crushable ash. |

# WOOL

**Wool** was one of the first fibers to be spun into yarns and woven into cloth. Wool was one of the most widely used textile fibers before the Industrial Revolution. Now, wool is more of a luxury fiber.

The high initial cost of wool products and the cost of their care have led many customers to classify wool garments and furnishings as investments. These factors have encouraged the substitution of acrylic, polyester, or wool/synthetic blends in many end-use products. However, wool has a combination of properties that are unequaled by any manufactured fiber: ability to be shaped by heat and moisture, good moisture absorption without feeling wet, excellent heat retention, water repellency, feltability, and flame retardance.

Sheep were probably among the first animals domesticated. The covering of primitive sheep consisted of a long, hairy outercoat (kemp) and a light, downy undercoat. The fleece of present-day domesticated sheep is primarily the soft undercoat. The Spanish developed the **Merino** sheep, whose fleece contains no kemp fiber. Some kemp is still found in wools of all breeds of sheep except the Merino.

Sheep raising on the Atlantic seaboard began in the Jamestown, Virginia, colony in 1609 and in the Massachusetts settlements in 1630. From these centers, the sheep-raising industry spread rapidly. In 1643, English wool combers and carders settled in the Massachusetts Bay colony, where they produced and finished wool fabric. This was the beginning of the New England textile industry. Following the U.S. Civil War, the opening of free grazing lands west of the Mississippi prepared the way for the expansion of sheep production. By 1884, the peak year, 50 million sheep were found in the U.S. The U.S. sheep population has declined steadily since then.

## Production of Wool

In 1995, major producers of wool were Australia (28.9 percent), Eastern Europe (11.8 percent), New Zealand (10.1 percent), and China (9.6 percent). The United States ranked tenth with only 1.3 percent of world production. Total amount produced was almost 5.8 billion pounds of raw wool.

Merino sheep produce the most valuable wool (Figure 5–1). About 43 percent of Merino wool comes from Australia. Good-quality ewes produce 15 pounds of wool per fleece, while rams produce 20 pounds. Australian Merino wool is 3–5 inches long and very fine. Merino wool is used to produce high-quality products with a soft hand and luster and good drape and wear.

Fine wool is produced in the United States by four breeds of sheep: Delaine-Merino, Rambouillet, Debouillet, and Targhee. More than half of this fine wool is produced in Texas and California. It is 2½ inches long. These fine wools are often used for good-quality products that compete with higher priced Merino wools.

The greatest share of U.S. wool production is of medium-grade wools removed from animals raised more for meat than fiber. These fibers have a larger diameter than the fine wools and a greater variation in length, from 1½ to 6 inches. These fibers are used for products, like carpet, where the coarser fiber contributes high resiliency and good abrasion resistance. Fifteen breeds of sheep are commonly found in the United States. The breeds vary tremendously in appearance and type of wool produced. Sheep are raised in every state of the United States, with the exception of Hawaii, but most sheep are raised in the western U.S.

**FIGURE 5–1** ❖ Merino rams. (COURTESY OF THE WOOL BUREAU, INC.)

Sheep are generally sheared once a year in the spring. The fleece is removed with power shears that look like large barber's shears. A good shearer can handle 100–225 sheep per day. An expert can shear a sheep in less than 5 minutes. The fleece is removed with long, smooth strokes, beginning at the legs and belly. A good shearer leaves the fleece in one piece. After shearing, the fleece is folded together and put in bags to be shipped to market.

As an alternative to shearing, a chemical additive to the sheep's diet has been tried. When the chemical is digested it causes the wool to become brittle. Several weeks later, the fleece can be pulled off the sheep.

The sheared (or pulled) wool is **raw wool** or **grease wool.** It contains impurities such as sand, dirt, grease, and dried sweat *(suint),* which account for 30–70 percent of the weight of the fleece. Once these impurities are removed, the wool is **clean,** or **scoured, wool.** The grease is a valuable byproduct; in its purified state, it is *lanolin* used in manufacturing creams, cosmetics, soaps, and ointments.

Grading and sorting are two marketing operations that group wools of like character together. In **grading,** the whole fleece is judged for fineness and length. Each fleece contains more than one quality of wool. In **sorting,** the individual fleece is pulled apart into sections of different-quality fibers. The best-quality wool comes from the sides, shoulders, and back; the poorest wool comes from the lower legs. Different qualities of wool are used differently. For example, fine wool may be used in a lightweight worsted fabric while a coarse wool could be used in carpets.

The quality of wool is based on fineness and length and does not necessarily imply durability because fine fibers are not as durable as coarse fibers. Fineness, color, crimp, strength, length, and elasticity are characteristics that vary with the breed of the sheep.

## Types and Kinds of Wool

Many different qualities of wool are available for the production of yarns and fabrics. Although breeds of sheep produce wools with different characteristics, labels on wool products almost never give that information; the fiber is simply identified as wool. The term *wool* legally includes fiber from various animals, such as sheep, Angora and Cashmere goats, camel, alpaca, llama, and vicuña.

Sheared wool is removed from live sheep. Pulled wool is taken from the pelts of meat-type sheep. Recycled wool is recovered from worn clothing and cutters' scraps. **Lamb's wool** comes from young animals technically defined as less than 7 months old. This wool is finer and softer because it is the first shearing and the fiber has only one cut end: the other end is the natural tip (Figure 5–2). Lamb's wool is usually identified on a label.

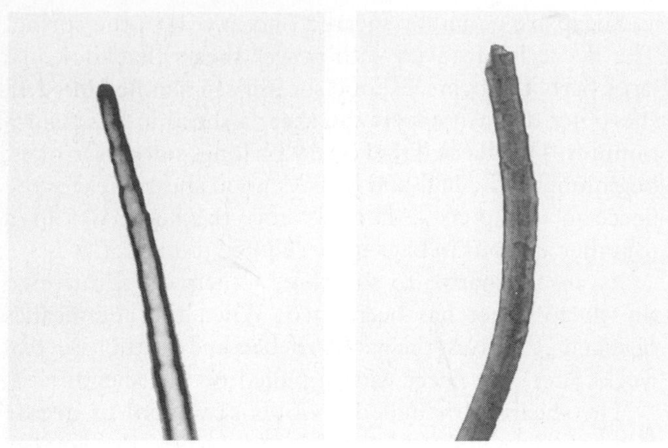

**FIGURE 5–2** ❖ Lamb's wool fiber natural tip (left); cut end of sheep fiber (right).

Wool is often blended with less expensive fibers to reduce the cost of the fabric or to extend its use. The terms that appear on the label of a garment made of wool fiber are defined by the Federal Trade Commission as follows:

1. Virgin wool—wool that has never been processed. If only the term "wool" is used, it implies a virgin wool. The phrase *virgin wool* on a label is a helpful marketing tool.
2. Wool—new wool or wool fibers reclaimed from knit scraps, broken thread, and noils. (Noils are the short fibers that are combed out in the making of worsted yarns.)
3. Recycled wool—scraps of new woven or felted fabrics that are **garnetted** (shredded) back to the fibrous state and used again in the manufacture of woolens. Shoddy wool comes from old clothing and rags that is cleaned, sorted, and shredded into fibers. Recycled wool may be blended with new wool before being respun and used in thick, boardy fabrics.

Recycled wool is important in the textile industry. However, these fibers lose some desirable properties during garnetting. Some fibers are broken by the mechanical action and/or wear. The fibers are not as resilient, strong, or durable as new wool, yet the fabrics made from them perform well. The terms **recycled wool** or **virgin wool** on a label do not refer to the quality of the fiber, but to the past use of the fiber.

Quality of wool is based on fiber fineness, length, scale structure, color, cleanliness, and freedom from damage caused by environment or processing. The best quality wools are white, clean, long, free of defects, fine in size, and with a regular scale structure.

## Physical Structure of Wool

**LENGTH** The length of Merino wool fibers ranges from 1½ to 5 inches, depending on the animal and the length of time between shearings. Long, fine wool fibers, used for worsted yarns and fabrics, have an aver-

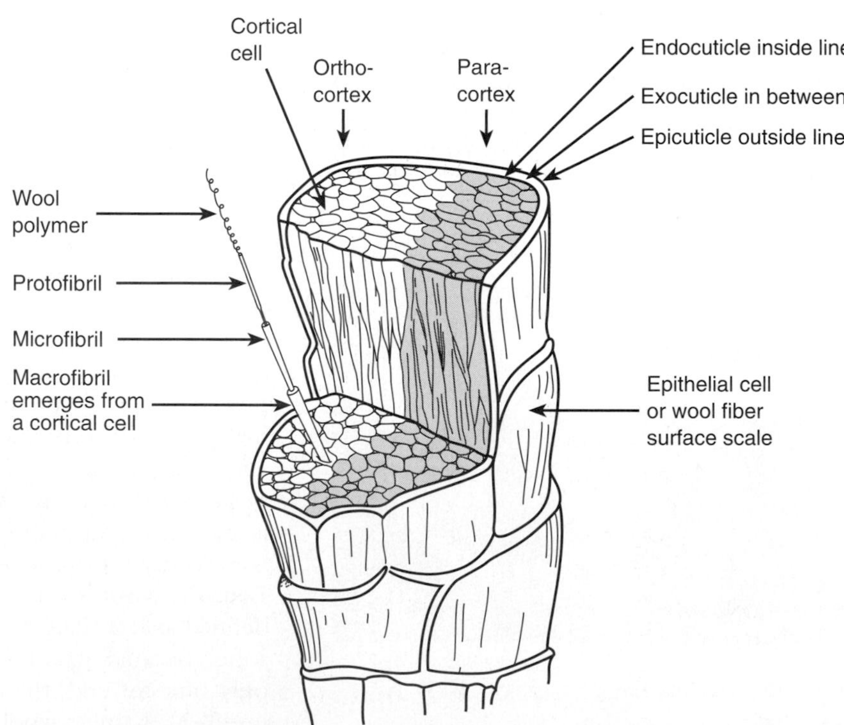


**FIGURE 5–3** ❖ Physical structure of wool fiber. [COURTESY OF E. P. G. GOHL. FROM *TEXTILE SCIENCE* (1983) BY E. P. G. GOHL AND L. D. VILENSKY. PUBLISHED BY LONGMAN CHESHIRE, NOW ADDISON WESLEY LONGMAN AUSTRALIA PTY. LIMITED.]

age length of 2½ inches. Worsted refers to a yarn type and implies long fibers, greater uniformity of fiber length, and more compact yarns. The shorter fibers, which average 1½ inches in length, are used in woolen fabrics. Woolen also refers to yarns and implies shorter, less parallel, softer, and looser yarns with greater variety of fiber length. Certain breeds of sheep produce coarse, long wools that measure from 5 to 15 inches in length. These long wools are used in specialty fabrics and hand weaving.

The diameter of wool fiber varies from 10 to 50 micrometers. Merino lamb's wool may average 15 micrometers in diameter. The wool fiber is made up of a cuticle, cortex, and medulla (Figure 5–3).

**MEDULLA** When present, the **medulla** is a honeycomblike core containing air spaces that increase the insulating power of the fiber. It may appear as a dark area when seen through the microscope, but is usually absent in fine wools.

**CORTEX** The **cortex** is the main part of the fiber. It is made up of long, flattened, tapered cells with a nucleus near the center. In natural-colored wools, the cortical cells contain *melanin,* a colored pigment.

The cortical cells on the two sides of the wool fiber react differently to moisture and temperature. These cells are responsible for wool's unique three-dimensional **crimp.** This irregular lengthwise waviness gives wool fabrics three very important properties: cohesiveness, elasticity, and loft. Figure 5–4 shows the crimp in wool fiber. Fine Merino wool may have as many as 30 crimps per inch. Lower-quality wools may have only 1–5 crimps per inch. Crimp helps individual fibers cling together in a yarn, which increases the strength of the yarn. Elasticity is increased because crimp helps the fiber act like a spring. As force is exerted on the fiber, the fiber straightens out from its naturally wavy state to a

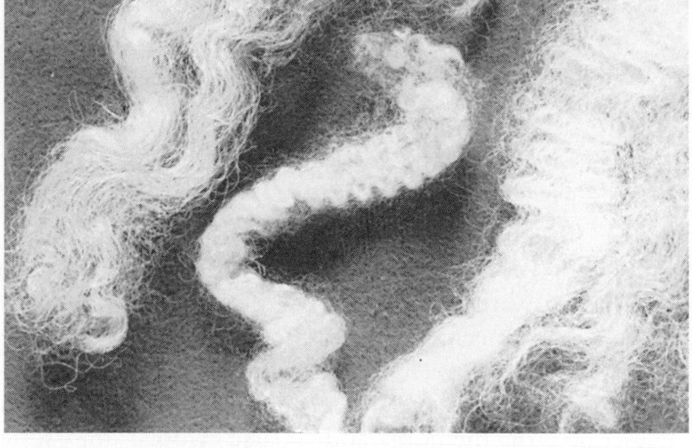

**FIGURE 5–4** ❖ Natural crimp in wool.

flat state, without any damage to the fiber. Once the force is released, the wool fiber gradually returns to its crimped position. Crimp also is an important factor in the loft or bulk that wool yarns and fabrics exhibit throughout use.

The crimp in wool is three-dimensional. As the fiber bends back and forth, it twists around its axis. This is shown in Figure 5–5. Because wool has two different cell types in the cortex, it is a **natural bicomponent fiber,** so called because the fiber has two components with slightly different properties. To illustrate this bicomponent nature, consider how a wool fiber reacts to moisture. One side of the fiber swells more than the other side, decreasing the natural crimp of the fiber. When the fiber dries, the crimp returns.

Wool can be described as a giant molecular coil spring with outstanding resiliency. This resiliency is excellent when the fiber is dry and poor when it is wet. If dry wool fabric is crushed, it tends to spring back to its original shape when the crushing force is released. Wool can be stretched up to 30 percent longer than its

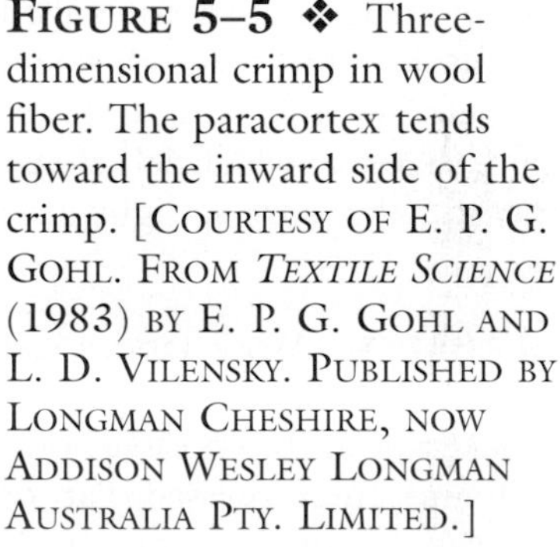

**FIGURE 5–5** ❖ Three-dimensional crimp in wool fiber. The paracortex tends toward the inward side of the crimp. [COURTESY OF E. P. G. GOHL. FROM *TEXTILE SCIENCE* (1983) BY E. P. G. GOHL AND L. D. VILENSKY. PUBLISHED BY LONGMAN CHESHIRE, NOW ADDISON WESLEY LONGMAN AUSTRALIA PTY. LIMITED.]

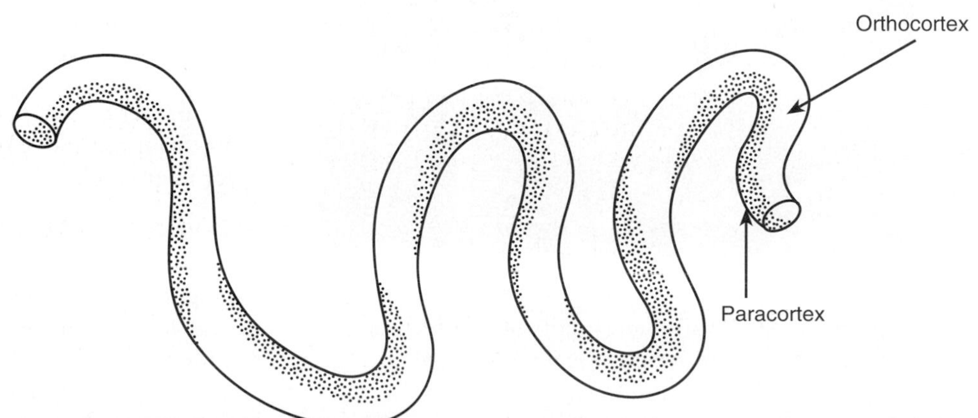

original length. Recovery from stretching is good, but it takes place more slowly when the fabric is dry. Steam, humidity, and water hasten recovery. This is why wool items lose wrinkles more rapidly when exposed to a steamy or humid environment.

**CUTICLE** The cuticle consists of an epicuticle and a horny, nonfibrous layer of **scales.** The *epicuticle* is a thin, nonprotein membrane that covers the scales. This layer gives water repellency to the fiber, but is easily damaged by mechanical treatment. In fine wools, the scales completely encircle the shaft and each scale overlaps the bottom of the preceding scale like parts of a telescope. In medium and coarse wools, the scale arrangement resembles shingles on a roof or scales on a fish (Figure 5–6). The free edges of the scales project outward and point toward the tip of the fiber. The scales contribute to wool's abrasion resistance and felting property, but they can cause skin irritation for some people.

**Felting,** a unique and important property of wool, is based on the structure of the fiber. Under mechanical action combining agitation, friction, and pressure with heat and moisture, the wool fiber tends to move rootward and the edges of the scales interlock. This prevents the fiber from returning to its original position and results in shrinkage, or felting, of the fabric.

The movement of the fibers is speeded up and felting occurs more rapidly under extreme or severe conditions. Wool items can be shrunk to half their original size. Lamb's wool felts more readily than other wool. In soft, fluffy fabrics the fibers are not firmly held in position and are free to move, so these fabrics are more susceptible to felting than are the firmly woven worsteds. The felting property is an advantage in making felt fabric directly from fibers without spinning or weaving, yet it can be a disadvantage because it makes the laundering of wool more difficult. Treatments to prevent felting shrinkage (see Chapter 18) are available.

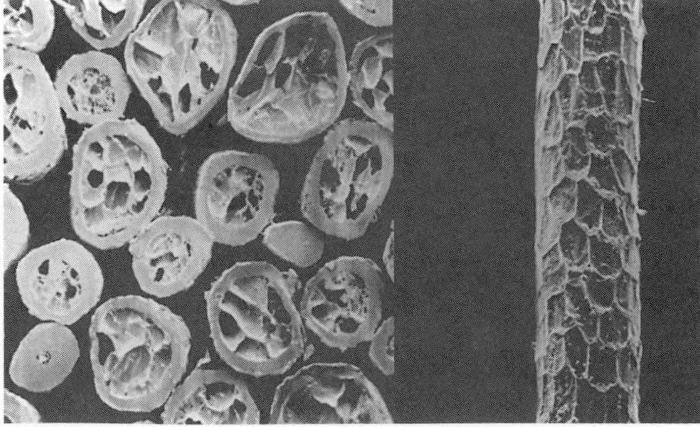

**FIGURE 5–6** ❖ Photomicrograph of wool: cross-sectional view (left) and longitudinal view (right). (COURTESY OF THE BRITISH TEXTILE TECHNOLOGY GROUP.)

## Chemical Composition and Molecular Arrangement of Wool

Wool fiber is a protein called **keratin.** It is the same protein that is found in human hair, fingernails, horns, and hooves. Keratin consists of carbon, hydrogen, oxygen, nitrogen, and sulfur. These combine to form over 17 different amino acids. Five amino acids are shown in Figure 5–7. The wool molecule consists of flexible molecular chains held together by natural cross-links—cystine (or sulfur) linkages and salt bridges—that connect adjacent molecules.

Figure 5–7 resembles a ladder, with the cross-links analogous to the crossbars of the ladder. This simple structure can be useful in understanding some of the properties of wool. Imagine a ladder made of plastic that is pulled askew. When wool is pulled, its inherent tendency is to recover its original shape; the cross-links are very important in this recovery. However, if the cross-links are damaged, the structure is destroyed and recovery cannot occur.

A more realistic model of the structure of wool molecules would show this ladderlike structure alternating with a helical structure. About 40 percent of the chains are in a spiral formation, with hydrogen bonding occurring between the closer parts. The ladderlike formation occurs at the cystine cross-links or where other bulky amino acids meet and the chains cannot pack closely together. The spiral formation works like a spring and is also important in the resilience, elongation, and elastic recovery of wool fibers. Figure 5–8 shows the helical structure of wool.

The cystine linkage is the most important part of the molecule. Any chemical, such as alkali, that damages this linkage can destroy the entire structure. In controlled reactions, the linkage can be broken and then reformed. Minor modifications of the cystine linkage that result from pressing and steaming have a beneficial effect; those from careless washing and exposure to light have a detrimental effect.

**SHAPING OF WOOL FABRICS** Wool fabrics can be shaped by heat and moisture—a definite aid in producing wool products. Puckers can be pressed out; excess fabric can be eased and then pressed flat or rounded as desired. Pleats can be pressed into wool cloth with heat, steam, and pressure, but they will not last through washing.

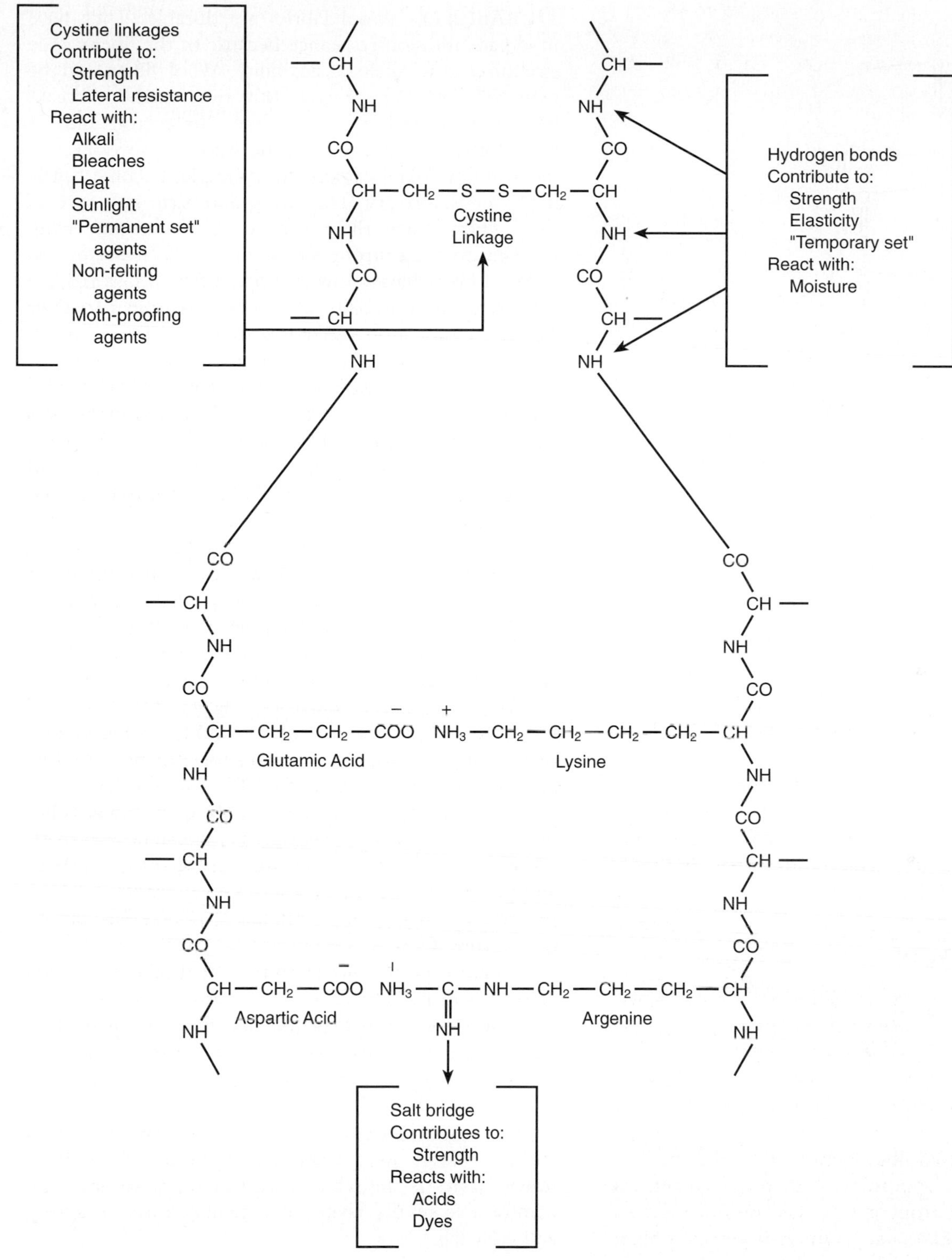


**FIGURE 5–7** ❖ Structural formula of the wool molecule.

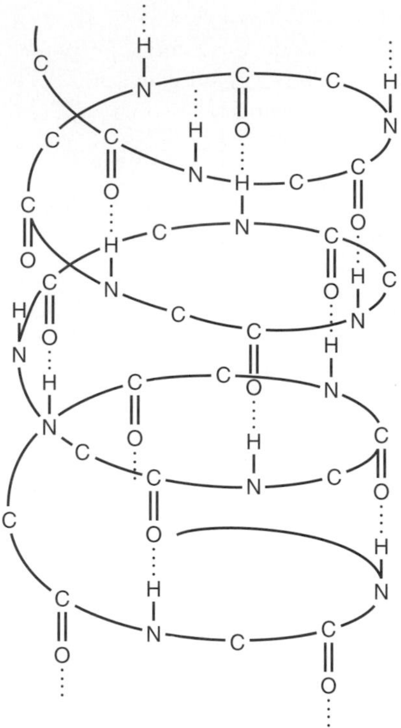

**FIGURE 5–8** ❖ Helical arrangement of the wool molecule. (COURTESY OF INTERNATIONAL WOOL SECRETARIAT.)

Hydrogen bonds are broken and reformed easily in the presence of steam (hot water vapor) pressing. The newly formed bonds retain their pressed-in shape until exposed to high humidity conditions, when the wool returns to its original shape.

## Properties of Wool

Reviewing the fiber property tables in Chapter 3 will help in understanding wool's performance.

**AESTHETIC** Because of its physical structure, wool contributes loft and body to fabrics. Wool sweaters, suits, carpets, and upholstery are the standard "looks" by which manufactured fiber fabrics are measured.

Wool has a matte appearance. Fibers are sometimes blended with wool from sheep that produce longer fibers, specialty hair fibers such as mohair, or other fibers to modify the fabric's luster or texture.

Drape, luster, texture, and hand can be varied by choice of yarn structure, fabric structure, and finish. Sheer-wool voile, medium-weight printed-wool challis, medium-weight flannels and tweeds, heavy-weight coating, upholstery fabrics, and wool rugs and carpets demonstrate the spectrum of possibilities.

**DURABILITY** Wool fabrics are durable. They have moderate abrasion resistance because of the fiber's scale structure and excellent flexibility. Wool fibers can be bent back on themselves 20,000 times without breaking, as compared to 3,000 times for cotton and 75 times for rayon. Atmospheric moisture helps wool retain its flexibility. Wool carpets, for example, become brittle if the air is too dry. The crimp and scale structure of wool fibers make them very cohesive so they cling together to make strong yarns.

Wool fibers have a low tenacity, 1.5 g/d dry and 1.0 g/d wet. The durability of wool fibers relates to their excellent elongation (25 percent) and elastic recovery (99 percent). When stress is put on the fabric, the crimped fibers elongate as the molecular chains unfold. When stress is removed, the cross-links pull the fibers back almost to their original positions. The combination of these properties, excellent flexibility, elongation, and elastic recovery, results in wool fabrics that can be used and enjoyed for many years.

**COMFORT** Wool is more hygroscopic than any other fiber. It has a moisture regain of 13–18 percent under standard conditions. Wool fibers are initially water repellent. In a light rain or snow, the water runs off or remains on the fabric surface.

Wool is a poor conductor of heat so that warmth from the body is not dissipated readily. Outdoor sports enthusiasts have long recognized the superior comfort provided by wool. Drying of wool occurs slowly enough that the wearer is more comfortable than in any other fiber. Wool's excellent resiliency is important in providing warmth. The wool fibers can recover from crushing and the fabrics will remain porous and capable of incorporating much air. This "still" air is an excellent insulator because it keeps body heat close to the body.

Some people are allergic to the chemical components of wool and itch, break out in a rash, or sneeze when they touch wool. Other people may find the harsh edges of coarse, low-quality wools irritating and uncomfortable.

Wool has a medium density (1.32 g/cc). People often associate heavy fabrics with wool since it is used in fall and winter wear when the additional warmth of heavy fabrics is desirable. Lightweight wools are very comfortable in the changeable temperatures of spring and early fall.

One way to compare fiber densities is to think of blankets. A winter blanket of wool is heavy and warm. An equally thick blanket of cotton would be even heavier (cotton has a higher density), but not as warm. A winter blanket of acrylic would be lighter in weight (acrylic has a lower density than either). Personal preferences will help determine which fiber to choose.

**APPEARANCE RETENTION** Wool is a very resilient fiber. It resists wrinkling and recovers well from wrinkles. It wrinkles more readily when wet. Wool maintains its shape fairly well during normal use. Often wool apparel is lined to maintain its shape.

When wool fabrics are dry cleaned, they retain their size and shape well. When wool items are hand washed, they need to be handled carefully to avoid shrinkage. Follow care instructions for washable woolens.

Wool has an excellent elastic recovery—99 percent at 2 percent elongation. Even at 20 percent elongation, recovery is 63 percent. Recovery is excellent from the stresses of normal usage. Wool carpet maintains an attractive appearance for years.

**CARE** Wool does not soil readily, and the removal of soil from wool is relatively simple. Grease and oils do not spot wool fabrics as readily as they do fabrics made of other fibers. Wool items do not need to be washed or dry cleaned after every use. Layer wool garments with washable ones to decrease odor pickup.

A firm, soft brush not only removes dust but also gently lifts matted fibers back to their natural springiness. Damp fabrics should be allowed to dry before brushing. Garments should have a period of rest between wearings to recover from deformations. Hanging the item in a humid environment or spraying a fine mist of water on the cloth speeds up recovery.

Wool is very susceptible to damage when it is wet. Its wet tenacity is a third lower than its relatively low dry strength. Wet elongation increases to 35 percent before breaking. Resiliency and elastic recovery decrease. The redeeming properties of dry wool that make it durable in spite of its low tenacity do not operate when it is wet. Handle wet wool very gently.

Dry cleaning is the recommended care method for most wool items. Dry cleaning minimizes potential problems that may occur during hand or machine washing. Incorrect care procedures can be disastrous and costly; the item can be ruined.

Some items can be hand washed if correct procedures are followed. Use warm water that is comfortable to the hand. Avoid agitation; squeeze gently. Support the item, especially if it is knit, so it does not stretch unnecessarily. Air dry flat. Do not machine or tumble dry or felting will occur. Woven or knit items that are labeled machine washable are usually blends or have been given a special finish so they can be laundered safely. Follow any special instructions given. These special instructions usually require using warm or lukewarm water and a gentle cycle for a short period of time, with line or flat drying recommended.

Chlorine bleach, an oxidizing agent, damages wool. Verify this by putting a small piece of wool in fresh chlorine bleach. What happens? The wool dissolves! Wool is also very sensitive to alkalis, such as strong detergents. The wool reacts to the alkali by turning yellow, then becoming slick and jellylike, and finally dissolving. If the fabric is a blend, the wool in the blend disintegrates, leaving only the other fibers.

Wool is attacked by moth larvae and other insects. Regular, liberal use of mothballs or crystals is discouraged due to the toxic nature of these pesticides. However, they should be used when evidence of insects is apparent, such as when moths or traces of larvae are seen. Moth larvae also eat, but do not digest, any fiber that is blended with wool.

Unless mothproofed, wool fabrics should be stored so that they will not be accessible to moths. Wool fabrics should be cleaned before storage.

Wool burns very slowly and is self-extinguishing. It is normally regarded as flame-resistant. This is one of the reasons why wool is so popular with interior designers. However, when wool is used in public buildings, a flame-retardant finish may be applied to meet building code requirements.

Table 5–2 summarizes wool's performance in apparel and furnishing fabrics.

## Environmental Impact of Wool

Since wool is a natural fiber, many consumers believe it is environmentally friendly. Although wool can be viewed as a renewable resource, it is not produced without any impact on the environment. Sheep graze pastures so closely that soil erosion can occur if care is not taken to avoid overgrazing. Disposal of animal waste is another concern. Sheep manure is frequently spread over the

**TABLE 5–2** ❖ Summary of the performance of wool in apparel and furnishing fabrics.

| | |
|---|---|
| **Aesthetic** | **Variable** |
| Luster | Matte |
| **Durability** | **High** |
| Abrasion resistance | Moderate |
| Tenacity | Poor |
| Elongation | High |
| **Comfort** | **High** |
| Absorbency | High |
| Thermal retention | High |
| **Appearance retention** | **High** |
| Resiliency | High |
| Dimensional stability | Poor |
| Elastic recovery | Excellent |
| **Recommended care** | Dry clean (apparel)<br>Steam clean (furnishings) |

ground to return nutrients to the soil. However, excessive applications can create problems with runoff contaminated with the manure. In addition, sheep producers have traditionally opposed programs that contribute to the survival of wolves and other natural predators.

Another issue is that sheep are susceptible to some diseases that can be transmitted to humans. Most diseases of this nature are of little concern and then only to sheep producers; consumers of wool products are not at risk. However, customs officials and importers examine imported wools from certain Third World countries to check for diseases that can be transmitted via contaminated fibers. Fibers contaminated in this way are not permitted to be imported. Consumers should not be concerned with imported items purchased in the U.S., but they should exercise caution when purchasing wool products in Third World countries.

Other environmental issues relate to the intensive use of water, energy, and chemicals to clean the fiber, produce wool fabrics, and finish and dye them. Many wool products require dry cleaning. Some dry cleaning solvents have been identified as possible carcinogens and restrictions regarding exposure in the workplace have been imposed. See Chapter 20 for more information on dry cleaning.

## Uses of Wool

Only a small amount of wool is used in the United States. In 1994 domestic consumption of wool was 243 million pounds, or approximately 1.4 percent of all fiber used in the United States. The most important use of wool is for adult apparel (see Table 5–3).

**TABLE 5–3** ❖ Uses of wool.

| PERCENT | END USE | MILLION POUNDS |
|---|---|---|
| 72.7 | Apparel | |
| | Lightweight suits, dresses | 3.5 |
| | Heavier weight suits, trousers, slacks, skirts | 121.2 |
| | Underwear and nightwear | 3.3 |
| | Sweaters | 13.5 |
| | Retail piece goods | 1.7 |
| | Socks | 3.6 |
| | Hand-knitting yarns | 2.6 |
| 23.0 | Home Furnishings | |
| | Carpets | 29.5 |
| | Upholstery | 9.8 |
| | Blankets | 3.8 |
| 4.2 | Industrial | |
| | Felts | 13.8 |

*Source: Fiber Organon 66* (9), Sept. 1995.

Wool suits perform well and look great. They fit well because they can be shaped through tailoring. The fabrics drape well and are durable. They are comfortable under a variety of conditions and retain their good looks during wear and care. Suits are usually dry cleaned to retain their best looks and because of the shaping components. Blends of synthetic fibers with wool for suiting materials are also important.

The Wool Bureau has adopted two symbols to assist in the promotion of wool: the Woolmark® used on all 100 percent wool merchandise that meets the Wool Bureau's specifications for quality and the Woolblend® mark for blends with at least 60 percent wool. Both symbols are shown in Figure 5–9.

Wool is extremely important for furnishings, even though the actual percentage of furnishing products that are wool is small. Wool is the standard by which carpet appearance is judged. A major use of wool is in carpets and custom rugs, often special-order or one-of-a-kind rugs. Many woven Axminster and Wilton rugs with complex designs are made from wool. More contemporary looks that are hand woven or hooked are also available. Most rugs are imported, although some are made in the United States. Wool carpets and rugs are more expensive than those made from other fibers, but people who prefer them like the patterns and appreciate the rich color, texture, and appearance of wool. Wool carpets and rugs account for a very small share of the floor coverings market.

Wool is also found in upholstery fabrics. Both wool and wool blend fabrics are used in upholstery because of their aesthetic characteristics, good appearance retention, durable nature, and natural flame resistance. For residential use no additional flame retardant treatment may be necessary, but for many commercial and contract uses the wool or wool blend upholstery fabric may require flame retardant treatment.

Handcrafted wall hangings and woven tapestries are often made of wool because textile artists prefer the way

**FIGURE 5–9** ❖ Woolmark® and Woolblend® symbols of quality. (COURTESY OF THE WOOL BUREAU, INC.)

**TABLE 5–4** ❖ Groupings of specialty wools.

| GOAT FAMILY | CAMEL FAMILY | OTHERS |
|---|---|---|
| Angora goat—mohair<br>Cashmere goat—cashmere | Camel's hair<br>Llama<br>Alpaca<br>Vicuña<br>Guanaco | Angora rabbit—angora<br>Fur fibers<br>Musk ox—qiviut |

the fiber handles and designers, artists, and consumers appreciate the way the finished item looks and wears.

Many school laboratories have fire blankets of wool for safety. Stadium blankets and throws are often made of wool for warmth and an attractive appearance.

In industrial uses, wool is important in felts, which are used under heavy machinery to help decrease noise, or for a variety of other uses. Wool is also used to clean up oil spills. Tiny balls of wool absorb up to 40 times their weight in oil. Wool mulch mats for landscape and horticultural weed control is another industrial end use.

❖

# Specialty Wools

Most specialty wools are obtained from the goat, rabbit, and camel families (see Table 5–4).

Specialty wools are available in smaller quantities than sheep's wool so they are usually more expensive. Like all natural fibers, specialty wools vary in quality. Most specialty wool products require dry cleaning.

Specialty wool fibers are of two kinds: the coarse, long outerhair and the soft, fine undercoat. Coarse fibers are used for interlinings, upholstery, and some coatings; the very fine fibers are used in luxury coatings, sweaters, shawls, suits, dresses, and furnishing fabrics.

## Mohair

**Mohair** is the hair fiber of the Angora goat. In 1994, 16 million pounds of mohair were produced worldwide. Major producers are South Africa and the U.S. Texas is the major producer in the United States. Most U.S. mohair is exported. The goats (see Figure 5–10) are usually sheared twice a year, in the early fall and early spring. Each adult yields about 5 lbs of fiber. The fiber length is 4 to 6 inches if sheared twice or 8 to 12 inches if sheared once. Approximately 12 percent of the crop is kid (baby goat) fiber and the remaining 88 percent is adult fiber.

Mohair fibers have a circular cross section. Scales on the surface are scarcely visible and the cortical cells show through as lengthwise striations. There are some air ducts between the cells that give mohair its lightness and fluffiness. Few of the fibers have a medulla.

Mohair is one of the most resilient fibers and has none of the crimp found in sheep's wool, giving it a silk-like luster and a smoother surface that is more resistant to dust than wool. Mohair has fewer scales than wool, so mohair fibers are smoother and more lustrous than wool fibers (see Figure 5–11). Mohair is very strong and

**FIGURE 5–10** ❖ Angora goats produce mohair fibers. (COURTESY OF THE MOHAIR COUNCIL OF AMERICA.)

**FIGURE 5–11** ❖ Photomicrograph of mohair: cross-sectional view (left) and longitudinal view (right). (COURTESY OF THE BRITISH TEXTILE TECHNOLOGY GROUP.)

has good affinity for dye. The washed fleece is a lustrous white. Mohair is less expensive than most of the other specialty wools.

Mohair's chemical properties are the same as those of wool. Mohair makes a better novelty loop yarn than wool or the other specialty hair fibers.

Mohair's good resiliency is used to advantage in hand-knitting yarns, pile fabrics, and suitings. Because it resists crushing and pilling, it is used in flat and pile upholstery fabrics and hand-produced floor coverings. Its natural flame resistance, insulation, and sound absorbency make it ideal for specialty drapery applications. Because it holds heat well, it is used in blends for blankets. Mohair is also used to produce human-hair substitute wigs and hairpieces.

Figure 5–12 shows the quality symbol used on all mohair products that meet performance standards established by the Mohair Council of America.

**FIGURE 5–13** ❖ The musk ox of Alaska produces qiviut fiber. (COURTESY OF FAIRBANKS CONVENTION AND VISITOR BUREAU.)

## Qiviut

**Qiviut,** a rare and luxurious fiber, is the underwool of the domesticated musk ox (see Figure 5–13). Successful musk ox domestication projects have been conducted in Alaska and Canada's Northwest Territories. A large musk ox provides 6 pounds of wool each year. The fiber can be used just as it comes from the animal, for it is protected from debris by the long guard hairs and has a low lanolin content. The fleece is not shorn but is shed naturally and is removed from the guard hairs as soon as it becomes visible. Qiviut is an expensive fiber, over $150 an ounce, used to produce handcrafted items by Inuit and other Native American people.

## Angora

**Angora** is hair of the Angora rabbit. These rabbits are raised in Europe, Chile, China, and the U.S. (see Figure 5–14). Each rabbit produces only a few ounces of fiber, which is very fine, fluffy, soft, slippery, and fairly long. It is pure white or a natural color.

Fiber is harvested up to four times a year by plucking or shearing. Annual yield varies with the rabbit, its health, and breed and usually ranges from 8 to 30 ounces. There are four breeds of Angora rabbits; the two most common types are English and French. The quantity and quality of fiber differs with the breed. English Angoras produce a fine silky fiber; French Angoras

**FIGURE 5–12** ❖ Mohair symbol of quality. (COURTESY OF THE MOHAIR COUNCIL OF AMERICA.)

**FIGURE 5–14** ❖ The Angora rabbit produces a soft, white fiber. (COURTESY OF AMICALE INDUSTRIES.)

produce a coarser fiber. Both breeds produce white and naturally colored fiber.

Angora does not take dye well and usually has a lighter color than other fibers with which it is blended. It is usually blended with wool to facilitate spinning because the slick fiber has poor cohesiveness. Angora is most often used in apparel such as sweaters.

## Camel's Hair

**Camel's hair** is obtained from the two-hump Bactrian camel. These camels are found from Turkey east to China and north to Siberia. Camel's hair is said to have the best insulation of any of the wool fibers. The hair is collected by a "trailer" who follows the camel caravan, picks up the hair as it is shed, and places it in a basket carried by the last camel. The trailer also gathers the hair in the morning at the spot where the camels lay down for the night. A camel produces about 5 pounds of hair a year.

Because camel's hair gives warmth without weight, the finer fibers are much prized for clothing fabrics. They are often used in blends with sheep's wool, which is dyed the tan color of camel's hair. Camel's hair is most often used in coats or jackets, scarves, and sweaters. Camel's hair and wool blend blankets are on the market.

## Cashmere

**Cashmere** comes from a small goat raised in Kashmir, China, Tibet, Mongolia, and New Zealand. The fibers vary in color from white to gray to brownish gray. The goat has an outercoat of long, coarse hair and an innercoat of down. The hair usually is combed by hand from the animal during the two molting seasons. In dehairing, the coarse hair is separated from the fine fibers. The downy fine fibers make up only a small part of the fleece, probably not more than one-half pound per goat. The fiber is solid with no medulla and fine scales. Cashmere is used in high-quality apparel, especially women's sweaters and coats and men's suits, coats, and jackets. Fabrics are warm, buttery in hand, and have beautiful draping characteristics. Cashmere is more sensitive to chemicals than wool.

**Cashgora** is a new fiber resulting from the breeding of feral cashmere goats with angora goats in New Zealand and Australia. Although the International Wool Textile Organization has adopted cashgora as a generic fiber term, it is not recognized around the world. The fiber is coarser than cashmere and not as lustrous. It is used primarily in less expensive coatings and suitings.

## Llama and Alpaca

**Llama** and **alpaca** are domesticated animals of the South American branch of the camel family. The fiber is 8–12 inches in length and is noted for its softness, fineness, and luster. The natural colors are white, light fawn, light brown, dark brown, gray, black, and piebald. Both fibers are used for clothing, handcrafts, and rugs. Because alpaca is softer, it is used more often for apparel. Its soft hand, beautiful luster, and good draping characteristics are appreciated by fashion designers. As with wool, fibers from the younger animals are finer and softer.

## Vicuña and Guanaco

**Vicuña** and **guanaco** are wild animals of the South American camel family. They are very rare. In the past, the animals were killed to obtain the fiber. Vicuña and guanaco are now protected. Vicuña is the softest, finest, rarest, and most expensive of all textile fibers. The fiber is short, very lustrous, and light cinnamon in color. Research is underway to produce genetic crosses of alpaca and vicuña. As of mid-1996, it was illegal to bring into the U.S. any items containing vicuña because of the Endangered Species Act.

# SILK

**Silk** is a natural protein fiber. It is similar to wool in that it is composed of amino acids arranged in a polypeptide chain. Silk is produced by the larvae of a moth.

According to Chinese legend, silk culture began in 2640 B.C. when Empress Hsi Ling Shi became interested in silkworms and learned how to reel the silk and make it into fabric. Through her efforts China developed a silk industry and a 3,000-year monopoly. Silk culture later spread to Korea and Japan, westward to India and Persia, and then to Spain, France, and Italy. Silk fabrics imported from China were coveted in other countries; in India, the fabrics were often picked apart and rewoven into looser fabrics or combined with other fibers to provide more yardage from the same amount of silk filament. Several attempts at sericulture were made in the U.S., but none were successful. Today, major producers of silk are China (54 percent), India (14 percent), and Japan (11 percent).

Silk is universally accepted as a luxury fiber. The International Silk Association of the United States emphasizes the uniqueness of silk by its slogan "Only silk is silk." Silk has a combination of properties not possessed by any other fiber: It has a dry tactile hand, unique natural luster, good moisture absorption, lively suppleness and draping qualities, and high strength.

The beauty and hand of silk and its high cost are probably responsible for the manufactured fiber industry. Silk is a solid fiber with a simple physical structure. It is this physical nature of silk that some modifications of manufactured fibers attempt to duplicate. Manufactured fibers with a triangular cross section and fine size are the most successful.

## Production of Silk

**Sericulture** is the production of cultivated silk, which begins when the silk moth lays eggs on specially prepared paper. The cultivated silkworm is usually *Bombyx mori*. When the eggs hatch, the caterpillars, or larvae, are fed fresh, young mulberry leaves. After about 35 days and 4 moltings, the silkworms are approximately 10,000 times heavier than when hatched and ready to begin spinning a cocoon, or chrysalis case. A straw frame is placed on the tray and the silkworm starts to spin the cocoon by moving its head in a figure eight (see Figure 5–15). The silkworm produces silk in two glands and forces the liquid silk through openings, *spinnerets,* in its head. The two strands of silk are coated with a water-soluble protective gum, **sericin.** When the silk comes in contact with the air, it solidifies. In 2 or 3 days, the silkworm has spun approximately 1 mile of filament and has completely surrounded itself in a cocoon. The silkworm then begins to change into a chrysalis and then into a moth. Usually the silkworm is killed (stifled) with heat before it reaches the moth stage.

If the silkworm is allowed to reach the moth stage, it is used for breeding additional silkworms. The moth secretes a fluid that dissolves the silk at one end of the cocoon so that it can crawl out. Cocoons from which the moths have emerged cannot be used for filament silk yarns and the staple silk from these cocoons is less valuable.

To obtain filament silk from the cocoon after stifling, the cocoons are sorted for fiber size, fiber quality and defects, then brushed to find the outside ends of the filaments. Several filaments are gathered together and wound onto a reel. This process, referred to as **reeling,** is performed in a manufacturing plant called a *filature*. Each cocoon yields approximately 1,000 yards of silk filament. This is **raw silk,** or **silk-in-the-gum,** and it has not yet been processed into a fabric. Several filaments are combined to form a yarn. The operators in the filature must be careful to join the fibers so that the diameter of the reeled silk remains uniform in size. Uniformly reeled filament silk is the most valuable (see Figure 5–16).

As the fibers are combined and wrapped onto the reel, twist can be added to hold the filaments together. Adding twist is referred to as *throwing* and the resulting yarn is called a *thrown yarn*. There are several types of thrown yarns. The type of yarn and amount of twist relate to the type of fabric desired. The simplest type of thrown yarn is a singles. In a *singles,* three to eight filaments are twisted together to form a yarn. Commonly used for filling yarns in many silk fabrics, singles may have two or three twists per inch.

Much usable silk is not reeled because long filaments cannot be taken from a damaged cocoon. Cocoons in which the filament broke or the moth was allowed to mature and silk from the inner portions of the cocoon yield staple silk, often referred to as **silk noils,** or *silk waste*. This silk is degummed (the sericin is removed) and spun like any other staple fiber or blended with

**FIGURE 5–15** ❖ Silk caterpillar spinning silk fibers to form cocoon. (COURTESY OF STOCK, BOSTON. © CARY WOLINSKY, 1984.)

**FIGURE 5–16** ❖ Reeling of silk. (COURTESY OF THE TEXTILE INSTITUTE.)

another staple fiber and spun into a yarn. Spun silk is less expensive, less durable, of lower quality than filament silk, and tends to pill.

**Wild silk** production is not controlled as is production of cultivated silk. Although many species of wild silkworms produce wild silk, the two most common are *Antheraea mylitta* and *Antheraea pernyi*. The silkworms feed on oak and cherry leaves and produce fibers that are much less uniform in texture and color. The fiber may be brown, yellow, orange, or green, with brown the most common color. Current research is investigating the feasibility of producing fabrics of these naturally colored silks.

Since the cocoons are harvested after the moth has matured, the silk cannot be reeled and must be used as spun silk. **Tussah silk** is the most common type of wild silk. It is coarser, darker, and cannot be bleached. Hence, white and light colors are not available in tussah silk. *Tasar* is a type of wild silk from India. Some fabrics are sold simply as wild silk. "Raw silk" is sometimes used incorrectly to describe these fabrics. **Duppioni silk** results when two silkworms spin their cocoons together. The yarn is irregular in diameter with a thick-thin appearance. It is used in linenlike silk fabrics like shantung.

Silk fabric descriptions may include the term **momme,** the standard way to describe silk fabrics. Momme, pronounced like "mummy" and abbreviated mm, describes the weight of the silk. One momme (momie or mommie) weighs 3.75 grams. Most silk fabrics are produced in several weights. Higher numbers describe heavier fabrics. Other terms, such as *habutai* or *crepe,* describe the yarn and fabric structure. Silk fabrics are often graded for their degree of evenness, fiber or yarn size, and freedom from defects. Grade A refers to the highest grade, only about 10 percent of the silk produced.

Japan is known for its high-quality silks. India is known for its handwoven wild silks with a pronounced texture. Thailand produces handwoven iridescent silks created by using two colors of yarn in weaving the fabric. With over 30 countries producing silk, there is a wide range of silk types and qualities on the market. Pure silk and pure dye silk describe 100 percent silk fabrics that do not contain any metallic weighting compounds. See Chapter 21 for more information on labeling silk fabrics.

## Physical Structure of Silk

Silk is the only natural filament fiber. It is a solid fiber, smooth but irregular in diameter along its shaft. The filaments are triangular in cross section with rounded corners (Figure 5–17). Silk fibers are very fine—1.25 denier/filament. Wild silks may be slightly coarser and have slight striations along the longitudinal length of the fiber.

**FIGURE 5–17** ❖ Photomicrographs of silk fiber: cross-sectional view (left); longitudinal view (right). (COURTESY OF THE BRITISH TEXTILE TECHNOLOGY GROUP.)

## Chemical Composition and Molecular Structure of Silk

The protein in silk is **fibroin** with 15 amino acids in polypeptide chains. Silk has reactive amino ($NH_2$) and carboxyl (COOH) groups. Silk has no cross-linkages and no bulky side chains. The molecular chains are not folded as in wool, but are almost fully extended and packed closely together. Thus silk is highly oriented, contributing to its strength. As with all fibers, there are some amorphous areas between the crystalline areas, giving silk its elasticity.

## Properties of Silk

The fiber property tables in Chapter 3 will aid in comparing the performance of silk to that of the other fibers. Table 5–5 compares silk and wool.

**AESTHETIC** Silk can be dyed and printed in brilliant colors. It is adaptable to a variety of fabrication methods, thus it is available in a wide variety of fabric types for furnishing and apparel uses. Because of cultivated silk's smooth but slightly irregular surface and triangular cross section, the luster of this fiber is soft with an occasional sparkle. It is this luster that has been the model for many manufactured fibers. Fabrics made of cultivated silk usually have a smooth appearance and a luxurious hand.

Wild silks have a duller luster because of their coarser size, less regular surface, and presence of sericin. Fabrics made of wild silk have a more pronounced texture.

**TABLE 5–5** ❖ Comparison of wool and silk.

| PROPERTY | WOOL | SILK |
|---|---|---|
| Abrasion resistance | Moderate | Moderate |
| Breaking tenacity (dry; wet) | 1.5 g/d; 1.0 g/d | 4.5 g/d; 2.8–4.0 g/d |
| Breaking elongation (dry; wet) | 25%; 35% | 20%; 30% |
| Absorbency | 13–18% | 11% |
| Thermal retention | Excellent | Moderate |
| Specific gravity | 1.32 g/cc | 1.25 g/cc |
| Resiliency | Excellent | Moderate |
| Elastic recovery at 3% stretch | 99% | 90% |
| Resistance to strong acids | More resistant | More sensitive |
| Resistance to alkalis | Harmed | Harmed |
| Resistance to light | Poor | Poor |
| Fiber length | 1.5–5 inches | Natural filament; available in staple form |
| Fiber fineness (micrometers) | 10–50 | 11–12 |

In filament form, silk does not have good covering power. Before the development of strong synthetic fibers, silk was the only strong filament and silk fabrics were often treated with metallic salts such as tin, a process called **weighting,** to give the fabric better drape, covering power, and dye absorption. Unfortunately, these historic weighted silks aged quickly. Figure 5–18 shows a 19th-century silk bodice that has shattered (disintegrated). Silk has **scroop,** a natural rustle, which can be increased by treatment with an organic acid such as acetic or tartaric acid.

**DURABILITY** Silk has moderate abrasion resistance. Because of its end uses and cost, silk seldom receives harsh abrasion.

Silk is one of the strongest natural fibers, with a tenacity of 4.5 g/d dry. It may lose up to 20 percent of its strength when wet. Its strength is excellent in relation to its fineness.

Silk has a breaking elongation of 20 percent. It is not as elastic as wool because there are no cross-linkages to retract the molecular chains. When silk is elongated by 2 percent, its elasticity is only 90 percent. Thus, when silk is stretched a small amount it does not return to its original length, but remains slightly stretched.

**COMFORT** Silk has good absorbency with a moisture regain of 11 percent. Silk may develop static cling resulting from the smoothness of the fibers and yarns and the fabric weight. Silk fabrics are comfortable in summer. Like wool, silk is a poor conductor of heat so that it is comfortably warm in the winter. The weight of a fabric is important in heat conductivity—sheer fabrics, possible with filament silk, are cool whereas heavy fabrics are warm. Silk is smooth and soft and thus not irritating to the skin. The density of silk is 1.25 g/cc, producing strong and lightweight silk products. Weighted silk is not as durable as regular silk and wrinkles more readily.

**APPEARANCE RETENTION** Silk has moderate resistance to wrinkling. Because silk's recovery from elongation is low, it does not resist wrinkling as well as some other fibers.

Silk fibers do not shrink. Because the molecular chains are not easily distorted, silk swells only a small amount when wet. Fabrics made from true crepe yarns shrink if laundered, but this is due to the yarn structure, not the fiber content.

**CARE** Dry cleaning solvents do not damage silk. In fact, dry cleaning often is recommended for silk items because of yarn structures, dyes that have poor fastness to water or laundering, or product or fabric-construction methods. Washable silk items can be laundered in a mild detergent solution with gentle agitation. Since silk may lose up to 20 percent of its strength when wet, care should be taken with wet silks to avoid any unnecessary stress. Silk items should be pressed after laundering.

**FIGURE 5–18** ❖ Shattered bodice (c. 1885) of weighted silk.

Pure dye silks should be ironed damp with a press cloth. Wild silks should be dry cleaned and ironed dry to avoid losing sericin, which gives the fabric its body. Silk furnishings are generally cleaned by the dry extraction method.

Silk may water-spot easily. Before hand or machine washing, test in an obscure place of the item to make sure the dye or finish does not water-spot. Silk can be damaged and yellowed by strong soaps or detergent (highly alkaline compounds) and high temperatures. Chlorine bleaches should be avoided. Cleaning agents containing hydrogen peroxide and sodium perborate are safe to use if the directions are followed carefully.

Silk is resistant to dilute mineral acids and organic acids. A crepelike surface effect may be created by the shrinking action of some acids.

Silk is weakened and yellowed by exposure to sunlight and perspiration. Many dyes used to color silk are damaged by sunlight and perspiration. Furnishing fabrics of silk should be protected from direct exposure to sunlight.

Silks may be attacked by insects, especially carpet beetles. Items should be stored clean because soil may attract insects that do not normally attack silk.

Weighted silks deteriorate even under good storage conditions and are especially likely to break at the folds. Historic items often exhibit a condition known as *shattered silk,* in which the weighted silk is disintegrating. (See Figure 5–18.) The process cannot be reversed.

Table 5–6 summarizes silk's performance in apparel and furnishing fabrics.

**TABLE 5–6** ❖ Summary of the performance of silk in apparel and furnishing fabrics.

| | |
|---|---|
| **Aesthetic** | **Variable** |
| Luster | Beautiful and soft |
| **Durability** | **High** |
| Abrasion resistance | Moderate |
| Tenacity | High for natural fibers |
| Elongation | Moderate |
| **Comfort** | **High** |
| Absorbency | High |
| Thermal retention | Good |
| **Appearance Retention** | **Moderate** |
| Resiliency | Moderate |
| Dimensional stability | High |
| Elastic recovery | Moderate |
| **Recommended Care** | Dry clean (apparel) or dry extraction clean (furnishings) |

## Environmental Impact of Silk

Silk is a natural fiber and a renewable resource. Sericulture uses leaves of the mulberry tree. These trees grow in regions where the soil may be too poor to grow other crops or in small and irregular spaces. The trees help retain soil and contribute to the income of small farms. Mulberry trees are severely pruned when the leaves are harvested and the trees do not achieve a natural shape. Since mulberry trees are deciduous, leaves are available for only part of the year and silk production is limited to one generation each year.

Silkworms are susceptible to disease and changes in temperature. Research to increase silk production is aimed at developing disease-resistant varieties, producing artificial diets, and controlling internal environments to induce silk moths to breed and lay eggs year round. Research is also examining the possibility of producing naturally colored silks that do not require use of chemical dyes.

Silkworms are raised for the silk they produce. Most are killed before they have matured in order to harvest filament silk. Because of this, some animal rights activists avoid purchasing or using silk items. Silk production is labor intensive and is concentrated in regions where labor costs are low. When silk prices fall, these regions suffer accordingly. Child labor may be used in producing silk. However, in many areas, silk production allows families to work together and each member's work contributes to a better economic situation for the family. Efforts to mechanize the production of silkworms could have a pronounced impact on regions that have traditionally relied on hand labor to produce silk.

Silk production makes extensive use of water and other chemicals to clean the fiber and remove sericin. Although the use of chemical finishes is relatively small for silk, use of dyes is high. Dyeing silk requires use of heat, water, dye, and other chemicals. Environmental regulations are minimal in some parts of the world where silk is processed, and disposal of chemicals is done with little regard for the environment. Although not all silk products require dry cleaning, many do. Dry cleaning solvents may harm the environment, and their use and disposal are restricted. For more information on dry cleaning, see Chapter 20.

## Uses of Silk

Silk has a drape, luster, and texture that may be imitated by synthetic fibers, but cannot be duplicated exactly. Because of its unique properties and high cost, silk is used primarily in apparel and furnishing items. Other factors that contribute to the continued popularity of silk are its appearance, comfort, and strength. Silk is extremely versatile and can be used to create a variety of fabrics from sheer, gossamer chiffons to heavy, beautiful brocades and velvets. Because of silk's absorbency, it is appropriate for warm weather wear and active sportswear. Because of its low heat conductivity, it is also appropriate for cold weather wear. Silk underwear, socks, and leggings are popular due to silk's soft hand, good absorbency, and wicking characteristics. Silk is available in a range of apparel from one-of-a-kind designer garments to low-priced discount store T-shirts.

Silk and silk blends are equally important in furnishings. Silk blends are often used in window treatment and upholstery fabrics because of the soft luster and drape silk contributes. Silk is also frequently used by itself in upholstery, wall covering fabrics, and wall hangings. Some designers are so enamored with silk that they drape entire rooms in silk. The texture and drape of wild and duppioni silks make them ideal for covering ceilings and walls. Occasionally, beautiful and expensive handmade rugs are made of silk. Liners for sleeping bags, blankets, and bed sheets of silk feel warm, soft, and luxurious next to the skin.

Silk has limited application beyond apparel and furnishings. However, silk is used in the medical field for sutures and prosthetic arteries.

## Identification of Natural Protein Fibers

Natural protein fibers can be identified with a microscope fairly easily. The wool fibers have scales that are visible along the edge and, if the fiber is white or pastel, may be seen throughout the length of the fiber. It is difficult to distinguish among the wool fibers because of their similar appearance. For example, it is easy to distinguish wool from cotton, but it is difficult to distinguish sheep's wool from camel hair. Silk can be identified with the microscope, but with greater difficulty. Since silk is a natural fiber, its surface is not as regular as that of most manufactured fibers. The trilobal cross section may not be apparent, but the fiber has slight bumps or other irregularities. Natural protein fibers are soluble in sodium hypochlorite. In the burn test, these fibers smell like burning hair. However, the odor is so strong that a very small percentage of protein fiber produces a noticeable hair odor. Hence, the burning test is not reliable for blends, nor will it distinguish among the protein fibers.

## Key Terms

Hygroscopic
Wool
Merino
Raw or grease wool
Scoured or clean wool
Grading wool
Sorting wool
Lamb's wool
Garnetted
Recycled wool
Virgin wool
Medulla
Cortex
Crimp
Natural bicomponent fiber
Scales
Felting
Keratin
Mohair
Qiviut
Angora
Camel's hair
Cashmere
Cashgora
Llama
Alpaca
Vicuña
Guanaco
Silk
Sericulture
Sericin
Reeling
Raw silk
Silk-in-the-gum
Silk noils
Wild silk
Tussah silk
Duppioni silk
Momme
Fibroin
Weighting
Scroop

## Questions

1. Describe the similarities in the properties common to all protein fibers.
2. For the products listed below, describe the properties of wool and silk that some manufactured fibers attempt to duplicate.

   carpeting
   blanket
   blouse
   interview suit (wool)
   interview suit (silk)

3. How is the processing of wool and silk different?
4. Identify a natural protein fiber that would be appropriate for each of the end uses listed below and describe the properties that contribute to that end use:

   area rug in front of a fireplace
   upholstery for corporate boardroom
   suit for business travel
   tie with small print pattern

5. To what fiber aspects are the differences in properties among the natural protein fibers attributed?

## Suggested Readings

Burroughs, James (1993, November). "Making a Case for Mohair Fashions." *Knitting Times,* pp. 11, 13, 15.

Feltwell, John (1990). *The Story of Silk.* London: Alan Sutton Publishing.

Grayson, Martin, ed. (1984). *Encyclopedia of Textiles, Fibers, and Nonwoven Fabrics.* New York: John Wiley & Sons.

Hyde, Nina (1988, May). "The Fabric of History: Wool." *National Geographic, 173,* pp. 552–591.

Hyde, Nina (1984, January). "The Queen of Textiles." *National Geographic, 165,* pp. 2–49.

McCarthy, Brian (1991). "Specialty Animal Fibres." *Textiles,* no. 1., pp. 6–8.

Parker, Julie (1991). *All about Silk: A Fabric Dictionary and Swatchbook.* Seattle, WA: Rain City Publishing.

Rheinberg, L. (1991). "The Romance of Silk." *Textile Progress, 21* (4), pp. 1–43.

Trotman, E. R. (1984). *Dyeing and Chemical Technology of Textile Fibers,* 6th ed. New York: John Wiley & Sons.

Chapter 6

# The Fiber Manufacturing Process

## OBJECTIVES

- To understand the concepts related to manufacturing fibers.
- To understand common fiber modifications, how they are achieved, and the functions they serve.
- To understand the differences and similarities among natural and manufactured fibers.
- To relate production processes to fiber modifications.
- To understand how fibers are engineered for end uses.

Manufactured fibers are produced to satisfy a market or supply a special need. The first manufactured fibers made it possible for consumers to have silklike fabrics at low cost. Synthetic fibers produce fabrics with properties unlike those of natural fiber fabrics.

In 1664, Robert Hooke suggested that if the proper liquid were squeezed through a small aperture and allowed to congeal, a fiber like silk might be produced. In 1889, the first successful manufactured fiber (made in 1884 from a solution of cellulose by a Frenchman, Count de Chardonnet) was shown at the Paris Exhibition. In 1910, rayon fibers were commercially produced in the United States. Acetate was produced in 1924. In 1939, the first noncellulosic, or synthetic, fiber—nylon—was made. Since that time, many more generic fibers and modifications or variants of these generic fibers have appeared on the market.

Fiber manufacturers use generic names to identify particular fibers, whereas trade names are companies' names for their fibers, used to promote and market a company's fibers over competitors' fibers. Certification requirements for use of a trade name or trademark allow the owner to set minimum performance standards for a product that carries the trade name or trademark. The number of fiber names appearing on labels can create confusion for the consumer. See Table 6–1 for a list of generic names for manufactured fibers.

With increased competition worldwide and environmental regulations, fiber producers are reducing the variety of generic fibers they produce. Generic fiber trade names, like Dacron polyester, are being used less often to market products to consumers. However, trade names for special fiber modifications, like Supplex nylon, are more often used to promote products.

The impact of manufactured fibers on the consumer and the industrial market has far exceeded original predictions. The first manufactured fibers were aimed at people who could not afford the expensive natural fibers, like silk. Yet manufactured fibers have caused tremendous changes in the way people live and the things they do. End uses that simply were not possible or practical are now commonplace due to the use of manufactured fibers. Many fashions are directly related to manufactured fibers. The combination of fit and performance found in spandex and nylon biking shorts, swimwear, and leotards is not possible with any natural fiber or any combination of natural fibers. The common use of carpeting in homes, businesses, and other facilities is related to the low cost and good performance characteristics of nylon, olefin, and other manufactured fibers. Carpets of wool are too expensive and do not possess the characteristics appropriate for the many ways carpets are used today. The use of manufactured fibers in roadbed underlays, communication cables, and replacement body parts are examples of end uses that are not possible with natural fibers. Manufactured fibers have literally revolutionized daily life!

**TABLE 6–1** ❖ Generic names for manufactured fibers.

| CELLULOSIC | NONCELLULOSIC OR SYNTHETIC | | MINERAL |
|---|---|---|---|
| Acetate | Acrylic | Olefin | Glass |
| Triacetate* | Anidex* | PBI | Metallic |
| Rayon | Aramid | Polyester | |
| Lyocell | Azlon* | Rubber | |
| | Lastrile* | Saran | |
| | Modacrylic | Spandex | |
| | Novoloid* | Sulfar | |
| | Nylon | Vinal* | |
| | Nytril* | Vinyon* | |

* Not produced in the United States.

Manufactured fibers possess the unique ability to be engineered for specific end uses. For that reason, many of these fibers are highly versatile and found in an amazing array of products. With our expanded understanding of polymer chemistry and fiber production, many problems in the original fiber have been overcome through changes in the polymer, production, or finishing steps.

With current lifestyles, it is not possible to return to the use of natural fibers only. Table 6–2 summarizes the use of manufactured fibers in the U.S. in 1994. Worldwide, manufactured fibers comprise 50 percent of the market. In the U.S., that number is 64 percent; 42 percent for apparel, 73 percent for furnishings, and 89 percent for industrial products. Those numbers are especially amazing when one realizes that the manufactured fiber industry uses only 1 percent of the nation's oil and natural gas supplies. The industry is highly efficient. One 300-acre polyester facility can produce as much fiber as 600,000 acres of cotton.

❖

# FIBER SPINNING

It took many years to develop the first **fiber spinning** solutions and invent mechanical devices to convert the solutions into filaments. The first solutions were made by dissolving cellulose in certain substances. It was not until the 1920s and 1930s that we first learned how to build long-chain molecules from simple substances.

**TABLE 6–2** ❖ Use of manufactured fibers.

| USE CATEGORY | PERCENTAGE |
|---|---|
| Sheer hosiery | 96 |
| Socks/anklets | 40 |
| Sweaters | 64 |
| Craft yarn | 81 |
| Underwear | 13 |
| Lingerie | 43 |
| Robes and loungewear | 50 |
| Pile fabrics | 100 |
| Linings | 66 |
| Apparel lace | 84 |
| Narrow fabrics | 67 |
| Top weight apparel | 44 |
| Bottom weight apparel | 37 |
| Other apparel | 76 |
| Bedspreads and quilts | 39 |
| Blankets | 35 |
| Sheets | 37 |
| Towels | 2 |
| Window treatments | 43 |
| Upholstery | 52 |
| Carpet | 99 |
| Other furnishings | 76 |
| Tires | 99 |
| Hose | 95 |
| Belting | 79 |
| Medical, surgical uses | 88 |
| Nonwovens | 100 |
| Fiberfill | 100 |
| Felts | 69 |
| Filtration | 93 |
| Rope, etc. | 91 |
| Sewing thread | 70 |
| Reinforcement, paper and tape | 41 |
| Reinforcement, plastic and electrical | 37 |
| Coated fabrics | 82 |
| Transportation fabrics | 97 |
| Narrow fabrics, industrial | 88 |
| Bags, bagging | 96 |
| Miscellaneous | 86 |

All manufactured fiber spinning processes are based on these three general steps:

1. Preparing a viscous or syrupy dope.
2. Forcing or extruding the dope through an opening in a spinneret to form a fiber.
3. Solidifying the fiber by coagulation, evaporation, or cooling.

The *raw material* may be a natural product such as cellulose or protein, or it may be synthetic chemicals formed into resins. These raw materials are made into solutions by dissolving them with chemicals or by melting. The solution is referred to as the **spinning solution** or **dope.**

**Extrusion** is a very important part of the spinning process. It consists of forcing or pumping the spinning solution through the tiny holes of a spinneret.

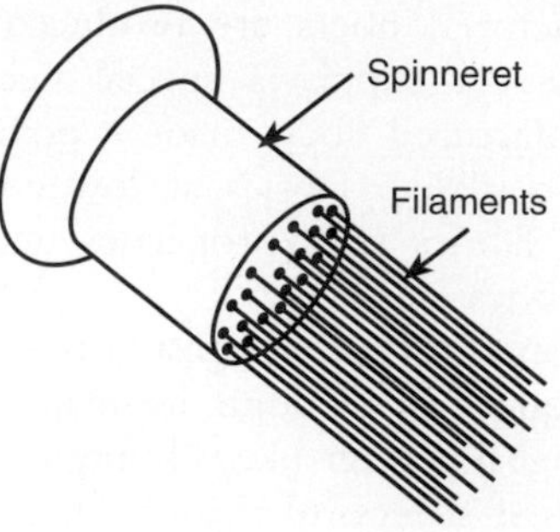


**FIGURE 6–1** ❖ Spinneret with filament fibers being extruded.

A **spinneret** is a small thimblelike nozzle made of platinum for rayon or stainless steel for the other fibers (Figure 6–1). Spinnerets are costly and new developments are closely guarded secrets. The making of the tiny holes is the critical part of the process. Fine hairlike instruments or laser beams are used. Round holes are most common, but other shapes are used for special fiber types (see Figure 3–3).

Each hole in the spinneret forms one fiber. **Filament fibers** are spun from spinnerets with 350 holes or less. When these fibers are grouped together and slightly twisted, they make a filament yarn. **Filament tow** is an untwisted rope of thousands of fibers. This rope is made by combining the fibers from many spinnerets, each of which may have thousands of holes. The tow is given a crimp and is ready to be converted into staple by cutting or breaking to the desired length. (See Chapter 10 for methods of breaking filament tow into staple.)

## Spinning Methods

Spinning is done by four different methods, which are compared briefly in Figure 6–2. Details of the methods are given in later chapters.

The process of developing a new fiber is long and expensive, and millions of dollars must be invested before any profit can be realized. First, a research program develops the new fiber. Then a pilot plant is built to translate laboratory procedures to commercial production. Fibers produced by the pilot plant are tested to determine end uses and evaluate suitability. When the fiber is ready, a commercial plant is built.

A patent on the process gives the producer 17 years of exclusive right to the use of the process—time to recover the initial cost and make a profit. The price per pound during this time is high, but it drops later. The patent owner can license other producers to use the process. Continuing research and development programs address problems that arise and produce modifications for special end uses.

*Wet Spinning: Acrylic, Rayon, Spandex*

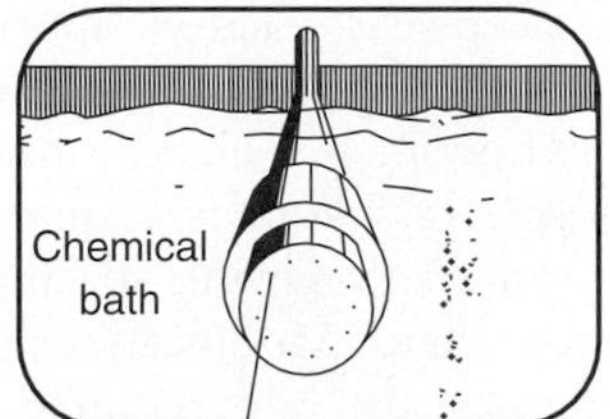


1. Raw material is dissolved by chemicals.
2. Fiber is spun into chemical bath.
3. Fiber solidifies when coagulated by bath.

Oldest process
Most complex
Weak fibers until dry
Washing, bleaching, etc., required before use

*Dry Spinning:*
*Acetate, Acrylic, Modacrylic, Spandex (Major Method)*

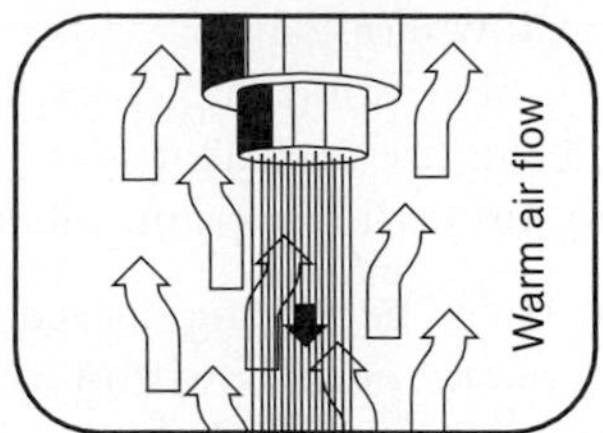


1. Resin solids are dissolved by solvent.
2. Fiber is spun into warm air.
3. Fiber solidifies by evaporation of the solvent.

Direct process
Solvent required
Solvent recovery required
No washing, etc., required

*Melt Spinning: Nylon, Olefin, Polyester, Saran*

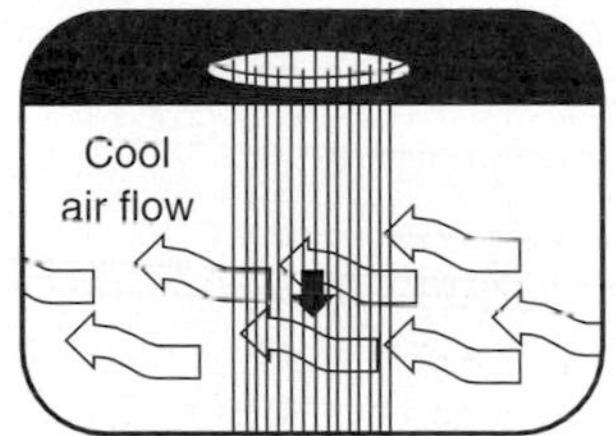


1. Resin solids are melted in autoclave.
2. Fiber is spun out into the air.
3. Fiber solidifies on cooling.

Least expensive
Direct process
High spinning speeds
No solvent, washing, etc., required
Fibers shaped like spinneret hole

*Solvent Spinning: Lyocell*

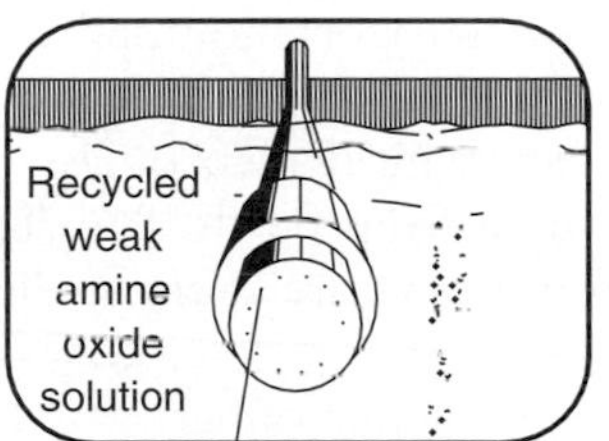


1. Raw material dissolved in amine oxide.
2. Fiber spun into weak amine oxide solution.
3. Fiber precipitates out of solution.

Newest process
Relatively simple fiber production method
Solvent recovered
Fibers must be washed and dried before use

**FIGURE 6–2** ❖ Major methods of spinning manufactured fibers. (COURTESY OF AMERICAN FIBER MANUFACTURERS ASSOCIATION, INC.)

❖

# COMMON FIBER MODIFICATIONS

One advantage of the manufactured fibers is that each step of the production process can be precisely controlled to modify the parent fiber. These modifications are the result of a producer's continuing research program to address any limitations, explore the potential of its fibers, and develop properties that will give greater versatility in the end uses of the fibers.

The **parent fiber** is the fiber in its simplest form. It is often sold as a commodity fiber by generic name only, without benefit of a trade name. Other terms for parent fiber include regular, basic, standard, conventional, or first-generation fiber.

Modifications of the parent fiber may be sold under a brand or trade name. Modifications may also be referred to as types, variants, or *x* generation fibers where the *x* could be any number. Some fiber producers are identifying tenth and higher generation modifications.

The following are some **fiber modifications** of the second generation:

1. Modification of fiber size and shape: cross section, thick and thin, hollow
2. Modification of molecular structure and crystallinity: high tenacity, low pilling, low elongation
3. Additives to polymer or fiber solution: cross dye, antistatic, sunlight resistance, fire retardant
4. Modifications of spinning procedures: crimp, fiberfill

Complex modifications have been engineered to combine two polymers as separate entities within a single fiber or yarn. These have been referred to as third-generation fibers and include two types. Bicomponent fibers are discussed towards the end of this chapter. Blended filament yarns are discussed in Chapter 10.

## Fiber Size

Fiber size is generally easy to control. The simplest way is by changing the size of the opening in the spinneret. Fiber size often dictates end use. Finer fibers, those with a denier of less than 7, are most often used for apparel. Deniers ranging from 5 to 25 are used in furnishings. Industrial applications have the widest range of denier, ranging from deniers of 1 for transportation upholstery and sewing thread to several thousand for ropes and fishline. **Microdenier** are fibers with deniers of less than 1.0. These fibers tend to range from 0.5 to 0.8 denier per filament *(dpf)*. **Ultrafine fibers** are even smaller—less than 0.3 dpf.

A yarn of microdenier fibers or microfibers may have as many as four times more fibers than a regular fiber yarn of the same size. Microdenier generic fibers on the market include polyester, nylon, acrylic, and rayon. These fibers are used in apparel and furnishings. Fabrics made from these fibers are softer and are more drapeable, silklike, comfortable, and water repellent.

Microfibers may be present by themselves in fabrics or in blends with natural or other manufactured fibers. Both filament and staple forms are available. In blends, at least 40 percent microfiber is needed to retain the microfiber's characteristics. These fibers are used in coats, blouses, suits, sleepwear, active sportswear, hosiery, upholstery, window treatments, bedding, and wall coverings. Microfiber women's hosiery has been especially successful. These very fine fibers required that yarn spinning frames, looms and sewing machines be modified in order to handle them. Modifications in dyeing and finishing techniques also are required. Both designers and consumers are enthusiastic about these fibers, in spite of their higher price.

Microfibers and ultrafine fibers are produced by modifying the spinning technique or by splitting or separating the filaments. Figure 6–3 shows several techniques that have been used to produce these very fine fibers. Polyester ultrafine fibers with modified cross sections and occasional fiber irregularities are sometimes referred to as ***shin-gosen***, a Japanese term that means new synthetic fiber. Although not a new generic fiber type, these fibers use technical innovations in fiber production and processing and result in products with exceptional consumer performance characteristics. Used primarily in women's wear, these fibers mimic the appearance aspects of natural fibers, especially silk.

**Mixed denier filament bundling** combines fibers of several denier sizes in one yarn (Figure 6–4). Fibers of micro size (0.5 dpf) contribute the buttery hand to the fabric while the macro or regular denier fibers (2.0 dpf) contribute drape, bounce, and durability to the fabric. When the resulting fabric is laundered, the macro fibers shrink 10 percent more than the microfibers. This forces the microfibers to the surface of the fabric.

Larger sized fibers are used where greater strength, abrasion resistance, and resiliency are required. For example, carpet fibers with deniers in the range of 15 to

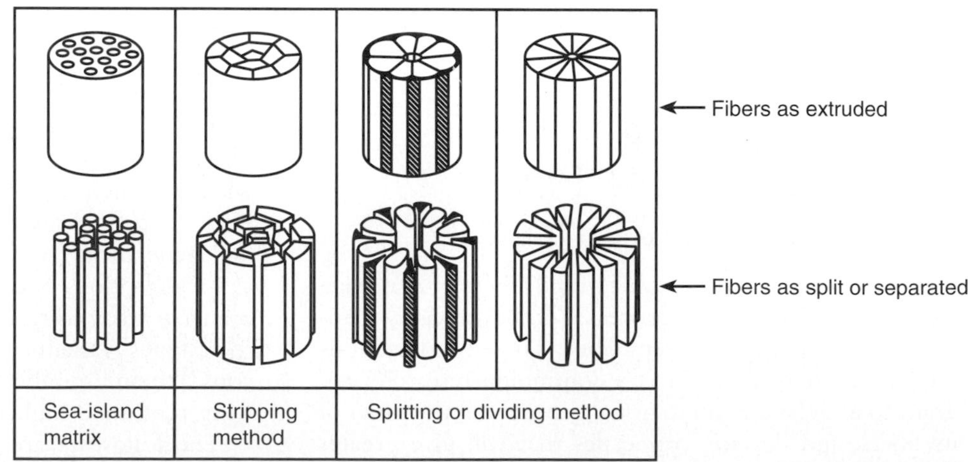


FIGURE 6–3 ❖ Typical methods of splitting or separating microfibers. (COURTESY OF AMERICAN ASSOCIATION OF TEXTILE CHEMISTS AND COLORISTS.)

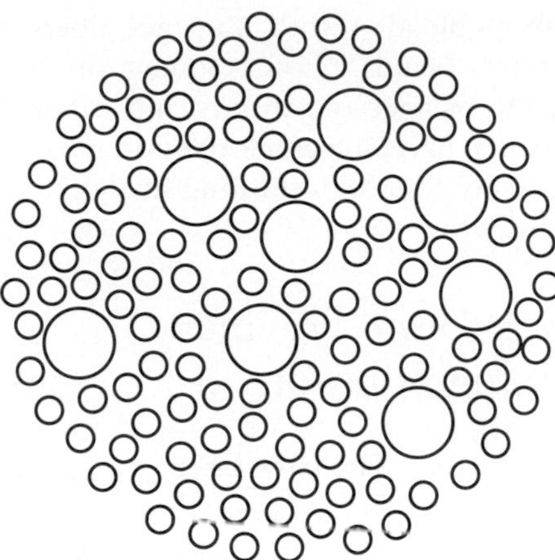

**FIGURE 6–4** ❖ Cross section of yarn combining micro and macro fibers.

24 give better resiliency. Higher denier fibers resist crushing better than lower denier fibers.

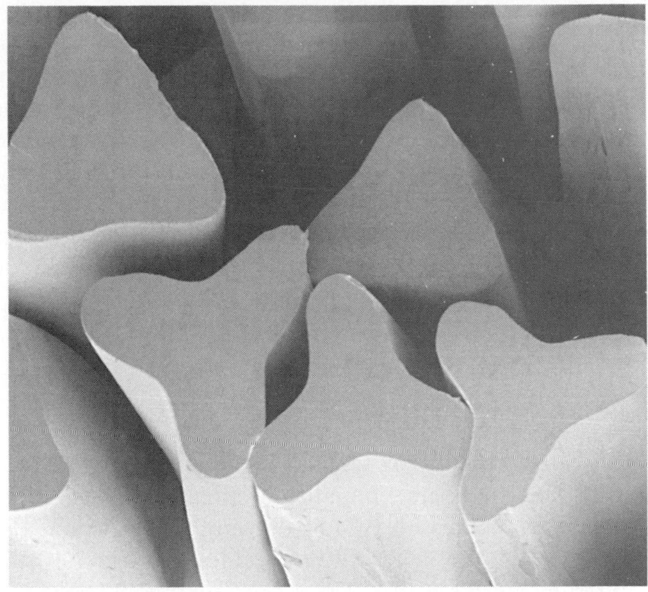

**FIGURE 6–5** ❖ Stereoscan of trilobal nylon. (COURTESY OF E. I. DUPONT DE NEMOURS & COMPANY.)

## Fiber Shape

**SOLID FIBERS** Changing the cross-sectional shape is the easiest way to alter the mechanical and aesthetic properties of a fiber. This is usually done by changing the shape of the spinneret hole to produce the fiber shape desired. All kinds of shapes are possible: flat, trilobal, quadralobal, pentalobal, triskelion, cruciform, cloverleaf, and alphabet shapes such as Y and T (see Figure 3–3).

The *flat shape* was one of the first variations produced. "Crystal" acetate and "sparkling" nylon are ribbonlike fibers that are extruded through a long, narrow spinneret hole. Flat fibers tend to reflect light much as a mirror does, so fabrics have a glint or sparkle.

The **trilobal shape** has been widely used in both nylon and polyester fibers (Figure 6–5). It is spun through a spinneret with three triangularly arranged slits. The trilobal shape produces a fabric with a beautiful silklike hand (depending on end-use requirements), subtle opacity, soil-hiding capacity, built-in bulk without weight, heightened wicking action, silklike sheen and color, crush resistance in heavy deniers, and good textured crimp.

Other fiber shapes that produce similar characteristics are *triskelion* (a three-sided configuration similar to a boat propeller), *pentalobal* (see Figure 6–6), *octolobal,* and *Y-shaped.*

**Thick-and-thin fiber types** vary in their diameter along their length as a result of uneven drawing or stretching after spinning. Fabrics woven of these fibers have a duppioni silklike or linenlike texture. The thick areas, or nubs, dye a deeper color to create interesting tone-on-tone color effects. Many surface textures are possible by changing the size and length of the nubs or slubs.

**HOLLOW OR MULTICELLULAR FIBER TYPES** The hair or fur of many animals contains air cells that provide insulation in cold weather. The feathers of birds are hollow to give them buoyancy. Similar air cells and hollow filaments are possible in manufactured fibers by the use of gas-forming compounds added to the spinning solution, by air injection at the jet face as the fiber is forming, or by the shape of the spinneret holes.

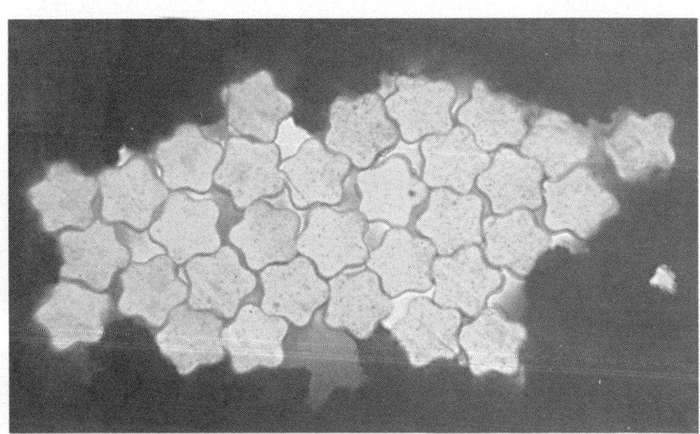

**FIGURE 6–6** ❖ Trevira® polyester pentalobal cross section. (COURTESY OF TREVIRA.)

**Hollow** melt-spun fibers can be formed by pyrolizing a portion of the polymer flowing to the spinneret to form gas and then extruding the bubble containing polymer as hollow filaments. The spinneret hole can be shaped to produce hollow fibers. When extruded through a C-shaped hole, the fiber closes immediately. Other spinneret holes spin the fiber as two halves that immediately close to make the hollow fiber (see Figure 6–7). Examples of trade names of hollow fibers include Hollofil and Quallofil by DuPont.

## Molecular Structure and Crystallinity

**High-tenacity fibers** are produced by a controlled stretching of fibers immediately after extrusion. Fiber strength is increased by (1) drawing or stretching the fiber to align or orient the molecules, thus strengthening the intermolecular forces, and/or by (2) chemical modification of the fiber polymer to increase the degree of polymerization. These procedures will be discussed in more detail in Chapters 7 and 8.

**Low-pilling fibers** are engineered to reduce their flex life by slightly reducing the molecular weight of the polymer chains. When flex-abrasion resistance is reduced, the fiber pills break off almost as soon as they are formed and the fabric retains its smooth appearance. These low-pilling fibers are not as strong as other types but are durable enough for apparel uses and are particularly suited to soft knitting yarns. (Review the discussion of molecular weight in Chapter 3.)

**Binder staple** is a semidull, crimped polyester with a very low melting point. (Melting point relates to molecular structure.) Binder staple develops a thermoplastic bond with other fibers under heat and pressure. It sticks at 165°F and shrinks 55–75 percent at 200°F.

**Low-elongation fiber types** are used as reinforcing fibers to increase the strength and abrasion resistance of weaker fibers blended with stronger fibers as in cotton/polyester blends. Low elongation results from changing the balance of tenacity and extension. High-tenacity fibers have lower elongation properties. End uses are mainly for work clothing and other items that receive hard wear.

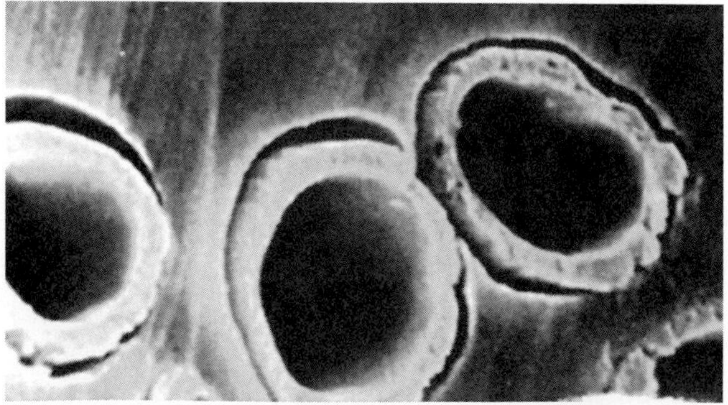

FIGURE 6–7 ❖ Cross section of hollow rayon fibers. (COURTESY OF COURTAULDS FIBERS, INC.)

## Additives to the Polymer or Spinning Solution

**DELUSTERING** The basic fiber reflects light from its smooth, round surface. It is referred to as a **bright fiber.** (Note that here bright refers to high luster, not intense color.) To **deluster** a fiber, titanium dioxide—a white pigment—is added to the spinning solution before the fiber is extruded. In some cases, the titanium dioxide can be mixed in at an earlier stage, while the resin polymer is being formed. The degree of luster can be controlled by varying the amount of delusterant, producing dull or semidull fibers. Figure 6–8 shows three yarns of different lusters.

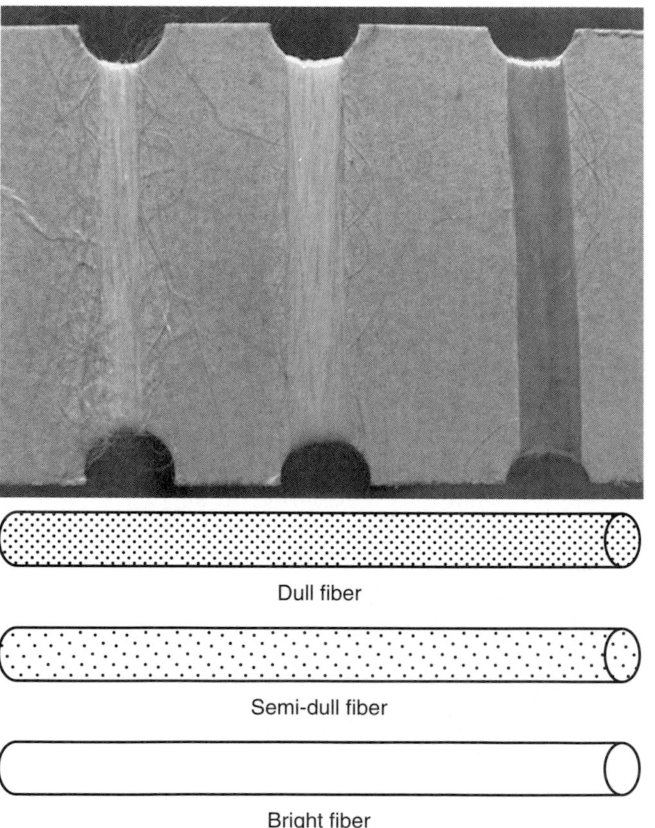


FIGURE 6–8 ❖ (Top) Polyester yarns (left to right: dull, semidull, bright). (Bottom) Fibers as they would look under a microscope.

Delustered fibers can be identified microscopically by the presence of dark spots within the fiber (Figure 6–8). The particles of pigment absorb light or prevent reflection of light. Absorbed light causes degradation, or tendering, of the fiber. For this reason, bright fibers that reflect light suffer less light damage and are better for use in window treatment fabrics. The strength of a delustered fiber is slightly less than that of a bright fiber. Rayon, for example, is 3–5 percent weaker when it is delustered.

**SOLUTION DYEING OR MASS PIGMENTATION** Solution dyeing, or **mass pigmentation,** was developed in response to the fading of many dyes used to dye some of the earliest manufactured fibers. **Solution dyeing** is the addition of colored pigments or dyes to the spinning solution. Thus, the fiber is colored when it emerges from the spinneret. These fibers are also referred to as *solution dyed, mass pigmented, dope dyed, spun dyed,* or *producer colored.* If the color is added before the fiber hardens, the term *gel dying* may be used. Solution dyeing provides color permanence that is not obtainable in any other way. The lightfastness and washfastness are unchanged for the life of the item. Because the color is uniformly distributed throughout the fiber, crocking and other color changes with use are not problems.

Because of the difficulty in obtaining a truly black dye that has reasonable colorfastness properties, black pigments are usually the first ones to be used. Other colors are produced as suitable colorfast pigments are developed.

Solution-dyed fibers cost more per pound than uncolored fibers. This difference may be offset later by the cost of yarn or piece (fabric) dyeing. The solution-dyed fibers are used in all kinds of end uses, such as upholstery, window treatments, and apparel. One disadvantage of the solution-dyed fibers is that the manufacturer must carry a large inventory to be able to fill orders quickly. The manufacturer is also less able to adjust to fashion changes in color, because it is not possible to strip color from these fibers and redye them.

**WHITENERS AND BRIGHTENERS** **Whiteners** and **brighteners** are added to the spinning solution to make fibers that look whiter or that resist yellowing. The additive used is an optical bleach or fluorescent dye that reflects more blue light from the fabric, thus masking yellowing. These whiteners are permanent in washing and dry cleaning. They also eliminate the necessity for bleaching.

**DYE AFFINITY** Dye affinity or **cross-dyeable fibers** are very different from solution-dyed fibers. Solution-dyed fibers have colored pigment added to the spinning solution, so they are colored as they emerge from the spinneret. Dye affinity fibers are not colored when they emerge from the spinneret.

Cross-dyeable fibers are made by incorporating dye-accepting chemicals into the molecular structure. Some of the parent fibers are nondyeable; others have poor acceptance of certain classes of dyes. The cross-dyeable types were developed to correct this limitation. The dye affinity fibers are far easier to dye than their parent fibers.

**ANTISTATIC FIBER TYPES** Static is a result of the flow of electrons. Fibers conduct electricity according to how readily electrons move in them. If static builds up in a fiber so that it has an excess of electrons, it is negatively charged and it is attracted to something that is positively charged—something that has a deficiency of electrons. This attraction is illustrated by the way clothing clings to the body. Water dissipates static. Because many synthetic fibers have such low water absorbency, static charges build up rapidly but dissipate slowly during dry weather or when fabrics have been rubbed or tumbled together. If the fibers can be made wettable, the static charges will dissipate quickly and there will be no annoying static buildup.

The **antistatic fiber types** give durable protection because the fiber is made wettable by incorporating an antistatic compound—a chemical conductor—as an integral part of the fiber. The compound is added to the fiber-polymer raw material so that it is evenly distributed throughout the fiber dope or spinning solution. It changes the fiber's hydrophobic nature to a more hydrophilic one and raises the moisture regain so that static is dissipated more quickly. The moisture content of the air should be kept high enough to provide moisture for absorption—even cotton will build up static if the air is dry enough. Static control is also achieved by incorporating a conductive core into the fiber (Figure 6–9). Table 6–3 lists trade names and end uses of some antistatic fiber variants.

The soil-resistant benefits of the antistatic fiber types are outstanding. The antistatic fibers retard soiling by minimizing the attraction and retention of dirt particles, and the opacity and luster in the yarn have soil-hiding properties. Soil redisposition in laundry is dramatically reduced. Oily stains, even motor oils, are released more easily.

**SUNLIGHT-RESISTANT FIBERS** Ultraviolet light causes fiber degradation as well as color fading. When ultraviolet light is absorbed, the damage results from a reaction between the radiant energy and the fiber or dye. Stabilizers such as nitrogenous compounds may be added to the dope to increase light resistance. These stabilizers must be carefully selected for the fiber-dye com-

**FIGURE 6–9** ❖ Antistatic polyester. (COURTESY OF E. I. DU PONT DE NEMOURS & COMPANY.)

bination. Estron SLR is a **sunlight-resistant** acetate fiber. These fibers are especially important for window treatments and other furnishings in glass office buildings. SLR fibers are also important for car interiors because of the amount of exposure to sunlight. Delustered fibers are more sensitive to sunlight than bright fibers.

**FLAME-RESISTANT FIBERS** **Flame-resistant fibers** give better protection to consumers than do topical flame-retardant finishes (see Chapter 18). Some manufactured fibers are inherently flame retardant because of their chemical composition. These include aramid, novoloid, modacrylic, glass, PBI, saran, sulfar, and vinyon. Other manufactured fibers can be modified by changing their polymer structure or by adding water-insoluble compounds to the spinning solution. These fiber modifications make the fibers inherently flame resistant, but they may vary in their resistance to flame.

## Fiber Spinning Procedure

When producers started to make staple fiber, mechanical crimping was done to broken filaments and later to filament tow to make the fibers more cohesive and thus easier to spin into yarns. Other techniques were developed to give permanent crimp to rayon and acetate and to provide bulk or stretch to all fibers—filaments as well as staple.

Crimping of fibers is important in many end uses: for cover and loft in bulky knits, blankets, carpets, battings for quilted items, and pillows and for stretch and recovery from stretch and recovery from stretch in hosiery and sportswear.

For wet spun fibers, crimp can be produced by coagulating the fiber in a slightly modified bath. A skin forms around the fiber, bursts, and a thinner skin forms over the rupture. The crimp develops when the fiber is immersed in water. Melt-spun fibers with a helical or spiral crimp are produced by cooling one side of the fiber faster than the other side as the fiber is extruded. This uneven cooling causes a curl to form in the fiber. The same effect can be achieved by heating one side of the fiber during the stretching or drawing process. This helical crimp has more springiness than the conventional mechanical sawtooth crimp. These fibers are used where high levels of compressional resistance and recovery are needed.

## Third-Generation Fiber Types

**BICOMPONENT FIBERS** A **bicomponent fiber** is a fiber consisting of two polymers that are chemically different, physically different, or both. If the two components would fall into two different generic classes, the term **bicomponent-bigeneric** may be used. Bicomponent fibers may be of several types. Bilateral fibers are spun with the two polymers side by side. In core-sheath fibers, one polymer is surrounded or encircled by another polymer. In matrix-fibril fibers, short fibrils of one polymer are embedded in another polymer (see Figure 6–10).

**TABLE 6–3** ❖ Antistatic fiber variants.

| PARENT FIBER | TRADEMARK | FIBER MODIFICATION | END USE | PRODUCER |
|---|---|---|---|---|
| Nylon | Antron III | Three filaments of carbon-black core surrounded by sheath of nylon | Apparel | DuPont |
| Nylon | Ultron | Conjugate spun 95 percent nylon 6,6 and 5 percent nylon/carbon-black polymer stripe | Carpets | Monsanto |
| Nylon | Hydrofil | | Apparel | Allied-Signal |
| Polyester | Dacron III (Figure 6–9) | Polymeric conductive core | Carpets | DuPont |

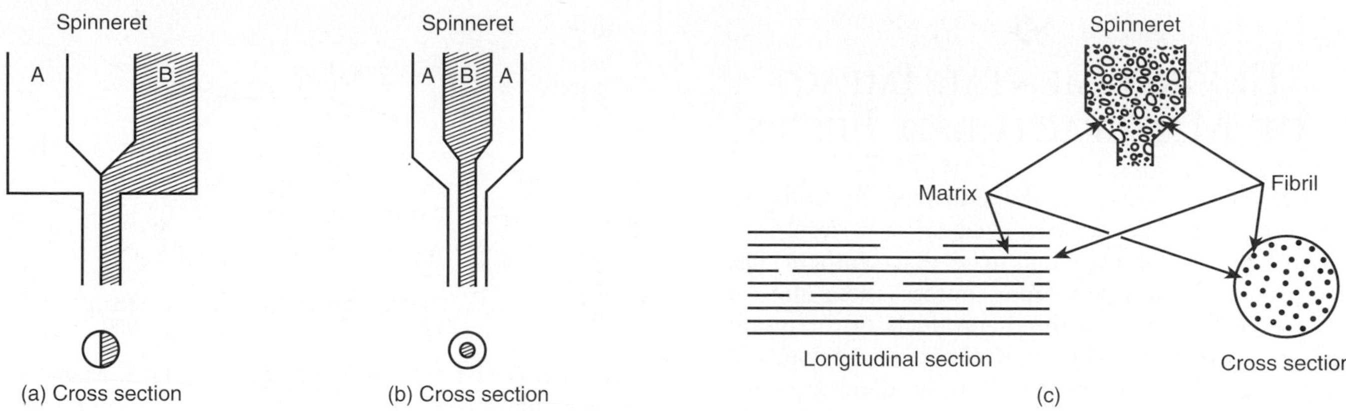


**FIGURE 6–10** ❖ Bicomponent fiber structure: (a) bilateral; (b) core-sheath; (c) matrix-fibril.

The original discovery that the two sides of a fiber can react differently when wet was made during studies of wool in 1886. In 1953, it was discovered that the difference in reaction was the result of the bicomponent nature of wool, which results from a difference in growth rate and in chemical composition. This differential behavior is used to advantage in producing bilateral bicomponent fibers with latent or inherent crimp.

For example, acrylic fibers can be spun straight and made into a garment such as a sweater, which is then exposed to heat; one side of the fiber shrinks and the fiber takes on a helical crimp. The reaction of the fibers to water occurs during laundering. As the fiber gets wet, one side swells and the fiber uncrimps. As the crimp relaxes, the sweater increases in size. The crimp returns as the sweater dries and it will regain its original size if properly handled. Sweaters of this type should not be drip-dried or placed on a towel to dry because the weight of the water and the resistance of the towel prevent the sweater from regaining its original size. The correct way to dry the sweater is either to machine dry it at a low temperature or to place it on a smooth, flat surface and bunch it in to help the crimp recover.

A bicomponent-bigeneric antistatic fiber has been developed with a polyester core surrounded by a sheath of a polyester copolymer impregnated with black carbon particles. This fiber is intended for applications where static can create a potential explosion hazard or where static creates a nuisance. It can be used in furnishing, apparel, and industrial applications.

Cordelan is a vinal/vinyon bicomponent-bigeneric flame-resistant fiber from Kohjin of Japan. It is a matrix-fibril–type fiber used in flame-retardant furnishings and blankets in airplanes.

## Performance Fibers

Fiber modifications that provide comfort and improve human performance are important in active sportswear. With recent advances in fiber and fabric technology, more efficient materials produce lighter weight and more comfortable products. Several materials may be combined into one product: One layer manages moisture or wicks perspiration away from the body's surface, a second layer provides warmth or insulation to keep the body warm, and a third layer protects from wind, rain, or snow.

The moisture management layer may be a synthetic fiber with good wicking characteristics, like polyester or olefin. An alternative is a fiber with hydrophilic molecules permanently grafted onto the surface that allow for cooling by evaporation during vigorous exercise. Fiber research and development continues to focus on the insulation layer. While fiber insulators build on the principle of trapped air for warmth, advances in fiber size, configuration, and placement have resulted in a variety of products that are soft, breathable, and fashionable. Microfibers, such as DuPont's Microloft and 3M's Thinsulate, provide incredibly warm, soft, and lightweight insulation. These fibers are used in outerwear, pillows, quilts, blankets, sleeping bags, and window treatments to minimize heat transfer. Shell fabrics may be made of microfibers with a special finish to further enhance the fabric's performance so that it is both waterproof and breathable.

More information on specific fiber performance and trade names is provided in the appropriate sections of Chapters 7, 8, and 9. Finishes that enhance these performance fibers are discussed in Chapter 18. Additional aspects of performance fabrics are discussed in Chapters 12 through 15 with fabrication methods.

❖

# Environmental Impact of Manufactured Fibers

Manufactured fibers may be criticized by consumers because these fibers are perceived to be harmful to the environment. Although it is true that synthetic fibers are processed from petroleum sources, these fibers use only a small fraction of the by-products of the production of gasoline and fuel oils. Fibers like nylon, polyester, and olefin are produced from natural gases or from butadiene, a by-product of refining crude oil. Fibers from naturally occurring polymers like rayon, which are produced from wood pulp, may contribute to excess acid in the air and surface water. Some practices of harvesting trees to be processed into wood pulp, such as clear-cutting timber, cutting old growth forests, and overharvesting national forests, are criticized by environmentalists.

Concerns with manufactured fibers regarding crude oil and hazardous chemical spills, recycling, health, and safety are real and cannot be ignored or minimized. Government regulations, concern for safety, the economic necessity of reducing costs, and public image concerns have resulted in significant efforts on the part of fiber producers to minimize the negative environmental aspects of fiber production. Fiber production processes and record-keeping practices have been modified to use fewer hazardous chemicals, recycle chemicals, and document the production and disposal of waste materials. Materials that were disposed of ten years ago are now recycled within the firm or sold to other firms for their use. The generation of hazardous waste and the problems related to waste disposal have been reduced significantly. Besides minimizing the impact on the environment, these practices also keep costs lower and benefit the consumer with lower retail prices. Some fiber modifications enhance fiber finishing and further minimize use of hazardous chemicals.

Consumers also are concerned with the disposal of manufactured fibers that do not degrade naturally. Natural fibers will degrade eventually, if exposed to nature. However, with current waste disposal methods such as landfills, fibers do not degrade. This is as true for cotton as it is for polyester. Although the concern for synthetics in landfills is valid, consumers should be equally concerned with natural fibers.

Recycling of synthetic fibers is very important to the fiber industry. Polyester fibers produced from pre- and postconsumer waste are being recycled. Finished products made from recycled fibers range from underwear to carpeting. Items with trade names, like Polartec Recycled, DyerSport E.C.O., and Fortrel EcoSpun, are popular with consumers who are interested in environmentally sound items. Some products labeled "100 percent recyclable" will be taken back by the manufacturer and recycled when the consumer is ready to dispose of them.

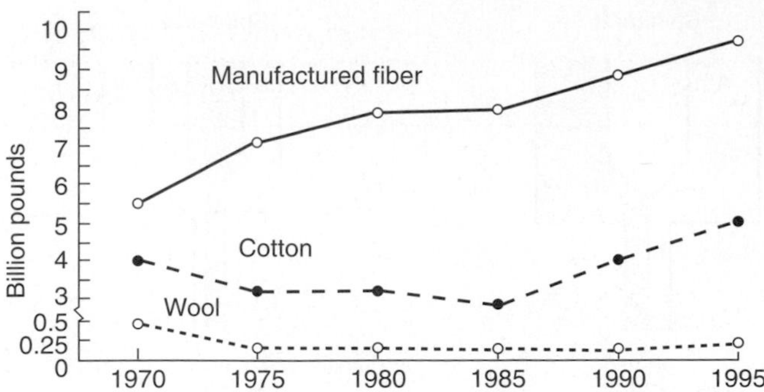


**FIGURE 6–11** ❖ Domestic consumption: Manufactured fiber, cotton, and wool. (COURTESY OF FIBER ORGANON.)

❖

# Manufactured Fiber Consumption

In 1928, manufactured fibers accounted for 5 percent of fiber consumption in the United States; by 1994, manufactured fibers comprised over 57 percent of U.S. textile consumption. See Figure 6–11, which compares domestic consumption of manufactured fiber, cotton, and wool, and Table 6–4, which lists U.S. manufactured fiber production in millions of pounds.

❖

# Manufactured Versus Natural Fibers

A comparison of natural and manufactured fibers is made in Table 6–5.

**TABLE 6–4** ❖ U.S. manufactured fiber production in millions of pounds in 1994

| | |
|---|---|
| Acetate, lyocell, and rayon | 498 |
| Acrylic and modacrylic | 442 |
| Nylon | 2,727 |
| Olefin | 2,408 |
| Polyester | 3,858 |

*Source: Fiber Organon*, January 1995, p. 4.

**TABLE 6–5** ❖ Comparison of natural and manufactured fibers.

| CATEGORY | NATURAL | MANUFACTURED |
|---|---|---|
| Production | Seasonal; stored until used | Continuous |
| Quality | Varies due to weather, nutrients, insects, or disease | Uniform |
| Uniformity | Lacking | Can be uniform or nonuniform depending on end use |
| Physical structure | Dependent on natural growth of plant or animal | Dependent on fiber-spinning processes and after treatments |
| Chemical composition and molecular structure | Dependent on natural growth | Dependent on starting materials |
| Properties | Inherent; but can be changed by yarn, fabrication, and finishes | Inherent; but can be changed by varying spinning solutions and spinning conditions, fabrication, or finishes |
| Length | Mostly staple; only silk is available in filament | Any length |
| Versatility | Not as versatile | Versatile; changes can be made quickly |
| Absorbency | Highly absorbent | Most have low absorbency* |
| Heat sensitivity | Not heat sensitive | Most are heat sensitive** |
| Heat setability | Require fabric finish | Most can be heat-set* |
| Research, development, and promotion | By trade organizations | By individual companies as well as by trade organizations |
| Size | Dependent on type and variety | Any size can be produced |

* Rayon and acetate are exceptions.
** Rayon is an exception.

## KEY TERMS

Manufactured fiber
Fiber spinning
Dope or spinning solution
Extrusion
Spinneret
Filament fiber
Filament tow
Parent fiber
Fiber modification
Microdenier
Ultrafine fiber
*Shin-gosen*
Mixed denier filament bundling
Trilobal shape
Thick-and-thin fibers
Hollow fibers
High-tenacity fibers
Low-pilling fibers
Binder staple
Low-elongation fibers
Bright fibers
Delustering
Mass pigmentation
Solution dyeing
Whiteners or brighteners
Cross-dyeable fibers
Antistatic fibers
Sunlight-resistant fibers
Flame-resistant fibers
Bicomponent fibers
Bicomponent-bigeneric fibers

## QUESTIONS

1. Explain, in general terms, how a manufactured fiber is produced.
2. What are the three most common spinning methods used to produce manufactured fibers? Explain briefly how they differ and give an example of a fiber produced by each of these methods.
3. What characteristics of manufactured fibers can be modified? Give an example of an end use that would benefit from each modification. How are these modifications achieved?
4. Do fiber modifications cause any negative effects? If so, what are they?
5. What modifications would be appropriate for each end use listed below?

   carpeting for restaurant floor
   window treatment for office building
   woman's slip
   ski coat
   fiberfill for quilt batting
   tow rope

## SUGGESTED READINGS

American Fiber Manufacturers Association (1988). *Manufactured Fiber Fact Book.* Washington, D.C.: American Fiber Manufacturers Association.

Dockery, Alfred and Plott, Monte (January, 1990). "Fiber Producers in the '90s: In Style." *America's Textiles International,* pp. 50–59.

Grayson, Martin, ed. (1984). *Encyclopedia of Textiles, Fibers, and Nonwoven Fabrics.* New York: John Wiley & Sons.

"Magical Microfibers." (1994, July/August). *Compressed Air Magazine,* pp. 38–43.

Matsuda, Mitsuo (1993). "The Preparation and Dyeing of Shin Gosen: Processing Problems and Solutions by Applying Multifunctional Surfactants." *Book of Papers.* Research Triangle Park, NC: American Association of Textile Chemists and Colorists.

Rawnitzkey, Michael (1994, September). "How Synthetics Became Real." *Industrial Fabric Products Review,* pp. 49–50, 52, 54.

Chapter 7

# Manufactured Regenerated Fibers

## OBJECTIVES

- To be aware of the complex procedures to produce manufactured regenerated fibers.
- To understand the properties of rayon, lyocell, and acetate.
- To relate fiber properties to end uses for rayon, lyocell, and acetate.

Manufactured regenerated fibers are produced from naturally occurring polymers. These polymers do not naturally occur as fibers; thus, processing is needed to convert them into fiber form. These fibers may also be referred to as regenerated fibers. There are two groups of manufactured or regenerated fibers: cellulosic and protein. The manufactured protein fibers, azlon, are no longer produced in the U.S. and will not be discussed in this chapter. (See Appendix B.) The manufactured cellulosic fibers—rayon, lyocell, and acetate—are used in apparel, furnishings, and industrial products. These fibers met 5.8 percent of the worldwide fiber demand in 1994. In 1994, 496 million pounds of rayon, lyocell, and acetate were produced in the U.S. In the U.S., 55 percent of the manufactured cellulosic fibers are used in apparel, 28 percent in industrial products, and 17 percent in furnishings. Table 7–1 describes the uses of regenerated cellulosic fibers.

## Identification of Manufactured Fibers

The manufactured cellulosic fibers appear similar microscopically. Rayon and acetate have striations and irregular cross sections. Lyocell is more rounded and smoother. Rayon and lyocell burn like cotton or flax.

**TABLE 7–1** ❖ Uses of manufactured cellulosic fibers (1994).

| CATEGORY* | % OF TOTAL FIBER USE |
|---|---|
| Apparel | 4 |
| Robes | 6 |
| Lingerie | 3 |
| Lining | 50 |
| Top weight | 2 |
| Bottom weight | 2 |
| Other | 71 |
| Furnishings | 3 |
| Sheets | 1 |
| Window treatments | 12 |
| Upholstery | 5 |
| Other | 6 |
| Industrial | 5 |
| Tires | 3 |
| Hose | 15 |
| Medical/surgical/sanitary | 11 |
| Nonwovens | 14 |
| Filtration | 8 |
| Transportation | 3 |
| Misc./consumer goods | 5 |

* Categories in which fiber usage is less than 1% are not listed.

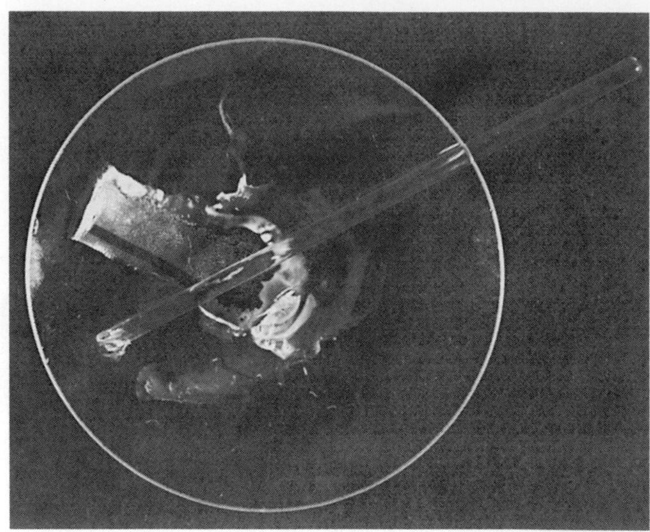

**FIGURE 7–1** ❖ Acetone test for identification of acetate fiber.

Acetate burns freely, melts, and decomposes to a black char. The solubility test is easy to use to identify acetate.

The **acetone test** is a specific identification test for acetate, since none of the other fibers dissolves in acetone. Figure 7–1 shows a procedure for testing the acetate content of a fabric. Work in a well-ventilated room or chemical hood. Use a dropper bottle, glass rod, watch glass, and tissue. Test individual yarns first to determine the presence of other fibers. Add a small amount of acetone to the watch glass. Place the fabric in the solution and stir. Work quickly: acetone evaporates easily. The structure does not disintegrate if only a small amount of acetate is present, but as the solvent evaporates it feels sticky and stiffens permanently. If the fabric dissolved completely, it was 100 percent acetate.

## Rayon

**Rayon** was the first manufactured cellulosic fiber. It was developed before scientists knew how molecular chains were developed in nature or how they could be produced in the laboratory. The developers of rayon were trying to make artificial silk. Frederick Schoenbein discovered in 1846 that **cellulose** pretreated with nitric acid would dissolve in a mixture of ether and alcohol, but the resulting fiber was highly explosive. In 1884 in France, Count Hilaire de Chardonnet made the first successful rayon by changing the nitrocellulosic fiber back to cellulose. This process was dangerous and difficult and discontinued in 1949.

**TABLE 7–2** ❖ Spinning process for viscose rayon.

| REGULAR OR STANDARD | | HIGH-WET-MODULUS |
|---|---|---|
| 1. Blotterlike sheets of purified cellulose | | 1. Blotterlike sheets of purified cellulose |
| 2. Steeped in caustic soda | | 2. Steeped in weaker caustic soda |
| 3. Liquid squeezed out by rollers | | 3. Liquid squeezed out by rollers |
| 4. Shredder crumbles sheets to alkali crumbs<br>5. Crumbs aged 50 hours<br>6. Crumbs treated with carbon disulfide to form cellulose xanthate, 32 percent $CS_2$ | | 4. Shredder crumbles sheets to alkali crumbs<br>5. No aging<br>6. Crumbs treated with carbon disulfide to form cellulose xanthate, 39–50 percent $CS_2$ |
| 7. Crumbs mixed with caustic soda to form viscose solution | | 7. Crumbs mixed with 2.8 percent sodium hydroxide to form viscose solution |
| 8. Solution aged 4–5 days<br>9. Solution filtered | | 8. No aging<br>9. Solution filtered |
| 10. Pumped to spinneret and extruded into sulfuric acid bath | | 10. Pumped to spinneret and extruded into acid bath |
| 10 percent $H_2SO_4$<br>16–24 percent $Na_2SO_4$<br>1–2 percent $ZnSO_4$ | Spinning bath | 1 percent $H_2SO_4$<br>4–6 percent $Na_2SO_4$ |
| 120 meters/minute | Spinning speed | 20–30 meters/minute |
| 45–50°C | Spinning bath temperature | 25–35°C |
| 25 percent | Filaments stretched | 150–600 percent |

In 1890, Louis Despcissis discovered that cellulose would dissolve in a cuprammonium solution, and in 1919 J. P. Bemberg made a commercially successful cuprammonium rayon. In 1892, in England, Cross, Bevan, and Beadle developed the viscose method.

Commercial production of viscose rayon in the United States began in 1911. The fiber was sold as artificial silk until the name "rayon" was adopted in 1924. Viscose filament fiber, the first form of the fiber to be made, was a very bright, lustrous fiber. In 1932, machinery was designed especially for making filament tow that was to be crimped and cut into staple fiber. Rayon was originally used in crepe and linenlike apparel fabrics. The high twist that was required to make the crepe yarn reduced the bright luster of the fibers. Other early rayon fabrics included transparent velvet, sharkskin, tweed, challis, and chiffon.

The physical properties of rayon remained unchanged until 1940, when high-tenacity rayon was developed. It proved to be superior to cotton for tire cord, and by 1957 had replaced cotton in that market. After high-tenacity tire cord and heavy-denier carpet fiber were developed, 65 percent of the rayon produced went into industrial and home furnishings uses and less went into apparel.

Continued research and development led to what has been considered the greatest technological breakthrough in rayon—**high-wet-modulus rayon.** Production in the United States started in 1955. This modification expanded the use of rayon into sheets and towels. Used in blends with cotton, it stimulated a resurgence in the use of rayon in apparel.

High-wet-modulus rayon is frequently referred to as HWM rayon to distinguish it from regular or viscose rayon. In fact, HWM rayon is a viscose rayon, but in common usage viscose rayon refers to the weaker fiber. HWM rayon is also called high-performance (HP) rayon, or polynosic rayon. Polynosic is used as a generic name for HWM rayon in Europe.

It is likely that the output of rayon will not be increased significantly because of the high cost of replacement machinery and the cost of wet spinning. Rayon is no longer the inexpensive fiber it once was—now it is generally comparable in price to cotton.

## Production of Rayon

In the most common method of producing rayon, purified cellulose is chemically converted to a viscous solution, forced through spinnerets into a bath, and returned to solid 100 percent cellulose filaments. This is done by the **wet-spinning** process (see Figure 6–2). Table 7–2 (p. 83) describes processes for making regular and high-wet-modulus rayon. The differences in the spinning process produce fibers with different properties. The high-wet-modulus process maintains maximum chain length and fibril structure as much as possible.

Regular rayon produced in the U.S. is a **viscose rayon.** Some imported rayon is made using the **cuprammonium** process and labeled as cupro rayon under the trade name Bemberg.®

## Physical Structure of Rayon

Regular viscose is characterized by lengthwise lines called **striations.** The cross section is a *serrated* or indented circular shape (Figure 7–2). The shape of the fiber results from loss of the solvent during coagulation.

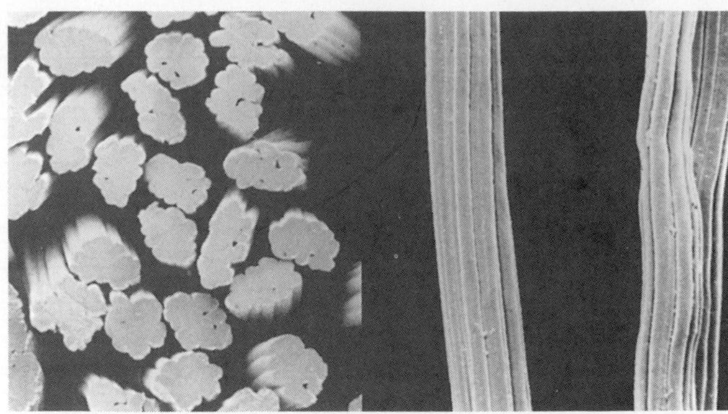

**FIGURE 7–2** ❖ Photomicrographs of viscose rayon: cross-sectional (left); longitudinal (right). (COURTESY OF THE BRITISH TEXTILE TECHNOLOGY GROUP.)

This serrated shape is an advantage in dye absorption because of an increase in surface area. High-wet-modulus rayon has a rounder cross section. Because the process is different, cupra rayon also has a rounder cross section compared to viscose rayon and no striations. Note the differences among them.

Filament rayon yarns have from 80 to 980 filaments per yarn and vary in size from 40 to 5,000 denier. Staple fibers and tow have a range of 1.5 to 15 denier. Staple fibers are crimped mechanically or chemically.

Rayon fibers are naturally very bright, which limits use to more formal apparel and furnishing items. The addition of delustering pigments (see Chapter 6) remedies this problem. Solution-dyed fibers are also available.

## Chemical Composition and Molecular Arrangement of Rayon

*Rayon—a manufactured fiber composed of regenerated cellulose, as well as manufactured fibers composed of regenerated cellulose in which substituents have replaced not more than 15 percent of the hydrogens of the hydroxyl groups.*

—*FEDERAL TRADE COMMISSION.*

Rayon is 100 percent cellulose and has the same chemical composition and molecular structure as the natural cellulose found in cotton or flax, except that the rayon chains are shorter and are not as crystalline. The cellulose breaks down when the alkali cellulose and the viscose solutions are aged. When the solution is spun into the acid bath, regeneration and coagulation take place rapidly. Stretching aligns the molecules to give strength to the filaments.

In high-wet-modulus rayon, the aging is eliminated and the molecular chains are not shortened as much.

**TABLE 7–3** ❖ Comparison of cotton, rayon, and lyocell.

| PROPERTIES | COTTON | REGULAR RAYON | HWM RAYON | LYOCELL |
|---|---|---|---|---|
| Fibrils | Yes | No | Yes | Yes |
| Molecular chain length | 10,000 | 300–450 | 450–750 | — |
| Swelling in water, percent | 6 | 26 | 18 | — |
| Average stiffness | 57–60 | 6–50 | 28–75 | 30 |
| Tenacity, grams/denier | | | | |
| Dry | 4.0 | 1.0–2.5 | 2.5–5.0 | 4.3–4.7 |
| Wet | 5.0 | 0.5–1.4 | 3.0 | 3.8–4.2 |
| Breaking elongation, percent | 3–7 | 8–14 | 9–18 | 14–16 |

Because the acid bath is less concentrated, there is slower regeneration and coagulation so that more stretch and greater orientation of the molecules can be achieved. HWM rayon retains its microfibrilar structure. This means its performance is more similar to that of cotton than to that of regular rayon. Table 7–3 compares cotton with the rayons. Modal is a trade name for a HWM rayon produced by Lenzing Fibers Corp.

## Properties of Rayon

Rayon fibers are highly absorbent, soft, comfortable, easy to dye, and versatile. Fabrics made of rayon have a unique soft drape that designers love. Rayon is used in apparel, furnishings, and industrial products. Table 7–4 summarizes rayon's performance in apparel and furnishings. Review the tables in Chapter 3 to understand the performance of rayon compared to that of the other fibers.

**AESTHETIC** Since the luster, fiber length, and diameter of the fiber can be controlled, rayon can be made into fabrics that resemble cotton, linen, wool, and silk. Rayon can be engineered to have much the same physical characteristics as the other fiber in a blend. If it is chosen instead of cotton or to blend with cotton, rayon can give a fabric the look of mercerized long-staple cotton. Rayon has an attractive, soft, fluid drape. Sizing may be added to increase the body and hand. Cupra rayon has a more silklike hand and luster and may be found in smaller deniers.

**DURABILITY** Regular rayon is a weak fiber that loses about 50 percent of its strength when wet. The breaking tenacity is 1.0–2.5 g/d. Rayon has a breaking elongation of 8–14 percent dry and 20 percent wet. It has the lowest elastic recovery of any fiber. All of these factors are due to the amorphous regions in the fiber. Water readily enters the amorphous areas, causing the molecular chains to separate as the fiber swells, breaking the hydrogen bonds and distorting the chains. When water is removed, new hydrogen bonds form, but in a distorted state. Cupra rayon is not as strong as HWM rayon, but stronger than viscose rayon.

HWM rayon has a more crystalline and oriented structure so that the dry fiber is relatively strong. It has a breaking tenacity of 2.5–5.0 g/d, a breaking elongation of 9–18 percent dry and 20 percent wet, and an elastic recovery greater than that of cotton.

**COMFORT** Rayons make very comfortable, smooth, soft fabrics. They are absorbent, having a moisture regain of 11.5–12.5 percent. This eliminates any static except under the most extreme conditions. Thermal retention is low.

**APPEARANCE RETENTION** The resiliency of rayon is low. This can be improved in HWM rayon fabrics by adding a wrinkle-resistant finish. However, the finish

**TABLE 7–4** ❖ Summary of the performance of rayon in apparel and furnishing fabrics.

| | REGULAR RAYON | HWM RAYON |
|---|---|---|
| **Aesthetic** | **Variable** | **Variable** |
| **Durability** | **Poor** | **Moderate** |
| Abrasion resistance | Poor | Moderate |
| Tenacity | Poor | Moderate |
| Elongation | Moderate | Poor |
| **Comfort** | **Excellent** | **Excellent** |
| Absorbency | High | Excellent |
| Thermal retention | Poor | Poor |
| **Appearance Retention** | **Poor** | **Moderate** |
| Resiliency | Poor | Poor |
| Dimensional stability | Poor | Moderate |
| Elastic recovery | Poor | Moderate |
| **Recommended Care** | Dry clean | Machine wash<br>Dry clean |

may decrease strength and abrasion resistance. The dimensional stability of regular rayon is low. Fabrics may shrink or stretch. The fiber is very weak when wet and has low elastic recovery. The performance of HWM rayon is better. It exhibits moderate dimensional stability that can be improved by shrinkage-control finishes. The fiber is not likely to stretch out of shape and elastic recovery is moderate.

**CARE** Regular rayon fabrics have limited washability because of their low strength when wet. Unless resin treated, rayon fabrics have a tendency to shrink progressively that cannot be controlled by finishes. Regular rayon fabrics generally should be dry cleaned. Another reason to dry clean rayon is the presence of sizings that increase the body and hand but may water-spot or streak after wetting with water.

HWM rayon fabrics have greater washability. They have stability equal to cotton and strength equal to or better than cotton; they can be mercerized and finished to minimize shrinkage; and they wrinkle less than regular rayon in washing and drying.

The care of interior textiles of rayon or rayon blends poses some real problems. Although many items can be cleaned with water-based compounds, the lack of labeling of many furnishings makes this a gamble. Items may shrink, water-spot, or lose color when cleaned. In addition, since manufacturers and suppliers of furnishings rarely distinguish among regular or HWM rayons, it is difficult for professionals to make recommendations regarding care of these products. Thus, as a general recommendation, furnishings of rayon should be cleaned when necessary, but with the realization that the results may not be completely satisfactory.

The chemical properties of rayon are similar to those of the other cellulosic fibers: harmed by acids, resistant to dilute alkalis, and not affected by organic solvents. They can be safely dry cleaned. Rayon may be damaged by silverfish and mildew.

Rayon is not greatly harmed by sunlight. It is not thermoplastic and thus can withstand a fairly high temperature for pressing. Rayon burns readily, like cotton.

## Environmental Impact of Rayon

Although rayon is produced from a naturally occurring polymer, significant processing is needed to produce a usable fiber. Most rayon is produced from wood pulp. Some of the wood is harvested from tree farms located on marginal agricultural land. However, other wood used to produce rayon is cut from mature forests. Environmental issues related to cutting trees include clear cutting—all trees in an area are cut and no trees remain to hold soil and provide habitat for birds, animals, insects, and other plants; cutting old growth forests that may provide habitat for endangered species; and harvesting trees in national forests at minimal cost to lumber companies.

The processing of wood pulp uses large quantities of acid and other chemicals that may contribute to water and air pollution. Regulations describing air and water quality have resulted in modifications of rayon production processes. Cuprammonium rayon is no longer made in the U.S. because producers could not meet water and air quality requirements. The chemicals used to process rayon into fiber and to clean rayon after fiber extrusion should be recovered and recycled, but these additional steps are costly to perform and monitor. Higher costs are reflected in higher prices in the market. U.S. producers are reducing pollutant emissions like hydrogen sulfide and carbon disulfide and decreasing wastewater effluent. Some rayon producers are working toward using a closed chemical system so that 99 percent of the waste liquor can be recovered.

Because rayon is a regenerated cellulose fiber, it is biodegradable. However, current landfill practices prevent natural degradation of buried materials. Rayon is not generally recycled. Since rayon fibers are used in many sanitary products, including disposable diapers, concerns related to disposal of these products continue to be an issue. Producing consumer goods from rayon makes extensive use of water, dyes, and finishing chemicals. Depending on how items have been finished, they may require dry cleaning. Solvents used in dry cleaning present additional hazards to the environment. See Chapter 20 for more information on dry cleaning.

## Uses of Rayon

Rayon is mostly used in woven fabrics, especially in apparel and furnishing products. Antique-satin drapery fabrics in a blend of rayon and acetate continue to be a classic fabric for interiors.

The second most important use of rayon is in nonwoven fabrics, where absorbency is important. Items include industrial wipes; medical supplies, including bandages; diapers; sanitary napkins and tampons. Hollow cuprammonium rayon is used in dialysis machines to filter waste products from blood.

## Types and Kinds of Rayon

The only way to determine a specific type of rayon is by the trade name, such as Modal or Bemberg. Unfortunately, trade names for rayon are seldom used as a marketing tool with consumers. Besides HWM rayons, other types include solution dyed, modified cross section, intermediate or high tenacity, optically brightened, high absorbency, hollow, and microfibers.

# LYOCELL

**Lyocell** is the first new generic fiber in decades. Its development was prompted in part by concern about rayon's negative environmental impact. When the fiber was first introduced in the early 1990s, it was marketed as a type of rayon. However, because of lyocell's unique combination of characteristics, Courtaulds Fibers requested a new generic classification for this fiber and the Federal Trade Commission granted the new fiber classification in 1996. Lyocell is produced in both Europe and the U.S.

## Production of Lyocell

Solvent spinning is the procedure used to produce lyocell (see Figures 6–2 and 7–3). In solvent spinning, the cellulose polymer is dissolved in amine oxide and spun into a well-diluted bath of the solvent. Amine oxide is a chemical with low toxicity and low skin irritation. It dissolves the cellulose in wood pulp without changing the nature of the cellulose. The major difference in the fiber spinning process between wet and solvent spinning is the formulation of the bath and the greater viscosity or thickness of the solution. In wet spinning, the bath is a weak acid solution; in solvent spinning, the bath is a weak solution of the amine oxide that causes the fiber to precipitate. After spinning, the fiber is washed and dried. The solvent is recovered, purified, and recycled. The solvent spinning process results in a fiber that is more like cotton than any other manufactured fiber. Table 7–3 compares the properties of cotton, rayon, and lyocell.

## Physical Structure of Lyocell

Because of the spinning process, lyocell does not collapse in on itself as rayon does and the resulting fiber has a more rounded cross section and smoother longitudinal structure (see Figure 7–4). Lyocell is available in a variety of deniers and lengths. Filament yarns are available in various numbers of filaments per yarn depending on end use. Staple fibers and tow range from approximately 1.0 to 15 denier per filament and are mechanically crimped for use in blends and other staple fiber products.

## Chemical Composition and Molecular Arrangement of Lyocell

*Lyocell—a manufactured fiber composed of solvent-spun cellulose.*

—FEDERAL TRADE COMMISSION.

Lyocell is 100 percent cellulose with the same chemical composition and molecular structure as that found in natural cellulose. The polymer chain length is longer than that of rayon, but not as long as that of cotton. Drawing the fibers after spinning increases the orienta-

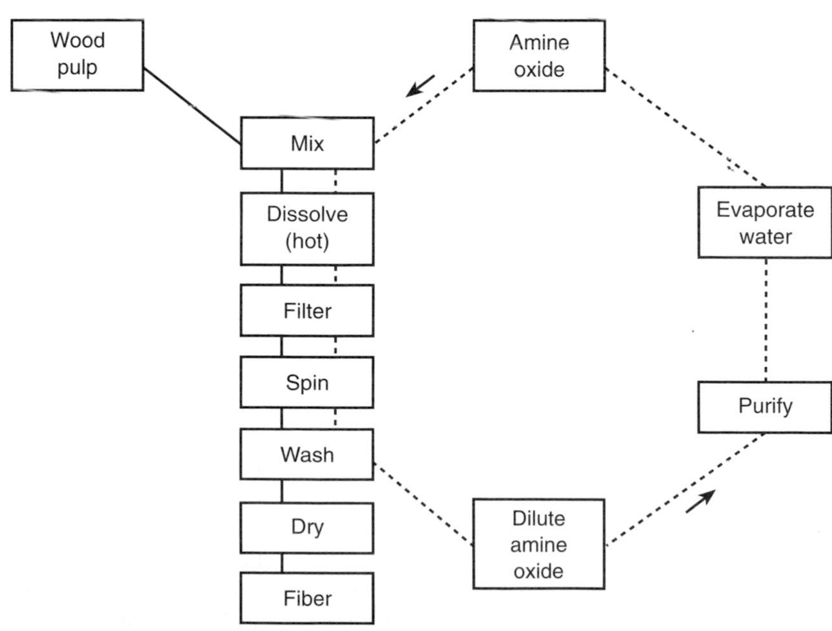


FIGURE 7–3 ❖ Solvent spinning. (COURTESY OF COURTAULDS FIBERS INC.)

**TABLE 7–6** ❖ Acetate manufacturing process.

1. Purified cellulose from wood pulp or cotton linters
2. Mixed with glacial acetic acid, acetic anhydride, and a catalyst
3. Aged 20 hours—partial hydrolysis occurs
4. Precipitated as acid-resin flakes
5. Flakes dissolved in acetone
6. Solution is filtered
7. Spinning solution extruded in column of warm air. Solvent recovered (see Fig. 7–6)
8. Filaments are stretched and wound onto beams, cones, or bobbins ready for use

(blue to pink, green to brown, gray to pink) when exposed to atmospheric fumes, now referred to as atmospheric pollutants. Solution dyeing was developed to correct this problem and is now used for many manufactured fibers. In 1955, an inhibitor was developed that greatly improved dye performance under all conditions that cause fading. However, **fume and pollution fading** continues to be a problem.

## Production of Acetate

The basic steps in the acetate manufacturing process are listed in Table 7–6. Triacetate was produced until the end of 1986, when the last triacetate plant was closed because the Environmental Protection Agency (EPA) banned use of the solvent methylene chloride. Some triacetate is imported into the United States, so it is important to know that triacetate is a thermoplastic fiber. It can be heat set for resiliency and dimensional stability and is machine washable.

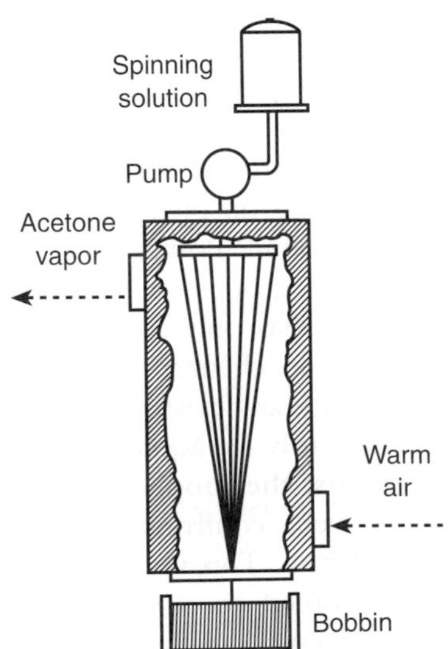


**FIGURE 7–6** ❖ Acetate spinning chamber. (COURTESY OF TENNESSEE EASTMAN CO.)

## Physical Structure of Acetate

Acetate is available as staple or filament. Much more filament is produced because it produces a silklike look. Staple fibers are crimped and usually blended with other fibers. The cross section of acetate is lobular or flower petal–shaped. The shape results from the evaporation of the solvent as the fiber solidifies in spinning. Notice in Figure 7–7 that the lobes may appear as a false lumen.

The cross-sectional shape can be varied. Y-shaped fibers may be used for fiberfill for pillows and battings; flat filaments give glitter to fabrics.

## Chemical Composition and Molecular Arrangement of Acetate

*Acetate—a manufactured fiber in which the fiber-forming substance is cellulose acetate. Where not less than 92 percent of the hydroxyl groups are acetylated, the term triacetate may be used as a generic description of the fiber.*

—*FEDERAL TRADE COMMISSION.*

Because acetate is an ester of cellulose, it has a different chemical structure from rayon or cotton. In acetate, two of the hydroxyl groups have been replaced by bulky acetyl groups (see Fig. 7–8) that prevent the molecules from packing into crystalline areas. There is less attraction between the molecular chains as a result of a lack of hydrogen bonding. Water molecules do not penetrate as readily, contributing to the lower absorbency of acetate. The changed chemical structure also explains acetate's different dye affinity. Acetate is thermoplastic.

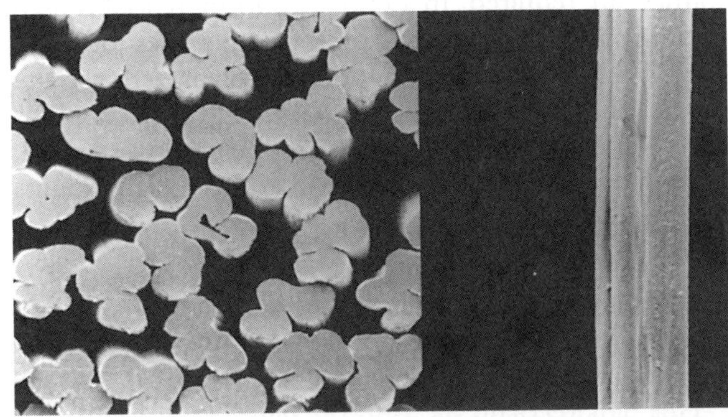

**FIGURE 7–7** ❖ Photomicrographs of acetate fiber: cross-sectional (left); longitudinal (right). (COURTESY OF THE BRITISH TEXTILE TECHNOLOGY GROUP.)

**FIGURE 7–8** ❖ Chemical structure of acetate.

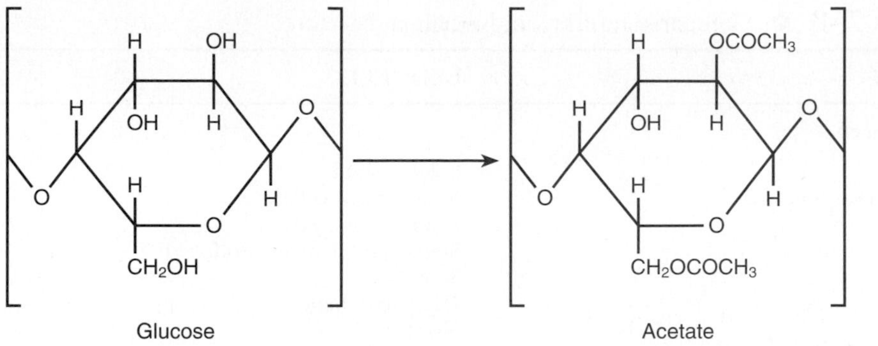

## Properties of Acetate

Acetate has a combination of properties that make it a valuable textile fiber. It is low in cost and has good draping qualities. Table 7–7 summarizes acetate's performance in apparel and furnishing fabrics. Reviewing the tables in Chapter 3 will help in comparing the performance of acetate with that of the other fibers.

**AESTHETIC** Acetate has been promoted as the beauty fiber. It is widely used in satins, brocades, and taffetas in which luster, body, and beauty of fabric are more important than durability or ease of care. Acetate has, and keeps, a good white color. This is one of its advantages over silk, which yellows readily.

**DURABILITY** Acetate is a weak fiber having a breaking tenacity of 1.2–1.4 g/d. It loses some strength when wet. Other weak fibers have some compensating factor, such as good elastic recovery in wool or spandex, but acetate does not. Acetate has a breaking elongation of 25 percent. Acetate also has poor resistance to abrasion. A small percentage of nylon may be combined with acetate to produce a stronger fabric.

**TABLE 7–7** ❖ Summary of the performance of acetate in apparel and furnishing fabrics.

| | |
|---|---|
| **Aesthetic** | **Excellent** |
| Luster | High |
| Drape | High |
| Texture | Smooth |
| Hand | Smooth |
| **Durability** | **Poor** |
| Abrasion resistance | Poor |
| Tenacity | Poor |
| Elongation | Moderate |
| **Comfort** | **Moderate** |
| Absorbency | Moderate |
| Thermal retention | Moderate |
| **Appearance Retention** | **Poor** |
| Resiliency | Poor |
| Dimensional stability | Moderate |
| Elastic recovery | Poor |
| **Recommended Care** | Dry clean |

**COMFORT** Acetate has a moisture regain of 6.3–6.5 percent and is subject to static buildup. The fiber is soft and has no allergenic potential. Thermal retention is poor.

**APPEARANCE RETENTION** Acetate fabrics are not very resilient and wrinkle during use. When washed, fabrics develop wrinkles that are difficult to remove. Acetate has moderate dimensional stability. The fibers are weaker when wet and can be shrunk by excess heat. Elastic recovery is low, 58 percent.

**CARE** Acetate should be dry cleaned unless other care procedures are identified on the care label. Acetate is resistant to weak acids and to alkalis. It can be bleached with hypochlorite or peroxide bleaches. Acetate is soluble in acetone. Acetate cannot be heat set at a temperature high enough to give permanent shape to fabrics or to ensure that embossing is durable.

Acetate is thermoplastic and heat sensitive; it becomes sticky at low temperatures (177–191°C, 350–375°F) and melts at 230°C (446°F). Triacetate has a higher melting point than acetate.

Acetate has better sunlight resistance than silk or nylon but less than the cellulose fibers. It is resistant to moths, mildew, and bacteria.

**COMPARISON WITH RAYON** Rayon and acetate are the two oldest manufactured fibers and have been produced in large quantities, filling an important need for less expensive fibers in the textile industry. They lack the easy care, resilience, and strength of the synthetics and have had difficulty competing in uses where these characteristics are important. Rayon and acetate have some similarities because they are made from the same raw material, cellulose. The manufacturing processes differ, so the fibers differ in their individual characteris-

**TABLE 7–8** ❖ Comparison of rayon, lyocell, and acetate.

| RAYON | LYOCELL | ACETATE |
|---|---|---|
| **Differences** | | |
| Wet spun | Solvent spun | Dry spun |
| Regenerated cellulose | Regenerated cellulose | Chemical derivative of cellulose |
| Serrated cross section | Round cross section | Lobular cross section |
| More staple produced | Staple and filament produced | More filament produced |
| Scorches | Scorches | Melts |
| High absorbency | High absorbency | Fair absorbency |
| No static | No static | Static |
| Not soluble in acetone | Not soluble in acetone | Soluble in acetone |
| Industrial uses—tires, absorbent products, dialysis | Industrial products, filters | Few industrial uses, fiberfill |
| Color may crock or bleed | Color may crock or bleed | Color may fume or pollution fade |
| Mildews | Mildews | Resists mildew |
| Moderate cost | Higher cost | Low cost |
| **Similarities** | | |
| Low strength | Higher strength | Low strength |
| Low abrasion resistance | Better abrasion resistance | Low abrasion resistance |
| Chlorine bleaches can be used | Chlorine bleaches can be used | Chlorine bleaches can be used |

tics and uses. Tables 7–8 and 7–9 compare rayon, lyocell, and acetate.

## Environmental Impact of Acetate

Acetate is produced from cellulose and requires a significant amount of processing to produce a usable fiber. The same concerns identified in the discussion of rayon apply to the wood pulp used to produce acetate. Because acetate is dry spun, it is easier for producers to reclaim and reuse the solvent. With current environmental regulations and economic pressures, solvent recovery and reuse is standard practice in the production of acetate. Acetate fiber is less likely to degrade naturally compared to rayon and is not recycled. Acetate is usually dyed with disperse dyes. Special chemical carriers may be used to move the dye into the fiber. Acetate items usually require dry cleaning. The solvents used in dry cleaning present additional hazards to the environment. See Chapter 20 for more information on dry cleaning.

## Uses of Acetate

Acetate is a minor fiber in terms of usage. Acetate is used in apparel, furnishings, and industrial products.

**TABLE 7–9** ❖ Performance of rayon, lyocell, and acetate.

| PROPERTY | VISCOSE RAYON | LYOCELL | ACETATE |
|---|---|---|---|
| Abrasion resistance | moderate | good | poor |
| Breaking tenacity, g/d (dry; wet) | 1.0–2.5; 0.5–1.4 | 4.8–5.0; 4.2–4.6 | 1.2–1.4; 1.0–1.3 |
| Breaking elongation, g/d (dry; wet) | 7–14; 20 | 14–16; 16–18 | 24–45; 35–50 |
| Absorbency | 12.5% | 11.5% | 6.3–6.5% |
| Specific gravity, g/cc | 1.48–1.54 | 1.56 | 1.32 |
| Resiliency | poor | moderate | poor |
| Elastic recovery at 3% stretch | 95% (at 2%) | unknown | 48–65% (at 4%) |
| Chemical resistance | | | |
| strong acids | harmed | harmed | harmed |
| alkalis | resistant | resistant | resistant |
| organic solvents | resistant to most | resistant to most | soluble in many |
| Light resistance | moderate | moderate | moderate |

An important use of acetate is in lining fabrics. The aesthetics of acetate—its luster, hand, and body—its relatively low cost, and its ease in handling contribute to its wide use here. However, since acetate is not a durable fiber, the fabric must be carefully selected for the end use or the consumer will be dissatisfied with the product.

Acetate is used in robes and loungewear in brushed-tricot and fleece fabrics. In knits, the fiber is washable and performs well. Acetate is very important in drapery fabrics. Sunlight-resistant modifications contribute to the fiber's popularity here as do its luster and soft drape. Antique-satin fabrics made of blends of acetate and rayon are very common. Fabrics of 50 percent acetate and 50 percent cotton are used where draperies need to match bedspreads or lightly used upholstery. Acetate and acetate-blend fabrics come in an amazingly wide assortment of colors—nearly any decor can be matched.

Another use of acetate is in fabrics for formal wear, such as dresses and blouses in moiré taffeta, satin, and brocade.

Other important uses of acetate fabrics include bedspreads and quilts, satin sheets, fabrics sold for home sewing, ribbons, and cigarette filters. MicroSafe AM acetate is an absorbent antimicrobial fiber produced by Hoechst Celanese Corp. for use in personal hygiene products, fiberfill, and filters. Celebrate! by Hoechst Celanese Corp. is used for both furnishings and apparel.

## Types and Kinds of Acetate

Types of acetate are solution dyed, flame retardant, sunlight resistant, fiberfill, textured filament, modified cross section, antimicrobial, and thick-and-thin slublike filament.

## Key Terms

| | |
|---|---|
| Manufactured regenerated fiber | Cuprammonium rayon |
| Acetone test | Striations |
| Rayon | Lyocell |
| Cellulose | Acetate |
| High-wet-modulus rayon | Triacetate |
| Wet spinning | Thermoplastic |
| Viscose rayon | Heat sensitive |
| | Fume or pollution fading |

## Questions

1. How do the properties of rayon and acetate differ from those of the natural cellulosic fibers?
2. Explain the difference in properties among viscose rayon, HWM rayon, and lyocell.
3. Why do the properties of rayon and acetate differ from those of the natural fibers?
4. How can the manufactured fibers be changed to enhance their performance for specific end uses?
5. For each end use listed below, identify a fiber discussed in this chapter that would be appropriate. Indicate why that fiber was selected as well as any fiber modifications that might enhance the fiber's performance for that end use.

   inexpensive kitchen wipes
   draperies for formal dining room
   lining for suit jacket
   summer-weight suit

## Suggested Readings


"Acetate Properties." (1994, Autumn). *Textiles Magazine*, p. 24.

Davidson, W. A. B. (1993, April). "Rayon Makers Clean Up Image." *America's Textiles International*, pp. 54–55.

Davies, Stan (February, 1989). "All You Need to Know About Tencel." *Textile Horizons*, pp. 62–63.

Ford, J. E. (1991). "Viscose Fibres." *Textiles*, no. 3, pp. 4–8.

Grayson, Martin, ed. (1984). *Encyclopedia of Textiles, Fibers, and Nonwoven Fabrics*. New York: John Wiley & Sons.

"Tencel Properties." (1994, Winter). *Textiles Magazine*, pp. 21–22.

Trotman, E. R. (1984). *Dyeing and Chemical Technology of Textile Fibers*, 6th ed. New York: John Wiley & Sons.

"Viscose Rayon Properties." (1994). *Textiles Magazine*, no. 2, p. 17.

Ward, Derek (August, 1988). "World's Largest Viscose Producers." *Textile Month*, pp. 23–24.

*Chapter 8*

# SYNTHETIC FIBERS

OBJECTIVES

- To know the properties common to most synthetic fibers.
- To understand the processes used in producing synthetic fibers.
- To integrate performance characteristics of the common synthetic fibers with end use requirements.
- To recognize the importance of synthetic fibers to the industrial products industry.
- To recognize the use of synthetics in apparel and furnishing products.

Synthetic fibers have helped shape the world as we know it. These fibers are a subset of manufactured fibers. The major difference between manufactured regenerated fibers and synthetic fibers is the raw material from which a fiber is formed. Regenerated fibers are produced from naturally occuring polymers. The polymers for **synthetic fibers** must be synthesized or made. Once the polymer is synthesized, the fiber is made; hence, the name synthetic fiber. Although other names like chemical fibers and noncellulosic manufactured fibers are used, these fibers are most often referred to as synthetic fibers.

# Overview of the Synthetic Fibers

In producing synthetic fibers, the fiber-forming compounds are made from basic raw materials. The procedures involved in creating the fiber-forming materials from the starting materials are complex and beyond the scope of this text. Many synthetic fibers are made from petrochemicals (petroleum-based chemicals). Even though the synthetic fiber industry is a huge one (see Table 8–1), the amount of petrochemicals used to produce fibers is less than 1 percent of the total petroleum consumed in the U.S. in one year.

Once the materials are available, they are polymerized or connected into one extremely large linear compound called a polymer. In many cases, the basic unit of the polymer, the monomer, is fairly simple; in other cases, the monomer is more complex. Two basic polymerization processes are used: addition and condensation. In addition polymerization, a double bond between 2 adjacent carbon atoms in a monomer is broken and many monomers are connected in a long chain. In condensation polymerization, small molecules (hydrogen, hydroxyl, or others) are removed by a chemical reaction from the compound and many monomers react to form the polymer. A small molecule, often water, is a byproduct of this reaction. (See Figure 8–1.)

(a) $3(A = B) \longrightarrow -A-B-A-B-A-B-$

Addition polymerization

(b) $3D-H + 3E-OH \longrightarrow D-E-D-E-D-E + 3H_2O$

Condensation polymerization

**FIGURE 8–1** ❖ Polymerization: (a) addition and (b) condensation.

**TABLE 8–1** ❖ Million pounds of fiber used.

| FIBER | (1994) | PERCENT |
|---|---|---|
| Cotton | 5,192 | 34.4 |
| Polyester | 3,858 | 25.6 |
| Nylon | 2,740 | 18.2 |
| Olefin | 2,419 | 16.0 |
| Acrylic | 442 | 2.9 |
| Rayon, lyocell, and acetate | 443 | 2.9 |
| Other | — | — |
| Total | 15,094 | 100 |

Different chemical compounds are used as the materials from which nylon, polyester, olefin, acrylic, and modacrylic are formed. These fibers are found in a wide variety of apparel, furnishing, and industrial applications and will be discussed in this chapter. The next chapter will focus on other synthetic fibers that have special uses or applications in the textile industry. The synthetic fibers have many properties and processes in common (see Table 8–2).

Synthetic fibers have acquired a negative image in the minds of many consumers for a variety of reasons: inappropriate end uses, poor fashion image, concern for the environment, and poor comfort characteristics. Marketing strategies have been developed to strengthen the industry and change the public's perception of these fibers. These fibers offer much in terms of high-tech versatility, easy care, durability, and high-fashion appeal. Research and development efforts continue to improve the performance and acceptability of these fibers.

## Common Properties of Synthetic Fibers

**HEAT SENSITIVITY** Many synthetic fibers used for apparel and furnishings are heat sensitive. **Heat sensitivity** refers to fibers that soften or melt with heat; those that scorch or decompose are described as being heat resistant. Awareness of heat sensitivity is important in manufacturing processes because of the heat in dyeing, scouring, singeing, and other finishing and production processing. Heat sensitivity is equally important to consumers because of heat encountered in washing, ironing, and dry cleaning.

Fibers differ in their level of heat sensitivity. This difference is reflected in Table 3–8. Because of the speed of the iron in normal ironing, the fabric never gets as hot as the sole plate of the iron. If the iron speed slows or the iron stands in one spot, the heat builds up. When heat-sensitive fabrics get too hot, the yarns soften and

**TABLE 8–2** ❖ Properties common to synthetic fibers.

| PROPERTIES | IMPORTANCE TO CONSUMERS |
|---|---|
| Heat sensitive | Fabrics will shrink and melt if exposed to excess heat. Holes may appear. Pleats, creases, and other three-dimensional fabric effects can be heat set. Fabric can be stabilized by heat setting. Yarns can be textured for bulk. Furlike fabrics can be produced. |
| Resistant to most chemicals | Used in industrial applications where chemical resistance is required. |
| Resistant to moths, fungi, and rot | Storage is no problem. Used in geotextiles, sandbags, fishlines, tenting, and other industrial applications |
| Low moisture absorbency | Products dry quickly, resist waterborne stains. Lack of comfort in humid weather. Increases possibility of static. Water does not cause shrinkage. Difficult to dye. |
| Oleophilic | Oil and grease absorbed by fibers must be removed by dry cleaning agents. |
| Electrostatic | Static cling may occur. May cause sparks that can cause explosions or fires. Shocks in cold, dry weather are unpleasant. |
| Abrasion resistance good to excellent (acrylics lowest) | Good appearance retained longer because holes and worn places do not appear as soon. Used in many industrial applications. |
| Strength good to excellent | Strongest fibers make good ropes, belts, and women's hosiery. Resist breaking under stress. |
| Resilience excellent | Easy-care apparel, packable for travel. Less wrinkling during wear. Resilient carpeting. |
| Sunlight resistance good to excellent (nylon modified to improve resistance) | Webbing for outdoor furniture. Indoor/outdoor carpet. Curtains and draperies. Flags, banners, and awnings. |
| Flame resistance | Varies from poor to excellent. Check individual fibers. |
| Density or specific gravity | Varies as a group but tend to the lightweight. More product per unit mass. |
| Pilling | May occur in products made of staple fibers. |

pressure from the iron flattens them permanently (Figure 8–2). This effect is referred to as **glazing.** Glazing can be used to achieve embossed and shiny surfaces on fabrics.

Alterations are difficult to make in heat-sensitive fabrics because creases, seams, and hems are hard to press in or out. Fullness cannot be shrunk out for shaping, so patterns have to be adjusted to remove some of the fullness in areas where fullness is sometimes controlled by shrinkage.

**PILLING** Fiber tenacity is a basic factor in **pilling,** the formation of tiny balls of entangled fiber ends on the surface of the fabric. Pilling occurs on staple fiber fabrics where fiber ends entangle due to abrasion. The pills may break off before the item becomes unsightly, but most synthetic fibers are so strong that pills accumulate on the fabric's surface. Pills are of two kinds: lint and fabric. *Lint pills* are more unsightly, because they contain not only fibers from the item but also fibers picked up during care, in use, through contact with other fabrics, and even through static attraction. Fabric pills consist of fibers from the fabric and are less apparent. Pilling can be minimized by fiber modification or finishes.

Fabric construction is an important factor in minimizing pilling. Close weaves, high yarn twist or plied yarns, and longer-staple fibers are recommended. Resin finishes of cotton and fulling of wool also help prevent pilling.

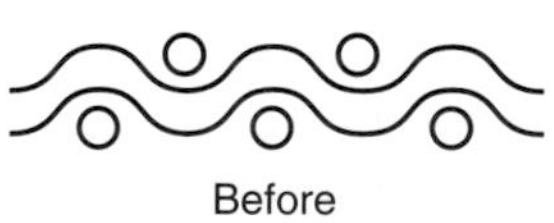

**FIGURE 8–2** ❖ Heat and pressure cause permanent flattening of the yarn; note the change in cross section (glazing.)

**STATIC ELECTRICITY** Static electricity is generated by the friction of a fabric when it is rubbed against itself or other objects. If the electrical charge is not removed, it builds up on the surface. When the fabric comes in contact with a good conductor, a shock, or electron transfer, occurs. This transfer may produce sparks that, in some environments, can cause explosions. Static tends to build up more rapidly in dry, cold regions. Problems involving static include the following:

1. Soil and lint cling to the surface of the fabric and dark colors become very unsightly. Brushing simply increases the problem.

2. Dust and dirt are attracted during storage and to furnishings.
3. Fabrics cling to equipment in production facilities and make cutting and handling very difficult. Static may contribute to increased defects resulting in a higher percentage of seconds.
4. Clothes cling to the wearer and cause discomfort and an unsightly appearance. Static can be minimized by the use of fabric softeners, when used as directed.

Antistatic finishes are applied to many fabrics at the factory, but they may not be permanent.

**OLEOPHILIC** Fibers that have low moisture absorption usually have a high affinity for oils and greases. They are **oleophilic.** Exposure to oily substances may cause these fibers to swell. Oily stains are very difficult to remove and may require prespotting with a concentrated liquid soap or a dry cleaning solvent.

## Common Manufacturing Processes

**MELT SPINNING** Many synthetic fibers are melt spun. The basic steps in the melt-spinning process for filament and staple fiber made from filaments are shown in Figure 8–3. **Melt spinning** is essentially a simple process. It can be demonstrated by a simple and entertaining laboratory experiment. A flame, a pair of tweezers, and a piece of nylon fabric are needed. Heat the fabric until some of it has melted, then quickly draw out the melt with tweezers as shown in Figure 8–4.

Commercial melt spinning consists of forcing the melt through the holes of the stainless-steel plate of a heated spinneret. The fiber cools in contact with the air, solidifies, and is wound on a bobbin.

**DRAWING** After extrusion of the fiber, its chainlike molecules are in an amorphous or disordered arrangement. The filament fiber must be *drawn* to develop the desirable strength, pliability, toughness, and elasticity properties. Some fibers are cold drawn; others must be hot drawn. Drawing aligns the molecules, placing them parallel to one another and bringing them closer together so they are more crystalline and oriented. The amount of draw or the draw ratio varies with intended use, determines the decrease in fiber size, and controls the increase in strength.

**HEAT SETTING** **Heat setting** is a process that uses heat to stabilize yarns or fabrics made of heat-sensitive fibers. The yarn or fabric is heated to bring it almost to the melting point specific for the fiber being heat set or the glass transition temperature (Tg). At this temperature the fiber molecules move freely to relieve stress within the fiber. The fabric is kept under tension until cool to lock this shape into the molecular structure of the fiber. After cooling, the fabric or yarn will be stable to any heat lower than that at which it was set, but changes can be made by higher temperatures. Heat setting may be done at any stage of finishing, depending on the fiber's heat resistance and other qualities (see Table 8–3).

## Identification of Synthetic Fibers

Burn tests identify the presence of several synthetic fibers if the product is all synthetic because of the melting and dripping that occur. However, the burn test is not good for blends or for fibers that are flame retardant. The burn test also cannot be used to identify a specific generic fiber since the differences may be minimal or masked by fiber additives or finishes. See Table 3–15 for the slight differences in the burn test results for each synthetic fiber.

Microscopic appearance is not a reliable method of identification for these fibers. Since these are synthetic fibers, fiber appearance can be easily modified. Fibers in this group have no unique visible characteristics at either the microscopic or macroscopic level. Photomicrographs included in this chapter clearly illustrate this.

Solubility tests are the only procedures that differentiate among the synthetic fibers. Table 3–16 lists solvents commonly used to identify synthetic fibers. Several solvents used in identification of fibers are toxic and hazardous. Appropriate care should be taken when using any solvent.

## Common Fiber Modifications

**FIBER SHAPE AND SIZE** Since many synthetic fibers are melt spun, changing the fiber's cross-sectional shape is relatively easy. Fiber shape can be changed by altering the shape of the spinneret hole. Many modifications are possible. Figure 3–3 illustrates some of the more common ones. Hollow fibers for fiberfill provide better thermal properties and lighter weight aspects. Trilobal, pentalobal, and multilobal fibers are used for apparel and furnishings, especially carpeting. Voided fibers help hide soil on carpeting. Flat ribbon fibers are used in formal and special occasion apparel. Channel fibers like DuPont's CoolMax are used in active sportswear to wick moisture away from the skin's surface. Fiber size can range from very large for industrial applications to very small for apparel and furnishings.

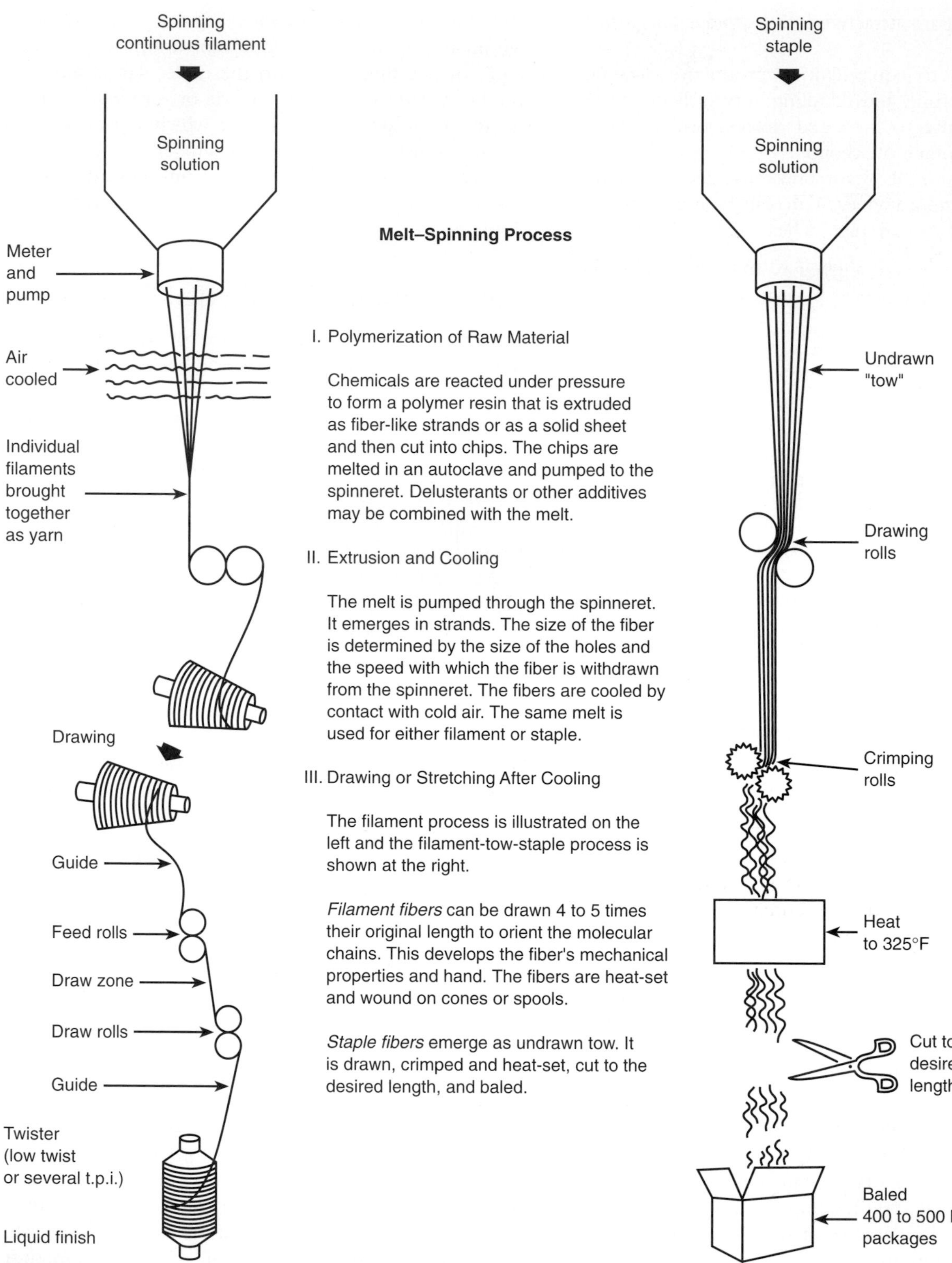


**FIGURE 8–3** ❖ The melt-spinning process.

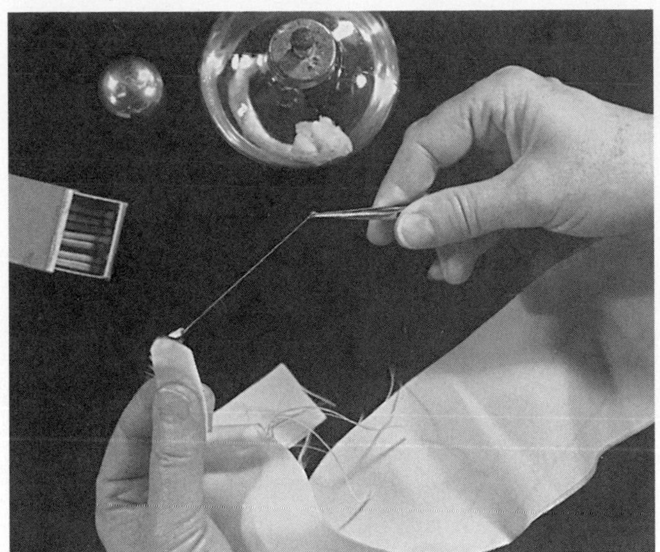

**FIGURE 8–4** ❖ Spinning a melt-spun fiber by hand.

Microfibers are filament or staple fibers with a denier per filament (dpf) of less than 1.0; most are in the range of 0.5 to 0.7 dpf. Many synthetic microfibers are available; the most common are nylon and polyester varieties. These fibers are produced by conventional melt spinning, splitting bicomponent fibers, or dissolving one of the components of bicomponent fibers (Figure 6–3). All three techniques provide commercially important microfibers for apparel, furnishing, and industrial applications. End uses include fashion apparel, intimate apparel, performance athletic apparel, upholstery, wall coverings, bedding, window treatment fabrics, medical uses, and wiping cloths for the precision and glass industries.

**LOW-PILLING FIBERS** Low-pilling fibers are engineered to minimize pill formation. By reducing the molecular weight slightly, the fiber's flex life is decreased. When the flex abrasion resistance is reduced, fiber pills break off almost as soon as they are formed, thus maintaining the fabric's original appearance. The low-pilling fibers are not as strong as other fiber types, but are durable enough for most apparel and furnishing uses. They are especially applicable for soft knitting yarns. Some low-pilling fiber modifications are designed for blending with natural fibers. For example, polyester low-pilling types blend well with cotton, rayon, or lyocell.

**TABLE 8–3** ❖ Heat setting.

| ADVANTAGES | DISADVANTAGES |
|---|---|
| Embossed designs are permanent. | "Set" creases and wrinkles are hard to remove in ironing or in garment alteration. |
| Pleats and shape are permanent. | Care must be taken in washing or ironing to prevent setting wrinkles. |
| Size is stabilized. | |
| Pile is crush resistant. | |
| Knits do not need to be blocked. | |
| Clothing resists wrinkling during wear. | |

**HIGH-TENACITY FIBERS** Stretching a fiber will change its stress/strain behavior. Fiber strength is increased in several ways. Drawing or stretching the fiber to align or orient the molecules strengthens the intermolecular forces. Chemical modifications of the fiber polymer increase the degree of polymerization, the length of the polymer chain. Some high-tenacity fibers are produced by combining drawing with chemical modification.

In synthetic fibers, the molecular chain length can be varied by chemical modification or by changes in time, temperature, pressure, and catalysts used in the process. Long molecules are harder to pull apart than short molecules.

**LOW-ELONGATION FIBERS** Fibers with low elongation reinforce the strength and abrasion resistance of cellulosic-blend fabrics. The low elongation is a result of changing the balance of tenacity and extension. High-tenacity fibers have lower elongation properties. Primary end uses are apparel and furnishing items that get hard use like work clothing and heavy-duty upholstery fabrics.

## NYLON

**Nylon** was the first synthetic fiber and the first fiber developed in the United States. In 1928, the DuPont Company established a fundamental research program as a means of diversification. DuPont hired Dr. Wallace H. Carothers, an expert on high polymers, to direct a team of scientists. The team created many kinds of polymers, starting with single molecules and building them into long molecular chains. One team member discovered that a solution could be formed into a stable solid filament. This stimulated the group to concentrate on textile fibers. By 1939, DuPont was making a polyamide fiber in a pilot plant. This fiber, nylon 6,6, was introduced to the public in women's hosiery where it was an instant success. The name *nylon* was chosen for the fiber, but the reason for that choice is not known. At that time there were no laws specifying generic names for fibers.

Nylon had a combination of properties unlike any other fiber in use in the 1940s. It was stronger and more resistant to abrasion; it had excellent elasticity and could be heat set. Permanent pleats became a reality. For the first time, gossamer-sheer fabrics were durable and machine washable. Nylon's high strength, light weight, and resistance to chemicals made it suitable for ropes, cords, sails, parachutes, and other industrial products.

As nylon entered more end-use markets, its disadvantages became apparent—static buildup, poor hand, lack of comfort in skin-contact fabrics, and low resistance to sunlight. As each problem appeared, ways were developed to overcome the disadvantages.

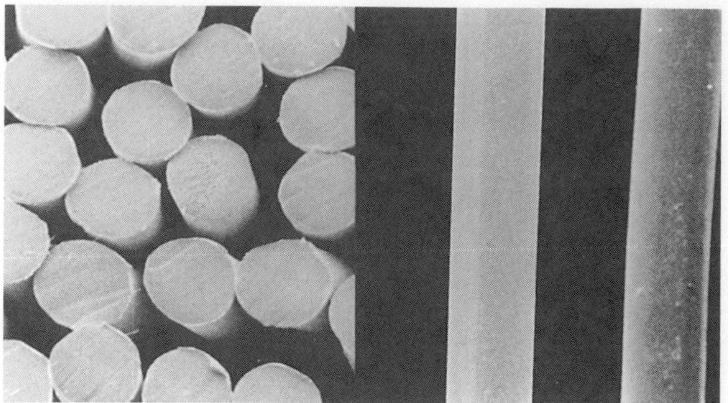

**FIGURE 8–5** ❖ Photomicrograph of nylon fiber: cross-sectional view (left); longitudinal view (right). (COURTESY OF THE BRITISH TEXTILE TECHNOLOGY GROUP.)

## Production of Nylon

Nylon or polyamides are made from various substances. The numbers after the word nylon indicate the number of carbon atoms in the starting materials. Nylon 6,6 is made from hexamethylene diamine, which has six carbon atoms, and adipic acid, which also has six carbon atoms.

While nylon 6,6 was being developed in the United States, scientists in Germany were working on nylon 6. It is made from a single substance, caprolactam, which has six carbon atoms.

**FIGURE 8–6** ❖ Photomicrograph of trilobal nylon. (COURTESY OF E. I. DU PONT DE NEMOURS & COMPANY.)

## Physical Structure of Nylon

Nylon is available in multifilament, monofilament, staple, and tow in a wide range of deniers and shapes and as partially drawn or completely finished filaments. Many staple lengths are also available. Fibers are produced in bright, semidull, and dull lusters, with varying degrees of polymerization and strengths.

Regular nylon has a round cross section and is perfectly uniform throughout the filament (Figure 8–5). Microscopically, the fibers look like fine glass rods. They are transparent unless they have been delustered or solution dyed.

At first, the uniformity of nylon filaments was a distinct advantage over the natural fibers, especially silk. However, the perfect uniformity of nylon produced woven fabrics with a dead, unattractive feel. This condition is reduced by changing the fiber's shape. Melt-spun fibers, like nylon, tend to retain the shape of the spinneret hole. Thus, where performance is influenced by fiber shape, producers can adjust the shape as needed. For example, in nylon carpets, trilobal fibers and square fibers with voids give good soil-hiding characteristics (see Figures 8–6 and 8–7).

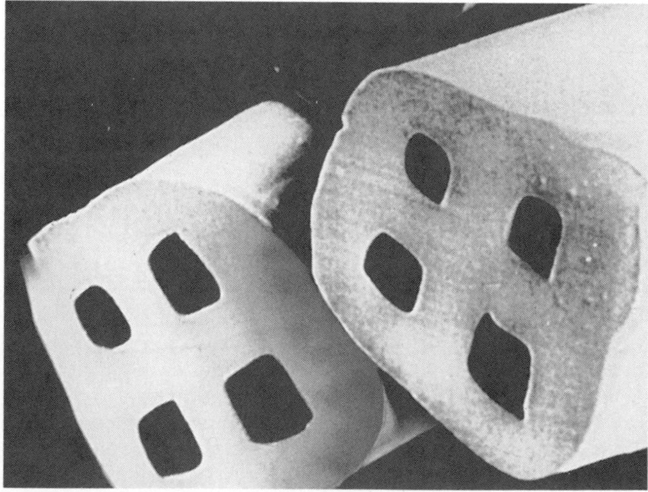

**FIGURE 8–7** ❖ Nylon fiber with voids. (COURTESY OF E. I. DU PONT DE NEMOURS & COMPANY.)

## Chemical Composition and Molecular Arrangement of Nylon

*Nylon—a manufactured fiber in which the fiber-forming substance is any long-chain, synthetic polyamide in which less than 85 percent of the amide linkages*

$$\left[ \begin{array}{c} -\underset{\underset{\displaystyle O}{\|}}{C}-NH- \end{array} \right]$$

*are attached directly to two aromatic rings.*

—FEDERAL TRADE COMMISSION.

Nylons are **polyamides;** the recurring amide groups contain the elements carbon, oxygen, nitrogen, and hydrogen. Nylons differ in their chemical arrangement and this accounts for slight differences in some properties.

The molecular chains of nylon are long, straight chains of variable length with no side chains or cross-linkages. Cold drawing aligns the chains so that they are oriented with the lengthwise direction and are highly crystalline. High-tenacity filaments have a longer chain length than regular nylon. Staple fibers are not cold drawn after spinning, have lower degrees of crystallinity, and have lower tenacity than filament fibers.

Nylon is related chemically to the protein fibers silk and wool. Both have amino dye sites that are important in dyeing, but nylon has far fewer dye sites than wool.

## Properties of Nylon

Nylon's performance in apparel and furnishing fabrics is summarized in Table 8–4. Compare the performance of nylon to that of other fibers by reviewing the tables in Chapter 3.

**TABLE 8–4** ❖ Summary of the performance of nylon in apparel and furnishing fabrics.

| | |
|---|---|
| **Aesthetic** | **Variable** |
| **Durability** | **Excellent** |
| Abrasion resistance | Excellent |
| Tenacity | Excellent |
| Elongation | High |
| **Comfort** | **Poor** |
| Absorbency | Poor |
| Thermal retention | Moderate |
| **Appearance Retention** | **High** |
| Resiliency | High |
| Dimensional stability | High |
| Elastic recovery | Excellent |
| **Recommended Care** | Machine wash (apparel)<br>Dry extraction method (furnishings) |

**AESTHETIC** Nylon has been very successful in hosiery and in knitted fabrics such as tricot and jersey because of its smoothness, light weight, and high strength. The luster of nylon can be selected for the end use—it can be lustrous, semilustrous, or dull. Trilobal nylons have a pleasant luster.

The drape of fabrics made from nylon can be varied, depending largely on fiber and yarn size and fabric structure selected. High-drape fabrics are found in draperies, in sheer overlays for nightgowns, and in formals. Stiff fabrics are found in taffetas for formal wear, parkas, furnishings, or industrial uses. Very stiff fabrics include webbing for luggage handles and seat belts. These also vary in filament size.

Smooth textures are frequently found. These too can be varied by using spun yarns or by changing the knit or woven structure. The hand frequently associated with nylon fabrics is smooth because of the filament yarn and flat tricot-knit construction. Textured-yarn fabrics are bulkier.

Nonround fibers are generally used in upholstery and carpets. Trilobal, pentalobal, and voided fibers are used for several reasons. Round fibers tend to magnify soil and look dirty very quickly. The nonround fibers hide the soil. Even though the product may be quite dirty, it may not look soiled at all. In addition, voids and flat sides of the fibers scatter light, which assists in hiding the soil and more closely duplicates the matte luster of wool and other natural fibers (see Figures 8–6 and 8–7).

**DURABILITY** Nylon has outstanding durability. High-tenacity fibers are used for seat belts, tire cords, ballistic cloth, and other industrial uses. Regular-tenacity and staple fibers are used in apparel and furnishings. (See Table 8–5.)

High-tenacity fibers are stronger, but have lower elongation than regular-tenacity fibers. During production the high-tenacity fibers are drawn to a greater degree than the regular-tenacity fibers. Thus, the HT fibers are more crystalline and oriented. HT nylon fibers are used in industrial products, like tow ropes, where high strength and low elongation is essential.

In addition to excellent strength and high elongation, nylon has excellent abrasion resistance. For example, nylon carpet fibers outwear all other fibers including wool (see Table 8–6).

A major end use for nylon is carpet. The ideal carpet is durable, resilient, and resistant to pilling, shedding, fading, traffic, abrasion, soil, and stains. Nylon meets or exceeds many of these demands. In terms of durability,

**TABLE 8–5** ❖ Comparison of nylon 6,6 and nylon 6.

| NYLON 6,6 | NYLON 6 |
|---|---|
| Made of hexamethylene diamine and adipic acid | Made of caprolactam |
| $\left[ \overset{\displaystyle O}{\overset{\|}{C}} (CH_2)_4 \overset{\displaystyle O}{\overset{\|}{C}} NH(CH_2)_6NH \right]_n$ | $\left[ NH(CH_2)_5 \overset{\displaystyle O}{\overset{\|}{C}} \right]_n$ |
| **Advantages** | **Advantages** |
| Heat setting 205°C (401°F)<br>Pleats and creases, can be heat set at higher temperatures<br>Softening point 250°C (482°F)<br>Difficult to dye | Heat setting 150° (302°F)<br>Softening point 220°C (428°F)<br>Better dye affinity than nylon 6,6; takes deeper shades<br>Softer hand<br>Greater elasticity, elastic recovery, and fatigue resistance<br>Better weathering properties, including better sunlight resistance |

| **Performance** (Nylon 6,6) | | | | **Performance** (Nylon 6) | | |
|---|---|---|---|---|---|---|
| *Tenacity dry/wet* | *Breaking elongation, %* | *Elastic recovery, %* | *Fiber type* | *Tenacity dry/wet* | *Breaking elongation, %* | *Elastic recovery, %* |
| 5.9–9.8/ 5.1–8.0 | 15–28/ 18–32 | 89 | High-tenacity filament | 6.5–9.0/ 5.8–8.2 | 16–20/ 19–33 | 99–100 |
| 2.3–6.0/ 2.0–5.5 | 25–65/ 30–70 | 88 | Regular-tenacity filament | 4.0–7.2/ 3.7–6.2 | 17–45/ 20–47 | 98–100 |
| 2.9–7.2/ 2.5–6.1 | 16–75/ 18–78 | 82 | Staple | 3.5–7.2/ — | 30–90/ 42–100 | 100 |
| — | — | — | Bulked continuous filament | 2.0–4.0/ 1.7–3.6 | 30–50/ 30–60 | — |

nylon is unexcelled in abrasion resistance. Nylon pile upholstery fabrics are popular because of their good durability properties.

This combination of properties makes nylon the fiber for women's hosiery. No other fiber has been able to compete with nylon in pantyhose. The high elongation and excellent elastic recovery of nylon account for its outstanding performance here. Hosiery is subjected to high degrees of elongation; nylon recovers better after high elongation than other fibers do. Another factor that helps it retain its shape during wear is that the shape of hosiery can be heat or steam set. Filament hosiery develops runs because the fine yarns break and the knit loop is no longer secure. Sheer hosiery is less durable than opaque hosiery.

Nylon is used for lining fabrics in some coats and jackets. Nylon linings are more durable; however, the cost is greater because of the greater difficulty in sewing them and their higher costs compared to acetate fabrics.

Nylon is not very durable as a curtain or drapery fabric because it is weakened by the sun. Sunlight- or ultraviolet-resistant modifications are available. These modified fibers are used in sheer glass curtains, draperies, car interiors, seat belts, and other industrial applications.

**COMFORT** Nylon has low absorbency. Even though its moisture regain is the highest of the synthetic fibers (4.0–4.5 percent for nylon 6,6 and 2.8–5.0 for nylon 6), nylon is not as comfortable a fiber to wear as the natural fibers.

Compact yarns of filament nylon originally were used in men's woven sports shirts. The shirts became transparent when wet from perspiration and felt like a plastic sheet wrapped around the body. They were especially uncomfortable in warm, humid weather. Later, open-structure woven fabrics and crimped yarns were used to improve comfort.

Because of this early and inappropriate use, fiber producers began to develop certification and quality-control programs through which they could exercise control over the final product and thus protect the image of their fibers. Today, textured and spun yarns used in knit

**TABLE 8–6** ❖
Comparison of wool and manufactured carpet fibers.

| FIBER CHARACTERISTIC | WOOL | MANUFACTURED |
|---|---|---|
| Fiber diameter | Coarse blends of various wools | 15–18 denier or blend of various deniers |
| Fiber length | Staple | Staple or filament blend of various lengths |
| Crimp | 3D crimp | Sawtooth crimp, 3D crimp, bicomponent, textured filament |
| Cross section | Oval | Round, trilobal, multilobal, square with voids, 5-pointed star |
| Resiliency and resistance to crushing | Good | Medium to excellent depending on fiber |
| Resistance to abrasion | Good | Good to excellent |
| Resistance to waterborne stains | Poor | Good to excellent |
| Resistance to oily stains | Good | Poor |
| Fire retardancy | Good | Modified fiber or topical finish |
| Static resistance | Good | Poor to good depending on fiber |

fabrics result in more comfortable shirts. Knit fabrics of nylon are more comfortable than woven nylon fabrics because the additional air spaces within the fabric structure allow heat and moisture to escape more readily.

The very factors that make nylon uncomfortable under one set of conditions make it very comfortable under a different set. Nylon is widely used for wind- and water-resistant jackets, parkas, tents, and umbrellas. The smooth, straight fibers pack closely together into yarns that can be woven into a compact fabric with very little space for wind or water to penetrate.

With a density of 1.14, nylon is one of the lightest fibers on the market. Compared to polyester, nylon yields 21 percent more yardage per pound of fabric. This lighter weight corresponds to lighter products and lower costs of moving fabrics and finishing fabrics. Actionwear and sports gear take advantage of nylon's light weight and high durability.

Another disadvantage of low absorbency is the development of static electricity by friction at times of low humidity. This disadvantage can be overcome by using antistatic-type nylon fibers, or antistatic finishes, and by blending with high-absorbency, low-static fibers.

Antistatic fiber modifications and finishes are common carpet modifications. Metallic and carbon fibers may be used to minimize static in carpets. Static creates problems with comfort, soiling, and function.

**APPEARANCE RETENTION** Nylon fabrics are highly resilient because they have been heat set. The same process can be used to make permanent pleats, creases, and embossed designs that last for the life of the product.

Nylon carpet yarns are heat set before they are incorporated in the carpet. Heat setting improves the compressional resiliency of the fibers in the pile yarns. Compressional resiliency refers to the ability of the carpet fibers to spring back to their original height after being bent or otherwise deformed. Nylon has excellent compressional resiliency. Thus, traffic paths do not develop quickly. In addition, depressions from heavy furniture are less likely to be permanent. Marks from heavy furniture can be minimized by steaming these areas. In addition, most carpet fibers are made in a large denier, often 15 or greater. Larger denier fibers have improved compressional resiliency and appearance retention.

Shrinkage resistance is also high because the heat setting and the low-absorbency fiber are not affected by water. Elastic recovery is excellent. Nylon recovers fully from 8 percent stretch; no other fiber does as well. At 16 percent elongation, it recovers 91 percent immediately. This property makes nylon an excellent fiber for hosiery, tights, ski pants, swimsuits, and other actionwear (see Table 8–5). Nylon does not wrinkle much in use, it is stable, and it has excellent elastic recovery, so it retains its appearance very well during use.

Solution-dyed carpet fibers are available for areas where fading, especially from exposure to sunlight, may be a problem. These carpets are specifically aimed at the low-priced contract/commercial markets and for automotive interiors.

**CARE** Nylon introduced the concept of easy-care garments. In addition to retaining their appearance and shape during use, nylon fabrics retain their appearance and shape during care.

The wet strength of nylon is 80–90 percent of its dry strength. Wet elongation increases slightly. Little swelling occurs when nylon is wet. This is in marked contrast to the swelling of cellulosic fibers: nylon, up to

14 percent; cotton, 40–45 percent; and viscose rayon, 80–110 percent.

To minimize wrinkling, warm wash water, gentle agitation, and gentle spin cycles are recommended. Hot water may cause wrinkling in some fabrics. Wrinkles set by hot wash water can be permanent. Hot water will help to remove greasy and oily stains.

Nylon is a *color scavenger.* White and light-colored nylon fabrics pick up color from other fabrics or dirt that is in the wash water. A red sock that loses color into the wash water of a load of whites will turn the white nylon fabrics a dingy pink-gray. This extra color may be extremely difficult to remove. Prolonged use of chlorine bleach may cause yellowing of white nylon. Discolored nylon and grayed or yellowed nylon can be avoided by following correct laundry procedures.

Since nylon has low absorbency, it dries quickly. Hence, fabrics need to be dried only for a short time. Do not overdry the fabrics. Dryer temperatures should be warm or low. Avoid using the hot setting on commercial gas dryers. Figure 8–8 shows the melted and fused result of a nylon garment dried in an overheated gas dryer with socks of a different fiber content.

Nylon does have problems with static, particularly when the air is dry, so a fabric softener may be used in the washer or dryer. Nylon should be pressed or ironed at a low temperature setting, 270–300°F, to avoid glazing. Home-ironing temperatures are not high enough to press seams, creases, and pleats permanently in items or to press out wrinkles acquired in washing.

The chemical resistance of nylon is generally good. Nylon has excellent resistance to alkali and chlorine bleaches but is damaged by strong acids. Pollutants in the atmosphere can damage nylon or create problems with dyes used on nylon. Certain acids, when printed on the fabric, create a puckered effect. Nylon dissolves in formic acid and phenol.

Nylon is resistant to the attacks of insects and fungi. Food soil on carpet may attract insect damage.

Nylon has low resistance to sunlight. Better resistance is achieved in end uses where sunlight exposure is a concern by using bright rather than delustered fibers so that damaging energy is reflected and not absorbed. In addition, sunlight-resistant modifications of nylon are available.

Carpet soiling can be a real problem. Soiling in carpets is related to fiber cross section, carpet color, and fiber opacity/translucence. Round cross sections tend to magnify soil. Nonround cross sections, such as trilobal, pentalobal, and voided, hide soil (see Figures 8–6 and 8–7). Soil resistant fiber modifications are used in carpeting to minimize soil adherence and permanent staining. In addition, many carpets now combine soil-resistant fiber modifications with soil-resistant finishes. See Chapter 18 for information on soil-resistant finishes for carpets.

## Environmental Impact of Nylon

Nylon is resistant to molds, mildew, rot, and many chemicals—it is resistant to natural degradation and does not degrade quickly. Although most nylon is sensitive to sunlight damage, the damage does not occur quickly enough to minimize disposal problems with nylon products. Nylon is processed from petrochemicals, so there are concerns regarding drilling in sensitive environments, oil spills, refinement and production of the chemicals from which nylon is made, and use of and disposal of hazardous chemicals.

The processing of nylon from raw fiber into finished product uses few, if any, chemicals to clean the fiber.

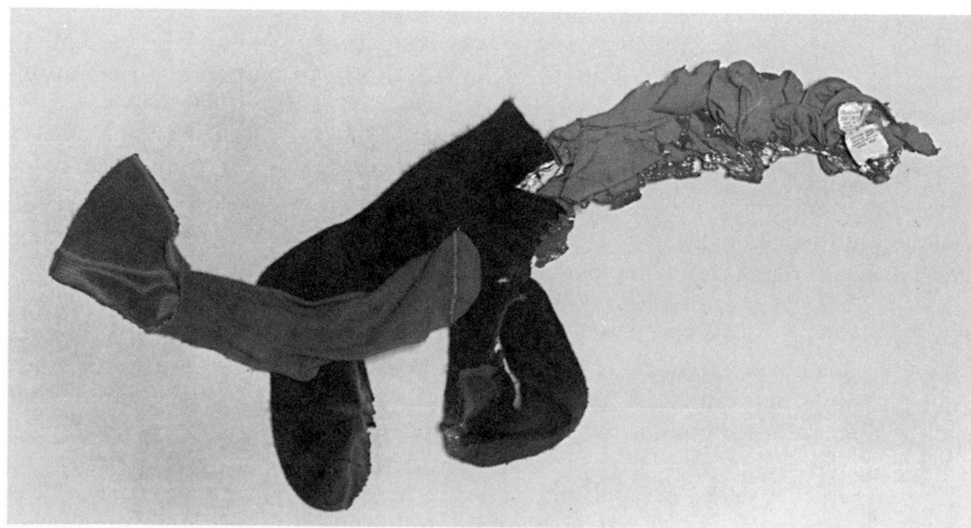

**FIGURE 8–8** ❖ The melted and fused remains of nylon garments dried in an overheated gas dryer.

This is because synthetic fibers like nylon, unlike the natural fibers, are not contaminated with soil and other materials like leaf bits. Since nylon is a melt-spun fiber, no residue from chemical baths needs to be rinsed from the fiber and no solvents, like those used with solvent or dry-spun fibers, need to be reclaimed. In addition, less water, salt, and acid is used to dye the fiber. Removal of excess dye from nylon fabrics uses less water than for some common dyes used for natural and regenerated cellulose fibers. Chemical finishes are rarely needed to enhance consumer satisfaction with nylon products because the fiber can be engineered for specific end uses. Thus, once nylon fiber is produced, further processing of nylon has minimal impact on the environment.

Nylon is made from materials that are by-products of oil refineries. Thus nylon makes use of raw materials that were once considered waste products. Although nylon is not extensively recycled at present, nylon producers are working on ways to make nylon recycling a reasonable alternative to disposal. Two problems with recycling nylon relate to the presence of other materials added to the melt in producing the original material and the wide variety of nylon polymers on the market.

BASF has developed a commercial carpet recycling program, "6ix Again," that economically converts BASF nylon carpet fiber to caprolactam (a nylon 6 raw material). Carpet eligible for this recycling program is identified with a 6ix Again logo on the back. In DuPont's recycling program for some of its nylon carpet fiber, the fiber is shaved from the carpet's surface and mixed with plastic and concrete. These composite materials of fiber and plastic or concrete are light weight and durable. They are used to make products like recycled picnic tables and and poured concrete foundations.

## Uses of Nylon

Nylon is the third most widely used fiber in the United States. It follows cotton and polyester in pounds used.

The single most important use of nylon is for carpets. In 1995, almost 65 percent of nylon fibers were used for carpets. Tufted carpets are an excellent end use for nylon because of its aesthetic appearance, durability, appearance retention, and ability to be cleaned in place. The combination of nylon fiber and the tufting process results in relatively low-cost and highly serviceable carpeting, contributing to the widespread use of carpeting in both residential and commercial buildings.

A second important use of nylon is for apparel. Lingerie fabrics are an end use for which nylon is an important fiber. The fabrics are attractive and durable; they retain their appearance well and are easy-care. Panties, bras, nightgowns, pajamas, and lightweight robes are frequently made from nylon. A copolymer absorbent nylon by Allied-Signal Fibers, Hydrofil, is used in sports bras and panties for greater comfort.

Women's sheer hosiery is an important end use of nylon. No other fiber has the combination of properties that make it so ideal for that use. The very sheer hosiery is often 12–15 denier instead of a heavier denier yarn or monofilament. Sheers give the look that is wanted, but they are less durable. Hosiery yarns may be monofilament or multifilament-stretch nylon. They may be plain or textured.

Short socks or knee-high socks are sometimes made from nylon. More frequently they are nylon blends with cotton or acrylic, with the nylon adding strength and stretch.

Active sportswear and actionwear in which comfort stretch is important—leotards, tights, swimsuits, and ski wear—is another end use for nylon. Nylon-taffeta windbreakers and parkas are commonly seen in cooler weather. Lining fabrics, especially for jackets and coats, are sometimes made of nylon.

Some performance fibers that have been modified to have a cottonlike hand with improved pilling resistance are used in the inner layers of workwear, hunting apparel, and mountaineering apparel. Other nylons have been modified to be stain and tear resistant, quiet, quick drying, and warm. These fabrics are used in outer layers of workwear and hunting and hiking apparel. Cordura by DuPont is a trade name for many of these products. Supplex is a DuPont microfiber nylon that has been modified to be softer, more supple, and less bulky compared to regular nylon so that it provides greater freedom of movement in outerwear, beachwear, and actionwear. Supplex is wind resistant, water repellent, breathable, and durable.

Industrial uses for nylon are varied. Within this group, an important use of nylon is for tire cord. The nylon or polyester fibers that are used in the cord of radial tires go rim to rim over the curve of the tire. Nylon is facing stiff competition in this specialized market and may lose the market to polyester, aramid, and/or steel.

Although nylon is strong and abrasion resistant, with high elongation and high elasticity, it has a tendency to "flat spot." Flat spotting occurs when a car has been stationary for some time and a flattened place forms on the tire. The car will have a bumpy ride for the first mile or so until the tire recovers from flattening. With the advent of belted-radial tires and the availability of heat-resistant aramid and steel, the market is changing.

Car interiors are another example of the varied uses for nylon. The average car uses 25 pounds of fiber, a good share of which may be nylon. Upholstery fabric (called body cloth), carpet for the interior, trunk lining, door and visor trims, head liners on the interior of the car roof, and seat belt webbing may be nylon fabrics of one kind or another. Some may be modified to be sunlight resistant, heat resistant, or high tenacity. In addition, clutch pads, brake linings, and yarns to reinforce radiator hoses and other hoses are needed. Allied-Signal Fibers' nylon, StayGard, is used in airbags.

Additional industrial uses include parachute fabric, cords and harnesses, glider tow ropes, ropes and cordage, conveyor belts, fishing nets, mail bags, and webbings.

The category of industrial uses also includes consumer uses, sporting goods, and leisure fabrics. Consumer uses include umbrellas, clotheslines, toothbrush and hairbrush bristles, paintbrushes, and luggage. Leisure goods include soft luggage, backpacks, book bags, camera bags, golf bags, hunting gear, and horse blankets. Cordura nylon by DuPont is used in many leisure goods. Blends of Cordura with other fibers are used in protective apparel, work wear, and career apparel.

Nylon is important in sporting goods. It is used for tents, sleeping bags, spinnaker sails, fishing lines and nets, racket strings, backpacks, and duffle bags.

Nylon microfibers are used in apparel and furnishings. These fibers are 26–36 percent softer than regular nylon fibers and range in size from 0.7 to 1.0 dpf, compared to a denier of 2.0 for regular nylon. The micro nylons are available from several manufacturers and are used in a variety of applications. These fibers are water repellent, wind and wear resistant, and vapor permeable and comfortable. They are used in 100 percent nylon formations and in blends with natural fibers like wool and cotton (see Table 8–7).

**TABLE 8–7** ❖ Nylon microfibers.

| PRODUCER | FIBER TRADE NAME | FIBER SIZE | END USE |
|---|---|---|---|
| BASF | Silky Touch | 0.8 dpf | Lingerie, swimwear |
| DuPont | Supplex<br>MicroSupplex | 1.0 dpf<br>0.7 dpf | Woven fabrics in actionwear |

## Types and Kinds of Nylon

It has been said that as soon as a new need arose, a new type of nylon was produced to fill the need. This has led to a large number of types of nylon that are identified by trademarks.

The list in Table 8–8 illustrates many modifications of nylon. Table 8–9 lists trade names for several producers of nylon.

**TABLE 8–8** ❖ Types and kinds of nylon.

| CROSS SECTION | DYEABILITY | CRIMP OR TEXTURED | OTHERS |
|---|---|---|---|
| Round | Acid dyeable | Mechanical crimp | Antistatic |
| Heart-shaped | Cationic dyeable | Crimp-set | Soil hiding |
| Y-shaped | Disperse dyeable | Producer textured | Bicomponent |
| 8-shaped | Deep dye | Undrawn | Faciated |
| Delta | Solution dye | Partially drawn | Thick and thin |
| Trilobal | Heather | Steam crimped | Antimicrobial |
| Triskelion | Optically whitened | Bulked continuous filament | Sunlight resistant |
| Trinode | | Latent crimp | Flame resistant |
| Pentagonal | | | Delustered |
| Hollow | | | High tenacity |
| Voided | | | Cross-linked |
| Microfibers | | | |

**TABLE 8–9** ❖ Some trademarks and producers.

| NYLON 6,6 | | NYLON 6 | |
|---|---|---|---|
| Trade Names | Producer | Trade Names | Producer |
| Antron, Cordura, Supplex | DuPont | Anso, Caprolan, Captiva, Hydrofil, StayGard, A.C.E. | Allied-Signal |
| Ultron, Wear-Dated | Monsanto | Natural Touch, Silky Touch, Zeftron | BASF Fibers |
| | | Shareeen | Courtaulds |

❖

# POLYESTER

The first polyester fiber, Terylene, was produced in England. It was first introduced in the U.S. in 1951 by DuPont under the trade name Dacron (pronounced day′kron). The outstanding resiliency of polyester, whether dry or wet, coupled with its excellent dimensional stability after heat setting made it an instant favorite.

Sometimes referred to as the workhorse fiber of the industry, polyester is the most widely used synthetic fiber. The filament form of the fiber is extremely versatile and the staple form can be blended with many other fibers, contributing its desirable properties to the blend without destroying those of the other fiber. Its versatility in blending is one of the unique advantages of polyester.

The polyester polymer is endlessly engineerable, with many physical and chemical variations possible. These modified fibers improve the performance of the original polyester. One important physical difference has been changing from the standard round shape to other shapes to give different properties. A high-tenacity staple polyester was developed for use in durable-press fabrics to reinforce the cotton fibers, which had been weakened by the finishing process. Other polyesters have a hand and absorbency more like the natural fibers.

The properties of polyester are listed in Table 8–10.

## Production of Polyester

**Polyester** is produced by reacting dicarboxylic acid with dihydric alcohol. The fibers are melt spun by a process that is very similar to the one used to make nylon. The polyester fibers are hot drawn to orient the molecules and improve strength, elongation, and the stress/strain properties. Since polyester is melt spun, it retains the shape of the spinneret hole. Modifications in cross-sectional shape are inexpensive and easy to produce.

**TABLE 8–10** ❖ Properties of polyester.

| PROPERTIES | IMPORTANCE TO CONSUMERS |
|---|---|
| Resilient—wet and dry | Easy-care and packable apparel, furnishings |
| Dimensional stability | Machine washable |
| Sunlight resistant | Good for glass curtains and draperies |
| Durable, abrasion resistant | Industrial uses, sewing thread, work clothes |
| Aesthetics superior to nylon | Blends well with other fibers, silklike |

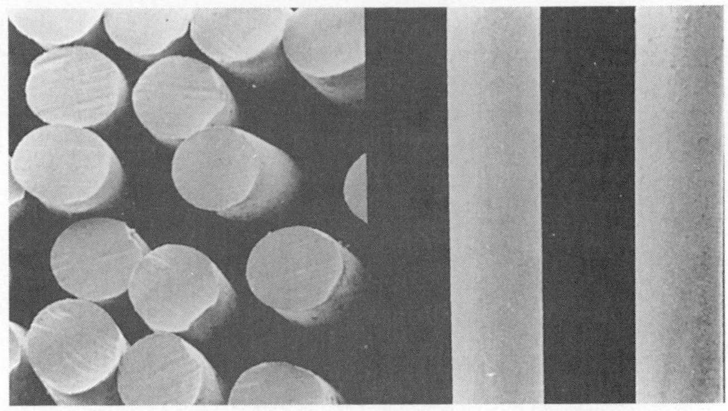

**FIGURE 8–9** ❖ Photomicrograph of polyester: cross-sectional view (left); longitudinal view (right). (COURTESY OF THE BRITISH TEXTILE TECHNOLOGY GROUP.)

## Physical Structure of Polyester

Polyester fibers are produced in many types. Filaments are high tenacity or regular, bright or delustered, white or solution dyed. Staple fibers are available in deniers from less than 1.0 to 10 and are delustered. They may be regular, low pilling, or high tenacity. Regular polyester fibers are smooth rodlike fibers that have a circular cross section (Figure 8–9). The fibers are not as transparent as nylon fibers. They are white, so they normally do not need to be bleached. However, whiter types of polyester fibers have been produced by the addition of optical whiteners to the fiber-spinning solution. The speckled appearance of the fiber may be due to delusterant.

A variety of cross-sectional shapes are produced: round, trilobal, octolobal, oval, hollow, voided, hexalobal, and pentalobal (star-shaped).

## Chemical Composition and Molecular Arrangement of Polyester

*Polyester fibers—manufactured fibers in which the fiber-forming substance is any long-chain synthetic polymer composed of at least 85 percent by weight of an ester of a substituted aromatic carboxylic acid, including but not restricted to substituted terephthalate units,*

$$p(-R-O-\underset{\underset{O}{\|}}{C}-C_6H_4-\underset{\underset{O}{\|}}{C}-O-),$$

*and para substituted hydroxybenzoate units,*

$$p(-R-O-C_6H_4-\underset{\underset{O}{\|}}{C}-O-).$$

—*FEDERAL TRADE COMMISSION.*

**TABLE 8–11** ❖ Comparison of PET and PCDT fibers.

| PET | PCDT |
|---|---|
| 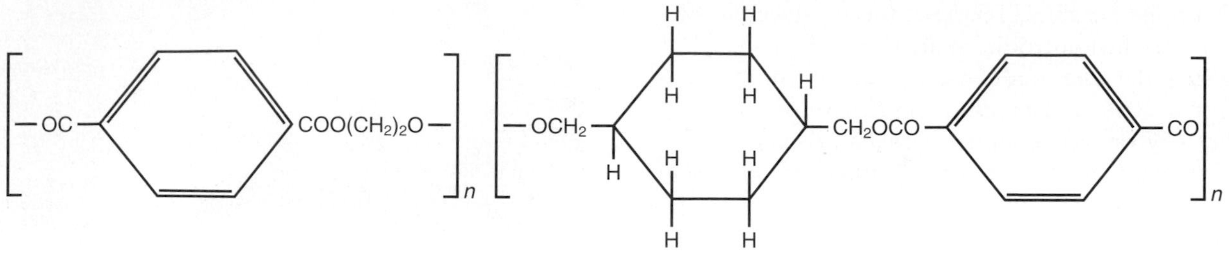 $\left[-OC-\quad-COO(CH_2)_2O-\right]_n$ | $\left[-OCH_2-\quad-CH_2OCO-\quad-CO\right]_n$ (H, H, H, H, H, H, H, H, H, H) |
| **PET Polyester** | **PCDT Polyester** |
| Dacron, Fortrel, Trevira | Kodel |
| Filaments are hot drawn | Drawn at higher temperatures |
| Filament or staple | Filament or staple |
| Textured yarns | Textured yarns |
| Stronger, more resistant to abrasion | More elastic |
| | Greater bulking properties |
| | Greater resiliency |
| Higher density, 1.38 | Lower density, 1.22 |
| Lower melting point, 480°F | Higher melting point, 540°F |

Most polyester fibers are made from two kinds of terephthalate polymers: polyethylene terephthalate (PET) and 1,4 cyclohexylene-dimethylene terephthalate (PCDT). The differences are listed in Table 8–11. Both PET and PCDT polymers may be homopolymers or copolymers. Most copolymers are pill-resistant, lower-strength staple fibers used primarily in knits, blends, and carpets.

Polyester fibers have straight molecular chains that are packed closely together and are well oriented with very strong hydrogen bonds.

## Properties of Polyester

Polyester's performance in apparel and furnishing fabrics is summarized in Table 8–12. To understand polyester's performance in comparison to that of the other fibers, examine the tables in Chapter 3.

**TABLE 8–12** ❖ Summary of the performance of polyester in furnishings and apparel fabrics.

| Aesthetic | Variable |
|---|---|
| **Durability** | **Excellent** |
| Abrasion resistance | Excellent |
| Tenacity | Excellent |
| Elongation | High |
| **Comfort** | **Poor** |
| Absorbency | Poor |
| Thermal retention | Moderate |
| **Appearance Retention** | **High** |
| Resiliency | Excellent |
| Dimensional stability | High |
| Elastic recovery | High |
| **Recommended Care** | Machine wash (apparel)<br>Dry extraction (furnishings) |

**AESTHETIC** Polyester fibers blend well, maintaining a natural fiber look and texture with the advantage of easy care for apparel and furnishings. The fabrics look like the natural fiber in the blend; their appearance retention during use and care clearly illustrates the influence of polyester.

Thick-and-thin yarns of polyester and rayon give a linen look to apparel and furnishing fabrics. Wool-like fabrics are found in both summer-weight and winter-weight men's suiting fabrics.

Silklike polyesters have been very satisfactory in appearance and hand. The trilobal polyester fibers resulted when DuPont tried to find a manufactured filament that would have the aesthetic properties of silk. In cooperation with a silk-finishing company, DuPont began by investigating the effect of silk-fin-

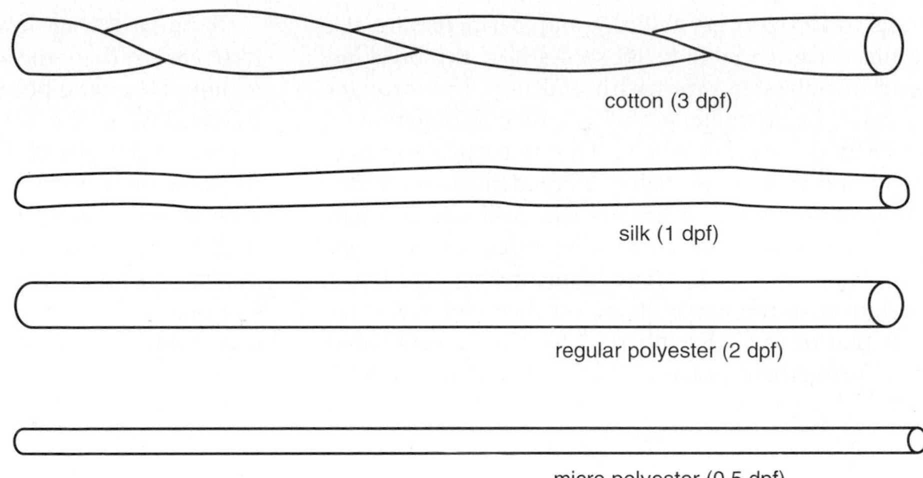


**FIGURE 8–10** ❖ Comparison of fiber size: cotton, silk, regular polyester, microfiber polyester.

ishing processes on the aesthetic properties of silk fabrics, since silk seemed to acquire richness in the fabric form.

The silk fabric study found that the unique properties of silk—liveliness, suppleness, and drape of the fabric; dry "tactile" hand; and good covering power of the yarns—resulted from (1) the triangular shape of the silk fiber; (2) the fine denier per filament; (3) the loose, bulky yarn and fabric structure; and (4) the highly crimped fabric structure. These results were applied to polyester. Silklike polyesters are spun with a trilobal shape and made into fabrics processed by a silk-finishing treatment. They are unique because they can be treated with a caustic soda that leaves a thinner, less uniform fiber, yarn, or fabric without basically changing the fiber.

Polyester microfibers are particularly suited to high fashion apparel and furnishing items because of the versatility and durability of the fibers. Designers find the microfibers' drape and hand exciting and challenging. Consumers have been willing to pay the additional cost of products incorporating microfibers. Microfibers yield softer and more drapeable fabrics than conventional fibers do. Figure 8–10 illustrates the differences among fiber sizes. Items of polyester microfibers, both 100 percent polyester and blends with other fibers, include coats, suits, blouses, dresses, active sportswear, wall coverings, upholstery, sleeping bags, tents, filters, and toweling (see Figure 8–11). Micromattique and Micromattique XF (0.3–10.7 dpf) by DuPont, and Trevira Finesse and Microfinesse (0.55–0.9 dpf) by Trevira are examples of microfibers used for a variety of apparel and furnishings. These fibers exhibit unparalleled softness, fluidity, drape, and appearance. *Shin-gosen* polyesters are Japanese fibers that are the most silklike of the very fine polyesters because of slight irregularities along the fiber. Some modifications combine a microchannel with the trilobal cross section; others have tiny microcraters along the fiber's surface. Although the techniques used to produce the microfibers and *shin-gosen* fibers are similar, they are not identical and the resultant fibers have slightly different performance and appearance characteristics.

**DURABILITY** The abrasion resistance and strength of polyesters are excellent. Wet strength is comparable to dry strength. The high strength is produced by hot

**FIGURE 8–11** ❖ Velvet gown by Nicole Miller made of Micromattique™ microdenier polyester. (COURTESY OF E. I. DU PONT DE NEMOURS & COMPANY)

drawing to develop crystallinity and by increasing the molecular weight. Table 8–13 shows how the breaking tenacity of polyester varies with end use. The stronger fibers have been stretched more; their elongation is lower than the weaker fibers. This is particularly dramatic in the case of partially oriented filament fibers, which are sold to manufacturers who will stretch them more during the production of textured yarns. Their tenacity is 2.0–2.5 g/d. These filament fibers are lower in strength than the staple fibers, yet their elongation far exceeds that of the other fibers, 120–150 percent! Sold in yarn form, these polyesters are referred to as POY, partially oriented yarn.

**COMFORT** Absorbency is quite low for the polyesters, 0.4–0.8 percent. Poor absorbency lowers the comfort factor of skin-contact apparel and upholstery. Woven fabrics made from round polyester fibers can be very uncomfortable to use in warm, humid weather. Moisture does not escape easily from between the skin and the fabric, and the fabric feels slick and clammy.

To increase comfort, select blends with absorbent fibers or comfort-modified fibers, a thin and somewhat open fabric design, spun rather than filament yarns, trilobal rather than round fibers, and finishes that absorb, or wick, moisture. Soil-release finishes have improved the wicking characteristics of polyester, thus improving fabric breathability and comfort. Finishes and fiber modifications also increase the comfort of polyester.

Blends of polyester and cotton are more comfortable in humid weather than are 100 percent polyester fabrics. Moisture is wicked along the outer surface of the polyester fibers to the fabric surface, where it evaporates. Polyester is resilient when it is wet, so the fabric does not mat down. Polyester is light in weight and dries quickly.

Polyester exhibits moderate thermal retention. It is generally not as comfortable as wool or acrylic for cold-weather wear. Blends with wool are very successful in increasing its comfort. Polyesters have been specifically engineered for fiberfill. Fiber modifications—including hollow fibers, binder staple, and crimped fibers—perform very well.

Because of their low absorbency, polyesters are more *electrostatic* than the other fibers in the heat-sensitive group. The static potential of polyester can be lowered by modifying the fiber's cross section, incorporating special water-absorbing compounds in the spinning solution prior to extrusion, or adding topical finishes such as soil-release and antistat finishes. Cross-sectional modifications may incorporate compounds that make a porous fiber surface that traps moisture. Other cross-sectional modifications expand the surface area per unit mass ratio, thus slightly increasing the absorbency. The density of polyester fibers ranges from 1.22 to 1.38. Hollow variants for fiberfill are lower in density.

A new antistatic modification of polyester is available from ICI Fibres in Europe. This bicomponent core-sheath fiber combines a polyester core and a polyester isophthalate copolymer sheath that is impregnated with carbon-black particles. Since the sheath has a significantly lower melting point than the core, the carbon particles are permanently embedded in the softened sheath. Epitropic polyester blends well with other fibers and creates no problems during the processes that convert a fiber into a finished product. Incorporating as little as 2 percent epitropic fiber in blends significantly reduces static buildup compared to other methods, such as incorporating metal fibers. Besides having applications in carpeting and upholstery, epitropic fibers have potential for use in filters, protective outerwear, felts, electrical components, ropes, and other applications where static buildup can be hazardous or annoying.

A new polyester called 3GT, developed by DuPont and Genencor International Inc., should be on the market by 2001. It has the ability to stretch 10 to 15 percent with good recovery. This is substantially better than that of regular polyester. With better stretch and softer hand, it will be ideal for many apparel products.

**APPEARANCE RETENTION** *Resiliency* refers to the extent and manner of recovery from deformation. Polyester has a high recovery when the elongation is low, an important factor in the apparel and furnishings markets. When only small deformations are involved, as in wrinkling, polyester recovers better than nylon. This

**TABLE 8–13** ❖
Performance aspects of modified polyester fibers.

| FIBER MODIFICATION | TENACITY, g/d | BREAKING ELONGATION, % | END USE |
|---|---|---|---|
| High-tenacity filament | 6.8–9.5 | 9–27 | Tire cord, industrial uses |
| Regular-tenacity filament | 2.8–5.6 | 18–42 | Apparel and furnishings |
| High-tenacity staple | 5.8–7.0 | 24–28 | Durable-press items |
| Regular-tenacity staple | 2.4–5.5 | 40–45 | Apparel and furnishings |

**TABLE 8–14** ❖ Tensile recovery from elongation.

| FIBER | 1% | 3% | 5% | 15% |
|---|---|---|---|---|
| Polyester 56 (regular) | 91 | 76 | 63 | 40 |
| Nylon 200 (regular) | 81 | 88 | 86 | 77 |

*Source:* E. I. du Pont de Nemours & Company. *Technical Bulletin X-142* (September 1961).

recovery is similar to that of wool at higher elongations, which helps explain the suitability of polyester and wool blends. Nylon exhibits better recovery at higher elongations, so it performs better in products that are subject to greater elongation—hosiery, for example (see Table 8–14).

Polyester has an advantage over wool in many uses, since wool has poor wrinkle recovery when wet. Under conditions of high humidity, polyester fabrics do not shrink and are very resistant to wrinkling. However, when polyester products wrinkle and where body heat and moisture set wrinkles, they may be difficult to remove, even with pressing.

Resiliency makes the polyesters especially good for fiberfill in quilted fabrics such as quilts, bedspreads, parkas, and robes, and in padding for furniture, futons, and mattresses.

The heat properties of the polyesters are used to advantage in fiberfill for pillows, quilts, and linings. If the fiber is flattened on one side or made asymmetrical, it takes on a tight spiral curl of outstanding springiness. Fiberfill of a blend of fiber deniers gives different levels of support. Lumpiness in pillows can be prevented by running hot needles through the batt to spot weld the fibers to each other. Fiberfills with 1, 4, or 7 hollow channels are available. (See Figure 8–12.)

To summarize, the resiliency of polyester is excellent; it resists wrinkles and, when wrinkled, it recovers well whether wet or dry. Elastic recovery is high for most apparel items. The dimensional stability of polyester is high. When properly heat set, it retains its size. It can be permanently creased or pleated satisfactorily.

Pilling was a severe problem with fabrics made from the unmodified polyesters. Low-pilling fiber types minimize the problem and are suitable for use in blends. The finishing process of singeing also helps control pilling.

**CARE** Polyester has revolutionized consumer laundering. This revolution occurred because of heat setting and the advent of durable-press or wrinkle-resistant finishes. Care instructions for polyester/cotton durable-press fabrics can be relatively simple: Wash in warm water; dry with medium heat in a dryer; remove promptly when the cycle is over; hang; and touch up with a steam iron if necessary.

The excellent abrasion resistance and tenacity, and the high elongation of polyester are unaffected by water; there is no difference in wet or dry performance. The low absorbency of polyester (0.4 percent) means that it resists waterborne stains and is quick to dry. The excellent resiliency of polyester keeps it looking good during use and minimizes wrinkling during care so only light pressing may be required. Because of heat setting, dimensional stability is excellent.

Warm water is generally recommended to minimize wrinkling. Hot water may cause fabrics to wrinkle more and may cause color loss. However, hot water (120–140°F) may be needed to remove greasy or oily stains or built-up body soil. Polyester is oleophilic and tends to retain oily soil. A familiar example of this is "ring around the collar." In polyester shirts or polyester/cotton blends, the soil usually responds to pretreatment, then laundering.

The oleophilic nature of polyester may result in redisposition of oily soil on fabrics, making them look dingy. However, polyester is not the color scavenger that nylon is. Soil-release finishes improve soil removal.

Another problem with polyester, especially noticeable with apparel, is a tendency to exhibit bacterial odor. This problem occurs when soil has built up on the fabric; bacteria grow there and an odor results. Use of hot

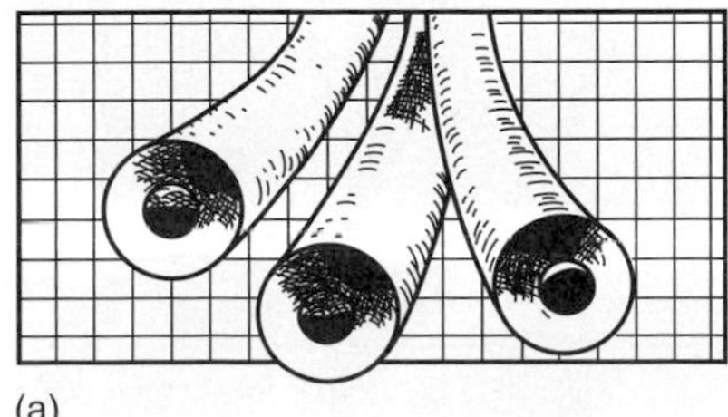
(a)

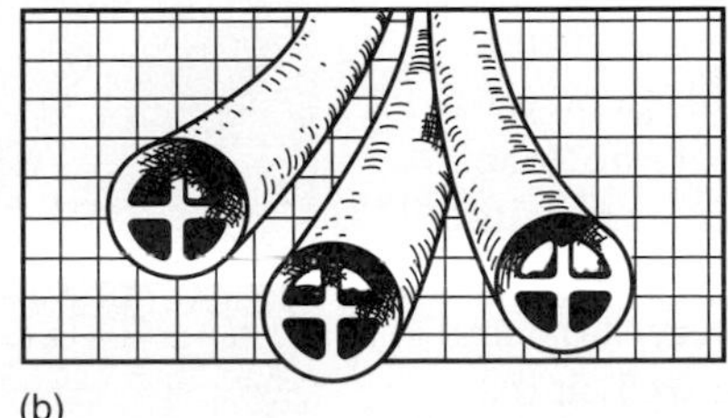
(b)

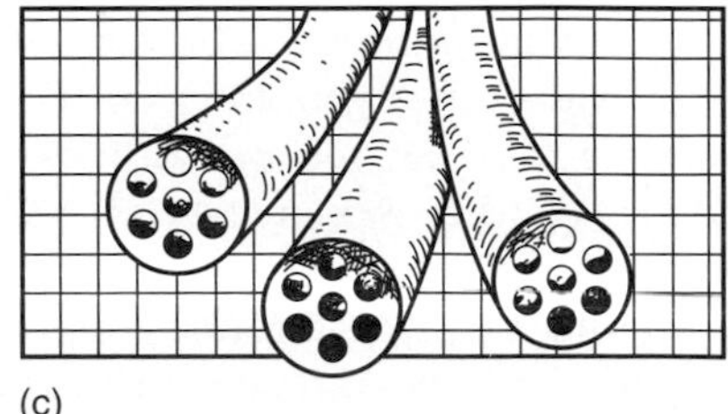
(c)

**FIGURE 8–12** ❖ Hollow polyester fibers: (a) 1-Hollofil, (b) 4-Qallofil, and (c) 7-Hollofil. (COURTESY OF E. I. DU PONT DE NEMOURS & COMPANY)

water wash, laundry agents such as borax, which minimizes odor, or bleach to remove the soil buildup and kill the bacteria may minimize the odor. Several detergents are available that focus on this problem.

Polyester fibers are resistant to both acids and alkalis and can be bleached with either chlorine or oxygen bleaches. Polyester fibers are resistant to biological attack and to sunlight damage, especially important for sheer drapery casement fabrics.

## Environmental Impact of Polyester

Many of the environmental issues discussed with nylon also apply to polyester. One main area of difference between the two fibers is that polyester is extensively recycled. Many recycled fibers are produced primarily from bottle-grade polyester, not from fiber-grade polyester. Recycled polyesters produce significantly less environmental pollution during production than do virgin fibers or those that are made from new raw materials. Air pollution, for example, may be reduced by as much as 85 percent. Challenges that needed to be overcome in the production of these recycled polyesters included achieving appropriate levels of purity of the polyester polymer and improved methods of spinning to make fibers of appropriate quality and with a comfortable hand.

Examples of trade names for recycled polyester fibers include Fortrel EcoSpun and Ecofil by Wellman, Inc. and Polartec Recycled by Malden Mills. Products made from recycled polyester include apparel and carpeting. Consumers like these products, even though the price is usually greater than that of virgin fiber products. The United Nations Environmental Programme has presented Wellman, Inc. with the Fashion Industry Award for Environmental Excellence for its pioneering developments in this area.

## Uses of Polyester

Polyester is the most widely used manufactured fiber in the United States. In 1995, 3.9 million pounds of polyester fiber were used.

Polyester is very important in woven fabrics for apparel and furnishings. Frequently, spun yarns blended with cotton or rayon are seen. Polyester filament yarns may be used in one or both directions of the fabric. Many of the woven fabrics are blends made into durable-press fabrics. These blended fabrics are attractive, durable, comfortable (except in very hot and humid conditions), retain their appearance well, and are easy care. Their excellent performance has resulted in their widespread use and continued popularity. Woven fabrics are used in top weight and bottom weight apparel, sheets, blankets, bedspreads, curtains and draperies, mattress ticking, table linens, and upholstery fabrics. Filaments are used in sheer curtains, where their excellent light resistance and fine denier make them particularly suitable for ninon and marquisette.

A second important use of polyester is in knitted fabrics. Polyester as well as polyester/cotton blend yarns are used. Knit fabrics of polyester wear well, are comfortable, retain their appearance well, and are easy care.

The first use of polyester filaments was in knit shirts for men and blouses for women. The use of filament polyester increased tremendously when textured yarns were developed. Both smooth and textured filaments are used in career apparel such as uniforms and in furnishings such as tricot sheets, warp knit upholstery, and warp knit window treatment fabrics.

A third important use of polyester is in fiberfill. Used in pillows, comforters, bedspreads, furniture padding, placemats, and winter apparel, polyester dominates the market. Other fiberfill materials include down, feathers, or acetate. The polyester used for fiberfill is engineered for resiliency and loft. The durability, comfort, and easy care of polyester also make it appropriate for this end use. Fiberfill is not visible during use—but poor performance shows up in lumpy products or hollow areas. Newer fiberfills create the soft, feathery feel of down. Primaloft is the trade name of a thermal insulation developed by Albany International Research Co. The mixture of an ultrafine polyester with more conventionally sized polyester mimics the large and small components of duck down (Figure 8–13). This combination of fiber sizes produces the same warmth characteristics of down, but at lower costs. In addition, Primaloft does not lose loft nor gain weight when wet.

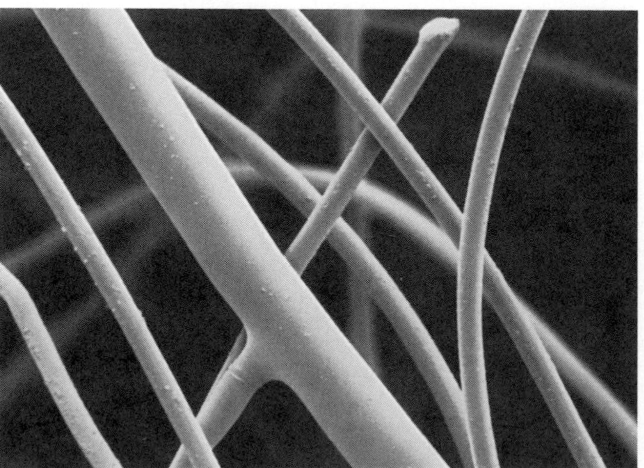

**FIGURE 8–13** ❖ Primaloft thermal insulation. (COURTESY OF ALBANY INTERNATIONAL RESEARCH CO.)

**TABLE 8–15** ❖ Variants of polyester.

| CROSS SECTION | DYEABILITY | CRIMP OR TEXTURED | TENACITY | SHRINKAGE | OTHER |
|---|---|---|---|---|---|
| Round | Disperse dyeable | Producer textured | Regular tenacity | High shrinkage | Pill resistant |
| Trilobal | Cationic dyeable | Partially oriented | Intermediate tenacity | Normal shrinkage | Homopolymer |
| Triangular | Solution dyed | Undrawn filament | High tenacity | Low shrinkage | Copolymer |
| Trilateral | Optically whitened | | High elongation | Heat stabilized | Bicomponent |
| Pentalobal | Deep dye | | Mid-modulus | Chemically stabilized, adhesive activated | Bigeneric |
| Scalloped oval | Extra bright | | High-modulus | | Polished high luster |
| Octolobal | Bright heather | | | | Binder fiber |
| Heptalobal | Dark heather | | | | Soft luster |
| Hollow (1, 4, or 7 channels) | | | | | |

Nonwoven or fiberweb fabrics are a fourth important use of polyester. Interfacings or interlinings, pillow covers, and furniture and mattress interlinings are examples of uses for nonwoven fabrics. They are used where the durability of rayon is inadequate and where absorbency is not needed. Olefin is a strong competitor in many industrial uses. Nonwoven polyester is used in medical softgood applications including nonabsorbent bandages and EKG pads. Other fiberweb products include base fabrics for coatings and laminates.

Tire cord is a fifth important use of polyester. Polyester tires do not "flat spot" as nylon tires do.

A small percentage of carpets that are produced are polyester; they have a softer hand than most nylon carpets. Polyester carpets are not quite as traffic resistant as nylon carpets. However, polyester carpets perform well in low-use areas like bedrooms. Polyester carpets suffer from a "walked down" look after a period of wear in heavy traffic areas. Autoclave heat setting the fibers minimizes the problem. Trevira has a polyester carpet fiber, Trevira XPS, with enhanced resistance to matting and crushing.

Polyester is chosen for many other consumer and industrial uses: pile fabrics, tents, ropes, cording, fishing line, cover stock for disposable diapers, garden hoses, sails, seat belts, filters, fabrics used in road building, seed and fertilizer bags, sewing threads, and artificial arteries, veins, and hearts. Research continues to increase industrial applications.

## Types and Kinds of Polyester

Fortrel by Wellman, Inc., Dacron by DuPont, and Trevira by Trevira are some common trade names and producers. Tables 8–15 and 8–16 describe fiber modifications and fibers engineered for special end uses. A large variety of specific fibers or yarns may combine one or more modifications.

**TABLE 8–16** ❖ Polyester for specialized uses.

| PRODUCER | TRADE NAME | USE |
|---|---|---|
| Allied-Signal | A.C.E. | Tire cord, furniture webbing |
| DuPont | Hollofil, Quallofil | Fiberfill and insulating fibers |
| | Sontara | Spunlaced nonwoven fabrics |
| | Thermoloft | Fiberfill and insulating fibers |
| Trevira | ESP | Apparel and furnishings |
| | Celwet | Nonwovens |
| | Comfort Fiber | Staple fiber for apparel uses |
| | Loftguard | Staple fiber for industrial uses |
| | Polar Guard | |
| | Lambda | Filament yarns with spun-yarn characteristics |
| | Serene | |
| | Superba | |
| | Trevira HT | Marine & military uses; ropes, cordage |
| | Trevira ProEarth | Recycled-content geotextiles |
| | Trevira XPS | Carpeting |
| | BTU | Cold-weather apparel |

# OLEFIN

Many attempts were made to polymerize ethylene, a by-product of the natural gas industry, in the 1920s. Ethylene was polymerized and used as an important plastic during World War II, but filaments made from it did not have sufficiently consistent properties for use in textile fibers. In 1954, Karl Ziegler in Germany developed a process in which the melting point of polymerized ethylene filaments was raised, but it still was too low for many uses. In Italy, Giulio Natta worked with polypropylene and was successful in making linear polymers of high molecular weight that proved to be suitable for most textile applications. By 1957, Italy was producing olefin fibers; U.S. production of olefin fibers started in 1960.

**Olefin** fibers have a combination of properties that make them good for furnishings, apparel that does not need ironing, and industrial uses. Olefin fibers are strong and resistant to abrasion, inexpensive, chemically inert, and thermoplastic but static resistant.

## Production of Olefin

Two processes are used to produce olefin. The high-pressure system, at a pressure of 10 tons per square inch, is used to produce polyethylene film and molded materials. The low-pressure system, at a lower temperature and in the presence of a catalyst and hydrocarbon solvent, is less expensive and produces a polymer (polyethylene) more suitable for textile uses. The extrusion process is similar to that of nylon and polyester. Olefin is melt spun into water or cool air and cold drawn to six times its spun length. Olefins differ from polyester and nylon in that the solution crystallizes very rapidly (undrawn fibers are crystalline), so that the spinning conditions and aftertreatments greatly affect the fiber properties. Olefin is an inexpensive fiber with extremely good performance characteristics for many end uses. The low price of olefin, coupled with its properties, explains its widespread use in industrial uses, furnishings, and apparel. Olefin is one synthetic fiber with a growing market (see Table 8–17).

**Gel spinning** is a relatively new spinning method in which the dissolved polyethylene polymer forms a viscous gel in the solvent. The gel is extruded through the spinneret, the solvent is extracted, and the fiber is drawn. This process produces fibers with very high strength characteristics. Spectra is a trade name for an olefin fiber by Allied-Signal produced by gel spinning.

## Physical Structure of Olefin

Olefins are produced as monofilament, multifilament, staple fiber, and tow with variable tenacities. The fibers are colorless, usually round in cross section, and have a somewhat waxy feel (Figure 8–14). The cross section can be modified depending on end use.

**TABLE 8–17** ❖ Production of synthetic fibers (millions of pounds).

| FIBERS | 1995 | 1990 | 1985 | 1980 | (PEAK YEAR) |
|---|---|---|---|---|---|
| Acrylic | 432 | 506 | 631 | 779 | 1981 |
| Nylon | 2,703 | 2,662 | 2,343 | 2,358 | 1989 |
| Olefin | 2,428 | 1,822 | 1,249 | 748 | still growing |
| Polyester | 3,887 | 3,195 | 3,341 | 3,989 | 1980 |

*Source: Chemical and Engineering News,* June 9, 1986, p. 38 and June 24, 1991, p. 34; *Fiber Organon,* June 24, 1996, p. 44.

## Chemical Composition and Molecular Arrangement of Olefin

*Olefin fibers—manufactured fibers in which the fiber-forming substance is any long-chain synthetic polymer composed of at least 85 percent by weight of ethylene, propylene, or other olefin units except amorphous (non-crystalline) polyolefins qualifying . . . as rubber.*

—*FEDERAL TRADE COMMISSION.*

Olefin may be referred to as polypropylene or polyethylene. **Polyethylene** is a simple linear structure of repeating $-CH_2-$ units. **Polypropylene** has a three-dimensional structure with a backbone of carbon atoms and methyl groups ($-CH_3$) protruding from the chain. Giulio Natta observed that three configurations could be developed when propylene was polymerized and that when all the methyl groups were on one side of the chain, the molecular chains could pack together and

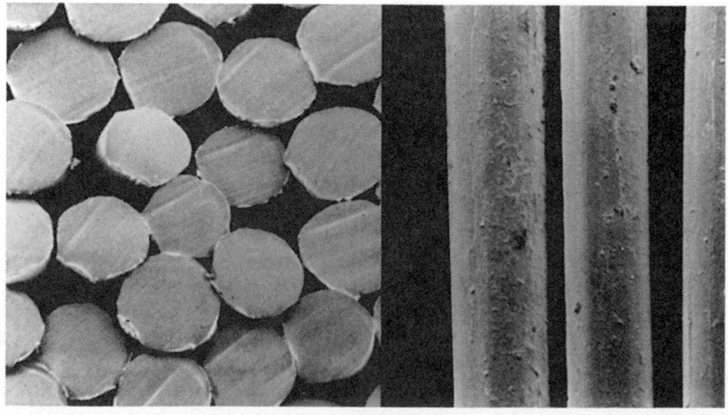

**FIGURE 8–14** ❖ Photomicrograph of olefin: cross-sectional view (left); longitudinal view (right). (COURTESY OF THE BRITISH TEXTILE TECHNOLOGY GROUP.)

crystallize. Natta developed the process in which polymerization would take place in this manner and, together with Karl Ziegler, received the Nobel Prize in Chemistry in 1963 for their work.

Karl Ziegler's work on catalysts to polymerize ethylene and Giulio Natta's discovery of steriospecific polymerization made it possible to obtain high-molecular-weight crystalline polypropylene polymers. *Steriospecific polymerization* means that the molecules are specifically arranged in space so that all the methyl groups have the same spatial arrangement. Natta called this phenomenon **isotactic.** In the atactic form, the methyl groups are randomly arranged, resulting in an amorphous polymer that would qualify as rubber.

```
       H       H       H
       |       |       |
   H   C   H   C   H   C
  \ | /  | \ | /  | \ | /  | \
   C   H   C   H   C   H
   |       |       |
  CH3     CH3     CH3
     ↖     ↑     ↗
      Methyl groups
```

Olefin fibers have no polar groups. The chains are held together by crystallinity alone; the fiber is highly crystalline. The absence of polar groups makes dyeing a problem. Solution dyeing is expensive and less versatile than other methods of adding color to fibers or fabrics. An acid-dyeable olefin has been developed, but dyed olefins comprise a tiny fraction of the market.

## Properties of Olefin

Olefin's performance in apparel and furnishing fabrics is summarized in Table 8–18. Review the fiber property tables in Chapter 3 to help understand the performance of olefin in comparison to that of the other fibers.

**TABLE 8–18** ❖ Summary of the performance of olefin in apparel and furnishing fabrics.

| | |
|---|---|
| **Aesthetic** | **Variable** |
| Luster | Medium |
| **Durability** | **High** |
| Abrasion resistance | Very good |
| Tenacity | High |
| Elongation | Variable |
| **Comfort** | **Moderate** |
| Absorbency | Poor |
| Thermal retention | Good |
| **Appearance Retention** | **Excellent** |
| Resiliency | Excellent |
| Dimensional stability | Excellent |
| Elastic recovery | Excellent |
| **Recommended Care** | Machine wash, dry at low temperature (apparel)<br>Dry extraction method (furnishings) |

**AESTHETIC** Olefin is usually produced with a medium luster and smooth texture, but the luster and texture can be modified depending on the end use. Many sizes of olefin fibers are available. Smaller fibers are becoming increasingly available in furnishings and apparel. Finer denier fibers produce a softer, natural drape.

Olefin has a waxy hand; crimped fibers with modified cross sections have a much more attractive hand. Fibers modified in this manner are most often used for apparel and furnishings. Drape can be varied relative to end use by selection of fiber modification, fabric construction method, and finish.

Current olefins do not look artificial as the early olefins did. Contemporary olefins are modified easily by changing cross section, fiber size, crimp, and luster. Olefin fibers are most often solution dyed; many producers provide a wide variety of color choices for olefins designed for furnishings or apparel. Some interior designers prefer olefin to most other fibers because of its attractive appearance and other positive performance aspects coupled with its relatively low price compared to similar products of different fibers.

**DURABILITY** Olefins may be produced with different strengths suited to the end use. The tenacity of polypropylenes ranges from 3.5 to 8.0 g/d; that of polyethylenes ranges from 1.5 to 7.0 g/d. Wet strength is equal to dry strength for both types. An ultra-high-strength olefin, Spectra by Allied-Signal, has a tenacity of up to 30 g/d and is used in industrial products. Fibers produced for less demanding end uses have tenacities ranging from 4.5 to 6.0 g/d. Olefin fibers have very good abrasion resistance. Elongation varies with the type of olefin. For olefins normally used in apparel and furnishings, the elongation is 10–45 percent with excellent recovery. Upholstery and commercial carpets of olefin and olefin blends combine excellent performance with low cost.

Olefin products are durable and strong. With olefin's low density, it is possible to produce highly durable, lightweight products. Resistance to abrasion and chemicals is excellent. This combination of characteristics and low cost means that olefin is very competitive with other fibers with equal or superior durability characteristics. In end uses where durability, low cost, and low density are critical, such as ropes and cables of great size or length, olefin is often selected.

**COMFORT** Olefins are essentially nonabsorbent with a moisture regain of less than 0.1 percent. Color is normally added during fiber production; most olefin fibers are solution dyed.

Olefins are nonpolar in nature and are not prone to static electricity problems. Because of its excellent wicking abilities, olefin is becoming more important in some end uses, such as active sportswear and as a cover stock in disposable diapers. It does not absorb moisture and minimizes leakage.

Olefin has good heat retention. However, it is olefin's ability to wick moisture that dictates its use in active sportswear, socks, and underwear. It wicks perspiration away from the body and aids in heat loss. In cold-weather wear and active sportswear, olefin keeps the skin dry by wicking moisture away from the skin's surface.

Olefin fibers are the lightest of the textile fibers. Polypropylene has a specific gravity of 0.90 to 0.91; polyethylene, 0.92 to 0.96. This low specific gravity provides more fiber per pound for better cover. As producers learn to deal with its low softening and melting temperatures, difficulty in dyeing, and unpleasant hand, olefins are becoming more popular in warmth-without-weight sweaters and blankets. It takes 1.27 pounds of nylon or 1.71 pounds of cotton to cover the same volume as 1 pound of olefin.

ComforMax IB is a new inner-layer barrier fabric by DuPont used in activewear. The barrier fabric combines wind resistance with air permeability and a good moisture vapor transport rate. **Moisture vapor transport rate** (MVTR) measures how quickly moisture vapor, such as evaporated perspiration, moves from the side of the fabric next to the body to the fabric's exterior side. A high MVTR describes a fabric with good comfort characteristics, especially when the wearer is active.

With modifications of cross section, crimp, and fiber size, olefin upholstery fabrics can be extremely comfortable. In upholstery, olefins with deniers of 1.7 produce comfortable textures. Most other upholstery fibers have a denier of 2. Olefin fibers with a similar small denier are used in apparel. Soft and lightweight olefin fibers with excellent wicking are prized by both amateur and professional athletes for the edge they contribute to performance.

**APPEARANCE RETENTION** Olefin has excellent resiliency and recovers quickly from wrinkling. Shrinkage resistance is excellent as long as it is not heated. It also has excellent elastic recovery. Olefin retains its attractive appearance for years. Since the fiber can be heat set, wrinkles are minimal. Crimp and other three-dimensional effects are permanent. The fiber does not react with most chemicals, so it does not soil or stain readily. Designers find olefin carpeting and upholstery fabrics ideal for a wide variety of end uses.

**CARE** Olefins have easy-care characteristics that make them suited to a number of end uses. They dry quickly after washing. Dry cleaning is seldom recommended because olefins are swollen by common dry cleaning solvents such as perchloroethylene. Petroleum dry cleaning solvents are acceptable for cleaning olefins, but if perchloroethylene is used, the damage cannot be reversed.

Since olefin is not absorbent, waterborne stains are not a problem. The fiber does not pick up color from stains or items that bleed in the wash. The major problems with olefin relate to its oleophilic and heat-sensitive nature. Oily stains are extremely difficult to remove. Exposure to oil may cause the fiber to swell. Exposure to excess heat causes the fiber to shrink and melt. Furnishing items of olefin should never be treated with soil removal agents that contain perchloroethylene since this solvent causes the fiber to swell and alters the appearance of any treated areas.

Olefins have excellent resistance to acids, alkalis, insects, and microorganisms. They are affected by sunlight, but stabilizers can be added to correct this disadvantage. Indoor/outdoor carpeting made of olefin fibers can be hosed off.

Olefins have a low melting point (325–335°F), which limits their use in apparel. Warm or cold water should be used for spot cleaning or washing. Olefin fabrics should be air dried. Olefins should be dried and ironed at low temperatures.

## Environmental Impact of Olefin

Many environmental issues discussed with nylon also apply to olefin. Olefin is an easier fiber to recycle than most other fibers. It is extensively used in a basic unmodified form to protect bales of fiber and rolls of fabrics used in the apparel and furnishings industry. Many packaging materials and industrial products used in other industries are also used in a basic form. These wraps and industrial products can be melted and reused with minimal effort to purify and process them back into fiber form. Tyvek ProtectiveWear by DuPont is an example of a product made of 25 percent postconsumer polyethylene.

Since most olefin is mass pigmented—the pigment is added to the fiber before extrusion—olefin is rarely dyed. The environmental problems related to dyeing generally do not exist for olefin. Because the fiber can be engineered for specific end uses, the problems related to recycling or disposing of finishing chemicals are of little concern for olefin.

Probably one of the most significant impacts of olefin on the environment is its use in industrial products that protect the environment. Erosion control fabrics used in landscaping and along highways protect newly seeded areas and prevent soil erosion. Weed barrier fabrics and protective covers for vegetables and flowers minimize use of herbicides and insecticides by farmers, gardeners, and home owners. Hazardous waste transport containers are lined with Tyvek, an olefin product by DuPont.

## Uses of Olefin

The American Polyolefin Association (APA) promotes the use of olefin and a positive image of the fiber. Olefin is found in an ever-widening array of end uses. In apparel, it is used for underwear, socks, sweaters, glove liners, and active sportswear. Telar by Filament Fiber Technology, Inc. is a fine-denier olefin used in blends for pantyhose, saris, and swimwear. ComforMax IB by DuPont is a microdenier olefin used as a wind, water, and cold barrier layer in active and outdoor wear. Thinsulate is a low-bulk, ultra-fine-microdenier fiberfill of olefin produced by 3M and used in footwear, ski jackets, and other outerwear where a slim silhouette is desired.

In furnishings, olefin is used in carpeting as face yarns and in tufted carpets as backing; as nonwoven, needle-punched carpets and carpet tiles; and as upholstery, draperies, and slipcovers.

Olefin is used in furnishings, by itself and in blends with other fibers. Olefin has almost completely replaced jute in carpet backing because of its low cost, easy processing, excellent durability, and suitability to a wide variety of face yarns, end uses, and finishing procedures. Duon olefin by Phillips Fiber Corp. is used for nonwoven fabrics for furniture webbing because it is versatile, efficient, easy to handle, and economic.

It is in industrial applications that olefin really proves itself. Olefin's continued growth, at a time when the market for most other fibers is stable or receding, is due to its versatility, serviceability, and low cost in a wide array of applications. Olefin makes an ideal geotextile, those textiles that are used in contact with the soil. It is used to produce roadbed support fabrics, like Petromat and Petrotak, that provide a water and particle barrier between road surfaces and the underlying soil foundation. Roadbed support fabrics are used on highways and streets, rail lines, and parking lots to extend their life.

Alpha olefin by Phillips Fiber Corp. is used in car interiors: floor coverings, upholstery, headliners, sun visors, instrument panels, arm rests, package shelf fabric, door and side panels, and carpeting in trunks and cargo areas. It is also a popular fiber in boats for furnishings and finishing fabrics and as surface coverings on docks and decks. Alpha olefin is also used in apparel.

In industrial end uses, olefin is found in dye nets, cover stock for diapers, filter fabrics, laundry and sand bags, banners, geotextiles, ground-control fabrics such as Mirafi and Supac, substrate for coated fabrics, ropes and twines, and roadbed stabilizer fabrics such as Petromat. Tyvek is used in wallpanel fabrics, envelopes and protective clothing. Figure 8–15 shows a rice bag of olefin. Typar by Reemay is used for coating substrates, geotextiles, carpet backing, landscape fabric, rags, and filtration fabrics.

Tables 8–19 and 8–20 list modifications, trade names, and producers of olefin. Table 8–21 compares the characteristics of nylon, polyester, and olefin, the three melt-spun fibers discussed in this chapter.

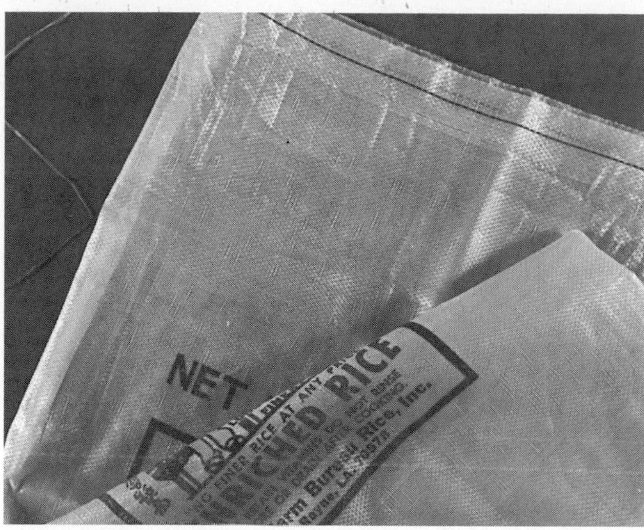


**FIGURE 8–15** ❖ Bag woven with slit-olefin yarns.

**TABLE 8–19** ❖ Types and kinds of olefin fibers.

| | |
|---|---|
| Heat stabilized | Acid dyeable |
| Light stabilized | Solution dyed |
| Modified cross section | Bicomponent |
| Pigmented | Fibrillated |
| | Soil blocking |

**TABLE 8–20** ❖ Some trade names and producers of olefins.

| Trade Name | Producer |
|---|---|
| Patlon, Marquessa Lana, Propex III | Amoco Fabrics & Fibers Co. |
| Tyvek | DuPont |
| Fibrilawn, Fibrilon | Fibron Corp. |
| Herculon | Hercules, Inc. |
| Duraguard, Evolution, Evolution III | Kimberly-Clark |
| Marvess, Duon, Petromat | Phillips Fibers |
| Polyloom | Polyloom Corp. |
| Typar, Biobarrier | Reemay, Inc. |
| Spectra 900, Spectra 1000 | Allied-Signal, Inc. |

# ACRYLIC

Acrylonitrile, the substance from which **acrylic** fibers are made and from which the generic name is derived, was first made in Germany in 1893. It was another chemical used by Carothers and his team in their fundamental research on high polymers for the DuPont Company.

DuPont developed an acrylic fiber in 1944 and started commercial production of this fiber in 1950. DuPont ceased acrylic production in 1991.

The marketing of acrylic fibers frequently takes advantage of its wool-like characteristics. Terms like "virgin acrylic," "mothproof," and "moth-resistant" apparently appeal to consumers. These terms do not convey anything significant since acrylics are inherently moth resistant and are not recycled in the same way that wool is recycled.

## Production of Acrylic

Some acrylic fibers are dry or solvent spun and others are wet spun. In **dry spinning,** the polymers are dissolved in a suitable solvent, such as dimethyl formamide, extruded into warm air, and solidified by evaporation of the solvent. After spinning, the fibers are stretched hot, three to ten times their original length, and then crimped, and marketed as cut staple or tow. In **wet spinning,** the polymer is dissolved in solvent, extruded into a coagulating bath, dried, crimped, and collected as tow for use in the high-bulk process or cut into staple and baled.

## Physical Structure of Acrylic

The cross-sectional shape of acrylic fibers varies as a result of the spinning method used to produce them (Figure 8–16). Dry spinning produces a dog-bone shape. Wet spinning imparts a round or lima bean shape to some fibers. Differences in cross-sectional shape affect physical and aesthetic properties and thus can be a factor in determining appropriate end use. Round and lima bean shapes have a higher bending stiffness, which contributes to resiliency, and are appropriate for bulky sweaters and blankets. Dog-bone shape gives the softness and luster desirable for other uses.

All the production of acrylic fibers in the United States is staple fiber and tow. Staple fiber is available in deniers and lengths suitable for all spinning systems. Acrylic fibers also vary in shrinkage potential. Bicomponent fibers were first produced as acrylics. Some filament yarn acrylic fabrics are imported, mostly in window treatments.

## Chemical Composition and Molecular Arrangement of Acrylic

*Acrylic fibers—manufactured fibers in which the fiber-forming substance is any long-chain synthetic polymer composed of at least 85 percent by weight of acrylonitrile units*

$$\left[ \begin{array}{c} -CH_2-\underset{\displaystyle CN}{\underset{|}{CH}}- \end{array} \right]$$

—FEDERAL TRADE COMMISSION.

**TABLE 8–21** ❖ Comparison of melt-spun fibers.

| | NYLON | POLYESTER | OLEFIN |
|---|---|---|---|
| Breaking tenacity g/d | 2.3–9.8 filament<br>2.9–7.2 staple | 2.8–9.5 filament<br>2.4–7.0 staple | 3.5–8.0 filament |
| Specific gravity | 1.14 | 1.22 or 1.38 | 0.91 |
| Moisture regain % | 4.0–4.5 | 0.4–0.8 | Less than 1 |
| Melting point | 482° or 414°F | 540° or 482°F | 325°–335°F |
| Safe ironing temperature | 270°–300°F | 325°–350°F | 250°F–lowest setting |
| Effect of light | Poor resistance | Good resistance | Poor resistance |

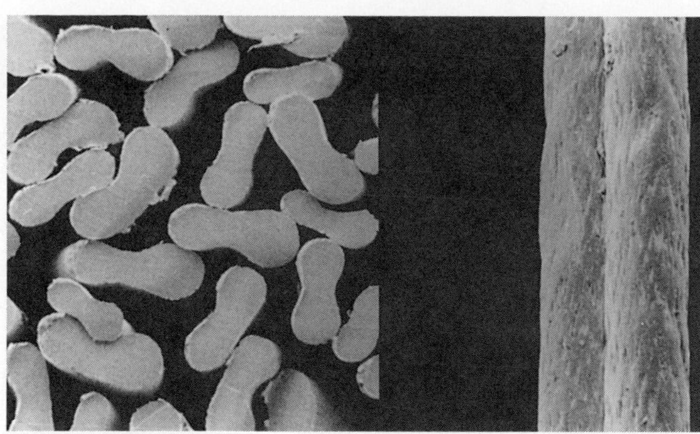

**FIGURE 8–16** ❖ Photomicrograph of acrylic: cross-sectional view (left); longitudinal view (right). (COURTESY OF THE BRITISH TEXTILE TECHNOLOGY GROUP.)

Fibers of 100 percent polyacrylonitrile have a compact, highly oriented internal structure that makes them virtually undyeable. They are an example of a **homopolymer,** a fiber composed of a single substance. Schematically, a homopolymer could be diagrammed:

x x x x x x x x x x x x x x x **Homopolymer**

Since this structure in acrylic fibers makes dyeing so difficult, acrylics are produced as **copolymers** with up to 15 percent additives. This results in a more open structure and permits dye to be absorbed into the fiber. The additives furnish dye sites that can be modified for specific dye classes so that cross dyeing is possible. Copolymer fibers are composed of two or more compounds and could be diagrammed:

O x O x O x O x O x O x O x **Copolymer**

or:

x x O x x x x O x x **Copolymer**

depending on the percentage of substances and their arrangement in relation to each other.

In graft polymerization, the additive does not become a part of the main molecular chain. It is a side chain that is attached to the backbone chain of the molecule. This gives the molecular chains a more open structure and less crystallinity; dye receptivity is increased.

Some fibers have molecules with chemically reactive groups; others are chemically inert. A chemically inert molecule can be made reactive by grafting reactive groups onto the backbone. It could be diagrammed:

```
x x x x x x x x x x x x x x x x x x x x x x
    |             |           |     |
    c             c           c     c
```

**Graft polymer**

Copolymer acrylics are not as strong as the homopolymers or **graft polymer** acrylics. Since the end uses for acrylics are mostly apparel and furnishings, the reduced strength is not a major concern.

## Properties of Acrylic

Acrylic fibers are soft, warm, lightweight, and resilient. They make easy-care fabrics. Because of their low specific gravity and high bulk properties, the acrylics have been called the "warmth without weight" fibers. Acrylics have been very successful in end uses such as sweaters and blankets that had been dominated by wool. They are superior to wool in their easy-care properties and are nonallergenic. Bulky acrylic yarns are popular in socks, fleece fabrics, fake-fur fabrics, and craft yarns. Table 8–22 summarizes the performance characteristics of acrylics. The fiber property tables in Chapter 3 compare acrylic properties to those of other fibers.

**AESTHETIC** Acrylic fibers possess favorable aesthetic properties. They are attractive and have a soft, pleasant hand. Bulky spun yarns are usually textured to be wool-like. Indeed, acrylic fabrics imitate wool fabrics more successfully than any of the other manufactured fibers.

Apparel and furnishing items of all acrylic or acrylic blends are attractive. Their luster is matte due to delustering, the irregular cross-sectional fiber shape, and fiber crimp. Since these products are almost always staple fibers, their wool-like appearance is maintained. Bulky yarns and bicomponent fibers also contribute to the wool-like appearance.

**TABLE 8–22** ❖ Summary of the performance of acrylic in apparel and furnishing fabrics.

| | |
|---|---|
| **Aesthetic** | **Wool-like** |
| **Durability** | **Moderate** |
| Abrasion resistance | Moderate |
| Tenacity | Moderate |
| Elongation | Moderate-high |
| **Comfort** | **Moderate** |
| Absorbency | Poor |
| Thermal retention | Moderate |
| **Appearance Retention** | **Moderate** |
| Resiliency | Moderate |
| Dimensional stability | Moderate |
| Elastic recovery | Moderate |
| **Recommended Care** | Machine wash; follow care label (apparel)<br>Dry clean or dry extraction method (furnishings) |

Cytec, Inc. produces an acrylic microfiber, Micro-Supreme, with a denier per filament of 0.8. It is used in fine-gauge knitted and woven apparel, hosiery, and furnishings.

**DURABILITY** Acrylics are not as durable as nylon, polyester, or olefin fibers, but, in apparel and furnishings, the strength of acrylics is satisfactory. Dry tenacity is moderate, ranging from 2.0 to 3.0 g/d. Abrasion resistance is also moderate. The elongation at break is 35 percent. Elongation increases when the fiber is wet. The overall durability of acrylic fibers is moderate, similar to that of wool and cotton.

Furnishings of acrylic or acrylic blends are highly durable. They provide reasonable resistance to abrasion for upholstery fabrics. They are sufficiently strong to withstand laundering (table linens), dry cleaning (draperies), and dry extraction cleaning (carpet). Pilling can be a noticeable problem with these staple fiber fabrics. However, some low-pilling fiber modifications are available. Some fabric finishes reduce pilling.

Monsanto has introduced a Wear Dated Traffic Control Carpet of 88 percent nylon/12 percent acrylic. The carpet has high bulk and is more durable than nylon alone. Both fibers are blended together in the carpet yarn, twisted, and heat set. Since the acrylic is a high shrinkage modification, it shrinks and tightens the yarn tuft, producing good durability characteristics.

Because of its exceptional resistance to weathering, acrylic is widely used in awnings and tarpaulins. Table 8–23 shows that acrylic is comparable to wool in durability properties.

**COMFORT** The fiber surface of acrylic fibers is much less regular than that of other synthetic fibers. Photomicrographs show irregularities and indentations on the surface (see Figure 8–17). In spite of the relatively low moisture regain of 1.0–2.5 percent, acrylics are moderately comfortable because of the irregular fiber surface. Instead of absorbing moisture and becoming wet to the touch, acrylic fibers wick moisture to the fabric's exterior where it evaporates more readily and cools the body.

**TABLE 8–23** ❖ Comparison of acrylic with wool—Durability.

| FIBER PROPERTY | ACRYLIC | WOOL |
|---|---|---|
| Abrasion resistance | Good | Fair |
| Breaking tenacity | 2.0–3.0 g/d dry | 1.5 g/d dry |
| | 1.8–2.7 g/d wet | 1.0 g/d wet |
| Elongation at break | 35 percent | 25 percent |
| Elastic recovery | 92 percent | 99 percent |

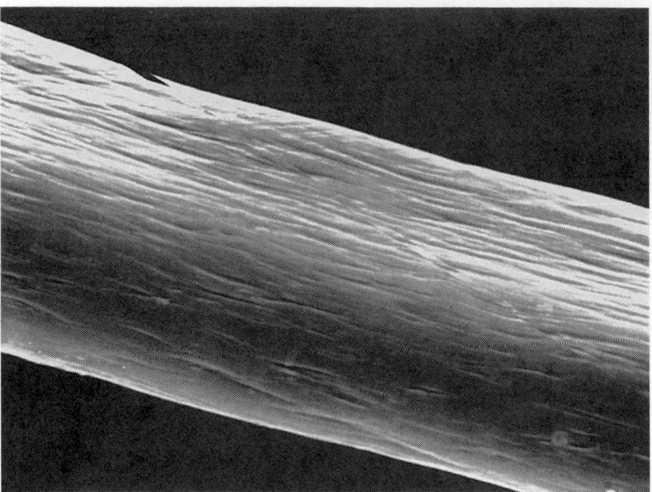

**FIGURE 8–17** ❖ Acrylic that is magnified 3,000 times shows a pitted and irregular surface.

Another factor that makes acrylics comfortable is that the fibers and yarns can be made with high bulk. Acrylic fibers can be produced with a *latent shrinkage potential* and retain the bulk indefinitely at room temperature. The resulting bulky fabrics retain body heat well so they are warm in cold temperatures. Bulky knit sweaters are a familiar example of this.

The structure of the yarn and fabric can be varied to make a warmer or cooler product, depending on how it is used. In general, acrylics are more comfortable than nylon and polyester, but not as comfortable as cotton in hot, humid weather, or as wool in very cold or cold, humid weather.

The density of acrylic is similar to that of nylon. Thus, the fabrics are lightweight with good durability. In apparel, this means bulky sweaters of acrylic are not as heavy as wool sweaters. Acrylic blankets are lighter than similar wool blankets.

**APPEARANCE RETENTION** Acrylic fibers exhibit moderate resiliency and recovery from bending, thus they resist wrinkling during use and care. They have moderate dimensional stability. When proper yarn and fabric structures are utilized, the dimensional stability of acrylic fabrics is good. Acrylics shrink when exposed to boiling water, so high temperatures and steam should be avoided. The fibers have poor hot-wet properties.

Acrylic fibers cannot be heat set like nylon and polyester because acrylic does not melt, but decomposes and discolors when heated. However, some acrylics can have pleats or creases set in that are not affected by normal use or care. With the application of heat and/or steam, the crease or pleats can be removed.

Acrylics also differ from nylon and polyester with poorer dimensional stability. Fabrics may shrink or stretch during care.

Pills form on some acrylic fabrics. Acrylics tend to fibrillate, or crack, with abrasion, which may contribute to pilling.

Acrylics and blends with acrylic maintain their appearance well. The bulk characteristics are permanent if the product receives the appropriate care. These fibers are less likely to mat than some fibers. With solution dyeing of some upholstery, drapery, and awning fabrics, colors are permanent. Awning fabrics of solution-dyed acrylic are popular in finishing window exteriors, entries, and outdoor entertainment areas.

**CARE** In caring for items made of acrylic, it is especially important to follow the instructions found on care labels. Table 8–24 compares care aspects of acrylic to those of wool. There are several basic acrylic fibers with slightly differing properties due to the polymer composition and manufacturing methods. With the additional variations available through shrinkage potentials of acrylic fibers, as well as of bicomponent fibers, many factors can affect appropriate care.

The acrylics have good resistance to most chemicals except strong alkalis and chlorine bleaches. This is not surprising; fibers containing nitrogen are usually susceptible to damage from alkali and chlorine. Except for the furlike fabrics, acrylic fabrics have good wash-and-wear characteristics. They do not wrinkle if handled properly and if directions on the care label are followed.

Some items made from high-bulk yarns of bicomponent fibers need to be machine dried to regain their shape after washing. If they are blocked, dried flat, or drip dried, they may be too large or misshapen. Rewashing and tumble drying the knit should help it recover its original shape.

Some acrylics can be dry cleaned. However, with some fabrics the finish is removed, resulting in a harsh feel. Thus, care labels should be followed. Acrylics are resistant to moth damage and mildew, and have excellent resistance to sunlight.

Following the recommended care procedures for acrylic or acrylic blend products is especially true for electric blankets of acrylic. Electric blankets should never be dry cleaned. Dry cleaning solvents dissolve the protective coating on the wiring of the blanket, resulting in a high risk of electric shock or fire. Steam cleaning of draperies, upholstery, and carpeting is generally not recommended because acrylics may shrink.

Mann Industries has developed a new antimicrobial fiber, Biokryl, to be used in apparel, furnishing, and industrial applications. Products include nursing uniforms, socks, shoe liners, sportswear, contract carpet and upholstery, surgical barrier fabrics, and industrial filters.

## Environmental Impact of Acrylic

Acrylic is resistant to natural sources of degradation including molds, mildew, rot, and many chemicals. Because acrylic is processed from petrochemicals, related concerns include drilling in sensitive environments, oil spills, and disposal of hazardous chemicals. The chemicals from which acrylic is made require significant processing before they can be used to produce the raw materials that are polymerized to form acrylic. With wet or dry spun fibers, recycling of solvents is necessary to minimize environmental impact. Wet-spun acrylics also require washing and drying to remove

**TABLE 8–24** ❖
Comparison of acrylics and wool—Care.

| FIBER PROPERTY | ACRYLIC | WOOL |
|---|---|---|
| Effect of alkalis | Resistant to weak alkalis | Harmed |
| Effect of acids | Resistant to most acids | Resistant to weak acids |
| Effect of solvents | Can be dry cleaned | Dry cleaning recommended |
| Effect of sunlight | Excellent resistance | Low resistance |
| Stability | Can be heat set for shape retention | Subject to felting, shrinkage |
| Permanence of creases | Creases can be set and removed by heat | Creases set by heat and moisture—not permanent |
| Effect of heat | Thermoplastic—sticks at 450–490°F | Scorches easily, becomes brittle at high temperature |
| Resistance to moths and fungi | Resistant | Harmed by moths; mildew forms on soiled, stored wool |
| Effect of water | None | May felt or mat, noticeable odor when wet |

chemicals from the coagulating bath. Different types of acrylic are made from slightly different raw materials. Potential hazards to the environment will differ depending on which raw materials and processes are used in production. Acrylic is not recycled. Because acrylics can be engineered for specific end uses, chemical finishing is not a concern. Acrylics may be dyed; processing of dye wastes is a concern.

## Uses of Acrylic

Acrylic accounted for approximately 4 percent of the fiber produced in the United States in 1995, approximately 432 million pounds. Although more acrylic is used in apparel, it is also important in furnishings and industrial products. Knitted apparel items of acrylic include fleece fabrics, sweaters, and socks. Socks of Duraspun by Monsanto are supposed to keep feet drier and last 35 percent longer. Fleece fabrics, available in many colors and prints, are frequently used in jogging outfits and active sportswear. Acrylic pile fabrics and thick, snuggly fun furs are used for coats, jackets, linings, or soft, cuddly stuffed animals.

Craft yarns are another important end use of acrylic fibers. Craft yarns are often made of a heavier denier (5–6 denier). Many sweaters, vests, and afghans are knit or crocheted with these yarns. Acrylic yarns are also used for embroidery, weaving, and other crafts.

Upholstery fabrics have a wool-like appearance and may be flat-woven fabrics or velvets with good durability and stain resistance. Drapery fabrics of acrylic have good sunlight resistance and weathering.

Acrylics are used in blankets, in a variety of fabric construction methods. Both lightweight and winter-weight blankets are available. Blankets are an appropriate use for acrylics because the cost is lower, the bulky fabrics are lighter weight, and the care is easier than for wool blankets.

Carpets and rugs of acrylic or blends look more wool-like than several other synthetic fibers and have easier care requirements and lower cost than wool carpets.

Acrylics are found in a number of industrial uses for which their chemical and abrasion resistance and good weathering properties make them suitable: awnings and tarpaulins, luggage, boat and other vehicle covers, outdoor furniture, tents, carbon fiber precursors, office room dividers, and sandbags (Figure 8–18). When exposed to chemicals, fibers with good chemical resistance show little or no loss of physical structure or fiber properties. Sunbrella mass-pigmented acrylic awnings by Glen Raven Mills, Inc. withstand exposure to sun, wind, and rain for years without fading, cracking, hardening, peeling, or rotting.

## Types and Kinds of Acrylic

Each company that produces acrylic in the United States identifies its fiber by a trade name:

| TRADE NAME | COMPANY | TYPE |
|---|---|---|
| Acrilan, Acrilan II, Bi-Loft, Du-Rel, Duaspun, Fi-Lana Pa-Qel, So-Lara | Monsanto Chemical Co. | Staple and tow |

**FIGURE 8–18** ❖ Acrylics are used for luggage and outdoor furniture because of their abrasion resistance and good weathering properties. (COURTESY OF BASF CORP. FIBERS DIVISION.)

| | | |
|---|---|---|
| Creslan, MicroSupreme | Cytec, Inc. | Staple and tow |
| Zefran, Biokryl, Mann Aeryl, Acry Pulp | Mann Industries, Inc. | Staple |

Fiber variants that are tailored for a specific end use or differ in performance are also produced. See Table 8–25 for a list of fiber and yarn types available. Trade names and modifications for one producer, Monsanto Chemical Co., are:

| | |
|---|---|
| Acrilan | |
| Bi-Loft | high bulk |
| So-Lara | producer colored |
| Fi-Lana | ultrasoft |
| Pa-Qel | bicomponent, high bulk |
| So-Qel | producer colored, bicomponent |
| Du-Rel | fade resistant pigmented fiber (upholstery) |
| Pil-Trol | pill resistant for specialty uniforms |

# Modacrylic Fibers

**Modacrylic** fibers are modified acrylics. They are made from acrylonitriles, but a larger proportion of other polymers are added to make the copolymers. Production of modacrylic fibers started in the United States in 1949.

Modacrylics were the first inherently flame-retardant synthetic fibers; they do not support combustion, are very difficult to ignite, are self-extinguishing, and do not drip. This inherent flame retardancy makes them good for end uses such as protective clothing and contract furnishings.

**Table 8–25** ❖ Types and kinds of acrylic fibers and yarns.

| |
|---|
| Homopolymer |
| Copolymer |
| Graft polymer |
| Bicomponent |
| Blends of various deniers |
| Blends of homopolymer and copolymer |
| Helical, nonreversible crimp |
| Reversible crimp |
| Surface modified |
| Variable cross section—round, acorn, dog-bone |
| Variable dyeability—cationic, disperse, acidic, basic |
| Solution dyed |

## Production of Modacrylic Fibers

The modacrylic fibers are produced by polymerizing the components, dissolving the copolymer in acetone (dry spun), pumping the solution into a column of warm air, and stretching while hot. Currently Monsanto Chemical Co. is the only producer in the U.S. The trade name S.E.F. (self-extinguishing flame) is used.

## Physical Structure of Modacrylic Fibers

The modacrylics are creamy white and are produced as staple or tow. They have a dog-bone or irregular cross section (Figure 8–19). Various deniers, lengths, crimp levels, and shrinkage potentials are available.

## Chemical Composition and Molecular Arrangement of Modacrylic Fibers

*Modacrylic fibers—manufactured fibers in which the fiber-forming substance is any long-chain synthetic polymer composed of less than 85 percent but at least 35 percent by weight acrylonitrile units except when the polymer qualifies as rubber.*

—*Federal Trade Commission.*

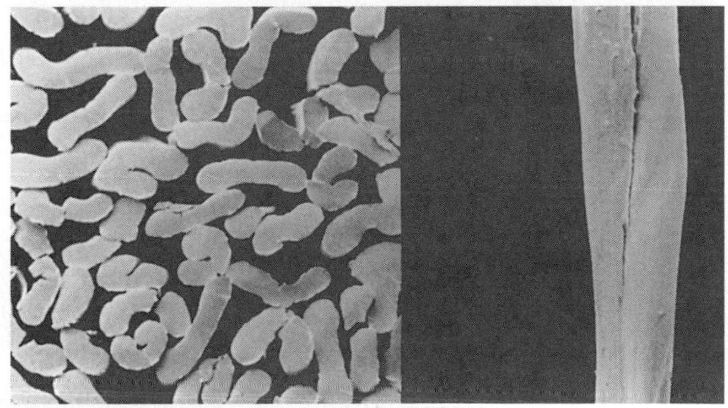

**Figure 8–19** ❖ Photomicrograph of modacrylic: cross-sectional view (left); longitudinal view (right). (Courtesy of the British Textile Technology Group.)

The chemicals used as copolymers include vinyl chloride ($CH_2CHCl$), vinylidene chloride ($CH_2CCl_2$), or vinylidene dicyanide ($CH_2CCN_2$).

## Properties of Modacrylic Fibers

Modacrylic has properties similar to acrylic. Major differences are that modacrylic is flame retardant and has better heat resistance compared to acrylic.

**AESTHETIC** Furlike fabrics, wigs, hairpieces, and fleece-type pile fabrics are produced of modacrylic fibers with different amounts of crimp and shrinkage potential. By mixing different fiber types it is possible to obtain fibers of different pile heights: long, polished fibers (guard hairs), and soft, highly crimped undercoat fibers much like real fur (Figure 8–20). Fabrics can be sheared, embossed, and printed to resemble fur.

Modacrylic has an attractive appearance similar to that of acrylic. It can be made to resemble wool with a soft, matte luster, or it can be made with a more intense luster to resemble the shiny guard hairs of fur.

**DURABILITY** Modacrylics are less durable than acrylics, but they have adequate durability for their end uses. The strength of modacrylics is similar to that of wool. Abrasion resistance is similar to acrylic. Elastic recovery is superior to that of acrylic.

**COMFORT** Modacrylics are poor conductors of heat. Fabrics are soft, warm, and resilient, but have a tendency to pill. Their absorbency is low, varying from 2 to 4 percent moisture regain.

Modacrylics combine flame retardancy with a relatively low density (1.35). This means that protective apparel need not be uncomfortably heavy. Flame-retardant furnishings, especially draperies, can be produced without great weight.

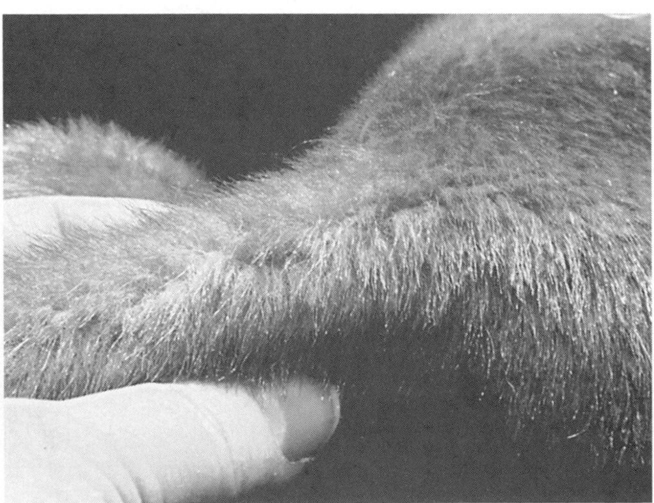

**FIGURE 8–20** ❖ Furlike fabric of modacrylic. Notice how the sleek guard hairs and the soft, fine underhairs simulate the appearance of fur.

**APPEARANCE RETENTION** Modacrylic fibers exhibit moderate resiliency. In typical end uses, they do not wrinkle. They have moderate dimensional stability and high elastic recovery.

Modacrylics pill more quickly, are more sensitive to heat, mat more readily, and are not as resilient as acrylics. Modacrylics tend to retain color well.

**CARE** Modacrylics are resistant to acids, weak alkalis, and most organic solvents. They are resistant to mildew and moths. They have very good resistance to sunlight and very good flame resistance.

Modacrylics can be washed or dry cleaned, but special care must be taken. Fibers are heat sensitive; they shrink at 250°F and stiffen at temperatures over 300°F. If fabrics are machine washed, use warm water and tumble dry at a low setting. The lowest iron setting should be used. Some furlike fabrics are dry cleanable; some require special care in dry cleaning (no steam, no tumble, tumble cold); and some should be cleaned by a furrier method.

Modacrylics are more sensitive to loss of appearance from improper care than the acrylics. The precautions regarding steam cleaning discussed with acrylics also apply to modacrylics.

## Environmental Impact of Modacrylic Fibers

Modacrylic is resistant to natural degradation. The concerns expressed for acrylic generally apply to modacrylic. Modacrylic has less of an impact on the environment compared to acrylic for two reasons. One, modacrylic is only produced using dry spinning, so concerns are limited to one process. The solvent, acetone, is relatively easy to reclaim and recycle in the spinning process. Two, modacrylic is a relatively minor fiber in terms of amount produced.

## Uses of Modacrylic Fibers

Modacrylics are used primarily in those applications where environmental resistance is needed or where flame retardancy is necessary or required by law or building codes (see Chapter 21). The primary end use is in outdoor fabrics and awnings. Other end uses include protective clothing such as shirts and trousers for electric line personnel; furnishings including upholstery, window treatment fabrics, and blankets; and industrial applications including filters and outdoor furnishings and awnings. Because of its heat sensitivity, modacrylic may be used to produce realistic fake furs and wigs or hairpieces that can be curled with a curling iron. Many modacrylics are mass pigmented rather than dyed.

## Key Terms

Synthetic fibers
Heat sensitivity
Glazing
Pilling
Oleophilic
Melt spinning
Heat setting
Nylon
Polyamides
Polyester
Olefin
Polyethylene
Gel spinning
Isotactic
Polypropylene
Moisture vapor transport rate
Acrylic
Dry spinning
Wet spinning
Homopolymer
Copolymer
Graft polymer
Modacrylic

## Questions

1. Explain the differences in chemical composition between these groups of fibers:

   polyethylene and polypropylene
   acrylic and modacrylic

2. Identify the differences in properties between the pairs of fibers listed in question 1.
3. What are the major performance characteristics of each of these fibers: nylon, polyester, olefin, acrylic, and modacrylic?
4. What spinning process is used to produce each of these fibers: nylon, polyester, olefin, acrylic, modacrylic? How does the spinning process relate to the fiber's cross-sectional shape?
5. How do the characteristics of these fibers differ from those of the natural fibers and those produced from naturally occurring polymers?
6. Identify a synthetic fiber that would be an appropriate choice for each end use listed below and explain, using performance characteristics, why that fiber was selected:

   carpet for department store boutique area
   pantyhose
   man's sweater vest
   geotextile for use as roadbed underlay
   lead rope for horses or ponies
   upholstery fabric for theater seats

## Suggested Readings

Borman, Stu. (1989, October 16). "New Fibers Offer Alternatives to Waterfowl Down." *Chemical and Engineering News*, pp. 25–26.

Davidson, W. A. B. (1993, April). "Wellman Launches Fortrel EcoSpun." *America's Textiles International*, pp. 80, 82.

Ford, J. E. (1992). "Acrylic Fibres." *Textiles*, no. 2, pp. 10–14.

Fukuhara, Mototada (1993). "Innovation in Polyester Fibers: From Silk-like to New Polyester." *Textile Research Journal, 63*, pp. 387–391.

Jerg, Gunter, and Baumann, Josef (1990). "Polyester Microfibers: A New Generation of Fabrics." *Textile Chemist and Colorist, 22* (12), pp. 12–14.

Kalogeridis, Carla (1992, August). "Microfibers: All Dressed Up and Everywhere to Go." *Textile World*, pp. 37–40, 43, 44, 47, 48.

Mansfield, Richard G. (1994, January). "Polypropylene Use in Apparel Grows." *Knitting Times* (Apparel Section), pp. 8, 10.

Mansfield, Richard G. (August, 1990). "Polypropylene: Strong Backing in Carpets." *America's Textiles International*, pp. 46–48.

Moore, Ronald A. F. (1989). "Nylon 6 and Nylon 6,6: How Different Are They?" *Textile Chemist and Colorist, 21* (2), pp. 19–22.

"The Polycotton Story." (1994, Winter). *Textiles Magazine*, pp. 8–11.

Trotman, E. R. (1984). *Dyeing and Chemical Technology of Textile Fibers*. New York: John Wiley & Sons.

Zeronian, S. Haig, and Collins, Martha J. (1988). "Improving the Comfort of Polyester Fabrics." *Textile Chemist and Colorist, 20* (4), pp. 25–28.

Chapter 9

# Special-Use Fibers

## OBJECTIVES

- To differentiate among special-use fibers based on their elastomeric or protective characteristics.
- To recognize the importance of these fibers in apparel, furnishings, and industrial products.
- To integrate properties of special-use fibers with their uses.

This chapter focuses on fibers with unique characteristics. Some of these fibers are in common consumer products, but consumers may not be aware of them. Other fibers are used in applications so specialized that most consumers would have little contact with them. These textiles contribute significantly to the technological advances we accept as commonplace and necessary for the lives we lead. The fibers are grouped by the purposes they serve: elastomeric or protective.

These fibers are produced in relatively small quantities compared to the majority of the fibers discussed in previous chapters. Special-use fibers comprise about 1 percent of the fibers used in the U.S. They are used either in small quantities in products or in items with a relatively small market segment. For example, spandex may comprise as much as 20 percent of the fiber in a swimsuit or leotard. Graphite fiber may be used in the frame of a bicycle to add structural support. The potential for growth in this segment of the textile industry is excellent. The price per pound of these fibers can be very high compared to that of common apparel and furnishing fibers. The environmental impact of these fibers is relatively small because of their small production levels. Several of the protective fibers that will be discussed later in this chapter are frequently used to remove harmful chemicals from the environment.

# Elastomeric Fibers

According to the American Society of Testing and Materials (ASTM), an **elastomer** is a natural or synthetic polymer that, at room temperature, can be stretched repeatedly to at least twice its original length and that, after removal of the tensile load, will immediately and forcibly return to approximately its original length. Elastomeric fibers include spandex, rubber, and anidex. Anidex is no longer produced in the United States.

Many textile products need some stretch or elasticity. There are two kinds of stretch: power stretch and comfort stretch. **Power stretch** is important in end uses where holding power and elasticity are needed. Elastic fibers that have a high retractive force must be used to attain this kind of stretch. Some end uses are foundation garments, surgical-support garments, swimsuits, garters, belts, and suspenders.

**Comfort stretch** is important in products where only elasticity is desired. Comfort-stretch fabrics look no different from nonstretch fabrics. They may be lighter weight than power-stretch fabrics and can be found in apparel and furnishings.

## Rubber

*Rubber—manufactured fiber in which the fiber-forming substance is comprised of natural or synthetic rubber, including:*

1. *A manufactured fiber in which the fiber-forming substance is a hydrocarbon such as natural rubber, polyisoprene, polybutadiene, copolymers of dienes and hydrocarbons, or amorphous (noncrystalline) polyolefins.*
2. *A manufactured fiber in which the fiber-forming substance is a copolymer of acrylonitrile and a diene (such as butadiene) composed of not more than 50 percent but at least 10 percent by weight of acrylonitrile units*

$$(\text{—CH}_2\text{—}\underset{\displaystyle \text{CN}}{\underset{|}{\text{CH}}}\text{—}).$$

*The term* lastrile *may be used as a generic description for fibers falling in this category.*

3. *A manufactured fiber in which the fiber-forming substance is a polychloroprene or a copolymer of chloroprene in which at least 35 percent by weight of the fiber-forming substance is composed of chloroprene units*

$$(\text{—CH}_2\text{—}\underset{\displaystyle \text{Cl}}{\underset{|}{\text{C}}} = \text{CH—CH}_2\text{—}).$$

—*Federal Trade Commission.*

Natural **rubber** is the oldest elastomer and the least expensive. It is obtained by coagulation of the latex from the rubber tree *Hevea brasiliensis.* In 1905, sheets of rubber were cut into strips that made the yarns used in foundation garments and the like. During and shortly after World War II, synthetic rubbers were developed. These synthetic rubbers are cross-linked diene polymers, copolymers containing dienes, or amorphous polyolefins. Both synthetic and natural rubbers must be vulcanized or cross-linked with sulfur in order to develop elastomeric properties. Natural and synthetic rubbers are large in cross section. The shape of the cross section is round if extruded as a fiber or rectangular if cut from an extruded film.

Rubber has excellent elongation characteristics of 700–900 percent with excellent recovery. Its low tenacity ranges from 0.5 to 1.0 g/d and limits its use in lightweight garments. The finest rubber yarns must be three times as large as spandex yarns to be comparable in strength. Because of rubber's low dye acceptance, hand, and appearance, it is almost always covered by a yarn of another fiber or by other yarns used to produce the fabric.

Rubber has been replaced in many uses by spandex, but it continues to be used in narrow elastic fabrics.

Synthetic rubber is more common in these elastic fabrics than is natural rubber.

Although antioxidants are incorporated in the spinning solution, rubber still does not have good resistance to oxidizing agents and is damaged by aging, sunlight, oil, and perspiration. Rubber's resistance to alkali is generally good, but it is damaged by heat, chlorine, and solvents. It should be washed with care and should not be dry cleaned.

Neoprene, a type of synthetic rubber made from polychloroprene, is used as an elastomeric fiber or a supported elastic film. It is resistant to acids, alkalis, alcohols, oils, caustics, and solvents. It is found in a variety of products including protective gloves and clothing, wetsuits, framing for window glass, industrial hoses and belts, anticorrosive seals and membranes, and coatings for wiring.

## Spandex

After many years of research, DuPont introduced the first manufactured elastic fiber, a spandex fiber called Lycra, in 1958. Spandex generated much interest because it was superior to rubber in strength and durability. Spandex is produced by DuPont under the trade name of Lycra and by Globe Manufacturing Company under the trade names of Glospan and Cleerspan.

**PRODUCTION** **Spandex** fibers are made by reacting preformed polyester or polyether molecules with di-isocyanate and polymerizing them into long molecular chains. Filaments are obtained by wet or solvent spinning. The spinning solution may contain delustering agents, dye receptors, whiteners, and lubricants.

**PHYSICAL STRUCTURE** Spandex is produced as monofilament or multifilament yarns in a variety of deniers. Monofilaments are round in cross section, whereas multifilaments are coalesced or partly fused together at intervals and are found in fibers with deniers of 40 and above (Figure 9–1). When sewing multifilament yarns, the needle goes between the fine filaments rather than breaking them. When sewing monofilament yarns with a ballpoint needle, the needle pushes the monofilament aside rather than rupturing it. Spandex is delustered and usually white or gray.

Deniers range from 20 to 4,300. Twenty-denier spandex is used in lightweight support hosiery where a large amount of stretch is desirable. Much coarser yarns, 1,500 to 2,240 denier, stretch less and are used for support in hosiery tops, swimwear, and foundation garments. (See Figure 9–2.)

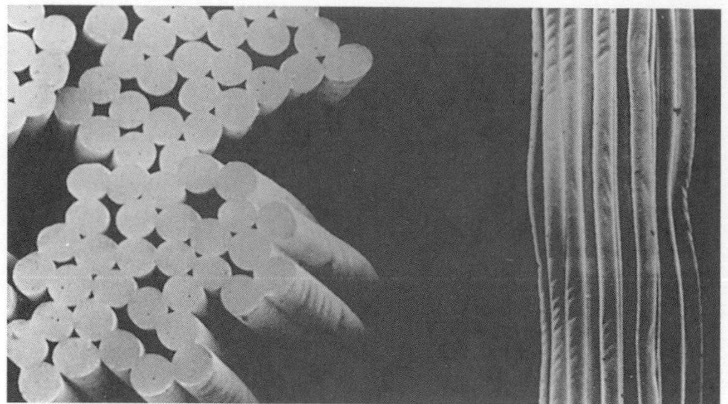

**FIGURE 9–1** ❖ Photomicrograph of spandex: cross-sectional view (left); longitudinal view (right). (COURTESY OF THE BRITISH TEXTILE TECHNOLOGY GROUP.)

**CHEMICAL COMPOSITION AND MOLECULAR ARRANGEMENT**

*Spandex—a manufactured fiber in which the fiber-forming substance is a long-chain synthetic polymer consisting of at least 85 percent of a segmented polyurethane.*

*—FEDERAL TRADE COMMISSION.*

Spandex is a generic name, but it is not derived from the chemical nature of the fiber as are most of the manufactured fibers. The name was coined by shifting the syllables of the word *expand*.

Spandex consists of rigid and flexible segments in the polymer chain; the soft segments provide the stretch and the rigid segments hold the chain together. When force is applied, the folded, or coiled, segments straighten out; when force is removed, they return to their original posi-

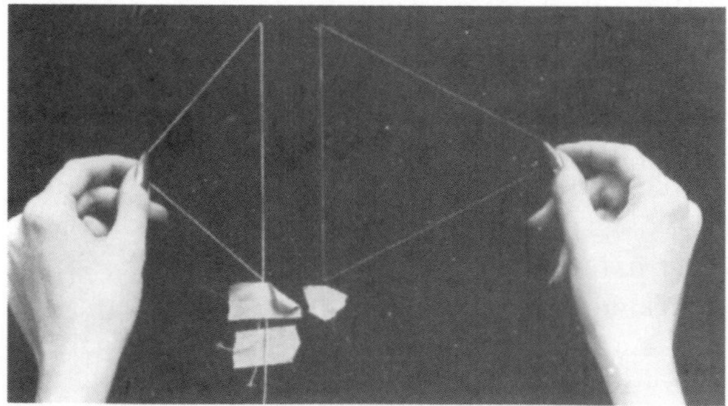

**FIGURE 9–2** ❖ Comparison of heavy 1,500 denier Lycra spandex fibers (left) and fine 20 denier yarn (right). (COURTESY OF E. I. DU PONT DE NEMOURS & COMPANY.)

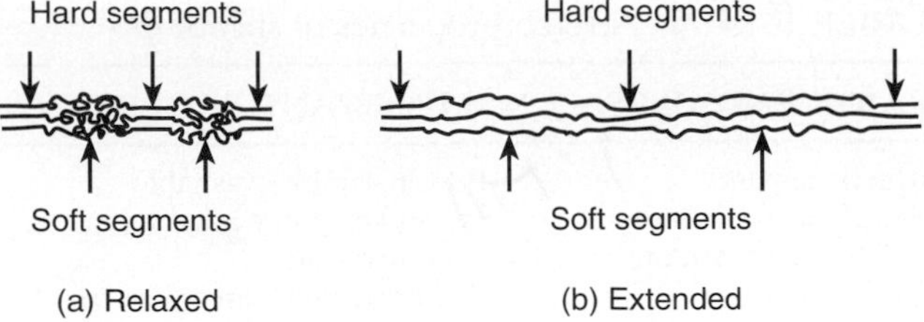


**FIGURE 9–3** ❖ Spandex molecular chains: (a) relaxed; (b) extended.

tions (Figure 9–3). Varying proportions of hard and soft segments control the amount of stretch.

**PROPERTIES** Table 9–1 compares the performance of spandex and rubber in apparel and furnishing fabrics. The tables in Chapter 3 include the performance characteristics of all the fibers.

**TABLE 9–1** ❖ Summary of the performance of spandex and rubber in apparel and furnishing fabrics.

| | SPANDEX | RUBBER |
|---|---|---|
| **Aesthetic** | **Moderate** | **Poor** |
| **Durability** | **Moderate** | **Poor** |
| Abrasion resistance | Poor | Poor |
| Tenacity | Poor | Poor |
| Elongation | Excellent | Excellent |
| **Comfort** | **Moderate** | **Poor** |
| **Appearance Retention** | **Good** | **Good** |
| Resiliency | Good | Good |
| Dimensional stability | Good | Good |
| Elastic recovery | Excellent | Excellent |
| **Recommended Care** | Machine wash or dry clean | Wash with care |

*Aesthetic* Spandex is seldom used alone in fabrics. Other yarns or fibers produce the desired hand and appearance. Even in power-stretch fabrics for foundation garments and surgical hose, where beauty is not of major importance, nylon, cotton, or other yarns are used. The characteristics of spandex that contribute to beauty in fabrics are dyeability of the fiber and good strength, making it possible to have fashionable colors and prints in sheer garments.

Spandex needs no cover yarns since it takes dye. Eliminating the cover yarn reduces the cost and results in lighter-weight garments. This is important not only for beauty but also for comfort. However, in uses where spandex will come in contact with the skin, it is normally covered.

*Durability* As Table 9–2 shows, spandex is more durable than rubber because it does not deteriorate with age. (Nylon is included in the table because it has more stretch than other manufactured filaments and illustrates the difference between a hard fiber and an elastomeric fiber.)

Spandex is resistant to body oils, perspiration, and cosmetics, which cause degradation of rubber. It also has good shelf life and does not deteriorate with age. Its flex life is ten times greater than that of rubber.

*Comfort* Spandex fibers have a moisture regain of 0.75–1.3 percent, making them uncomfortable for skin contact. Lighter-weight foundation garments of spandex have the same holding power as heavy garments of rubber. Spandex has a specific gravity of 1.2–1.25, which is greater than that of rubber. However, because of the greater tenacity of spandex, smaller denier yarns are used and lightweight products are available.

*Care* Spandex is resistant to dilute acids and to alkalis. It has good resistance to cosmetic oils and lotions. Spandex is resistant to bleaches. It has good resistance to dry cleaning solvents. Spandex is thermoplastic, with a melting point of 446–518°F.

Spandex has superior aging resistance compared to rubber, resists soiling, and has superior elasticity and elongation properties. Spandex items retain an attractive appearance. However, over time the coarser spandex

**TABLE 9–2** ❖ Durability factors of spandex, rubber, and nylon.

| FIBER PROPERTY | SPANDEX | RUBBER | NYLON |
|---|---|---|---|
| Breaking tenacity g/d | 0.6–0.9 | 0.34 | 3.0–9.5 |
| Breaking elongation | 400–700 percent | 500–600 percent | 23 percent |
| Flex life | Excellent | Fair | Excellent |
| Recovery from stretch | 99 percent | 97 percent | 100 percent |

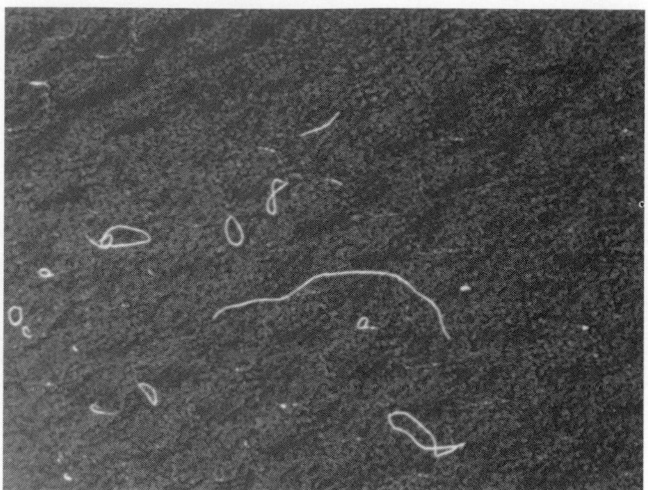

FIGURE 9–4 ❖ Grin-through in a swimsuit made of nylon and spandex.

fibers may rupture and work through the fabric so that short, thick gray-white fibers show. In these areas, the fabric loses its elasticity and elongation properties because the fiber has ruptured. This problem is sometimes referred to as **grin-through** because the broken ends of spandex appear on the surface. Once the problem has developed, it cannot be remedied. It occurs most often in products that have aged or have been stressed to extremes (see Figure 9–4).

USES Spandex is used to support, shape, or mold the body or to keep textiles from stretching out of shape during use. Spandex is used in foundation garments, active sportswear, hosiery, furnishings, and narrow fabrics. It is used in swimwear, skiwear, leotards and other dancewear, leggings, biking shorts, and other body-fitting apparel. Higher percentages of spandex in these products provide greater body contouring or support properties. It also has medical uses, such as surgical and support hose, bandages, and surgical wraps. It is used in fitted sheets and slipcovers. It is almost always used in blends from 2 to 40 percent with other fibers. These fabrics should not be referred to as spandex fabrics since they are not 100 percent spandex. They are spandex blends.

See Tables 9–3 and 9–4 for fiber modifications and a summary of end uses related to stretch properties.

## Other Elastomers

An elastomer based on polyether-ester has been introduced by the Japanese textile firm Teijin, Ltd. under the trade name Rexe. The stretch fiber received fiber classification from the Federal Trade Commission but the name has not been decided. The fiber has an elongation potential of 600 percent, a tenacity of 1.0 g/d, and elasticity of 80 percent at elongations over 200 percent. Those properties are slightly less than the properties of spandex. However, Rexe has superior strength retention in wet heat and after treatment with alkalis. It is also superior in its resistance to chlorine bleach. It may be treated to increase dyeability and print clarity and to achieve a more silklike hand. It is used in fashion outerwear and fitted furnishings.

TABLE 9–3 ❖ Stretch properties of spandex.

| MAJOR END USES | IMPORTANT PROPERTIES |
|---|---|
| Athletic apparel | Power stretch, washable |
| Foundation garments (power net, tricot) | Power stretch, washable, lightweight |
| Bathing suits | Power stretch, resistance to salt and chlorine, dyeable |
| Outerwear and sportswear | Comfort stretch |
| Support and surgical hose | Power stretch, lightweight |
| Elastic webbing | Power stretch |
| Slipcovers, bottom sheets | Comfort stretch, washable |

❖

# FIBERS WITH CHEMICAL, HEAT, OR FIRE RESISTANCE

The protective fibers are produced for specialized applications. In almost all cases, their costs are prohibitive for normal apparel and furnishing products. Some of these fibers cost over $60 per pound. Compare that to prices of less than $1 per pound for the fibers generally found in apparel and furnishings like cotton and polyester. Clearly, these fibers provide sufficient performance for their cost or they would not be used. With their unique resistance to chemicals, heat, and flame, these fibers have generated products not previously possible. The field of industrial textiles is very much related to these specialty fibers. Many of these fibers are described as high-temperature fibers. These fibers can be used con-

TABLE 9–4 ❖ Types and kinds of spandex.

| |
|---|
| White—delustered |
| Transparent—clear luster |
| 20–210 denier—support hosiery |
| 140–560 denier (core spun)—men's hosiery |
| 70–2240 denier—laces, foundation garments, swimwear, narrow fabrics, hosiery tops, fitted sheets |
| Bicomponent |

**TABLE 9–5** ❖ Properties of aramid.

| PROPERTY | m-ARAMID | p-ARAMID |
|---|---|---|
| Breaking tenacity, dry | 4.3–5.1 g/d—filament<br>3.7–5.3 g/d—staple | 21.5 g/d |
| Specific gravity | 1.38 | 1.44 |
| Moisture regain | 6.5 percent | 3.5–7.0 percent |
| Effect of heat | Decomposes at 700°F | Decomposes at 900°F |
| | Very resistant to flame<br>Does not melt | |
| Resistance to acids | | |
| Resistance to alkalis | Good | |
| Resistance to organic solvents | Excellent | |
| Resistance to sunlight | Moderate | |
| Oleophilic | Yes, unless special finishes are used | |
| Static buildup | Yes, unless special finishes are used | |

**m-aramid** $\left[-\overset{O}{\overset{\|}{C}}-C_6H_4-\overset{O}{\overset{\|}{C}}-\overset{H}{\overset{|}{N}}-C_6H_4-\overset{H}{\overset{|}{N}}-\right]_n$

**p-aramid** $\left[-\overset{O}{\overset{\|}{C}}-C_6H_4-\overset{O}{\overset{\|}{C}}-\overset{H}{\overset{|}{N}}-C_6H_4-\overset{H}{\overset{|}{N}}-\right]_n$

tinuously at temperatures over 200°C without serious decomposition while retaining major portions of their physical properties.

## Aramid

*Aramid—a manufactured fiber in which the fiber-forming substance is a long-chain synthetic polyamide in which at least 85 percent of the amide linkages*

$$\left(-\underset{O}{\underset{\|}{C}}-NH-\right)$$

*are attached directly to two aromatic rings.*

—FEDERAL TRADE COMMISSION.

Nylon is a polyamide fiber; **aramid** is an aromatic polyamide fiber. DuPont introduced a nylon variant with exceptional heat and flame resistance in 1963 under the trade name Nomex nylon. The development of aramid is attributed to Stephanie Kwolek, a chemist at DuPont. Another variant of nylon was introduced by DuPont in 1973 as Kevlar. This fiber had exceptional strength in addition to fire resistance. The Federal Trade Commission established the generic classification of aramid in 1974 for these fibers. An aromatic ring is a six-sided carbon compound with alternating double and single bonds. The location at which the amide linkages are attached determines the type of aramid and its properties. Nomex is a meta-aramid or m-aramid; Kevlar is a para-aramid or p-aramid. (See Table 9–5.)

Aramid can be wet or dry spun and is usually round or dog-bone shaped (Figure 9–5). Aramid fibers have

**FIGURE 9–5** ❖ Photomicrograph of aramid: cross-sectional view (left); longitudinal view (right). (COURTESY OF THE BRITISH TEXTILE TECHNOLOGY GROUP.)

high tenacity and high resistance to stretch, to most chemicals, and to high temperatures. The fiber can be produced as a high-tenacity fiber. Table 9–5 compares normal-tenacity aramids with high-tenacity aramids. These fibers maintain their shape and form at high temperatures. Aramid fibers have excellent impact and abrasion resistance.

Hollow aramid fibers are used to produce fresh water from sea water through reverse osmosis. The thin, dense skin of the fiber allows only water to pass through. Aramids are difficult to dye and have poor resistance to acids. Trade names for aramid fibers are Nomex, Kevlar, Conex, Fenilon, and Kermel. Nomex and Kevlar, trade names owned by DuPont, are the most common trade names found in the United States. Solution-dyed forms of Nomex and Kevlar are used extensively in the military.

Kevlar aramid is lightweight and fatigue and damage resistant. It is five times stronger than steel on an equal weight basis and 43 percent lower in density than fiberglass. Kevlar is used primarily in reinforcements of radial tires and other mechanical rubber goods. Kevlar 29 is found in protective apparel, cables, and cordage, and as a replacement for asbestos, such as in brake linings and gaskets. A 7-layer body-armor undervest of Kevlar 29 weighing 2.5 pounds can deflect a knife slash and stop a .38-caliber bullet fired from 10 feet (Figure 9–6). Unfortunately, as fiber technology advances, so does munitions technology. Bullets with a Teflon™ coating will penetrate body armor. Kevlar 49 has the highest tenacity of the aramids and is found as a plastic-reinforcement fiber for boat hulls, aircraft, aerospace uses, and other composite uses.

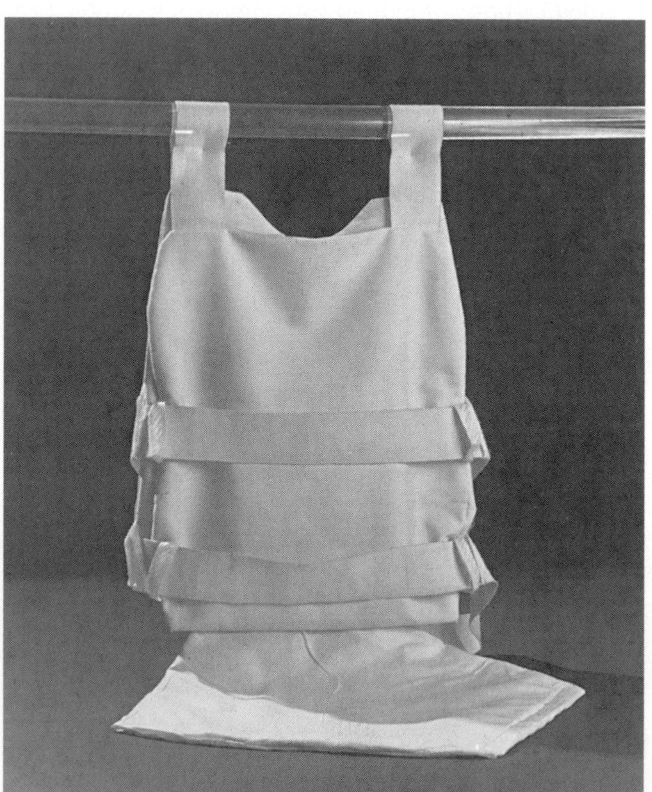

**FIGURE 9–6** ❖ Body armor of aramid fibers.

Nomex is used where resistance to heat and combustion with low-smoke generation are required. Protective clothing, such as firefighters' apparel and race-car drivers' suits, and flame-retardant furnishings for aircraft are made of Nomex. Nomex Omega by DuPont includes an expanding air layer that helps insulate firefighters from heat. Hot-gas filtration systems and electrical insulation are constructed of Nomex. This heat-resistant fiber is also found in covers for laundry presses and ironing boards.

Composites of aramid fibers intermixed in resins are being investigated for use in civil engineering structures like bridges and elevated highway support structures.

## Glass

*Glass—a manufactured fiber in which the fiber-forming substance is glass.*

—FEDERAL TRADE COMMISSION.

**Glass** is an incombustible textile fiber; it does not burn. This makes it especially suitable for end uses where the danger of fire is a problem—such as in draperies for motels, nursing homes, public buildings, and homes. The problems of severe skin irritation from tiny broken fibers has limited the use of glass fibers in apparel.

The process of drawing out glass into hairlike strands dates back to ancient times. It is thought that Phoenician fishermen noticed small pools of molten material among the coals of the fires they built on the sands of the Aegean beaches, and while poking at the strange substances, they drew out a long strand—the first glass fiber. Glass fiber was first used commercially in the 1920s.

The raw materials for glass are sand, silica, and limestone, combined with additives of feldspar and boric acid. These materials are melted in large electric furnaces (2,400°F). For filament yarns, each furnace has holes in the base of the melting chamber. Fine streams of glass flow through the holes and are carried through a hole in the floor to a winder in the room below. The winder revolves faster than the glass comes from the furnace, thus stretching the fibers and reducing them in size before they harden. The round rodlike filaments are shown in Figure 9–7. When staple yarn is spun, the glass flows out in thin streams from holes in the base of the furnace, and jets of high-pressure air or steam break the

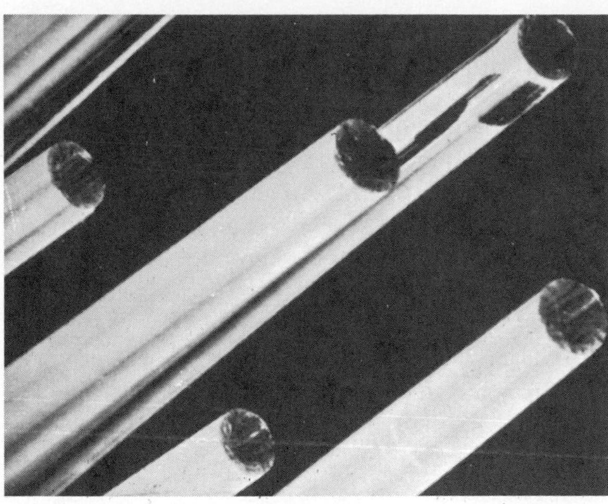

FIGURE 9–7 ❖ Photomicrograph of fiberglass. (COURTESY OF OWENS CORNING.)

strands into fibers 8–10 inches long. These fibers are collected on a revolving drum and made into a thin web, which is then formed into a sliver, or soft, untwisted yarn.

Beta Fiberglas, by the Owens-Corning Fiberglas Corporation, has one-sixth the denier of common glass fibers. The extremely fine filaments are resistant to breaking and thus more resistant to abrasion. Beta Fiberglas has about half the strength of regular glass fiber, but its tenacity of 8.2 is still greater than that of most fibers. It is used in products like window treatment fabrics, where greater fiber flexibility is needed.

Owens-Corning has a new bicomponent fiber of two forms of glass fused together into a single filament. As the fiber cools, the two glass types cause the filament to twist in an irregular fashion along its length. The resulting fiber is soft, resilient, flexible, and form filling.

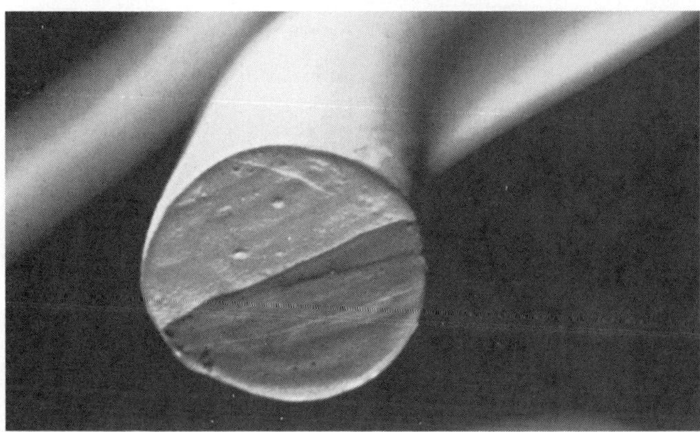

FIGURE 9–8 ❖ Bicomponent glass fiber. (COURTESY OF OWENS CORNING.)

TABLE 9–6 ❖ Types of glass fiber.

| TYPE | COMMENTS |
| --- | --- |
| A | Alkali containing glass used in fibers |
| AR | Alkali-resistant glass used in reinforcing cement |
| C | Chemically resistant glass used in fibers |
| E | Almost universally accepted formulation used in many fibers and related products; high electrical resistance; used in glass-reinforced plastics |
| HS | Magnesium-alumina-silica glass; high strength |
| S | Similar in composition to HS glass; used in composites |

Sold as Miraflex, it can be carded or needled to make a fiber batt. It is being used in home insulation, but it has potential for composites and other uses. (See Figure 9–8.)

Several types of glass fibers are produced. Table 9–6 summarizes the types and end uses for these fibers.

Glass has a tenacity of 6–10 g/d dry and 5–8 g/d wet. Glass has a low elongation of only 3–4 percent but excellent elasticity in this narrow range. Glass fibers are brittle and break when bent; they exhibit poor flex resistance to abrasion. These fibers are very heavy, with a specific gravity of 2.5. The fibers are nonabsorbent and are resistant to most chemicals. Trade names include Fiberglas, Beta glass, Chemglass, J M fiberglass, PPG fiberglass, and Vitron.

Hand washing is preferred to machine washing, which causes excessive breaking of the fibers. Figure 9–9 shows the remnants of a fiberglass laundry bag that was machine washed. A residue of tiny glass fibers in the washing machine will contaminate the next load and cause severe skin irritation for people who use those textiles. Even with hand washing, severe skin irritation can occur. Care labels should disclose this possibility.

Glass textiles should not require frequent washing, however, because glass fibers resist soil; spots and stains can be wiped off with a damp cloth. No ironing is necessary. Items can be smoothed and hung to dry. Oils used in finishing may gray white fabrics. Oil holds the dirt persistently and oxidizes with age. Washing has not proved to be a very satisfactory way to whiten the material, and dry cleaning is not recommended.

Glass fiber is used in furnishings such as flame-retardant draperies. Here the fiber performs best if bending and abrasion can be limited. Thus, movement from drafts, opening/closing the fabric, and abrasion from people and pets should be kept to a minimum. The weight of the fabrics may mean that special rods are necessary (see Table 9–7).

Glass fiber has wide industrial use where noise abatement, fire protection, temperature control (insulation),

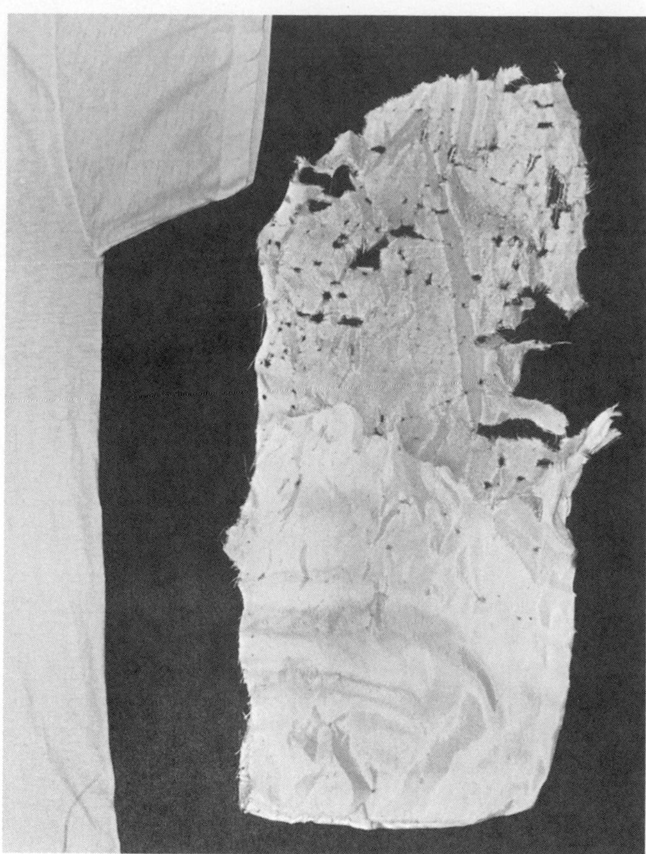

**FIGURE 9–9** ❖ Glass fiber laundry bag after being washed with regular family wash.

and air purification are needed. Glass is commonly used in insulation for buildings. Care should be exercised when working with glass. It has been identified as a possible carcinogen. Glass is common as a reinforcement fiber in molded plastics in boat, car, and airplane parts. Current research in civil engineering is evaluating glass fibers in resin as a repair material for highways and bridges. Insulation in buildings and vehicles, such as boats and railway cars, are made of glass. In addition, glass is found in ironing-board covers and space suits. Flame-resistant-glass mattress covers are produced for hotels, dormitories, and hospitals. A silica-glass quilt called AFRSI (Advanced Flexible Reuseable Surface Insulation) was used on several space shuttles. Glass is used in geotextiles. Filters, fire blankets, and heat- and electrical-resistant tapes and braids are other industrial products made of glass. A lightweight, durable, water-resistant cast material in several fashion colors is available from 3M for supporting broken bones as they heal. Owens-Corning is researching glass yarns suitable for apparel.

**TABLE 9–7** ❖ Glass fiber properties important in draperies.

| Property | |
|---|---|
| Flexibility | Breaks easily |
| Specific gravity | Heavy |
| Absorbency, percent of moisture regain | None |
| Effect of sunlight | None |
| Effect of acid and alkali | None |
| Effect of heat | Flameproof |

Additional end uses are the optical fibers, very fine fibers of pure glass. Laser beams, rather than electricity, activate the fibers. Glass optical fibers are free of electrical interference. Optical fibers are found in communication and medical equipment.

## Metal and Metallic Fibers

*Metallic—a manufactured fiber composed of metal, plastic-coated metal, metal-coated plastic, or a core completely covered by metal.*

—FEDERAL TRADE COMMISSION.

Gold and silver have been used since ancient times as yarns for fabric decoration. More recently, aluminum yarns, aluminized plastic yarns, and aluminized nylon yarns have replaced gold and silver. **Metallic** filaments can be coated with transparent films to minimize tarnishing. A common film is polyester with the trade name of Lurex. Metal fibers are used to add a decorative touch to apparel and furnishings.

Two processes are used to make these fibers. The *laminating process* seals a layer of aluminum between two layers of acetate or polyester film, which is then cut into strips for yarns (see Figure 9–10). The film may be colorless so the aluminum foil shows through, or the film and/or the adhesive may be colored before the laminating process. The *metalizing process* vaporizes the

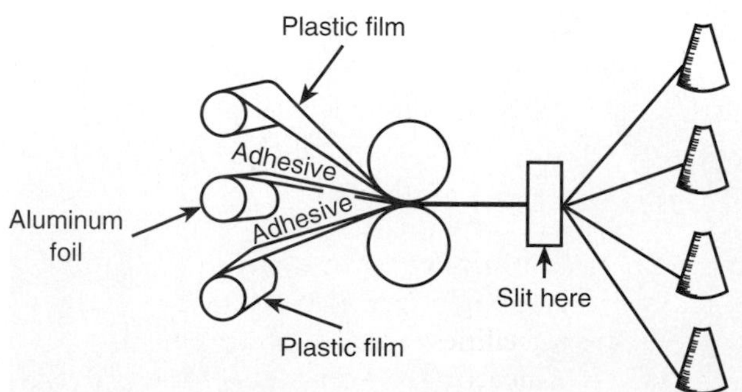


**FIGURE 9–10** ❖ Laminating layers to produce a metal yarn.

aluminum under high pressure and deposits it on the polyester film. The metalizing process produces thinner, more flexible, more durable, and more comfortable fibers. Monsanto has a line of metallized fiber, fabrics and film called Flectron. The fine layers of metal are bonded to almost any fiber or film surface for fabrics in computer rooms and specialized composites.

Fabric containing a large amount of metal can be embossed. Ironing is a problem when metallic film yarns are used because a high temperature melts the plastic. The best way to remove wrinkles is to set the iron on its end and draw the edge of the fabric across the sole plate of the iron.

**Stainless-steel fibers** were developed in 1960, and other metal fibers have also been made into fibers and yarns. Stainless steel has had the most extensive development.

The use of stainless steel as a textile fiber was an outgrowth of research for fibers to meet aerospace requirements. Superfine-stainless-steel filaments (3–15 micrometers) are a bundle of fine wires (0.002 inch) pickled in nitric acid and drawn to their final diameter. Several problems had to be solved, one of which involved twist. Each filament tended to act like a tiny coil spring, so the yarns required special treatment to deaden the twist.

Stainless-steel fibers are produced as both filament and staple. They can be used in complex yarns and either woven or knitted. The staple fiber can be blended with other fibers to reduce static permanently. Only 1–3 percent of the stainless-steel fiber is needed. The limitation on the use of stainless steel in clothing is its inability to be dyed, although some producers claim that such a small amount will not affect the color of white fabrics. Stainless steel is used in carpets to reduce static.

Static is one of the annoying problems associated with carpets in terms of comfort (static shock) and soiling. Brunsmet, a stainless-steel fiber from 2 to 3 inches long, can be mixed throughout any kind of spun yarn to make the yarn a good conductor. Only one or two fibers per tuft will carry the static from the face fiber to the backing. This kind of carpet yarn is used where static is a special problem, such as in rooms where sensitive computer equipment is kept. It is also suitable for upholstery, blankets, and work clothing. Stainless-steel fibers are used for tire cord, wiring, and missile nose cones, and in corrective heart surgery.

Metal fibers are blended with other fibers to produce static-free clothing worn in clean rooms in computer-production facilities and in other places where static creates nuisance or hazardous conditions. Metals do not have many of the properties usually attributed to textile fibers. They are much heavier than the organic materials that compose most fibers—the specific gravity of metal fibers is 7.88 g/cc as compared to 1.14 for nylon. They cannot bend without leaving permanent crease lines, have very little or no drape characteristics, and do not have the hand associated with textiles. Reduction in the denier of the fiber improves its properties, but the finer fibers are more expensive. Metal fibers are used in industrial products like wiring and cables. Metallic fibers are also used in cut-resistant gloves for butchers and meat cutters. Figure 9–11 shows a copper braid used in wiring.

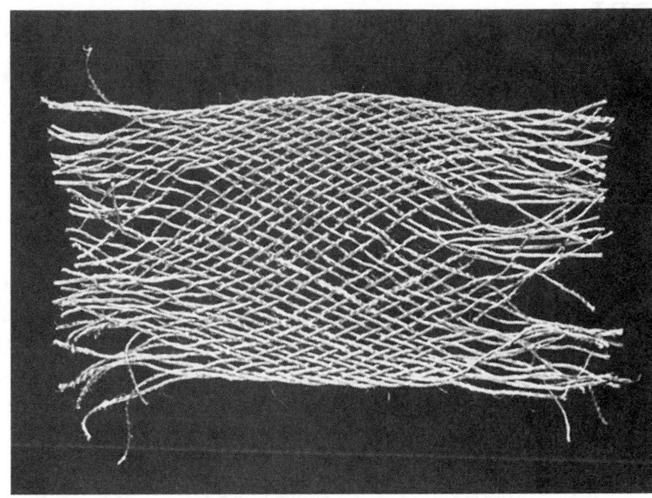

**FIGURE 9–11** ❖ Copper braid used in wiring.

## Novoloid

*Novoloid—a manufactured fiber in which the fiber-forming substance contains at least 35 percent by weight of cross-linked novolac (a cross-linked phenolformaldehyde polymer).*

—*FEDERAL TRADE COMMISSION.*

Commercial production of novoloid began in 1972. **Novoloid** shows outstanding flame resistance to a blaze of 2500°C from an oxyacetylene torch. Rather than melt, burn, or fuse, the yarns carbonize while maintaining their construction.

Novoloid has an elasticity of 35 percent. It has good resistance to sunlight and is inert to acids and organic solvents but susceptible to highly alkaline substances. Novoloid has a tenacity of 1.5–2.5 g/d, a specific gravity of 1.27 g/cc, and a regain of 6.0 percent. It is used for protective clothing and fabrics, chemical filters, gaskets, and packing materials. Fierce competition from carbon and aramid fibers may force novoloid out of the market.

When the fibers are extruded, they are water soluble. The fibers must be treated with formaldehyde in order to form cross-links, which make the fiber nonwater soluble. The fiber has a smooth, slightly grainy appearance with a U-shaped cross section. Vinal has a tenacity of 3.5–6.5 g/d, an elongation of 15–30 percent, and is 25 percent weaker when wet. The specific gravity of vinal is 1.26. It has a moisture regain of 5.0 percent. It does not support combustion, but softens at 200°C (390°F) and melts at 220°C (425°F). It has good chemical resistance and is unaffected by alkalis and common solvents. Concentrated acids harm the fiber. Vinal has excellent resistance to biological attack. Mass pigmentation is used to color the fiber.

In other countries, vinal is used in protective apparel. Major uses in the United States are industrial: fishing nets, filter fabrics, tarpaulins, and brush bristles. In water-soluble forms, the fiber is used as a ground fabric to create laces and other sheer fabrics. Once the fabric has been produced, the vinal ground is dissolved and the sheer fabric remains.

Vinal is used in film form, often labeled vinyl. It is used for rainwear, umbrellas, clear table coverings and upholstery protectors in showrooms.

## Polytetrafluoroethylene

**Polytetrafluoroethylene (PTFE)** is not defined by the Textile Fiber Products Identification Act. Polytetrafluoroethylene is common as a coating for cookware under the trade name Teflon. It is also used as a coating in plastic forms.

PTFE is polymerized under pressure and heat in the presence of a catalyst. Emulsion spinning can be used. In *emulsion spinning*, polymerization and extrusion occur simultaneously. (See Figure 9–15.) PTFE has the following repeat unit ($—CF_2—CF_2—$). It has a tenacity of 1.6 g/d, with low elongation and good pliability. The fiber is heavy, with a specific gravity of 2.3, and it can withstand temperatures up to 260°C (500°F) without damage. It is resistant to chemicals, sunlight, weathering, and aging. The fibers are chemically inert. PTFE does produce electrical charges. It is tan in color, but can be bleached white with sulfuric acid.

Gore-Tex is a trade name for fabrics that have a thin microporous film of PTFE applied to a fabric for use in outerwear. It is wind and liquid water resistant, but water vapor permeable. Gore-Tex can be dry cleaned but needs to be rinsed well to prevent impairment of the film's functions. Teflon by DuPont is used in haz-mat protective clothing. DuPont is examining potential apparel markets for Teflon. Because consumers expect to see generic fiber names, DuPont applied for a generic fiber classification in 1996. PTFE is used industrially in filter fabrics (to reduce smokestack emissions), packing fabrics, gaskets, industrial felts, covers for presses in commercial laundries, electrical tape, and as a layer of some protective fabrics.

*Emulsion Spinning.*

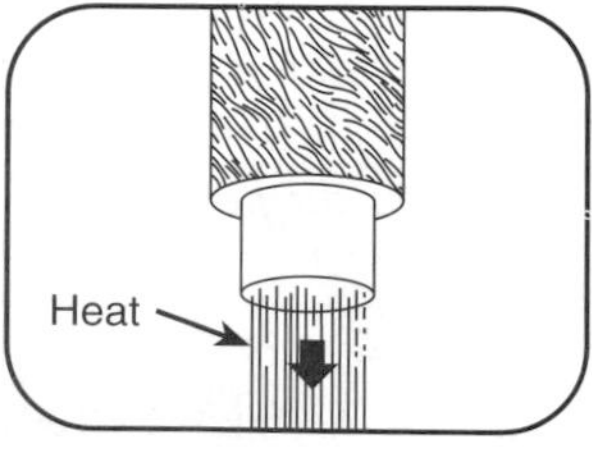


1. Polymer is dispersed as fine particles in a carrier.
2. Dispersed polymer is extruded through a spinneret and coalesced by heating.
3. Carrier is removed by heating or dissolving.

Expensive
Used only for those fibers that are insoluble
Carrier required

**FIGURE 9–15** ❖ Emulsion spinning.

## Carbon

**Carbon** is a fiber that is at least 96 percent pure carbon. It is made from precursor fibers such as rayon and polyacrylonitrile. These fibers are heated to remove oxygen, nitrogen, and hydrogen. The fiber has exceptional heat resistance and does not ignite or melt. It maintains its full strength of 1.5 g/d after prolonged exposure to temperatures of more than 200°C. Carbon has a density of 1.4, a moisture regain of 10 percent, and an elongation of 10 percent. Carbon fibers have very low coefficients of thermal expansion, are chemically inert, and biocompatible. They also dissipate static quickly. Because of these properties and its comfortable hand, carbon is used in protective clothing, to reinforce lightweight metal components in golf clubs and bicycle bodies, in aerospace uses, in bone grafts, and as a substitute for asbestos in industrial products. (See Figure 9–16.) Civil engineers are evaluating carbon fibers in resins for use in repairing bridge and highway support columns. It is proving to be a strong competitor against other high-performance fibers, such as novoloid. It is produced by Amoco Performance Products and Akzo Fortafil Fibers, Inc. It also is used as a coating of nylon for carpeting, upholstery, apparel, and industrial brushes and belts. It is used in radar-transparent military aircraft communication satellites and rocket motor nozzles.

Table 9–8 compares selected properties of aramid, glass, PBI, sulfar, PTFE, and carbon.

**FIGURE 9–16** ❖ Tennis racket with carbon fiber (graphite) reinforcement.

❖

## OTHER SPECIAL-USE FIBERS

Melamine is produced by BASF as Basofil. It has a dry tenacity of 1.8 g/d, a 12 percent elongation at break, 5 percent regain, a specific gravity of 1.44, fair abrasion resistance, and good to excellent resistance to chemicals except concentrated acids. Basofil is known for its very high flame and heat resistance. It is moderate in cost. It is used in products that require high temperature resistance and is expected to compete at a lower cost with meta-aramids, PBI, sulfar, and polyimide. Basofil received a temporary generic fiber classification number (BC0001) in 1996 from the Federal Trade Commission as a step toward becoming a separate generic fiber.

Polyimide has a dry tenacity of 3.7 g/d, a 20 percent elongation at break, 3 percent regain, a specific gravity of 1.41, good abrasion resistance, and good to excellent resistance to chemicals except alkalis. It is moderately high in cost. It is used in filtration devices for hot air or gas and corrosive liquids and in gaskets and seals, protective clothing, and fire block seating (a layer between the upholstery and the padding to minimize flame spread).

Ceramic fibers are composed of metal oxide, metal carbide, metal nitride, or other mixtures. The fibers were developed because aerospace, metallurgical, nuclear, and chemical industries required fibers with better thermal resistance than glass fibers could give. These fibers are used where high strength, high thermal structural stability, and stiffness are required.

A polytrimethylene terephthalate (PTT) polymer developed by Shell Chemical Co. and sold as Corterra

**TABLE 9–8** ❖ Comparison of selected chemical, heat, and fire resistant fibers: Aramid, glass, PBI, sulfar, PTFE, and carbon.

| FIBER | TENACITY g/d | ELONGATION % DRY | ELASTICITY % | REGAIN % | SPECIFIC GRAVITY | HEAT/CHEMICAL RESISTANCE |
|---|---|---|---|---|---|---|
| Aramid | 23 | 4.0 | 100 | 4.3 | 1.44 | Difficult to ignite, does not melt, decomposes at 900°F, resistant to dilute acids and bases, degraded by strong mineral acids, excellent solvent resistance |
| Glass | 15.3 | 4.8 | 100 | 0 | 2.48 | Does not burn, softens at +1350°F, resists most acids and alkalis, unaffected by solvents |
| PBI | 2.6–3.0 | 25–30 | — | 15 | 1.43 | Does not ignite or melt, chars at 860°F, unaffected by most acids, alkalis, and solvents |
| Sulfar | 3.0–3.5 | 35–45 | 100 | 0.6 | 1.37 | Outstanding heat resistance, melts at 545°F, outstanding resistance to most acids, alkalis, and solvents |
| PTFE | 0.9–2.0 | 19–140 | — | 0 | 2.1 | Extremely heat resistant, melts at + 550°F, most chemically resistant fiber known |
| Carbon | 15.9 | 0.7 | 100 | — | 1.75–2.2 | Does not melt, excellent resistance to hot, concentrated acids and alkalis, unaffected by solvents, degraded by strong oxidizers (chlorine bleach) |

exhibits the elastic recovery of nylon and the chemical resistance of polyester. It has good stain resistance and colorfastness, low water absorption, and low static generation. It will be marketed to the textile and carpet markets in both staple and continuous filament yarns. It also is a chemically recyclable fiber.

## Key Terms

Elastomer
Power stretch
Comfort stretch
Lastrile
Rubber
Spandex
Grin-through
Aramid
Glass
Metallic fibers
Stainless steel
Novoloid
PBI
Sulfar
Saran
Vinyon
Vinal
Polytetrafluoroethylene (PTFE)
Carbon

## Questions

1. Compare the performance characteristics of rubber and spandex.
2. What are the differences and similarities between power and comfort stretch?
3. Explain why glass and metal are included as textiles.
4. Identify a fiber from this chapter that would be an appropriate choice for each end use listed below and explain, using performance characteristics, why that fiber was selected. (Some of these fibers may actually be used in blend form in the product.)

    insulation for electrical wiring
    support hosiery
    theater costume for a performance of *King Lear*
    apron for welder
    firefighting suit
    particle filter for smokestack
    support fiber in resin for auto body repair

## Suggested Readings

Butler, Nick (1995, March). "Specialty Fibres to Continue to Flourish." *Technical Textiles International,* pp. 12–15.

Coffee, D. R., Serad, G. A., Hicks, H. L., and Montgomery, R. T. (1982). "Properties and Applications of Celanese PBI-Polybenzimidazole Fiber." *Textile Research Journal, 52,* pp. 466–472.

Grayson, Martin, ed. (1984). *Encyclopedia of Textiles, Fibers, and Nonwoven Fabrics.* New York: John Wiley & Sons.

Mukhopadhyay, S. K. (1993). "High-Performance Fibres." *Textiles Progress, 25* (3/4), pp. 1–71.

Pfister, Fred V. (January, 1991). "Technology Trends." *Textile Month,* pp. 8–10.

Smith, William C. (1995, April). "Hi-Temperature Fibers Gain in Performance, Market." *Textile World,* pp. 31–32, 37–38.

Trotman, E. R. (1984). *Dyeing and Chemical Technology of Textile Fibers,* 6th ed. New York: John Wiley & Sons.

# Section Three

# YARNS

Chapter 10

**YARN PROCESSING**

Chapter 11

**YARN CLASSIFICATION**

Chapter 10

# YARN PROCESSING

## OBJECTIVES

- To understand the processes used in producing yarns from filament and staple fibers.
- To recognize the different types and qualities of yarns.
- To relate yarn type to end use performance.
- To relate yarn properties to processing method.
- To integrate fiber properties with yarn properties.
- To understand the reasons for blending fibers and their effects on product performance.

Most apparel and furnishing fabrics are produced from yarns. A **yarn** is a continuous strand of textile fibers, filaments, or materials in a form suitable for knitting, weaving, or otherwise intertwining to form a textile fabric (ASTM, p. 54). This chapter explores the process of making a yarn from fibers or other starting materials. For filament yarns, this is a relatively quick and easy process. Spun yarns need a series of operations to make the fibers parallel and cohesive.

Yarn processing attracts a great deal of industry attention, but not much consumer interest. However, yarn type and quality have a great deal to do with product cost and performance. Thus, a general understanding of the making of yarn will help in understanding products made from yarns.

Many changes continue to occur in the ways yarns are made. Current efforts relate to ways of improving productivity, decreasing costs, increasing uniformity and quality, solving problems with current systems, and developing new systems or approaches to deal with changes in other segments of the industry. For example, yarn processing systems were modified to work with microfibers and yarn characteristics were modified to cope with the faster and faster production speeds of fabrication equipment. In fact, yarns may be the limiting factor in fabric production rates. Computer systems monitor yarn production and quality of yarns. Computerization of yarn processing continues with computers becoming more function specific and more user friendly.

# Filament Yarns

**Filament yarns** are primarily manufactured fibers because silk, the only natural filament, accounts for less than 1 percent of fiber and yarn production. Manufactured filament yarns are made by extruding a polymer solution through a spinneret. The polymer is solidified in fiber form. Then the individual filaments are brought together with or without a slight twist (see Figure 8–3). The grouping of the filaments with the addition of twist creates the filament yarn. The spinning machine winds the yarn on a bobbin. The yarn is then rewound on spools or cones and is a finished product unless some additional treatment is required, such as crimping, twisting, texturing, or finishing.

**Throwing,** originally a process for twisting silk filaments, evolved into the twisting of manufactured fibers and then into texturing. Throwing provides the fabricator with the kind of yarn needed for a particular product. The throwster performs a service for the industry; some throwsters place trade names on products made from their yarns. Some fiber producers texture yarns as a final step in the fiber-spinning process.

## Smooth-Filament Yarn

Filament yarns are more expensive per pound than staple fibers; however, the cost of making tow into staple and then mechanically spinning it into yarn usually makes the final cost about equal. The number of holes in the spinneret determines the number of filaments in the yarn.

Regular or conventional filament yarns are **smooth** and silklike as they come from the spinneret. Their smooth nature gives them more luster than spun yarns, but the luster varies with the amount of delustering agent used in the fiber and the amount of twist in the yarn. Maximum luster is obtained by the use of bright filaments with little or no twist. Very high twist yarns, like crepe yarns, reduce the luster of the filaments. With thermoplastic fibers, the twist can be heat set. Filament yarns generally have either high twist or low twist.

Filament yarns have no protruding ends, so they do not shed lint; they resist pilling; and fabrics made from them tend to shed soil. Filaments of round cross section pack well into compact yarns that give little bulk, loft, or cover to fabric. Compactness is a disadvantage in some end uses, where bulk and absorbency are necessary for comfort. Nonround filaments create more open space for air and moisture permeability and give greater cover. Compact yarns are used in wind- and water-resistant fabrics.

The strength of a filament yarn depends on the strength of the individual fibers and on the number of filaments in the yarn. Filament fiber strength is usually greater than that of staple fibers. Using polyester as an example, staple strength is 3–5.5 g/d (grams per denier); filament strength is 5–8 g/d.

The strength of each filament is fully utilized. In order to break the yarn, all the filaments must be broken. It is possible to make very sheer strong fabrics of fine filaments. Filament yarns reach their maximum strength at a low twist of about 3–6 turns per inch; then strength remains constant or decreases.

Fine-filament yarns are soft and supple. However, they are not as resistant to abrasion as coarse filaments, so for durability it may be desirable to have fewer but coarser filaments in the yarn.

## Monofilament Yarns

*Monofilament yarns* are found primarily in industrial uses. These yarns are made of a single coarse-filament fiber. End uses include sewing thread, fishline, fruit and vegetable bags, nets, and other woven or knitted fabrics for which low cost and high durability are the most important characteristics.

## Tape and Network Yarns

**Tape yarns** are inexpensive yarns produced from extruded polymer films (see Figure 10–1). *Extrusion*—forcing a liquid through a spinneret to form fine strands—is the standard method of spinning fibers and some films. The *split-fiber method* is less expensive than the traditional fiber extrusion process and can be done with a minimum investment in equipment. Some fiber polymers cannot be processed by the split-fiber method. However, polypropylene is used extensively in this way because of its ease of processing and economic factors. Tape yarns are ribbonlike in appearance but can take on the more rounded appearance of traditional yarns.

Pellets of polypropylene with appropriate additives are melted, then extruded as a film 0.005 to 0.020 inch thick onto a chilled roll or cooled quickly by quenching in water. The film is slit into tapes approximately 0.1 inch wide. The slit tapes are heat-stretched to orient the molecular chains. The stretching can be carried to a point where the film fibrillates (splits into fibers), or the film is passed over needles to slit it. Twisting or other mechanical action completes the fibrillation. Split-fiber yarns are strong.

Yarns as low as 250 denier have been made from split fibers. Tape yarns are coarse and usually used in carpet backing, rope, cord, fishnets, bagging, and furnishings where ribbonlike yarn is needed.

Olefin films are slit into yarns that are used for the same textile products as split-fiber olefin. Slit-film-tape yarns are much more regular than fibrillated film-tape yarns and they may be thicker. However, fibrillated yarns are less expensive and quicker to produce. Film-tape yarns are found most often in industrial textiles such as carpet backing and bagging.

Network yarns are made of fibers that are connected in a network arrangement. They have a ribbonlike characteristic similar to tape yarns, but are bulkier and less dense. These yarns are produced by incorporating air into the polymer to create a foam. When the foam is extruded and stretched, tiny air cells rupture, forming an interconnected fibrous web. Although strength is not as high as for multifilament, monofilament, or tape yarns, these network yarns have interesting bulk and comfort characteristics. Uses include industrial products where bulk and low density are more important than high strength.

## Bulk Yarns

A **bulk yarn** is a yarn that has been processed to have greater covering power or apparent volume than that of a conventional yarn of equal linear density and of the same basic material with normal twist (ASTM). Often these bulk yarns are referred to as **bulk-continuous-filament yarns.** A common shorthand notation used when referring to these yarns is **BCF.** BCF yarns include any continuous-filament yarn whose smooth, straight fibers have been displaced from their closely packed, parallel position by the introduction of some form of crimp, curl, loop, or coil (Figure 10–2).

The characteristics of bulk yarns are quite different from those of smooth-filament yarns. Bulking gives filaments the aesthetic properties of spun yarns by altering the surface characteristics and creating space between the fibers. Fabrics are more absorbent and comfortable and have better bulk, cover, and elasticity. They are more breathable and permeable to moisture. Static buildup is lower. Bulk yarns do not pill or shed.

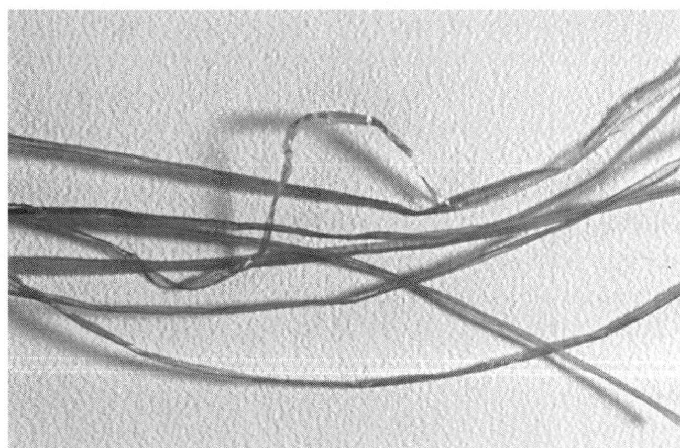

**FIGURE 10–1** ❖ Tape yarns used in industrial products.

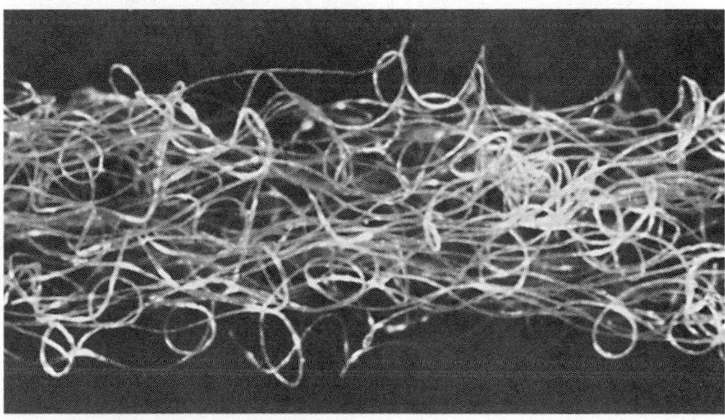

**FIGURE 10–2** ❖ Typical bulk yarn. (COURTESY OF THE FIBERS DIVISION OF MONSANTO CHEMICAL CO., A UNIT OF MONSANTO CO.)

There are three classes of bulk yarns: bulky yarns, stretch yarns, and textured yarns. These three classes will be discussed after texturing processes are discussed.

**TEXTURING FILAMENT YARNS** The **texturing** processes discussed here are mechanical texturing methods based on the use of thermoplastic fibers and heat and chemical methods of achieving texture by means of bicomponent fibers.

***False-Twist*** The false-twist spindle whirls at 600,000 revolutions per minute and generates such an intense sound that its effect on health and hearing is an industry concern. The process is continuous; the yarn is twisted, heat set, and untwisted as it travels through the spindle (Figure 10–3). The filaments form a distorted helical coil. When the yarn is pulled at each end, the coils straighten out—thus the stretch. This is one of the most important and cheapest processes used to add bulk and stretch to filament yarns.

***Draw-Texturing*** In draw-texturing unoriented filaments or partially oriented filaments are fed directly through the double-heater false-twist spinner, eliminating a separate stretching process. The false-twisted yarn is stretched slightly and heat set. Draw-texturing is a much faster and cheaper way of making textured bulk yarns. Finished yarns are as good as or better than those made by some other means.

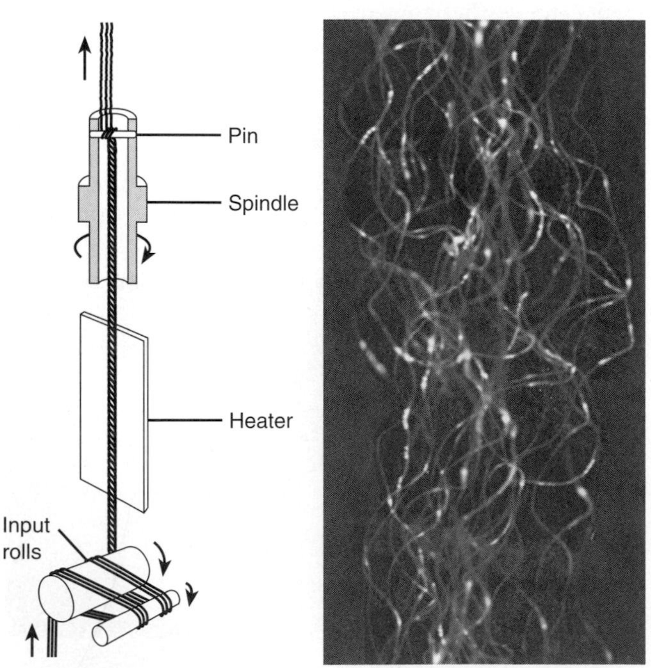


**FIGURE 10–3** ❖ False-twist process (left); yarn (right). (COURTESY OF THE FIBERS DIVISION OF MONSANTO CHEMICAL CO., A UNIT OF MONSANTO CO.)

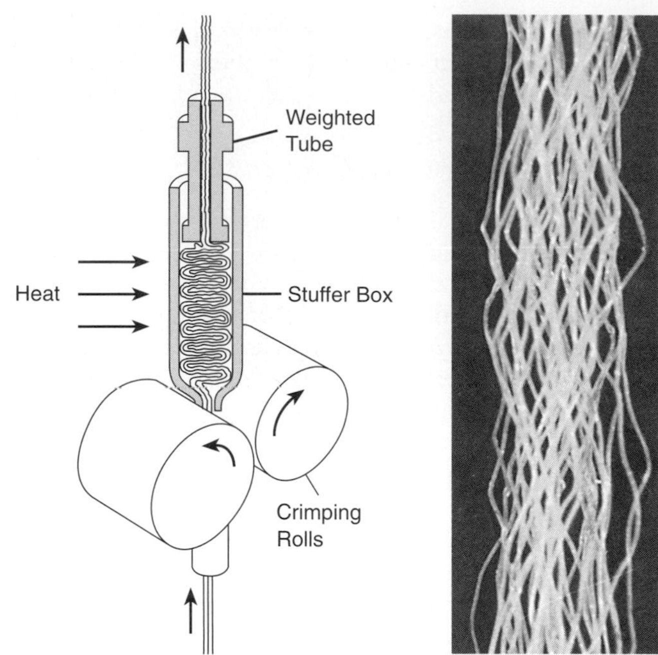


**FIGURE 10–4** ❖ Stuffer-box process (left); bulky yarn used in apparel (right). (COURTESY OF THE FIBERS DIVISION OF MONSANTO CHEMICAL CO., A UNIT OF MONSANTO CO.)

***Stuffer Box*** The stuffer box produces a sawtooth crimp of considerable bulk. Straight-filament yarns are literally stuffed into one end of a heated box (see Figure 10–4) and then withdrawn at the other end in crimped form. The apparent volume increase is 200–300 percent, with some elasticity. The stuffer box is a fast, inexpensive, and popular method for carpeting yarns.

***Air Jet*** Conventional filaments of any type are fed over an air jet (Figure 10–5) at a faster rate than they are drawn off. The blast of air forces some of the filaments into very tiny loops; the velocity of the air affects the size of the loops. This is a slow, relatively costly, but versatile process. Volume increases with little or no stretch. Air-jet yarns maintain their size and bulk under tension because the straight areas bear the strain and the loops remain relatively unaffected.

***Knit-Deknit*** A small-diameter tube is knit at a rapid speed (Figure 10–6). It is heat set, unraveled, and wound on cones. Crimp size and frequency can be varied by changing stitch size and tension. The gauge used to make the fabric must be different from that used to make the tube, or pinholes will form where the crimp gauge and knit gauge match.

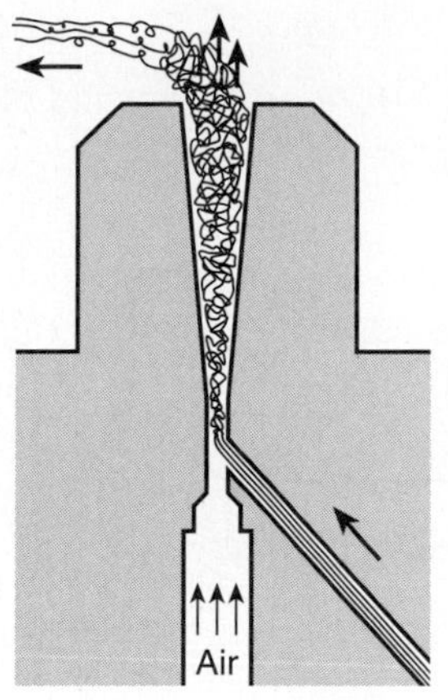


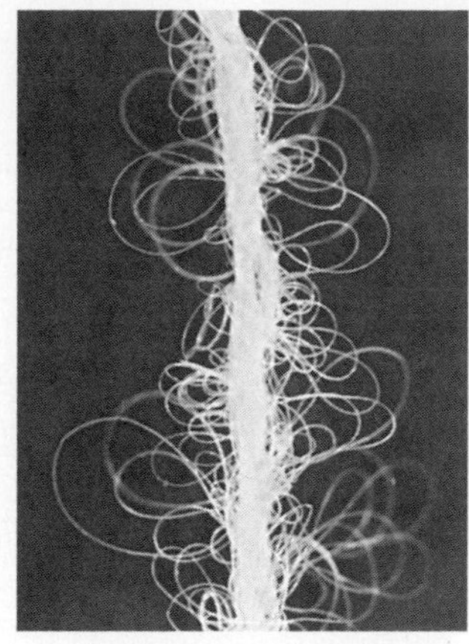

**FIGURE 10–5** ❖ Air-jet process (left); bulky yarn (right). (COURTESY OF THE FIBERS DIVISION OF MONSANTO CHEMICAL CO., A UNIT OF MONSANTO CO.)

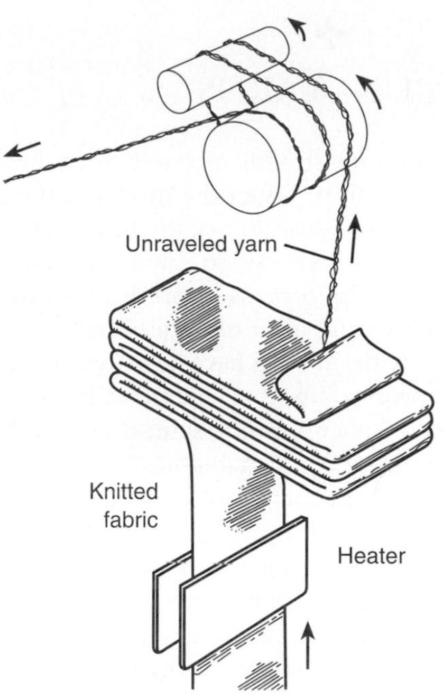


**FIGURE 10–6** ❖ Knit-deknit fabric is heat set, then unraveled.

## BULK YARN TYPES

***Bulky Yarns*** **Bulky yarns** are yarns formed from inherently bulky fibers, such as manufactured fibers that are hollow along part or all of their length, or yarns formed from fibers that cannot be closely packed because of their cross-sectional shape, fiber alignment, stiffness, resilience, or natural crimp (ASTM).

Bulky texturing processes can be used with any kind of filament fiber or spun yarn. The yarns have less stretch than either stretch or textured yarns. Bulky yarns are used in a wide array of products from carpeting to lingerie and sweaters to shoelaces.

***Stretch Yarns*** Stretch yarns are thermoplastic filament or spun yarns with a high degree of potential elastic stretch (300–500 percent), rapid recovery, and a high degree of yarn curl (ASTM). Stretch yarns have moderate bulk. **Stretch yarns** of nylon are used extensively in men's and women's hosiery, pantyhose, leotards, swimwear, leggings, football pants and jerseys. Stretch yarns make it possible to manufacture fewer sizes so that one-size items fit wearers of different sizes. Stretch yarns are not the same as yarns made with elastomeric fibers.

***Textured Yarns*** **Textured or bulked yarns** are filament or spun yarns with notably greater apparent volume than a conventional yarn of similar fiber (filament) count and linear density (ASTM). These yarns have much lower elastic stretch than stretch yarns, but greater stretch than bulky yarns. They are stable enough to present no unusual problems in subsequent processing or in use by the ultimate consumer. Fabrics made from these yarns maintain their original size and shape during wear and care.

Table 10–1 summarizes the three major types of bulk-filament yarns.

**TABLE 10–1** ❖ Comparison of bulk yarns.

| CHARACTERISTIC | BULKY YARNS | STRETCH YARNS | TEXTURED YARNS |
|---|---|---|---|
| Nature | Inherently bulky | High degree of yarn curl | High degree of bulk |
| Fiber type | May be hollow or crimped fibers | Any thermoplastic fiber | Any fiber that develops crimp with moisture, heat, or chemical treatment |
| Stretch | Little stretch | 300–500 percent stretch | Moderate amount of stretch |
| characteristics | Sawtooth, loops in individual fibers | Torque and nontorque | Loopy, high bulk, crimped |
| Processes | Stuffer box, air jet, draw-texturing, friction texturing | False-twist, knit-deknit, draw-texturing, friction texturing | Air jet, flat-drawn textured, draw-texturing, friction texturing |

# Spun Yarns

**Spun yarns** are continuous strands of staple fibers held together by some mechanism. Often the mechanism is a mechanical twist that takes advantage of the fiber's irregularities and natural cohesiveness to bind the fibers together into one yarn. The process of producing yarns from staple fibers by twisting is an old one. Methods of producing spun yarns without twist have been developed.

Spun yarns have protruding fiber ends that hold the yarn away from close contact with the skin; thus a fabric made of spun yarn is more comfortable next to the skin than a fabric of smooth-filament yarns that does not allow perspiration to evaporate.

Many of the insulating characteristics of a fabric are due to the structure of the yarns used to produce that fabric. There is more space between fibers in a spun yarn than in a filament yarn. A spun yarn with low twist has more air spaces than a spun yarn with a high twist. A spun yarn with low twist is better at insulating than a highly twisted yarn. For that reason, most fabrics designed for warmth have lower twist yarns. If wind resistance is desired, fabrics with high-twist compact yarns and a high count are more desirable because air permeability is reduced.

**Carded yarns** of short-staple fibers have more protruding fiber ends than **combed yarns,** which are made of long-staple fibers. Protruding ends contribute to greater comfort and warmth, a dull, fuzzy appearance, the shedding of lint and the formation of surface pills. Fuzzy fiber ends can be removed from the surface of the fabric by singeing (Chapter 16).

The strength of the individual staple fiber is a less important factor in spun yarn strength than it is in filament yarns. Spun yarn strength is dependent on the cohesiveness or clinging power of the fibers and on the points of contact resulting from twist or other binding mechanisms used to produce the spun yarn. The greater the number of points of contact, the greater the resistance to fiber slippage within the yarn. Fibers with crimp or convolutions have a greater number of points of contact. The friction of one fiber against another also gives resistance to lengthwise fiber slippage. A fiber with a rough or irregular surface—wool scales, for example—creates more friction than a smooth fiber.

The mechanical spinning of staple fibers into yarns is one of the oldest manufacturing arts and has been described as an invention as significant as that of the wheel. The basic principles of spinning are the same now as they were when yarns were first made.

Primitive spinning consisted of drawing out fibers held on a stick called a distaff, twisting them by the rotation of a spindle that could be spun like a top, and

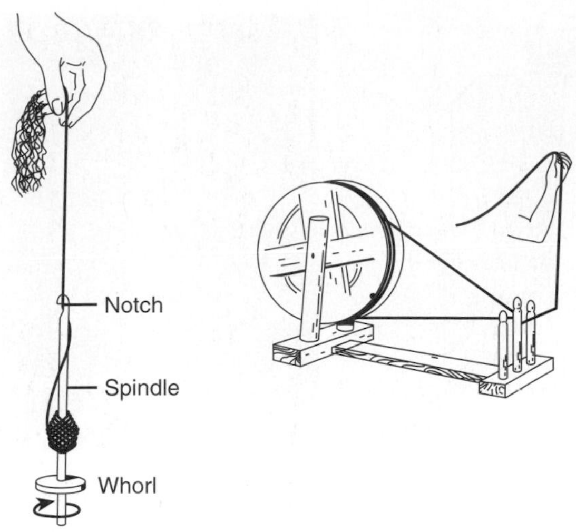


**Figure 10–7** ❖ Hand spinning (left); early spinning wheel (right).

winding up the spun yarn (Figure 10–7). The spinning wheel was invented in India and was introduced into Europe in the 14th century. The factory system began in the 18th century when James Hargreaves invented the first spinning jenny—a machine that could turn more than one spinning wheel at a time. Other inventions for improving the spinning process followed and led to the Industrial Revolution, when power machines took over hand processes and made mass production possible. Machines were developed for each separate step in the spinning process.

Spinning continues to evolve. Progress has been made in reducing the number of steps involved, in automating the process, and in making it faster, simpler, and more economical with higher production speeds and more user-friendly computerization. Spun-yarn processes are shown in Table 10–2.

## Processing Staple Fibers

**Ring or Conventional Spinning** **Ring or conventional spinning** consists of a series of operations designed to (1) clean and make parallel staple fibers, (2)

**Table 10–2** ❖ Spun yarn processes.

| FROM STAPLE FIBER | FROM FILAMENT TOW |
|---|---|
| Conventional ring | Tow-to-top |
| Direct | Tow-to-yarn |
| Open-end | High-bulk yarns |
| Friction | |
| Twistless | |
| Self-twist | |

**TABLE 10–3** ❖
The cotton system.

| OPERATION | PURPOSE |
|---|---|
| Opening | Loosens, blends, cleans, forms lap. |
| Carding | Cleans, aligns, forms carded sliver. |
| Drawing | Parallels, blends, forms drawn sliver. |
| Combing | Parallels, removes short fibers, forms combed sliver (used for long-staple cotton only). |
| Roving | Reduces size, inserts slight twist, forms roving. |
| Spinning | Reduces size, twists, winds the finished yarn on a bobbin. |
| Winding | Rewinds yarn from bobbins to spools or cones. |

draw them out into a fine strand, and (3) twist them to keep them together and give them strength. Ring spinning remains the standard by which spun yarns are judged. Even with continuous spinning, higher speeds, and automation, spinning remains a long and expensive process. Ring spun yarns are finer, have better quality, are more uniform, and create fewer problems in fabrication. Ring spinning is more automated than alternate spinning systems. Approximately half of the spun yarns are processed by this system.

Spinning may be done by any one of five conventional systems (cotton, woolen, French, Bradford, and American) that are adapted to the characteristics of the fiber—length, cohesiveness, diameter, elasticity, and surface contour. Because the cotton system is representative of the rest, it is discussed here in detail. Table 10–3 summarizes the steps in producing a spun yarn.

***Opening*** Machine-picked cotton contains a high percentage of trash and dirt. The fibers have been compressed very tightly in a bale and may have been stored in this state for a year or more. **Opening** loosens, cleans, and blends the fibers. Cotton varies from bale to bale, so the fibers from several bales are blended together to achieve more uniform quality in the finished yarn. It is important for manufacturers to produce yarns with consistent characteristics and performance so that basic fabrics do not differ by season or year.

Two types of opening units are used: a chute-feed system and a rotating carousel (Figure 10–8). In both systems bale pluckers (Figure 10–9) pull small tufts of fiber from the bales and drop the tufts on a screen or lattice. High-velocity air removes dirt and trash. The loosened, cleaned fibers are fed to the carding machine in sheet form.

**FIGURE 10–8** ❖ Karousel opener-picker machine. (COURTESY OF THE REITER COMPANY, INC.)

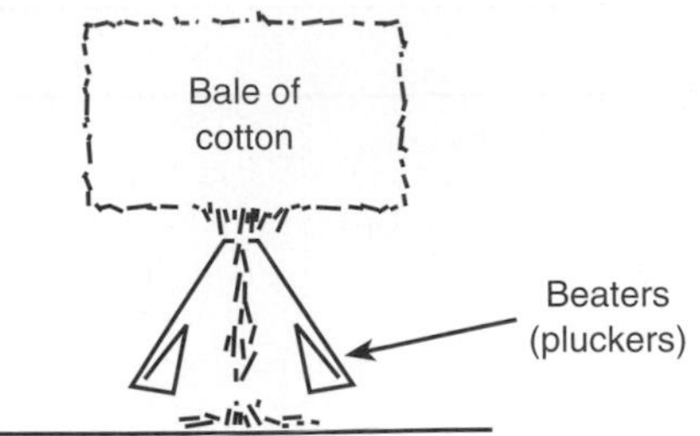


**FIGURE 10–9** ❖ Beaters (pluckers) pull fibers from the bale.

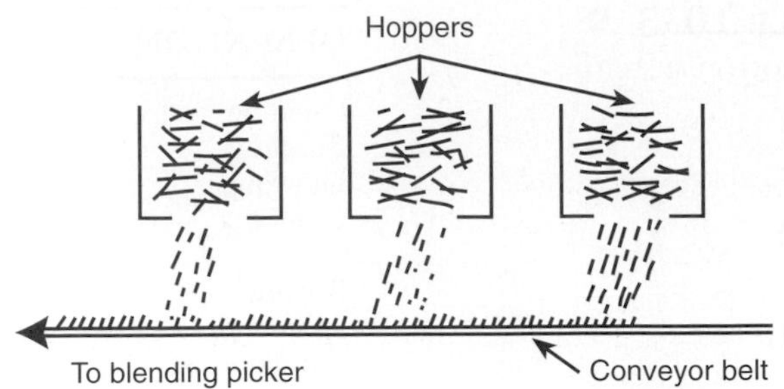


**FIGURE 10–10** ❖ Fibers from various hoppers are blended on a conveyor belt.

Material removed from the bale of fiber in the opening step includes very short fibers, soil, plant debris, and other foreign matter. This waste may be discarded or purchased and recycled into yarns and other textile products such as fiber batts.

There are several possibilities for blending fiber types in the opening operation. In one method, several bales of fiber are laid around the picker and fibers from each bale are fed alternately into the machine. Another method is called *sandwich blending*. The desired amounts of each fiber are weighed out and a layer of each is spread over the preceding layer to build up a sandwich composed of many layers. Vertical sections are then taken through the sandwich and fed into the picker. *Feeder blending* is an automatic process in which each type of fiber is fed to a mixing apron from individual hoppers (Figure 10–10).

***Carding*** **Carding** partially aligns the fibers and forms them into a thin web that is brought together as a soft, very weak rope of fibers called a *carded sliver* (Figure 10–11). The carding machine consists of revolving cylinders covered with heavy fabric embedded with specially bent wires or with granular cards that are covered with a rough surface similar to rough sandpaper.

***Drawing*** **Drawing** increases the parallelism of the fibers and combines several carded slivers into one *drawn sliver.* This is a blending operation that contributes to greater yarn uniformity. Drawing is done by sets of rollers, each set running successively faster than the preceding set (Figure 10–12). As **slivers** are combined, their size is reduced and a small amount of twist is added.

**FIGURE 10–11** ❖ Carding. (COURTESY OF COATS & CLARK INC.)

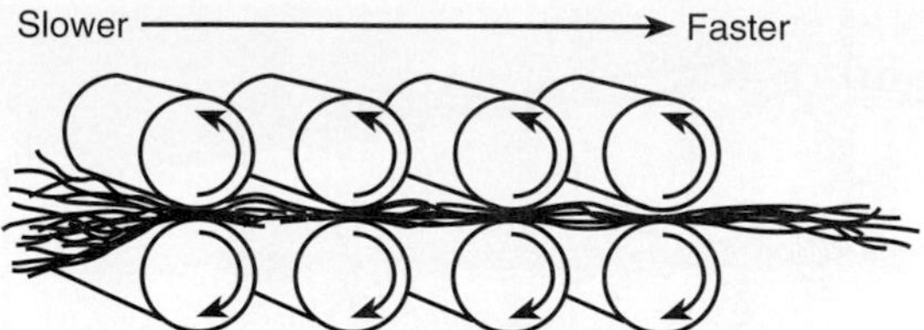


**FIGURE 10–12** ❖ Drawing rolls.

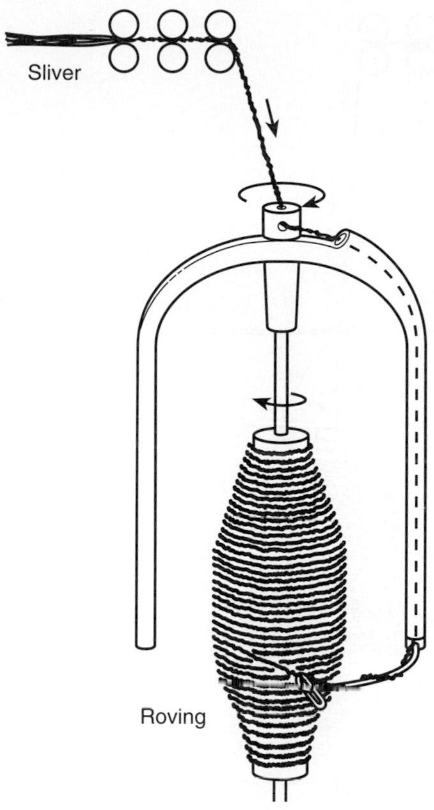


**FIGURE 10–13** ❖ Roving.

The drawing process may be repeated more than once. It is at this stage that fibers of different generic types often are combined into a blended drawn sliver. Because of differences in each fiber's physical properties, operating conditions for the carding and initial drawing steps differ for each fiber in a blend. Blending during the drawing process also eliminates mixed wastes.

***Combing*** If long-staple fibers are to be spun, another step is added to the process. *Combing* is done to achieve a yarn that is superior to a carded yarn in smoothness, fineness, evenness, and strength. Combing aligns fibers in a parallel arrangement. It also removes short fibers so that the fibers in the *combed sliver* will be more uniform in length. The combing operation and the long-staple fiber are costly. As much as one-fourth of the fiber is combed out as waste and reprocessed into short-staple carded yarns. When working with cotton or cotton blends, the term *combed yarn* is used. When working with wool or wool blends, the term **worsted yarn** is used. Yarns that have not received this process are called carded (cotton and cotton blends) or woolen (wool or wool blends).

***Roving*** The **roving** process reduces the drawn sliver, increases the parallel alignment of the fibers, and inserts a small amount of twist in the strand, now called the roving. The roving is a softly twisted strand of fibers about the size of a pencil (see Figure 10–13). Successive roving operations that gradually reduce the size of the strand may be used.

***Spinning*** **Spinning** adds the twist that makes a single-spun yarn. Ring spinning draws, twists, and winds in one continuous operation. The traveler (Figure 10–14) carries the yarn as it slides around the ring, thus inserting the twist. Ring spinning is a slow textile process in terms of productivity, with rates of 25,000 to 30,000 rpm compared to rates of 110,000 to 120,000 rpm for open-end spinning. Figure 10–15 shows a ring-spinning frame—a multiple-spinning machine that holds a number of individual units.

Blending can also take place during roving or spinning because several fiber strands are combined in these processes. Blending is usually done during roving or spinning to achieve a blending of color.

Ring-frame spinning is most commonly used for woolen yarns. It is similar to ring spinning of cotton yarns.

**COMPARISON OF CARDED-COMBED AND WOOLEN-WORSTED YARNS** The length and parallel alignment of fibers in spun yarns is a major factor in the kind of fabric produced, the cost of the yarns and fabrics, and the terminology used to designate these characteristics.

Yarns made from carded sliver are called *carded* yarns. Carded sliver of short wool fibers is made into **woolen yarns** and the fabrics are called *woolen* fabrics. (The term *woolen* refers to yarn type and is not a synonym for wool.)

Yarns made from combed sliver are called *combed* yarns. With wool, the combed sliver is referred to as **top** and the yarns made from top are called *worsted* yarns. The short fibers that are combed out are called *noils* and

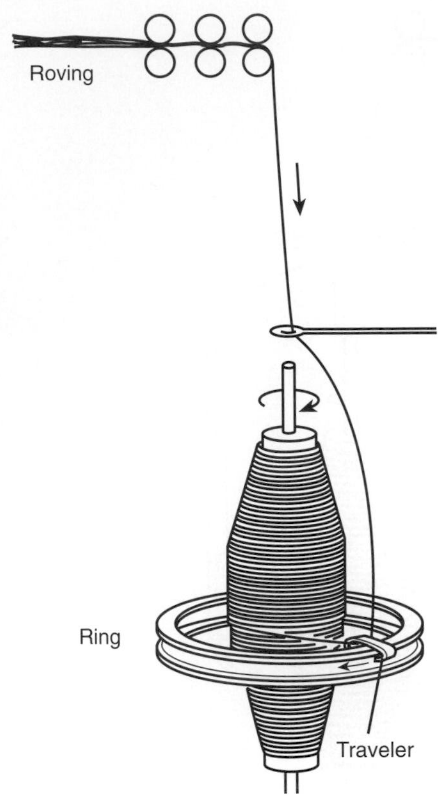


FIGURE 10–14 ❖ Ring spinning.

FIGURE 10–15 ❖ A spinning frame holds multiple ring spinners.

are a source of fibers for woolen yarns (see Figure 10–16). Fine-combed cotton yarns are made from the fibers that are more than 1⅛ inches long.

Carded and combed yarns are compared in Table 10–4.

## Alternate Spun Yarn Processes

These procedures focus on shortening or simplifying yarn spinning by eliminating or bypassing some of the steps in the conventional ring-spinning system. Most processes focus on eliminating one or more of these steps: drawing, roving, ring spinning, and rewinding.

**OPEN-END ROTOR SPINNING** **Open-end rotor spinning** eliminates the roving and twisting by the ring. Knots are eliminated, larger packages of yarn are formed, less operator supervision is needed, and production speeds are about four times that of ring spinning, but the yarns produced are coarser.

In the rotor-air-jet spinning process, sliver is broken up so that individual fibers are fed by an air stream and deposited on the inner surface of a rotating device driven at high speed. As the fibers are drawn off, twist is inserted by the rotation of the rotor, making a yarn (Figure 10–17). Rotor-spun yarns have a higher twist at the center of the yarn.

Friction spinning, a modification of open-end rotor spinning, combines the rotor and air techniques. The sliver is separated into fibers that are spread into carding or combing rolls and delivered by air to two cylinders that rotate in the same direction. These two cylinders pull the fibers into a yarn. The feed angle into the cylinder controls fiber alignment. Friction-spun yarns are

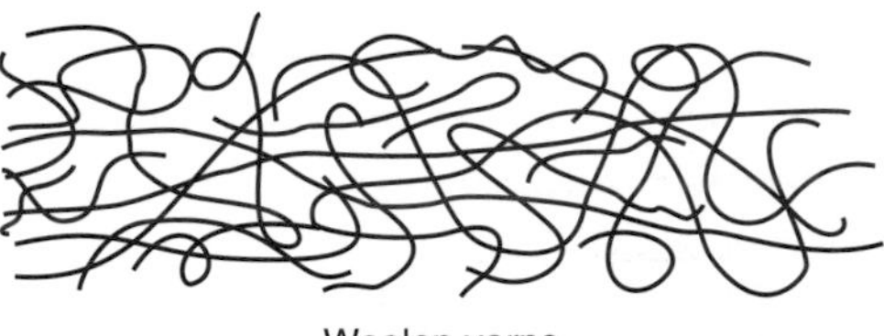

FIGURE 10–16 ❖ Woolen and worsted yarns: short-staple wool fibers in carded or woolen yarn (top); long-parallel wool fibers in combed or worsted yarn (bottom).

**TABLE 10–4** ❖ Comparison of carded and combed yarns.

| CHARACTERISTIC | CARDED | COMBED |
|---|---|---|
| Fibers used | Short staple | Long staple |
| Yarns | Less regular in size and appearance<br>Medium to low twist<br>More protruding ends<br>Bulkier, softer, fuzzier<br>More fibers present | More regular in size and appearance<br>Medium to high twist<br>Fewer protruding ends<br>Parallel fibers, finer count<br>Longer wearing, stronger<br>Fewer fibers present |
| Fabrics | May become baggy in areas of stress<br>Fabrics may be soft to firm<br>Blankets always carded<br>Wide range of uses<br>Less expensive | Smoother surface, lighter weight<br>Do not sag<br>Take and hold press<br>Fabrics range from sheers to suitings<br>More expensive |

more even, freer of lint and other debris, and loftier, but they are weaker when compared to conventional yarns. Friction spinning may be used to process very short waste staple fiber into yarns.

**AIR-JET SPINNING** The **air-jet spinning** process is similar to the rotor process except that an even, regular yarn is formed by moving air rather than a rotor. Air-jet yarns are less elastic and rougher than either ring- or rotor-spun yarns.

Table 10–5 compares ring spinning, rotor spinning, and air-jet spinning.

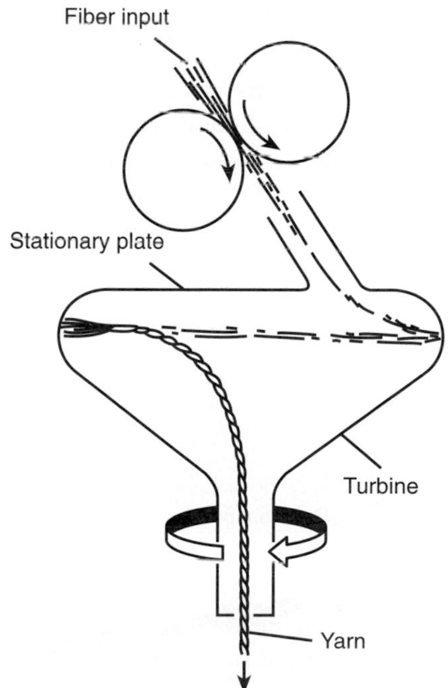


**FIGURE 10–17** ❖ Open-end, or rotor, spinning.

**DIRECT SPINNING** *Direct spinning* eliminates the roving but still uses the ring-spinning device for inserting the twist (see Figure 10–18). The sliver is fed directly to the spinning frame. This machine is used to make heavier yarn for pile fabrics and carpets.

**TWISTLESS SPINNING** *Twistless spinning* eliminates the twisting process. A roving is wetted, drawn out, sprayed with sizing or adhesive, wound on a package, and steamed to bond the fibers together. The yarns are ribbonlike in shape and stiff because of the sizing. They lack strength as individual yarns but gain strength in the fabric from the pressure between the warp and filling. The absence of twist gives the yarns a soft hand, good luster, and opacity after the sizing is removed. The yarns are easy to dye and have good durability but are not suitable to very open fabric structures.

**SELF-TWIST SPINNING** In *self-twist spinning*, two strands of roving are carried between two rollers that draw out the roving and insert twist. The yarns have areas of S-twist and areas of Z-twist. When the two twisted yarns are brought together, they intermesh and entangle, and, when pressure is released, the yarns ply over each other (Figure 10–19). This process can be used to combine staple plies, filament plies, or staple and filament plies.

## Spinning Filament Tow into Spun Yarns

Filament tow of any manufactured fiber can be made into spun yarns by direct spinning without disrupting the continuity of the strand. The two systems are tow-to-top or tow-to-yarn.

**TABLE 10–5** ❖ Comparison of ring-spun, rotor-spun, and air-jet-spun yarns.

| YARN CHARACTERISTIC | RING SPUN | ROTOR SPUN | AIR-JET SPUN |
|---|---|---|---|
| Parallelism of fibers | High | Medium | High at yarn core, less at yarn edge |
| Orientation of fibers | Helical in all areas | Helical in yarn core | Axial orientation in yarn core |
| Yarn structure | Compact | Less compact | Less compact |
| Insulation | Low | Moderate | Good |
| Yarn hairiness | High | Lower | Lower |
| Yarn stiffness | Low | More rigid | Depends on structure |
| Abrasion resistance | Medium | Low | High |
| Pilling propensity | Low | Pronounced | Less than rotor spun |
| Yarn strength | Good | Low | Medium |
| Surface roughness | Low | Medium | Medium |
| Yarn size | Wide range | Not as fine as ring | Not as fine as ring, but finer than rotor |
| Yarn evenness | Least even | Most even | Less even than rotor |
| Hand | Medium softness | Not as soft as ring | Soft |
| End uses | All end uses | Heavier weight apparel, furnishings | Bedding, furnishings |

**FIGURE 10–18** ❖ Mackie direct spinner turns sliver into finished yarn—eliminates roving. (COURTESY OF MACKIE INTERNATIONAL LTD.)

**TOW-TO-TOP (SLIVER) SYSTEM** The **tow-to-top system** bypasses the opening, picking, and carding steps of conventional spinning. In this system the filament tow is reduced to staple and formed into sliver (or top) by either diagonal cutting or break stretching. The sliver is made into regular-spun yarn by conventional spinning.

The diagonal cutting stapler changes tow into staple of equal or variable lengths and forms it into a crimped sliver. In the break-stretch process, the tow is stretched and the fibers break at their weakest points without disrupting the strand's continuity. The resultant staple is of various lengths.

**TOW-TO-YARN SYSTEM** **Tow-to-yarn spinning** is done by a machine called a direct spinner. Light tow (4,400 denier) passes between two pairs of nip rolls. The second pair of nip rolls breaks the fibers at their weakest points. The resulting strand is drawn out to

**FIGURE 10–19** ❖ Self-twist spinning.

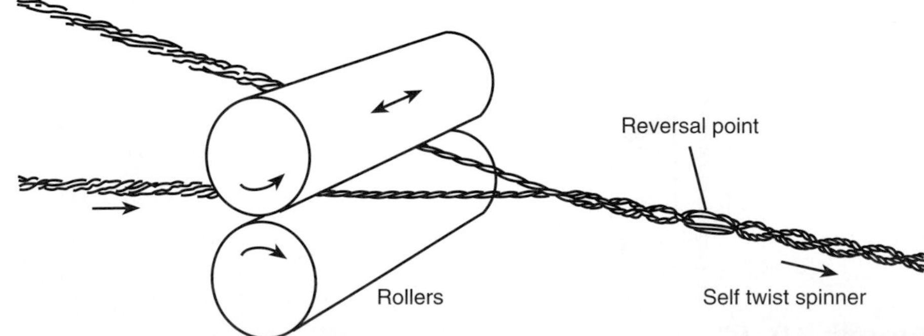

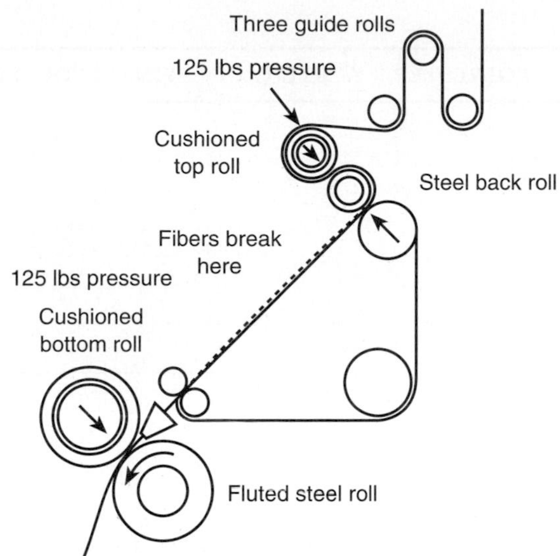


**FIGURE 10–20** ❖ Direct spinning of yarn from filament tow.

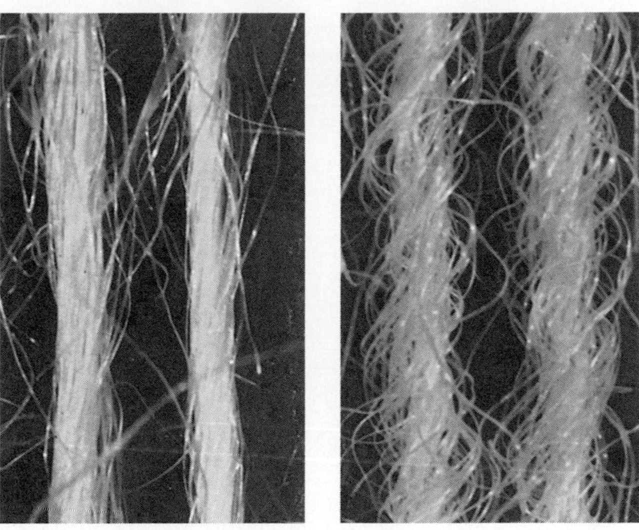

**FIGURE 10–21** ❖ High-bulk yarn before (left) and after (right) steaming.

yarn size, twisted, and wound on a bobbin (Figure 10–20).

## HIGH-BULK YARNS

**High-bulk yarns** are yarns essentially free from stretch. Some of the fibers have assumed a relatively high random crimp caused by shrinkage of low-crimp fibers.

Some fibers can be produced with a *latent shrinkage potential* and retain their bulk indefinitely at room temperature. Latent shrinkage in a fiber is achieved by heating, stretching, and then cooling while in the stretched condition. These heat-stretched fibers are called *high-shrinkage fibers* and are combined with nonshrinkage fibers in the same yarn, which is made into a product. Heat treatment of the product causes the high-shrinkage fibers to relax or shrink, forcing the nonshrinkage fibers to bulk (see Figure 10–21). This makes high-bulk sweaters, knitting yarns, and other products. High-shrinkage fibers migrate to the center of the yarn. Thus, if fine-denier nonshrinkage fibers are combined with coarse-denier high-shrinkage fibers, the fine-denier fibers concentrate on the outer surface of the yarn. The bulk can be controlled by regulating the heat stretching.

The high-bulk principle can be used to achieve interesting effects, such as "guard hairs" in synthetic furs and sculptured high-low effects in carpets. Higher density carpet pile or furlike fabrics can be made by using a high-shrinkage-type fiber for the ground yarns. When the yarns shrink, the fibers are brought much closer together.

## FIBER BLENDS

A **blend** is an intimate mixture of fibers of different composition, length, diameter, or color spun together into one yarn. In intimate blends, both fibers are present in the same yarn in planned proportions. Fiber types cannot be separated; they are next to each other throughout the yarn. When intimate blend yarns are untwisted and examined through a microscope, both fibers are visible within the viewing area.

**Mixture** refers to yarns of different generic types within a fabric. In a mixture, yarns of one fiber type are used in the warp and yarns of another type are used in the filling. When fabrics of this type are unraveled, the fibers can be separated by placing all warp yarns in one pile and all filling yarns in another pile. In a **combination,** ply yarns are used. At least one component of the ply yarn is of a different generic fiber type from the other components of the ply yarn. For example, many fabrics that incorporate a metallic component are combinations because the metallic component is part of a plied fancy yarn.

**TABLE 10–6 ❖ Fiber properties.**

| PROPERTIES | COTTON | RAYON | WOOL | ACETATE | NYLON | POLYESTER | ACRYLIC | OLEFIN | LYOCELL |
|---|---|---|---|---|---|---|---|---|---|
| Bulk and loft | – | – | +++ | | – | – | +++ | | – |
| Wrinkle recovery | – | – | +++ | ++ | ++ | +++ | ++ | ++ | – |
| Press (wet) retention | – | – | – | + | ++ | +++ | | | – |
| Absorbency | +++ | +++ | +++ | + | – | – | – | – | +++ |
| Static resistance | +++ | +++ | ++ | + | + | – | + | ++ | +++ |
| Resistance to pilling | +++ | +++ | + | +++ | + | | | ++ | + |
| Strength | ++ | + | + | + | +++ | +++ | + | +++ | +++ |
| Abrasion resistance | + | – | ++ | – | +++ | +++ | + | +++ | – |
| Stability | ++ | – | – | +++ | +++ | +++ | +++ | +++ | ++ |
| Resistance to heat | +++ | +++ | ++ | + | + | + | ++ | – | +++ |

+++, excellent; ++, good; +, moderate; –, low

Blends, mixtures, and combinations produce fabrics with properties that are different from those obtained with one fiber only. This discussion relates to blends because they are most common, but these comments also apply to mixtures and combinations.

Blending is done for several reasons:

1. To produce fabrics with a better combination of performance characteristics. Although blends never perform as well in the areas of positive performance as fabrics of only one fiber, blends help compensate for poor performance. In end uses where durability is important, nylon or polyester blended with cotton or wool increase strength and resistance to abrasion, while the wool or cotton look is maintained. For example, 100 percent cotton fabrics are not as durable as polyester/cotton blends, and polyester/cotton blends are less absorbent than 100 percent cotton fabrics.
2. To improve spinning, weaving, and finishing efficiency and to improve uniformity.
3. To obtain better texture, hand, or fabric appearance. A small amount of a specialty wool may be used to give a buttery or slick hand to wool fabrics, or a small amount of rayon may give luster and softness to a cotton fabric. Fibers with different shrinkage properties are blended to produce bulky, lofty fabrics or more realistic furlike fabrics.
4. To minimize fiber cost. Expensive fibers can be extended by blending them with less expensive fibers. Labeling requirements help protect consumers from unscrupulous labeling practices.
5. To obtain cross-dyed or unique color effects such as heather. Fibers with unlike dye affinity are blended together but dyed at a later stage in processing.

Blending is a complicated and expensive process, but the combination of properties it provides are permanent. Blends offer better serviceability of fabrics as well as improved appearance and hand.

Table 10–6 rates selected fiber properties. Notice that each fiber is deficient in one or more important properties. Try different fiber combinations to see how a blend of two fibers might be used to produce a fabric with satisfactory performance in all properties.

## Blend Levels

A blend of fibers that complement each other may give more satisfactory all-round performance than a 100 percent fiber fabric. For example, compare two fabrics, one of Fiber A and the other of Fiber B, across 5 properties. A fabric made of 50 percent A and 50 percent B will have values for each property that are neither as high as possible nor as low as possible (Caplan) (see Table 10–7). By blending the fibers, a fabric with intermediate values is obtained. Unfortunately, in a blend the real values do not come out in the same proportion as their respective percentages.

**TABLE 10–7 ❖ Effect of blending on performance.**

| PROPERTY | KNOWN VALUES A | KNOWN VALUES B | PREDICTED VALUES 50/50 A AND B |
|---|---|---|---|
| 1 | 12 | 4 | 8 |
| 2 | 9 | 12 | 10.5 |
| 3 | 15 | 2 | 8.5 |
| 4 | 7 | 9 | 8 |
| 5 | 12 | 8 | 10 |

Fiber manufacturers have conducted research to determine the percentage of each fiber necessary in various products. It is very difficult to generalize about percentages, because the percentage varies with the kind of fiber, the fabric construction, and the expected performance. For example, a small amount of nylon (15 percent) improves the strength of wool, but 60 percent nylon is needed to improve the strength of rayon. For stability, 50 percent acrylic blended with wool in a woven fabric is satisfactory, but 75 percent acrylic is necessary in knitted fabrics.

Fiber producers have controlled blend levels fairly well by setting standards for fabrics identified with their trademarks. For example, the DuPont Company recommends a blend level of 65 percent Dacron polyester/35 percent cotton in light- or medium-weight fabrics, whereas 50/50 Dacron/cotton is satisfactory for suiting-weight fabrics. This assures satisfactory performance of the fabric and maintains a positive fiber image for Dacron. The fabric manufacturer profits from the large-scale promotion by the fiber producer.

By using specially designed fiber variants, it is possible to obtain desired performance and appearance in fabrics. For example, fading, shrinkage, and softening over time are desirable characteristics for denim jeans, but are undesirable in most other apparel. For this market DuPont has developed a Dacron polyester variant that, when blended with cotton, fades, shrinks uniformly, and becomes softer.

## Blending Methods

Blending of staple can be done at any stage prior to the spinning operation including opening-picking, drawing, or roving. One of the disadvantages of direct spinning is that blending cannot be done before the sliver is formed.

The earlier the fibers are blended in processing, the better the blend. Figure 10–22 shows a cross section of yarns in which the fibers were blended in opening and in which the fibers were blended at the roving stage. Long, fine fibers tend to move to the center of a yarn, whereas coarse, short fibers migrate to the outside edge of a yarn (see Figure 10–22c).

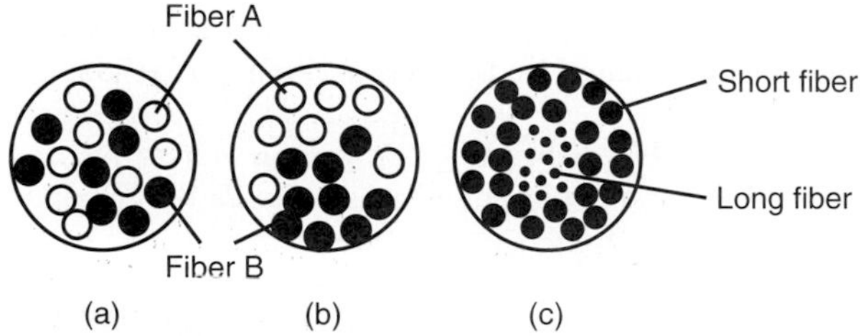


**FIGURE 10–22** ❖ Cross section of yarn showing the location of the fiber in the blend: (a) blended at the opening stage; (b) blended at the roving stage; (c) blend of short and long fibers.

Fabrics are also produced that are mixtures of bulk-filament yarns and spun yarns. These fabrics may have filament yarns in only one direction and spun yarns in the other, or they may have different yarns in bands in the warp or filling to create a design in the fabric.

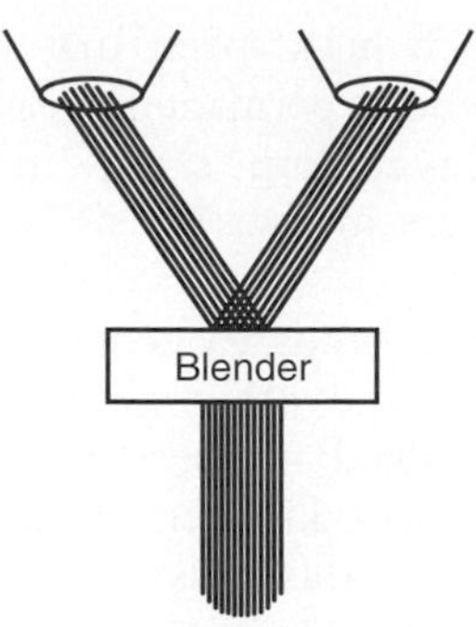


**FIGURE 10–23** ❖ Blended filament yarn. Different fibers are spun, then blended to form a yarn.

## Blended Filament Yarns

A *blended filament yarn* is one in which unlike filaments of different deniers or generic types are blended together. This is usually done to improve the performance and appearance of fabrics (see Figure 10–23). The yarns are used in apparel and furnishings.

**FASCIATED OR ROTOFIL YARNS** These yarns give better texture and hand to fabrics. The yarns are combinations of coarse filaments for strength and fine broken filaments for softness. The yarn has a staple fiber core with little or no twist wrapped with surface fibers that add integrity to the yarn. Air-jet spinning is used to produce these yarns.

❖

# ENVIRONMENTAL IMPACT OF YARN PROCESSING

Yarn processing may not be recognized as having significant environmental impact. However, several concerns regarding the environment should be discussed. The rotors used in false-twist texturing of filament yarns rotate at such high speed that workers in these areas have experienced permanent hearing losses. Current regulations regarding safety in the workplace require that workers in these areas wear hearing protection.

The opening step tends to generate large quantities of dust, fiber bits, and other airborne contaminants. Operators who worked in these parts of mills often developed respiratory disorders resulting from prolonged exposure to this dust. Current regulations regarding safety in the workplace require that dust in these areas be controlled. Opening areas and other parts of mills are significantly cleaner now. Small vacuum heads move through these parts of the mill removing dust, loose fiber, and other airborne debris. Humidity levels are regulated to minimize dust or the buildup of static electricity, which may create problems with equipment operation.

Opening, carding, and combing steps for spun yarn production generate a significant amount of waste that includes very short fibers, entangled fibers, plant debris, soil, and other foreign matter. At one time, this waste material was considered unusable and was discarded. Now, mills sell this waste to specialists who produce yarns and other fiber products from recycled waste fiber for use in apparel, furnishings, and industrial products.

Ring spinning tends to be concentrated in more low-labor-cost countries because the technology available in those countries is not highly advanced and less skilled labor can service and maintain ring-spinning equipment. In addition, spare parts for ring-spinning machines are more readily available and are relatively inexpensive. Power disruptions that may be experienced in less-developed countries do not create significant problems with ring spinning. Open-end and rotor spinning require higher energy consumption, more skilled labor, more expensive replacement parts, and more expensive technology.

# Key Terms

Yarn
Filament yarn
Throwing
Smooth-filament yarn
Tape yarn
Bulk yarn
Bulk-continuous-filament yarn
BCF
Texturing
Bulky yarn
Stretch yarn
Textured or bulked yarn
Spun yarn
Carded yarn
Combed yarn
Ring or conventional spinning
Opening
Carding
Drawing
Sliver
Combing
Worsted yarn
Roving
Spinning
Woolen yarn
Top
Open-end rotor spinning
Air-jet spinning
Tow-to-top system
Tow-to-yarn system
High-bulk yarn
Blend
Mixture
Combination

# Questions

1. Explain the processes used to produce each of these yarns: smooth filament, BCF, carded spun yarn, worsted spun yarn.
2. Using the serviceability concepts, explain why cotton and polyester are often blended for furnishing and apparel items.
3. Compare and contrast the appearance, processing, and performance of the yarn pairs listed:
   carded and combed yarns
   smooth and bulk filament yarns
   woolen and worsted yarns
4. How would the performance of two similar products differ if one were made of filament yarns of polyester and the other of spun yarns of polyester?
5. What are the differences between these two products: a blend of nylon and wool and a mixture of nylon and wool?

# Suggested Readings


American Society for Testing and Materials (1995). *Annual Book of ASTM Standards, Vol 7.01.* Philadelphia, PA: American Society for Testing and Materials.

Caplan, M. J. (1959). "Fiber Translation in Blends." *Modern Textile Magazine, 40,* p. 39.

Deussen, Helmut (1991, March). "How to Match Fibers to Your Rotor Spinning Needs." *Textile World,* pp. 61–62, 64.

Douglas, Keith (1995, February). "Producing Marketable Quality Ring- and Rotor-Spun Yarns." *Textile World,* pp. 61–63.

Krause, H. W., and Soliman, H. A. (July, 1990). "Do Higher Speeds Demand Better Yarns?" *Textile Month,* pp. 19–22.

Morris, Bill (1991). "Yarn texturing." *Textiles,* no. 1, pp. 10–13.

Nikolic, Momir, Cerkvenik, Janez, and Stjepanovic, Zoran (1994). "Influence of a Spinning Process on Spun Yarn Quality and Economy of Yarn Production." *International Journal of Clothing Science and Technology, 6*(4), pp. 34–40.

"The Polycotton Story." (1994, Winter). *Textiles Magazine,* pp. 8–11.

"Slit Film Extrusion of Polypropylene Yarns." (May, 1990). *Textile Month,* pp. 53–54.

Tortora, Phyllis G., and Merkel, Robert S. (1996). *Fairchild's Dictionary of Textiles,* 7th ed. New York: Fairchild Publications.

Wilson, D. K., and Kollu, T. (1991). "The Production of Textured Yarns by the False-Twist Technique." *Textile Progress, 21* (3), pp 1–42.

Chapter 11

# YARN CLASSIFICATION

OBJECTIVES

- To understand the classification of yarns based on their appearance and structure.
- To classify and name yarns when seen in fabrics and products.
- To explain performance of yarns in textile products.
- To understand relationships between yarn characteristics and fiber performance.
- To integrate yarn selection with end use and expected performance.
- To identify characteristics related to yarn quality.

Yarns can play a significant role in fabric and product performance. Many factors determine how a yarn is classified. Factors that assist in **yarn** identification include fiber length (staple/filament), yarn twist, yarn size, and yarn regularity/irregularity along its length.

Fabric producers select from a wide variety of yarns based on end use. For example, yarns with high twist create the texture in true crepe apparel and furnishing fabrics, and yarns with low twist are napped in flannel fabrics and blankets. Yarn may enhance good fiber performance or partially compensate for poor fiber performance. The effectiveness of a finish may depend on the yarn choice. Most yarns can be easily identified.

## Fiber Length

The names of most common yarns are based on the length of the fibers within them and the appearance and alignment of those fibers. When a typical yarn is unraveled from a fabric and examined, it may appear uniformly smooth, uniformly bulky, or fuzzy with protruding fiber ends. It can be untwisted until it separates into individual fibers. These fibers are either short, typically ½–2½ inches, or as long as the piece of fabric from which the yarn was pulled.

A **spun yarn** is composed of short-staple fibers that are twisted or otherwise bonded together, resulting in a fuzzy yarn with protruding fiber ends. Better quality and more expensive spun yarns are produced from longer staple fibers. Spun yarns of felted wool are available in some specialty sweaters.

A **filament yarn** is composed of long fibers that are grouped together or slightly twisted together. Filament yarns may be smooth—with straight, almost parallel fibers—or uniformly bulky, in which case they are called **textured-bulk-filament yarns** or just **textured-bulk yarns.** Table 11–1 summarizes the properties that result from the use of these three types of yarns in fabrics. Processing of spun yarns, smooth filament yarns, and textured bulk yarns was discussed in Chapter 10.

**Table 11–1** ❖ Comparison of spun, smooth-filament, and textured-bulk yarns.

| SPUN YARNS | SMOOTH-FILAMENT YARNS | TEXTURED-BULK YARNS (BCF) |
|---|---|---|
| I. Fabrics are cottonlike or wool-like. | I. Fabrics are silklike. | I. Fabrics have the strength of filament yarns and an appearance resembling spun yarns. |
| II. Strength of fibers is not completely utilized. | II. Strength of fiber is completely utilized. | II. Strength may or may not be completely utilized. |
| III. Short fibers twisted into continuous strand, has protruding ends.<br>1. Dull, fuzzy look.<br>2. Lint.<br>3. Subject to pilling.<br>4. Soil readily.<br>5. Warm (not slippery).<br>6. Loft and bulk depend on size and twist.<br>7. Do not snag readily.<br>8. Stretch depends on amount of twist.<br>9. More cover (more opaque). | III. Long continuous, smooth, closely packed strand.<br>1. Smooth, lustrous.<br>2. Do not lint.<br>3. Do not pill readily.<br>4. Shed soil.<br>5. Cool, slick.<br>6. Little loft or bulk.<br>7. Snagging depends on fabric construction.<br>8. Stretch depends on amount of twist.<br>9. Less cover (less opaque). | III. Long continuous, irregular, porous, flexible strand.<br>1. Bulky, dull.<br>2. Do not lint.<br>3. Pill less readily than spun yarns.<br>4. Soil more easily than smooth filament.<br>5. Warmer than smooth filament.<br>6. Lofty, bulky, and/or stretchy.<br>7. Snag easily.<br>8. Stretch depends on method of processing.<br>9. More cover (more opaque). |
| IV. Absorbency depends on fiber content. Most absorbent type.<br>1. Good for skin contact (most absorbent).<br>2. Less static buildup. | IV. Absorbency depends on fiber content.<br>1. Thermoplastics are low in absorbency.<br>2. Static buildup high in thermoplastics. | IV. More absorbent than smooth-filament yarns of same fiber content.<br>1. Most manufacturing processes require thermoplastic fibers.<br>2. Static buildup. |
| V. Size often expressed in yarn number. | V. Size in denier. | V. Size in denier. |
| VI. Various amounts of twist used. | VI. Usually very low or very high twist. | VI. Usually low twist. |
| VII. Most complex manufacturing process. | VII. Least complicated manufacturing process. | VII. Manufacturing process is more complex than for smooth filament. |

❖

# Yarn Twist

**Twist,** the spiral arrangement of the fibers around the axis of the yarn, is produced by rotating one end of a fiber strand while the other end is held stationary. Twist binds the fibers together and contributes strength to the spun yarn.

The number of twists has a direct bearing on the cost of the yarn. Higher twist yarns are more expensive because yarn yield is lower. Twist is identified by the number of turns per unit length: **turns per inch (tpi)** or turns per meter (tpm).

## Direction of Twist

The direction of twist is described as S-twist or Z-twist. A yarn has **S-twist** if, when held in a vertical position, the spirals conform to the direction of slope of the central portion of the letter "S." It is called **Z-twist** if the direction of spirals conforms to the slope of the central portion of the letter "Z." Z-twist is most common for weaving yarns (Figure 11–1).

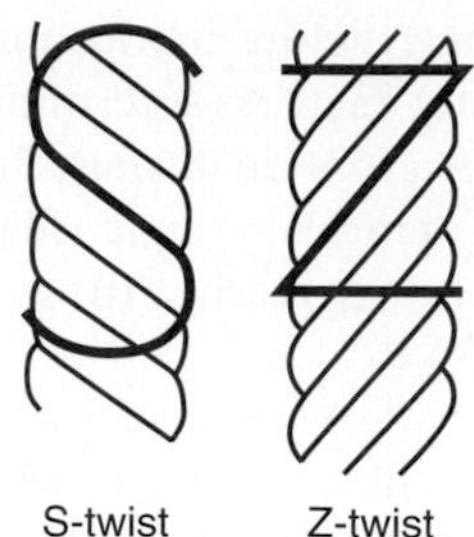


**Figure 11–1** ❖ S- and Z-twist yarns.

## Amount of Twist

The amount of twist varies with (1) the length of the fibers, (2) the size of the yarn, and (3) its intended use. Increasing the amount of twist to the point of perfect fiber-to-fiber cohesion increases the strength of the yarn. However, excess twist places the fibers at right angles to the axis of the yarn, causing a shearing action between fibers; the yarn loses strength (Figure 11–2). Increasing the amount of twist also affects yarn hairiness, comfort, cost, and linting. Yarns with lower twist tend to be hairier, pill and lint more, have better skin contact comfort, and cost less.

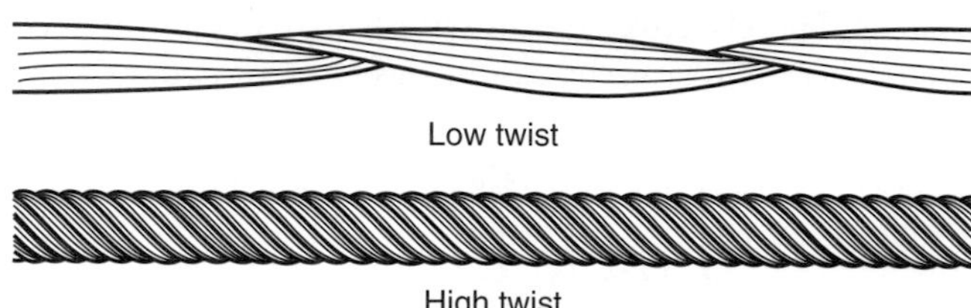


**Figure 11–2** ❖ Twist in yarns: low and high.

Combed yarns with long fibers do not require as much twist as carded yarns with short fibers. Long, parallel fibers have more points of contact per unit length, producing a stronger yarn for the same amount of twist. Fine yarns require more twist than coarse yarns. Knitting yarns have less twist than filling yarns used in weaving. In better quality yarns, twist is evenly distributed throughout the yarn and the tpi is toward the high end of the range for that yarn type. Table 11–2 and the following discussion give examples of uses for yarns with different amounts of twist.

**Napping twist** in spun yarns produces lofty yarns. They are used in filling yarns of fabrics that are to be napped. Napping teases out the ends of the staple fibers and creates the soft, fuzzy surface. (See "Napped," Chapter 17.) **Low twist** is used to maintain integrity within smooth-filament yarns. One to two turns per inch keep filament yarns from separating into individual fibers. See Figures 11–3b and 11–3c.

**Table 11–2** ❖ Amount of twist.

| AMOUNT | EXAMPLE | CHARACTERISTICS |
|---|---|---|
| Low twist | Filament yarns: 2–3 tpi* | Smooth and slick or bulky; may be difficult to recognize any twist. |
| Napping twist | Blanket warps: 12 tpi<br>Filling: 6–8 tpi | Bulky, soft, fuzzy, may be weak. |
| Average twist | Percale warps: 25 tpi<br>Filling: 20 tpi<br>Nylon hosiery: 25–30 tpi | Most common, smooth, regular, durable, comfortable. Produces smooth, regular fabrics. |
| Voile twist | Hard-twist singles: 35–40 tpi are plied with 16–18 tpi | Strong, fine yarns. Fabrics have harsher hand due to yarn twist. |
| Crepe twist | Singles: 40–80 or more tpi are plied with 2–5 tpi | Lively yarns tend to kink and twist in fabric. Creates good drape and texture in fabrics. |

* Turns per inch.

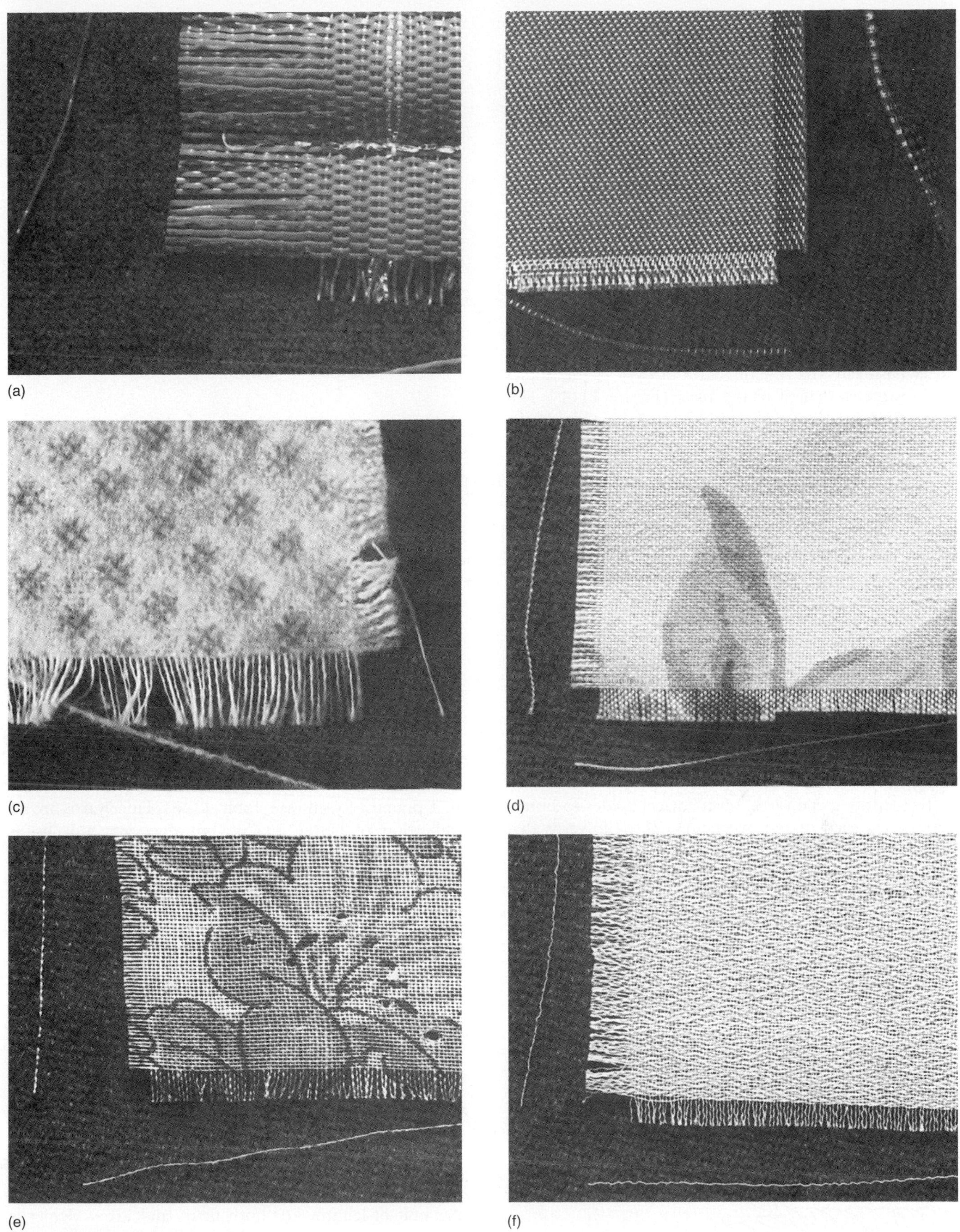


**FIGURE 11–3** ❖ Examples of yarn twist and fabrics of these yarns: (a) monofilament, (b) low twist, (c) napping twist, (d) average twist, (e) voile twist, and (f) crepe twist.

**Average twist** is used most commonly for yarns made of staple fibers and is very seldom used for filament yarns. Yarns with average twist are the most durable type of spun yarns. These yarns can be of long-staple fibers with a parallel arrangement as in combed and worsted yarns, or they can be of short-staple fibers with a less parallel arrangement (carded and woolen yarns). See Figure 11–3d.

**Hard twist** or **voile twist** yarns have a harsher hand and more turns per inch. The hardness of the yarn results when twist brings the fibers closer together and makes the yarn more compact. This effect is more pronounced when a twist-on-twist ply yarn is used. **Twist-on-twist** means that the direction of twist in the singles is the same as that of plying twist (Figure 11–4). This results in a buildup of the total amount of twist in the yarn. (See discussion of voile under "Lightweight Sheer Fabrics," Chapter 12.) See Figure 11–3e.

**Crepe yarns** are made of either staple or filament fiber and have the highest number of turns per inch (40–80) inserted in the yarn. These yarns are also referred to as unbalanced yarns since they tend to twist and kink when removed from the fabric. These yarns are so lively that they must be twist-set before they can be woven or knitted. **Twist-setting** is a yarn-finishing process.

Increasing the amount of crepe yarn twist and alternating the direction of twist increases the amount of crinkle in a crepe fabric. For example, a fabric made of 6S filling yarns followed by 6Z filling yarns gives a more prominent crinkle than 2S filling yarns followed by 2Z filling yarns.

To identify crepe yarns, ravel adjacent sides to obtain a fringe on each of the two edges. Test the yarns that are removed by pulling on the yarn and then letting one end go. The yarn will twist something like what is shown in Figure 11–5. Also see Figure 11–3f.

Do not confuse kink with yarn crimp. Examine the fringe of the fabric. If yarns other than crepe yarns are used in the fabric, they will probably be of very low twist. The majority of crepe fabrics have crepe yarns in the crosswise direction, although some are in the lengthwise direction, and some have crepe yarns in both directions. Crepe fabrics are discussed in Chapters 12 and 13.

**FIGURE 11–4** ❖ Twist-on-twist two-ply yarn.

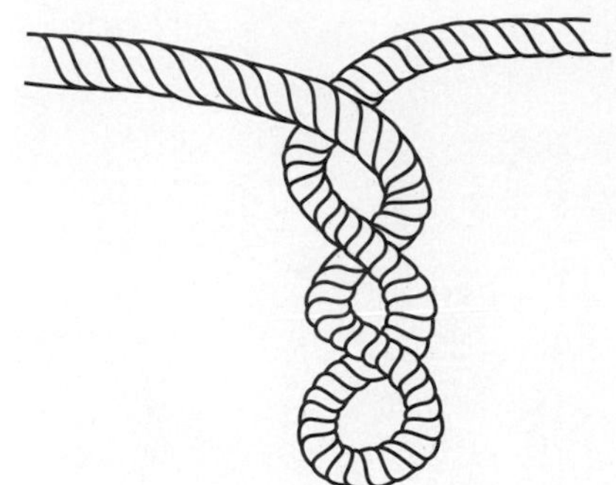

**FIGURE 11–5** ❖ Crepe yarns knot, twist, or curl when removed from a fabric.

# YARN SIZE

## Yarn Number

Yarn size or fineness is referred to as **yarn number.** For filament yarns it is expressed in terms of weight per unit length. For spun yarns, it is expressed in terms of length per unit weight. For spun yarns, the precise weights and lengths differ according to the fiber in the yarn. The cotton system is discussed here since many yarns are numbered by the cotton system. It is an indirect or fixed-weight system: the finer the yarn, the larger the number. Thus, a fine yarn would be a 70 and a coarser yarn would be a 20. The yarn number or cotton count is based on the number of hanks (1 hank is 840 yards) in 1 pound of yarn (see Table 11–3). Finer yarns are an indication of better quality, but they may not be as durable as slightly coarser yarns. Some examples that show how the size of the weaving yarn affects the weight of the fabric are presented in the lower half of the table.

The woolen and worsted systems are similar to the cotton system, except that hanks are of different lengths.

## Denier

**Denier** describes yarns made from filament fibers. The term is used for both smooth and bulky-textured yarns.

The size of filament yarns is based on the size of the individual fibers in the yarn and the number of those fibers grouped into the yarn. The size of both filament fibers and filament yarns is expressed in terms of weight per unit of length. For both fibers and yarns, denier is the weight in grams of 9,000 meters. In this system, the unit of length remains constant. The numbering system is direct, also referred to as a fixed-length system,

**TABLE 11–3** ❖ Cotton system.

| NUMBER OR COUNT OF SPUN YARN | NUMBER OF HANKS (TOTAL YARDAGE) | WEIGHT (POUNDS) |
|---|---|---|
| No. 1 | 1 (840 yards) | 1 |
| No. 2 | 2 (1,680 yards) | 1 |
| No. 3 | 3 (2,520 yards) | 1 |

| EXAMPLES OF FABRIC WEIGHT | YARN SIZE | |
|---|---|---|
| | Warp | Filling |
| Sheer lawn (2.0 oz/yd$^2$) | 70s* | 100s |
| Medium-weight print cloth (4.5 oz/yd$^2$) | 30s | 40s |
| Heavyweight sailcloth (7.5 oz/yd$^2$) | 13s | 20s |

* The "s" after the number means that the yarn is single.

because the finer the yarn, the smaller the number. See Table 11–4 for examples of filament yarns made in a specific denier for certain end uses.

Yarn denier is often used to describe filament yarn fabrics because it provides additional information to fabric specialists. Higher numbers describe larger yarns. For example, a 160 denier fabric has finer yarns than a 330 denier fabric. The 160 denier fabric will be softer and more comfortable in skin contact uses and less durable than the 330 denier fabric.

Yarn denier helps determine end use performance. When denier is listed as a fraction, the first number describes the size of the yarn and the second number describes the number of filament fibers in the yarn. When individual fiber size is important, it can be determined by dividing the first number by the second number. For example, an industrial Cordura nylon fabric by DuPont is described as 1,000/280. The yarn is a 1,000 denier yarn; there are 280 filament fibers present. Each fiber is approximately 3.6 denier in size. This would be a relatively tough, durable, and stiff fabric. End uses for such a fabric might include upholstery, briefcases, or tool pouches. This method of describing yarn denier and number of filaments is used for all types of fabrics made of filament yarns, including microfiber yarns used in apparel and furnishings.

**TABLE 11–4** ❖ Filament yarn size.

| YARN DENIER | USE | YARN TEX |
|---|---|---|
| 20 | Sheer hosiery | 2.2 |
| 40–70 | Tricot lingerie, blouses, shirts, support hosiery, glass curtains | 4.4–7.8 |
| 140–520 | Outerwear, draperies | 15.6–57.8 |
| 520–840 | Upholstery | 57.8–93.3 |
| 1,040 | Carpets, some knitting yarns | 115.6 |

## Tex System

The International Organization for Standardization has adopted the **tex** system, which determines yarn count or number in the same way for all yarns and uses metric units (weight in grams of 1 thousand meters of yarn). One tex is equal to 0.11 denier (tex = denier/9). Because the size can be small, the term *decitex (dtex)* may be used. One dtex is 10 times larger than one tex. This system is becoming more widely used in the United States.

❖

# YARN REGULARITY

Yarn regularity describes the uniformity of the yarn throughout its length in terms of its appearance and structure. Regular yarns have a similar appearance and structure throughout. There may be some slight variation due to uniformity of fiber distribution and fiber length, degree of parallelism of fibers within the yarn, and regularity of fiber size or diameter. For example, yarns with a wide variety of fiber length, unparalleled fibers, or fibers from bast sources like flax or ramie may be slightly less regular than other yarns. Yarn quality is related to the degree of uniformity within the yarn.

Fancy or novelty yarns have deliberately introduced appearance and structural variations. These irregularities tend to appear at a regular interval due to processing. Composite yarns have components that differ from each other. All three general yarn types will be discussed in more detail in this section.

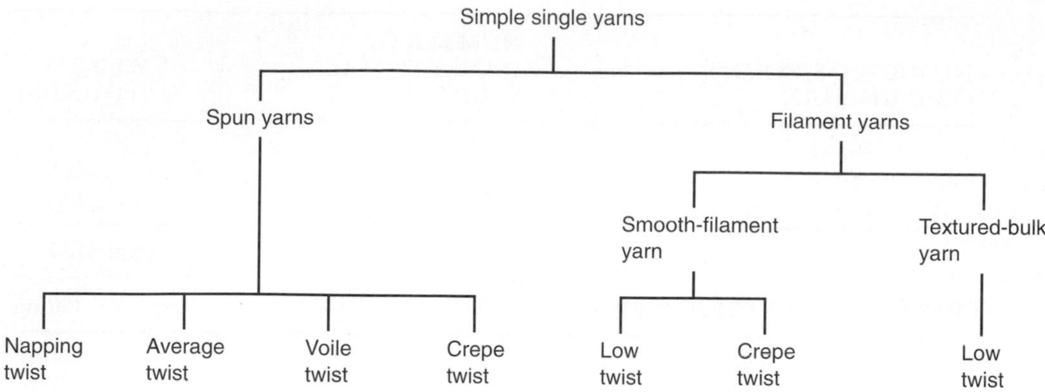


**FIGURE 11–6** ❖ Classification of simple single yarns.

## Simple Yarns

A **simple yarn** is alike in all its parts. It can be described as a spun or filament yarn based on the length of the fibers. A simple yarn also can be described by the direction and amount of twist in the yarn and by the size of the yarn. Figure 11–6 outlines the relationship of yarns in this category to each other. The number of strands used to produce the yarn is another means of classifying yarns.

Simple yarns are classified as single, ply, or cord yarns. A **single yarn** has one strand and is the simplest type. It is the product of the first twisting operation that is performed by the spinning machine (Figure 11–7a). These simple single yarns require no additional processing once the individual yarns have been formed.

Spun, filament, and textured yarns are each examples of simple single yarns. Since these three yarns are most commonly found in apparel and furnishing fabrics, they usually are referred to as spun, filament, or textured-bulk yarns. They are simple yarns, alike in all parts. They are single yarns, consisting of one strand of fibers.

A **ply yarn** is made by a second twisting operation that combines two or more singles (Figure 11–7b). Each part of the yarn is called a ply. The twist is inserted by a machine called a twister. Most ply yarns are twisted in the opposite direction to the twist of the singles from which they are made; thus the first few revolutions tend to untwist the singles and straighten the fibers somewhat from their spiral position and the yarn becomes softer.

Plying tends to increase the diameter, strength, uniformity, and quality of the yarn. Ply yarns sometimes are used in the warp direction of woven fabrics to increase strength. Two-ply yarns are found in the best-quality men's broadcloth shirts. Ply yarns are frequently seen in knits and furnishings. Two-ply and three-ply yarns are found in sewing thread and string used to tie packages. When simple ply yarns are used only in the filling direction, they are used for some fabric effect other than strength.

A **cord** is made by a third twisting operation, which twists ply yarns together (Figure 11–7c). Some types of sewing thread and some ropes belong to this group. Cord yarns are seldom used in apparel and furnishing fabrics, but are used in industrial-weight fabrics such as duck and canvas.

## Fancy Yarns

**Fancy yarns** are yarns that deliberately have unlike parts and that are irregular at regular intervals. The regular

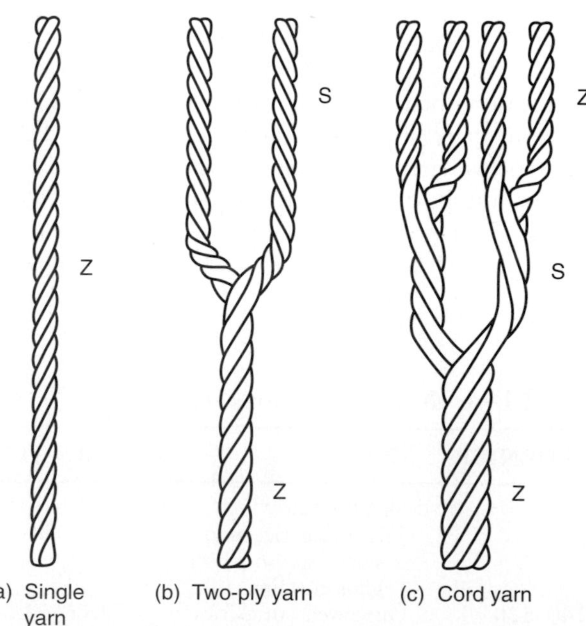


**FIGURE 11–7** ❖ Parts of a yarn: (a) single yarn; (b) two-ply yarn; (c) cord yarn.

intervals may or may not be obvious at first to the observer.

Fancy yarns may be single, plied, or cord yarns. They may be spun, filament, or textured yarns—or any combination of yarn types. They are called fancy yarns or **novelty yarns** because of their appearance: They lend an interesting or novel effect to fabrics made with them. Their structure may be complex and consist of several yarn plies combined into one yarn.

Fancy yarns are classified according to the number of parts and named for the effect that dominates the fabric. Usually more common in furnishing fabrics than in apparel fabrics, fancy yarns also are used by artists and craft people to create interest in otherwise plain fabrics of many fiber types.

Fancy yarns are made on twisters with special attachments for producing different tensions and rates of delivery in the different plies (parts), thus allowing loose, curled, twisted, or looped areas in the yarn. Slubs and flakes of short-staple fibers of different color are introduced into the yarn by special attachments. Knots or slubs are made at regular cycles of the machine operation.

Fancy or novelty yarns are used for a variety of reasons. Characteristics and performance vary widely by type and fiber content.

- Fancy yarns are usually plied yarns, but they seldom add strength to the fabric. Novelty yarns are often weak and sensitive to abrasion damage.
- When fancy yarns are used in one direction only, they are usually in the filling direction. They are more economical in that direction because there is less waste. Filling yarns are subject to less strain and are easier to vary for design purposes.
- Fancy yarns add permanent interest to plain-weave fabrics at lower cost than if the visual effects were obtained from variations in weave.
- Fancy yarns that are loose and bulky give crease resistance to a fabric, but they sometimes make the fabric spongy and hard to handle.
- The durability of fancy yarn fabrics is dependent on the size of the ply effect, how well it is held in the yarn, fiber content of the various parts, and on the firmness of the fabric structure. Generally speaking, the smaller the novelty effect, the more durable the fabric, since the yarns are less affected by abrasion and do not snag as readily.
- The quality of fancy yarns is related to the quality of the fibers and plies or components from which the yarn is made, the manner in which the unique visual component is produced in the finished yarn, and the regularity of the yarn structure. The cost of fancy yarns generally reflects the quality of the yarn.

Figure 11–8 classifies the most common fancy yarns according to whether they are typically single or ply yarns.

Tweed yarn is an example of a single, spun, fancy yarn. Flecks of color from short fibers twisted into the yarn add interest. The cohesiveness of wool fibers explains why tweeds are often made of wool. Tweed yarns are found in apparel, upholstery, and draperies.

A **slub yarn** is another single, spun, fancy yarn. This thick-and-thin yarn is made by varying the amount of twist in the yarn at regular intervals. The thicker part of the yarn is twisted less; the thinner part of the yarn is twisted more. Slub yarns can be found in shantung, drapery, and upholstery fabrics as well as in hand-knitting yarns and sweaters.

Other fancy yarns have two plies. One ply may be of one color, the other of a different color. The plies may be of differing thicknesses. A two-ply fancy yarn may have one spun ply combined with a filament ply.

Frequently fancy yarns have three basic parts:

1. The ground, or foundation, or core ply
2. The effect, or fancy ply
3. The binder ply

As a fancy yarn is examined, the **binder** is the first ply that can be unwound from the yarn. Its purpose is to hold the effect ply in place. The **effect ply** is mainly responsible for the appearance of the yarn, as well as the name given to the yarn. The **ground ply** forms the foundation of the yarn. Figure 11–9 shows a three-ply novelty yarn. For clarity in the illustration, each ply

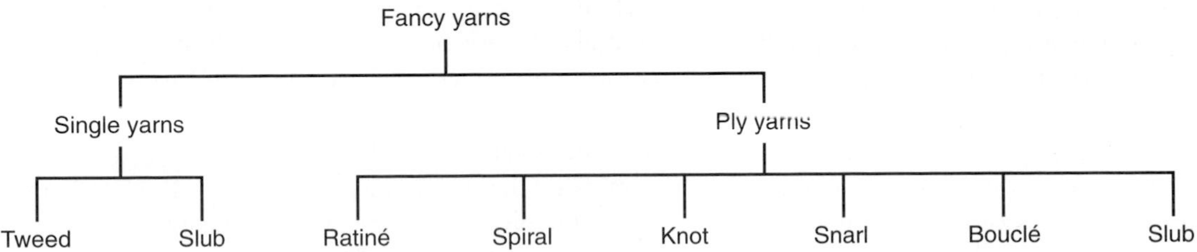


**FIGURE 11–8** ❖ Classification of fancy yarns.

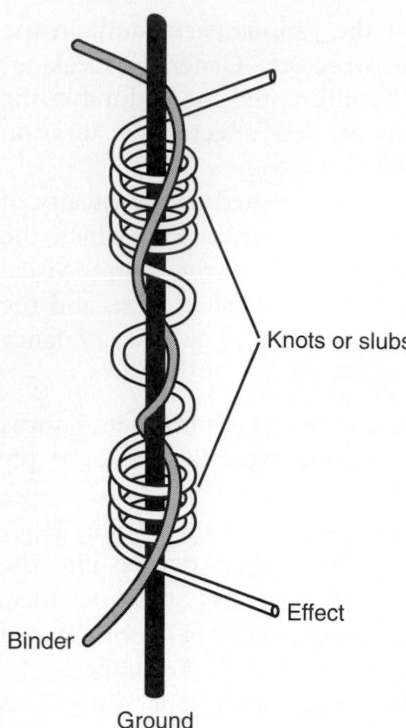


**FIGURE 11–9** ❖ Fancy yarn, showing the three basic parts.

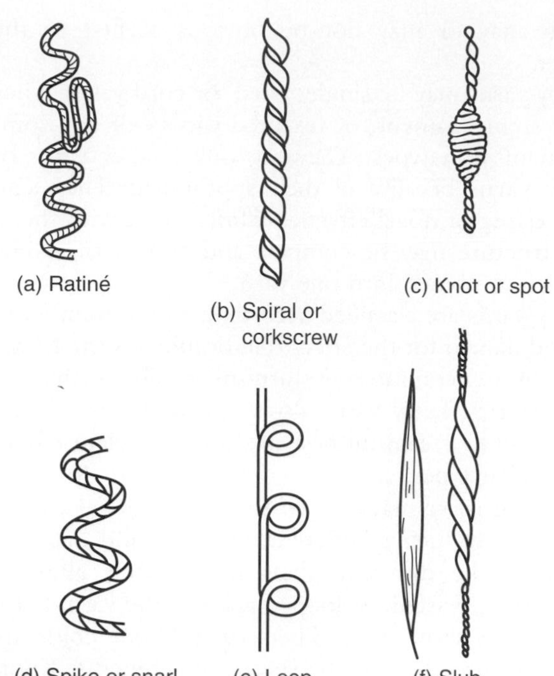


**FIGURE 11–10** ❖ Effect ply of several kinds of fancy yarns.

appears to be a simple, single, monofilament (single-fiber) yarn. In actuality, each ply could be spun, filament, BCF, or complex. Metallic components also may be used. For example, the ground may be a simple, single, filament yarn; the effect could be two-ply, with one ply a monofilament metallic yarn and the other ply a spun yarn; and the binder could be a simple, single, spun yarn. Each ply in two or more ply fancy yarns may have a different fiber content. Endless variations are possible!

The following are typical novelty yarns:

1. In **ratiné yarns,** the effect ply is twisted in a somewhat spiral arrangement around the ground ply. At intervals, a longer loop is thrown out, kinks back on itself, and is held in place by the binder (Figure 11–10a). These yarns are used primarily in furnishings.
2. The **spiral** or **corkscrew yarn** is made by twisting together two plies that differ in size, type, or twist. These two parts may be delivered to the twister at different rates of speed (Figure 11–10b). These yarns are used in furnishings and apparel.
3. The **knot, spot, nub,** or **knop yarn** is made by twisting the effect ply many times in the same place (Figure 11–10c). Two effect plies of different colors may be used and the knots arranged so the colored spots alternate along the length of the yarn. A binder is added during the twisting operation. These yarns are used in apparel and furnishings.
4. In the **spike** or **snarl yarn,** the effect ply forms alternating unclosed loops along both sides of the yarn (Figure 11–10d). These yarns are used in apparel and furnishings.
5. The **loop, curl,** or **bouclé yarn** has closed loops at regular intervals along the yarn (Figure 11–10e). These yarns are used in fabrics to create a looped pile that resembles caracul lambskin and is called **astrakhan cloth.** They are also used to give textured effects to other fabrics. Mohair, rayon, and acetate are often used for the effect ply. These yarns are used in apparel and furnishings.
6. **Slub effects** are achieved in two ways (Figure 11–10f). True slubs are made by varying the amount of the twist at regular intervals. Intermittently spun flake or slub effects are made by incorporating soft, thick, elongated tufts of fiber into the yarn at regular intervals. A core or binder is needed in the latter situation. Slub effects yarns are used in furnishings and apparel.
7. **Metallic yarns** have been used for thousands of years. See Chapter 9 for processing and use information. Metallic yarns may be monofilament fibers or combined in ply yarns. Metallic fancy yarns are used primarily in apparel.

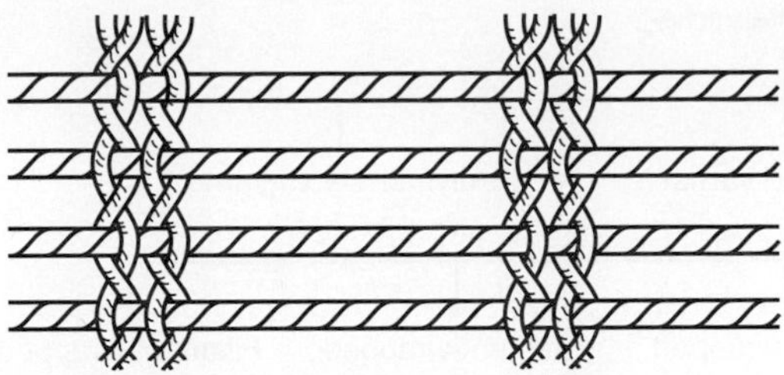

**FIGURE 11–11** ❖ Fabric from which chenille yarn is cut.

8. **Chenille yarn** is made by cutting a specially woven ladderlike fabric into warpwise strips (Figure 11–11). The cut ends of the softly twisted yarns loosen and form a fringe. This fringed yarn may be woven to produce pile on one side or on both sides of the fabric. If the pile is on one side only, the yarn must be folded before it is woven. This yarn is sometimes referred to as a "caterpillar" yarn. Chenille-type yarns can also be made by flocking or gluing short fibers on the surface of the yarn. Other chenille-type yarns are made by twisting the effect yarn around the core yarn, securing it in place with the binder, and cutting the effect so it forms a fringe or pile. Chenille yarns are used in furnishings and apparel.

Table 11–5 summarizes information about yarns relative to aesthetics, durability, comfort, and care. Use it to review the major yarns and compare their performance.

## Composite Yarns

**Composite yarns,** regular in appearance along their length, have several unlike components; they have both staple-fiber and filament-fiber components. Composite

**TABLE 11–5** ❖ Performance of yarns in fabrics.

| YARN TYPE | AESTHETICS | DURABILITY | COMFORT | CARE |
|---|---|---|---|---|
| Spun yarns | Fabrics are cottonlike or wool-like in appearance<br>Fabrics lint and pill | Weaker than filament yarns of same fiber<br>Ply yarns stronger than simple yarns<br>Yarns are more cohesive, so fabrics tend to resist raveling and running | Warmer<br>More absorbent because of larger surface area | Yarns do not snag readily<br>Soil readily |
| Smooth-filament yarns | Fabrics are smooth and lustrous<br>Fabrics do not lint or pill readily | Stronger than spun yarns of same fiber<br>Fabrics ravel and run readily | Cooler<br>Least absorbent but more likely to wick moisture | Yarns may snag<br>Resist soiling |
| Bulk yarns | Fabrics are less lustrous; more similar to those made of spun yarns<br>Fabrics do not lint but may pill | Stronger than spun yarns of same fiber<br>Yarns are more cohesive, so fabrics ravel and run less than those made with filament yarns but more than those made with spun yarns | Bulkier and warmer than smooth-filament yarns<br>More absorbent than filament yarns<br>Stretch more than other yarns | Yarns likely to snag<br>Soil more readily than filament yarns |
| Fancy yarns | Interesting texture<br>Larger novelty effects show wear sooner than smaller novelty effects<br>Fabrics lint and pill | Weaker than filament yarns<br>Most resist raveling<br>Less abrasion-resistant | Warmer<br>More absorbent if part is spun | Yarns likely to snag<br>Soil readily |
| Composite | Varies; yarns may be large, may have spun or filament appearance | Related to process | May have stretch; larger than many other yarns | Large yarns may snag |

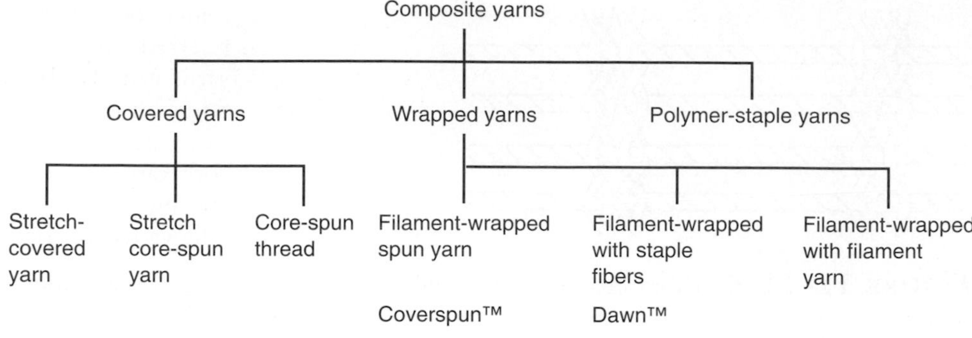


**FIGURE 11–12** ❖ Classification of composite yarns.

yarns include covered yarns, core-spun yarns, filament-wrapped yarns, and molten-polymer yarns. The relationship of the basic composite yarns is shown in Figure 11–12. The quality of composite yarns is related to fiber and component ply quality, finished yarn structure, and yarn uniformity.

**Covered yarns** have a central yarn that is completely covered by fiber or another yarn. These yarns were developed to produce more comfortable rubber foundation garments and surgical hose. Stretch-covered yarns consist of a central core of rubber or spandex covered with yarns. There are two kinds: single covered and double covered. Single-covered yarns have a single yarn wrapped around them. They are lighter, more resilient, and more economical than double-covered yarns and can be used in satin, batiste, broadcloth, and suiting as well as for lightweight foundation garments. Most ordinary elastic yarns are double-covered to give them balance and better coverage. Fabrics made with these yarns are heavier and thicker. A double-covered yarn is shown in Figure 11–13. Covered yarns are subject to "grin-through" (see Figure 9–4). Although these yarns include spandex, they should not be referred to as spandex yarns.

An alternate way of making a stretch yarn is to make a stretch **core-spun yarn** by spinning a sheath of staple fibers (roving) around a core. When working with elastomeric cores, the core is stretched while the sheath is spun around it so that the core is completely hidden. The sheath adds aesthetic properties to the yarn, and the core provides just enough stretch for comfort. Core-spun yarns in woven fabrics produce an elasticity more like that of the knits.

Polyester/cotton core-spun thread has a sheath of high-quality cotton and a high-strength filament polyester core. The cotton outer cover gives the thread excellent sewability, and the polyester core provides high strength and resistance to abrasion. Polyester/cotton thread provides the slight stretch that is necessary in knits.

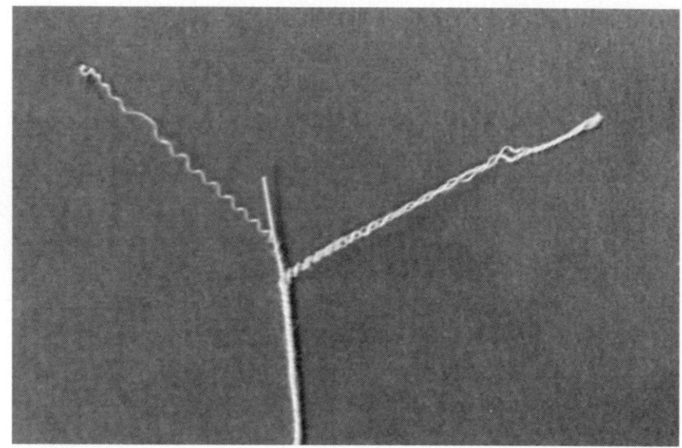

**FIGURE 11–13** ❖ Double-covered stretch yarn.

In **wrap-spun yarns,** a core of staple fibers (often a twistless yarn) is wrapped with filament fibers that serve as a binder. These yarns are economical and have good evenness, strength, appearance, and finishing properties.

**Fasciated yarns** are made of a grouping of filament fibers wrapped with staple fibers. The yarns are combinations of coarse filaments for strength and fine stretch-broken filaments for softness (Figure 11–14). Production of these yarns is very fast. These yarns give better texture and hand to fabrics. Another variation is a filament-wrapped filament yarn (Figure 11–15).

Yarns can be produced by pressing staple fibers of any length or generic class into a molten polymer stream. As the polymer solidifies, the fibers that are partially embedded become firmly attached and form a sheath of staple fiber. The resultant yarn is about two-thirds staple fiber and one-third coagulated polymer. The polymer, which is extruded as manufactured fibers are, is a less expensive product than other melt-spun filaments.

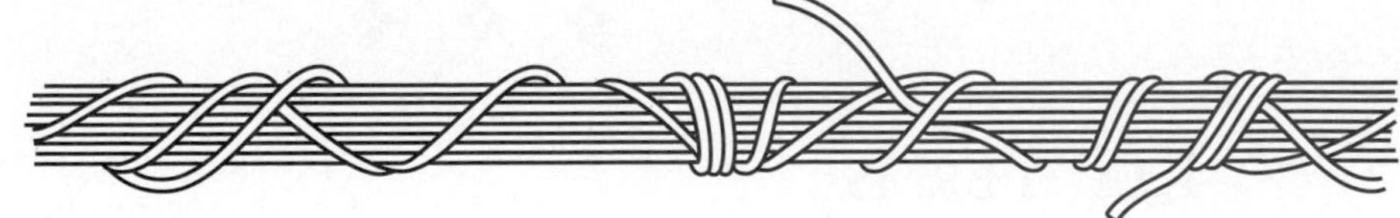

**FIGURE 11–14** ❖ Fasciated yarn.

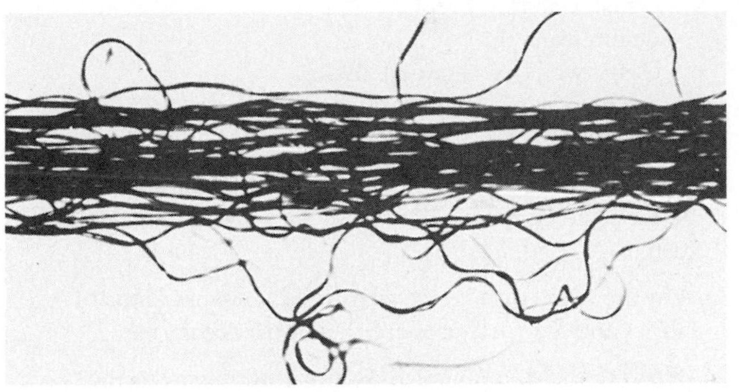

**FIGURE 11–15** ❖ Filament-wrapped filament yarn. (COURTESY OF HERCULES, INC.)

## YARN PERFORMANCE AND YARN QUALITY

Yarn characteristics and performance are identified and measured so that the right yarn is used in the fabric and product. Standard test methods determine yarn size, twist, bulk, evenness, appearance, and performance. Yarn strength is determined by measuring the load that breaks a yarn and the percent of elongation at that load. Tolerances or variations allowed in a yarn of a given type are also measured so that consistency in performance and appearance can be evaluated.

Yarn quality is an important factor related to the quality of the resultant fabric and product. Yarn quality refers to various factors such as yarn strength and thin spots within yarns. Thin spots tend to be weaker and are likely to break when the yarn is under stress. These thin spots or nips also create thin, weak areas in fabrics or unacceptable fabric appearance variations. Stresses can be substantial during the making of a fabric; yarn breaks are costly to repair and decrease fabric quality. Yarns must be strong enough to withstand the stresses of looms and knitting machines. Strength demands on yarns depend on the structure of the fabric and its end use. In addition, fabric producers demand high yarn quality and consistency of yarn characteristics at lower prices. Yarn producers are responding to these demands by incorporating on-line yarn defect detection systems so that yarn defects can be solved as soon as they begin to develop in the spinning process.

Many factors determine the quality of a yarn. Better quality yarns have more parallel fibers, tighter twist, and are more regular than lower quality yarns. High-quality yarns are strong enough to withstand additional processing (warping, weaving, knitting, etc.) and to provide adequate end-use performance. High-quality yarns are regular in structure with few thin spots. Their appearance and performance makes the finished material suitable for the end use and target market. The yarns facilitate subsequent dyeing and finishing steps. They are relatively free of unacceptable neps and hairiness. A **nep** is a small knot of entangled fibers, which may be immature or dead and subsequently create problems by not accepting dye. Neps may create thick spots on yarns or uncolored flecks in finished fabrics. **Hairiness** describes excessive fiber ends on the surface of a yarn. Figure 11–16 shows differences in yarn hairiness due to spinning method. Hairy yarns may create problems in fabrication or in consumer use because they tend to be more sensitive to abrasion and pilling. Yarn quality affects fabric quality, performance, and cost.

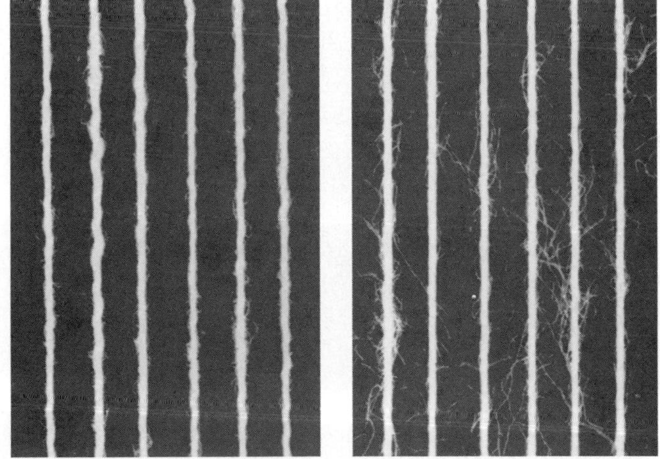

**FIGURE 11–16** ❖ Yarn hairiness. (COURTESY OF *TEXTILE WORLD*.)

## Key Terms

Yarn
Spun yarn
Filament yarn
Textured-bulk-filament yarn
Textured-bulk yarn
Twist
Turns per inch (tpi)
S-twist
Z-twist
Napping twist
Low twist
Average twist
Hard twist
Voile twist
Twist-on-twist
Crepe yarn
Twist setting
Yarn number
Denier
Tex
Simple yarn
Single yarn
Ply yarn
Cord
Fancy yarn
Novelty yarn
Slub yarn
Binder
Effect ply
Ground ply
Ratiné yarn
Spiral or corkscrew yarn
Knot, spot, nub, or knop yarn
Spike or snarl yarn
Loop, curl, or bouclé yarn
Astrakhan cloth
Slub effects
Metallic yarn
Chenille yarn
Composite yarn
Covered yarn
Core spun yarn
Wrap-spun yarn
Fasciated yarn
Neps
Hairiness

## Questions

1. Describe the type of yarn (in terms of fiber length, yarn twist, yarn complexity, regularity, and size) that would likely be found in each of the following products. Explain the performance of each yarn selected.
   percale sheeting in luxury hotel suite
   muslin sheeting in budget motel room
   tweed for woman's blazer
   carpet for family room
   upholstery for antique formal settee
   casual T-shirt
   denim jeans
   elastic wrap for sprained ankle
   casement cloth for draperies in medical center waiting room
2. What differences in fiber length and turns per inch would be expected between a low-twist yarn and an average-twist yarn?
3. Why are fancy or novelty yarns used? In what kinds of fabrics and for what uses are they most common?
4. What are the differences and similarities between the denier and tex systems?
5. What are the characteristics that differentiate a yarn of average quality and one of high quality?

## Suggested Readings

American Society for Testing and Materials (1995). *Annual Book of ASTM Standards, Vol 7.01.* Philadelphia, PA: American Society for Testing and Materials.

Merkel, Robert S. (1991). *Textile Product Serviceability.* New York: Macmillan Publishing Co.

Tortora, Phyllis G., and Merkel, Robert S. (1996). *Fairchild's Dictionary of Textiles,* 7th ed. New York: Fairchild Publications.

Wiberley, James S. (1984) "The Analysis of Textile Structure." In William J. Weaver, ed., *Analytical Methods for a Textile Laboratory.* Research Triangle Park, SC: American Association of Textile Chemists and Colorists.

# Section Four

# FABRICATION

Chapter 12

# Basic Weaves and Fabrics

OBJECTIVES

- To understand the loom, the process of weaving, and the three basic weaves.
- To identify fabrics made using the three basic weaves.
- To name basic fabrics.
- To predict performance of fabrics based on fabrication, yarn structure, and fiber.

A **fabric** is a pliable, planelike structure that can be made into two- or three-dimensional products that require some shaping and flexibility. Fabrics are used in apparel, furnishings, and many industrial products. The four chapters in this section focus on methods used to produce fabrics and introduce many fabrics by name for each method. Not all fabrics will be discussed for each process. Many fabrics have very specialized applications; others are no longer popular due to changes in fashion or lifestyles. Some fabrics are no longer commercially available due to changes in consumer expectations, different lifestyles, or cost of production. Some remain important, but their names have changed. Current names, especially names used in the industry, will be identified.

The fabric-forming process or fabrication method contributes to the fabric's appearance, texture, suitability for end use, performance, and cost. The process may determine the name of the fabric, like felt, lace, double knit, and tricot. The cost in relation to fabrication process depends on the number of steps involved and the speed of production. The fewer the steps and the faster the process, the cheaper the fabric. Changes in the textile industry have focused on increased automation; production flexibility that lets a firm produce a variety of fabrics with the equipment available; quick response to consumer needs; and improved quality.

Textile producers describe the shortest length of fabric they will produce to sell to another firm as minimums or minimum yardage. Some firms specialize in high-quality fabrics, special fabric types, or high-volume basic fabrics. Minimum yardage depends on the firm and its area of specialization. For example, 5,000 yards may be a minimum order for a basic fabric in a basic color, but 200 yards may be a minimum from a European specialty fabric producer.

Fabrics can be made from a wide variety of starting materials: solutions (films and foams), fibers (felts and fiberwebs or nonwovens), yarns (braids, knits, laces, and wovens), and fabrics (composite fabrics combining solutions, fibers, yarns, or fabrics to produce a fabric). The first three chapters of this section focus on fabrics made from yarns: woven and knitted fabrics. The final chapter focuses on all the other processes. Fabric names discussed in these chapters were selected because they are basic, commonly used fabrics. Many, many more named fabrics exist and can be found in the market. However, these other fabrics will not be discussed in this book. Several references listed at the end of this chapter are excellent for additional information on fabrics not described in this book.

**Fabric quality** is important to textile producers, designers, retailers, and consumers because it describes many characteristics: freedom from defects, uniform structure and appearance, and performance during production and in consumers' hands. Fabric quality influences product cost, suitability for a target market, aesthetic characteristics, and consumer appeal and satisfaction. Assessment of quality can be made by inspecting or examining fabric with the eye or an instrument to identify visible irregularities, defects, or flaws. Computer-aided fabric evaluation (CAFE) systems are being developed to speed this process and increase the accuracy of fabric inspection. Defects are assigned a point value based on their length or size. Fabric quality is **graded** by totaling the defect points of a piece of fabric. Production firms have developed lists or examples of defects or flaws and guidelines for grading fabrics (see Figure 12–1). Manufacturers of cut and sewn products determine the quality level suitable for their product line and target market and purchase fabric accordingly.

A second means of determining fabric quality assesses fabric performance. Standard test methods have been developed by several professional organizations to aid in performance assessment so that fabric evaluation is consistent. Fabric performance procedures exist to assess abrasion resistance, strength, wrinkle resistance, shrinkage during laundering or dry cleaning, colorfastness to light or perspiration, snagging resistance, flammability, water repellency, consistency of color throughout a length of fabric, soil resistance, and many other characteristics. Fewer manufacturers assess fabric quality from a performance perspective than from a visual examination. Unfortunately, many consumer problems with textile products stem from minimal performance evaluation by manufacturers.

With the exception of triaxial fabrics, all woven fabrics are made with two or more sets of yarns interlaced at

**FIGURE 12–1** ❖ The defect in the center of this fabric decreases its quality and performance.

right angles to each other. Sometimes these fabrics are referred to as biaxial. The yarns running in the lengthwise direction are called **warp** yarns or *ends,* and the yarns running crosswise are called **filling,** *weft,* or *picks.* The right-angle position of the warp to filling yarns gives the fabric more firmness and rigidity than yarn arrangements in knits, braids, or laces. Because of this structure, yarns can be raveled from adjacent sides. Woven fabrics vary in the ways the yarns interlace, the pattern formed by the yarns as they interlace, the number of yarns per inch, and the ratio of warp to filling yarns.

Woven fabrics are widely used, and weaving is one of the oldest methods of making fabric. Some fabric names are based on an earlier end use (hopsacking used in bags for collecting hops; tobacco cloth as shade for tobacco plants; cheesecloth to wrap cheeses; and ticking in mattress covers, which were called "ticks"); the town in which the fabric was woven originally (bedford cord from New Bedford, Massachusetts; calico from Calcutta, India; chambray from Cambrai, France; and shantung from Shantung, China); or the person who originated or was noted for that fabric (batiste for Jean Baptiste, a linen weaver; and jacquard for Joseph Jacquard).

Weaving is one of the most widely used construction techniques. Woven fabrics are used in apparel, furnishings, and industrial products. Woven fabrics generally have these characteristics:

- Two or more sets of yarns are interlaced at right angles to each other.
- Many different interlacing patterns give interest and texture to the fabric.
- Yarns can be raveled from adjacent sides.
- Fabrics have grain.
- Fabrics are relatively stable—they do not have much stretch in warp or filling.

## Weaving and the Loom

Weaving is done on a machine called a **loom.** All the weaves that are known today have been made for thousands of years. The loom has undergone significant modifications, but the basic principles and operations remain the same. Warp yarns are held taut within the loom, and filling yarns are inserted and pushed in place to make the fabric.

In primitive looms, the warp yarns were kept upright or horizontal (Figure 12–2). Backstrap looms, used for hand weaving in many countries, keep the warp yarns taut by attaching one beam to a tree or post and the other beam to a strap that fits around the weaver's hips as the weaver stands, squats, or sits (Figure 12–2). Filling yarns are inserted by a shuttle batted through raised warp yarns. To separate the warp yarns and weave faster, alternate warp yarns were attached to bars that could be raised, bringing the alternate warp yarns up. A toothed device very much like a comb pushed the filling yarns in

**FIGURE 12–2** ❖ Hand looms: backstrap (left) and horizontal (right). (COURTESY OF MARY LITTRELL.)

place. The bar developed into heddles and harnesses attached to foot pedals so the weaver could separate the warp yarns by stepping on the pedals, leaving the hands free for inserting the filling yarns.

During the Industrial Revolution, mass production high-speed looms were developed. The modern loom consists of two beams, a warp beam and a cloth or fabric beam, holding the warp yarns between them (Figure 12–3). The warp is raised and lowered by a harness-heddle arrangement. A **harness** is a frame to hold the heddles. The harness position and the warp yarns that are controlled by each harness determine the weave pattern or interlacing. A **heddle** (headle) is a wire with a hole in its center through which the warp yarn is threaded. There are as many heddles as there are warp yarns in the cloth, and the heddles are held in two or more harnesses. As can be seen in Figure 12–3, a simple two-harness loom, as one harness is raised the other harness remains in its original position, and the yarns form a **shed** through which the filling can be inserted.

Filling yarns are carried through the shed by carriers of several types. The name of the loom often refers to the carrier used to insert the filling yarn. Originally, these carriers were fairly large, somewhat oval wooden shuttles with a bobbin of yarn in the center. In the shuttle loom, a **shuttle** is thrown through the shed by picker sticks at both sides of the loom. These sticks bat the shuttle first from one side and then, after the shed has changed, back to the other side so quickly the shuttle is a blur. Shuttle looms are limited to about 200 picks or filling insertions per minute. The noise of the picker sticks striking the shuttle is deafening. Looms with quieter and more efficient carriers, called shuttleless looms, will be discussed later in this chapter.

A **reed,** or *batten,* beats or pushes the filling yarn into place to make the fabric firm. A reed is a set of wires in a frame; the spaces between the wires are called **dents.** Warp yarns are threaded through the dents in the reed. The spacing in the reed is related to the desired number of warp yarns per inch in the woven fabric. Reeds are available with a wide variety of spacings related to the density of the yarns in the finished fabric and the size of the yarns. For example, 20-dent reeds are used for low-density fabrics where the yarns are often large; 80-dent reeds are used for higher density fabrics where the yarns are finer. The way the reed beats the filling yarn in place helps determine the density of filling yarns and the grain characteristics of the finished fabric.

Weaving consists of the following steps:

1. **Shedding:** raising one or more harnesses to separate the warp yarns and form a shed.
2. **Picking:** passing the shuttle through the shed to insert the filling.
3. **Beating up:** pushing the filling yarn into place in the fabric with the reed.
4. **Take-up:** winding finished fabric on the fabric beam.

The most frequent type of commercial loom is a four-harness loom. This loom is extremely versatile and can be used to produce most simple woven fabrics. These fabrics comprise the greatest percentage of woven fabrics currently on the market and explain the popularity of the four-harness loom. Additional harnesses or other devices that control the position of the warp yarns are used to make more intricate designs. However, generally six harnesses is the limit in terms of efficiency. Patterns that require more than six harnesses are usually made on looms that utilize other devices to control the warp yarns. These other devices will be discussed later in this chapter.

## Preparing for Weaving

**WINDING** Yarns are repackaged so that they can be used on a particular loom to be used in making the fab-

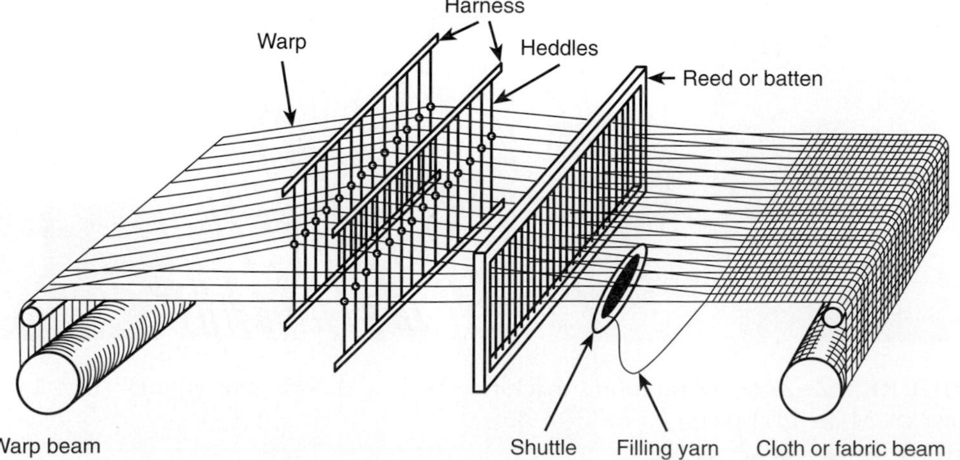


**FIGURE 12–3** ❖ Simplified drawing of a two-harness shuttle loom.

ric. This repackaging step is called *winding*. In this process, some spun yarns are given more twist or combined with other singles to make ply yarns.

**CREELING** Yarn packages are placed on a large frame called a *creel* (Figure 12–4). The creel holds the yarn as it is wound onto a warp beam. To protect warp yarns from damage during weaving, they are treated with a sizing agent. After weaving, the fabric is removed from the beam, washed to remove the sizing, finished to specification, and wound on bolts or tubes for sale to manufacturers or consumers. (See Chapters 16–19.)

## Loom Developments

Loom developments over the years have centered on (1) devices to weave intricate designs; (2) computers and electronic monitoring systems to increase speed, patterning capabilities, and quality; and (3) quicker and more efficient means of inserting filling yarns.

**PATTERNING CAPABILITIES** Devices that control the position (up or down) of the warp yarns have included dobby, doup, lappet, and leno attachments, and the jacquard loom. These have become so sophisticated that pictures can be woven in cloth (see Chapter 13). In some looms now available warp yarns are individually controlled by microcomputers. These looms may be referred to as electronic jacquards.

**COMPUTER SYSTEMS** *Computer* and *electronic devices* play an important part in developing design tables for setting up "maximum weavability" properties, such as tightness and compactness in wind-repellent fabrics or tickings. CAD systems (computer-aided design) are used extensively in textile design. Designs can be controlled by microcomputers that control the operation of individual warp yarns. Quick Style Change (QSC) and electronic jacquards allow quick changes from one fabric style to another, in 30 minutes or less compared to the several hours or more required with traditional jacquard looms. With QSC, shorter minimum yardage orders are possible.

Computerization of weaving has made tremendous advances in the past few years. Automation of weave rooms is an important goal in applying computer systems and robotics to fabric production. Some mills perform weaverless weaving. This refers to the use of automatic looms with microcomputers that function in many ways. The computer can alter loom operation so that high speeds of filling insertion are maintained while adjusting for minor changes in tension of both warp and filling yarns and winding up woven fabric. These computers also detect incorrect filling insertions, remove the incorrect insertion, correct the problem, and restart the weaving operation. All these steps occur without the assistance of a human operator.

Automation also helps reduce the chances of a fabric defect. Weaving quality and efficiency are improved.

**LOOM EFFICIENCY** Because of the noise and slower speeds, shuttle looms continue to be replaced with faster, quieter, more versatile shuttleless looms. Four types of shuttleless looms—air-jet, rapier, water-jet, and projectile—have higher weaving speeds and reduced noise levels. These factors are of great importance to the worker. In these looms, the filling yarns are measured, inserted, and cut, leaving a fringe along the side. These ends may make a fused selvage if the yarns are thermoplastic, or the ends may be tucked into the cloth. Shuttleless looms are more common than shuttle looms. Most shuttleless looms are air-jet or rapier types. Water-jet and projectile looms are less common.

***Air-Jet Loom*** In the **air-jet loom** the filling is premeasured and guided through a nozzle, where a blast of

FIGURE 12–4 ❖ Creeling: Spools of yarns are placed on a large creel and wound onto a warp beam. (COURTESY OF WEST POINT FOUNDRY AND MACHINE COMPANY.)

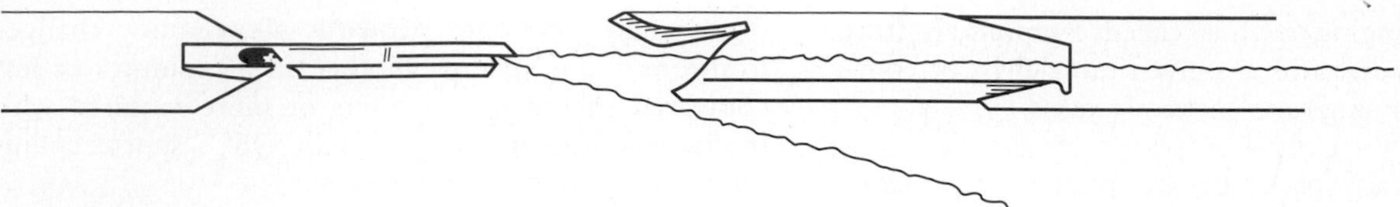

**FIGURE 12–5** ❖ Carrier arms of a rapier shuttleless loom.

air sends it through the shed. The loom operates at speeds up to 1,000 picks per minute and is suitable for spun yarns. Good warp preparation is required. There are limitations related to yarn bulk and weight in the types of filling yarns this loom can handle. Air-jet looms weave fabrics up to 400 centimeters (157 inches) in width.

***Rapier Loom*** The **rapier loom** weaves primarily spun yarns at up to 650 picks per minute. The double-rapier loom has two metal arms about the size of a small penknife, called carriers or "dummy shuttles," one on the right side and the other on the left side of the loom. A measuring mechanism on the right side of the loom measures and cuts the correct length of filling yarn to be drawn into the shed by the carriers. The two carriers enter the warp shed at the same time and meet in the center. The left-side carrier takes the yarn from the right-side carrier and pulls it across to the left side of the loom. Figure 12–5 shows the carrier arms. This loom is widely used to produce basic cotton and woolen/worsted fabrics. It is more flexible than the air-jet loom.

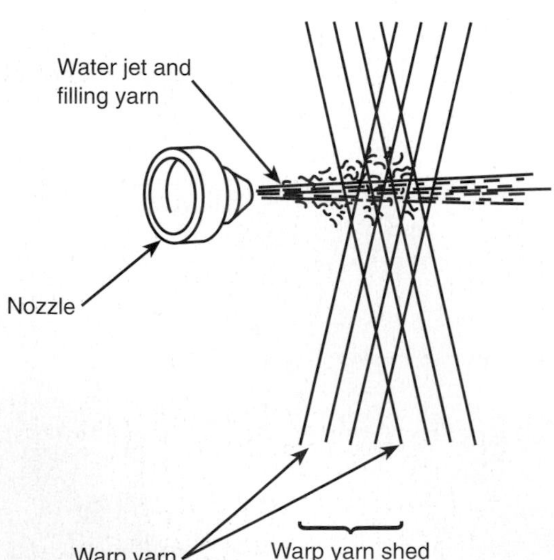


**FIGURE 12–6** ❖ Water jet carries filling yarn through warp shed.

***Water-Jet Loom*** The **water-jet loom** uses a high-pressure jet of water to carry the filling yarn across the warp (Figure 12–6). It produces fabrics without yarn streaks or barré (a type of yarn streak).

The water is removed from the loom by suction. Since water from the jet dissolves regular warp sizings, water-resistant sizings are used. The fabric is wet when it comes from the loom, so drying is an added expense. This loom is more compact, less noisy, and takes up less space than the conventional loom. It operates at 400–600 picks per minute—two or three times faster than the conventional loom.

***Projectile Loom*** In the **projectile loom,** one projectile with grippers carries the yarn across the full width of the shed. The yarn may be inserted from one or both sides. This loom is also called the missile or gripper loom.

***Double-Width Loom*** In double-width looms, twin warp beams allow two widths of fabric to be woven side by side. Because changing sheds is a time-consuming step in weaving, this loom makes optimal use of that time. Denim is often made on double-width looms.

***Multiple-Shed Loom*** In each of the looms discussed so far one shed forms at a time. In **multiple-shed weaving** more than one shed is formed at a time. In warp-wave looms, as a yarn carrier enters one portion of the warp, a shed is formed; as the carrier leaves that area, the shed changes. This action may occur simultaneously across the width of the warp several times. In weft-wave looms, several sheds form along the length of the warp yarns and open at the same time, one filling yarn is inserted into each shed, and then the sheds change.

As many as 16 to 20 filling carriers insert the precut filling in a continuous process instead of the intermittent process of single-shed weaving. Beating up and shedding arrangements are different. In this continuous-weaving process, the number of picks per minute (ppm) is doubled. However, multiphase looms have never been extensively used in the industry.

***Circular Loom*** Most looms weave flat widths of fabric. Circular looms weave tubular fabric. The **circular loom** in Figure 12–7 weaves sacks of split-film polypropylene. Some pillowcases are also tubular woven.

FIGURE 12–7 ❖ Circular loom used to weave bags. (COURTESY OF AMOCO FABRICS & FIBERS CO.)

***Triaxial Loom*** This system weaves three sets of yarns at 60° angles to each other (see Figure 12–8). These **triaxial** fabrics are stable in all directions—horizontally, vertically, and on the bias. Biaxial fabrics with two sets of yarns at right angles to each other are not stable on the bias.

In triaxial weaving, all the yarns are usually alike in size and twist. Two yarn sets are warp and the other set is filling. Fabrics can be produced more quickly than other weaves because there are fewer picks per inch and speed of weaving is based on the number of picks per minute. Triaxial fabrics are used for industrial products, such as balloons, air structures, sailcloth, diaphragms, and truck covers.

## Environmental Impact of Weaving

Environmental problems associated with weaving may be related to the type of loom used to produce a fabric. For example, shuttle looms are incredibly noisy. Loom

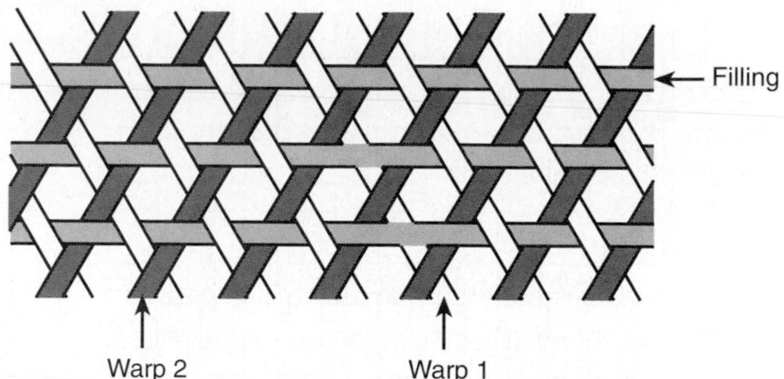


FIGURE 12–8 ❖ Triaxial weave pattern.

operators in shuttle weaving rooms wear hearing protectors to minimize hearing loss. Water-jet looms require the use of clean water to carry the filling yarn across the fabric. This water is reclaimed and recycled. Fabrics produced with this loom must be dried before storage to reduce problems with mildew, and the energy used in drying fabrics is great.

Energy use varies significantly with the type of loom. For example, rapier looms use almost twice the energy of projectile looms, and air-jet looms use almost three times the energy of projectile looms.

Warp yarns are treated with sizing or lubricating compounds to minimize problems with abrasion in weaving. Sizing and lubricating compounds are removed after the fabric has been produced and are often reclaimed, but reclamation is not 100 percent efficient and disposal of the residue is necessary. In addition, static electricity can build up in the weaving room, especially if synthetic fibers are used. Humidity is controlled to minimize static charges. Lint can also be a problem as a result of yarn abrasion during weaving. Lint can create fabric quality and respiratory problems. Vacuum heads attached to flexible tubing move through weaving rooms to remove lint and minimize health, quality, and equipment problems.

The industrywide trend of producing better-quality fabric improves efficiency and lessens environmental impact. Fewer fabric flaws means less recutting of product pieces. Improved fabric quality means fewer seconds from cut-and-sew production facilities.

# CHARACTERISTICS OF WOVEN FABRICS

All yarns in woven fabrics interlace at right angles to one another (Figure 12–9). An **interlacing** is the point at which a yarn changes its position from one side of the fabric to the other. When a yarn crosses over more than

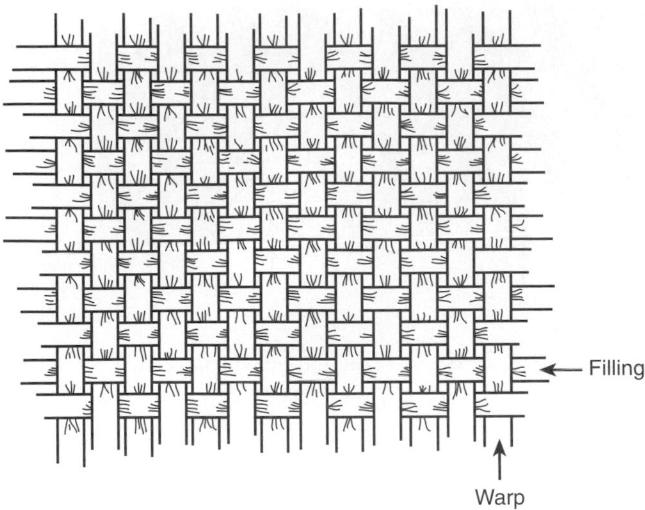


**FIGURE 12–9** ❖ Warp and filling yarns in woven fabrics. Note that the yarns in this diagram interlace at 90° angles.

one yarn at a time, **floats** are formed and the fabric has fewer interlacings.

## Warp and Filling

*Warp* and *filling yarns* have different demands placed on them and often differ in their makeup or structure. Thus, a fabric may not have the same performance characteristics for warp and filling. The warp must withstand the high tensions of the loom and the abrasion of weaving, so the warp yarns are stronger and more uniform with higher twist. Filling yarns are more apt to be fancy or special-function yarns, such as high-twist crepe yarns, low-twist napping yarns, or bouclé yarns.

It is possible to differentiate between warp and filling by carefully examining both the fabric and the lengthwise and crosswise yarns.

1. The selvage always runs in the lengthwise (warp) direction of all fabrics.
2. Most fabrics have lower elongation in the warp direction.
3. The warp yarns lie straighter and are more parallel in the fabric because of loom tension.
4. Fancy or special-function yarns are usually in the filling direction.
5. Specific fabric characteristics may indicate the warp and filling directions. For example, poplin has a filling rib and satin has warp floats.
6. Warp yarns tend to be smaller, are more uniform in structure and appearance, and have higher twist.
7. Fabric crimp is usually greater for filling yarns since they must bend or flex over or under warp yarns due to the way the loom operates.

## Grain

**Grain** refers to the geometry or position of warp yarns relative to filling yarns in the fabric. A fabric that is *on-grain* has warp yarns parallel to each other and perpendicular to the filling yarns, which move straight across the fabric. Lengthwise grain is parallel to the warp yarns. Crosswise grain is parallel to the filling yarns. Fabrics are almost always woven on-grain. Handling, finishing, or stress due to yarn twist, weave, or other fabric aspects may cause fabrics to distort and lose their on-grain characteristic. These fabrics are off-grain. Quality of fabrics has increased significantly and it is rare to find fabrics as badly off-grain as those illustrated.

**Off-grain fabrics** create problems in production and for consumers. During finishing, off-grain causes reruns or repeating finishing steps and lowers fabric quality. Products do not drape properly or hang evenly and printed designs are not straight. Figure 12–10 shows a design that has been printed off-grain—the print does not follow the yarns or a torn edge.

There are two kinds of off-grain. **Skew** occurs when the filling yarn is at an angle other than 90° to the warp.

**FIGURE 12–10** ❖ Skewed fabric.

**FIGURE 12–11** ❖ Bowed fabric. Note the horizontal lines traced on the fabric. The darker line traces a yarn in the fabric; the lighter and straighter line indicates the crosswise grain of the fabric.

It usually results in finishing when one side of the fabric travels ahead of the other (see Figure 12–10) **Bow** occurs when the filling yarns dip in the center of the fabric and usually develops when the center of the fabric lags behind the two sides as the fabric is finished (see Figure 12–11).

Fabrics should always be examined for grain. On-grain fabrics usually indicate high quality standards and minimize problems in matching designs or patterns, cutting, or sewing.

## Fabric Count

*Fabric count,* or **count,** is the number of warp and filling yarns per square inch of gray goods (fabric as it comes from the loom). Count may increase due to shrinkage during dyeing and finishing. Count is written with the warp number first, for example, 80 × 76 (read as 80 by 76); or it may be written as the total of the two, or 156. Count is not synonymous with yarn number. In some instances, density may be used to refer to or describe fabric count.

Count is an indication of the quality of the fabric—the higher the count, the better the quality for any one fabric. Higher count also may mean less potential shrinkage and less raveling of seam edges. Catalogs sometimes give count because the customer must judge the quality from printed information rather than from the fabric itself.

Count can be determined with a fabric counter (Figure 12–12) or by hand. The number of yarns in each direction are counted for an inch.

Count may vary depending on the end use or quality of fabric. Often it is listed as a total and may be described on labels as thread count even though yarns, not threads, are counted. For example, two plain-weave fabrics often used in bed sheets are percale and muslin. Percale is a higher quality fabric made of combed yarns in counts of 160, 180, 200, or more. Higher numbers describe better quality fabrics. Muslin is a harder wearing fabric designed for lower price points. It is usually made of carded yarns in counts of 112, 128, or 140. It is frequently used in bed linens for budget motels and hospitals. The 140-count fabric is the highest quality of the three.

## Balance

**Balance** is the ratio of warp yarns to filling yarns in a fabric. A balanced fabric has approximately one warp yarn for every filling yarn, or a ratio of 1:1 (read as one to one). An example of a balanced fabric is 78 × 78 print cloth. An unbalanced fabric has significantly more of one set of yarns than the other. A typical unbalanced fabric is broadcloth, with a count of 144 × 76 and a ratio of about 2:1.

Balance is helpful in recognizing and naming fabrics and in distinguishing the warp direction of a fabric. Balance plus count is helpful in predicting slippage. When the count is low, there will be more slippage in unbalanced fabrics than in balanced fabrics.

Balance can be determined by examining a fabric carefully. If the fabric can be raveled, unravel several

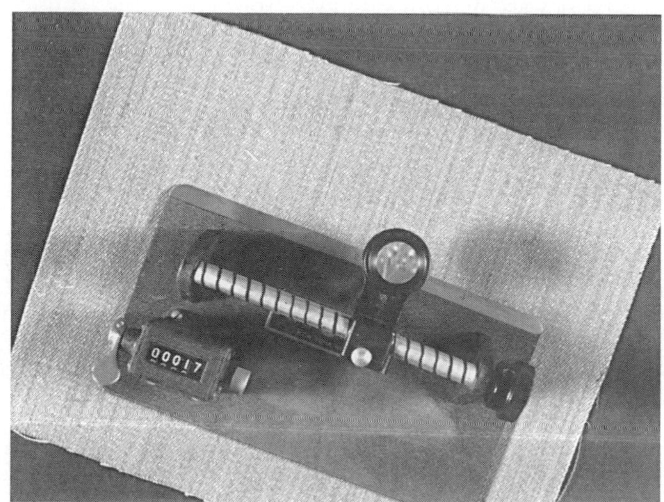


**FIGURE 12–12** ❖ Fabric yarn counter. (COURTESY OF ALFRED SUTER CO.)

yarns on adjacent edges and compare the density and size of yarn ends protruding from the fabric. In a balanced fabric, warp and filling yarns are nearly identical in size and count. In fact, in balanced fabrics, it may be difficult to differentiate between warp and filling yarns when the selvage is not present. In unbalanced fabrics, warp and filling yarn size may be significantly different or the density between warp and filling yarns may be different.

## Selvages

A **selvage** is the lengthwise self-edge of a fabric. On conventional shuttle looms, it is formed by the filling yarn when it turns to go back across the fabric. The conventional loom makes the same kind of selvage on both sides of the fabric, but shuttleless looms have different selvages because the filling yarn is cut and the selvage looks like a fringe. In some fabrics, different yarns or interlacing patterns are used in the selvage.

*Plain selvages* are similar to the structure of the rest of the fabric. They do not shrink and can be used for seam edges. *Tape selvages* used in sheeting are made with larger or plied yarns for strength. They are wider than the plain selvage and may be a different weave to maintain a flat edge. *Split selvages* are used when narrower items such as towels are woven so that two or more items are produced side by side and cut apart after weaving. These edges require hemming. *Fused selvages* are found in narrow fabrics of thermoplastic fibers cut from wide fabric.

## Fabric Width

The loom determines the width of the fabric. Handwoven fabrics are narrow, often 27–36 inches wide. Fabric widths have been increasing because wide fabrics are more economical to weave and allow for more efficient use of fabric in products. Traditional fabric widths are related to fiber type: cotton fabrics 45 or 60 inches wide, wool fabrics 54–60 inches wide, and silk-type fabrics 40–45 inches wide. However, some basic fabrics, regardless of fiber type, are 60 inches wide or wider.

## Fabric Weight

Fabric **weight** describes how much a fabric weighs for a given area or length of fabric. Fabric weight is important because it is used to identify fabric appropriateness for end use and in naming fabrics. Both length and area weight values are used in the textile industry. For example, yards per pound may be used in trade publications to identify current prices for basic fabrics, but fabric width is crucial in this system. Another system uses weight in ounces per square yard (oz/yd$^2$). The metric equivalent is g/m$^2$ (grams per square meter). This book will use oz/yd$^2$.

Lightweight or top-weight fabrics are usually described as those that weigh less than 4.0 oz/yd$^2$. These fabrics tend to be softer and more comfortable next to the skin and have better drape. Top weight fabrics are used for shirts, blouses, dresses, apparel linings, bedsheets, curtains, sheer draperies, substrates for industrial products, and backing fabrics for wall coverings and bonded and quilted fabrics.

Medium-weight fabrics weigh from 4.0 to 6.0 oz/yd$^2$. These fabrics are widely used for heavier and stiffer shirts, blouses, dresses, apparel linings, winter-weight bedsheets, draperies, upholstery, wall coverings, and table linens. Many medium-weight fabrics are used in quilted and bonded fabrics and as substrates for industrial products.

Heavyweight fabrics are often described as bottom-weight goods because they are used for apparel bottoms like pants and skirts. These fabrics weigh more than 6.0 oz/yd$^2$. They are durable, stiff fabrics used for outerwear, work clothing, upholstery, draperies, and bedspreads.

**TABLE 12–1** ❖ Properties of woven fabrics.

| FABRIC CHARACTERISTIC | PROPERTIES |
|---|---|
| High count | Firm, strong, good cover and body, compact, stable, more rigid drape, wind and water repellent, less edge raveling. |
| Low count | Flexible, permeable, pliable, softer drape, higher shrinkage potential, more edge raveling. |
| Balanced | Less seam slippage, warp and filling wear more evenly. |
| Unbalanced (usually more warp) | Seam slippage with low count; surface yarns wear out first, leaving slits (common in upholstery fabrics). Add visual and tactile interest. |
| Floats | Lustrous, smooth, flexible, resilient, may ravel and snag, seam slippage with low count. |

## Properties of Woven Fabrics

Fabric properties resulting from weaving variables are summarized in Table 12–1.

The weave or interlacing pattern influences fabric properties as well as fabric appearance. Table 12–2 summarizes the various weaves. This chapter and Chapter 13 deal with woven fabrics.

# Plain Weave

The **plain weave** is the simplest of the three basic weaves. Basic weaves are those that are made on a loom without any modification. The plain weave is formed by yarns at right angles passing alternately over and under each other. Each warp yarn interlaces with each filling yarn to form the maximum number of interlacings (Figure 12–13). Plain weave requires only a two-harness loom and is the least expensive weave to produce. It is described as a $\frac{1}{1}$ weave, read as one harness up and one harness down or as one up, one down, which describes the position of the harness when forming the shed.

Figure 12–13 shows several ways of diagramming a plain weave. The top drawing is a cross-sectional view of a fabric cut parallel to a filling yarn. The cut ends of the warp yarns appear as black circles. The filling yarn goes over the first warp yarn and under the second warp yarn. In a plain-weave fabric, this same pattern is repeated until the filling yarn has interlaced with all the warp yarns across the width of the loom. The second filling yarn goes under the first warp yarn and over the second. This pattern also is repeated across the width of the loom. Notice how these two filling yarns interlace with the warp yarns to achieve the maximum number of interlacings. In a plain weave, all odd-numbered filling yarns have the same interlacing pattern as the first filling yarn, and all even-numbered filling yarns have the same interlacing pattern as the second filling yarn.

The photograph of the fabric at the bottom of Figure 12–13 shows the same interlacing pattern as in the cross section. In the photograph, the yarns are opaque and only yarns on the surface are visible. Hence, a pattern of dark warp yarns and light filling yarns develops.

The checkerboard pattern in the center of Figure 12–13 is a simple representation of the photograph of the plain-weave fabric. In the checkerboard pattern, each square represents one yarn on the surface of the fabric; dark squares represent warp yarns on the surface and light squares represent filling yarns on the surface. Starting at the upper left-hand corner of the checkerboard and moving across the row, a filling yarn is on the surface, then a warp yarn is on the surface, and so on. The second row is just the opposite and represents the interlacing pattern of the second filling yarn. All woven fabrics can be diagrammed using this technique. These diagrams are an easy way to represent the interlacing patterns and help identify the weave in a fabric.

Plain-weave fabrics have no technical face or back due to the weave. Printing and some surface finishes may create a technical face or "right" side. Plain weave's uninteresting surface serves as a good ground for printed designs and many finishes. Because there are many interlacings per square inch, plain-weave fabrics tend to wrinkle more, ravel less, and be less absorbent than other weaves. Interesting effects can be achieved by varying fiber types or using novelty or textured yarns, yarns of different sizes, high- or low-twist yarns, filament or staple yarns, and finishes.

## Balanced Plain Weave

The simplest plain weave is one in which warp and filling yarns are the same size and the same distance apart so they show equally on the surface—**balanced plain weave** (see Figure 12–13). Balanced plain-weave fabrics have a wider range of end uses than fabrics of any other weave and are the most widely used type of woven fabric. They can be made in any weight, from very light to very heavy (see Table 12–3).

One convenient way of grouping fabrics is by fabric weight. Balanced plain-weave fabrics will be discussed in five groups: lightweight sheer, lightweight opaque, low-count sheer, medium weight, and heavyweight.

**Lightweight Sheer Fabrics** Lightweight sheer fabrics are very thin, lightweight, and transparent or semitransparent. High-count sheers are transparent as a result of the fineness of yarns. Fabric weight is less than 4.0 oz/yd$^2$. Fabrics are used for lightweight apparel and curtains.

Filament-yarn sheers may be described in part by fiber content; for example, polyester sheer or nylon sheer. **Ninon** is a filament sheer that is widely used for glass curtains. It is usually 100 percent polyester because of that fiber's resistance to sunlight, excellent resiliency, and easy washability. Although ninon is a plain weave, warp yarn spacing is not uniform across the fabric. Pairs of warp yarns are spaced close to each other. Space between adjacent warp yarn pairs is greater than the space between the two yarns in the pair. Ninon has medium body and hangs well.

**Georgette** and **chiffon** are made with filament yarns, the latter being smoother and more lustrous. In georgette, the direction of the crepe twist (S or Z) for warp and filling yarns alternates. For example, even-numbered warp and filling yarns may be S-twist and odd-num-

**Table 12–2** ❖ Basic weaves.

| NAME | INTERLACING PATTERNS | GENERAL CHARACTERISTICS | TYPICAL FABRICS | CHAPTER REFERENCE |
|---|---|---|---|---|
| Plain<br>$\frac{1}{1}$ | Each warp interlaces with each filling. | Most interlacings per square inch. Balanced or unbalanced. Wrinkles. Ravels. Less absorbent. | Batiste<br>Voile<br>Percale<br>Gingham<br>Broadcloth<br>Crash<br>Cretonne<br>Print cloth<br>Glazed chintz | 12 |
| Basket<br>$\frac{2}{1}$<br>$\frac{2}{2}$<br>$\frac{4}{4}$ | Two or more yarns in warp, filling, or both directions woven as one in a plain weave. | Looks balanced. Fewer interlacings than plain weave. Flat looking. Wrinkles. Ravels more. | Oxford<br>Monk's cloth<br>Duck<br>Sailcloth | 12 |
| Twill<br>$\frac{2}{1}$<br>$\frac{2}{2}$<br>$\frac{3}{1}$ | Warp yarns float over two or more filling yarns in a regular progression of one to the right or left. | Diagonal lines or wales. Fewer interlacings than plain weave. Wrinkles. Ravels more. May be more pliable than plain weave. Higher counts possible. | Serge<br>Surah<br>Denim<br>Gabardine<br>Herringbone<br>Flannel | 12 |
| Satin<br>$\frac{4}{1}$<br>$\frac{1}{4}$ | Warp yarns float over four or more filling yarns in a progression of two to the right or left. | Flat surface. Most are lustrous. High counts possible. Fewer interlacings. Long floats subject to slippage and snagging. Ravels. | Satin<br>Sateen<br>Antique satin<br>Peau de soie | 12 |
| Momie or crepe | An irregular interlacing of yarns. Floats of unequal lengths in no discernible pattern. | Rough-looking surface. Crepelike. | Granite cloth<br>Moss crepe<br>Sand crepe<br>Bark cloth | 13 |
| Dobby | Many different interlacings. Possible to create geometric patterns. | Cord-type fabrics. Simple patterns. | Shirting madras<br>Huck toweling<br>Waffle cloth<br>Piqué | 13 |
| Jacquard | Each warp yarn controlled individually. An infinite number of interlacings is possible. | Intricate patterns. | Damask<br>Brocade<br>Tapestry | 13 |
| Doublecloth | Several possible patterns use three, four, or five sets of yarns. | Thick, stiff, durable, warm fabrics. | Doublecloth<br>Suitings<br>Coatings | 13 |
| Pile | Extra warp or filling yarns are woven in to give a cut or an uncut three-dimensional fabric. | Plush or looped surface. Warm. Wrinkles less. Pile may flatten. | Velvet<br>Velveteen<br>Corduroy<br>Furlike fabrics<br>Wilton rugs<br>Terrycloth | 13 |
| Slack-tension | A variation of pile weave. Some warp yarns are released from tension in the loom to create texture or pile. | Crinkle stripes or pile surface. Absorbent. Nonwrinkling. | Seersucker<br>Terrycloth<br>Friezé | 13 |
| Leno | A doup attachment on the loom crosses one of two warp yarns over other warp yarns on alternate passages of the filling yarns. | Meshlike fabric. Lower count fabrics resist slippage. | Marquisette<br>Sheer curtain fabrics | 13 |
| Swivel | An attachment to the loom. Small shuttles with extra filling yarns weave in small dots. | Dots on both sides of fabric as filling floats. | Dotted swiss | 13 |

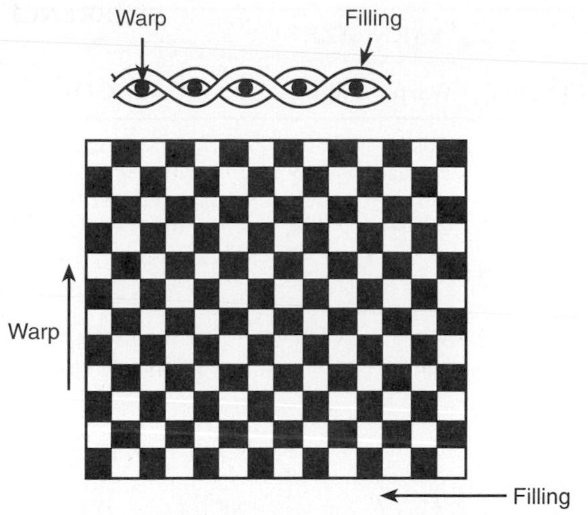


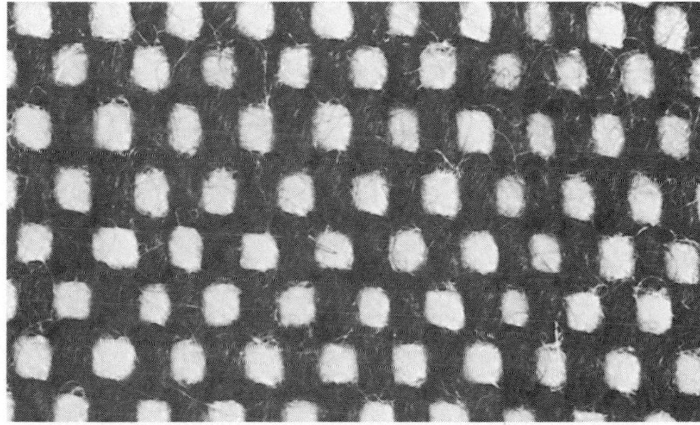

**FIGURE 12–13** ❖ Three ways to show the yarn-interlacing pattern of plain weave: cross section (top); checkerboard (center); photograph (bottom).

bered yarns may be Z-twist. Chiffon has smaller yarns in a hard twist. Both fabrics can be solid color or printed. Both are very lightweight, drape well, and are used in apparel. Both fabrics were originally made of silk but now often are made from manufactured filament yarns.

**Voile** is a sheer made with special high-twist spun yarns. The yarns may be combed or worsted. Voile can be solid color or printed. Voile was originally a cotton or wool fabric, but it is now found on the market in many fiber contents.

**Organdy** is the sheerest cotton cloth made. Combed yarns contribute to its sheer appearance. Its sheerness and crispness are the result of an acid finish on lawn gray goods (see Chapter 17). Because of its stiffness and fiber content, it wrinkles badly. Organza is the filament-yarn counterpart to organdy. It has a lot of body. These sheer fabrics are used for glass curtains and for summer-weight apparel. Both fabrics are available in solid colors or prints.

**LIGHTWEIGHT OPAQUE FABRICS** Lightweight opaque fabrics are very thin and light but are not as transparent as sheer fabrics. The distinction between the two groups of fabrics is not always pronounced. Fabric weight is less than 4.0 oz/yd$^2$. End uses include apparel and furnishings.

Organdy (a sheer fabric), lawn, and batiste are finished from the same gray goods, lawn gray goods. They differ from one another in the way they are finished. The two opaque fabrics, lawn and batiste, do not receive the acid finish and, thus, remain opaque. Better quality fabrics are made of combed yarns. **Lawn** is often printed and is usually all cotton or cotton/polyester.

**Batiste** is the softest of the lightweight opaque fabrics. Batiste fabrics are made of cotton, wool, polyester, or a blend. **Tissue ginghams** and **chambray** are similar in weight but are yarn-dyed.

**China silk** is similar to batiste, except that it is made from slightly irregular fine-filament yarns. It is a soft fabric that was originally made of silk and used for women's suit linings and matching blouses. **Habutai** is slightly heavier than China silk. The most common weight is 10 momme (see Chapter 5). Both fabrics can be dyed or printed.

**Challis** (shal′ee) tends to be heavier than the fabrics discussed so far and, depending on fiber content and fashion, it may be a medium-weight fabric. Challis is usually made with spun carded yarns and may be slightly napped so that a few fiber ends are raised to the surface. A classic challis fabric is wool in a paisley print. It is soft and drapes well. Challis usually is printed and slightly napped and frequently is made from rayon.

**LOW-COUNT SHEER FABRICS** Low-count sheer fabrics are characterized by open spaces between the yarns, making them transparent. They are made of carded yarns of size 28s and 30s in the warp and 39s and 42s in the filling. Count ranges from 10 × 12 to 48 × 44. These fabrics are neither strong nor durable, are seldom printed, and differ in the way they are finished. They are functional fabrics that may be used for decorative and industrial purposes, or as shaping or support fabrics in apparel and furnishings. Included in this group are cheesecloth, crinoline, buckram, and bunting. (See the Glossary at the end of the book for more information about these fabrics.)

**MEDIUM-WEIGHT FABRICS** Medium-weight fabrics comprise the most widely used group of woven fabrics. These fabrics have medium-sized yarns and a medium count with carded or combed yarns. They may be finished in different ways or woven from dyed yarns. They may be called top-weight fabrics because they are frequently used for blouses and shirts. Medium-weight

**TABLE 12–3 ❖** Balanced plain-weave fabrics.

| FABRIC | RANGE IN COUNT | YARN SIZE Warp | Filling | CATEGORY |
|---|---|---|---|---|
| Lawn | 88 × 80 | 70s* | 100s* | Lightweight opaque |
| Organdy | Similar to lawn | Similar to lawn | | Lightweight sheer |
| Batiste | Similar to lawn | Similar to lawn | | Lightweight opaque |
| Print cloth, carded or combed (muslin, percale, plissé, calico, chintz) | 80 × 80 to 64 × 60 | 28s | 42s | Medium weight |
| Combed cotton | 96 × 80 | 40s | 50s | Medium weight |
| Gingham, cotton | 64 × 76 | Same as print cloth | | Medium weight |
| Carded | to 64 × 60 | | | |
| Combed | 88 × 84 to 84 × 76 | | | |
| Cotton suiting | 48 × 48 to 66 × 76 | 13s to 20s | | Heavyweight |

* The "s" after the number means that the yarn is a single yarn.

fabrics are also used to produce many furnishing items, such as wall and window-treatment fabrics, bed and table linens, and some upholstery fabrics. Fabric weight ranges from 4.0 to 6.0 oz/yd$^2$.

The fabrics in this group are converted from a gray goods cloth called **print cloth.** Yarns can be carded or combed depending on the count, quality, and cost desired for the finished fabric. Yarn size ranges from 28s to 42s. Count ranges from 64 × 60 to 80 × 80. Figure 17–1 shows the variety of ways these fabrics can be finished. Use Chapter 17 as a supplement in understanding some of the differences in fabrics due to finishing. For example, two fabrics converted from print cloth are plissé and embossed.

**Percale** is a smooth, slightly crisp, printed or plain-colored fabric made of combed yarns. In percale bed sheets, counts of 160, 180, 200, and 250 are available. Percale is called **calico** if it has a small, quaint, printed design; **chintz** if it has a printed design; and **cretonne** if it has a large-scale floral design. When a fabric is given a highly glazed calendar finish, it is called **polished cotton.** When chintz is glazed, it is called **glazed chintz.** Glazed chintz is made in solid colors as well as prints. These fabrics are often made with blends of cotton and polyester or rayon. They are used for shirts, dresses, blouses, pajamas, matching curtains and bedspreads, upholstery, slipcovers, draperies, and wall coverings.

Any plain-woven, balanced fabric of carded yarns ranging in weight from lawn to heavy bed sheeting may be called **muslin.** It is usually available in counts of 112, 128, or 140. Muslin is also a name for medium-weight fabric that is unbleached or white.

Napped fabrics may be either medium- or heavy-weight. **Flannelette** can be found as both balanced and unbalanced plain-weave fabrics that are lightly napped on one side. It is available in several weights ranging from 4.0 to 5.7 oz/yd$^2$. It is used for sheets, blankets, and sleepwear. **Outing flannel** is heavier and stiffer than flannelette; it may be napped on one or both sides. It is used for shirts, dresses, lightweight jackets, and jacket linings. Some outing flannels are made with a twill weave. Both fabrics may be solid color, yarn dyed, or printed.

**Ginghams** are yarn-dyed fabrics in checks, plaids, or solids (Figure 12–14). *Chambrays* are yarn dyed. They may look solid color but have white filling and colored-warp yarns, or they may have darker yarns in the filling *(iridescent chambray),* or they may have stripes. Some chambray is unbalanced with high warp count and a filling rib similar to that of broadcloth and poplin.

Ginghams and chambrays are usually made of cotton or cotton blends. Better-quality fabrics are made with combed yarns. When they are made of another fiber, the fiber content is included in the name; for example, silk gingham. When filament yarns are used, these fabrics are given a crisp finish and called **taffetas.** In wool, similar fabrics are called wool checks, plaids, and shepherd's checks. **Madras,** or **Indian madras,** is frequently all

**FIGURE 12–14** ❖ Gingham fabrics: yarn-dyed checks and plaids.

cotton, often of a lower count than gingham. True madras is made with natural vegetable dyes that bleed when wet.

Stripes, plaids, and checks present problems that do not occur in solid-colored fabrics. Ginghams may have a design with an up and down, a right and left, or both. More time is needed to cut out an item in plaid than in plain material, more attention must be given to the choice of design, and more care must be taken during production to match seams.

Imitations of yarn dyed fabrics are made by printing. There is, however, a technical face (front or right side) and a technical back (back or wrong side) to the print, whereas true yarn-dyed fabrics are the same on both sides. Lengthwise printed stripes are usually on grain, but the crosswise stripes may be off-grain. These printed fabrics may be percale if the fabric was converted from a print cloth.

**Pongee** is a filament-yarn, medium-weight fabric. It has a fine warp of regular yarns with filling yarns that are irregular in size. It was originally silk with slub-filling yarns, but is now made of a variety of fibers. **Honan** is similar to pongee, but it is characterized by slub yarns in both the warp and the filling.

Plain-weave fabrics with crepe yarns in either warp or filling or in both warp and filling are often referred to as **true crepe.** These fabrics can be any weight, but are most often found in medium-weight or heavyweight fabrics. Because of their interesting texture and lively drape, these fabrics are frequently used by designers for apparel and furnishings. In apparel, true crepes are found in both weights and are most commonly used in suits, coats, and dresses. In furnishings, true crepes are common in upholstery, draperies, and wall coverings. True crepes are also found in table linens but are not as common in that use.

**HEAVYWEIGHT FABRICS** Heavyweight fabrics are also known as **suiting-weight** or **bottom-weight fabrics.** These fabrics weigh more than 6.0 oz/yd$^2$ and are heavy enough to tailor and drape well. Their filling yarns are usually larger than the warp yarns and have slightly lower twist. Because of their weight, these fabrics are more durable and more resistant to wrinkling than sheer or medium-weight fabrics, but they tend to ravel more because of the lower count.

**Weaver's cloth** is a more general name for cotton suiting, which is converted from a gray goods called *coarse sheeting.* Cotton suiting is plain in color or printed.

*Homespun* is a name used for furnishing fabrics with slightly irregular yarns, a lower count, and a handwoven look.

**Crash** is made with yarns that have thick-and-thin areas, giving it an uneven nubby look. It is often linen or a manufactured fiber or fiber blend that looks like linen. The irregular surface shows wrinkles less than a plain surface does.

*Butcher rayon* or butcher cloth is a crashlike fabric of 100 percent rayon or rayon/polyester. In heavier weights it looks like linen suiting.

**Burlap** or hessian has a much lower count than crash, and is used in furnishings, such as wall coverings, rather than apparel. It has characteristic coarse thick-and-thin yarns and is made of jute.

**Osnaburg** is a variable-weight fabric most often found in suiting weight. Like muslin, it may be unbleached or bleached. In general it is a lower-quality fabric than muslin, with a lower count and bits of leaf and bark from the cotton plant giving it a characteristic spotted appearance. It is a utility fabric that occasionally becomes fashionable. It is seen as a drapery-lining or upholstery support fabric. It is also frequently used as a substrate for tufted upholstery fabrics. When printed or dyed, it may be used in upholstery and drapery fabrics.

**Flannel** is a plain-weave suiting fabric that is napped. Made in woolen yarns of several fiber types, it is used for women's suits, slacks, skirts, and jackets. It may have a plain or twill weave.

**Tweed** is made of any fiber or mixture of fibers and is always characterized by novelty yarns with nubs of different colors. Harris tweed is handwoven in the Outer Hebrides Islands, and Donegal tweed is handwoven in Donegal County, Ireland. True Harris tweeds will carry a certified registered trademark.

*Tropical worsted suitings* are made from long-fiber worsted yarns and typically range in weight from 6 to

10 oz/yd$^2$. They are wool-like fabrics made for men's suits, intended for use in tropical countries or for summer use in temperate climates. They frequently are made of fiber blends.

Heavyweight balanced plain-weave fabrics are often used in furnishings. They are used in wall coverings, upholstery, and draperies. Often producers give these fabrics a company name.

## Unbalanced Plain Weave

In an **unbalanced plain weave,** there are significantly more yarns in one direction than the other. Increasing the number of warp yarns in a plain-woven fabric until the count is about twice that of the filling yarns creates a crosswise ridge called a filling **rib.** In such a fabric, the warp yarns completely cover the filling yarns. This type of fabric may be called a *warp-faced* fabric because the warp yarns form the surface of the fabric. Warp faced fabrics are more durable than filling faced fabrics. Ribs in fabric can be produced by increasing the reed pressure (pushing more yarns into the same area) or by changing yarn size. Small ridges are formed when the warp and filling yarns are the same size; larger ridges are formed where the filling yarns are larger than the warp. Yarn sizes are given in Table 12–4.

When the yarns are of different colors, the color showing on the surface will be that of the yarn with the greater count. Figure 12–15 shows an unbalanced plain-weave fabric and the checkerboard diagram.

Identification of an unbalanced fabric may not be easy. To assist in identification, ravel adjacent sides until a yarn fringe can be seen. Observe the difference in den-

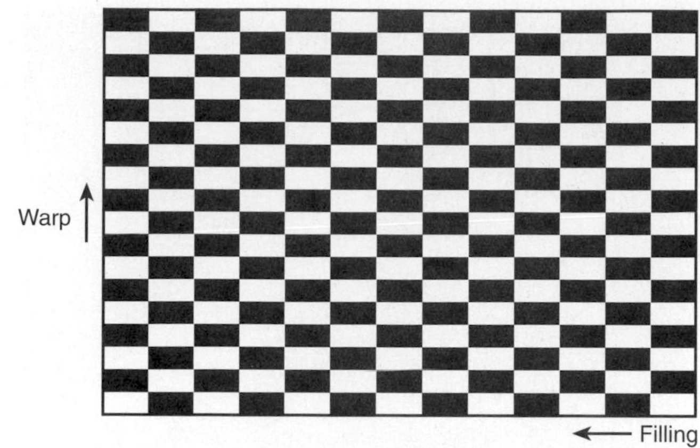


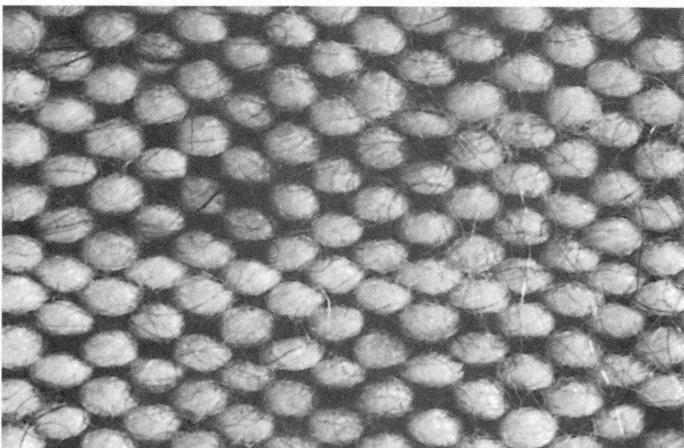

**FIGURE 12–15** ❖ Unbalanced (1:2) plain-weave fabric (top diagram and bottom). Compare this to the balanced plain-weave fabric in Figure 12–13 woven with the same size yarns.

**TABLE 12–4** ❖ Unbalanced plain-weave fabrics.

| FABRIC | COUNT* | YARN SIZE Warp | YARN SIZE Filling | CATEGORY |
|---|---|---|---|---|
| **Staple Fiber** | | - | | |
| Combed broadcloth | 144 × 76 | 100/2 | 100/2 | Medium weight |
| Carded broadcloth | 100 × 60 | 40s | 40s | Medium weight |
| **Filament Fiber** | | | | |
| Rayon taffeta | 60 × 15 | 10/2 | 3s | Medium weight |
| Acetate taffeta | 140 × 64 | 75 denier | 150 denier | Medium weight |
| Faille | 200 × 64 | 75 denier | 200 denier | Medium weight |
| Rep | 88 × 31 | 30/2 | 5s | Heavyweight |
| Bengaline | 92 × 40 | 150 denier | 15s spun | Heavyweight |
| Shantung | 140 × 44 | 150 denier | 30/2 | Heavyweight |

* Counts may be high for polyester/cotton and durable-press fabrics.

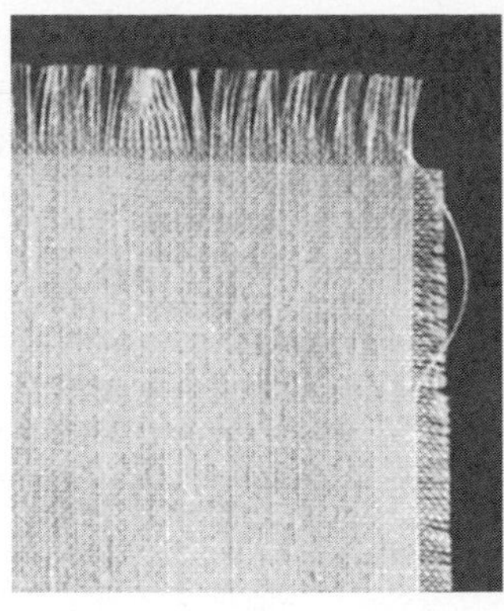

**FIGURE 12–16** ❖ Compare the count and balance of the print cloth (percale) (left) and broadcloth (right).

sity of warp and filling yarns. Broadcloth has a very thick fringe of warp yarns (144 × 76). Percale (78 × 78) has a fringe of equal density for both warp and filling (see Figure 12–16).

Slippage is a problem in ribbed fabrics made with filament yarns, especially those of lower quality and lower count (see Figure 12–17). Slippage occurs when one set of yarns is pushed to one side, exposing the yarns that are normally covered. It usually happens at points of wear and tension, such as at seams, but with low-count fabrics, one can create slippage with a thumbnail.

Wear occurs on the surface of the ribs. The warp yarns wear out first and splits occur in the fabric. Filling yarns, which are covered by the warp, are protected from wear.

Ribbed fabrics with fine ribs are softer and more drapeable than comparable balanced fabrics—broadcloth is softer than percale. Fabrics with large ribs have more body and are stiffer. A few sheer rib fabrics are used in glass curtains.

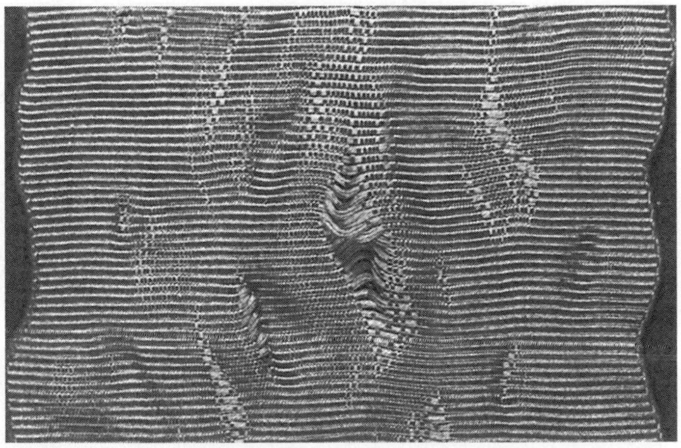

**FIGURE 12–17** ❖ Slippage of yarns in a ribbed fabric.

**LIGHTWEIGHT RIBBED FABRICS** **Crepe de chine,** traditionally a filling crepe-silk fabric, drapes beautifully. It has a dry and very pleasant hand and medium luster. The fabric is more commonly found now as a filament polyester for blouses and fine linings with filament warp and fine crepe-twist filling. There are many more warp yarns per inch than filling yarns, but it does not have a noticeable rib. Crepe de chine can be dyed or printed.

**MEDIUM-WEIGHT RIBBED FABRICS** Medium weight (4.0 to 6.0 oz/yd$^2$) is the largest group of ribbed fabrics. **Broadcloth** has the finest rib of any of the staple-fiber fabrics because the warp and filling yarns are the same in size. Better quality fabrics are made of long-staple combed cotton, plied yarns and may be mercerized for luster. Slub broadcloth is made with a yarn that contains slubs at regular intervals. Silk broadcloth has filament warp and staple filling.

*Taffeta* is a fine-rib, filament-yarn fabric with crispness and body. Note that the term *taffeta* is used to describe both balanced and unbalanced plain-weave fabrics. Iridescent taffeta has warp and filling yarns of different colors. *Moiré taffeta* has a water-marked, embossed design (Figure 12–18).

**Shantung** has an irregular rib surface produced by long, irregular areas in filling yarns. It may be made in medium or suiting weight and of various fiber types.

**FIGURE 12–18** ❖ Moiré taffeta.

**HEAVYWEIGHT RIBBED FABRICS** The fabrics in this grouping usually weigh more than 6.0 oz/yd$^2$. **Poplin** is similar to broadcloth, but the ribs are heavier and more pronounced because of larger filling yarns. It is usually suiting weight. Polyester/cotton blends are widely used.

**Faille** (pronounced file) has a fine, subtle rib and is made of filament-warp and spun filling yarns. **Rep** or repp is a heavy, coarse fabric with a pronounced rib effect. **Bengaline** is similar to faille but with a slightly more pronounced rib and is often made with rayon warp and cotton filling. It is sometimes woven with two warps at a time to emphasize the rib. **Ottoman** has alternating large-and-small ribs that are adjacent to each other, created by using filling yarns of different sizes or using different numbers of filling yarns in adjacent ribs. **Grosgrain** (pronounced grow´-grane), usually produced in ribbon width, also has a rounded rib.

**Bedford cord** is seen occasionally in apparel fabrics, but more commonly in furnishing fabrics like bedspreads. It has spun warp yarns that are larger than the filling yarns. Other ways of producing bedford cord will be discussed in Chapter 13.

## Basket Weave

**Basket weaves** are made with two or more adjacent warps controlled by the same harness, and with two or more fillings placed in the same shed. The interlacing pattern is similar to a plain weave, but two or more yarns follow the same parallel path. A full basket would have the basket feature used in both warp and filling: both warp and filling are grouped. A half basket would have the basket feature in only warp or filling; only one yarn set would be grouped. (See Figure 12–19.) The most common basket weaves are 2 × 2 or 4 × 4, but variations of the basket weave include 2 × 1 and 2 × 3. Basket-weave fabrics have greater flexibility and more wrinkle resistance because there are few interlacings per square inch. The fabrics have a flatter appearance than a comparable regular plain-weave fabric would have. However, long floats snag easily.

**Dimity** is a sheer unbalanced fabric used for apparel and window treatments. It has heavy-warp cords at intervals across the fabric. The cords may be formed by yarns larger than those used elsewhere in the fabric, or by grouping yarns together in that area. Either tech-

4 × 4 Full basket

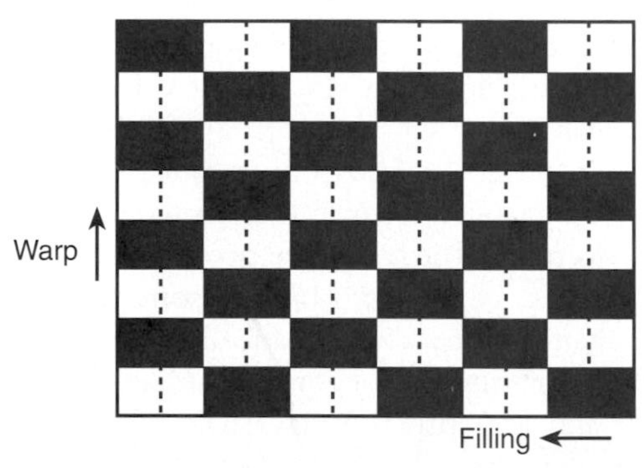


2 × 1 Half basket

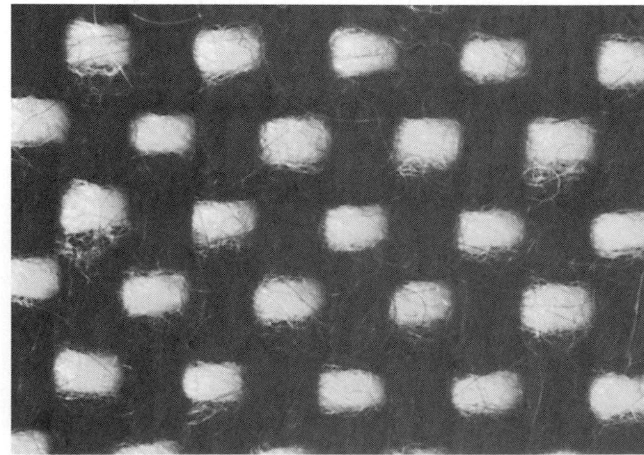

**FIGURE 12–19** ❖ Basket weaves: 4 × 4 full basket (left), 2 × 1 half basket (right).

nique produces the unique narrow band or stripe indicative of dimity. Dimity is white or printed.

**Oxford** is usually a 2 × 1 or 3 × 2 basket weave. It is most common as a 2 × 1 half basket weave. It may have a yarn-dyed warp and white filling and be called *oxford chambray.* Oxford looks like a balanced fabric because the warp yarns are finer and have higher twist than the filling. Because of soft yarns and loose weave, yarn slippage is likely to occur at seams and within the fabric itself. Oxford fabrics are medium weight, soft, porous, and lustrous.

Most basket weaves are heavyweight fabrics. Common ones include sailcloth, duck, or canvas. Sailcloth is lighter weight than duck or canvas. Canvas is the heaviest of the three. Sailcloth is used in slacks, skirts, summer-weight suits, and furnishings. Furnishings and industrial variations of these fabrics come in many different weights and range from soft to stiff in drape. They are usually 2 × 1 or 3 × 2 basket weaves that are used for slipcovers, boat covers, shoe fabrics, and house and store awnings.

**Hopsacking** is a coarse open basket-weave fabric of spun yarns. It is primarily used for coats, suits, upholstery, and wallcoverings.

**Monk's cloth,** friar's cloth, druid's cloth, and mission cloth are some of the oldest full-basket-weave fabrics. They are usually brownish white or oatmeal color. These fabrics are usually found in square counts: 2 × 2, 3 × 3, 4 × 4, or 6 × 6. They are used primarily in furnishings.

# Twill Weave

In a **twill weave,** each warp or filling yarn floats across two or more filling or warp yarns with a progression of interlacings by one to the right or left, forming a distinct diagonal line, or **wale.** A **float** is the portion of a yarn that crosses over two or more yarns from the opposite direction. Twill weaves require three or more harnesses, depending on the complexity of the weave. Twill weave is the second basic weave that can be made on the simple loom. Although it is possible to create fairly elaborate patterns using a twill weave, this chapter will focus only on basic fabrics and patterns.

Twill weave is often designated as a fraction—such as $\frac{2}{1}$—in which the numerator indicates the number of harnesses that are raised, in this example 2, and the denominator indicates the number of harnesses that are lowered when a filling yarn is inserted, in this example 1. The fraction $\frac{2}{1}$ would be read as "two up, one down." The minimum number of harnesses needed to produce a twill can be determined by totaling the numbers in the fraction. For the example described, the number of harnesses is 3.

In order to weave any twill, the loom must be properly warped. To weave a $\frac{2}{1}$ twill, the threading and shedding processes described here must be followed. Any change in this process will produce something other than a $\frac{2}{1}$ twill. The first warp yarn is threaded through a heddle in the first harness, the second warp yarn through a heddle in the second harness, and the third warp yarn through a heddle in the third harness. This process repeats until the entire set of warp yarns are threaded through the three harnesses. In weaving the first filling yarn, the first two harnesses are raised and the third harness is lowered. For the second filling yarn, the shed changes so that harnesses 2 and 3 are raised, harness 1 is lowered, and the yarn is inserted. The third filling yarn is inserted into a shed created by raising harnesses 1 and 3 and lowering harness 2. This pattern is repeated until the entire fabric has been woven. Thus, by following the steps of threading and shedding, the $\frac{2}{1}$ twill has been made. A $\frac{2}{1}$ twill is shown in Figure 12–20. The distance between the arrows demonstrates the length of the float. The floats on the surface of the technical face are warp yarns, making it a warp surface; it is classified as a warp-faced twill.

## Characteristics of Twill Weave

Twill fabrics have a technical face and a technical back. The technical face is the side of the fabric with the most pronounced wale. It is usually more durable, more attractive, and most often used as the fashion side of the fabric. The face usually is the side visible on the loom during weaving. If there are warp floats on the technical face, there will be filling floats on the technical back. If the twill wale goes up to the right on one side, it will go up to the left on the other side. Twill fabrics have no up and down as they are woven. Check this fact by turning a fabric end to end and then examining the direction of the twill wale.

Sheer fabrics are seldom made with a twill weave. Because a twill surface has interesting texture and design, printed twills are much less common than printed plain weaves. When twills are printed, they are more likely to be lightweight fabrics. Soil shows less on the uneven surface of twills than it does on smooth surfaces such as plain weaves. Thus, twills are often used for sturdy work clothing or durable upholstery where soils and stains are less noticeable.

Fewer interlacings permit the yarns to move more freely and give the fabric more softness, pliability, and wrinkle recovery than a comparable plain-weave fabric. When there are fewer interlacings, yarns can be packed

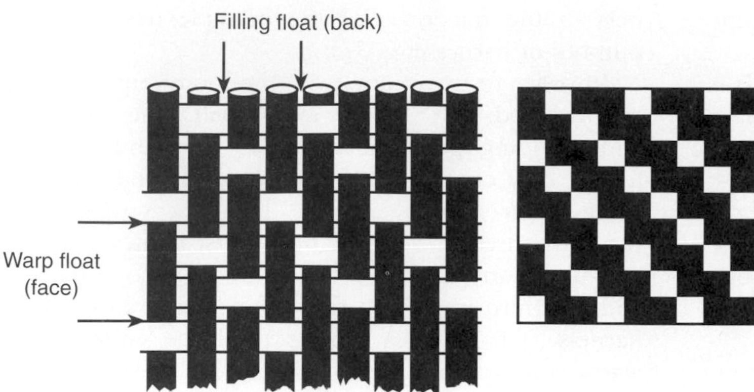


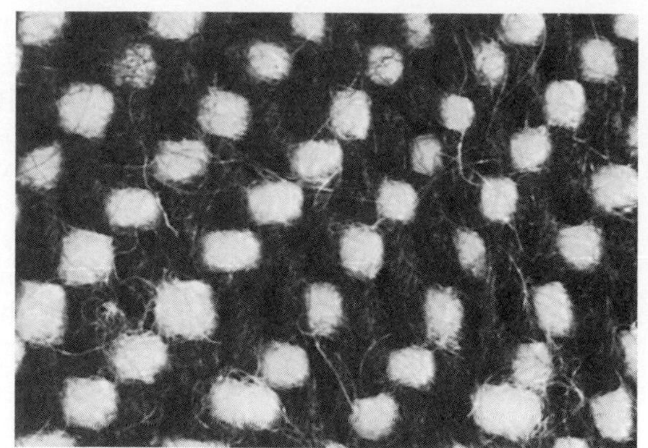

**FIGURE 12–20** ❖ A $\frac{2}{1}$ twill weave.

closer together to produce a higher-count fabric (Figure 12–21). If a plain-weave fabric and a twill-weave fabric have the same kind and number of yarns, the plain-weave fabric would be stronger because it has more interlacings. In twills with higher counts, the fabric is more durable and air or water resistant.

The prominence of a twill wale may be increased by the use of long floats, combed or worsted yarns, plied yarns, hard-twist yarns, twist yarns opposite to the direction of the twill line, and high counts. Fabrics with prominent wales, such as gabardine, may become shiny because of wale flattening caused by wear.

The direction of the twill wale traditionally goes from lower left to upper right in wool and wool-like fabrics—right-hand twills—and from lower right to upper left in cotton or cottonlike fabrics—left-hand twills. This fact is important only in determining the face or back of a twill fabric. In some fabrics that have a very prominent wale or are made with white and colored yarns, design implications relative to the wale should be considered. The distinction between direction of the wale by fiber type has become less significant over the past 20 or so years.

The angle of the wale depends on the balance of the cloth or the warp to filling ratio. The twill line may be **steep, regular,** or reclining. The greater the difference between the number of warp and filling yarns, the steeper the twill line. Steep-twill fabrics have a high warp count and therefore are stronger in the warp direction. The importance of the angle is that it serves as a guide in determining the strength and name of a fabric. Figure 12–21 shows how the twill line changes in steepness when the warp yarn density increases and the filling yarn density remains the same. Note that all three dia-

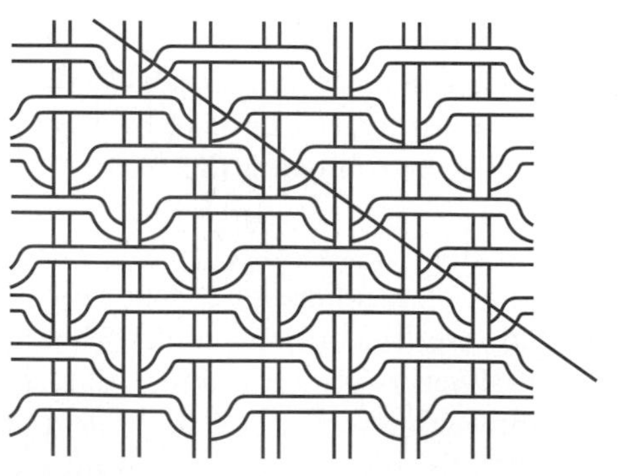

Reclining twill
35° angle
Warp yarns per inch = 6
Filling yarns per inch = 8

Regular twill
45° angle
Warp yarns per inch = 7
Filling yarns per inch = 8

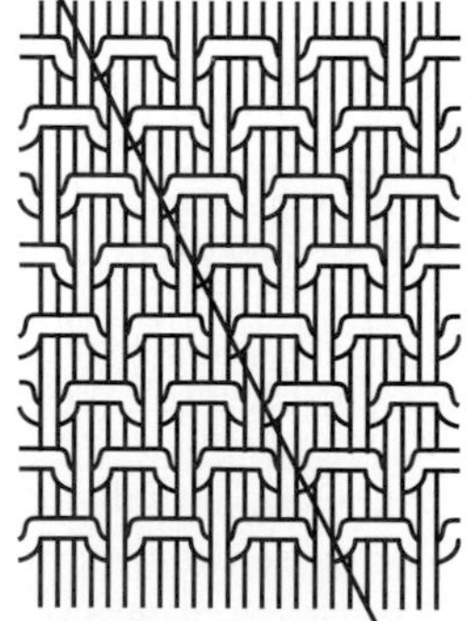

Steep twill
63° angle
Warp yarns per inch = 12
Filling yarns per inch = 8

**FIGURE 12–21** ❖ Twill angle depends on ratio of warp to filling. These diagrams show left-handed twills.

grams are for a $\frac{2}{1}$ left-handed twill. The only change is in the number of warp yarns, yet the wale angle changes drastically.

**Filling-faced twills** are not discussed in this text because they are seldom used. They are usually reclining twills and are less durable than the others.

## Even-Sided Twills

**Even-sided twills** have an equal percentage of warp and filling yarn exposed on both sides of the fabric. They are sometimes called *reversible twills* because they look alike on both sides, although the direction of the twill line differs. Better-quality filling yarns must be used in these fabrics than in the warp-faced twills because both sets of yarn are exposed to wear. They are most often $\frac{2}{2}$ twills and have the best balance of all the twill weaves (see Table 12–5).

**Foulard** or **surah** is a printed filament-twill fabric of $\frac{2}{2}$ construction that is used in silklike dresses, linings, ties, and scarves. It is soft, smooth, and lightweight. Sometimes it is piece dyed instead of printed.

**Serge** is a $\frac{2}{2}$ twill with a rather subdued wale and a clear finish (not napped or brushed). Cotton serge of fine yarn and high count may have a water-repellent finish and is used for jackets, snowsuits, and raincoats. Heavy-yarn cotton serge is used for work pants. Wool serge is used in apparel. Serge is a heavier weight fabric, often 10 or more oz/yd$^2$.

**Twill flannel** is a $\frac{2}{2}$ or $\frac{2}{1}$ twill. The filling yarns are larger low-twist yarns, specially made for napping. They may be either woolen or worsted. Worsted flannels have less nap, take and hold a sharp crease better, and are less apt to show wear or get baggy, as compared with woolen flannels. These are found in both apparel and furnishings, most often in upholstery.

*Sharkskin* is a $\frac{2}{2}$ twill with a sleek appearance. It has a small-step pattern because yarns in both the warp and the filling alternate one white yarn with one colored yarn. Sharkskin is used primarily for slacks and suits.

**Herringbone** fabrics have the twill line reversed at regular intervals to give a design that resembles the backbone of a fish, hence the name herringbone (Figure 12–22). Two different color yarns may be used to accentuate the pattern. Herringbone patterns can be very subtle or very pronounced. Herringbone is used in both apparel and furnishings.

Another woven-in pattern is **houndstooth.** This $\frac{2}{2}$ twill fabric is basically a check but is unique in appearance because it is pointed—rather like an eight-point star (see Figure 17–15). Two contrasting colors of yarn in the warp and filling are used in groups of four to create the distinctive pattern. Houndstooth fabrics also are used in apparel and furnishings.

## Warp-Faced Twills

**Warp-faced twills** have a predominance of warp yarns on the face of the fabric. Since warp yarns are made with higher twist, these fabrics are stronger and more resistant to abrasion and pilling. Table 12–6 summarizes warp-faced twills.

**Lining twill** is a medium-weight $\frac{2}{1}$ fabric made from filament yarns and usually piece dyed or printed in a small pattern. It is similar to foulard in appearance and use.

**Denim** is a yarn-dyed cotton twill made in several weights, ranging from 6 oz/yd$^2$ to 14 or more oz/yd$^2$ in a $\frac{2}{1}$ or $\frac{3}{1}$ interlacing pattern. Its use in casual wear has

**TABLE 12–5** ❖ Even-sided twills.

| FABRIC | COUNT | RANGE IN YARN SIZE | |
|---|---|---|---|
| | | Warp | Filling |
| Serge | 48 × 34 to 62 × 58 | Varies with fiber content | |
| Flannel | 56 × 30 to 86 × 52 | Varies with fiber content | |

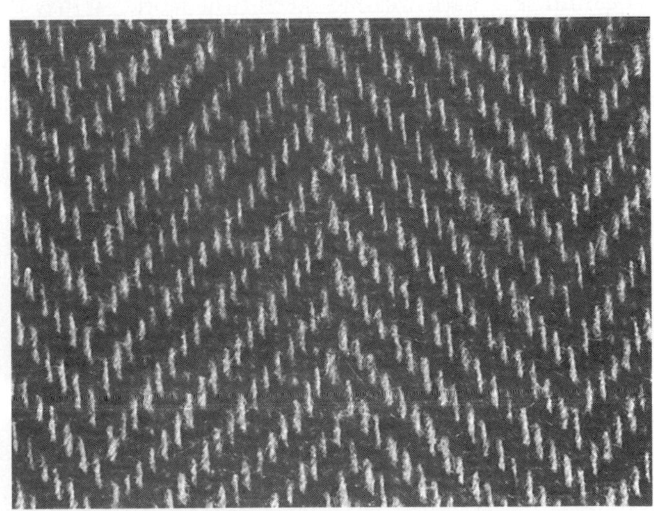

**FIGURE 12–22** ❖ Herringbone.

**TABLE 12–6** ❖ Warp-faced twills.

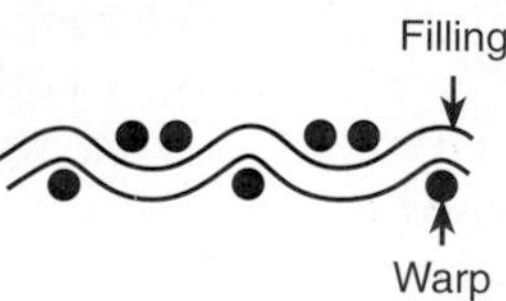


| FABRIC | COUNT | RANGE IN YARN SIZE Warp | Filling |
|---|---|---|---|
| Jean | 84 × 56 to 100 × 64 | 21s to 24s | 24s to 30s |
| Denim | 60 × 36 to 72 × 44 | 7s to 16s | 8s to 23s |
| Gabardine | 110 × 76 to 130 × 80 | 15s to 39/2 | 15s to 26s |

been popular for decades, and the nature of denim has also changed. It may be napped, printed, made with stretch yarns, or otherwise modified for a current fashion look.

*Jean* is a piece-dyed or printed medium-weight twill used for children's playclothes, draperies, slipcovers, and work shirts. Jean is not heavy enough for work pants.

**Drill** is a strong, medium- to heavyweight twill fabric. It is a $\frac{2}{1}$ or $\frac{3}{1}$ twill that is piece dyed. It is usually seen in work clothing and industrial fabrics.

*Covert* is a twill fabric with a mottled appearance resulting from two colors of fibers being used in the yarns or from two colors of plies twisted together to form the yarns. It is usually a $\frac{2}{1}$ heavyweight twill made of hard-twist worsted yarns.

**Chino** is a hard-wearing steep-twill fabric. It has a slight sheen and is frequently made from combed yarns. Usually combed two-ply yarns are used in both the warp and the filling directions. Chino is typically a summer-weight military uniform fabric.

**Gabardine** is a warp-faced steep or regular twill with a very prominent, distinct wale that is closely set together and raised. It always has many more warp than filling. It can be made of carded or combed single or ply yarns. The long-wearing fabric may be heather, striped, plaid, or solid color.

*Cavalry twill* also has a pronounced steep-twill line. Its unique characteristic is that it has a double-twill line; that is, two diagonal lines that are very close together separated by a little space from the next pair of diagonal lines.

Fancy twill interlacings are used to create more interesting textures and patterns in the fabric for uses in upholstery, window treatment fabrics, wall coverings, and apparel. These twills may be altered so that the wale is not continuous, such as broken twills, or so that fairly elaborate pronounced wales are created within the fabric (see Figures 12–23 and 12–24).

❖

## SATIN WEAVE

In a **satin weave,** each warp yarn floats over four filling yarns ($\frac{4}{1}$) and interlaces with the fifth filling yarn, with a progression of interlacings by two to the right or the left (Figure 12–25); or each filling yarn floats over four warps and interlaces with the fifth warp ($\frac{1}{4}$) with a progression of interlacings by two to the right or left (Figure 12–26). In certain fabrics each yarn floats across seven yarns and interlaces with the eighth yarn. Satin weave is the third basic weave that can be made on the simple loom; however, this weave requires at least five harnesses to achieve the interlacing pattern. Thus, basic four-harness looms cannot be used to produce a satin

**FIGURE 12–23** ❖ Examples of broken twill fabrics.

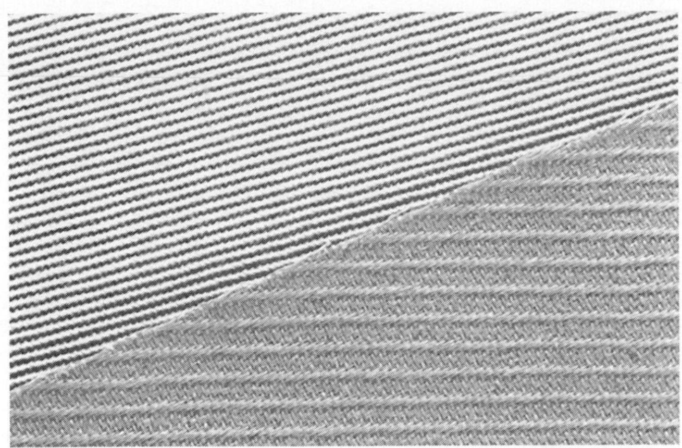

**FIGURE 12–24** ❖ Examples of twill fabrics with pronounced wales.

weave. Basic fabrics made with this weave are **satin** and **sateen.**

Satin-weave fabrics are characterized by luster due to the long floats that cover the surface. Note in Figure 12–25 the checkerboard designs show few interlacings;

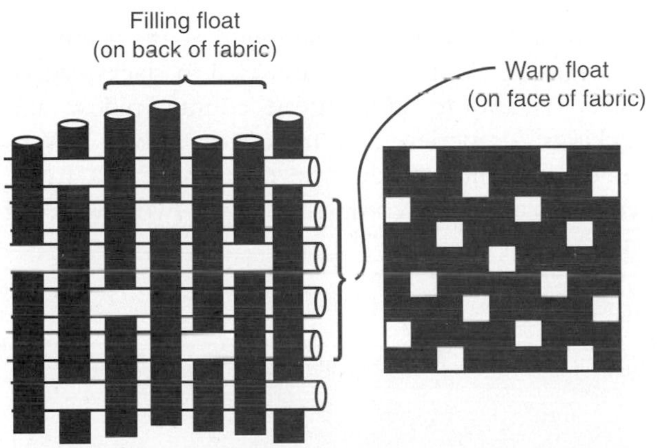


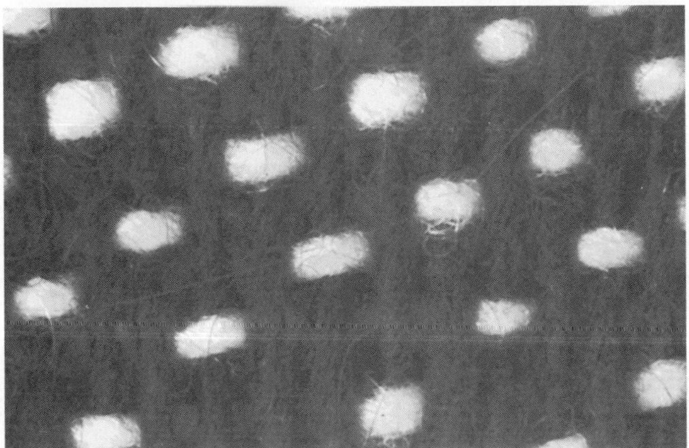

**FIGURE 12–25** ❖ Warp-faced satin weave: $\frac{4}{1}$ yarn arrangement.

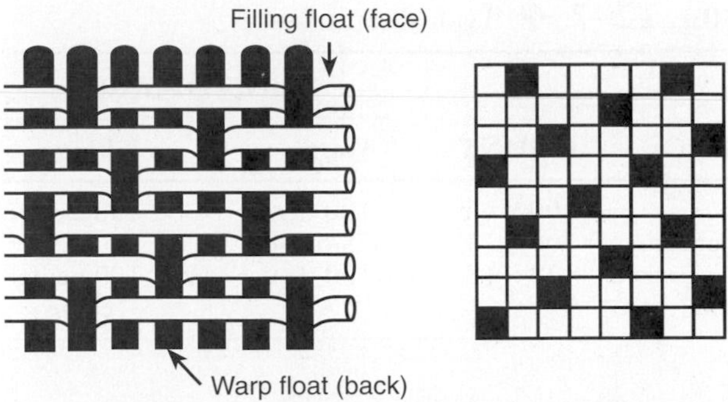


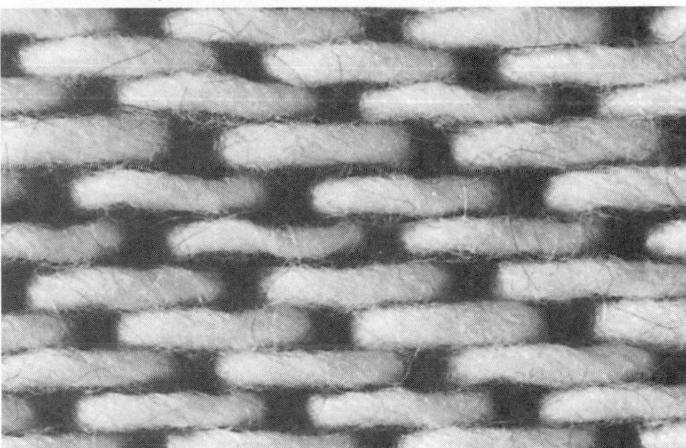

**FIGURE 12–26** ❖ Filling-faced satin weave: $\frac{4}{1}$ yarn arrangement.

the yarns can be packed close together to produce a very high-count fabric. Also note that no two interlacings are adjacent to each other. However, unless examined carefully, satin weaves may resemble twill weaves on the back. This is especially common when the count is high.

When warp yarns cover the surface, the fabric is a warp-faced fabric and the warp count is high. When filling floats cover the surface, the fabric is a filling-faced fabric and the filling count is high. These fabrics are unbalanced, but the high count compensates for the lack of balance.

All these fabrics have a face and back side with a significantly different appearance for each side. A high count gives them strength, durability, body, firmness, and wind repellency. Fewer interlacings give pliability and resistance to wrinkling but may permit yarn slippage and raveling.

## Satin Fabrics

Satin fabrics are usually made of bright filament yarns with very low twist. Satin is almost always warp faced; warp floats cover the surface. Because of the bright fibers, low twist, and long floats, satin is one of the most lustrous fabrics made. It is made in many weights (see

**TABLE 12–7** ❖ Typical satin fabrics.

| FABRIC | COUNT | KIND OF YARN | |
|---|---|---|---|
| | | Warp | Filling |
| Satin | 200 × 65 | 100 denier | 100 denier |
| Slipper satin | 300 × 74 | 75 denier | 300 denier |
| Crepe-backed satin | 128 × 68 | 100 denier | 100 denier crepe |

**TABLE 12–8** ❖ Typical sateen fabrics.

| FABRIC | COUNT | KIND OF YARN | |
|---|---|---|---|
| | | Warp | Filling |
| Filling sateen | 60 × 104 carded | 32s | 38s |
| | 84 × 136 carded | 40s | 50s |
| | 96 × 108 combed | 40s | 60s |
| Warp sateen | 84 × 64 carded | 12s | 11s |
| | 160 × 96 carded | 52s | 44s |

Table 12–7) for use in dresses, linings, lingerie, draperies, drapery linings, and upholstery. It seldom has printed designs. It is especially good for linings because the high count makes it very durable and smooth. Satin makes a more pliable lining than taffeta and thus does not split as readily at hems. Quality is particularly important in linings. Low-count satins pull at the seams and rough up in use. Floats may shift in position and bubble or wrinkle.

In **crepe-back satin,** crepe yarns are used in the filling, and the low-twist warp floats give the smooth, satiny surface to the fabric. The crepe yarns give softness and drapeability. In antique satin, novelty filling yarns add visual interest to the fabric. Antique satin often is used with the technical back as the fashion side in furnishings, especially upholstery and window treatments.

## Sateen

Sateen is a lustrous fabric made of spun yarns. In order to achieve luster with staple fibers, medium-twist yarns form the float surface. Finishes are used to enhance the luster and durability. (See Chapter 17.)

**Filling sateen** is a smooth, lustrous cotton fabric used for draperies, drapery linings, and apparel. It is often made with carded yarns with a high filling count. Yarns are similar in size to those used in print cloth, but the filling yarns are larger in size than the warp yarns. Combed sateens are usually finished for added luster. (See Chapter 17.)

**Warp sateens** are cotton fabrics made with warp floats in a $\frac{4}{1}$ interlacing pattern. They may have a rounded wale effect that resembles a twill fabric. They are stronger and heavier than filling sateens because of the high warp count. They are less lustrous than filling sateen and used where durability is more important than luster. Warp sateens are used in slacks, skirts, bedsheets of 250 to 300 thread counts, pillow and bed tickings, draperies, and upholstery fabrics. Warp sateens are the most likely type of satin fabrics to be printed. Table 12–8 compares these two types of sateen.

# KEY TERMS

Fabric
Fabric quality
Fabric grading
Warp
Filling
Loom
Harness
Heddle
Shed
Shuttle
Reed
Dents
Shedding
Picking
Beating up
Take-up
Air-jet loom
Rapier loom
Water-jet loom
Projectile loom
Multiple-shed weaving
Circular loom
Triaxial
Interlacing
Floats
Grain
Off grain
Skew
Bow
Count
Balance
Selvage
Weight
Plain weave
Balanced plain weave
Ninon
Georgette
Chiffon
Voile
Organdy
Organza
Lawn
Batiste
Tissue gingham
Chambray
China silk
Habutai
Challis
Print cloth
Percale
Calico
Chintz
Cretonne
Polished cotton
Glazed chintz
Muslin
Flannelette
Outing flannel
Gingham
Taffeta
Madras
Pongee
Honan
True crepe

Suiting-weight fabrics
Bottom-weight fabrics
Weaver's cloth
Crash
Burlap
Osnaburg
Flannel
Tweed
Unbalanced plain weave
Rib
Crepe de chine
Broadcloth
Shantung
Poplin
Faille
Rep
Bengaline
Ottoman
Grosgrain
Bedford cord
Basket weave
Dimity
Oxford cloth
Hopsacking
Monk's cloth
Twill weave
Wale
Float
Steep twill
Regular twill
Filling-faced twill
Even-sided twill
Foulard
Surah
Serge
Twill flannel
Herringbone
Houndstooth
Warp-faced twill
Lining twill
Denim
Drill
Chino
Gabardine
Satin weave
Satin
Sateen
Crepe-back satin
Filling sateen
Warp sateen

# Questions

1. Describe how a loom produces a woven fabric.
2. Diagram the interlacing patterns for the three basic weaves. Use both the cross section diagram and the checkerboard.
3. What are the criteria to use in determining the name of a fabric?
4. Identify the similarities and differences between these paired groups of fabrics:
   gingham and plissé
   flannelette and challis
   organdy and georgette
   oxford cloth and monk's cloth
   herringbone and gabardine
   denim and chambray
   satin and sateen
5. Compare and contrast the characteristics of fabrics made from the three basic weaves.
6. Predict the performance of the following textile products:
   100 percent olefin tweed upholstery with large-flake filling yarns and fine-filament warp yarns
   50 percent cotton/50 percent polyester broadcloth shirt/blouse with combed yarns of similar size in both warp and filling
   100 percent acetate antique satin drapery
   100 percent nylon taffeta backpack with BCF yarns in the warp and filling
   100 percent rayon challis skirt and blouse
7. Describe four factors that influence fabric quality.

# Suggested Readings


Cahill, Neil, and Isaacs, McAllister (1991, January). "World Class Manufacturing Goal: No-Break Weaving." *Textile World,* pp. 60–63.

Dockery, Alfred (1994, January). "Weaving Automation and the Quality Factor." *America's Textiles International,* pp. 58, 60.

Emery, Irene (1980). *The Primary Structures of Fabrics.* Washington, D.C.: The Textile Museum.

Humphries, Mary (1996). *Fabric Glossary.* Upper Saddle River, NJ: Prentice Hall.

Krause, H. W., and Soliman, H. A. (July, 1990). "Do Higher Speeds Demand Better Yarns?" *Textile Month,* pp. 19–22.

Schwartz, Peter, Rhodes, Trevor, and Mohamed, Mansour (1982). *Fabric Forming Systems.* Park Ridge, NJ: Noyes Publications.

Suzuki, Hajime (February, 1990). "Automated Weaving: A Japanese Perspective." *Textile Month,* pp. 26–28.

Tortora, Phyllis G., and Merkel, Robert S. (1996). *Fairchild's Dictionary of Textiles,* 7th ed. New York: Fairchild Publications.

"Weave from Yarn to Fabric." (1994, Spring). *Textiles Magazine,* pp. 11–12.

Chapter 13

# Fancy Weaves and Fabrics

OBJECTIVES

- To understand the production of fancy woven fabrics.
- To identify the technique or process used to produce fancy woven fabrics.
- To integrate fabrication, yarn type, and fiber in predicting product performance.
- To relate technological advances in fabric production to market availability and cost.

Fancy fabrics appear uniquely different from basic fabrics. This difference in appearance is an inherent and permanent structural part of the fabric and cannot be removed without dismantling the fabric. Some fabrics may require additional treatment in order for these differences to be fully developed, as in the pile fabrics that require shearing or napping.

The characteristics that all these **fancy weaves** have in common are that the production process is more involved than for the basic weaves, fabric costs are higher, and the fabric tends to have a more specialized application. The techniques used to obtain these fabrics vary in complexity and influence the cost and serviceability of the fabric. Recognition of the technique used in manufacturing the fabric assists in selecting a serviceable fabric for the intended end use.

*Woven figures* are made by changing the interlacing pattern between the design area and the background. The interlacing pattern is controlled by the warp yarns' position during weaving. In a three-harness loom there are three possible arrangements of the warp yarns; in a four-harness loom there are as many as 12 different arrangements. As the number of harnesses increases, the number of possible different interlacings also increases. But there is a limit to the number of harnesses that can be used efficiently. Consider the number of interlacings needed to make a figure: If the figure is ¼ inch in length, in an 80 × 80 fabric, it may require 20 different interlacings; if the figure is ½ inch long on a nylon-satin background (320 × 140), it may require 70 different interlacings. Special looms, attachments, or controls are necessary to make these fabrics competitive in price with imitations achieved by prints or finishes.

This chapter will discuss options for patterned fabrics and other fancy flat fabrics. Openwork woven fabrics will be described next. Fabrics made with additional yarn sets to create fabric layers or pile fabrics also will be discussed. Narrow fabrics of any woven structure will be the final topic.

FIGURE 13–1 ❖ Pattern roll that controls warp shedding on a dobby loom. (COURTESY OF CROMPTON & KNOWLES CORP.)

❖

# DOBBY WEAVES

Small-figured designs, which require fewer than 25 different yarn arrangements to complete one repeat of the design, are made on a loom with a dobby attachment—usually referred to as a **dobby loom.** Two methods are used to create the pattern.

In the older method, the weave pattern is controlled by a plastic tape with punched holes (Figure 13–1). These tapes resemble the rolls for a player piano. The holes control the position of each warp yarn in forming a shed. The newer method of creating a simple geometric pattern in the fabric uses a computer to control the position of the warp yarns. This system is faster, compatible with several computer-aided design systems (CADs), and allows for easy and quick pattern changes in the fabric.

Many designs made on either type of dobby loom are small geometric figures. There are many dobby fabrics; a few readily available and identifiable ones are discussed here. Figure 13–2 illustrates several generic patterned fabrics found in apparel and furnishings.

**Bird's-eye** has a small diamond-shaped filling-float design with a dot in the center that resembles the eye of a bird. This design was originally used in white silk fabric for ecclesiastical vestments. At one time, a cotton version was widely used for kitchen and hand towels and

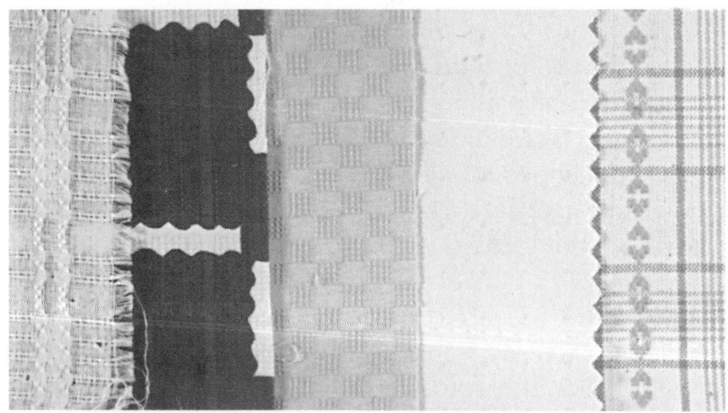

FIGURE 13–2 ❖ Dobby fabrics for use in apparel and furnishings.

**FIGURE 13–3** ❖ Bird's eye diaper (left) and huck (right).

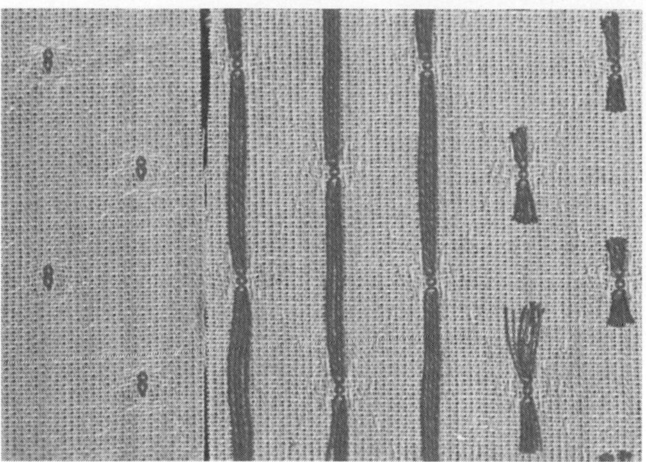

**FIGURE 13–4** ❖ Fabric made with extra warp yarns: face of fabric (left); back, before clipping (center) and after clipping (right).

diapers. **Huck** or **huck-a-back** has a pebbly surface made by filling floats. It is used primarily in roller, face, and medical-office towels. (See Figure 13–3.)

**Shirting madras** has small, satin-float designs on a ribbed or plain ground. **Waffle cloth** is made with a dobby attachment and has a three-dimensional honeycomb appearance. Waffle cloth is used for blankets, dish and bar cloths, upholstery, and apparel.

## Extra-Yarn Weaves

Yarns of different colors or types are woven into the fabric to create a pattern in an **extra yarn weave.** The figure portion has warp or filling floats. When not used in the figure, the extra yarns float across the back of the fabric and are usually cut away during finishing. In hand-woven fabrics the warp yarns are manipulated by hand and the extra yarns can be laid in where wanted by using small shuttles. But in power looms an automatic attachment must be used.

Extra-warp yarns are wound on a separate beam and threaded into separate heddles. The extra yarns interlace with the regular filling yarns to form a design and float behind the fabric until needed for the repeat. The floats are then clipped close to the design or clipped long enough to give an eyelash or fringed effect. Figure 13–4 shows a fabric before and after clipping.

Extra-filling yarns are inserted in several ways. **Clipped-dot designs** are made with low-twist filling yarns inserted by separate shuttles. The shedding is done so that the extra yarns interlace with some warp yarns and float across the back of other warp yarns. A box loom uses a wire along the edge to prevent the extra yarns from being woven into the selvage. Clipped-dot fabrics may have many yarn ends per dot. Figure 13–5 shows a clipped fabric, dotted swiss, before and after clipping.

Many of the fabrics that have small-dot designs are called dotted swiss. The dots may be structural designs: clipped-dot designs, as described above, or swivel-dot designs. **Swivel-dot designs** are made on a loom that has an attachment holding tiny shuttles. The fabric is woven so the shuttles and extra yarns are above the

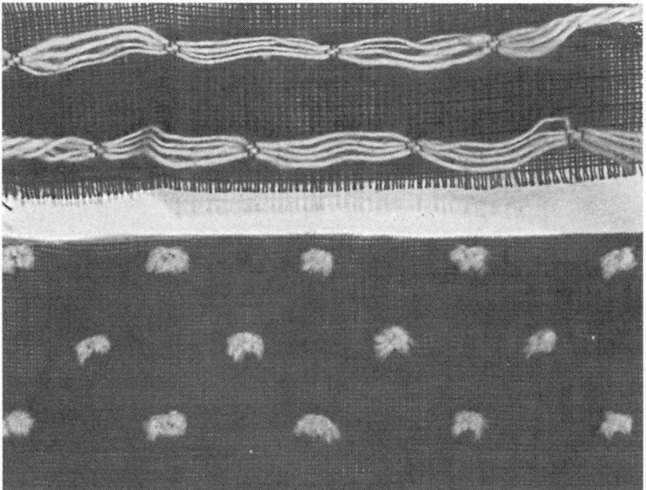

**FIGURE 13–5** ❖ Dotted swiss made with extra filling yarns: before (above) and after (below) clipping.

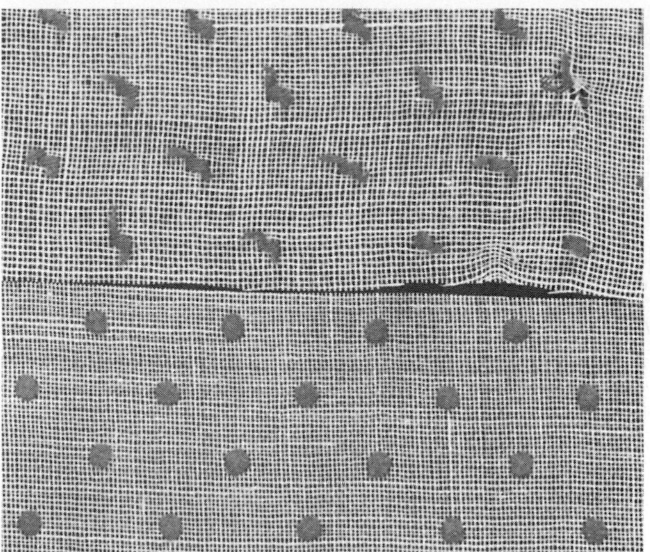

**FIGURE 13–6** ❖ Dotted swiss showing both sides of a swivel-dot fabric.

ground fabric. Each shuttle carrying the extra yarn wraps around the warp yarns in the ground fabric several times and then the yarn is carried along the surface to the next spot. The yarn is sheared off between the spots (Figure 13–6). Swivel-dot fabrics have only two yarn ends per dot. Swivel-dot fabrics are rarely seen in the United States, except as imported designer fabrics. Either side of swivel-dot fabrics, clipped-dot fabrics, and the larger clipped-spot fabrics may be the fashion side.

Dotted swiss may also be an applied design. (See Chapter 17 for more details.) A comparison of several different types of dotted swiss is an interesting exercise in determining the serviceability, quality, and cost of fabrics.

## Piqué Weaves

The word **piqué** comes from the French word meaning quilted because the raised effect in these fabrics is similar to that in quilts. Piqué weave produces a fabric with ridges, called wales or cords, that are held up by floats on the back. The wales vary in width. *Widewale piqué* (0.25 inch) is woven with 20 or more warp yarns in the face of the wale and then two warps form a valley in between. *Pinwale piqué* (0.05 inch) is a six-warp wale with two consecutive filling yarns floating across the back of the odd-numbered wales and then woven in the face of the even-numbered wales. The next two consecutive picks alternate with the first two by floating across the back of the even-numbered wales. Figure 13–7 shows a cross section diagram of a six-warp pinwale piqué.

Stuffer yarns are laid under the ridges in better-quality piqué fabrics to emphasize the roundness, and their presence or absence is one way of determining quality. The stuffer yarns are not interlaced with the surface yarns of the fabric and may be easily removed when analyzing a swatch of fabric. Piqué fabrics are woven on either a dobby or jacquard loom depending on the complexity of the design.

Cords or wales usually run in the lengthwise direction. In bird's-eye and bull's-eye piqués the cords run crosswise. Cord fabrics have a definite technical face and technical back. With abrasion, the floats on the wrong side usually wear out first. Figure 13–8 shows the face and back of a piqué fabric. Piqué fabrics are more resistant to wrinkling and have more body than flat fabrics. Better-quality piqué fabrics are made with long-staple combed yarns and have at least one stuffer yarn. Carded yarn piqués are made without the stuffer yarn and are sometimes printed.

Fabrics in this group are called piqué with the exception of bedford cord. *Bedford cord* is a heavy fabric with wide warp cords used for bedspreads, upholstery, window treatments, slacks, and uniforms. Its spun warp yarns are larger than the filling yarns. Cords located at intervals across the fabric are formed by extra filling yarns floating across the back, giving a raised effect. Stuffer yarns result in a more pronounced cord. The lengthwise cords may be the same size or alternately larger and smaller.

*Bird's-eye piqué* has a tiny design formed by the wavy arrangements of the cords and by the use of stuffer yarns. *Bull's-eye piqué* is made like bird's-eye but has a much larger scale design. Both fabrics have crosswise rather than lengthwise cords and are used for apparel and furnishings.

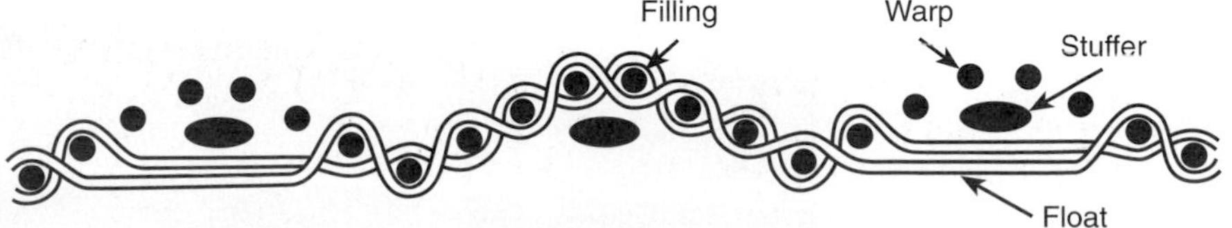


**FIGURE 13–7** ❖ Six-warp pinwale piqué.

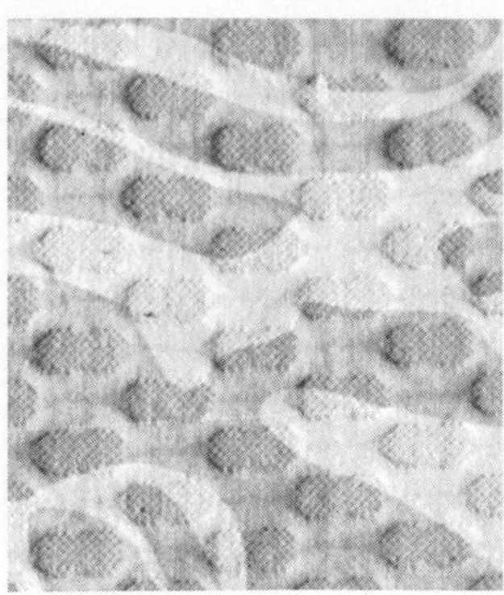

FIGURE 13–8 ❖ Piqué: face of fabric (left); back of fabric (right). Note stuffer yarns visible on the back and how the fabric flattens out at the bottom where the stuffer yarns have been removed.

FIGURE 13–9 ❖ Jacquard loom for weaving large-figured fabrics. (COURTESY OF CROMPTON & KNOWLES CORP.)

# JACQUARD WEAVES

Large-figured designs, which require more than 25 different arrangements of the warp yarns to complete one repeat design, are woven on the **jacquard loom.** Two types of looms are used to produce jacquard weaves. In the older type of loom (Figure 13–9), each warp is controlled independently by punched cards that are laced together in a continuous strip. The position of the warp yarns is controlled by rods attached to them. When the rods hit the cards, some go through the holes and raise the warp yarns; others remain down. In this manner the shed is formed for the passage of the filling yarn. Figure 13–10 shows a picture woven with fine silk yarns on a

FIGURE 13–10 ❖ Jacquard-woven picture.

**FIGURE 13–11** ❖ Electronic jacquard loom. (COURTESY OF BONAS USA, INC.)

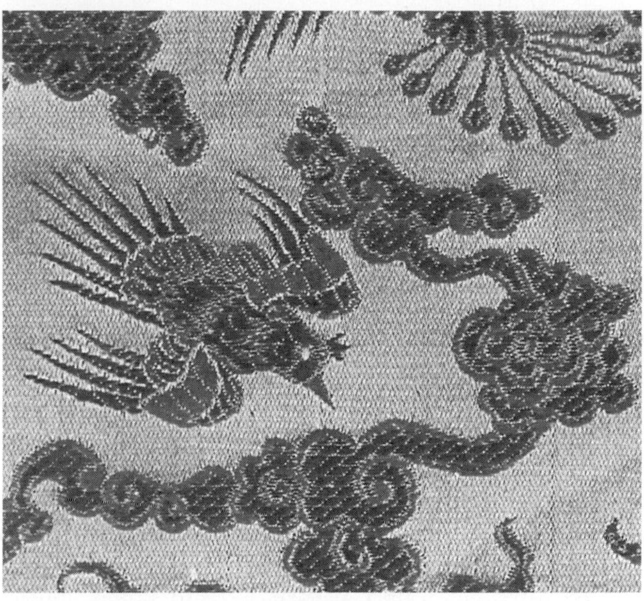

**FIGURE 13–13** ❖ Brocade.

jacquard loom. Notice that this pattern does not repeat from top to bottom or from side to side. The repeat would be another picture.

The newer method for producing these large patterns in the fabric uses a computer, often designed to be used with an air-jet loom and referred to as an electronic jacquard (Figure 13–11). The computer controls the position of the warp yarns and the insertion of different colored filling yarns. This system is fast with weaving speeds of 600 picks per minute, compatible with several computer-aided design systems (CADs), and allows for easy and quick pattern changes. Fabrics produced on the electronic jacquard looms include fancy mattress ticking, upholstery, and apparel.

Fabrics made on a jacquard loom include damask, brocade, tapestry, and a variety of other patterns (see Figure 13–12). **Damask** has satin floats on a satin background, with the floats in the design opposite those in the background. For example, if the pattern is warp-faced, the ground is filling-faced. Damask patterns are subtle but visible because of slight differences in light reflected from the two areas. Damask can be made from any fiber and in many different weights for apparel and furnishings. Damask is the flattest-looking of the jacquard fabrics and is often finished to maintain that flat look. Quality and durability are dependent on count. Low-count damask is not durable because the long floats rough up, snag, and shift during use.

**Brocade** has satin or twill floats on a plain, ribbed, twill, or satin background (Figure 13–13). Brocade differs from damask in that the floats in the design are more varied in length and are often of several colors.

**Brocatelle** fabrics are similar to brocade fabrics, except that they have a raised pattern. This fabric frequently is made with filament yarns, using a warp-faced pattern and

**FIGURE 13–12** ❖ Jacquard patterned fabrics for upholstery.

filling-faced ground. Coarse cotton stuffer filling yarns may be used to help maintain the three-dimensional appearance of the fabric when used for upholstery.

Originally, **tapestry** was an intricate picture that was handwoven with discontinuous filling yarns. It was usually a wall hanging and time consuming to weave. Today's jacquard tapestry is mass produced for upholstery, handbags, and the like. It is a complicated structure consisting of two or more sets of warp and two or more sets of filling interlaced so that the face warp is never woven into the back and the back filling does not show on the face. Upholstery tapestry is durable if warp and filling yarns are comparable. With lower quality fabrics, fine yarns are combined with coarse yarns, and the resulting fabric is not durable.

Wilton rugs are figured pile fabrics made on a jacquard loom. These rugs, once considered imitations of Oriental rugs, are so expensive to weave that the tufting industry has found a way to create similar figures through printing techniques.

## Momie Weaves

**Momie** (mō′mē) is a class of weaves that present no wale or other distinct weave effect but give the cloth the appearance of being sprinkled with small spots or seeds. The appearance resembles crepe made from yarns of high twist. Fabrics are made on a loom with a dobby attachment or electronic control. Some are variations of satin weave, with filling yarns forming the irregular floats. Some are even-sided and some have a decided warp effect. Momie weave is also called **granite** or **crepe weave.** Any fiber can be used to make crepe-weave fabrics. An irregular interlacing pattern of crepe weave is shown in Figure 13–14.

**Sand crepe** is a common medium to heavy weight momie-weave fabric of either spun or filament yarns. It has a repeat pattern of 16 warp yarns and 16 filling yarns and requires 16 harnesses. No float is greater than two yarns in length.

**Granite cloth** is made with a momie weave, based on the satin weave. It is an even-sided fabric with no long floats and no twill effect. It is used for furnishings and apparel.

**Moss crepe** is a combination of high-twist crepe yarns and crepe weave. The yarns are plied yarns with one ply made of a crepe-twist single yarn. Regular yarns may be alternated with the plied yarns, or they may be used in one direction while the plied yarns are used in the other direction. This fabric should be treated as a high-twist crepe fabric. Moss crepe is used in dresses and blouses.

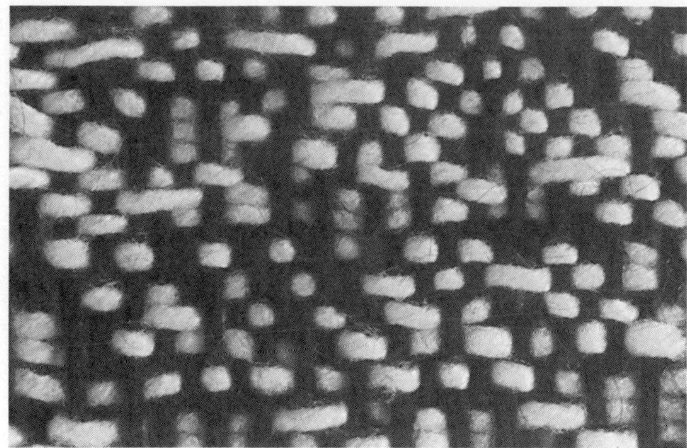

**Figure 13–14** ❖ Momie weave.

Bark cloth is a heavyweight momie weave fabric used primarily in furnishings. The interlacing pattern usually uses spun yarns and creates a fabric with a rough texture somewhat like that of tree bark, hence the fabric's name. The fabric may be printed or solid. The rough texture adds visual interest to the fabric and minimizes the appearance of soiling.

## Leno Weaves

**Leno** is a weave in which the warp yarns do not lie parallel to each other. Warp yarns work in groups, usually pairs of two; one yarn of each pair is *crossed* over the other before the filling yarn is inserted, as shown in Figure 13–15.

Leno is made with a **doup attachment** that may be used with a plain or a dobby loom. The attachment consists of a thin needle supported by two heddles. One yarn of each pair is threaded through an eye at the upper end of the needle, and the other yarn is drawn between the two heddles. Both yarns are threaded through the same dent in the reed. During weaving, when one of the two heddles is raised, the yarn that is threaded through the needle is drawn across to the left. When the other heddle is raised, the same yarn is drawn across to the right.

When looking at a leno fabric, one might think that the yarns were twisted fully around each other, but this is not true. Careful examination shows that they are *crossed* and that one yarn of the pair is always above the other.

Fabrics made by leno weave include **marquisette** (Figure 13–16), mosquito netting, agrotextiles to shade delicate plants, and some bags for laundry, fruit, and vegetables. Polyester marquisettes are widely used for sheer curtains. Casement draperies are frequently made

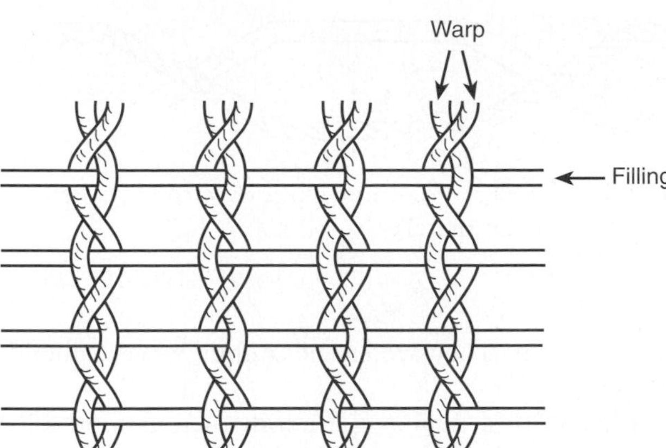

**FIGURE 13–15** ❖ Leno weave: diagram (top) and fabric (bottom).

with leno weave and novelty yarns. Thermal blankets are sometimes made of leno weave. All these fabrics are characterized by sheerness or open spaces between the yarns. The crossed-yarn arrangement gives greater firmness and strength than plain-weave fabrics of a similar low count and minimizes yarn slippage. Snagging may be a problem in use and care, however.

Chenille yarns (Chapter 11) are made using a leno weave. The fabric is produced with fine-warp, and low-twist filling. It is cut apart parallel to the warp, and the filling untwists to produce the fuzzy chenille yarn (Figure 11–11).

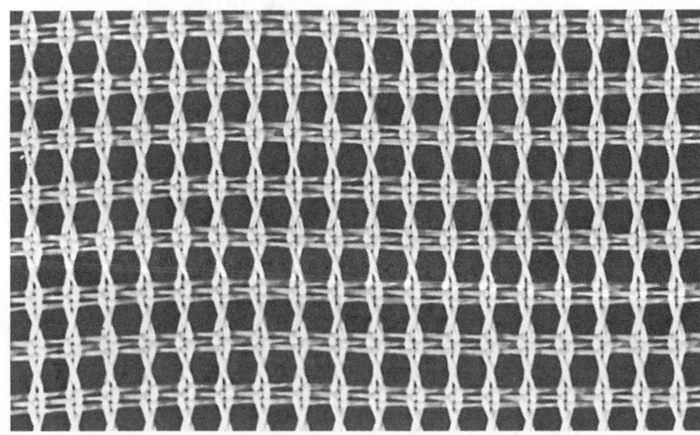

**FIGURE 13–16** ❖ Marquisette.

❖

## DOUBLE CLOTH

Double-cloth fabrics have a different appearance on the two sides due to the fabrication method. These fabrics tend to be heavier and have more body than single cloths. A single cloth, such as percale, is made from two sets of yarns; one set of warp yarns and one set of filling yarns. Double cloth is made from three or more sets of yarns.

There are three types of woven double cloth fabrics:

1. Double cloth—coat fabrics: melton and kersey.
2. Double weave—apparel and upholstery fabrics: matelassé.
3. Double-faced—blanket cloth, double-satin ribbon, lining fabric, and silence cloth.

**Double cloth** is made with five sets of yarns: two fabrics woven one above the other on the same loom with the fifth yarn (warp) interlacing with both cloths (Figure 13–17). This technique is used to produce vel-

**FIGURE 13–17** ❖ Double cloth made with five sets of yarns.

vet. (See "Pile Weaves," this chapter.) True double cloth can be separated by pulling out the yarns holding the two cloths together. It can be used in reversible garments such as capes and skirts.

Double cloth is expensive to make because it requires special looms and the production rate is slower than for single fabrics. Double cloth is more pliable than the same weight single fabric because finer yarns can be used. The two specific fabrics that may be either true double cloth or single cloth are melton and kersey. Both of these heavyweight-wool coating fabrics are twill-weave fabrics that have been heavily finished so that it is difficult to identify the weave.

**Melton** tends to have a smoother surface than kersey. **Kersey** is usually heavier than melton and has a shorter, more lustrous nap. Both fabrics are used in winter coats, overcoats, riding habits, and military uniforms.

## Double Weaves

**Double weave** is made with four sets of yarns, creating two separate layers of fabric that periodically reverse position from top to bottom, thus interlocking the two layers of fabric. Between the interlocking points the two layers are completely separate, creating pockets in the fabric (Figure 13–18).

Double-weave fabrics are also *pocket fabrics, pocket cloth,* or **pocket weave.** They are most commonly seen in high-quality upholstery fabrics. Their main advantages are the designs that can be achieved and their heavier weight. They are usually tightly woven, durable fabrics.

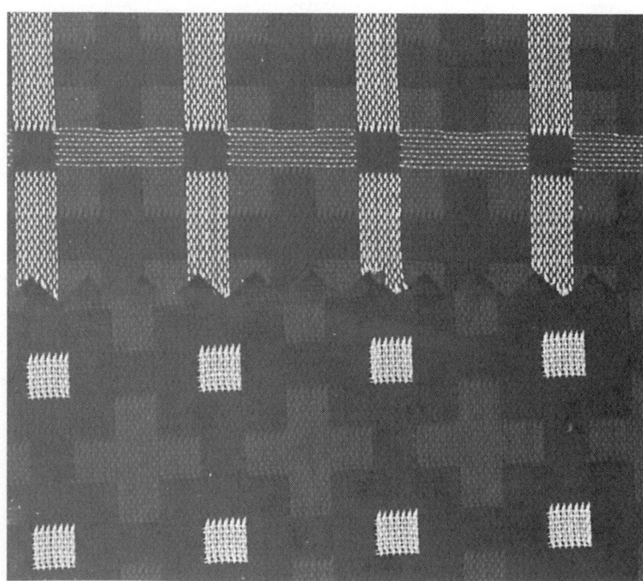

FIGURE 13–18 ❖ Double weave: face of fabric (bottom); back of fabric (top).

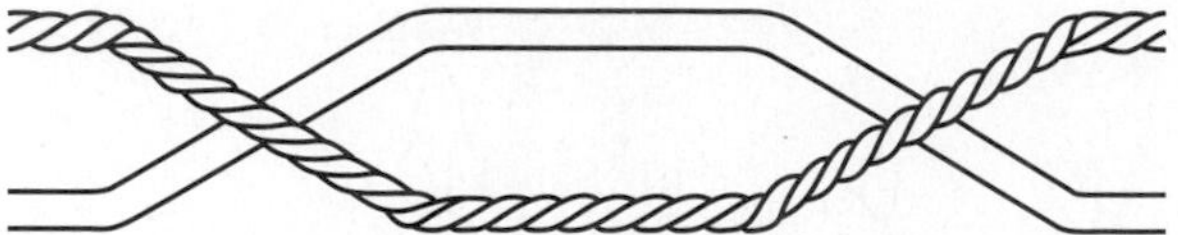

FIGURE 13–19 ❖ Interlacing of yarns between fabric surfaces of matelassé.

**Matelassé** is a double-cloth construction with either three or four sets of yarns woven on a jacquard or dobby loom. Two of the sets are the regular warp and filling yarns, and the others are crepe or coarse cotton yarns. They are woven together so that the two sets crisscross, as shown in Figure 13–19. When the fabrics are finished, the crepe or cotton yarns shrink, giving the fabric a puckered appearance. Heavy cotton yarns sometimes are used as stuffer yarns beneath the fabric face to emphasize the three-dimensional appearance of the fabric. Matelassé is used in apparel and upholstery (see Figure 13–20).

## Double-Faced Fabrics

**Double-faced fabrics** are made with three sets of yarns: two warp and one filling, or two sets of filling and one set of warp. Blankets, satin ribbons, interlinings, and silence cloth are made this way (Figure 13–21).

Blankets with one color on one side and another color on the other side are usually double-faced blankets. One set of warp yarns is used, with two sets of different-colored filling yarns. Sometimes designs are made by interchanging the colors from one side to the other. Double-faced blankets are usually expensive woven-wool blankets.

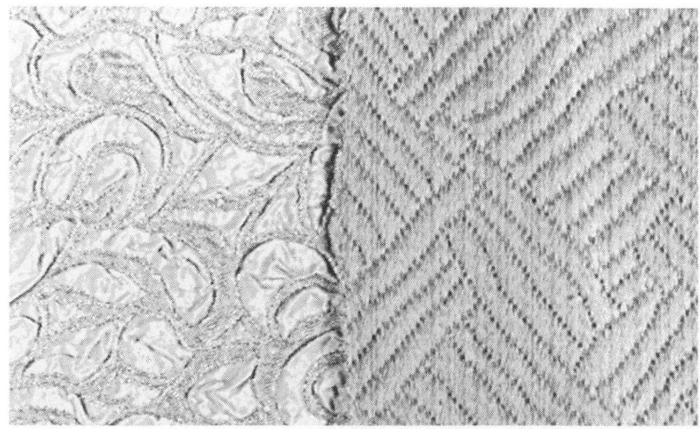

FIGURE 13–20 ❖ Two examples of matelassé: apparel weight (left) and upholstery weight (right).

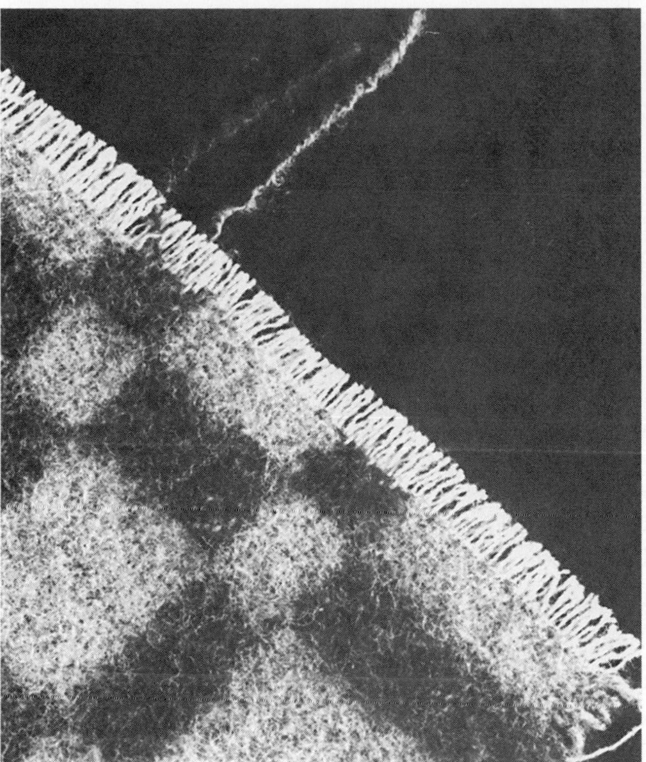

**FIGURE 13–21** ❖ Double-faced blanket. One set of warp yarns and two sets of filling yarns.

*Satin ribbons,* which have a lustrous satin face on both sides of the ribbon, are used in designer lingerie and evening wear. These ribbons have two sets of warp yarns that form the surface on both sides of the ribbon. They are interlaced with one set of filling yarns.

A double-faced interlining fabric is used to add warmth to winter jackets and coats. The face of the fabric is a filament-yarn satin weave that slides easily over other clothing. The back of the fabric uses a third set of low-twist yarns that are heavily napped for warmth. Thus the fabric functions as a combination lining and interlining fabric.

**Silence cloth** is a heavy cotton fabric that has been napped on both sides. Available in white, it is used under fine tablecloths to silence the noise of china and silverware while dining.

❖

## PILE WEAVES

Woven-pile fabrics are three-dimensional structures made by weaving an extra set of warp or filling yarns into the ground yarns to make loops or cut ends on the surface (Figure 13–22). Pile comes from the Latin word *pilus,* meaning hair. The pile is usually ½ inch or less in height. Woven-pile fabric is less pliable than other pile fabrics. Sometimes when the fabric is folded, the rows of pile tufts permit the back to show, or "grin-through." As tuft density increases, grin-through decreases.

Pile fabrics can be both functional and beautiful. A high and thick pile adds warmth as either the shell or the lining of coats, jackets, gloves, and boots. High-count fabrics produce beautiful and durable carpets, upholstery, and bedspreads. Low-twist yarns produce absorbent towels and washcloths. Other uses for pile fabrics are stuffed toys, wigs, paint rollers, buffing and polishing cloths, and decubicare pads for bedridden patients. Interesting effects can be achieved by combinations of cut and uncut pile (Figure 13–22), pile of various heights, high- and low-twist yarns, areas of pile on a flat surface, flattening pile, or forcing pile into a position other than upright.

In pile fabrics, the pile receives the surface abrasion and the base weave receives the stress. A durable base structure contributes significantly to a satisfactory pile fabric. A compact ground or base weave increases the resistance of a looped or uncut pile to snagging and of a cut pile to shedding and pulling out. A dense pile stands erect, resists crushing, and gives better cover. Care must be taken in cleaning and pressing to keep the pile erect. Cut pile may look better if dry cleaned, but some pile fabrics—such as pinwale corduroy—can be washed, depending on the fiber content. Incorrect pressing may flatten the pile and result in a fabric that appears lighter in color. Special pressing aids or techniques are used with pile fabrics, like steaming or using needleboards.

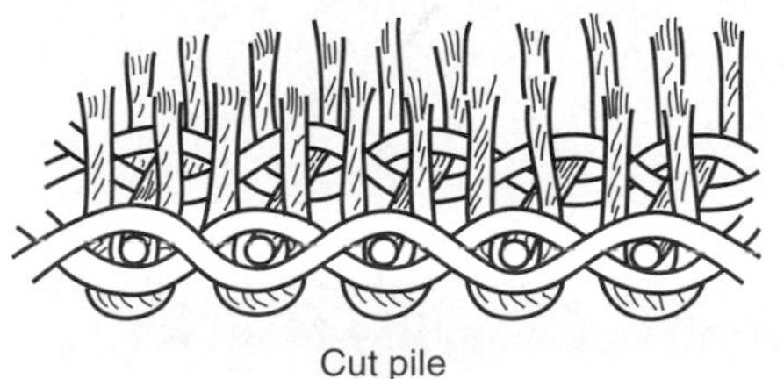



**FIGURE 13–22** ❖ Cut pile and loop pile: woven fabric.

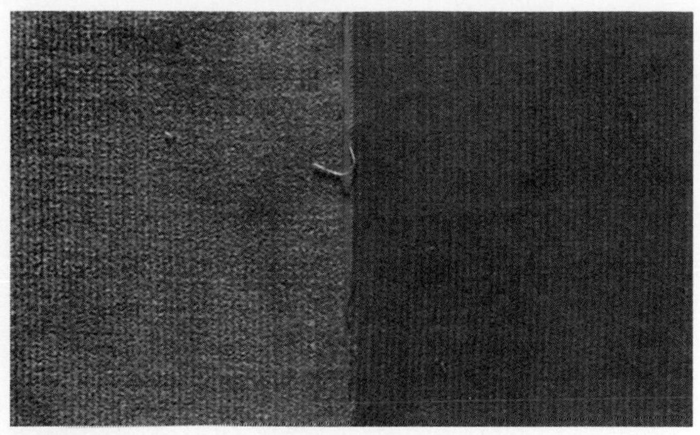

**FIGURE 13–23** ❖ Corduroy: Both pieces of fabric were cut from the same bolt. Differences in apparent color are due to differences in the lay of the nap.

Many pile fabrics are pressed during finishing so that the pile slants in one direction, giving an up and down. It is important that the pile be directed in the same way in all pieces of a product. Otherwise, light will be reflected differently and the product will appear to be made of two colors. (See Figure 13–23.)

## Filling-Pile Fabrics

The pile in **filling-pile fabrics** is made by long filling floats on the surface that are cut after weaving (Figure 13–24). Filling pile fabrics are always cut pile. Two sets of filling yarns and one set of warp are used. The ground fabric is made with one set of filling yarns and the warp yarn set. During weaving, the extra filling yarns float across the ground yarns, interlacing occasionally. In **corduroy,** the floats are arranged in lengthwise rows; in **velveteen,** they are scattered over the base fabric.

Cutting is done by a special machine consisting of guides that lift the individual floating yarns from the ground fabric and revolving knives that cut the floats (Figure 13–25). A gray-goods corduroy with some of the floats cut is shown in Figure 13–26. When widewale corduroy is cut, the guides and knives can be set to cut all the floats in one operation. For narrow corduroy and velveteen, the rows are so close together that alternate rows are cut with each pass and the fabric must be run through the machine twice.

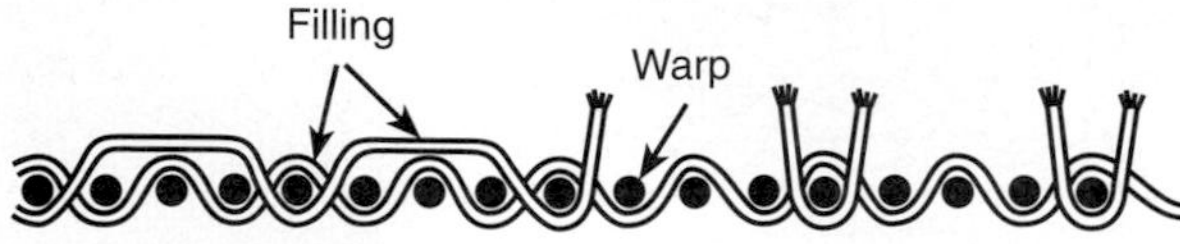


**FIGURE 13–24** ❖ Filling pile. Cross section of weave in corduroy.

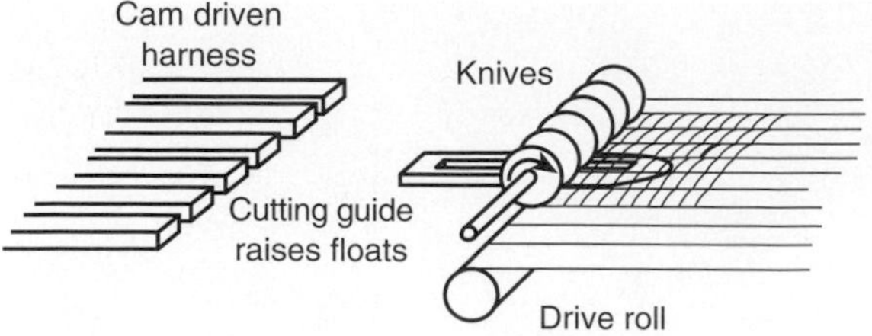


**FIGURE 13–25** ❖ Process for cutting floats to make corduroy.

After cutting, the surface is brushed crosswise and lengthwise to bloom open the yarn tuft, raise the pile, and merge the separate pile tufts. Finishing gives the fabric its final appearance.

Both velveteen and corduroy are made with long-staple combed cotton for the pile. In good-quality fabrics, long-staple cotton is used for the ground as well. Polyester/cotton blends are available with polyester in the ground yarns for strength. The ground may be made with plain- or twill-weave interlacing patterns. With the twill pattern, it is possible to have a higher count and a denser pile. Corduroy can be recognized by lengthwise wales. Velveteen has more body and less drapeability than velvet. The pile is not higher than ⅛ inch. Both corduroy and velveteen are available in both solid-color and printed fabrics. Table 13–1 describes characteristics of different types of corduroy.

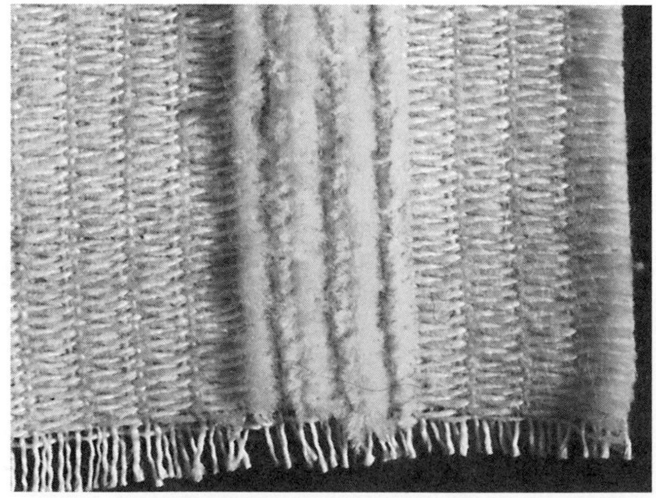

**FIGURE 13–26** ❖ Corduroy gray goods showing some of the floats cut and brushed open.

**TABLE 13–1** ❖ Types of corduroy.

| | WALES PER INCH | OUNCES PER SQUARE YARD | CHARACTERISTICS, USES |
|---|---|---|---|
| Featherwale | 18–19 | 5± | Shallow pile, flexible, tops & bottoms |
| Pinwale | 14–16 | 7± | Shallow pile, flexible, tops & bottoms |
| Midwale | 11 | 10± | Men's and women's outerwear & bottoms, upholstery |
| Widewale | 3–9 | 12± | Most durable corduroy made, coats, upholstery |

## Warp-Pile Fabrics

**Warp-pile fabrics** are made with two sets of warp yarns and one set of filling. Warp-pile fabrics can have cut or uncut pile. One set of warp yarns and the filling yarn set form the ground fabric. The extra set of warp forms the pile. Several methods are used.

**DOUBLE-CLOTH METHOD** Two fabrics are woven, one above the other, with the extra set of warp yarns interlacing with both fabrics. There are two sheds, one above the other, and one filling yarn is inserted in each shed. The fabrics are cut apart while still on the loom by a traveling knife that passes back and forth across the loom. With the *double-cloth method* of weaving, the depth of the pile is determined by the space between the two fabrics (Figure 13–27).

**Velvet** is made of filament yarns with a pile height of 1⁄16 inch or less. Velvet must be handled carefully so that there are no folds or creases in the fabric that would flatten the pile.

Velvet and velveteen can be distinguished by fiber length, since velvet is usually made with filaments and velveteen with staple. To identify warp directions in these fabrics, ravel adjacent sides. In velvet, the tufts are interlaced with a filling yarn (Figure 13–28). Another way to tell warp direction is to bend the fabric. In velveteen, the pile "breaks" into lengthwise rows because the filling tufts are interlaced with the warp yarns. In velvet, the pile breaks in crosswise rows because the warp tufts are interlaced with the ground-filling yarns. This technique works best with medium- to poor-quality fabrics. Sometimes it helps to unravel a fabric. In filling-pile fabrics, the pile is pushed out as individual tufts when a filling yarn is removed. But when a warp yarn is removed, the pile tufts cling to it and it looks a little like a woolly caterpillar (Figure 13–28). In warp-pile fabrics, the opposite occurs. Pile tufts cling to filling yarns.

**Crushed velvet** is made by mechanically twisting the wet cloth. The surface yarns are randomly flattened in different directions.

**Panné velvet** is an elegant fabric that has had the pile pressed flat by heavy pressure in one direction to give high luster. If the pile is disturbed or brushed in the other direction, the smooth, lustrous look is destroyed.

**Velour** is a warp-pile cotton fabric used primarily for upholstery and draperies. It has a deeper pile than velveteen and is heavier in weight. **Plush** has a deeper pile than velour or velvet and is usually longer than 1⁄4 inch.

*Furlike fabrics* may be finished by curling, shearing, sculpturing, or printing to resemble different kinds of real fur. (Most furlike fabrics are made by other processes; see Chapters 14 and 15.)

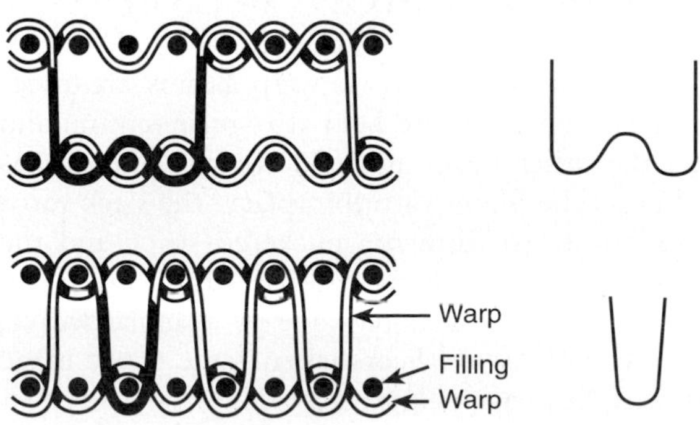


**FIGURE 13–27** ❖ Warp pile: double-cloth method. W-interlacing (above); V-interlacing (below).

**OVER-WIRE METHOD** In the **over-wire method** a single cloth is woven with wires placed across the width of the loom so that they are positioned above the ground warp and under the pile warp. For cut pile fabrics, each wire has a hook at one end with a knife edge that cuts all the yarns looped over it as it is withdrawn. Uncut pile is produced using wires without hooks or waste picks of filling yarns. The wires are removed before the cloth is removed from the loom, and the waste picks are removed after the fabric is off the loom. Friezé, mohair-pile plush, and most woven pile carpets or rugs are made in this way.

**Friezé**, an uncut or combination cut/uncut pile fabric, is an upholstery fabric that has fewer tufts per square

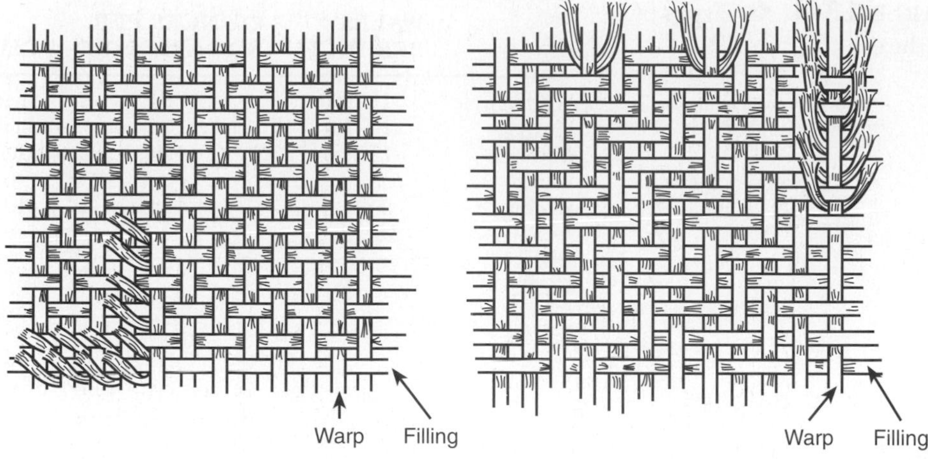


**FIGURE 13–28** ❖ Comparison of filling pile and warp pile. Velvet: warp-pile yarn is interlaced with ground filling (left). Velveteen: filling-pile yarn is interlaced with ground warp (right).

inch than most other pile fabrics. The durability of friezé depends on the closeness of the weave (Figure 13–29).

Velvet also can be made by the over-wire method. Complex patterns using different-color yarns and loops combined with cut pile result in a wide variety of fabrics.

**SLACK-TENSION PILE METHOD** The pile in **terrycloth** is formed by a special weaving arrangement in which three picks or fillings are inserted and beaten up with one motion of the reed. After the second pick in a set is inserted, there is a let-off motion that causes the yarns on the warp-pile beam to slacken, while the yarns on the ground-pile beam are held at tension. The third pick is inserted, the reed moves forward all the way, and all three picks are beaten up firmly into place (Figure 13–30). These picks move along the ground warp and push the pile-warp yarns into loops. The loops can be on one side only or on both sides. Loop height is determined by the let-off motion of the warp-pile beam.

Terrycloth is used for bath towels, beach robes, and sportswear. Each loop acts as a tiny sponge. When the loops are sheared and the surface is brushed to loosen and intermesh the fibers of adjacent yarns, the surface becomes more compact, less porous, and absorbs more slowly compared to loop-pile terry. Institutional cotton/polyester terry towels have blended ground yarns and cotton pile, the pile yarns for absorbency and the polyester ground yarns for strength and durability, especially in selvages.

There is no up and down in terrycloth unless the cloth is printed. Some friezés are made by the terrycloth method. Another slack tension fabric, **shagbark,** has widely spaced rows of loops.

**FIGURE 13–29** ❖ Friezé is woven over wires.

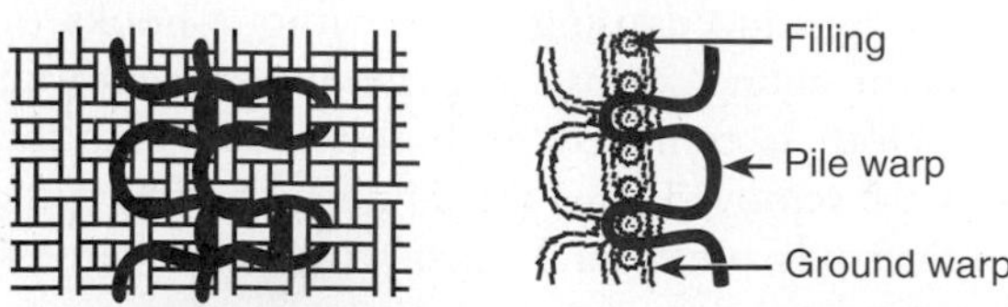


**FIGURE 13–30** ❖ Warp pile: slack-tension method for terrycloth.

❖

## SLACK-TENSION WEAVES

In **slack-tension weaving** two warp beams are used. The yarns on one beam are held at regular tension and those on the other beam are held at slack tension. As the reed beats the filling yarn into place, the slack yarns crinkle or buckle to form the puckered stripe and the regular-tensioned yarns form the flat stripe. Loop-pile fabrics, such as terrycloth, are made by a similar weave; see the previous section. **Seersucker** is the fabric made by slack-tension weave (Figure 13–31).

The yarns are wound onto the two warp beams in groups of 10 to 16 for a narrow stripe. The crinkle stripe may have slightly larger yarns to enhance the crin-

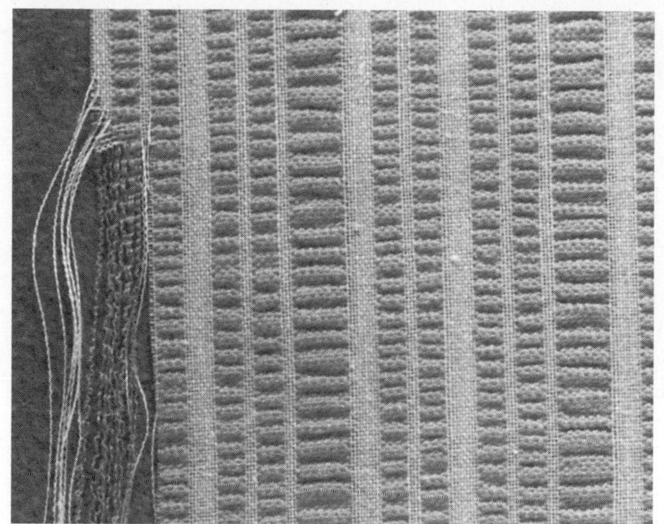

**FIGURE 13–31** ❖ Seersucker. Note that the lighter yarns from the flat portion of the fabric are smaller and straighter. The darker colored yarns from the puckered area are larger and more crimped.

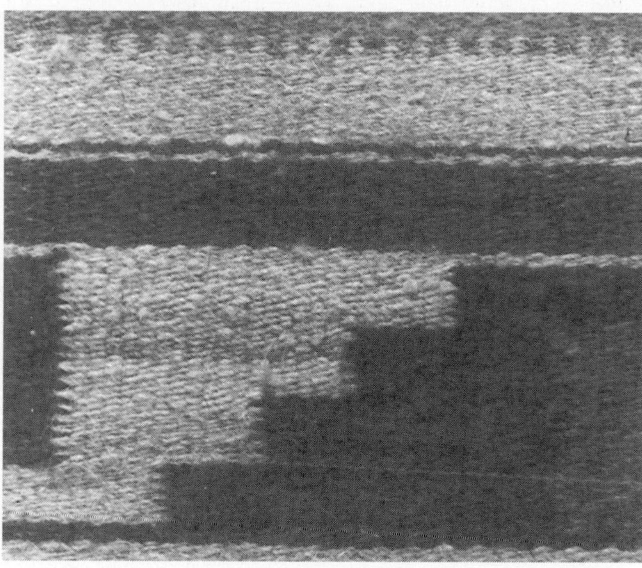

**FIGURE 13–32** ❖ Close-up of a tapestry rug from central Mexico. Note how the yarns dovetail where the pattern changes color. This is one method used to avoid producing slits in a tapestry.

kle. The stripes are always in the warp direction and on-grain. Seersucker is produced by a limited number of manufacturers. It is a low-profit, high-cost item to produce because of slow weaving speed. Seersuckers are made in 45- or 60-inch widths in plain colors, stripes, plaids, checks and prints. Seersucker is used in curtains and summer suiting, dresses, and sportswear.

## TAPESTRY WEAVE

A tapestry weave is a hand-produced, filling-faced, plain-weave fabric. The discontinuous filling yarns are arranged so that the color in the weave changes, thus creating the pattern. Discontinuous filling means that filling yarns rarely travel completely across the fabric from one side to the other. Each color of filling yarn moves back and forth in a plain-weave interlacing pattern as long as the pattern calls for that color; then another color is used. In tapestries, filling yarns are not always straight within the fabric and may interlace with the warp at an angle other than 90°. If the color changes along a vertical line, slits in the structure can develop. Different methods of structuring the fabric can enhance or eliminate the slit depending on the effect desired by the artist.

Two types of looms are used to create tapestries: horizontal and vertical. The differences between the looms relate to the size and end use of the tapestry. Fabrics made using this weave are one-of-a-kind rugs, wall hangings, and fiber art pieces. Sometimes they are referred to as true tapestries to differentiate them from the jacquard-patterned tapestry. True tapestries tend to have larger filling yarns than warp yarns. Warp yarns are covered completely by the filling. Although pictorial tapestries are common, there are many categories of tapestries based on the pattern and end use. Figure 13–32 shows a close-up of a tapestry rug from central Mexico.

## NARROW FABRICS

**Narrow fabrics** encompass a diverse range of products that are up to 12 inches wide and made by a variety of techniques. Woven narrow fabrics will be discussed here. Narrow fabrics include ribbons of all sorts, elastics, zipper tapes, Venetian-blind tapes, couturier's labels, hook and loop tapes such as Velcro, pipings, carpet-edge tapes, trims, safety belts, and harnesses (Figure 13–33). Webbings are an important group of narrow fabrics used in packaging, cargo handling, furniture, and for animal control, like leashes or lead ropes for dogs, horses, and show cattle.

Narrow-fabric looms weave many fabrics side by side. Each fabric has its own shuttle but shares all other loom

**FIGURE 13–33** ❖ Narrow fabric (left to right): woven fancy, grosgrain ribbon, woven satin ribbon, bias tape, zipper tape, and rickrack.

mechanisms. Plain, twill, satin, jacquard, and pile weaves are used.

Woven elastics are made using a variety of weaves. They are used in apparel where tight fit and holding power are needed, such as women's undergarments. They have better stability and rigidity than knit elastics and are less prone to riding up, but are more expensive.

Table 13–2 compares the characteristics of the fancy weaves discussed in this chapter.

**TABLE 13–2** ❖ Comparison of fancy weaves.

| WEAVE | FABRICATION DETAILS | APPEARANCE | USES/FABRICS |
|---|---|---|---|
| Dobby | Warp controlled in groups | Small geometric patterns | Apparel, furnishings, bird's-eye diaper, waffle cloth |
| Extra yarn | Additional yarn sets in warp or filling, excess removed or on back, yarn ends add interest | Small geometric patterns, yarn fringe | Apparel, furnishings, dotted swiss, eyelash |
| Piqué | Dobby or jacquard technique, raised pattern areas | Floats on back or stuffer yarns create raised areas | Apparel, furnishings, bedford cord, pinwale piqué, bull's-eye piqué |
| Jacquard | Warp controlled individually | Elaborate, intricate designs | Apparel, furnishings, brocade, damask, tapestry |
| Momie | Irregular interlacing | Pebbly, uneven surface | Apparel, furnishings, crepe, bark cloth, moss crepe |
| Leno | Warp yarns cross over each other | Stable, open fabric | Apparel, furnishings, leno, casement cloth, marquisette |
| Double | Three, four, or five sets of yarns used | Double-faced, pockets in fabric, or thick, heavy fabrics | Apparel, furnishings, matelassé, melton, blankets, upholstery |
| Pile | Extra yarns in warp or filling create surface pile | Thick, bulky, warm, durable fabrics | Apparel, furnishings, corduroy, velveteen, velvet, friezé, terrycloth, Wilton carpets |
| Slack tension | Warp bands under different tensions during weaving | Puckered stripes in warp direction | Apparel, furnishings, seersucker |
| Tapestry | Discontinuous filling | Pattern created by yarn color | One-of-a-kind rugs, wall hangings, fiber art |

# Key Terms

Fancy weaves
Dobby weave
Dobby loom
Bird's-eye
Huck or huck-a-back
Shirting madras
Waffle cloth
Extra yarn weave
Clipped-dot fabric
Swivel-dot fabric
Piqué
Jacquard loom
Damask
Brocade
Brocatelle
Tapestry
Momie weave
Crepe or granite weave
Sand crepe
Granite cloth
Moss crepe
Leno
Doup attachment
Marquisette
Double cloth
Melton
Kersey
Double weave
Pocket weave
Matelassé
Double-faced fabric
Silence cloth
Pile weave
Filling pile fabrics
Corduroy
Velveteen
Warp-pile fabrics
Velvet
Crushed velvet
Panné velvet
Velour
Plush
Over-wire method
Friezé
Terrycloth
Shagbark
Slack-tension weave
Seersucker
Narrow fabrics

# Questions

1. Explain why the fabrics in this chapter are referred to as fancy.
2. Summarize the structural characteristics of these weaves: dobby, jacquard, momie, leno, double cloth, pile, slack tension.
3. What performance differences would be expected among the weaves in question 2?
4. Name a fabric and end use for each of these weaves and discuss the appearance characteristics that are useful in recognizing that fabric. Why is that fabric appropriate for that end use?

# Suggested Readings

Emery, Irene (1980). *The Primary Structures of Fabrics.* Washington, D.C.: The Textile Museum.

Humphries, Mary (1996). *Fabric Glossary.* Upper Saddle River, NJ: Prentice Hall.

Mohamed, Mansour H. (1990, November/December). "Three-Dimensional Textiles." *American Scientist, 78,* pp. 530–541.

Schwartz, Peter, Rhodes, Trevor, and Mohamed, Mansour (1982). *Fabric Forming Systems.* Park Ridge, NJ: Noyes Publications.

Suzuki, Hajime (February, 1990). "Automated Weaving: A Japanese Perspective." *Textile Month,* pp. 26–28.

"Textile Machinery Technology." (April, 1991). *Textile World,* pp. 61–68.

Tortora, Phyllis G., and Merkel, Robert S. (1996). *Fairchild's Dictionary of Textiles,* 7th ed. New York: Fairchild Publications.

Chapter 14

# KNITTING AND KNIT FABRICS

OBJECTIVES

- To describe the differences between woven and knit fabrics.
- To differentiate between warp- and filling-knit fabrics.
- To understand the characteristics of warp- and filling-knit fabrics.
- To integrate fabrication, yarn type, and fiber with end use.
- To understand the versatility of knit fabrics for apparel, furnishing, and industrial products.

Knitting is the formation of a fabric by the interlooping of one or more sets of yarns. Knitting has been the traditional method of producing some items, such as sweaters, underwear, hosiery, and baby blankets. The trend toward a more casual lifestyle is reflected in increased uses of knits in furnishings and apparel.

Knitting is probably not as old a technique as weaving. Remnants of knit fabrics dating back to A.D. 250 were found near the borders of ancient Palestine. Knitting was a hand process until 1589, when the Reverend William Lee of England invented a flatbed machine for knitting cloth for hosiery. This machine produced cloth 10 times faster than hand knitting. The circular-knitting machine and the warp-knitting machine were developed about 200 years later. Other devices invented about that time include the ribbing device and the latch needle.

A unique advantage of knitting is that a complete product can be produced or fashioned directly on the knitting machine. Sweaters and hosiery are good examples. The knitting of a complete garment has been possible since 1863 when William Cotton invented a machine that could shape garment parts by adding or dropping stitches.

The rate of production of knitting machines is relatively high—about four times as many square yards or meters per hour as for looms since machine width is not related to operating speeds. This speed should be an economic factor in favor of knitting as a method of fabrication, but the increased cost of the yarn more than offsets any savings in the cost of manufacture. There are several reasons for this. First, because the looped position of the yarn imparts bulk, more yarn is required to produce a knit fabric than to produce a comparable woven fabric. Second, the looped structure is porous—has holes or spaces—and provides less cover than a woven fabric in which yarns lie side by side. So, in order to achieve an equal amount of cover, small stitches (finer gauge) and finer and more expensive yarns are used. Knitting yarns are more expensive because they must be much more uniform to prevent the formation of thick-and-thin places in the fabric.

Knitting is a very efficient and versatile method of making fabric. This versatility has resulted from the use of computer-aided design systems wherein electronic-patterning mechanisms and QSC modifications to machines permit rapid adjustment to fashion changes. In addition, microcomputers are being used in a manner similar to their use in pattern weaves. Electronic controls identify the type of stitch for each needle, the yarn to be used in the stitch, and the tension on the yarn. Electronic controls for knitting machines make knitting faster, more efficient, and more practical. These machines are more versatile than other machines and changing patterns is much simpler and quicker. There is now a knitted counterpart for almost every woven fabric—knitted seersucker, piqué, denim, crepe, satin, terrycloth, velour, and so on.

Other knitting machine technological developments helped broaden the range of end uses. Attachments to the knitting machine produce fabrics with stability more like that of wovens. The weft-insertion knitting machine introduced filling yarn for more crosswise stability and the warp-insertion knitting machine added warp yarns for greater lengthwise stability.

Other major advantages of knits are in comfort and appearance retention. Comfort is based on the ability to adapt to body movement. The loop structure provides the fabric with outstanding elasticity (stretch/recovery) that is distinct from any elastic properties of the fibers and yarns that are used. The loop can change shape by lengthening or widening to give stretch in any direction of the cloth (Figure 14–1). However, knits may sag, bag, or snag.

Quality in knit fabrics is assessed in much the same way as for woven fabrics. (See Chapter 12.) Procedures focus on inspecting for flaws and assessing how the fabric performs in specific areas of interest. Characteristics that are used to define a high-quality knit fabric include a heavy weight for the fabric type, fiber content, and end use. Yarns are regular in appearance and may be combed or worsted depending on the fiber. Pattern is incorporated into the fabric as part of its structure; jacquard or raschel fabrics are or higher quality than printed or embossed fabrics. Bow and skew are minimal. Garment parts are shaped on the knitting machine rather than being cut and sewn.

Because of the unique interlooped structure of knits, they are more prone to specific problems, such as snagging and sagging. Special procedures have been developed to assess these performance characteristics of knits. The next few paragraphs describe some of these procedures.

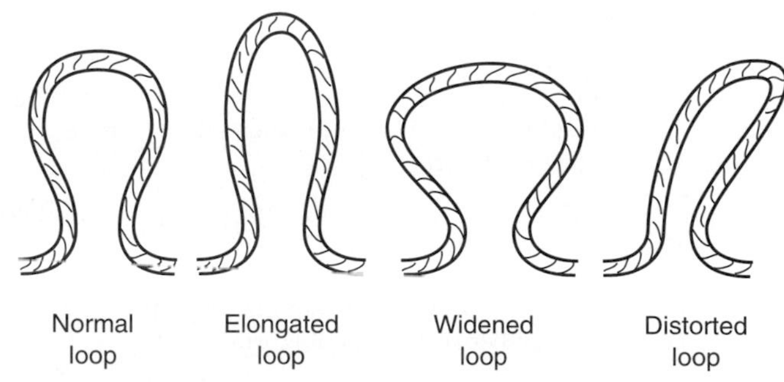


**FIGURE 14–1** ❖ The loop can change its shape to give stretch.

Skew (an off-grain characteristic first discussed in Chapter 12) is common with knits, especially circular knits, because of the way they are made. In assessing skew, a fabric is placed flat on a surface and one course is followed across the fabric. A right angle is used to measure the difference between a straight course and a skewed course in the fabric.

Knitted fabrics have higher potential shrinkage than woven fabrics. The accepted standard is 5 percent for knits, whereas 2 percent is standard for wovens. However, the performance specifications developed by the American Society for Testing and Materials list a recommended maximum shrinkage for both woven and knit products of 3 percent in both vertical and horizontal directions.

The bulky structure of a knit provides many trapped-air cells for good insulation in still air but a wind-repellent outer layer is needed to prevent chill winds from penetrating. On a warm, humid day, knits may be too warm because they tend to conform to the body and insulate too well.

Appearance retention means lack of wrinkles during use, care, and packing or storage. Wrinkle recovery is based somewhat on the loop structure, but it is also strongly influenced by fiber and yarn type. Snagging is probably the single most serious problem encountered in the use of knit fabric. When a yarn is snagged so it pulls out and stands away from the surface of the fabric, "shiners" or tight yarns are formed on either side of the snag. Finer yarns, smaller stitches, and higher yarn twist all contribute to snag resistance. Snag resistance can be evaluated using special equipment. (See Figure 14–2.) If

**FIGURE 14–2** ❖ ICI snag tester. (COURTESY OF SDL INTERNATIONAL LTD.).

**TABLE 14–1** ❖ Comparison of knit and woven fabrics.

| KNITTING | WEAVING |
|---|---|
| **Comfort and Appearance Retention** | |
| Mobile, elastic fabric. Adapts easily to body movement. Good recovery from wrinkles. | Stable to stress (unless made with stretch yarns). Varies with the weave. |
| **Cover** | |
| Porous, less opaque. More open spaces between yarns let winds penetrate. | Provides maximum hiding power and cover per weight of yarn. Less air permeable, especially if count is high. |
| **Fabric Stability** | |
| Less stable in use and care. Many shrink more than 5 percent unless synthetic fibers have been heat set. | More stable in use and care. Many shrink less than 2 percent. |
| **Versatility** | |
| Sheer to heavyweight fabrics. Plain and fancy knits. Can be made to look like many other fabrics. | Sheer to heavyweight fabrics. Many different textures and designs. |
| **Economics** | |
| Design patterns can be changed quickly to meet fashion needs. | Machinery becoming more adaptable to rapid changes in fashion. |
| Process is less expensive but is offset by more expensive raw material costs. Speedier regardless of fabric width. | Most economical method of producing a unit of cover. Wider looms weave slower. |
| **Fabric Structure and Characteristics** | |
| Series of interconnected loops made with one or more sets of yarns. Can be raveled from top or bottom depending on the knit type (warp knits cannot be raveled). May snag and run. | Two or more sets of yarns interlaced to form the fabric structure. Yarns are essentially straight in the fabric. Can be raveled from any cut edge. May snag and ravel. |

snags are cut off (rather than being worked back into their original position), a run may start in some knits, particularly in filling knits.

A **run** occurs when the stitches in a wale collapse or pull out. A run occurs in a stepwise fashion when one stitch after another in a wale collapses due to stress on the loop when a yarn is cut.

Table 14–1 summarizes some of the major differences between knitting and weaving and the fabrics made by them. Performance and appearance characteristics of knits include:

- One or more yarns are formed into a series of interlocking loops.
- Knitting is a faster technique than weaving, requiring more yarn per unit of cover. Knits may be bowed or skewed.
- Knits are stretchy, elastic fabrics.
- Knits are porous and resilient; they may be bulky.
- Knits are used for apparel, furnishing, and industrial products.
- Knits are usually heavier than comparable woven fabrics because greater quantities of yarn are used.

# KNITTING

**Knitting** is a fabrication process in which needles are used to form a series of interlocking loops from one or more yarns or from a set of yarns. **Filling,** or **weft, knitting** is a process in which one yarn or yarn set is carried back and forth (or around) and under needles to form a fabric. Yarns run horizontally in the fabric. **Warp knitting** is a process in which a warp beam is set into a machine and yarn sets are interlooped to form a fabric. Yarns run vertically in the fabric. These names were borrowed from weaving and refer to the direction the yarns move in the fabric. In knitted fabrics, yarns do not move in both directions as they do in weaving; there are no warp and no filling yarns in a knitted fabric. When a woven fabric is unraveled, both warp and filling yarns are removed. When a knit fabric is unraveled, a row of loops is removed. Try unraveling a knit and a woven to see the differences between the two structures.

## Needles

Knitting is done by needles: **spring-beard, latch,** or **compound,** which are shown in Figure 14–3. Most filling knits are formed with the latch needle. The spring-beard, or bearded, needle may be used to produce fully fashioned garments and knit-fleece fabrics. Spring-beard needles are usually used with fine yarns, whereas latch needles may be used in making coarse fabrics. A double-latch needle is used to make purl loops. The compound needle is used primarily in warp knitting.

## Stitches

Needles make **stitches** or loops. The stitches are named based on the way they are made. Stitches may be open or closed, depending on how the stitch is formed. Open stitches are most common in filling knitting. In warp knitting either kind may be found, depending on the design of the knit. Open or closed stitches are useful primarily in identifying the way the fabric was made and have little relationship to performance characteristics.

## Fabric Characteristics

Fabric density is defined by describing the number of stitches, not yarns, in a specific direction. **Wales** are vertical columns of stitches in the knit fabric. **Courses** are horizontal rows of stitches. In machine knitting, each wale is formed by a single needle. Wales and courses show clearly on filling-knit jersey (see Figures 14–4 and 14–5). Fabric density is often designated as wales by courses. For example, a T-shirt jersey might have 32 wales per inch and 44 courses per inch. This fabric would have a density of 32 × 44.

**Cut,** or **gauge,** indicates the fineness of the stitch; it is measured as the number of needles in a specific space on the needle bar and often expressed as needles per inch (npi). Cut is often used in the textile industry to describe knit fabrics.

The higher the cut, or gauge, the finer the fabric. The finished fabric may not have the same cut as the machine on which it was made because of shrinkage or stretching during finishing. A fine-cut, filling-knitting machine may have 28 npi or more. A coarse cut may have 13 npi or fewer.

It may be difficult to identify the technical face of the fabric. The following list identifies some characteristics that may help in determining the technical face of a knitted fabric (see Figures 14–4 and 14–5). **Technical face** refers to the outer side of the fabric as knitted. This may not be the side used as the fashion side in a product.

1. The technical face side has a better finish.
2. If two kinds of yarn or fiber are used, the more expensive one is used on the face side.
3. If floats are present, the least snaggable ones are on the face.
4. Finer yarns are on the face.
5. If the two sides differ, the design is on the face side.
6. If the fabric curls, it curls to the **technical back,** parallel to the wales.

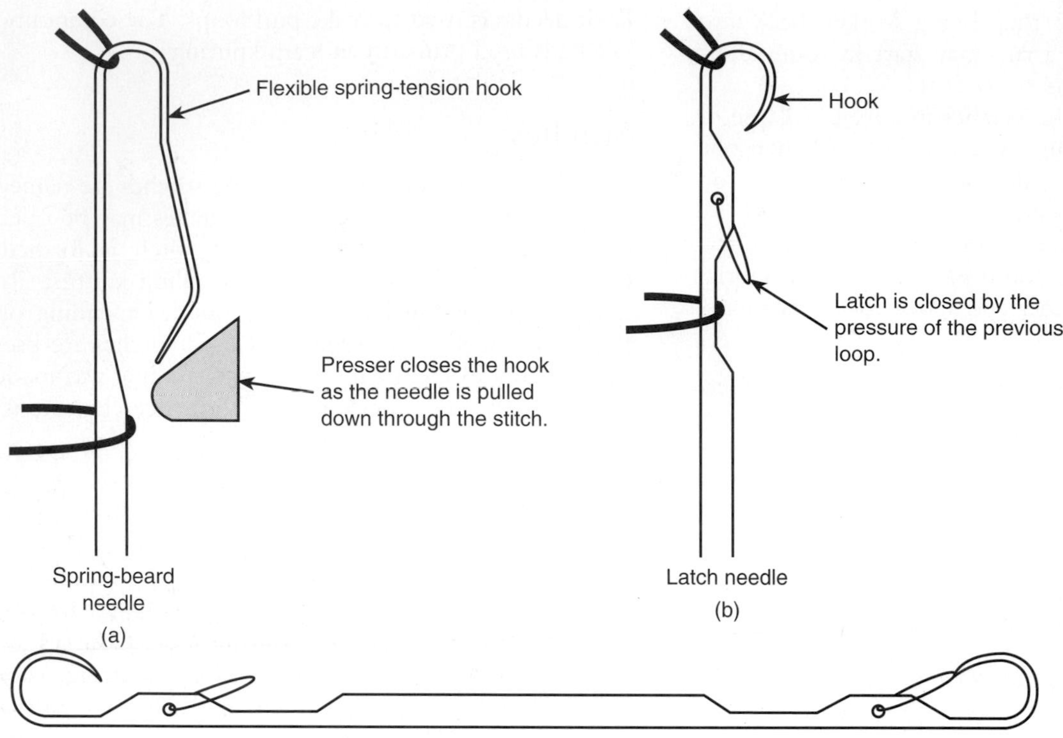


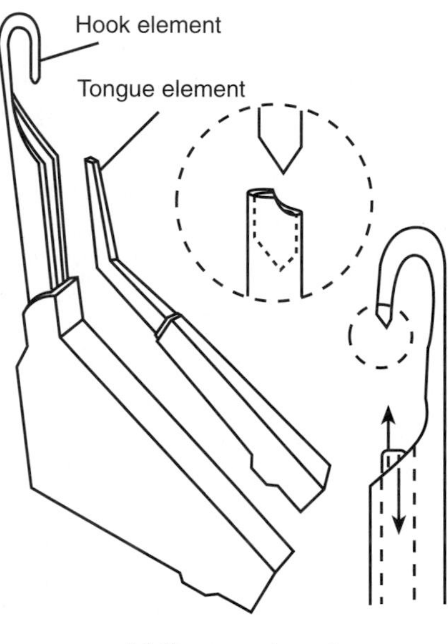


**FIGURE 14–3** ❖ Knitting needles: (a) spring-beard needle; (b) latch needle; (c) double-latch needle; (d) compound needle.

## Environmental Impact of Knitting

The process of knitting creates fewer environmental problems compared to weaving. Chemicals to minimize abrasion on yarns or generation of static charges are less likely to be used with knits. There is no knit equivalent to the water-jet loom. Knitting machines are quieter than shuttle looms. Knitting produces less vibration and lint. Knitting machines also use less energy in their operation than looms.

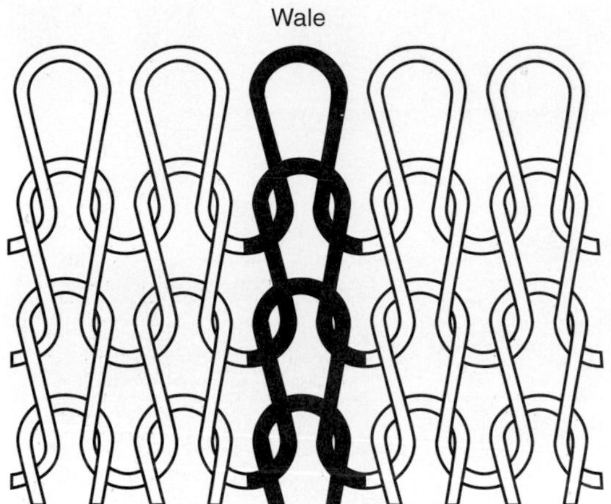


**FIGURE 14–4** ❖ Wale as seen from the technical face of a filling-knit jersey fabric.

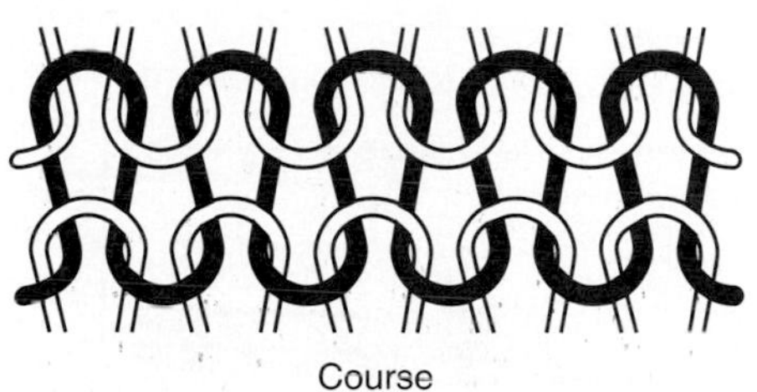


**FIGURE 14–5** ❖ Course as seen from the technical back of a filling-knit jersey.

## FILLING (OR WEFT) KNITTING

Filling knitting can be either a hand or a machine process. In *hand knitting,* a yarn is cast (looped) onto one needle, another needle is inserted into the first stitch, the yarn is positioned around the needle, and by manipulating the needle the new stitch is taken off onto the second needle. The process is repeated with all the stitches being taken off from one needle to the other.

In *machine knitting,* many needles (one for each wale) are set into a machine and the stitch is made in a series of steps. By the end of the series, one needle has gone through a complete up and down motion, and a new stitch has been formed (Figure 14–6). In the *running position,* the needle moves up and the old stitch begins to slide down the needle. In *clearing,* the old stitch is moved down to the stem or base of the needle and the needle is in its highest position. During the *yarn-feed step,* the new yarn is positioned in front of the hook part of the needle and the needle has begun its downward stroke. In the *knockover step,* the old stitch is removed from the needle. The final step is the *pulling step,* when the new stitch is formed at the hook of the needle and the needle is in its lowest position. These five steps are repeated in a continuous up and down motion to form a knit. Each needle in the machine is at a slightly different stage in this process so that, with knitting machines, one sees a wave or undulating motion across or around the machine.

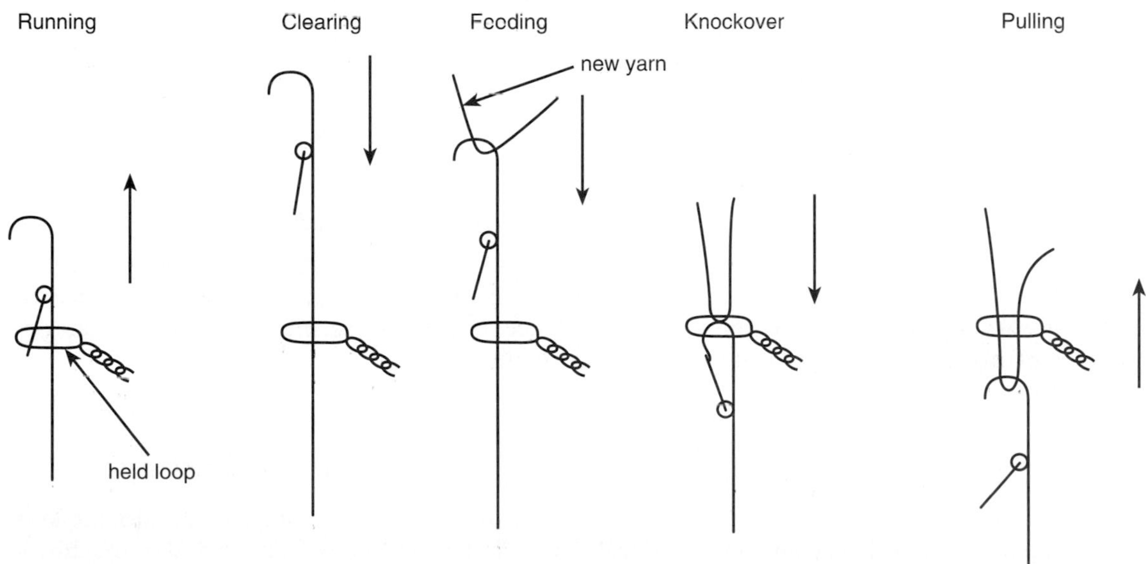


**FIGURE 14–6** ❖ Latch-needle knitting action.

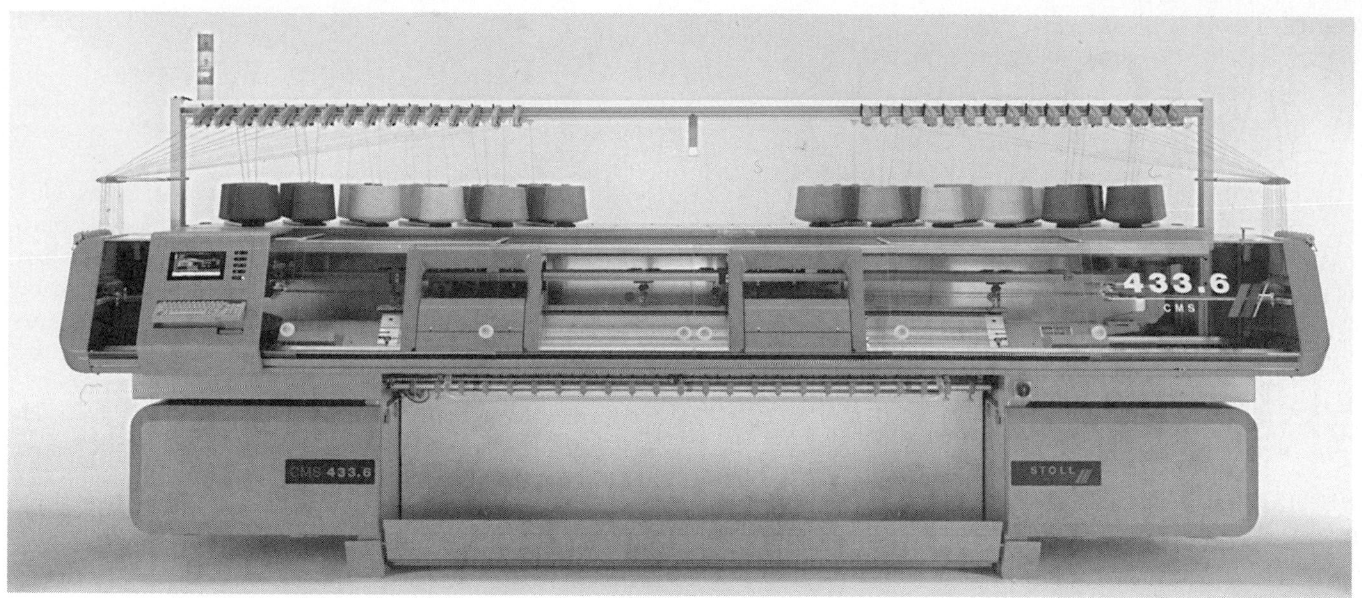


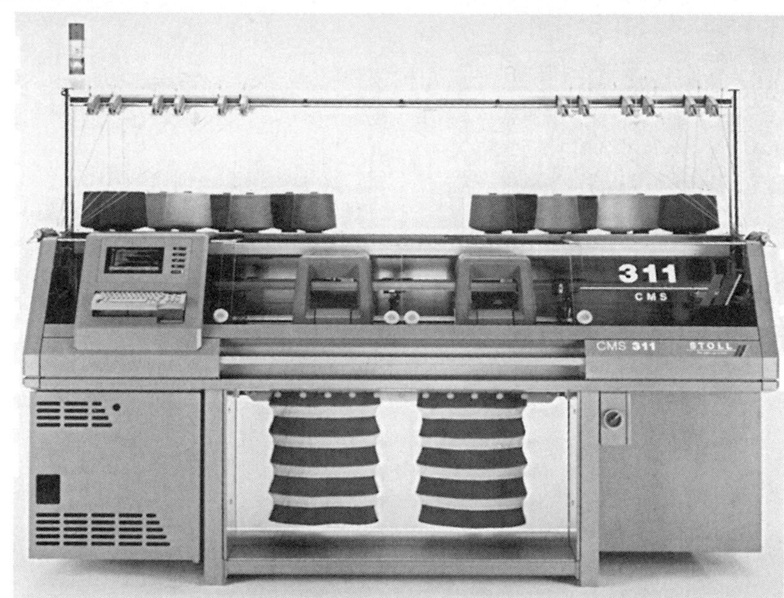


**FIGURE 14–7** ❖ Flatbed knitting machines for fabric (top) and garment parts such as collars (bottom). (COURTESY OF STOLL AMERICA KNITTING MACHINERY, INC.)

Knitting can be flat, in which the yarn is carried back and forth on a flatbed machine (see Figure 14–7), or circular, in which the yarn is carried in a spiral like the threads in a screw on a circular machine (see Figure 14–8). Figure 14–9 shows yarn movement in fabrics knit using these two types of machines. In hand knitting, many kinds of stitches can be made by varying the way the yarn is placed around the needle (in front or behind) and by knitting stitches together, dropping stitches, or transferring stitches. Special devices are used to obtain these variations in machine knitting.

Knits are classified by several factors: the machine on which the knit is made, the number of yarn sets in the knit, and the type of stitch or stitches used in the knit. Categorizing filling knits by the number of yarn sets is a carryover from hand knitting. Some fabrics, such as ribknits, are made with one set of yarns on a machine with two needle beds. Thus, ribknits could be categorized as single or double knits. In this book, knits are categorized by the machine used to produce them.

## Machines Used in Filling Knitting

Machine knitting is done on single- and double-knit circular and flatbed machines. The **circular machines** are faster in production. Circular machines are described

**FIGURE 14–8** ❖ Circular knitting machine. (COURTESY OF SULZER MORAT GMBH.)

by the diameter of the fabric tube they produce. Greater flexibility demands by the industry have resulted in machines that make a variety of tube diameters. Diameters can be changed with minimal down time. New yarns can be fed into the structure at any point on the diameter. Yarn feeds normally range from 3 to 4 feeds per diameter inch. With a tube diameter of only 13 inches and 3 feeds per diameter inch, there could be 39 courses between the point where a yarn began its circular pattern and where that yarn began its second course around the fabric. High yarn feeds per diameter inch allow knitting machines to be highly productive, but they produce fabrics with significant skew and potential problems in cutting, sewing, and consumer satisfaction.

Circular machines primarily make yardage, but are also used to make sweater bodies, panty hose, and socks.

**Flatbed machines** also knit a variety of fabric widths. Most *flatbed knits* are 100 or more inches across. These machines are slower than circular machines, but they produce less skew in the fabric and have the ability to fashion or shape garment or product parts.

Finally, knitting machines may be described by the type of fabric they produce, such as simple jersey for T-shirts or more complex fabrics such as knit terrycloth. Patterned knits may be produced on machines like mini-jacquards for simple patterns or jacquards for more complex patterns. Electronic controls decrease flaws in the structure, increase machine flexibility, and decrease time for changing patterns.

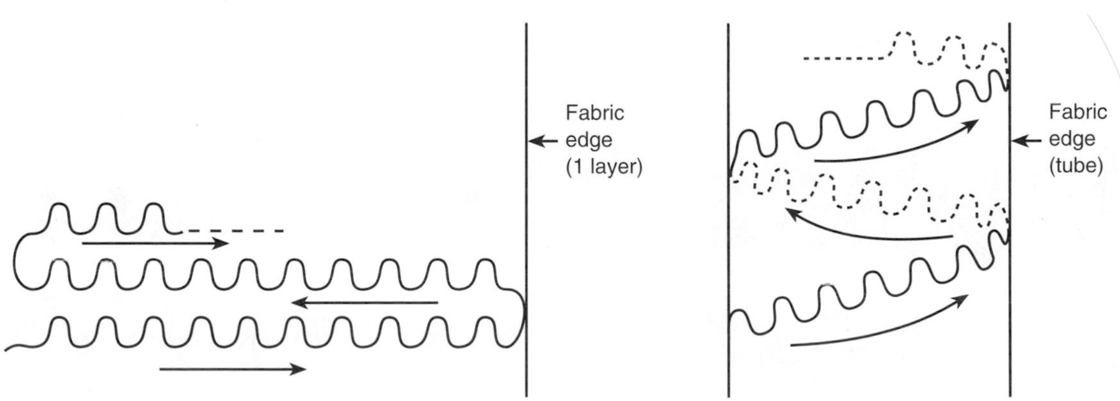


**FIGURE 14–9** ❖ Yarn motion in flatbed knits (left) and circular knits (right).

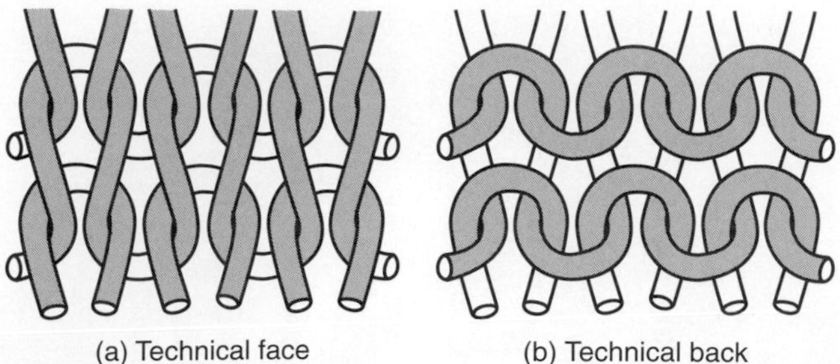


**FIGURE 14–10** ❖ Close-up of a plain jersey stitch: technical face (left); technical back (right). The gray part indicates the part of the yarn that can be seen from that side of the fabric.

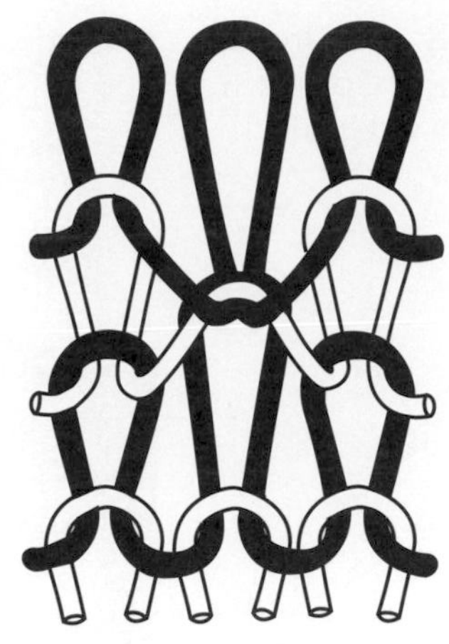


**FIGURE 14–12** ❖ Tuck stitch. (COURTESY OF *KNITTING TIMES*, THE OFFICIAL PUBLICATION OF NATIONAL KNITWEAR AND SPORTSWEAR ASSOCIATION.)

## Filling-Knit Structures—Stitches

Filling-knit fabrics are classified according to the stitch type used. There are four possible stitch types. Each is controlled by the selection of *cams,* or guides, that control the motion of the needle. The first stitch is the **knit stitch.** This is the basic stitch used to produce the majority of filling-knit fabrics (see Figure 14–10). These fabrics have greater elongation crosswise and less elongation lengthwise. The sides of the stitches appear on the face of jersey; the back is comprised of the tops and bottoms of the stitches. Figure 14–11 illustrates the appearance of both sides of the fabric. When jerseys are printed, they are printed on the face since that is the smoothest and most regular surface. However, many jerseys, especially the pile types, are used with the technical back as the fashion side because of the loop formation.

The **tuck stitch** is used to create a pattern in the fabric. In the tuck stitch, the old stitch is not cleared from the needle. Thus there are two stitches on the needle. Figures 14–12 and 14–13 show how the tuck stitch looks in a fabric. In a knit fabric with tuck stitches, the fabric is thicker and slightly less likely to stretch crosswise than a basic-knit fabric with the same number of stitches. Tuck stitches create bubbles, blisters, or puckers for visual interest, which may be incorporated in a pattern or added randomly to create texture. These are usually referred to as jacquard jerseys.

The **float** or **miss stitch** is also used to create a pattern in the fabric. In the float stitch, no new stitch is

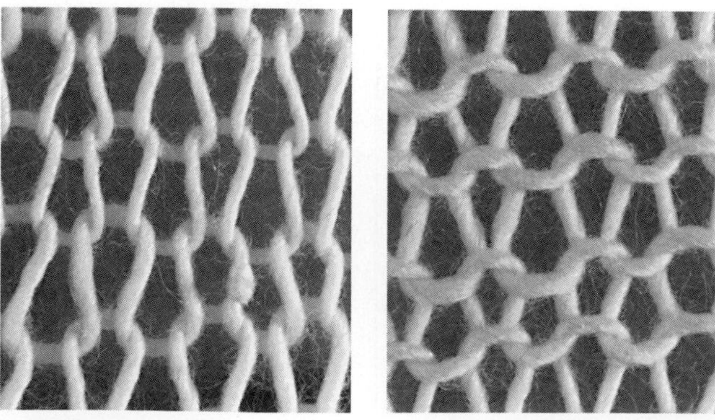

**FIGURE 14–11** ❖ Single jersey: (left) technical face; (right) technical back.

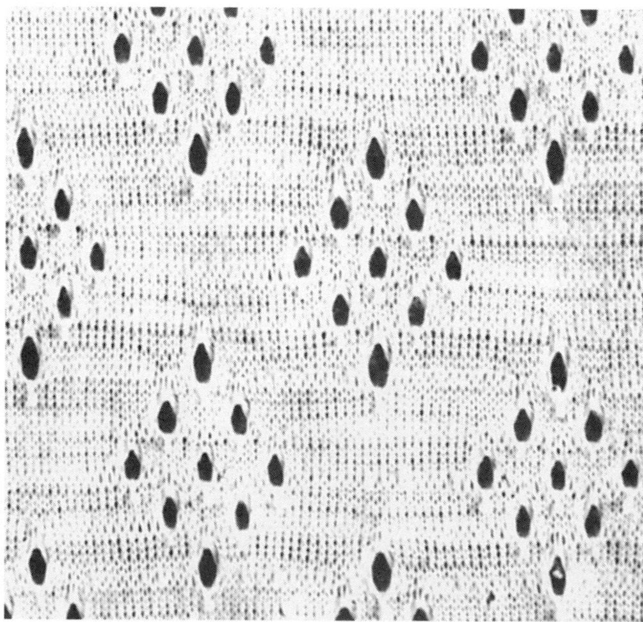

**FIGURE 14–13** ❖ Fabric knitted with tuck stitch.

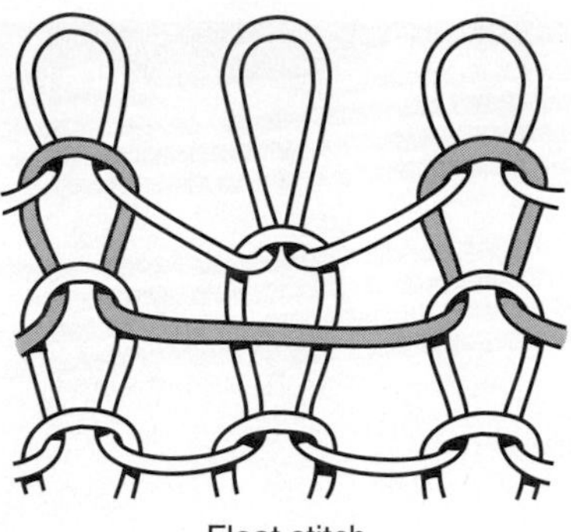


**FIGURE 14–14** ❖ Float, or miss, stitch. (COURTESY OF *KNITTING TIMES*, THE OFFICIAL PUBLICATION OF NATIONAL KNITWEAR AND SPORTSWEAR ASSOCIATION.)

formed at the needle while adjacent needles form new stitches. The float stitch can be used when yarns of different colors are used to create patterns. Figure 14–14 shows how the float stitch looks in a fabric. A knit fabric with float stitches is much less likely to stretch crosswise than a basic-knit fabric with the same number of stitches. In jacquard jerseys, float stitches are very common because of the combination of colors in the fabric. For example, if a fabric incorporates two or more colors in a pattern, float stitches are necessary as one color comes to the face and the other floats in this area. Figure 14–15 shows the face and back of a jacquard jersey with float stitches.

The **purl,** or **reverse, stitch** forms a fabric that looks like the technical back of a basic-knit fabric on both sides. The fabric is reversible (see Figure 14–16). Purl-knit fabrics are relatively slow fabrics to make and expensive to produce because they require special machines. Since the face and back of a purl fabric look like the back of a jersey, manufacturers often use the technical back of a jersey as the fashion side when a purl-like appearance is desired. These imitation "purl" fabrics pass casual inspection by consumers and are competitive in price with other knit structures, so the consumer does not pay more for this special look.

## Filling-Knit Fabrics

**SINGLE-FILLING KNITS** **Single-filling knits** are made using a machine with one set of needles. This machine is usually a circular one, but it may also be a flatbed one.

Single knits can be any pattern or weight. They are less stable than double knits, tend to curl at the edges, and run readily, especially if made of filament yarns.

***Single or Plain Jersey*** Single jersey fabric is the simplest of the filling-knit structures. The face side has prominent wales—columns of stitches running length-

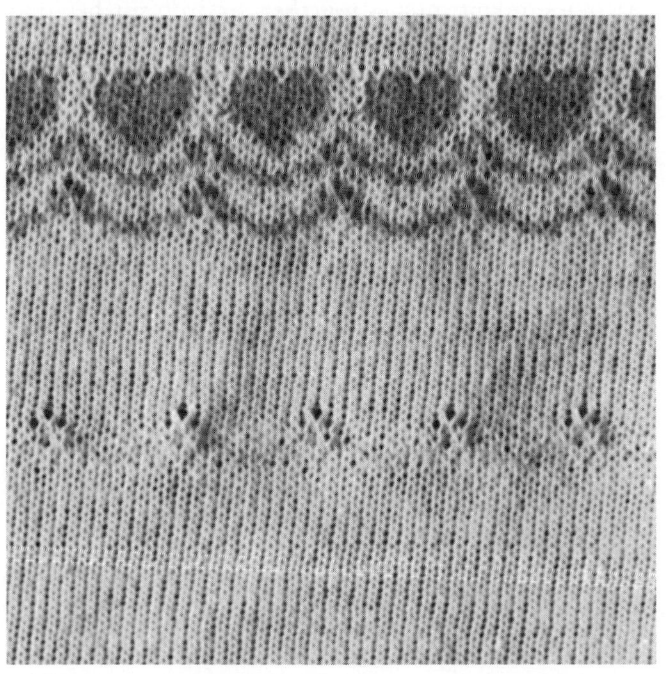

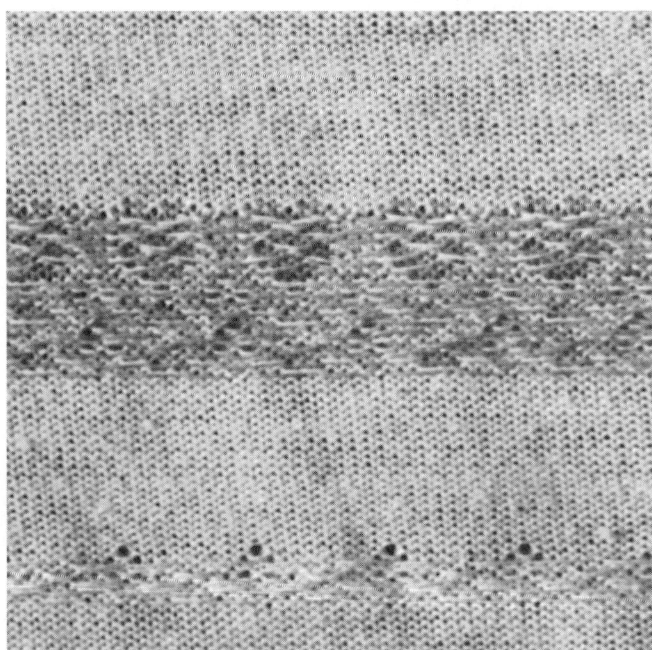

**FIGURE 14–15** ❖ Jacquard jersey: face (left) and back (right). Note the pattern on the face and the floats on the back.

**FIGURE 14–16** ❖ Purl stitch looks the same on both sides.

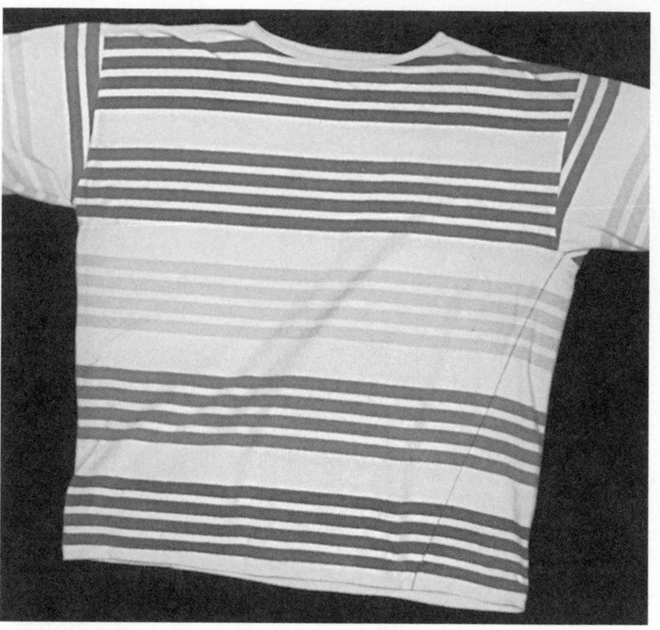

**FIGURE 14–17** ❖ T-shirt showing skew of the circular knit jersey fabric. Note how the side seam twists toward the front of the shirt.

wise. The back has prominent courses—rows of stitches running crosswise. Stretch a swatch of jersey crosswise and it will curl to the back at the lengthwise edges. The ends will curl toward the face. Yarns ravel crosswise because the yarns run horizontally in the fabric. Cut edges or broken yarns may create problems with runs. Single jerseys made of spun yarns resist running because of fiber cohesiveness.

The single-jersey structure, or plain knit, is widely used because it is the fastest method of filling knitting and is made on the least complicated knitting machine.

**Jersey** is a light- to heavyweight fabric usually knitted on a circular-jersey machine and sold in tubular form or cut and sold as flat goods. When tubular fabrics are pressed in finishing, the creases are seldom parallel to the wales of the fabric—they are off-grain. The tubular cloth does not need to be cut and opened out when cutting out product parts, unless there is a specific reason for doing so. T-shirts with no side seams are made from circular knit jersey. Tube socks are another common circular knit product.

Figure 14–17 shows a T-shirt that was cut from tubular cotton jersey with yarn-dyed crosswise stripes. When purchased, the strips were parallel and the side seam was perpendicular to the lower edge. After washing, the fabric assumed its normal position, causing the side seams to twist and the stripes to spiral.

Heavier weight jerseys are often used for simple solid color or striped sweaters, tops, and skirts. Fancy or multiple ply yarns add body, durability, warmth, cover, or texture. **Stockinette** or stockinet usually refers to a heavier knit jersey fabric made with a coarse spun yarn compared to regular jerseys.

**Lisle** (lyle) is a high-quality jersey made of fine two-ply combed cotton yarns. It can be found in several weights depending on its end use. Lisle is used for men's and women's socks, undergarments, shirts, skirts, and sweaters.

End uses for plain-knit structures include hosiery, underwear, shirts, T-shirts, dresses, and sweaters.

Variations in plain knit are made by programming the machines to knit stitches together, to drop stitches, and to use colored yarns to form patterns or vertical stripes. Extra yarns or slivers are used to make pile fabrics like terrycloth, velour, and fake-fur fabrics.

***Jacquard Jerseys*** **Figured-single jerseys** are made by a jacquard mechanism on circular-jersey machines. Electronic control of jacquard knitting machines is becoming more common every year. Patterns consist of combinations of stitches such as knit, tuck, and float, combinations of yarns that vary by color or texture, or incorporation of yarns in specific areas within the fabric, much like a true tapestry weave for woven fabrics. **Jacquard jerseys** are the simplest of these patterned fabrics. In a Jacquard jersey, the pattern develops because of different stitch types, yarn colors, or a combination of stitch type and yarn color. Figure 14–15 shows the face and back of a simple jacquard jersey where the color knit on the face changes to create the pattern.

In a more complicated patterned single-knit fabric, the yarn used to create a pattern in the fabric is knit into the fabric in that area only. This is the knit counterpart to a true tapestry weave. This fabric is referred to as an intarsia.

**Intarsia** designs in jersey are made by knitting in colored yarns. True intarsia designs have a clear pattern on both the right and wrong side of the cloth with no bird's-eye backing that is characteristic of jacquard designs. Fabrics have no extra weight, and the stretch is not impaired. Mock intarsia designs are made by knitting and float-knitting (float or miss stitch), which results in a heavier-weight fabric with floating yarns on the reverse side. These floating yarns reduce the elasticity of the fabric and may snag readily. Compare both fabrics in Figure 14–18.

***Pile Jerseys*** **Pile jerseys** are made on a modified circular jersey machine. The fabrics look like woven pile but are more pliable and stretchy. The pile surface may consist of (1) cut or uncut loops of yarn or (2) fibers (see the following discussion of sliver knits). In velour and knit terrycloth, the fabric is made with two sets of yarns. One yarn set is spun yarns and will eventually form the pile surface of the finished fabric. The other set is a BCF yarn that has been processed in such a way as to shrink when heated. Both yarn sets are knit together to form the fabric. At this point, the fabric looks like a very loose, poor-quality jersey. The fabric is heat set and the BCF yarn shrinks. The spun yarns form the pile and the fabric is finished to produce the appropriate look.

**Knitted terrycloth** is a loop pile fabric used for beachwear, robes, and babies' towels and washcloths. It is softer and more absorbent than woven terry but does not hold its shape as well. (See Figure 14–19.) **Velour** is a cut-pile fashion fabric used in men's and women's wear and in robes. Velour is knit with loops that are cut evenly. Then the yarn uncurls giving better coverage. The fabric is dyed, tentered, and steamed. (See Figure 14–19.)

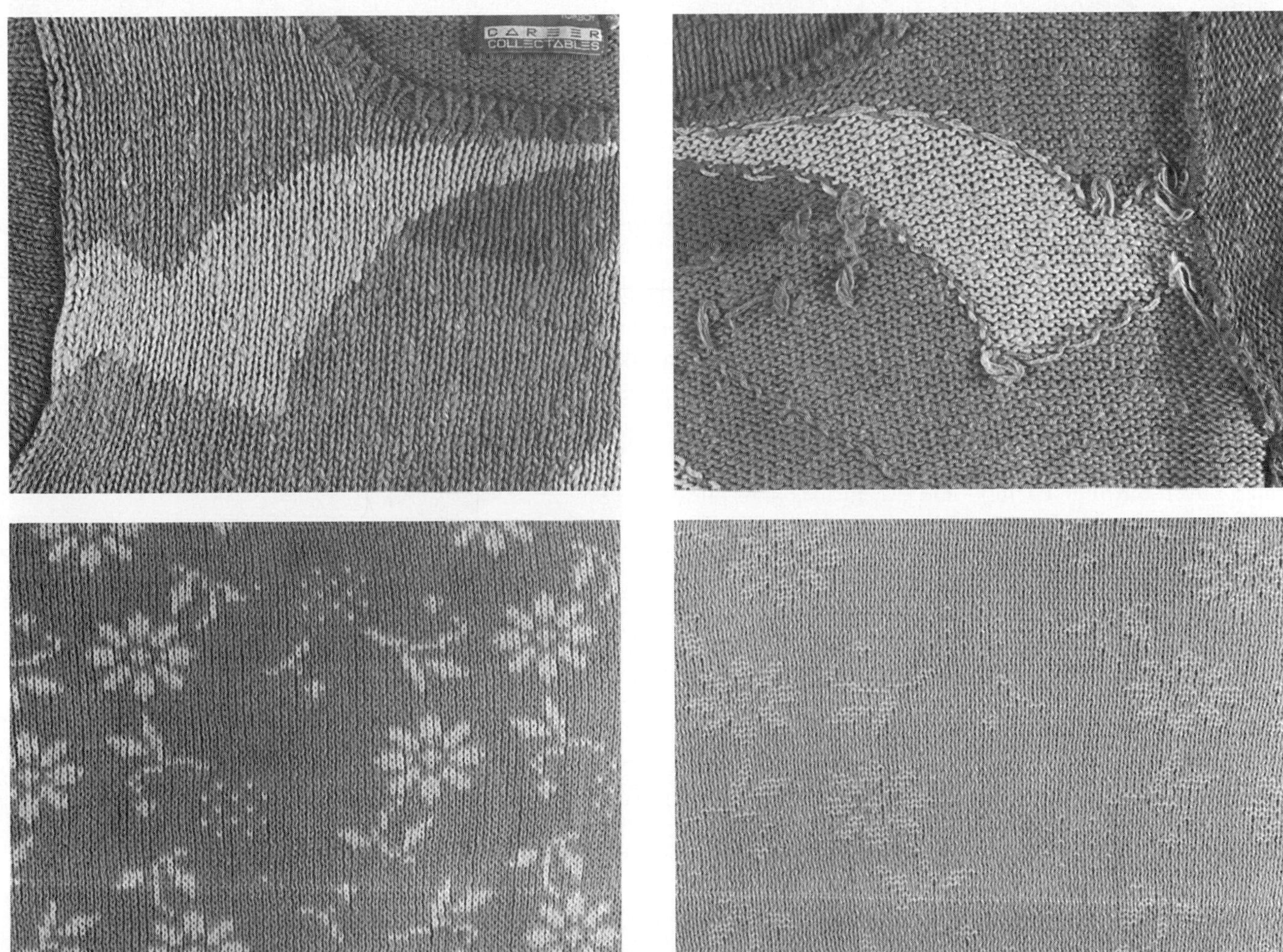


**FIGURE 14–18** ❖ Compare these two fabrics: true intarsia, face (top left) and back (top right); mock intarsia, face (bottom left) and back (bottom right).

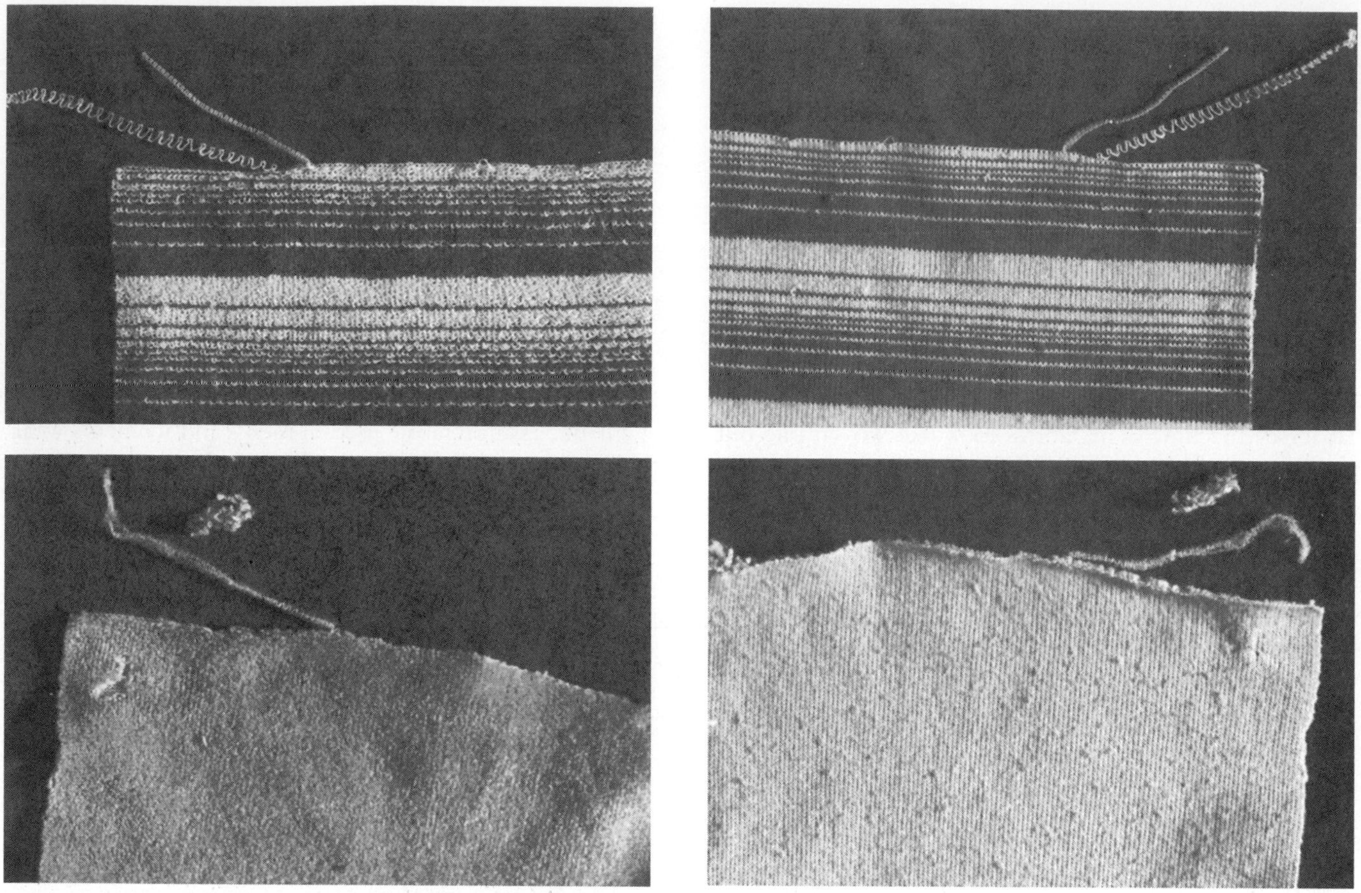

FIGURE 14–19 ❖ Pile filling knit fabrics: knit terry, face (top left) and back (top right); velour, face (bottom left) and back (bottom right). Note the yarns ravelled from each fabric and the side that forms the fashion side of the fabrics.

**Sliver-pile knits** are made on a special weft-knit, circular, sliver-knitting machine and are furlike high-pile, or deep-pile fabrics. Examine Figure 14–20 and notice that yarns are used for the ground; the *sliver* furnishes the fibers for the pile. Sliver is an untwisted rope of fiber and is the product of either carding, drawing, or combing (Chapter 10).

Fibers from the sliver are picked up by the knitting needles—along with the ground yarns—and are knit into place as the stitch is formed. A denser pile can be obtained with sliver than with yarn because the amount of face fiber is not limited by yarn size or by the distance between yarns.

The surface pile can be made with heat-sensitive manufactured fibers to resemble guard hairs for a more realistic look, printed to resemble more exotic protected species furs like jaguar or leopard, or used in other designs for fun furs. Fibers may be solution dyed or fiber dyed because piece dyeing distorts the pile. **Fake fur** fabrics are used for the shells (the outer layer) and

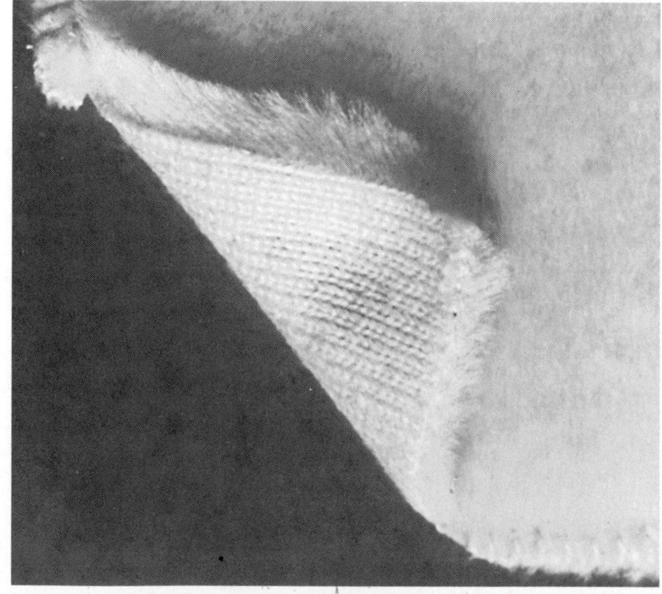

FIGURE 14–20 ❖ Sliver-knit furlike fabric.

for linings (the inner layer) of coats and jackets. Some sliver knits are also used for casual upholstery fabrics and for bath rugs.

Furlike fabrics are much lighter in weight, are much more pliable, and have better comfort characteristics than real fur. They require no special storage. A dry cleaner can successfully clean furlike fabrics by using a cold tumble dryer and combing the pile rather than steam pressing it.

***Weft-Insertion Jersey*** In **weft insertion,** a yarn of any type is laid in a course as that course is being knit. The yarn is not knit into stitches but is laid in the loops of the stitches as they are being formed. The yarn may be novelty, large, irregular, or very low twist and weak and not suitable for normal knitting. The laid-in yarn increases the crosswise stability of the fabric. This yarn may be used for decorative, strength, stability, or comfort reasons; it may be designed to produce a nap during finishing. In **french terry,** no special finishing is needed. The technical back is used as the fashion side. In **fleece** the technical back is napped. Fleece may be cotton, cotton/polyester, or cotton/acrylic blends in weights ranging from 7 to 11 oz/yd$^2$. French terry and fleece are used in sportswear, cardigans, dresses, and tops. (See Figure 14–21.)

**SHAPING ON THE KNITTING MACHINE** Garment parts—sweater bodies, fronts, backs, sleeves, skirts, socks, seamed hosiery, and collars—can be knitted to shape on flatbed machines. The stitch used for shaping is called a *loop transfer.* A knit stitch is transferred from one needle to another, usually near the end of a course, so that the width of the fabric is decreased. The process, called **fashioning,** is used to shape parts like armholes, neckline curves, collar points and finish edges.

**FIGURE 14–21** ❖ Weft-insertion weft or filling knit: napped side (left) and technical face with knit and laid-in yarn (right).

A **looping machine** is used to join the shoulders and sleeves of the shaped parts with the effect of continuous knitting rather than with an obvious seam line. This machine is also used to join collars to cut-and-sewn knit garments.

To identify fashioned garments, look for "fashion marks" accompanied by an increase or decrease in the number of wales. By closely examining Figure 14–22, one can see that the number of wales decreases from the bottom of the photo to the top. Mock fashion marks are sometimes put in the garment but they are not accompanied by an increase or decrease in the number of wales, so no shaping is done by the mock fashion marks. In Figure 14–23, one can see that there is no change in the number of wales in the photo. Full-fashioned sweaters are often made with a jersey stitch. Circular jersey sweaters are cut and sewn.

Full-fashioned garments do not necessarily fit better than cut-and-sewn garments because fit depends on the size and shape of the pieces. But full-fashioned garments are always on-grain, look better to the discerning eye, should not become misshapen during washing due to twisted seams, and are often better quality garments.

See Table 14–2 for a summary of the differences and similarities between flatbed and circular machines from a single- and double-knit perspective.

**HOSIERY** Fashion and manufactured fibers have been responsible for many of the developments in hosiery. Spun yarns are used for socks, of any fiber content. Spandex is used in the tops of socks. Nylon reinforces the heels and toes of socks. Filament nylon yarns are used in women's hosiery and lighter weight socks (see Figure 14–24).

All hosiery is a filling knit. The types include plain (or jersey), rib, mesh, and micromesh. The plain knit has stretch in both directions, and hose can be very sheer if made of fine-denier fibers or microfibers. Plain knit has the disadvantage of running readily when a loop is broken. Mesh hose are lacelike knits that do not run, but they snag and holes will develop. Micromesh has loops knitted so that a run goes up only. Mesh and micromesh stockings are not as elastic or as smooth as plain jersey. Rib stitches, jersey, and fancy knits such as cable and argyles are often used in socks or tights.

Shaping of socks and hosiery may be done by decreasing the size of the loop gradually from top to toe. If shaping is done at toe and heel, a circular fash-

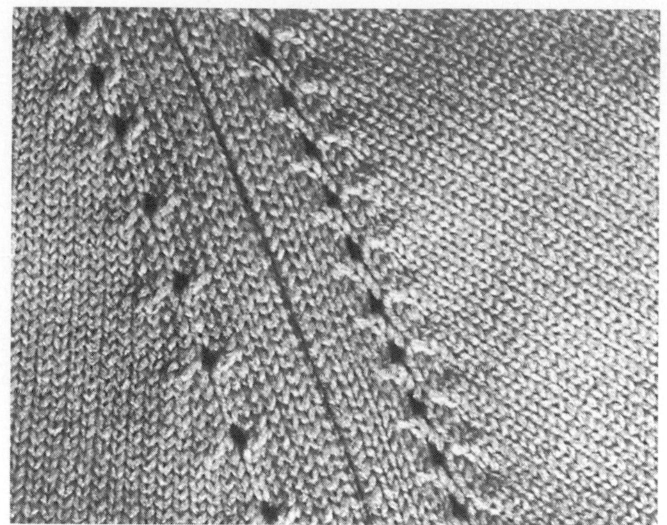

**FIGURE 14–22** ❖ Raglan sleeve portion of full-fashioned sweater. Note that stitches are dropped to shape the sleeve.

**FIGURE 14–23** ❖ Raglan sleeve portion of cut-and-sewn sweater. Note the mock full-fashion marks.

**TABLE 14–2** ❖ Filling-knitting machines and fabrics.

| | SINGLE KNIT | | DOUBLE KNIT | |
|---|---|---|---|---|
| | **Jersey—Flat** | **Jersey—Circular** | **Flat (Rib/Interlock)** | **Circular (Rib/Interlock)** |
| Description | Straight bar holds one set of latch needles | See Figure 14–8. One set of latch needles | Two flat needle beds formed in /\ position, see Figure 14–26 | See Figure 14–27. One set of needles mounted on dial, one set on cylinder |
| | Yarn carried back and forth | Yarn carried around | Yarns carried back and forth | Multiple-feed yarn carried around needle selection mechanism |
| | Purpose is to shape items | Electronic control patterns make range of designs | Stitch-transfer carriage can switch from one bed to another to make variety of stitches | Same as for flat double knit |
| Kinds of knits and end uses | Basic knit stitch | Workhorse of knitting industry | | Double knits—plain and jacquard double knits |
| | Fabric has different appearance on face and back | Fabric has different appearance face and back | Same appearance face and back | Face and back may look the same or different |
| | Full-fashioned garments | High-volume production<br>Seamless hose<br>Jersey, velour, terry | Used when fabric must have finished edge<br>Collars, trims | Double knit apparel and some furnishings |
| Advantages | Economical use of yarn<br>Garments always on grain<br>Design variations possible | Fastest method | Less waste than circular rib | High-speed production<br>Excellent design flexibility<br>Versatile in yarn usage |
| Limitations | Quite slow in production<br>Higher priced end product<br>Single-feed system | Variety of pattern possibilities available | Slow speed | Complex machine<br>Downtime can be a problem |

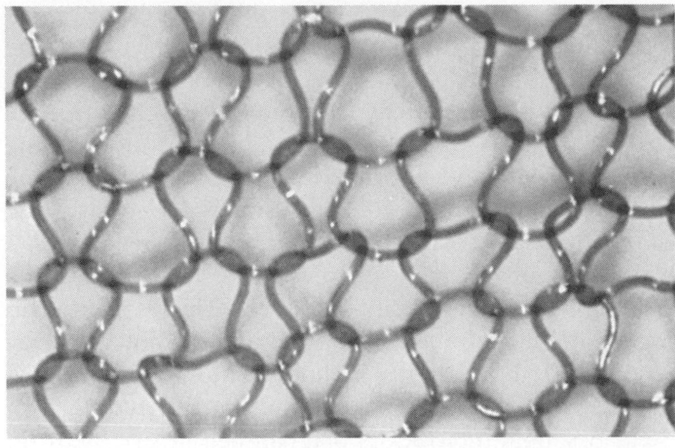

(a)

(b)

**FIGURE 14–24** ❖ Nylon hosiery: (a) stretched; (b) relaxed. (COURTESY OF E. I. DU PONT DE NEMOURS & COMPANY.)

ioning mechanism that drops stitches is used. Heavier yarn can be knit into toe and heel to give greater comfort and durability. Seamless hosiery is knit in one piece as a continuous operation. When knitting is finished, the toe is closed and the product is turned right side out.

Hosiery with shaped heels are *preboarded,* a process in which stockings are placed on metal leg forms of the correct size and shape and then steamed to press. Tube socks and stockings do not have shaped heels. They are seamed across the toe end.

Panty hose are usually made from textured stretch nylon. The panty portion may be heavier than the stocking portion. Panty hose are knitted in tube shape with a guide for slitting. After the panty section is slit, two tubes are stitched together in a U-shaped crotch seam with a firm, serged stitch. A separate crotch section may be inserted for better fit.

**DOUBLE-FILLING KNITS** **Double-filling knits** are made using a machine with two sets of needles, with the second bed or set of needles located at a right angle to the first bed of needles. Most double-knitting machines have the two needle beds arranged in an inverted V and are called **V-bed machines.** The double-knit fabric may be made with one or more sets of yarns. Double knits are categorized based on the arrangement of the needles in the double-knitting machine, or the *gait* of the machine. In a **rib-gait machine,** the two beds of needles are positioned so that both needles can be knitting at the same time. The needles of one bed are located opposite the spaces between the needles of the other bed. In **interlock gaiting,** the needles are positioned so that only one needle bed can be knitting at a time. The needles of one bed are located directly across from the needles of the other bed (see Figure 14–25 for rib and interlock gaiting).

Double-knit fabrics can be made with any combination of the four stitches: knit, tuck, float, or purl. In the flatbed machine, the needles from one bed pull the loops to the back and those in the other bed pull the loops to the front (Figure 14–26). In the circular machine, the loops are pulled to the face and back by setting one set of needles vertically in a cylinder and the other set of needles horizontally in a dial or cam (Figure 14–27).

Double-knit fabrics have two-way stretch and relatively high dimensional stability. They do not curl at the edges and are less apt to stretch out than single knits. They do not run. Double knits can resemble any woven structure and are often given the woven fabric name—denim, seersucker, double piqué, and the like.

A technique used to illustrate the production of double knits is a diagram based on the two needle beds

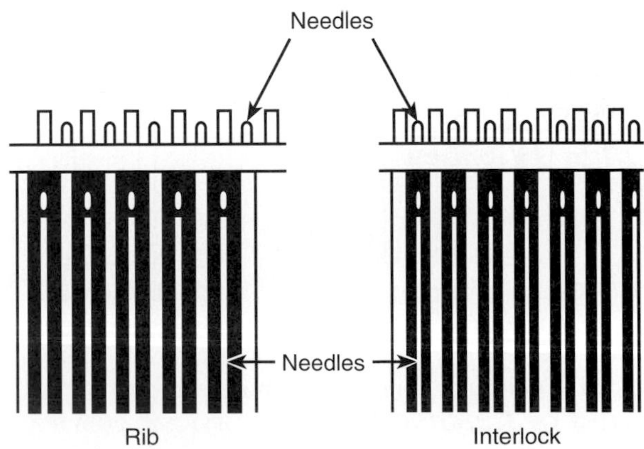


**FIGURE 14–25** ❖ Gaiting: rib (left); interlock (right).

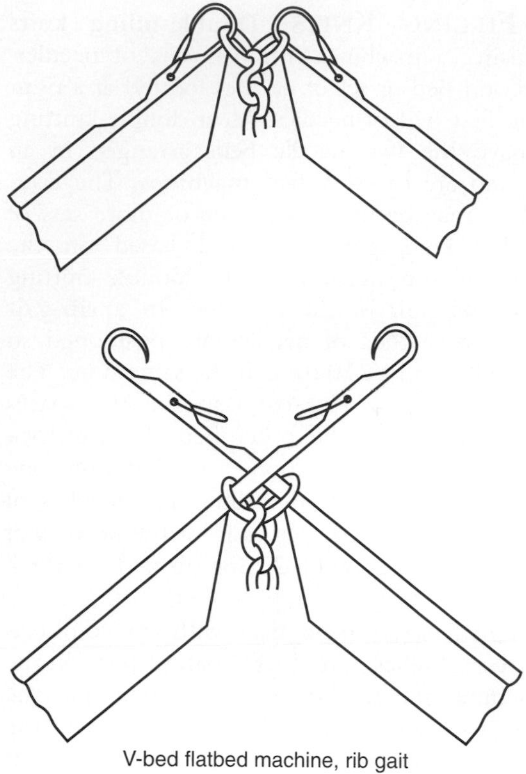


**FIGURE 14–26** ❖ Needle action in flatbed machine. (COURTESY OF *KNITTING TIMES*, THE OFFICIAL PUBLICATION OF NATIONAL KNITWEAR AND SPORTSWEAR ASSOCIATION.)

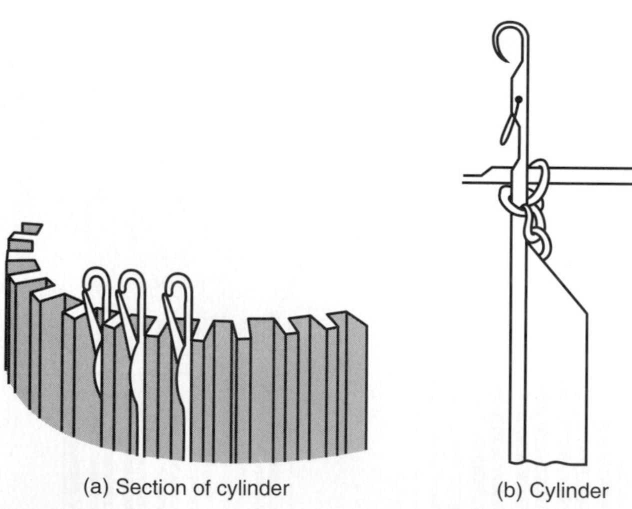


**FIGURE 14–27** ❖ (a) Needle beds and (b) knitting action in circular-knitting machine, rib gait. (COURTESY OF *KNITTING TIMES*, THE OFFICIAL PUBLICATION OF NATIONAL KNITWEAR AND SPORTSWEAR ASSOCIATION.)

and the type of gaiting. A center horizontal line represents the space between the beds. A short vertical line represents a needle. In **interlock gaiting,** the short vertical lines are directly opposite each other (Figure 14–28). In **rib gaiting,** the needle lines stop at the horizontal line and needle lines on one side of the line are staggered with needle lines on the opposite side (Figure 14–29). In the diagram, a loop represents a knit stitch, an inverted V represents a tuck stitch, and a — represents a float or miss stitch. Thus a 1 × 1 rib would be diagrammed on rib gaiting, as shown in Figure 14–30. Each course required to produce the pattern is diagrammed separately and is referred to as a step. A simple interlock is diagrammed in two steps on interlock gaiting because two steps are required to create the interlock fabric (see Figure 14–31). A double

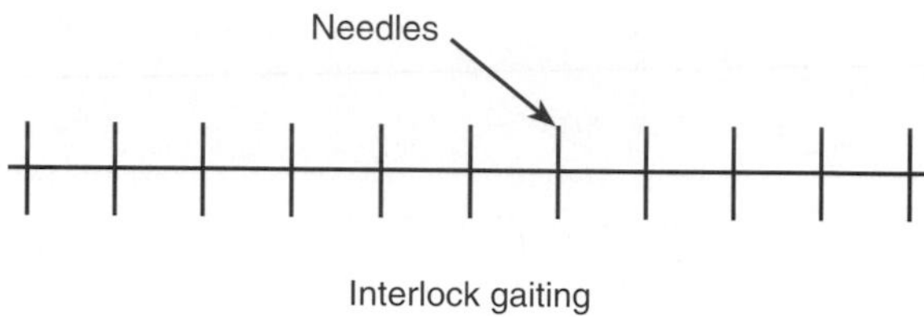


**FIGURE 14–28** ❖ Interlock gaiting.

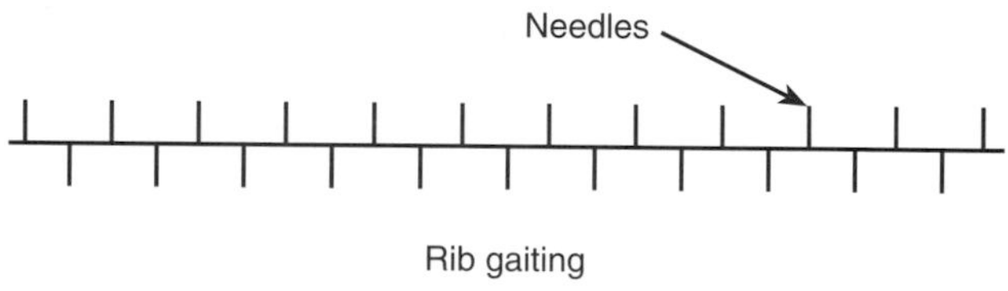


**FIGURE 14–29** ❖ Rib gaiting.

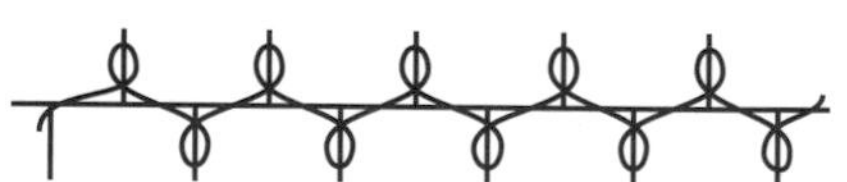

**FIGURE 14–30** ❖ 1 × 1 rib (rib gaiting).

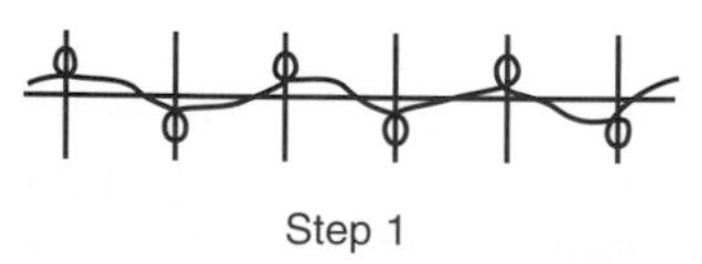


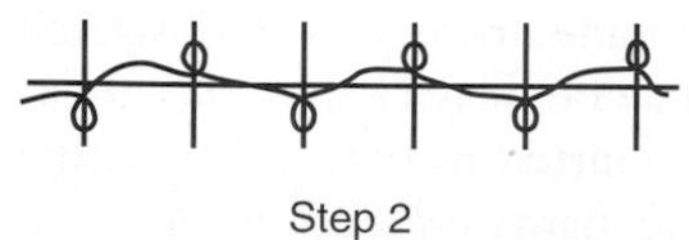


**FIGURE 14–31** ❖ Interlock diagram.

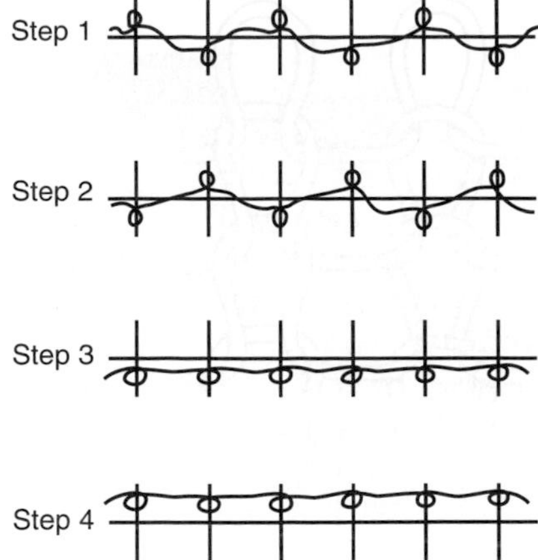


**FIGURE 14–32** ❖ Ponte de roma (interlock gaiting).

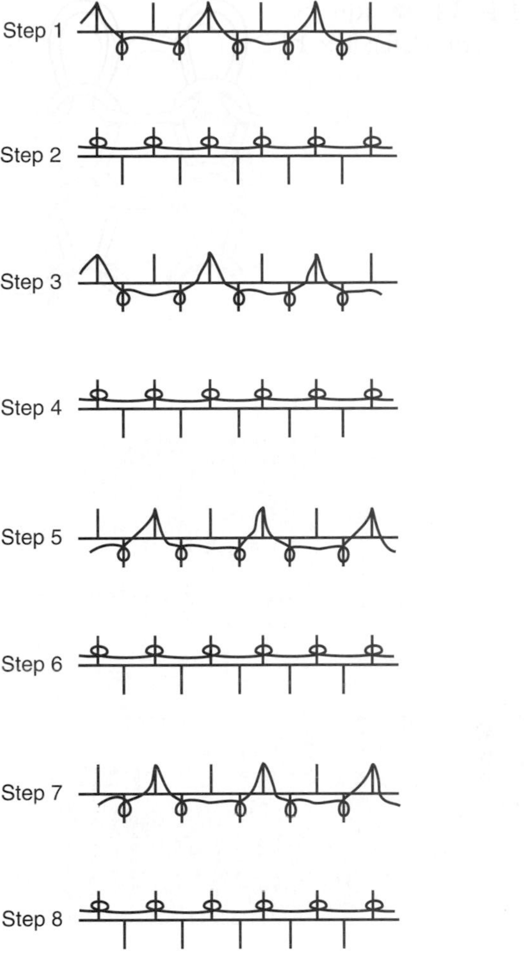


**FIGURE 14–33** ❖ La coste (rib gaiting).

knit on interlock gaiting might be a ponte de roma, which requires four steps to create the fabric (see Figure 14–32). A double knit on rib gaiting might be a la coste, which requires eight steps in knitting (see Figure 14–33). An easy way to identify a double knit is to look at the edge of the fabric parallel to a course. If all loops point in one direction, it is a single knit. If some of the loops point toward the front and some toward the back, it is a double knit. If the loops are directly opposite each other, it is made with interlock gaiting. If the loops are not directly opposite each other, it is made with rib gaiting. A magnifying glass or stereoscopic microscope aids identification.

**Double-knit jersey,** like *interlock jersey,* looks the same on both sides. It differs in that it is made on rib gaiting and needles from the cam and cylinder are not opposite each other but are positioned so that the needles from one bed work between the needles from the other bed. They knit a 1 × 1 rib. To distinguish between an interlock and a rib-gaiting fabric, cut along a course and stretch the edge widthwise. Examine the edge. If it is interlock, there will be a back stitch opposite each front stitch; if it is rib double knit, the back stitches will alternate between the front stitches. Interlock runs much easier than a rib double knit, but interlock is a softer, more fluid fabric.

***Rib Structure*** A **rib structure** is made of face wales and back wales. The lengthwise ridges are formed on both sides of the fabric by pulling stitches first to the face and next to the back of the fabric in adjacent stitches or groups of stitches. These may be in various combinations, 1 × 1, 2 × 2, 2 × 3, and so on (Figure 14–34). Sides of the stitches are darker to assist in seeing the structure and its face. Figure 14–35 shows a fabric in a combination plain and rib knit. The 1 × 1 rib is the simplest double-knit fabric produced using rib gaiting. It usually consists of one set of yarns.

Rib knits have the same appearance on the face and back. They generally have up to twice the extensibility crosswise as that of single jersey. Rib knits do not curl at the edges, but they run. They unravel from the end knit last. They are usually twice as thick as single jersey.

**Jacquard double knits** have almost limitless design possibilities. The intermeshing of the two yarns is the same as for the double-knit jersey but with added needle-selecting mechanisms (Figure 14–36). Although double knits are often named for the woven fabrics they resemble, more often the term double knit is the only name used to identify this type of fabric.

***Interlock Structure*** The *interlock* is the simplest double-knit fabric produced using interlock gaiting (see Figure 14–28). Interlock fabrics are composed of two

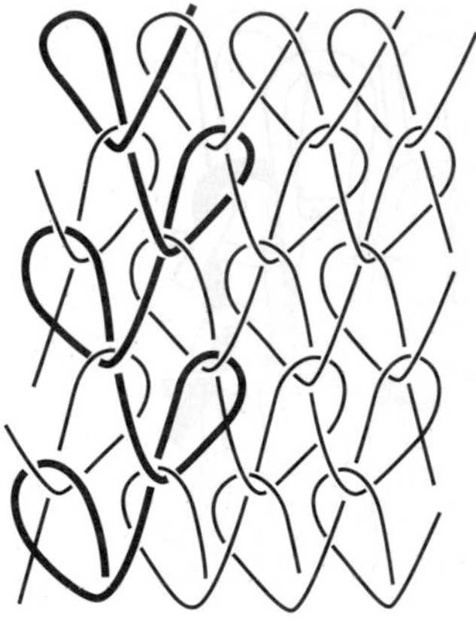

**FIGURE 14–39** ❖ Warp-knitting stitch.

and two or more guide bars, and so on: hence the terms *one-bar tricot* and *two-bar tricot.* Each yarn guide on the bar directs one yarn to the hook of one knitting needle. More guide bars give greater design flexibility. The loops of one course are all made simultaneously when the guide bar rises and moves sideways, laying the yarns around the needles to form the loops, which are then pulled down through the loops of the preceding course.

Warp knits usually are diagrammed using a **point-paper** notation. In this notation, each point in a horizontal row represents a needle. Arrows represent the movement of the guide bar that controls yarn movement. Thus the diagram for each row of points represents the movement of the guide bar that creates the yarn loops for a course. The next row of points represents the next course, and so on until one complete repeat has been represented. The diagram starts at the bottom row of points and moves up the paper from course to course as time progresses. Figure 14–39 is a diagram for a warp knit. Figure 14–40 shows the steps (a through g) that are needed to create that fabric. In (a) of Figure 14–41, the seven steps are combined in one diagram; in (b), the resulting yarn loop is shown; in (c), the two repeats of the pattern are shown. Yarn from the front bar usually predominates on the surface, whereas yarn from the back bars provides run resistance, elasticity, and weight.

Apparel end uses for warp knits include lingerie, underwear, sportswear, and outerwear. Warp knits are used in contract-grade carpet, some upholstery, some drapery and casement fabrics, and for face fabrics in wall partitions and miniblind slats. Industrial end uses are the most rapidly expanding area and include fabrics for sun and light protection, for controlling rock falls, for grass collection, for snow barriers and for dam reinforcement. Warp-knit fabrics also are used as medical implants such as artificial veins and tissue-support fabrics.

Even though warp knitting is fast, warp knits are not inexpensive because the process requires very regular yarns. The cost of the yarns offsets the fast speed of the process.

## Machines Used in Warp Knitting

Warp knits are classified by the machine used to produce the fabric and its characteristics. Tricot machines use a single set of spring-beard or compound needles. Tricot-knitting machines with computer-controlled guide bars, electronic beam control, and computerized take-up are able to knit 2,000 courses per minute. Raschel machines use one or two sets of vertically mounted latch needles. Jacquard raschel knitting machines with computer-controlled guide bars are used to produce complex structures used for apparel, furnishing, and industrial products. The differences between the fabrics produced by

**FIGURE 14–40** ❖ Guide-bar movements, step by step, for warp-knit stitch.

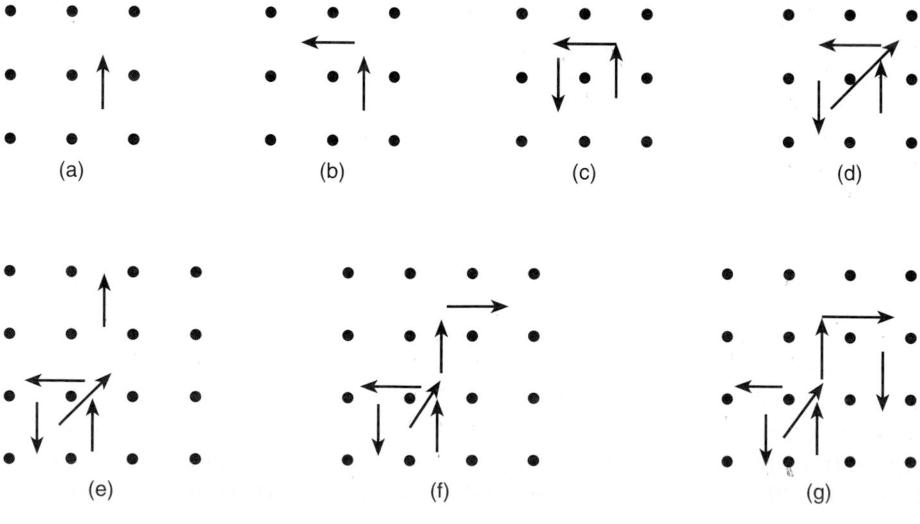

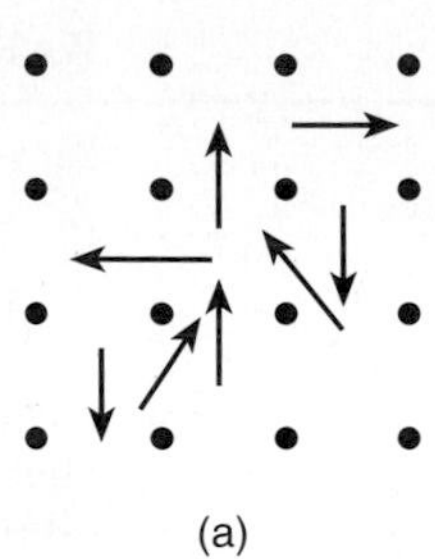

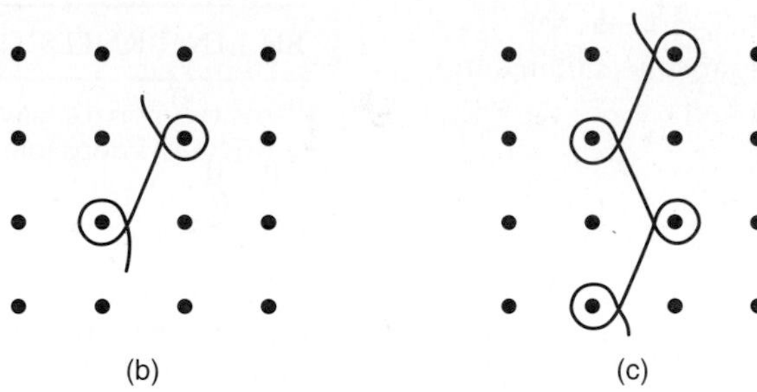

**FIGURE 14–41** ❖ Guide-bar movements: (a) all steps of the guide-bar movement; (b) yarn movement following the guide-bar movement; (c) series of yarn loops creating the warp-knit fabric.

these machines have become less distinct. Several types of warp knitting machine are listed in Table 14–3. Tricot and raschel machines, however, account for the manufacture of more than 95 percent of all warp-knit goods.

## Warp Knits versus Filling Knits

Warp and filling knits differ because of the different knitting techniques and the machines used in their manufacture. The major differences are summarized in Table 14–4.

## Warp-Knit Fabrics

**TRICOT WARP KNITS** The name **tricot** has been used as a generic name for all warp-knit fabric. Tricot comes from the French word *tricoter*, meaning *to knit.* It is the fabric produced on the tricot machine using the *plain stitch.*

The plain stitch and the lockstitch are shown in Figure 14–42. The plain stitch runs and is seldom used except for backings for quilts and bonded fabrics. The lockknit is used in other tricots. The face of the fabric is formed of the vertical portion of loops and the back has the horizontal portion of loops. The face has a much finer appearance than the back. Tricot is nonraveling. Lockknit tricots do not run. However, tricots may split or "zip" between wales. The fabric will curl just as filling-knit jersey does. Tricot is more stable compared to filling knits. It has little elasticity in the lengthwise direction and some elasticity in the crosswise direction. Some important end uses of tricot fabrics include lingerie, sleepwear, shirts, blouses, uniforms, dresses, and automotive upholstery.

The tricot machine is the mainstay of the warp-knitting industry (Figure 14–43). It is a high-speed machine that can knit flat fabric up to 170 inches wide. The machine makes a plain-jersey stitch or can be modified to make many designs. Another modification is the attachment for laying in yarn in a tricot structure.

**TABLE 14–3** ❖ Warp-knitting machines.

| TRICOT | RASCHEL | SIMPLEX | MILANESE |
|---|---|---|---|
| Single bed | One or two needle beds | Two sets of needles | Flat—spring-beard needles |
| Spring-beard needles or compound needles | Latch needles | Spring-beard needles | Circular—latch needles |
| | Coarse gauge | | |
| 2–3–4 bars indicate number of sets of warp yarns | May have as many as 78 guide bars | | Yarn travels diagonally from one side of material to the other |
| Simple fabric | Complex fabric | | |
| High-speed, high-volume | Great design possibilities | Seldom used | Seldom used |
| Usually filament yarns | Usually spun or spun and filament yarns | | |
| Wider fabric, 170 inches | Narrower fabric, 100 inches | | |
| | **End Uses** | | |
| Plain, patterned, striped, brushed fabric | Sheer laces and nets | Warp double knits | Underwear |
| Underwear | Draperies | Gloves | Outerwear |
| Outerwear | Power net | | |
| Upholstery | Thermal cloth | | |
| | Outerwear | | |
| | Upholstery | | |

**TABLE 14–4** ❖ Comparison of filling and warp knits.

| FILLING KNITS | WARP KNITS |
|---|---|
| Yarns run horizontally | Yarns run vertically |
| Loops joined one to another in the same course | Loops joined one to another in adjoining course |
| Connections are horizontal | Connections are diagonal |
| More design possibilities | Higher productivity |
| More open fabric | More compact fabric |
| Two-way stretch | Crosswise stretch, little lengthwise stretch |
| Run, most ravel | Most do not run or ravel |
| Hand or machine process | Machine process |
| Flat or circular | Flat |
| Can have finished edges | Seldom have finished edges |
| Can knit shaped garments, garment pieces, or yardage | Produced as yardage |

*Plain tricot* is made on a machine employing one set of needles and two guide bars. Filament yarns are used in either smooth or textured form. In the standard ranges of 15–40 denier, nylon tricot is lightweight (17.5–6.5 yards/pound), has exceptional strength and durability, and can be heat set for dimensional stability. One of the unique features of nylon tricot is that the same piece of gray goods can be finished under different tensions to different widths and different appearances; for example, 168-inch gray goods can be finished at 98, 108, 120, 180, or 200 inches wide.

**FIGURE 14–42** ❖ Two-bar tricot: technical face (top); technical back (bottom).

**Brushed tricots** have a velvetlike surface of fibers raised from the surface. The fabric is used in evening gowns, shoes, slacks, upholstery, and draperies.

The knit stitches have long underlaps. One set of yarns is carried over 3–5 wales to form floats; the second set of yarns interloops with adjacent yarns. Nylon is used for the adjacent looping to provide strength and durability. The long floats are broken when the fabric is finished. The napped side is used as the fashion side of the fabric even though it is the technical back (Figure 14–44).

*Satinlike* tricots are made in the same way as napped tricots except that the finishing processes differ. These fabrics are usually 100 percent nylon or polyester and the floats are longer.

*Tricot-net fabric* can be made by skipping every other needle so only half as much yarn is used and open spaces are created in the fabric. **Tulle** (tool) is a hexagonal net used for veiling, support fabrics, and as overlays for apparel.

*Tuck effects* use the same yarns as in the striped fabrics, but a change in the yarn arrangement forms a tuck. The tucks may be straight, wavy, irregular, intermittent, wide, or narrow.

*Automotive tricot upholstery* of a double-knit velvet is made in a manner similar to that of velvet. Two layers of fabric are knit face to face with a pile yarn connecting the two layers. The layers are separated when the pile yarn is cut. Pile height is related to the distance between the two layers.

**RASCHEL-WARP KNITS** The raschel-warp knitting machine has one or two needle beds with latch needles set in a vertical position and as many as 78 guide

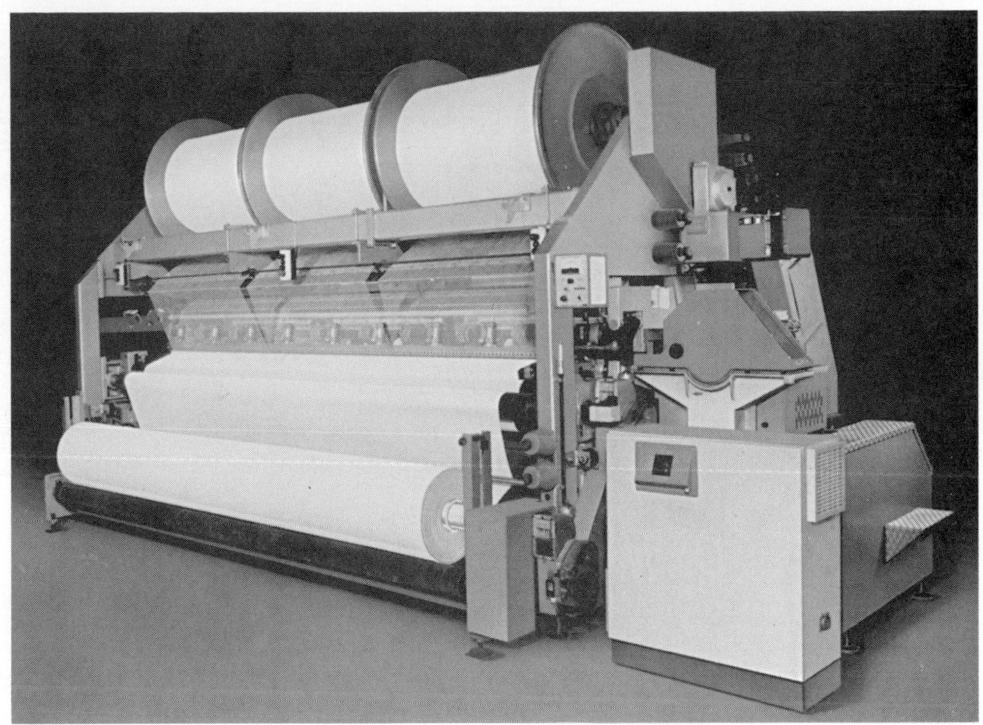

**FIGURE 14–43** ❖ Warp-knitting tricot machine. (COURTESY OF MAYER TEXTILE MACHINE CORP.)

bars. The fabric comes from the knitting frame almost vertically instead of horizontally as in the tricot machine. The various raschel machines knit a wide variety of fabrics from gossamer-sheer nets and veilings to very heavy carpets.

Raschel knits are used industrially for a variety of products including laundry bags, fish nets, dye nets, safety nets, and covers for swimming pools.

**Raschel fabrics** have rows of chainlike loops called *pillars,* with laid-in yarns in various lapping configurations (Figures 14–45 and 14–46). These fabrics can be identified by raveling the laid-in yarn and noticing that the fabric splits or comes apart lengthwise. Window treatment fabrics and outerwear fabrics are knitted on this standard-type machine.

Carpets have been knitted since the early 1950s. Since their production is faster, knitted carpets are cheaper to make than woven carpets. Another technique, tufting, is the most common method for producing carpet. (See Chapter 15.) Knitted carpets have two- or three-ply warps for lengthwise stability, laid-in crosswise yarns for body and crosswise stability, and pile yarns. Knitted carpets can be identified by looking for chains of stitches on the underside. They seldom have a secondary backing. These carpets are usually commercial or contract carpets.

**Lace** and curtain nets of the kind made on Leavers lace machines (see Chapter 15) can be made at much higher speeds on a raschel machine. Window-treatment nets with square, diamond, or hexagonal meshes are made on tricot machines. Laces are usually made of nylon or polyester. Many laces are now warp knits because the process is inexpensive and fast. Thus, light, delicate, and elaborate laces can be made quickly and inexpensively.

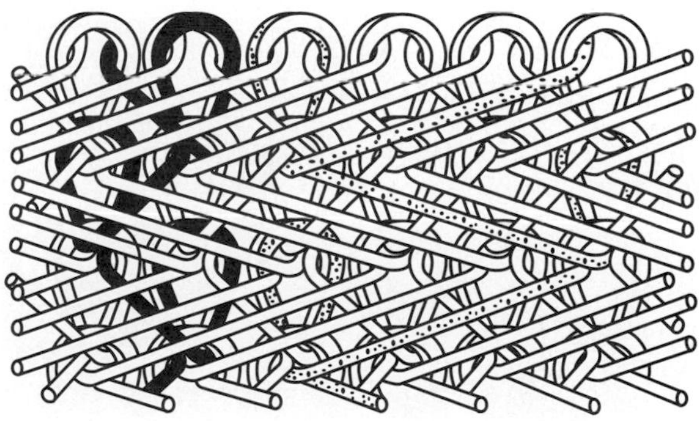

**FIGURE 14–44** ❖ Warp knit velour before napping. White and speckled yarns will be broken during napping. (COURTESY OF *KNITTING TIMES,* THE OFFICIAL PUBLICATION OF NATIONAL KNITWEAR AND SPORTSWEAR ASSOCIATION.)

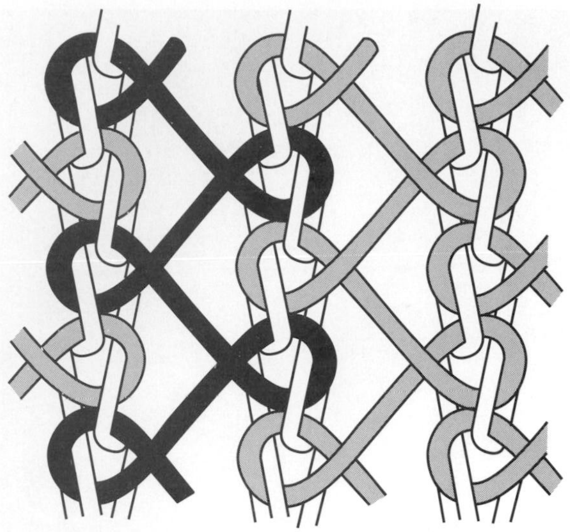

**FIGURE 14–45** ❖ Raschel knit. (COURTESY OF *KNITTING TIMES*, THE OFFICIAL PUBLICATION OF NATIONAL KNITWEAR AND SPORTSWEAR ASSOCIATION.)

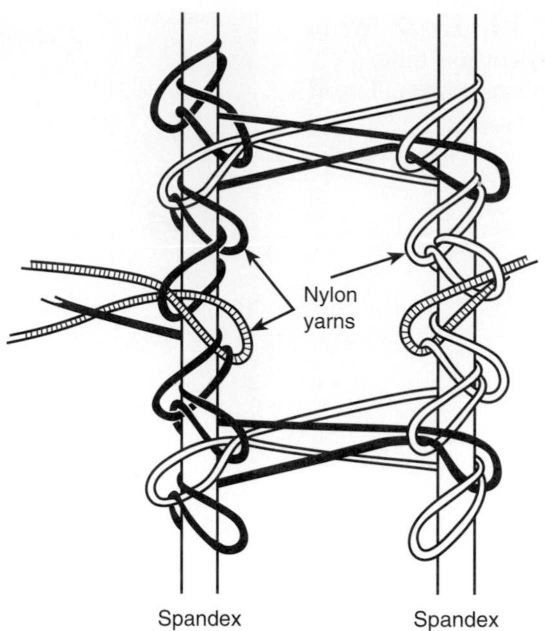


**FIGURE 14–47** ❖ Raschel power-knit stitch.

Knit meshes may be made using either tricot or raschel machines depending on their complexity, yarn size, and end use. (See Figure 14–46.)

*Thermal cloth* has pockets knitted in to trap heat from the body; it looks like woven waffle cloth and is used mainly for winter underwear. This knit is also used for some thermal blankets.

**Power net** is an elasticized fabric used for foundation garments and bathing suits. Nylon is used for the two-bar ground construction and spandex is laid in by two other guide bars (Figure 14–47). Although sometimes referred to as spandex, these fabrics are blends of nylon and spandex.

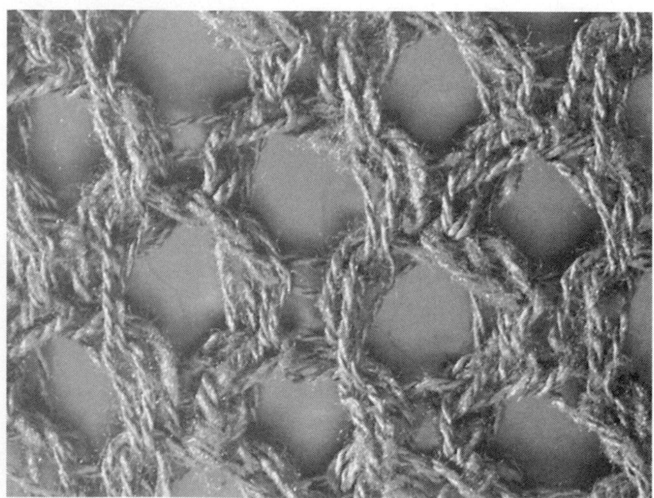

**FIGURE 14–46** ❖ Raschel mesh fabric.

**INSERTION WARP KNITS** Insertion of yarns in the warp knit structure is a relatively simple concept. Yarns are laid in the stitches during the knitting process but are not used to form any stitches. These laid-in yarns provide directional stability and can be in any direction or at an angle. Fabric characteristics can be engineered for desired properties. Yarns that are not appropriate for knitting can be used, such as extremely coarse, fine, or irregular yarns and yarns of fibers that have low flexibility, such as carbon or glass. Insertion fabrics are used in aircraft and aerospace components, automotive parts, boat hulls, ballistic protective clothing, structural building elements, interlinings for apparel, and window treatment and wall covering fabrics.

**Weft insertion** is done by a warp-knitting machine with a weft-laying attachment. An attachment carries a single filling yarn to and fro across the machine, and this yarn is fed steadily into the needle zone of the machine. A firm selvage is formed on each side.

More complex attachments supply a sheet of filling yarns to a conveyor that travels to and fro across the machine. The yarns are then fed into the stitching area of the machine. A cutting device trims filling yarn "tails" from the selvages and a vacuum removes the tailings.

Weft-insertion fabrics offer the best combination of properties of both woven and knitted cloth: namely, strength, comfort, cover without bulk, and weight. They are lighter weight than double knits but have more covering power. They have increased crosswise stability of weaves but retain the comfort of knits.

**FIGURE 14–48** ❖ Warp and weft insertion. Warp-knit casement fabric for windows.

In weft-insertion warp knits, the inserted yarn is caught in a vertical chain of stitching. These fabrics are used for hospital curtains and table linens, as well as for other furnishing and industrial uses.

The insertion of **warp** yarn into a knit structure gives the fabric the vertical stability of woven cloth while retaining the horizontal stretch of knit fabric.

Warp- and weft-insertion fabrics have characteristics very similar to woven fabrics. These fabrics can be much less expensive than woven fabrics and are available in wide widths. They are frequently used as window treatment fabrics (see Figure 14–48).

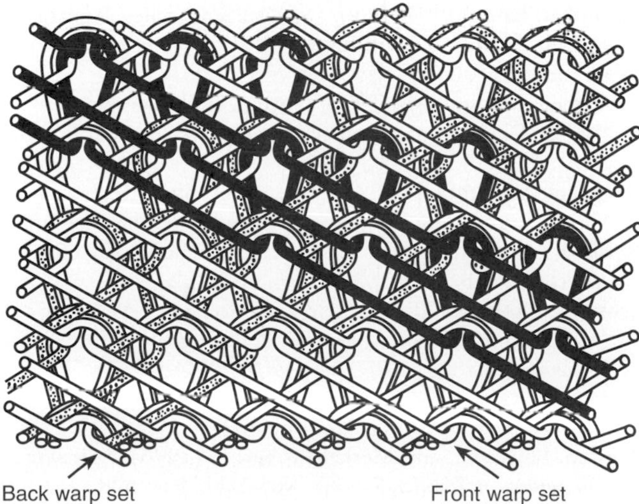


**FIGURE 14–49** ❖ Milanese. (COURTESY OF *KNITTING TIMES*, THE OFFICIAL PUBLICATION OF NATIONAL KNITWEAR AND SPORTSWEAR ASSOCIATION.)

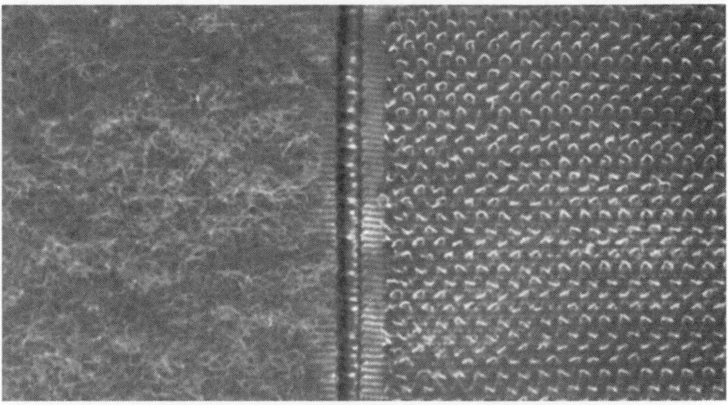

**FIGURE 14–50** ❖ Hook-and-loop closure fabric: looped fabric (left); hooked fabric (right).

## Minor Warp Knits

**SIMPLEX** The **simplex machine,** which is similar to the tricot machine, uses spring-beard needles, two needle bars, and two guide bars. It produces a two-faced fabric somewhat like circular double knits. End uses are fashion gloves, swimwear, and dresses.

**MILANESE** The **Milanese machine** is especially constructed to produce superior warp-knit fabrics. The machine can use both kinds of needles. The fabric it produces, equivalent to a two-bar tricot fabric, is made from two sets of warp yarns with one needle bar and one guide bar. But the lapping movements are arranged so each warp yarn moves across the full width of the fabric, one set knitting from right to left and the other from left to right. This results in a diagonal formation

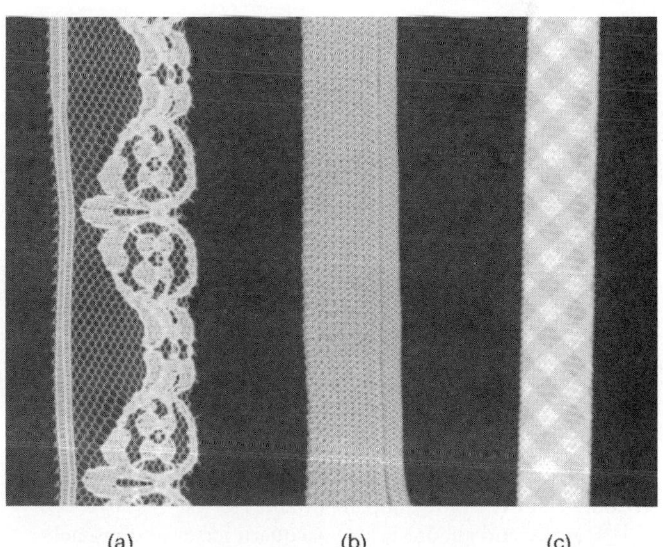


**FIGURE 14–51** ❖ Narrow fabrics: (a) raschel knit lace; (b) flat filling knit; (c) circular knit.

(Figure 14–49), which shows up on the back of the cloth. The face has a very fine rib. The fabric is runproof and is used for gloves and lingerie.

## Narrow Knitted Fabrics

*Narrow knitted fabrics* are made on a few needles on a multiknit machine, either filling or warp-knitting machines. One of the more important types of narrow knitted fabrics are knit elastics. Knit elastics account for 35–40 percent of the narrow elastic market and are used in underwear, running shorts, slacks, fleece products, and hosiery. Hook and loop tape fasteners are warp-knit narrow fabrics (see Figure 14–50). Other trim and knit elastics are shown in Figure 14–51.

Narrow knitted fabrics of thermoplastic fiber are made on regular machines in wide widths and slit with hot knives to seal the edges. These are much cheaper to produce and are satisfactory if the heat sealing is properly done.

# Key Terms

Run
Knitting
Filling or weft knitting
Warp knitting
Spring-beard needle
Latch needle
Compound needle
Stitch
Wale
Course
Gauge
Cut
Technical face
Technical back
Circular machines
Flatbed machines
Knit stitch
Tuck stitch
Float or miss stitch
Purl or reverse stitch
Single-filling knit
Jersey
Stockinette
Lisle
Single-figured jersey
Jacquard jersey
Intarsia
Pile jersey
Knitted terrycloth
Velour
Sliver-pile knit
Fake fur
Weft insertion
French terry
Fleece
Fashioning
Looping machine
Double-filling knit
V-bed machine
Gait
Rib gaiting
Interlock gaiting
Double-knit jersey
Rib
Jacquard double knit
Purl knits
Tricot machine
Point-paper notation
Tricot
Brushed tricot
Tulle
Raschel
Lace
Power net
Weft insertion warp knit
Warp insertion warp knit
Simplex machine
Milanese machine

# Questions

1. Compare the characteristics of woven and knit fabrics.
2. Compare the characteristics of filling and warp-knit fabrics.
3. Describe the differences in appearance and performance between the following pairs of knit fabrics:
   jersey and tricot　　jacquard jersey and raschel
   ribknit and interlock　　fleece and velour
4. Describe the performance that might be expected in the following products:
   100 percent combed cotton filling-knit jersey T-shirt
   100 percent modacrylic warp-insertion raschel casement drapery (smooth filament yarns and inserted thick-thin novelty yarns) for a public library
   100 percent olefin raschel warp-knit contract carpet of BCF yarns for hallway of office building
   80 percent nylon/20 percent spandex raschel-knit swimsuit
5. Describe the characteristics of a good quality jersey and a good quality tricot.

# Suggested Readings


Davidson, W. A. B. (1993, March). "Spotlight on Warp Knitting." *Knitting/Apparel* in *Knitting Times,* pp. 29–30.
Gross, David (1995, May). "Circular Machinery Sales Strong Leading to ITMA '95." *Knitting Times,* pp. 35–39.
Humphries, Mary (1996). *Fabric Glossary.* Upper Saddle River, NJ: Prentice Hall.
Leventhal, Larry (1994, July). "Specialized Niches Available to Knits in Home Furnishings." *Knitting Times,* pp. 33, 49.
Mohamed, Mansour H. (1990, November/December). "Three-Dimensional Textiles." *American Scientist, 78,* pp. 530–541.
Raz, Sam (September, 1989). "New Concepts in Technical Fabric Engineering." *Knitting Times,* pp. 65–68.
Reisfeld, A. (April, 1989). "Multi-Axial Machine for Weft-Insertion Knits." *Knitting Times,* pp. 21–22.
Schwartz, Peter, Rhodes, Trevor, and Mohamed, Mansour (1982). *Fabric Forming Systems.* Park Ridge, NJ: Noyes Publications.
Spencer, David J. (1983). *Knitting Technology.* New York: Pergamon Press.
Tortora, Phyllis G., and Merkel, Robert S. (1996). *Fairchild's Dictionary of Textiles,* 7th ed. New York: Fairchild Publications.

# Chapter 15

# OTHER FABRICATION METHODS

OBJECTIVES

- To understand fabrication processes beyond weaving and knitting.
- To recognize fabrics made using these techniques.
- To integrate the performance of film, foam, fiberweb and netlike structures, lace, braid, composite fabrics, leather, and fur with end use requirements.

Although woven and knit fabrics are common on the market, many other means of producing fabrics are also used. This chapter focuses on those fabrics and is organized according to the material from which the fabric is made: solutions, fibers, yarns, or fabrics. This chapter discusses all other fabrication methods beyond weaving and knitting. Many of these methods and fabrics do not fit the classic definition of a textile. These methods and fabrics are included in this text because they are used to produce textile products, they are used as substitutes for textiles, they are made of the same chemicals as textiles, or they are made of textile components like fibers, yarns, and fabrics. Many of these items are used for apparel and furnishings. They are equally, if not more, important to the industrial textile markets. This discussion begins with the simplest process and components and moves to the most complex. Assessing the performance of these fabrics is often similar to assessing the performance of woven or knit fabrics. Some special procedures may be used and will be discussed in the appropriate section.

# Fabrics from Solutions

## Films

**Films** are made directly from a polymer solution by melt-extrusion or by casting the solution onto a hot drum. The solutions are similar to the spinning solutions for fibers.

Most apparel and furnishing textile films are made from vinyl or polyurethane solutions. Both types are similar in appearance but vary in the care required. Vinyl films are washable but become stiff in dry cleaning solvents. Urethane films are both washable and dry cleanable. Urethane films remain soft in cold weather, whereas vinyl films become brittle and stiff.

There are several structures of films. **Plain films** are firm, dense, and uniform; they also are referred to as **nonreinforced films.** These films are usually impermeable to air and water. They have excellent soil and stain resistance and recover well from deformation.

**Expanded films** are spongier, softer, and plumper as a result of a blowing agent that incorporates tiny air cells into the compound. They are neither as strong nor as abrasion resistant as plain films. Expanded films also tend to be less impermeable to air and water. To increase the comfort characteristics of plain and expanded films, thousands of tiny pinholes called micropores may be punched in the fabric to permit air and water vapor, but not liquid water, to pass through the fabric. Nonporous films may be used for inexpensive upholstery. These films are uncomfortable, especially in hot weather and in direct contact with skin.

Because plain films and expanded films are seldom durable enough to withstand normal use, these products are usually attached to a woven, knit, or fiberweb support fabric or substrate. The end result is a **supported,** *coated,* or *reinforced* **film.** Supported films are composite fabrics and will be discussed later in this chapter. Supported films are more durable, more expensive, easier to sew, and less likely to crack and split than nonreinforced films.

Plastic films and coated fabrics are more waterproof than any other material. The finishing process can make them look like almost any other textile (see Figure 15–1). They can vary in thickness from very thin transparent film used to make a sandwich bag to heavy leatherette used to cover a dentist's chair. They have the advantage of being uniform in appearance and quality, they are available in long, uniformly wide lengths, and they are much cheaper and easier to make into products compared to leather.

This list briefly summarizes films:

- Solution is extruded through narrow slits into warm air or cast onto a revolving drum. Molding powders may be pressed between hot rolls.
- Films are waterproof, low cost, resistant to soil, nonfibrous.
- Films may lack permeability.

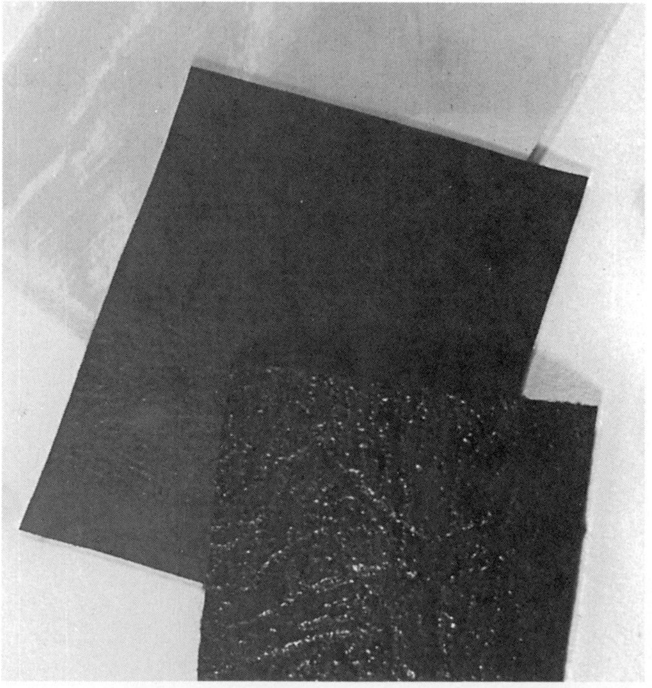

**Figure 15–1** ❖ Films.

- Films may lack strength unless supported by a fabric back.
- Films have low drapeability.
- Films can be finished to look like many other fabrics or to have their own characteristic appearance.
- Films are used for shoes, shower curtains, upholstery, and plastic bags.

Table 15–1 lists polymers that are used in both film and fiber form.

## Foams

**Foams** are made by incorporating air into an elastic-like substance. Rubber and polyurethane are most common. The outstanding characteristics of foams are their bulk and sponginess. They are used as carpet backings and underlays, furniture padding, and pillow forms, and are laminated to fabric for apparel and furnishing textiles (Figure 15–2). Shredded foam is used to stuff accent pillows and toys.

Polyurethane foam is available in a wide range of physical properties from very stiff to rubbery. The size of the air cells can be controlled. Foams will yellow on exposure to sunlight, but this does not decrease urethane foam's usefulness and durability. (Exposure to sunlight does, however, cause rubber to disintegrate.) Foams are relatively weak and are not used by themselves. Polyurethane is prepared by the reaction of diisocyanate with a compound containing two or more hydroxyl groups in the presence of a suitable catalyst. Chemicals and foaming agents are mixed thoroughly. After the foam is formed, it is cut into blocks 200–300 yards long, and strips of the desired thickness are cut from these blocks.

This list briefly summarizes foams:

- Foams are made by incorporating air into an elastic-like substance. Rubber and polyurethane are the most commonly used foams.

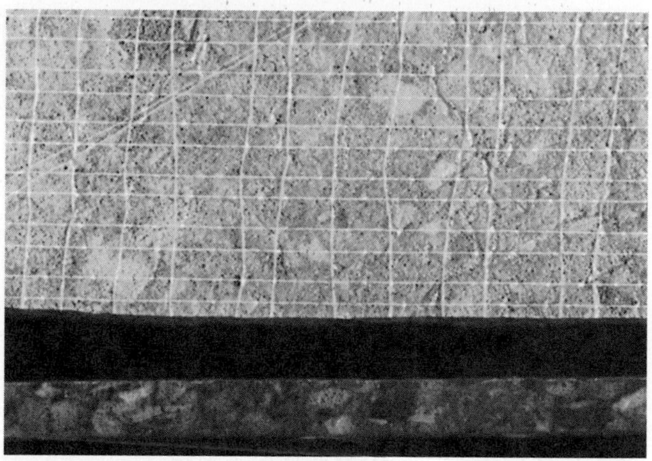

**FIGURE 15–2** ❖ Foam carpet pad with yarn-reinforced fiberweb surface layer: surface view (top) and cross-sectional view (bottom).

- Foams are lofty, springy, bulky material, too weak to be used without backing or covering.
- Foams are used in pillows, chair cushions, mattresses, carpet padding, and apparel.

# FABRICS FROM FIBERS

Some fabrics are made directly from fibers or fiber-forming solutions; thus there is no processing of fibers into a yarn. These operations include very old and very new processes. The origins of felt and tapa cloth are lost in antiquity; netlike structures used to bag fruits and vegetables use new technologies; composite fabrics are made by combining fibers with other materials to form fabrics.

The first fiberweb, tapa cloth, is made from the fibrous inner bark of the fig tree. It was used chiefly for

**TABLE 15–1** ❖ Films made from solutions.

| SOLUTION | FIBER | FILM | END USES FOR FILM |
|---|---|---|---|
| Acetate | Acetate | Acetate | Photographic film, projection film |
| Polyamide | Nylon | Nylon | Cooking bags |
| Polyester | Polyester | Mylar* | Packaging, metallic yarns, novelty balloons, computer disks |
| Polypropylene | Olefin | | |
| Polyethylene | | Polyethylene | Packaging, garment and shopping bags, squeeze bottles |
| Polyurethane | Spandex | Polyurethane | Leatherlike fabrics |
| Polyvinyl chloride | Vinal | Vinyl | Packaging, garment bags, leather-like fabrics for apparel and upholstery, seed tapes, water-soluble bags |
| Vinylidene chloride | Saran | Saran Wrap* | Packaging for food |
| Viscose (regenerated cellulose) | Rayon | Cellophane | Glitter weaving yarns—mostly in handwoven textiles |

* Trade names.

**FIGURE 15–3** ❖ Tapa cloth from Samoa.

clothing by people in many areas where the fig tree grows, the Pacific Islands, Central America, and elsewhere. The cloth is made by soaking the inner bark to loosen the fibers, beating them with a mallet, smoothing them out into a paperlike sheet, and decorating them with block prints (Figure 15–3).

Today, fabrics made from fibers are the fastest-growing area of the textile industry. These fabrics most often have industrial uses, but some are used in apparel and furnishing items. Much research and development work is being focused on industrial fabrics; new products provide expanded markets for fiber companies.

These fabrics are often referred to as **nonwovens,** meaning that they are not made from yarn. However, the term *nonwoven* creates confusion because knits are nonwovens as well. Nonwoven refers to a wide variety of fabric structures. In the textile industry, nonwoven usually refers to a fiberweb structure.

Increased usage of these fabrics is related to the increased cost of traditional textiles—especially the labor cost; fluctuating costs of natural fibers; production and promotion of some manufactured fibers; easier cutting and sewing, especially by unskilled labor; and new technologies that result in made-to-order inexpensive products.

## Nonwoven or Fiberweb Structures

**Nonwoven** or **fiberweb structures** include all textile-sheet structures made from fibrous webs, bonded by mechanical entanglement of the fibers or by the use of added resins, thermal fusion, or formation of chemical complexes. Fibers are the fundamental units of structure, arranged into a web and bonded so that the distances between fibers are several times greater than the fiber diameter. Nonwovens are not like paper; they are more flexible than paper structures of similar construction.

The properties of nonwovens are controlled by selection of the geometrical arrangements of the fibers in the web, the properties of the fibers used in the web, and the properties of any binders that may be used.

**PRODUCTION** Fiberwebs are quick and inexpensive to produce. When compared to woven fabrics, nonwovens of the same weight and fiber type are generally 50 percent cheaper.

The basic steps include selecting the fibers, laying the fibers to make a web, and bonding the web together to make a fabric. Any fiber can be used to make the web. The inherent characteristics of the fibers are reflected in the fabric. Filaments and strong staple fibers are used where strength and durability are important; rayon and cotton are used for absorbency; thermoplastics are used for spun-bonded webs.

Web formation can be a more involved process. The five techniques are dry laid, wet laid, spun bonded, spun laced, and melt blown. Fiber orientation is an important factor in controlling web characteristics. Fiber orientation describes both the degree of parallelism among fibers in the web and the degree of parallelism between the fibers and the machine direction. Machine direction describes the direction of movement of the supporting conveyor belt. Webs with fibers parallel to each other are *oriented.* Webs whose fibers are highly parallel to each other and are parallel to the machine direction are oriented in the lengthwise direction. Webs with fibers that are not parallel to each other are *random.* Lengthwise-oriented webs have a grain; strength and drape properties are related to their orientation.

**Dry-laid fiberwebs** are made by carding or air laying the fibers in either a random or oriented fashion. Carding is similar to the process used in producing yarns to achieve a parallel arrangement of fibers. Webs can be cross-laid by stacking the carded web so that one layer is oriented lengthwise and the next layer crosswise to give added strength and pliability. *Cross-laid webs* do not have a grain and can be cut more economically than woven or knitted fabrics. *Air-laid,* or *random, webs* are made by machines that disperse the fibers by air. This web is similar to the cross-laid web but has a more random fiber distribution. Oriented webs have good strength in the direction of orientation, but poor cross-orientation strength. Since random webs have the fibers oriented in a random fashion, strength is uniform in all directions. End uses for dry-laid fiberwebs include wipes, wicks, battery separators, backing for quilted fabrics, interlining, insulation, abrasive fabric bases, filters, and base fabric for laminating and coating.

**Wet-laid fiberwebs** are made from a slurry of short, paper-process–length and textile-length fibers and water. The water is extracted and reclaimed, leaving a random-oriented fiberweb. The advantage of these webs is their exceptional uniformity. Typical end uses for wet-laid fiberwebs include laminating and coating bases, filters, interlining, insulation, roofing substrates, adhesive carriers, wipes, and battery separators.

**Spun-bonded webs** are made immediately after fibers are extruded from spinnerets. The continuous hot filaments are laid down in a random fashion on a fast-moving conveyor belt and, in their semimelted state, fuse together at their cross points. They may be further bonded by heat and pressure. Spun-bonded fiberwebs have high tensile and tear strength and low bulk (Figure 15–4). Typical end uses for spun-bonded fiberwebs include carpet backings like Typar by Du Pont, geotextiles, adhesive carriers, envelopes like Tyvek by Du Pont, tents and tarps, wall coverings, house-wrap vapor barriers, tags and labels, bags, protective apparel, filters, insulation, and roofing substrate.

**Hydroentangled** or ***spunlace*** **webs** are similar to spun-bonded webs except that jets of water are forced through the web, shattering the filaments into staple fibers and producing a wovenlike structure (Figure 15–5). These webs have greater elasticity and flexibility than spun-bonded fabrics.

These fabrics are also known as water-needled fabrics. This technique makes products that are not possible with any other process. Water from high-pressure jets on both sides of the fabric entangle the fibers. The water is reclaimed, purified, and recycled. The degree

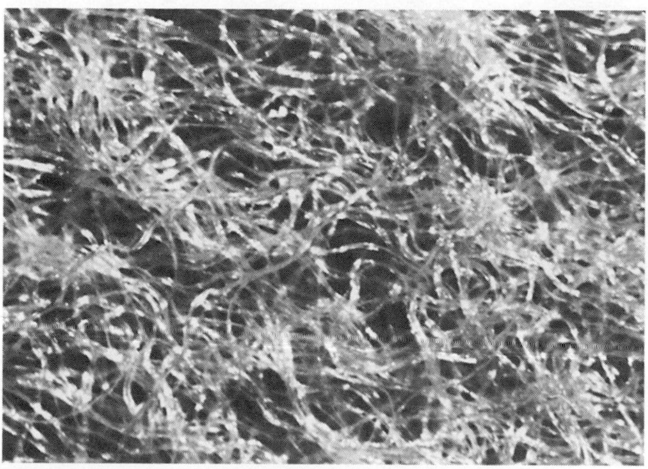

**FIGURE 15–4** ❖ Spun-bonded filament fabric.

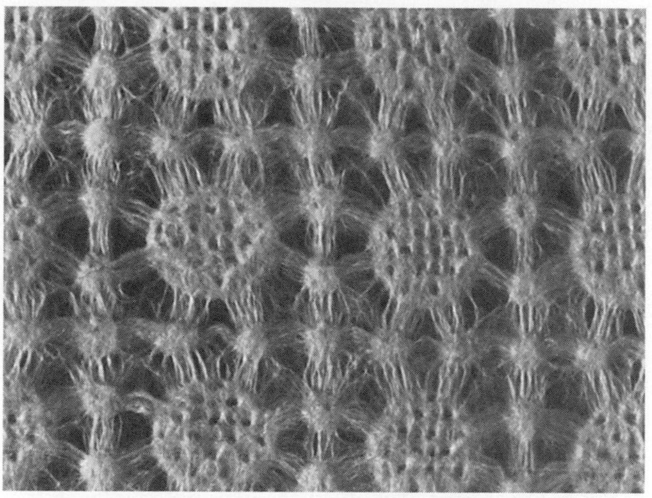

**FIGURE 15–5** ❖ Hydroentangled or spunlace fabric.

of entanglement is controlled by the number and force of jets and the fiber type. Computer controls maintain a uniform quality in the fabric. Hydroentangled textiles are used in medical gowns and drapes, battery separators, interlinings, roofing substrates, floppy disk liners, mattress pads, table linens, household wipes, wall coverings, window treatment components, protective clothing, and filters. Sontara is a hydroentangled polyester produced by DuPont. Another DuPont product, ComforMax IB, combines microdenier olefin and hydroentangling to produce a fabric that is impermeable to wind, cold, and liquid water. It is used in activewear.

**Melt-blown fiberwebs** are made by extruding the polymer through a single-extrusion orifice into a high-velocity, heated-air stream that breaks the fiber into short pieces. The fibers are collected as a web on a moving conveyor belt and are held together by a combination of fiber interlacing and thermal bonding. Because the fibers are not drawn, fiberweb strength is lower than might be expected for a specific fiber. Olefin and polyester are the fibers used commercially with this process to produce hospital/medical products and battery separators.

Webs become fabrics through the use of a mechanical needling process, the application of chemical substances or adhesives, or heat.

**Needle punching** or needling consists of passing a properly prepared dry-laid web over a needle loom as many times as is necessary to produce the desired strength and texture. A *needle loom* has barbed needles protruding 2 or 3 inches from the base (Figure 15–6). As the needles stitch up and down through the web, the barbs pull a few fibers through the web, causing them to

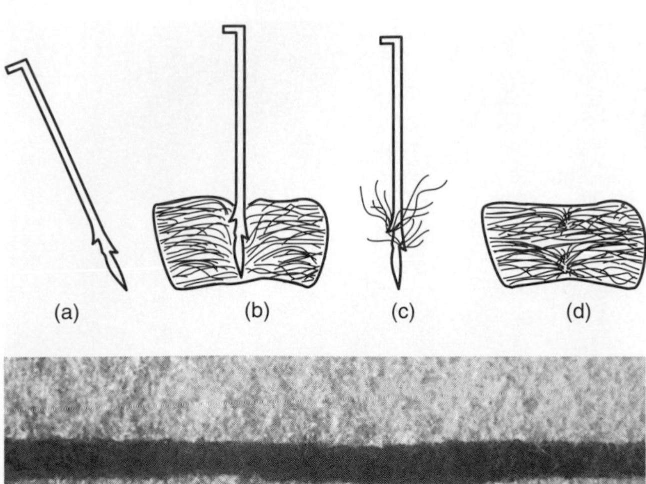

**FIGURE 15–6** ❖ Needle punch process: (a) Barbed needle, (b) needle pulling fibers through web, (c) entangled fibers in cross section of web, (d) needle punched web, (e) photo of fabric.

interlock mechanically with other fibers. The construction process is relatively inexpensive.

Blankets, carpeting, and carpet backing are examples of needle-punched products. Fiber denier, fiber type, and product loft may be varied. Indoor/outdoor needle-punched carpeting made of olefin is used extensively for patios, porches, pools, and putting greens because it is impervious to moisture. Needled carpet backings are used with some tufted carpets.

Needled fabrics can be made of a two-layer web with each layer a different color. By pulling colored fibers from the lower layer to the top surface, geometric designs can be made. If the fibers are pulled above the surface, a pile fabric results. The military has developed a ballistics-protective vest for combat use from needle-punched fabrics. Needle-punched fabrics are finished by pressing, steaming, calendering, dyeing, and embossing. Solution-dyed fibers are often used.

Other techniques include the use of a closed needle that penetrates the web, opens, grabs some fibers, and draws them back as a yarnlike structure that is then chain-stitched through the web. These fabrics are related to the stitch-through fabrics discussed later in this chapter.

**Chemical adhesives** are used with dry-laid or wet-laid webs to bond the fibers together. Although several options exist, acrylic emulsions are usually used.

*Heat* and pressure are used to bond thermoplastic-fiber webs. Mirafi 140 fabric is used for roadbed stabilization. This industrial fabric is a random mixture of heat-bonded polypropylene (olefin) homopolymer and bicomponent-polypropylene core-nylon sheath filaments (Figure 15–7).

**FIBERFILL** Batting, wadding, and fiberfill are not fabrics, but they are important components in apparel for snowsuits, ski jackets, quilted robes, and coats, and in furnishing textiles for quilts, comforters, furniture paddings, pillows, mattresses, and mattress pads.

**Batting** is made from new fiber, **wadding** is made from waste fiber, and **fiberfill** is a manufactured fiber staple made especially for these end uses. Carded fibers are laid down to the desired thickness and may be covered with a sheet of nonwoven fabric.

Fiber density describes the weight or mass per unit volume. Fiber density is important for batting, wadding, and fiberfill in order to produce lightweight, resilient products.

**Resiliency** is important because fabrics that maintain their loft incorporate more air space. When fibers stay crushed, the fabric becomes thinner and more compact, losing bulk, insulating power, and padding characteris-

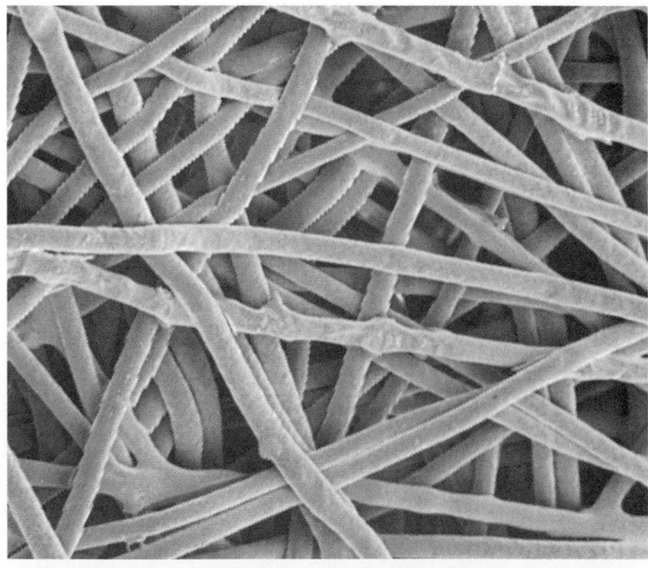

**FIGURE 15–7** ❖ Mirafi 140 fabric. (COURTESY OF DOMINION TEXTILES OF CANADA.)

tics. **Resistance to shifting** is important in maintaining uniformity of thickness in the fabric. For instance, down comforters need to be shaken often because the filling tends to shift to the outer edges. The thermoplastic-fiber batts can be run through a needle-punch machine where hot needles melt the parts of the fibers that they touch, fusing them and forming a more stable batt, often referred to as a bonded web. The thicker the batt, the warmer the fabric, regardless of fiber content. In apparel there is a limit to the thickness, however, because too much bulk restricts movement and limits styling. (See Table 15–2.) Several fiberfills are made from recycled polyester solutions.

Two polyester fiberfills by DuPont are Thermoloft, a high-loft insulation, and Thermolite, a thin insulation made with microfibers. Both types are used in apparel. Other DuPont fiberfills used in both apparel and furnishings include Hollofil and Quallofil. These two fiberfills incorporate voided areas to increase the loft and insulation while decreasing weight. Comforel by DuPont is made of polyester clusters for bedding and pillows. Primaloft is a microdenier polyester fiberfill by Albany International Research Company that mimics down in weight and loft and is used in bedding. Polarguard and Trevira Loft by Trevira are other trade name fiberfills used in apparel.

Although not fibers, down and feathers are used as fiberfill. These fills are defined by the Federal Trade Commission in the Code of Federal Regulations. Down refers to the undercoating of waterfowl and relates to the fine, bulky underfeathers. Items labeled 100 percent down must meet specified requirements relating to the condition of the down. Down-filled items must be 80 percent down or down fiber and may include up to 20 percent other feathers. Down is rated by its loft capacity, the volume one cubic ounce of down will fill. For example 650 down is warmer and more expensive than 550 down. The range is generally 300 to 800.

Down is lightweight and warm. However, it has a tendency to shift, and when wet, it mats and loses its warmth. Down may be difficult to clean and still maintain the original loft. People who are allergic to feathers may experience difficulty with down products. Down is used in apparel, bedding, and padding for pillows and soft furniture.

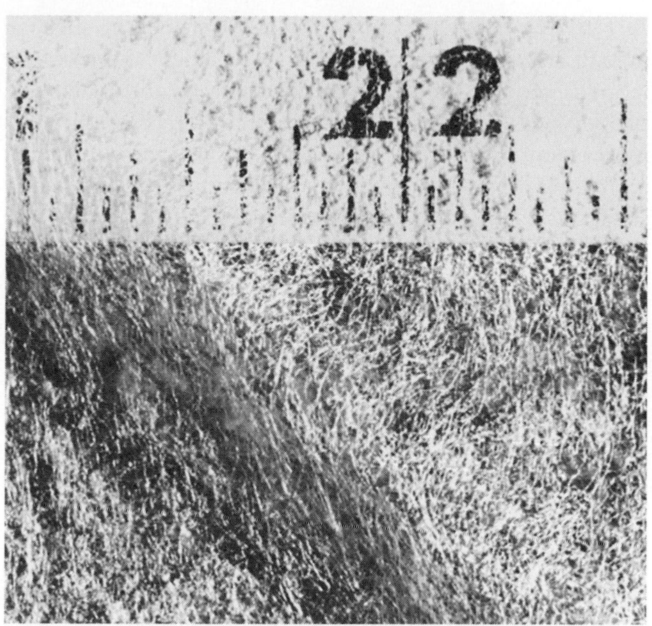


**FIGURE 15–8** ❖ Fusible interlining. Tape under web demonstrates its sheerness.

**FUSIBLE NONWOVENS** **Fusible nonwovens** contribute body and shape to garments as interfacing or interlinings in shirts, blouses, dresses, and outerwear.

A fusible is a fabric that has been coated with a heat-sealable, thermoplastic adhesive. It also may be a thin, spiderweblike fabric of thermoplastic filaments (Figure 15–8). The fusible fabric is applied to the back of a face fabric; the layers are bonded by heat and pressure.

The adhesives used are polyethylene, hydrolyzed ethylene vinyl acetate, plasticized polyvinyl chloride, and polyamides. The adhesive may be printed on the substrate in a precisely positioned manner to give the desired hand to the end product.

**TABLE 15–2** ❖ Comparison of properties of commonly used battings.

| FIBER | DENSITY | RESILIENCY | RESISTANCE TO SHIFTING | CARE |
|---|---|---|---|---|
| Down (high cost) | Lightweight | Excellent | Poor | Dry cleanable |
| Acetate (low cost) | 1.30 | Fair | Poor | Washable, dries more quickly than cotton |
| Polyester (medium cost) | 1.30–1.38 | Good | Good—can be bonded | Washable, quick drying |
| Cotton (low cost) | 1.52 | Poor | Poor | Washable, but slow drying |

Fusibles eliminate certain areas of stitching, such as zigzag stitches used in coat and suit lapels. Less skilled labor is required in garment production, and when the proper technique and correct selection are combined, increase productivity. However, fusibles may generate problems for producers and consumers. The layers may separate during care. Adhesives may bleed through to the face fabric. The layers may shrink differently during care. The change in hand and drape are difficult to predict.

**END USES OF NONWOVENS** Nonwovens are used for disposable goods, such as diapers and wipes, durable goods that are incorporated into other products, or alone for draperies, furniture, mattresses, mattress pads, and some apparel (see Table 15–3).

To summarize, nonwovens are:

- Produced by bonding and/or interlocking fibers by mechanical, chemical, thermal, or solvent means, or combinations of these processes.
- Cheaper than woven or knitted fabrics. Widely used for disposable or durable items. May have grain but usually do not.
- Used for apparel, furnishing, and industrial purposes.

## Felt

True **felt** is a mat or web of wool or part-wool fibers held together by the interlocking of the scales of the wool fibers. Felting is one of the oldest methods of making fabrics. Primitive peoples made felt by washing wool fleece, spreading it out while still wet, and beating it until it had matted and shrunk together in fabriclike form. Figure 15–9 shows a Numdah felt rug made in India. In modern factories, layers of wool or wool blends are built up until the desired thickness is attained and then heat, soap, and vibration are used to mat the fibers together. Finishing processes for felt resemble those for woven fabrics.

**FIGURE 15–9** ❖ Numdah felt rug.

Felts do not have grain; they are stiff and less pliable than other structures; they do not ravel. Felts are not as strong as other fabrics and vary in quality depending on the quality of the fiber used.

Felt has many industrial and some clothing uses. It is used industrially for padding, soundproofing, insulation, filtering, polishing, and wicking. In the past, felt was used under practically all machinery to absorb sound. Foams, being much cheaper, have replaced felt in this end use.

Felt is not used for fitted clothing because it lacks the flexibility and elasticity of fabrics made from yarns. Felt

**TABLE 15–3** ❖ Uses of nonwovens.

| DURABLE | TYPE | DISPOSABLE | TYPE |
|---|---|---|---|
| Bedding and coated fabrics, mattress ticking, backing for quilting, dust cloth for box springs | Spun bonded | Diapers, underpads, sanitary napkins/tampons | Dry laid |
| Carpet backing, coated fabrics | Needled, spun bonded, dry laid | Surgical packs and accessories | Dry laid, melt blown |
| Filters | | Wipes and towels | Dry laid, or wet |
| Interfacings | Dry or wet laid | Packaging, floppy disk liners | Spun bonded |
| Interlinings | Needled, dry laid | | |
| Draperies, upholstered furniture, backings, facings, dust covers, automotive, shoe parts, geotextiles, labels, backings for wall coverings, leatherlike fabrics | Dry and wet laid, spun bonded, hydroentangled, melt blown | | |

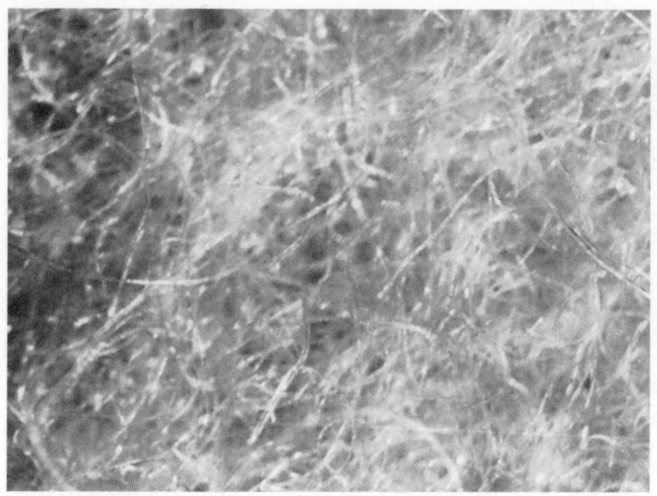

**FIGURE 15–10** ❖ Felt (magnified).

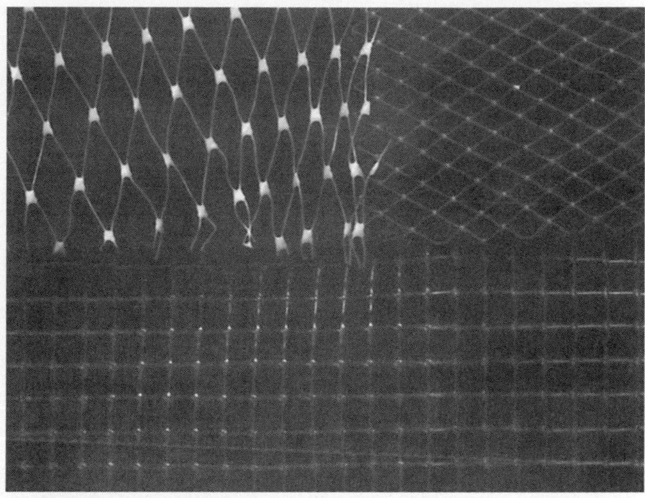

**FIGURE 15–11** ❖ Netlike structures.

has wide use in such products as hats, slippers, clothing decorations, and pennants. Because felt does not fray, it needs no seam finish. Colored felt letters or decorations on apparel often fade in washing and should be removed or the garments should be sent to a professional dry cleaner.

The following characteristics summarize felt:

- Wool fibers are carded (and combed), laid down in a thick batt, sprayed with water, and run through hot agitating plates that cause the fibers to become entangled (see Figure 15–10).
- Felt has no grain; it does not fray or ravel.
- Felt has poor pliability, strength, and stretch recovery.
- Felt is used in apparel accessories, crafts, and industrial matting.

## Netlike Structures

**Netlike structures** include all textile structures formed by extruding one or more fiber-forming polymers as a film or a network of ligaments or strands. In the integral-fibrillated-net process, the extruded and noncoagulated film is embossed by being passed through a pair of heated rollers that are engraved to form a pattern on the fabric. When the film is stretched biaxially, slits occur in the fabric, creating a netlike structure. In the integral-extruded-net process, the spinneret consists of two rotating dies. When the polymer is extruded, the fibers form as single strands that interconnect when the holes of the two rotating dies coincide. The process produces tubular nets that are used for packaging fruit and vegetables, agricultural nets, bird nets, and plastic fencing for snow and hazards (Figure 15–11).

# FABRICS FROM YARNS

## Braids

**Braids** are narrow fabrics in which many yarns are interlaced lengthwise and diagonally (see Figure 15–12). They have good elongation characteristics. They are very pliable, curve around edges nicely, and are used primarily for trims, shoelaces, and coverings on components in industrial products like wiring and hoses for liquids like gasoline and water. Three-dimensional braids are made with two or more sets of yarns.

**FIGURE 15–12** ❖ Braid.

**FIGURE 15–13** ❖ Braiding machine with mandrel. (COURTESY OF ALBANY INTERNATIONAL RESEARCH CO.)

Their shape is controlled by an internal mandrel (see Figure 15–13).

The characteristics of braid include the following:

- Yarns are interlaced both diagonally and lengthwise.
- Braid is stretchy and easily shaped.
- Braid can be flat or three-dimensional.
- Braid is used for trim and industrial products.

## Lace

**Lace** is another basic fabric made from yarns. Many fabrication methods may be used. Yarns may be twisted around each other to create open areas. Lace is an openwork fabric with complex patterns or figures, handmade or machine-made on special lace machines or on raschel knitting machines.

It can be difficult to determine the machine used to make a fine lace fabric without the aid of a microscope. However, it is a fairly simple matter to determine the origin of many laces. Some imitation lacelike fabrics are made by printing or flocking (Figure 15–14). Quality in lace is based on the fineness of yarns, number of yarns per square inch or closeness of background net, and intricacy of the design.

Lace was very important in men's and women's fashion between the 16th and 19th centuries, and all countries in Europe developed lace industries. Lace remains important today as a trim or accessory in apparel and furnishings. The names given to lace often reflect the town in which the lace was originally made. For example, the best-quality needlepoint lace was made in Venice in the 16th century—hence the name Venetian lace. Alençon and Valenciennes are laces made in French towns.

### HANDMADE LACE

**Handmade lace** has always been, as it is today, a prestige textile. With the contemporary interest in crafts, many of the old lace-making techniques are experiencing renewed interest. Handmade lace is used as wall hangings, belts, bags, shawls, afghans, bedspreads, and tablecloths.

Lace is classified according to the way it is made and the way it appears. Handmade laces include needlepoint, bobbin, crochet, and Battenburg.

***Needlepoint Lace*** **Needlepoint lace** is made by drawing a pattern on paper, laying down yarns over the pattern, and stitching over the yarns with a needle and thread. The network of fine threads making the ground is called *reseau* or *brides*. The solid part of the pattern is called *toile*. Needlepoint laces often include birds, flowers, and vases as the design.

***Bobbin Lace*** **Bobbin lace** is made on a pillow. The pattern is drawn on paper and pins are inserted at various points. Yarns on bobbins are plaited around the pins to form the lace (Figure 15–15).

***Crocheted Lace*** *Crocheted lace* is done by hand with a crochet hook. Crocheted laces are Irish lace and Syrian lace.

***Battenburg Lace*** This handmade lace is made with loops of woven tape caught together by yarn brides in patterns. Figure 15–16 shows a piece of **Battenburg**

(a) Machine-made cordonnet lace. Alençon.

(b) Raschel lace.

(c) Filling knitted lacelike fabric.

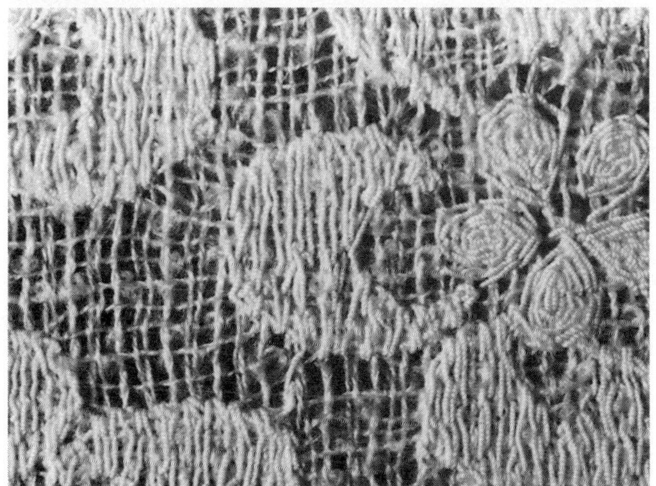

(d) Woven lacelike fabric.

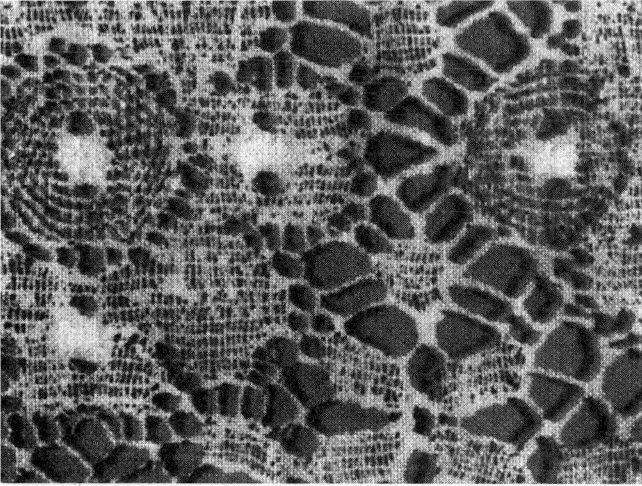

(e) Imitation lace.

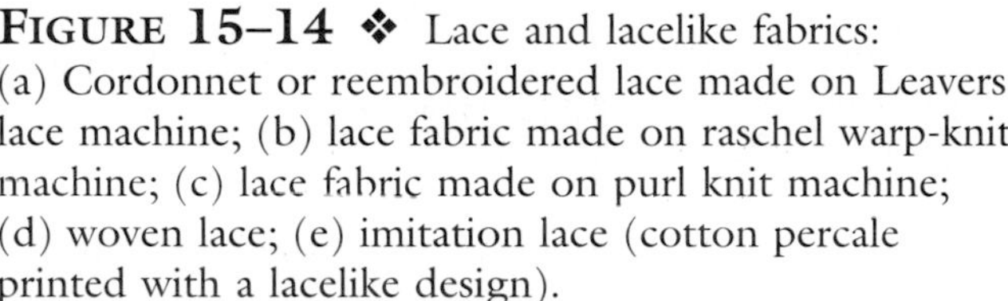

**FIGURE 15–14** ❖ Lace and lacelike fabrics: (a) Cordonnet or reembroidered lace made on Leavers lace machine; (b) lace fabric made on raschel warp-knit machine; (c) lace fabric made on purl knit machine; (d) woven lace; (e) imitation lace (cotton percale printed with a lacelike design).

**FIGURE 15–15** ❖ Bobbin lace: handmade (left); machine-made (right).

**lace.** Making Battenburg lace was a common hobby in the U.S. in the early part of the 20th century. Contemporary pieces are imported from Asia, especially China, for apparel and furnishing accessories.

**MACHINE-MADE LACE** In 1802 in England, Robert Brown perfected a machine that made nets on which lace motifs could be worked by hand. In 1808 John Heathcoat made the first true lace machine by developing brass bobbins to make bobbinet. In 1813, John Leavers developed a machine that made patterns and background simultaneously. A card system, similar to the technique used on card jacquard looms, made it possible to produce intricate designs with the Leavers machine.

***Leavers Lace*** The Leavers machine consists of warp yarns and oscillating bobbins that are set in frames called *carriages.* The carriages move back and forth with the bobbins swinging around the warp to form a pattern. These bobbins, holding 60 to 300 yards of yarn, are thin enough to swing between adjacent warp yarns and twist themselves around one warp before moving to another yarn (Figures 15–17 and 15–18). The Leavers machine has approximately 20 brass bobbins for each inch width of the machine. A machine 200 inches wide would have 4,000 brass bobbins side by side.

**Leavers laces** are fairly expensive, depending on the quality of yarns used and the intricacy of the design. On some fabrics, a yarn or cord outlines the design. These are called **Cordonnet,** or **reembroidered, lace** (Figure 15–14a).

***Raschel Lace*** Raschel knitting machines (see Chapter 14) are used to make patterned laces that look like Leavers lace. **Raschel laces** can be made at much higher speeds and thus are less expensive to produce. Filament yarns are commonly used to make coarser laces that are suitable for tablecloths, draperies, and casement fabrics, as in Figure 15–19.

**FIGURE 15–16** ❖ Close-up view of a Battenburg lace tablecloth.

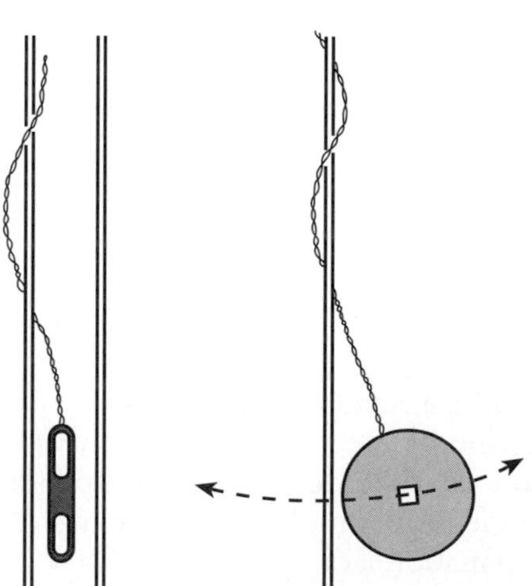

**FIGURE 15–17** ❖ Brass bobbins. (REPRODUCED FROM *TEXTILES,* 1973, VOL. 2, NO. 1, A PERIODICAL OF THE BRITISH TEXTILE TECHNOLOGY GROUP, UNITED KINGDOM, FORMERLY THE SHIRLEY INSTITUTE.)

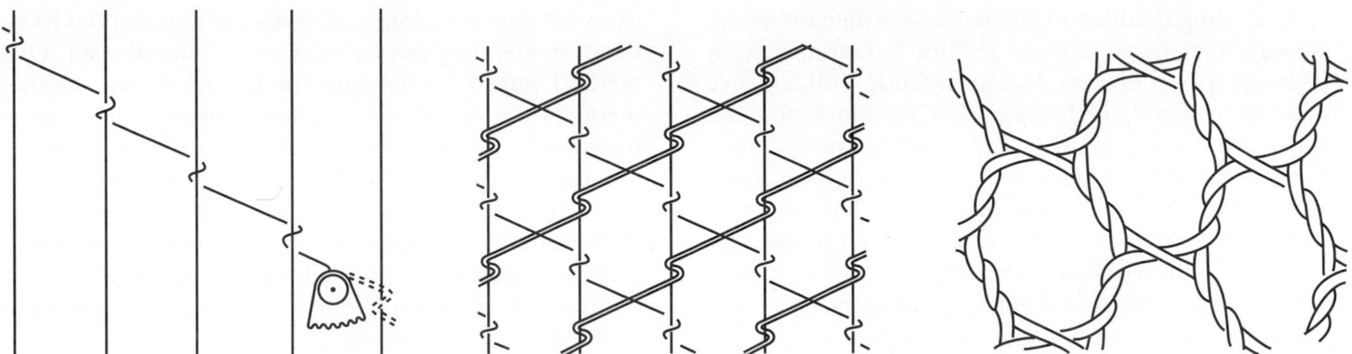

**FIGURE 15–18** ❖ Brass bobbins, carrying thread, twist around warp yarns. (REPRODUCED FROM *TEXTILES*, 1973, VOL. 2, NO. 1, A PERIODICAL OF THE BRITISH TEXTILE TECHNOLOGY GROUP, UNITED KINGDOM, FORMERLY THE SHIRLEY INSTITUTE.)

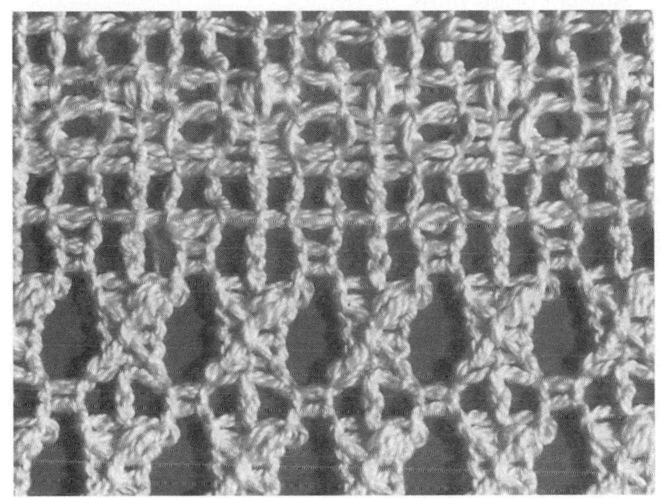

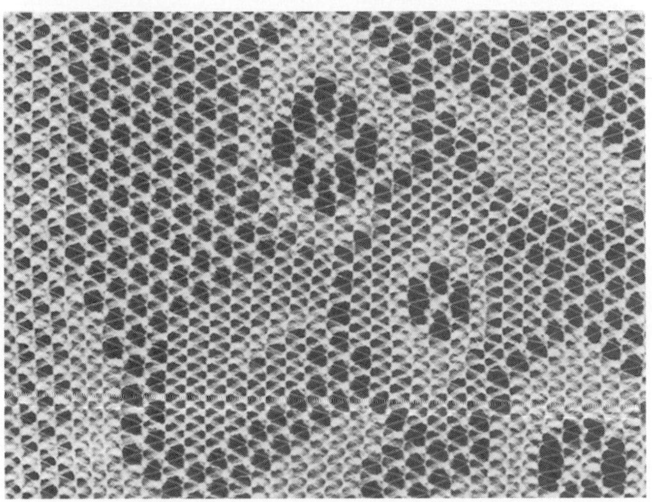

**FIGURE 15–19** ❖ Raschel crochet (top); raschel lace (bottom).

**CARE OF LACE** Because lace has open spaces, it can easily snag and tear. Fragile laces should be washed by hand-squeezing suds through the fabric rather than rubbing. Some laces can be put into a protective bag and machine washed. Dry cleaning is another option, providing similar precautions are followed.

# COMPOSITE FABRICS

**Composite fabrics** are fabrics that combine several primary and/or secondary structures, at least one of which is a recognized textile structure, into a single structure. This broad category includes such diverse fabrics as stitch-bonded structures, laminates, tufted and flocked structures, and coated fabrics.

## Coated Fabrics

A **coated fabric** combines the characteristics of a textile fabric with a polymer film. The woven, knit, or nonwoven fabric substrate provides such characteristics as strength and elongation control. The coating or film provides protection from environmental factors such as water, chemicals, oil, and abrasion. Commonly used films include rubber and synthetic elastomers such as polyvinyl chloride (PVC), neoprene, and polyurethane. PVC-coated fabrics are the most common; they are used in window shades, book covers, upholstery, wall coverings, apparel, shoe liners, and shoe uppers. Neoprene is used for protective clothing like chemical gloves and wetsuits. Most polyurethane-coated fabrics are used in shoe uppers and apparel. Heavier-weight polyurethane-coated fabrics are used in industrial tarpaulins.

The coating is added to the fabric substrate by several methods. The most common method is **lamination,** in which a prepared film is adhered to fabric with adhesive or heated to slightly melt the back of the film before the layers are pressed together. In the second method, calendering, the viscous polymer is mixed with filler, stabilizing agent, pigment, and plasticizer. The additives control the opacity, hand, color, and environmental resistance of the coating layer. The mixture is applied directly onto a preheated fabric by passing the fabric and the mixture between two large metal cylinders or calenders spaced close together. Another method is *coating,* in which a more fluid compound is applied by knife or roll. The degree of penetration of the mixture into the fabric substrate is controlled by allowing the mixture to solidify or gel slightly before it comes in contact with the substrate.

Other methods of coating include rotary screen, slot die, foam, spray, and transfer coating. In the rotary screen technique, the coating is applied to the fabric through a rotating open screen in contact with the fabric. A smoothing blade closes up and smoothes out the coating compound to produce a continuous surface. This technique is used for lightweight upholstery fabrics where flame retardancy is required or where some air permeability is desired. In the slot die technique, the solution is extruded over the substrate's full width at the desired thickness. The slot die technique is becoming increasingly important. Another technique applies the coating as a foam. This technique is often used for thermal drapery fabrics and blackout curtains. In the spray technique, a thin solution is sprayed onto the surface of the substrate. Under heat or pressure, the solution flows over the surface and forms a continuous layer. In transfer coating, the coating compound is applied to release paper, dried, and then applied to the substrate. Transfer coating is used only when other techniques cannot be used.

Coated fabrics are also referred to as supported films. Coated fabrics can be printed or embossed. They may resemble real leather and are being sold as "vegetarian" leather. They are used for apparel, shoe uppers and liners, upholstery, vinyl car tops, floor and wall coverings, window shades, bandages, acoustical barriers, filters, soft-sided luggage, awnings, pond and ditch liners, and air-supported structures and domes.

Bion II by Biotex Industries is a monolithic, or solid, polyurethane coating that is waterproof, breathable, and flame retardant. It is used in active sportswear such as running suits. outerwear such as parkas, diaper covers, mattress covers, and incontinence products. It can be applied to most fibers in woven or knit forms.

Coated fabrics can be impermeable to water in liquid and vapor forms. When used in clothing, they produce a hot, clammy feeling. When used in upholstery, they can stick to exposed skin. In order for these fabrics to be comfortable, they can be modified in several ways. One method punches tiny holes in the fabric. In another method, coated fabrics can incorporate a nonporous hydrophilic membrane or film. Sympatex by Akzo incorporates a hydrophilic polyester film. (Another method uses a microporous film, which will be discussed in the next section.) Sympatex can be laminated to an outer shell, a lining fabric, or a lightweight insert fabric such as tricot or fiberweb for use in skiwear. Sympatex is washable or dry cleanable.

A summary of coated fabrics includes these aspects:

- Coated fabrics are produced by applying semi-liquid materials to a fabric substrate. Neoprene, polyvinyl chloride, and polyurethane are usual coating materials (see Figure 15–20).
- Coated fabrics are stronger and more stable than unsupported films.
- Coated fabrics are used for upholstery, luggage and bags, and apparel (see Table 15–4).

## Poromeric Fabrics

**Poromeric,** or *microporous,* **fabrics** incorporate films, but they are classified in a separate category because the film is very thin and microporous. These two major distinctions determine many characteristics of the resulting fabric. The poromeric or membrane layer is stretched in both directions and annealed to impart micropores in the fabric that are small enough to allow the passage of water vapor, but not liquid water. Hence, they are water vapor–permeable. This factor greatly enhances comfort in apparel. These fabrics are effective because of the

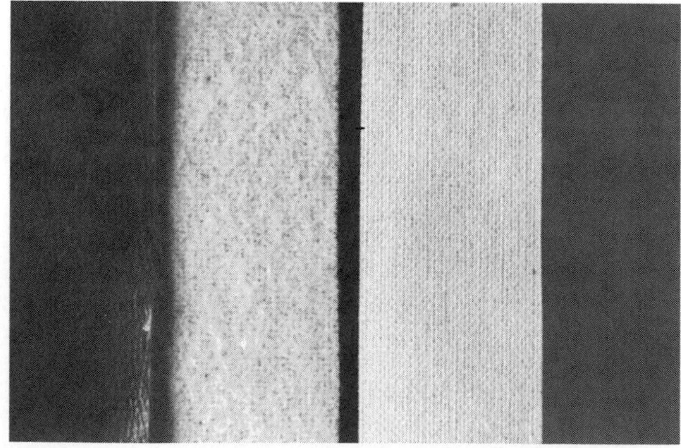

**FIGURE 15–20** ❖ Coated fabrics: (left) knitted base fabric; (right) woven base fabric. The outer portions show the technical face of each fabric. The inner portions show the technical back or base of each fabric.

**TABLE 15–4** ❖ End uses for films and coated fabrics.

| | |
|---|---|
| Air-supported roofings | Tablecloths and placemats |
| Self-lined draperies | Umbrellas |
| Hospital-bed coverings | Upholstery |
| Hose container for fuel and water | Waterproof apparel such as raincoats, boots, and mittens |
| Inflatable flood gates for water control | Wetsuits |
| Leather-like coats, jackets | Chemical protective clothing and gloves |
| Shower curtains | |

enormous size difference between a droplet of liquid water and the size of water vapor—the water vapor droplet is 250,000 times smaller!

Poromeric films can be made from polytetrafluoroethylene (Gore-Tex) or polyurethane (Figure 15–21). These products are waterproof, windproof, and breathable. The film can be applied to a wide variety of fabrics and fibers and is used primarily in apparel because of the need for comfort and protection. These fabrics are used for active sportswear and rugged outdoorwear such as hunting clothes. Other applications include tents, sleeping bags, medical products, filters, coatings for wires and cables, and protective apparel. Besides Gore-Tex, other poromeric fabrics include Dartexx, a warp knit with a polyurethane membrane, and Entrant and Breathe-Tex, with polyurethane membranes. Several of these fabrics are used in the medical field because they present a barrier to bodily fluids.

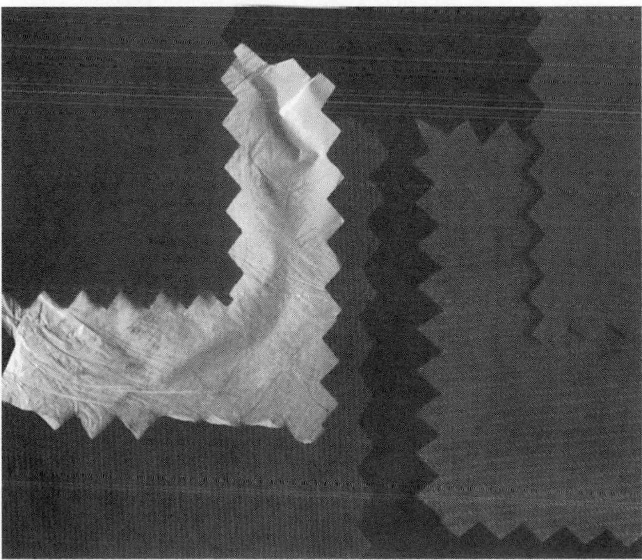

**FIGURE 15–21** ❖ Gore-Tex fabric: face fabric, polytetrafluoroethylene film, backing (left); face and back of fabric (right).

The enhanced performance of poromeric fabrics is reflected in their price. Fabrics that are both comfortable and waterproof incorporate expensive components and processes.

## Suedelike Fabrics

Because of the beautiful texture and hand of suede and the problems encountered in its care, **suedelike fabrics** have been developed. These fabrics are needle-punched fabrics made from microdenier fibers combined with a resin coating and nonfibrous polyurethane. The microdenier fibers are arranged in a manner that reproduces the microscopic structure of natural suedes. The fabric is dyed and finished. The process was developed by Toray Industries in Japan. Ultrasuede® and Ultraleather® are registered trade names of Springs Industries. Both are used in apparel and furnishings. Ultrasuede® is made of 60 percent microfine polyester and 40 percent polyurethane foam. Ultraleather® is 100 percent polyurethane with a knit back of 70 percent rayon and 30 percent nylon. The embossed fabric is lightweight, soft, and water repellent with comfort stretch. Ultrasuede® may be backed with a woven fabric when used for upholstery. Belleseime® is a similar fabric of 65 percent polyester/20 percent nylon matrix fiber on a 15 percent polyurethane-foam substrate produced by Kanebo Company of Japan.

Suede- and leatherlike fabrics are used in apparel, upholstery, wall coverings, and accessories. These fabrics are made in various ways (see Table 15–5). This process can be summarized as follows:

- Fibers and polyurethane solution are mixed together, cast on a drum, or forced through a slit to make fabric, which is napped on both sides.
- The fabric looks and feels like suede.
- The fabric is machine washable and dry cleanable.
- The fabric is uniform in thickness, appearance, and quality and sold by the yard or meter.

## Tufted-Pile Fabrics

**Tufting** is a process of making pile fabrics by stitching extra yarns into a fabric base or substrate. The ground fabric ranges from thin sheeting or nonwoven to heavy burlap or coarse warp knit and may be woven, knitted, or nonwoven. Tufting developed as a hand craft when early settlers worked candle wicks into bedspreads to create interesting textures and designs. The making of candlewick bedspreads and hooked rugs grew into a cottage industry. In the 1930s, machinery was developed to convert the hand technique to mass production

TABLE 15–5 ❖ Leather, suede, and imitations.

| CONSTRUCTION TECHNIQUE | CHARACTERISTICS | TRADE NAME |
|---|---|---|
| Composite fabric—polyester fibers and polyurethane mixed, cast on drum, napped or embossed | Washable, dry cleanable<br>Looks like leather or suede | Ultrasuede®<br>Ultraleather® |
| Composite fabric | Easy care<br>Looks like suede | Belleseime® |
| Woven cotton/polyester substrate, surface coating of polyurethane | Dry cleanable<br>Washable | |
| Substrate with polyurethane on both sides | | |
| 100 percent polyester-pile fabric with suedelike finish | Dry cleanable<br>Washable | |
| Flocked cotton | Least expensive and least effective imitation. Flock may wear off at edges | |
| 100 percent polyester-warp knit-napped | Washable, dry cleanable | Super-suede® |
| Leather (cow, pig, lamb, or other animal) | Natural product, irregular in nature, available in wide variety of finishes, cleanability may not be good | None |
| Suede (cow, pig, lamb, or other animal) | Natural product, irregular in nature, cleanability may not be good | None |

(see Figure 15–22). Carpets, rugs, bedspreads, and robes are produced in many patterns and colors at low cost.

Tufting is done by a series of needles (see Figures 15–23 and 15–24), each carrying a yarn from a number of spools held in a creel. The substrate is held in a horizontal position and the needles all come down at once and go through the fabric to a predetermined depth, much as a sewing machine needle goes through fabric. For each needle, a hook moves forward to hold the loop as the needle is retracted. In loop pile fabrics, the loop remains when the hook is removed. For cut-loop pile, a knife is incorporated with the hook and it moves forward as the needles are retracted to cut the loop. The fabric moves forward at a predetermined rate, and the needles move downward again to form another row of tufts.

With cut loops, the yarns ends must be teased open to hold the tuft in place. The tufts are held in place by blooming or untwisting the yarn, by shrinkage of the ground fabric in finishing, or by use of a coating on the back of the ground fabric.

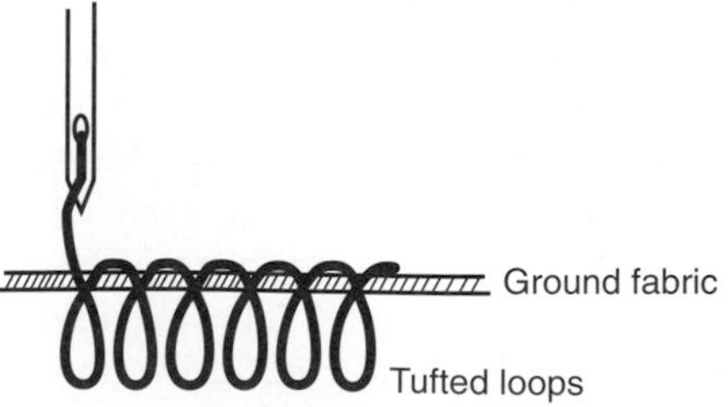


FIGURE 15–22 ❖ Tufting.

**Tuft density** refers to the number of tufts per square inch and is related to the number of needles per inch and the number of stitches per inch (needles/inch × stitches/inch = tuft density). Any pile fabric with low pile density is subject to grin-through, a problem of the ground

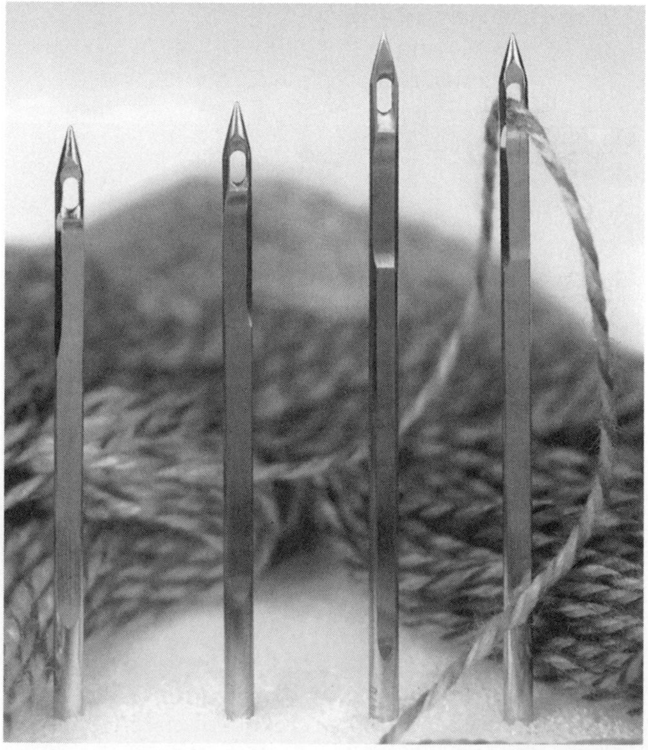

FIGURE 15–23 ❖ Tufting needles and yarn.

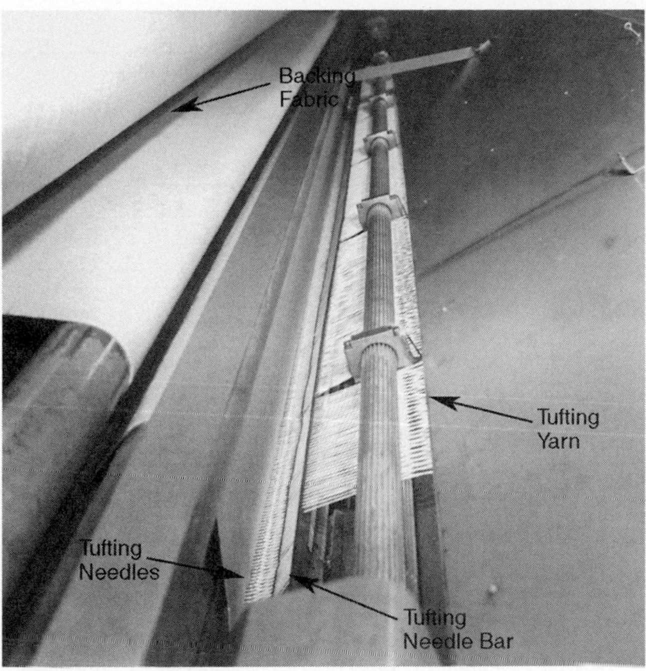


**FIGURE 15–24** ❖ Needle area of tufting machine.

structure showing through the pile. This problem is obvious when the fabric is bent or rolled and is common with carpets, especially when steps are carpeted.

Computers control the tufting process. Patterns can be created quickly and easily by changing yarn color or type, tuft depth, and tuft type (cut or uncut). Thousands of patterns are possible. The widespread use of carpets in homes, businesses, and industrial facilities is directly related to tufting, a low-cost method of producing carpet.

Tufting is a less costly method of making pile fabrics because it is extremely fast and involves less labor and time to create new designs. Tufted apparel fabrics are made on 5/64-gauge machines. **Gauge** refers to the distance in inches between the tufting needles. Tufting specifications on this gauge include 10–11 stitches per inch and a pile height of ⅛ inch.

Furlike tufted fabrics may be used for shells or linings of coats and jackets, but there are few other tufted apparel fabrics. Tufted bed-size blankets can be made in less than two minutes. Tufted blankets have not been successful in the United States but are used in Europe.

Tufted upholstery fabric is made in both cut and uncut pile and is widely available. The back is coated to hold the yarns in place.

Carpeting of room-width size was first made by tufting in 1950; in 1995, approximately 94 percent of broadloom carpeting was made by tufting. A tufting machine can produce approximately 650 square yards of carpeting per hour compared to an Axminster loom which can weave about 14 square yards per hour.

Gauge in carpets also describes the spacing of the needles in the tufting machine. Generally carpets for home or lower traffic use differ in gauge from carpets for commercial, industrial, and high-traffic uses. Typical carpet gauges for commercial carpets range from 5⁄32 inch (0.16 inch) to 1⁄16 inch (0.063 inch). Carpets of finer gauges are becoming more common.

Variations in texture are possible by varying loop height. Cut and uncut tufts can be combined. Tweed textures are made by using different-colored plies in the tufting yarns. Special dyeing and printing techniques produce colored patterns or figures where the color penetrates the tufts completely. A latex coating is put on the back of the carpet to help hold the tufts in place (Figure 15–25). *Face weight* refers to the mass or weight of the tuft yarns used in the carpet. In general, the higher the face weight, the more expensive and durable the carpet. Face weights of 25 oz/yd$^2$ or more are common for commercial carpets.

DuPont has developed a guide sheet for predicting carpet performance based on five factors: color, design, density, pile texture, and fiber. The guide sheet describes a way to quantify carpet characteristics and relate them to end use requirements. Color is included because it is an important factor in hiding soil. Design describes how colors are blended and also relates to hiding soil. Density refers to the number of tufts per unit area. The denser the carpet, the better it is at resisting soiling and compacting. Pile texture describes the tuft loop structure and yarn type used. This also influences resistance to soiling and compacting. Fiber addresses the performance of the fibers used in the carpet pile yarns. Almost all carpet fibers are specifically engineered for soil and static resistance.

Tufted fabrics can be summarized as follows:

- Yarns carried by needles are forced through a fabric substrate and formed into cut or uncut loops.

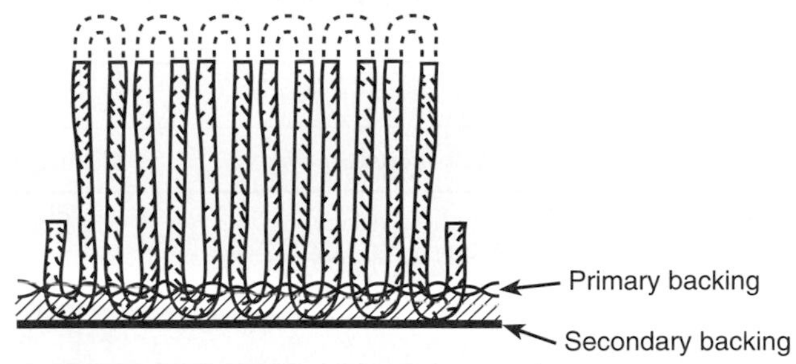


**FIGURE 15–25** ❖ Tufted carpet. Tufts are punched through primary backing. Secondary backing is bonded to primary backing to lock in pile.

**TABLE 15–6** ❖ Look-alike pile fabrics.

| | FURLIKE FABRICS—USED FOR COAT AND JACKET SHELLS, LININGS, DECUBICARE PADS, AND ACCENT RUGS | | |
|---|---|---|---|
| | **Woven-Warp Pile** | **Sliver Knit** | **Tufted** |
| **Fibers used** | Cotton ground. Wool, acrylic, rayon, polyester pile. | Cotton, olefin, or modacrylic ground. Acrylic, modacrylic pile. | Cheesecloth or soft, filled sheeting substrate of cotton or cotton/polyester. Acrylic, modacrylic pile. |
| **Cost** | Most expensive | Variable | Least expensive |
| **Characteristics** | Pile firmly held in place. Tendency to grin-through in low-count fabrics. | Most widely used<br>Dense underfibers and guard hairs possible, like real fur. Denser surface possible. | Mostly used for sheepskin-type goods. Blooming of yarns and shrinkage of ground holds tufts in place. |

| | CARPETS | | | | |
|---|---|---|---|---|---|
| | **Woven-Warp Pile** | **Filling Knit, Raschel Knit** | **Chenille Yarns** | **Tufted** | **Flocked** |
| **Types and kinds** | Wilton<br>Axminster<br>Velvet | Laid-in yarn | Usually woven to order | Most widely used. All kinds of textures.<br>Tufts held in by backings | Not very durable<br>Limited pile height |
| **Cost** | Most expensive | Raschel knits expensive | Expensive | Inexpensive to moderate in cost | Inexpensive |

| | VELOUR | | |
|---|---|---|---|
| | **Woven-Warp Pile** | **Filling Knit—Jersey** | **Warp Knit** |
| **Fiber content** | Cotton, wool, acrylic, blends | Cotton, polyester | Nylon, acetate |
| **Characteristics** | Heavy fabric, durable | Medium weight, soft, drapeable | Medium to heavyweight |
| **End uses** | Upholstery, draperies | Robes, shirts, casual apparel | Robes, nightwear |

| | VELVET | | |
|---|---|---|---|
| | **Woven-Warp Pile** | **Tufted** | **Flocked** |
| **Fibers** | Rayon, nylon, cotton, acetate, polyester | Nylon, olefin | Nylon |
| **Characteristics** | Filament—formal, pile flattens<br>Durability related to fiber and pile density<br>Rich looking—heavyweight fabric | Pile not held in as firmly as woven, less expensive | Least expensive |
| **End uses** | Apparel and upholstery | Upholstery | Upholstery, draperies, bedspreads |

| | TERRYCLOTH | |
|---|---|---|
| | **Stack-Tension Weave** | **Filling Knit—Jersey** |
| **Characteristics** | Usually cotton<br>Holds its shape | All fibers. Soft, stretchy. Cotton does not hold its shape well. Very pliable. |
| **End uses** | Towels, washcloths, robes | Baby towels and washcloths<br>Baby sleepers, adult sportswear, socks |

**TABLE 15–7** ❖
Comparison of pile fabrics.

| METHOD | TYPES AND KINDS | FABRICS—END USES | IDENTIFICATION |
|---|---|---|---|
| **Weaving** | 1. Filling floats cut and brushed up | 1. Velveteen, corduroy | Filling pile |
| | 2. Made as double cloth and cut apart | 2. Velvet, velour | Warp pile |
| | 3. Over wires | 3. Friezé, Wilton and velvet carpets | Warp pile |
| | 4. Slack tension | 4. Terrycloth, friezé | Warp pile |
| **Knitting** | Filling knit: laid-in yarn<br>Sliver knit | Velour, terry, fake fur, fleece | Stretchy—rows of knit stitches on back |
| | Warp knit: laid-in yarn or pile loops | | More stable |
| **Tufting** | Yarns punched into substrate | Rugs and carpets<br>Robes, bedspreads<br>Upholstery<br>Fake furs | Rows of stitches (like machine stitches) on wrong side |
| **Flocking** | Fibers anchored to substrate | Blankets, jackets<br>Designs on fabric<br>Upholstery | Fiber surface rather stiff |
| **Chenille yarns** | Pile-type yarns made by weaving<br>Chenille yarns woven or knitted into fabric | Upholstery<br>Outerwear fabric | Ravel adjacent yarns and examine novelty yarn |

- Tufted fabrics are cheaper than woven or knitted pile fabrics.
- Tufted fabrics are used in carpets and rugs, upholstery, coat linings, and bedspreads.

Tables 15–6 and 15–7 compare the different methods of producing pile fabrics.

## Laminates

**Laminates** include those fabrics in which two layers of fabric are combined into one fabric with an adhesive or foam. The term *laminate* refers to a fabric in which an adhesive was used; the term *bonded* refers to a fabric in which a foam was used. However, both terms are used interchangeably.

Introduced in 1958, bonding was originally a way to deplete inventories of tender (weak) or lightweight fabrics. Some converters were marginal operators who were not interested in quality. A bonder could buy two hot rolls discarded by finishers and be in business. The fabric could be stretched as it went through the rollers. Consequently, many problems were associated with these bonded fabrics. The layers separated (delaminated) or shrank unevenly. There were problems with blotchy colors when the adhesive bled through to the technical face. Because of these problems, laminated fabrics have a poor reputation. However, the textile industry improved the quality of laminated fabrics, and current laminates have greatly improved performance characteristics. Some advantages and limitations are given in Table 15–8.

**LAMINATING PROCESS** With knits, random nonwovens usually are used as the *backing* fabric because they give with the stresses applied to the face fabric. Acetate and nylon tricot often are used because of their low cost. The color of the backing can be a decorative feature in bonded laces.

Two methods of bonding are used (Figure 15–26):

1. Wet-adhesive method with aqueous acrylic adhesive or solvent urethane adhesive
2. Foam-flame method

In the **wet-adhesive method,** the adhesive is applied to the underside of the face fabric, and the liner fabric is joined by being passed through pressure rollers. The fabric is heated twice, the first time to drive out solvents and to give a preliminary cure, and the second time to produce permanent bond.

Monolithic membranes and microporous films are combined with fabrics in a laminated form. These durable and washable fabrics are breathable, drapeable, and comfortable. They are used for protective clothing and protect from heat, chemicals, biological organisms, radiation, abrasion, and particulates.

In the **foam-flame process,** polyurethane foam is the adhesive. Foam laminates consist of a layer of foam cov-

**TABLE 15–8** ❖ Laminated fabrics.

| ADVANTAGES | LIMITATIONS |
|---|---|
| Less costly fabrics are upgraded. | Top-quality fabrics are not bonded. |
| Self-lining gives comfort. | Backing does not prevent bagging, so a lining may be needed. |
| Stabilized if good quality. | Uneven shrinkage possible.* |
| Reduces time in sewing. | May be bonded off-grain. |
| Interfacings may be eliminated. | May delaminate.* |
| Underlinings, stay-stitching, and seam finishing are not needed. | Layered areas (hems, seams, etc.) may be stiff and boardy. |
| | Do not hold sharp creases. |

* These are the two major problems.

ered by another fabric or between two fabrics. The foam is made tacky first on one side and then on the other by passing under a gas flame. The final thickness of the foam is about 15/1,000 of an inch. This method gives more body but reduces the drapeability of the fabric. Another foam process generates the foam at the time it is to be applied, flowing it onto the fabric and curing on the fabric.

Foam laminates were first produced as thermal garments for outdoor workers because they were lightweight but warm. Foams were quilted to lining fabrics for a lining/interlining combination. Foam laminates

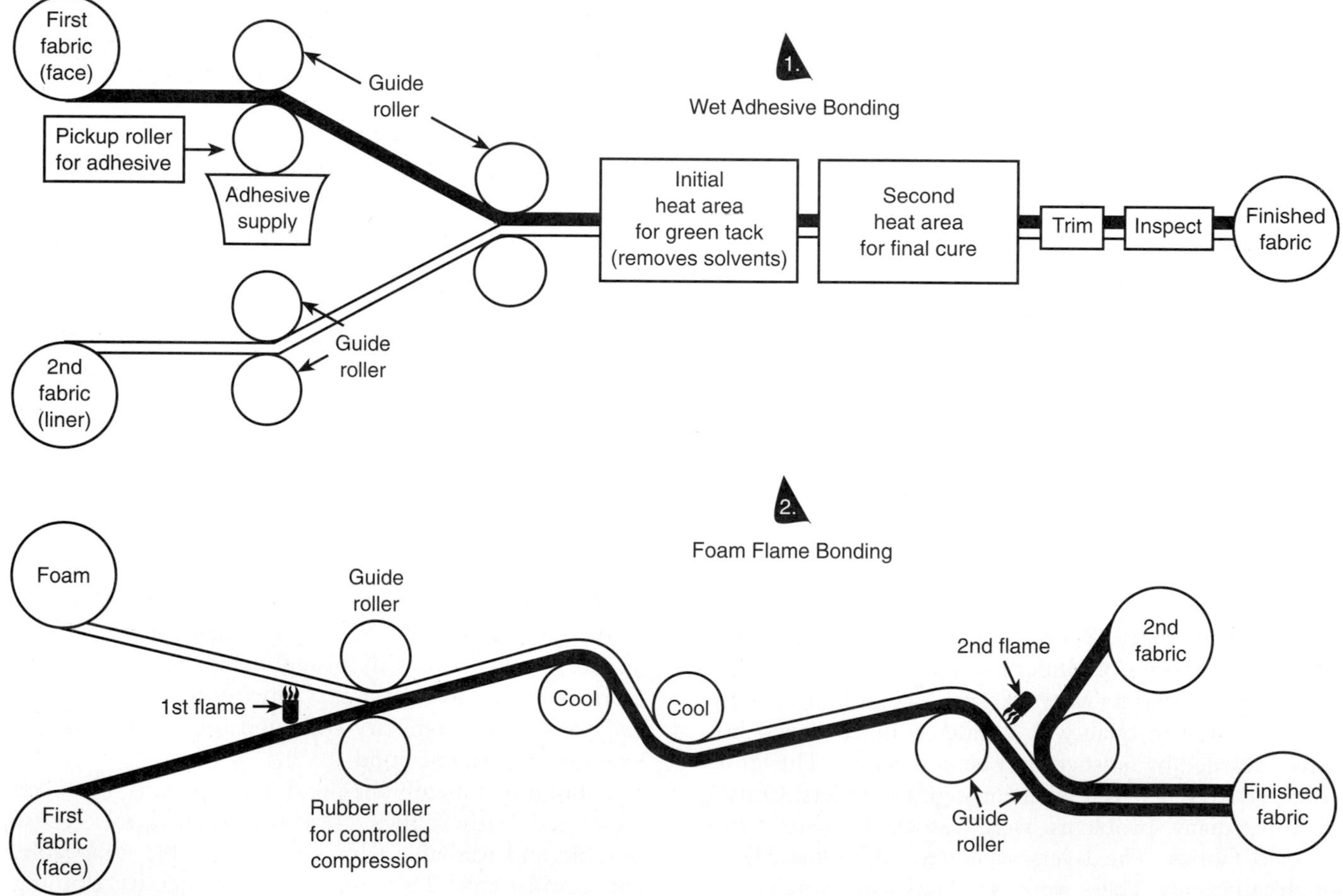


**FIGURE 15–26** ❖ Two basic methods for producing bonded textiles. (REPRINTED FROM *AMERICAN FABRICS & FASHIONS*, 1985, NO. 132. REPRINTED WITH PERMISSION FROM *BOBBIN MAGAZINE*. COPYRIGHT BOBBIN BLENHEIM MEDIA. ALL RIGHTS RESERVED.)

are made using all kinds and qualities of fabric with many different thicknesses of foam. Some firms will laminate or back upholstery fabrics for interior designers.

Flame laminates are widely used to produce automotive upholstery because the method is economical and produces a product with a soft hand and good compression strength and recovery power. Unfortunately, the technique also produces unacceptable volumes of pollutants from the melting and combustion of the foam, and alternate procedures are being developed that have less environmental impact.

Laminated fabrics can be summarized as follows:

- Two or more fabrics are made to adhere together by an adhesive or flame-foam process.
- The laminating process is less expensive than double-weave or double-knit processes.
- Laminating gives warmth without weight, when foam is one layer.
- Laminating makes possible the use of lightweight fabrics for outerwear.
- Laminated fabrics have body.
- Laminated fabrics do not hold sharp creases.
- Fabrics may be laminated off-grain and may delaminate.
- Laminates are used in apparel, furnishings, shoes, and industrial products.

## Stitch-Bonded Fabrics

**Stitch-bonded fabrics** include those fabrics that combine textile structures by adhering fabric layers with fiber or yarn loops, chemical adhesives, or fusion of thermoplastic fibers. Stitch-bonded fabrics are divided into knit-through fabrics and quilted fabrics. Stitch-bonded fabrics can be produced from nonwovens and any woven or knit fabric.

**Knit-through fabrics** are made in several ways. In the first process, a raschel warp-knitting machine knits yarns through a fiberweb or nonwoven structure. These fabrics also can be made by knitting fibers or knitting yarns around laid (not woven) warp and filling yarns. To make these knit-through fabrics, needles are used to create interconnected loops from yarns or fibers to stabilize the structure. These fabrics look like wovens, but careful examination shows that the lengthwise and crosswise yarns are not interwoven.

Araknit® is a knit-through fiberweb fabric used as a coating substrate. Arachne® and Maliwatt® are trade names for fabrics made by warp-knitting yarns through a fiberweb structure. These knit-through fabrics are produced at high speeds and are used for furnishing items—such as upholstery, blankets, and window treatment fabrics—and industrial uses—such as insulation and interlining. Malimo® uses warp or filling or warp and filling laid-in yarns with warp-knitting yarns (see Figure 15–27). These fabrics can be produced at very high speeds and are used for tablecloths, window treatment fabrics, vegetable bags, dishcloths, and outerwear. Another name for these fabrics is sew-knit fabrics.

Some knit-through fabrics utilize split-polymer films from recycled carbonated-beverage bottles. These fabrics are used in the carpet, geotextile, and bale-wrap industries.

## Quilted Fabrics

**Quilted fabrics** are composite fabrics consisting of three layers: face fabric, fiberfill or batting, and backing fabric. The three layers are stitch bonded with thread, chemical adhesive, or fusion by ultra-high-frequency sound. The bonding connects the layers in a pattern. The actual area physically bonded together is a very tiny percentage of

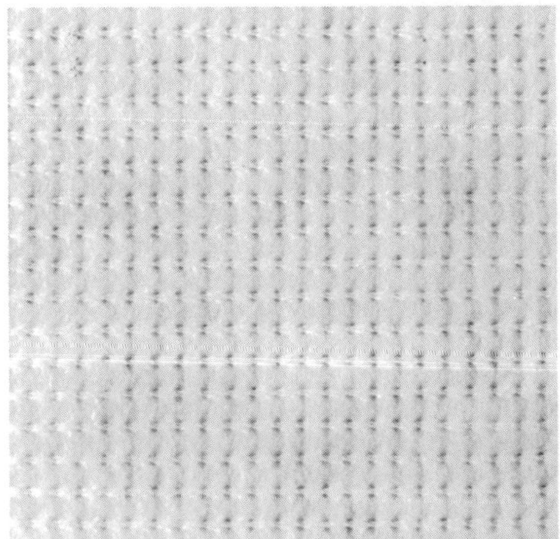

**FIGURE 15–27** ❖ Malimo® fabrics: drapery and casement fabrics.

the fabric's surface so that the high loft and bulky appearance desired in quilted fabrics are not sacrificed.

Most quilted fabric is made by stitching with thread. The thread and type of stitch used in quilting are good indicators of the quality and durability of the finished fabric. A durable quilt will have a lock-type stitch with a durable thread. Twistless nylon-monofilament thread is sometimes used because of its strength and abrasion resistance and because it is transparent and becomes hidden in the colors of the face fabric.

Almost any thread can be used, but those designed for quilting have different performance characteristics compared to regular sewing thread. Quilting threads must be durable. The disadvantage of thread stitches in quilting is that the threads may break from abrasion or snagging. Broken threads are unsightly and the loose fiberfill is no longer held in place.

Any fabric can be used for the shell or covering. A fashion fabric is used on one side. If the article is reversible or needs to be durable or beautiful on both sides, two fashion fabrics are used. If the fabric is to be lined or used as upholstery or a bedspread, the under layer is often an inexpensive fabric like cheesecloth, tricot, or a nonwoven fabric.

The batting may be foam, cotton, down, or fiberfill. Fiberfill is a manufactured fiber modified so that the loft is maintained.

Quilting is usually done in straight or curved lines. In upholstery, quilts, and comforters or bedspreads, the stitching may outline printed figures. This is a hand process in which the machine quilting is guided by hand. These fabrics are more costly.

Beauty of fabric is important for all end uses. For ski jackets and snowsuits, a closely woven water- and wind-repellent fabric is desirable; for comforters, resistance to slipping off the bed is important; for upholstery, durability and resistance to soil are important.

Chemical adhesive quilts seldom are used at present. Chemical adhesives can be applied in a pattern, but these fabrics are neither as appealing nor as durable as those produced by the other quilting methods.

Ultrasonic quilting requires thermoplastic fibers. Heat generated by ultra-high frequency sound or ultrasonic vibrations melts thermoplastic fibers, fusing several layers. Figure 15–28 shows a Pinsonic Thermal Joining machine that heat seals thermoplastic materials by ultrasonic vibrations. The machine quilts seven times as fast as conventional quilting machines. This process is used

**FIGURE 15–28** ❖ Pinsonic Thermal Joining machine (left) and close-up (right). (COURTESY OF BRANSON ULTRASONICS CORP.)

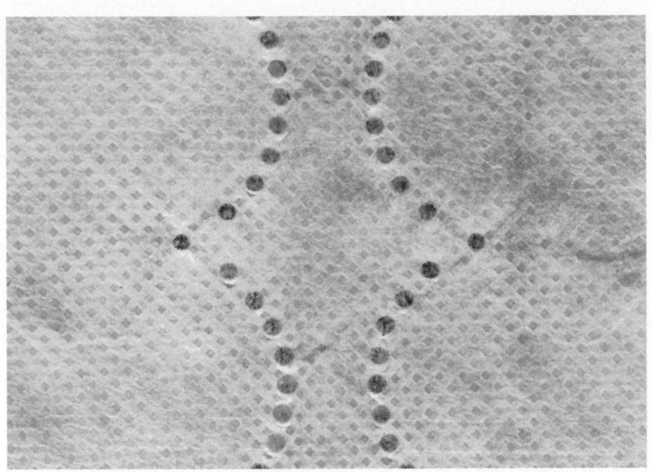

**FIGURE 15–29** ❖ Mattress pad. Two layers of fiberweb fabric and fiberfill batt joined by Pinsonic Thermal Joining machine.

on some mattress pads and lower priced bedspreads. It eliminates the problem of broken threads—a boon for institutional bedding in the hospitality industry. However, the outer layer may tear along the quilting lines. Figure 15–29 shows a **Pinsonic fabric.**

Quilted fabrics can be summarized as follows:

- One or two fabrics and wadding, batting, or foam are stitched together by machine or hand or welded by sonic vibrations.
- Quilted fabrics are bulky, warm, and decorative. However, stitches may break.
- Quilted fabrics are used in ski jackets, robes, comforters, quilts, and upholstery.

## Supported-Scrim Structures

**Supported-scrim structures** include the foam- and fiber-type blankets currently on the market. These fabrics use a lightweight nylon scrim, a loose warp-knit fabric, between two thin layers of polyurethane foam. A short nylon-flock fiber is adhered to the surface. These fabrics are attractive, durable, easy care, and inexpensive. Vellux and Vellux-Plus are two trade names.

Other types of supported-scrim fabrics include those that are needle punched with a scrim between the fiberweb layers. These fabrics are used industrially for roadbed-support fabrics and other applications requiring high stability.

## Fiber-Reinforced Materials

*Fiber-reinforced materials* are composites that include a fibrous component with a polymer resin, metal, or ceramic matrix. The reinforcing fiber adds strength and pliability, minimizes weight, and increases stability. These composite materials are very important in industrial applications and have contributed to major advances in transportation technology for lightweight automobiles and airplanes and more durable road surfaces.

A common example is the fiberglass-polymer resin used to make boat hulls and car bodies. Another example is an all-weather sport surface for horse racing in which fine sand is reinforced with polypropylene fibers. Polyester fibers are mixed with other materials to provide additional durability in concrete for poured road surfaces and building components.

❖

# Animal Products

The category of animal products includes leather and fur. These products are animals skins that are processed to maintain flexibility after being removed from the animal. In order to use the skin, the animal must be killed. Animal rights activists object to using animals in this way. Many people find products made of skins or hides attractive and functional regardless of the source of the product.

## Leather

**Leather** is processed from the skins and hides of animals, reptiles, fish, and birds. It is an organic substance derived from living animals and varies greatly in uniformity. Most leather in the U.S. is cow, pig, or lamb. These animals are raised primarily for meat or fiber, not for their hides or skins. Leather is a relatively unimportant by-product.

The hides from different animals differ in size, thickness, and grain. **Grain** is the marking that results from the skin formation and varies not only from species to species and from animal to animal but also within one hide. Other factors influence the surface of hides: Animals fight and bite or scratch each other, run into barbed-wire fences or nails, and are bitten by ticks and insects, causing scars that cannot be erased; brand marks or skin diseases also mar hides. In addition, vein marks, wrinkles, or pronounced grain marks may be viewed as undesirable irregularities. Of 100 hides, it is estimated that less than 5 percent are suitable for conversion into smooth top-grain leather in aniline finish, 20 percent are suitable for smooth leathers with a pigment finish, and the remaining 75 percent must be embossed, buffed, snuffed, or corrected in some fashion.

Dried skins and hides are stiff, boardy, nonpliable, and subject to decay. **Tanning** is the process in which skins and hides are treated with a chemical agent to make them pliable and water and rot resistant. *Vegetable tanning,* the most expensive process, is done with an extract leeched from the bark of various trees. *Chrome tanning,* a solution of bichromate of soda, sulfuric acid, and glucose, makes soft, pliable leather. *Oil tanning* is used to make chamois. *Alum tanning* is used for white leather. Because of environmental concerns, vegetable tanning is becoming more common since chromium-containing waste is highly toxic.

Skins go through many processes to become leather: salting; cleaning to remove the hair and epidermis; tanning; bleaching; stuffing; coloring or dyeing; staking; and finishing by glazing, boarding, buffing, snuffing, or embossing, depending on the desired end use. The many processes explain why leather is an expensive product.

The appearance of leather can be modified extensively in processing. Many finishes, including stuffing, snuffing, and buffing, are designed to camouflage flaws, scars, wrinkles, or irregularities in the skins. Fillers improve the appearance by covering these irregularities with a chemical compound much like cosmetics are used to hide flaws. Bleaching whitens the skin prior to dyeing. Staking is a tension drying process to minimize skin shrinkage. Dyeing, printing, glazing, and embossing are finishing steps to add color, gloss, or texture to the skin. Many of these finishes add greatly to the appeal of the leather item. Unfortunately, many of these finishes are not fast to leather dry cleaning processes and are removed or altered during cleaning. In addition, fillers may be removed, allowing hide irregularities to appear. Dyes and prints may not be fast. Most leather cleaners are adept at finishing or reworking leather items so that the consumer is never aware that the original appearance has been replaced. However, the high cost of leather cleaning clearly reflects the additional efforts required of the dry cleaner.

Leather is a nonseparable-fiber product. As shown in Figure 15–30, the fibers are very dense on the skin side and less dense on the flesh side. Thick hides are often split or shaved into layers to make them more pliable and economical (Figure 15–31).

The first layer is called **top grain** and has the typical animal grain on its outer surface. It takes the best finish and wears well. It is also the highest quality and the most expensive layer. **Splits** have a looser, more porous structure and are cut across the fibers. They are not as smooth as top grain and tend to rough up during wear. Most split leathers are given an embossed finish or a suede finish. Although splits are not identified as such on product labels, top grain is usually mentioned. Splits are less expensive and lower in quality. Quality of splits decreases with each layer; lowest quality leather is next to the animal's flesh.

**FIGURE 15–30** ❖ Cross-sectional drawing of a strip of leather, showing variations in density.

Leather is a durable product. It may have a noticeable odor. It varies greatly in quality—not only from skin to skin but within one skin. Like wool fibers, leather from the backs and sides of the animal is better, whereas that from the belly and legs tends to be thin and stretchy or very coarse.

Leather picks up oils and grease readily. It requires special care in cleaning since it is stiffened by solvents. Most dry cleaners send leather and suede items to a specialist for cleaning. Leather cleaning removes soil, odor, and oil from the skin. Unfortunately, screen prints, dyes, and fillers may also be removed. Scars and other flaws like wrinkles, vein marks, and texture differences may appear. The oil can be replaced fairly easily. Dry cleaners can redye to bring the item closer to its original appearance. Thus, it is always wise to have all items of the same color cleaned at the same time in case a problem develops. However, screen prints and wrinkles create problems that cannot be handled as easily (see Figure 15–32). Many consumers assume the dry cleaner is at fault when these problems occur. That may well be the

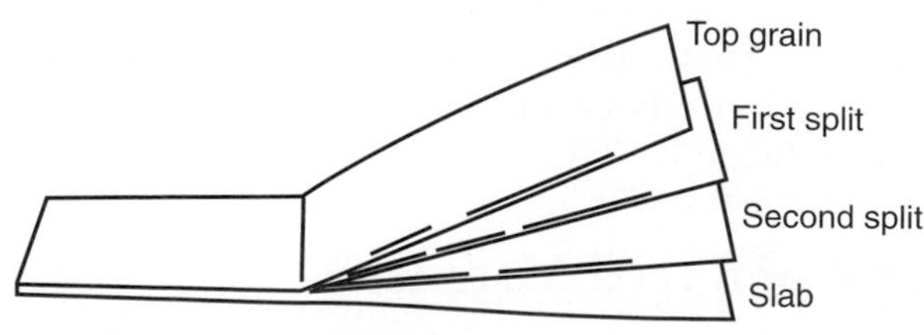


**FIGURE 15–31** ❖ Split leather.

**FIGURE 15–32** ❖ Pigskin suede after dry cleaning. The strip superimposed on the sample illustrates the original color and texture. Scars and other hide flaws are clearly visible.

case. Frequently, however, the problem lies with the manufacturer who selected the incorrect hide, process, chemical, or component to use in the item. For example, fusible interlinings in jackets may separate or shrink, causing bubbling or puckering of the leather. Screen prints may not be tested for fastness to dry cleaning before application to the leather.

Leathers are used for apparel, upholstery, wall coverings, athletic gear (balls, gloves, and saddles), luggage and bags, and accessories like wallets, lamp shades, and coasters. Product design is limited by the size of the skins. Leather products frequently include a greater number of seams compared to other materials because of this size limitation.

Reconstituted leathers have been made by grinding up leather, mixing it with urethane, and forming it into sheets. This "leather" product is uniform in thickness and quality and is not limited in length and width.

**SUEDE** **Suede** is a popular leather for coats, jackets, dresses, trims, and furnishings like upholstery and wall coverings. The soft, dull surface is made by napping (running the skin under a coarse emery sander) on the flesh side or on one side of a split to pull up the fibers. Suede is a very durable product, but it requires special care. Rain, wet snow, and other moisture damage suede. Cleaning of suede also should be done by specialists.

## Furs

A **fur** is any animal skin or part of an animal skin to which the hair, fleece, or fur fibers are attached. Most fur is used in apparel, but fur is also used for throws and rugs, wall hangings, and animal toys. Fur garments are considered luxury items by the United States government. Consumers usually purchase furs because of their beautiful appearance rather than for their warmth, durability, or easy care. It is important to know about the kinds of fur, how fur garments are made, and how to care for them in order to make wise selections and to maintain the beauty of the garment.

Furs are natural products and vary in quality. Good-quality fur has a very dense pile. If the fur has guard hairs, they are long and very lustrous. The fur is soft and fluffy. The quality depends on the age and health of the animal and the season of the year in which it is killed. Furs are usually harvested in late fall because the coat is most dense with minimal sun and abrasion damage.

Fur trapping has long been an important industry in all parts of the world. Fur farming, started in 1880, has been a boon to the fur industry because better pelts are produced as a result of scientific breeding, careful feeding and handling of the animals, and slaughtering them when the fur is in prime condition. Silver fox, chinchilla, mink, Persian lamb, and nutria are the common fur-bearing animals raised on ranches. By crossbreeding and inbreeding, new and different colored furs have been produced. However, efforts by animal rights activists to decrease use of furs have had a negative impact on fur farming and demands for fur products.

The cost of fur depends on fashion, the supply and demand for fashionable furs, and the work involved in producing the item. Chinchilla, mink, sable, platina fox, and ermine have always been very expensive. Skins are gathered together from all over the world and sold at public auction.

Furs go through many processes before they are sold as products. Dressing of fur is comparable to tanning of leather and the purpose is the same—to keep the skins from putrefying and make them soft and pliable. Dressing must be more carefully done than with leather so that the surface hairs or fibers are not damaged. After tanning, pelts are combed, brushed, and beaten. The final process is drumming in sawdust to clean and polish the hair and to absorb oil from the leather and fur. The sawdust is removed by brushing or vacuuming.

Many furs are dyed. Furs may be dyed to make less expensive furs look like the expensive ones. For example, muskrat may be dyed to resemble seal, and rabbit may be stenciled to look spotted. Furs are also dyed to improve their natural color as well as to give them unnatural colors—red or green, for example. Tip dyeing is brushing the tips of the fur and guard hairs with dye. Furs also are dip dyed, a process in which the entire skin is dipped in dye. Some furs are bleached and some are bleached and then dyed.

Furs require special care to keep them beautiful. They should not be stored in damp or hot, humid places and never in plastic bags. Between seasons, if possible, garments should be sent to a furrier for cold storage; the furs are kept in special vaults in which the temperature and humidity are controlled. To restore luster and clean the garment, it is usually best to send it to a furrier once a year. Furs should never be dry cleaned, unless the furrier method is used. In this method, the fur is tumbled in an oil-saturated, coarsely grained powder. The powder absorbs soil, adds oil to the fibers and skin, and cleans the fibers without excessive abrasion and matting. The item must be carefully brushed and vacuumed to remove the excess powder. Sometimes after furs have been cleaned, a small amount of the powder may be found in the pockets.

Furs should be protected from abrasion. Avoid sitting on fur garments. Hang them on a wide, well-constructed hanger and allow plenty of space between garments. Shake garments rather than brush them.

## Key Terms

Film
Plain film
Nonreinforced film
Expanded film
Supported film
Foam
Nonwoven
Fiberweb structure
Dry-laid fiberweb
Wet-laid fiberweb
Spun-bonded web
Hydroentangled web
Melt-blown fiberweb
Needle punching
Chemical adhesive
Batting
Wadding
Fiberfill
Resiliency
Resistance to shifting
Fusible nonwovens
Felt
Netlike structure
Braid
Lace
Handmade lace
Needlepoint lace
Bobbin lace
Battenburg lace
Leavers lace
Cordonnet lace
Reembroidered lace
Raschel lace
Composite fabric
Coated fabric
Lamination
Poromeric fabric
Suedelike fabric
Tufting
Tuft density
Gauge
Laminates
Wet-adhesive method
Foam-flame process
Stitch-bonded fabric
Knit-through fabric
Quilted fabric
Pinsonic fabric
Supported-scrim structure
Leather
Grain
Tanning
Top grain
Split leather
Suede
Fur

## Questions

1. Why are nonwoven or fiberweb structures so important in the industrial products markets?
2. From the list of fabrication methods in this chapter (film, foam, nonwoven, lace, braid, coated, tufted, bonded, quilted, leather, and fur) identify which are made from these materials:
   solutions
   fibers
   yarns
   fabrics
3. Identify the fabrication methods that combine two or more of the materials listed in question 2.
4. What performance can be expected from these products?
   a vinyl film (jersey supported) upholstered recliner chair
   a 100 percent polyester Leavers lace casement drapery for a master bedroom
   a quilted bedspread and matching draperies (50 percent polyester/50 percent cotton) for a hotel room
   a pair of leather slacks
   wall covering of a suedelike structure
   a poromeric raincoat of 65 percent polyester/35 percent cotton (outer fabric)
5. Explain the relationship of these methods to products likely to be encountered by professionals in the apparel or furnishing industry.

## Suggested Readings

Brown, Stephen G. (1994, July/August). "The Making and Coloration of Leather." *Journal of the Society of Dyers and Colourists, 10,* pp. 213–214.
Davies, Stan, and Owen, Phil (August, 1989). "Staying Dry and Keeping Your Cool." *Textile Month,* pp. 37–40.
E. I. du Pont de Nemours & Company. (no date). "A Formula for Gauging Carpet Performance." Wilmington, DE: Commercial Carpet Fibers Division, Fibers Marketing Center.
Earnshaw, Pat (1982). *A Dictionary of Lace.* Aylesburg, Bucks, United Kingdom: Shires Publications.
Ford, J. E. (1991). Nonwovens. *Textiles* (4), pp. 17–21.
Fulmar, T. D. (1992, June). "The How and Why of Coated Fabrics." *America's Textiles International,* pp. 80, 82, 84.

Grayson, Martin, ed. (1984). *Encyclopedia of Textiles, Fibers, and Nonwoven Fabrics.* New York: John Wiley & Sons.

Humphries, Mary. (1996). *Fabric Glossary.* Upper Saddle River, NJ: Prentice Hall.

Judd, Peter T. (1992). "Base Fabrics Used in Interlining Construction." *Textiles* (4), pp. 14–16.

Landmann, Axel (1994, July/August). "The Effect of 'Natural' Defects on Leather Dyeing." *Journal of the Society of Dyers and Colourists, 10,* pp. 217–219.

Lombard, Gerard, and Marcotte, Michel (1992, April). "Geotextiles: Engineered Synthetic Fabrics." *Canadian Textile Journal,* pp. 36–41.

Mohamed, Mansour H. (1990, November/December). "Three-Dimensional Textiles." *American Scientist, 78,* pp. 530–541.

Schwartz, Peter, Rhodes, Trevor, and Mohamed, Mansour (1982). *Fabric Forming Systems.* Park Ridge, NJ: Noyes Publications.

Senior, Colin, and Thorpe, Derek. (1994, July/August). "Leather Dyeing." *Journal of the Society of Dyers and Colourists, 10,* pp. 215–216.

Tortora, Phyllis G., and Merkel, Robert S. (1996). *Fairchild's Dictionary of Textiles,* 7th ed. New York: Fairchild Publications.

Wagner, J. Robert (1982). *Nonwoven Fabrics.* Norristown, PA: Author.

# Section Five

# FINISHING

Chapter 16

# FINISHING: AN OVERVIEW

## OBJECTIVES

- To understand the general steps and sequence involved in fabric finishing.
- To recognize the ways fabrics can be modified in finishing.
- To relate finishing to fabric quality, end-use suitability, and product performance.

The four chapters in this section focus on converting a fabric from a raw form to the form consumers expect. In this process, the fabric is finished and its performance and appearance are enhanced.

A **finish** is any process that is done to fiber, yarn, or fabric either before or after fabrication to change the *appearance* (what is seen), the *hand* (what is felt), or the *performance* (what the fabric does). All finishing adds to the cost of the end product and the time it takes to produce the item.

The sequence normally followed in textile processing is an involved one. Often several steps are repeated. A common sequence is fiber processing followed by yarn processing. Fabrication (producing a fabric) usually follows some preparation steps. In preparation, the yarn or fabric is made ready for additional steps in the sequence. Bleaching is almost always done before dyeing. Coloration usually is done before finishing and reworking (repairing). Figure 16–1 shows a diagram of a typical sequence used to produce a fabric.

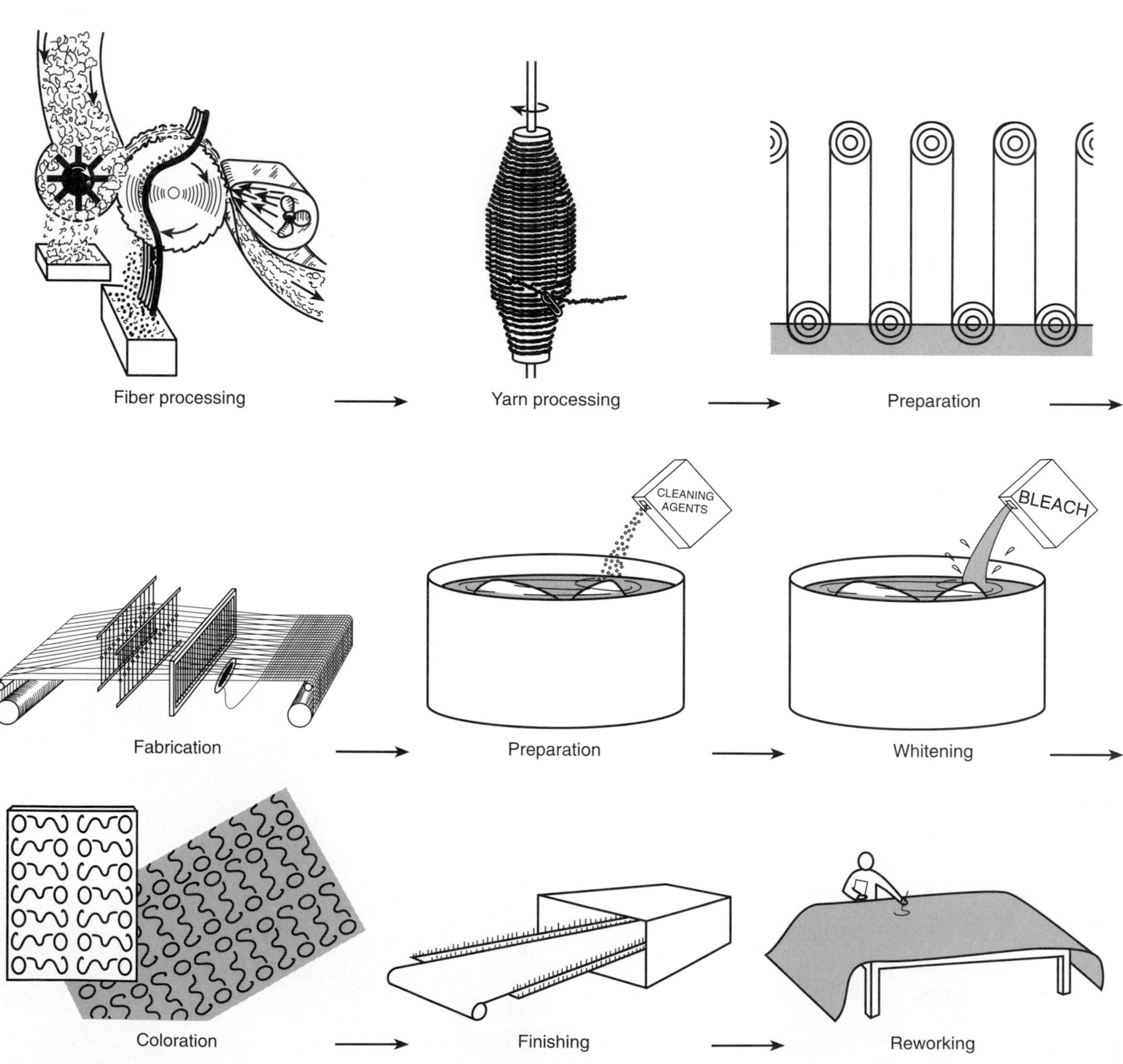


**FIGURE 16–1** ❖ Typical production sequence for textile fabrics.

Finishing may be done in the mill where the fabric is constructed or it may be done in a separate establishment by a highly specialized group called **converters.** Converters operate in two ways: They perform a service for a mill by finishing goods to order, in which case they are paid for their services and never own the fabric; or they buy the fabric from a mill, finish it according to their needs, and sell it under their trade name.

Vertically integrated firms are an important part of the industry and often direct and control every step of processing for the fabrics used in their products, from opening bales of raw fiber to cutting and sewing the finished products. Vertical firms convert or finish fabrics in-house in facilities they own and operate.

Finishes can be classified by how long they are effective on the fabric. A **permanent finish,** such as mercerization, lasts the life of the item. A **durable finish,** such as wrinkle resistance, lasts longer than a temporary finish, but not for the life of the item. These finishes often require some effort or manipulation on the part of the user, especially as the fabric ages. With wrinkle-resistant finishes, older items may require some touch-up ironing. A **temporary finish,** such as simple calendering, lasts until the item is washed or dry cleaned. A **renewable finish,** such as some water-repellent finishes, can be applied by the consumer, or it may be applied by the dry cleaner.

Some finishes—such as dyeing, printing, or embossing—are easy to recognize because they are visible. Other finishes—such as wrinkle resistance—are not visible but have an important effect on fabric performance. Consumers may have difficulty understanding the higher costs for fabrics with invisible finishes, like wrinkle- and soil-resistant finishes. Improved performance is expected, but the consumer needs to recognize the visible finishes and the need for nonvisible finishes, as well as the serviceability of the finish. The improved performance resulting from these finishes adds to the inherent value and the cost of the product.

Many finishing processes are used on all kinds of fabric. The processes are very similar regardless of fabric type. However, because of their importance and greater likelihood of being finished, the emphasis here will be on woven and knitted fabrics. The major differences that exist between finishing woven or knitted fabrics occur in the way the fabric is handled or transported. Woven fabrics have little give or stretch. Knits have a much greater potential for stretch; hence precautions need to be taken to minimize stretching during finishing of knits. Pile fabrics are handled so that pile matting is minimized.

**Gray goods** (grey, greige, or loom state) are fabrics (regardless of color) that have been produced but have received no wet- or dry-finishing operations. Some gray goods fabrics have names, such as print cloth and soft-filled sheeting, which are used only for the gray goods. Other gray goods names, such as lawn, broadcloth, and sateen, also are used as names for the finished cloth. Many of these terms can be found in commodity price listings in trade publications like the *Daily News Record* (see Figure 2–2).

**Converted,** or ***finished,*** **goods** have received wet- or dry-finishing treatments such as bleaching, dyeing, or embossing. Some converted goods retain the gray goods name. Others, such as madras gingham, are named for the place of origin; still others, such as silence cloth, are named for the end use. Figure 16–2 shows a print cloth gray goods and the various looks of the fabric with different finishing procedures.

**Mill-finished fabrics** can be sold and used without further finishing. Some may be sized before they are sold.

For years, **water-bath finishing** was standard because water is a good solvent, it is readily available, and it is relatively inexpensive. In water-bath finishing, the chemical is placed in a water solution and padded onto the fabric by immersing the fabric in the solution and squeezing out any excess. The fabric is heavy with water, often as much as five times heavier. Moving and drying the fabric requires a lot of energy. A great deal of water was used to scour or clean the fabric. Recently, with water pollution and environmental concerns and energy costs, **foam finishing** has become an alternative means of adding a finish. Foam finishing uses foam rather than a liquid in applying the finishing chemical to the fabric. A foam is a mixture of air and liquid that is lighter weight than a solution of the liquid. Foam finishing is used because of the low-wet pickup (a much smaller amount of liquid is used and absorbed by the fabric). In addition, energy is conserved in moving and drying the lighter fabric. The higher production speeds of foam

**FIGURE 16–2** ❖ Print cloth gray goods: as produced, bleached, printed, piece dyed (from lower left to upper right).

finishing mean that the costs of finishing can be kept low. In foam finishing less water is used in scouring and cleaning. Foam finishing is used to add both routine and special-purpose finishes to the fabric. One major limitation of foam finishing is that as the amount of water in the process decreases, the ability to apply a finish uniformly throughout the fabric also decreases.

Another development in finishing is the use of solvents other than water, referred to as **solvent finishing.** Solvent finishing was developed in response to a need to decrease water pollution and energy costs. In solvent finishing, a solvent is used to mix the solution. Solvent finishing is not as popular as foam finishing because of the cost of solvents, expensive reclaiming processes, environmental concerns, regulatory issues, and health problems.

Computer control of finishing is extremely important. Computers provide automatic correction of processes, fabric tension, and finishing solutions and temperatures. Computerization allows for ease of planning and incorporates built-in menus to facilitate changing of finish additives. Computer systems also result in minimizing negative environmental impact by allowing for efficient treatment of residue and recycling of recoverable chemicals from finishing.

Combining finishing steps is a recent innovation in the industry. Combining steps minimizes space, chemicals, energy, water, and costs. In single-stage preparation, desizing, bleaching, and scouring occur in one step rather than the three separate ones formerly required. Discussion of these processes will be done separately, but remember, all three often occur simultaneously.

This chapter discusses routine finishing. Routine finishing includes those steps in finishing that are done to most fabrics to prepare them for dying and special-purpose aesthetic and functional finishes. These routine finishes are often referred to as **preparation.** The normal order of production of a basic commodity cotton/polyester, bottom-weight, plain-weave fabric will be used as the basis for discussion. Because many steps of production are discussed in detail elsewhere, these steps are included in the discussion for continuity, but see other chapters for review. Routine finishing steps for other fiber or fabric types are discussed at the end of this chapter.

# Routine Finishing Steps

## Fiber Processing

In *fiber processing,* the cotton fibers are processed separately from the polyester fibers because of the differences in properties of the two fiber types. Synthetic fibers like polyester generally require little additional processing once the fiber has been produced if they are used in filament form. However, since this fabric is to be a cotton/polyester blend, the polyester fibers must be in staple form to be blended. Thus, the polyester fibers were produced as filament tow, crimped and cut or broken into staple fibers, baled, and shipped to the yarn spinning facility.

Since cotton is a natural fiber, considerably more processing is necessary. The fiber is grown, picked at the appropriate time, ginned, baled, and shipped to the yarn processing facility. The cotton's grade must be assessed because the suitability of the cotton fiber is matched to the end use based on its grade. Higher grades of cotton demand higher prices in the market. These prices fluctuate on a daily and seasonal basis, as do most agricultural commodities. Hence, the price of cotton is more likely to vary than that of the polyester fibers. The processing of these two fiber types is discussed in more detail in Chapters 4 and 8.

## Yarn Processing

In *yarn processing* the fibers are aligned, blended, and twisted. Both fiber bales must be opened and dirt and soil removed. The compact fibers must be loosened and aligned in a parallel fashion before the yarns can be produced. Several different bales of cotton will be blended to assure that fabric performance and quality will be consistent from season to season and year to year. However, since the properties of these two fibers differ significantly, the processing tends to be separate until well into the yarn production process; for blends, fibers are often combined at the roving stage. Once the fibers are blended, the appropriate amount of twist is added to the yarns. Generally, the warp yarns have slightly higher twist to facilitate the weaving process. After the yarns have been spun, they are wound on bobbins and shipped to the mill to be processed into fabric. Yarn processing is discussed in Chapter 10.

## Yarn Preparation

Preparation involves several steps. The first steps involve the yarns and will be discussed before the fabrication step.

**SLASHING** In **slashing** the warp yarns are treated before being threaded into the loom for weaving. These yarns are usually wound onto a creel and then coated with a mixture of natural starches or synthetic resins so that they resist the abrasion and tension of weaving. Slashing adds a protective coating to the yarn to obtain optimum weaving efficiency, increase yarn rigidity, and decrease yarn hairiness. This has become more important with faster, shuttleless looms. The sizing may contain a starch, metal-to-fiber lubricant, preservative, defoamer, or a combination of these ingredients. Recipes will vary with fiber type. For this cotton/polyester-blend fabric, the sizing is probably a mixture of a starch and a lubricant or poly (vinyl alcohol). The filling yarns generally receive little if any treatment prior to weaving. The sizing must be removed after weaving in order for dyes and finishes to bond with the fibers.

## Fabrication

**Fabrication** normally follows slashing. In fabrication the fabric is woven, knitted, or created in some other manner. At the mill the cotton/polyester yarns are repackaged into the appropriate size unit for weaving. Warp yarns are threaded through the heddles in the harnesses and the spaces in the reed after slashing. Filling yarns are packaged for the specific type of loom to be used in weaving. Since shuttleless looms are so common in the U.S. textile industry, assume that this fabric will be made on such a loom. Filling yarn length is measured during weaving and the yarns are cut so that only the length needed for one insertion is available at any one time. The filling yarn is inserted in a shed that has every other warp yarn raised to create a plain weave. When the length of warp yarns has been woven, the fabric is removed from the loom and the cloth beam is transported to the finishing plant for appropriate finishing steps. For a more detailed discussion of weaving see Chapter 12.

## Fabric Preparation

**HANDLING** **Handling** refers to the physical form of the fabric during finishing. The two components that influence how a fabric will be handled are its width and length. Choices made regarding handling influence cost, quality, and minimums. **Minimums** describe the smallest quantity of a fabric a buyer can purchase from a mill. Firms that allow for shorter minimums tend to charge higher prices because the cost per yard of finishing short pieces or short runs of fabrics tends to be higher. The term **run** is used to describe a quantity of fabric receiving the same processing at the same time. Generally, as the length of a run increases, the costs per yard decrease. Thus, in general, it is cheaper for a mill to process a longer piece of fabric than to process several shorter pieces of fabric.

In terms of fabric width, the first option is **open-width finishing** during which the fabric is held out to its full width. Open-width finishing is often done with the fabric mounted on a tenter frame. Tentering will be discussed later in this chapter. In the second option, the fabric is allowed to roll and fold in on itself to form a tube or rope. This form of finishing is referred to as **rope** or **tubular finishing.** Heavier-weight woven fabrics are usually finished at open width because of the likelihood of creasing and wrinkles or tube marks being set in the fabric if it were finished in rope form. Fabrics for prints or whites can be finished in tube form because rope marks will be removed or hidden in bleaching or printing. However, lighter-weight woven fabrics, especially polyester/cellulose blends, give better results if finished in open-width form. Knit fabrics are usually finished in tube form because of the difficulties in controlling the knit structure in open-width form.

Tube finishing is more economical, but it may create problems with penetration of finishes and dyes into interior portions of the rope or tube. Creasing and wrinkling tend to occur more readily when fabrics are finished in tube form, and some machine-induced creases, wrinkles, and marks may be permanent. New techniques and use of different processing chemicals may minimize these problems with tubular finishing. Continuous open-width processing consumes huge quantities of water and energy.

A second component of handling refers to whether the fabric is handled in a batch or continuous process. **Batch processing** describes when a relatively small amount of fabric, say several hundred yards, is processed as a unit at one time in one machine or piece of equipment. The entire quantity of fabric is immersed in a solution at the same time. **Continuous processing** describes working with longer pieces of fabric that move in and out of solution. Continuous processing is more economical but requires larger quantities of fabric to achieve its full potential for minimizing costs per yard. In addition, the size of the finishing equipment requires fairly long pieces of fabric in order to engage all parts of the equipment. Because the heavyweight-blend fabric used as the example in this chapter is a commodity fabric, continuous open-width processing will be used.

**DESIZING** In **desizing** the sizing added to the warp yarns in the slashing step is removed. Desizing is necessary so that dyes and finishes will bond to both warp and filling yarns. For desizing to be effective, the finisher needs to know the sizing agent used to select the best means of desizing. Physical, biological, or chemical desizing may be done depending on the sizing agents and the fiber content of the fabric. Although sizing is present only on the warp yarns, all yarns in the fabric are treated since they cannot be separated. In cotton-blend fabrics, physical desizing (agitation) with biological desizing using an enzyme to destroy the starch may be done.

**CLEANING** All gray goods must be **cleaned** and made ready to accept any finish. Gray goods contain a warp sizing, which makes the fabric stiff and interferes with the absorption of liquids. Sizing residue must be removed before further finishing can be done. Also, fabrics are often soiled during fabrication and storage and must be cleaned for that reason. Warp sizing, dirt, and oil spots are removed by a washing process—*degumming* of silk, *kier boiling* or boiling-off of cotton, and *scouring* of wool.

**SINGEING** **Singeing** burns any fiber ends projecting from the surface of the fabric. These protruding ends cause roughness, dullness, and pilling, and interfere with finishing. Singeing may be the first finishing operation for smooth-finished cotton or cotton-blend fabrics and for clear-finished wool fabrics. The fabric is passed between two gas flame bars or hot plates to singe it on both sides in one step. Fabrics containing heat-sensitive fibers such as cotton/polyester blends must be singed carefully and often are singed after dyeing because the melted ends of the polyester may cause unevenness in color. Singeing is one solution for pilling.

**BIO-POLISHING** **Bio-polishing** is the use of a cellulase enzyme treatment to hydrolyze the surface of any cellulosic fibers. At present, the process is most often applied to cotton or cotton/polyester blend fabrics. Bio-polishing, a trade name by Novo Nordisk, is a permanent finish that is used to remove surface fuzz from spun yarns of cellulose or cellulose blends. The finished fabric has a soft, smooth appearance with very little surface fuzz. Protruding fiber ends that would constitute the fuzz in most spun-yarn fabrics have been destroyed by the enzyme treatment. By removing the fiber ends, the potential for fabric pilling during use is decreased. Colors also look brighter because the fabric's smooth surface does not scatter the light as much as a fuzzy surface would. Although the surface properties and appearance of the fabric are improved, a slight decrease of 3–10 percent in tensile strength usually occurs. Some products may be marketed with a hang-tag indicating that they have been bio-polished.

**SCOURING** **Scouring** is a general term referring to removal of foreign matter or soil from the fabric prior to finishing or dyeing. The procedure is related to the fiber content of the fabric. The foreign matter involved may be processing oils, starch, natural waxes, soils, and tints or color added to aid in fiber identification during production. Scouring generally uses detergents and is done several times during finishing to wet out the fabric or to remove excess chemicals or soil. Wetted out fabrics are easier and more efficient to finish than dry fabrics.

## Whitening

**BLEACHING** **Bleaching** is the process of whitening fibers, yarns, or fabrics by removing color. Most bleaches are oxidizing agents; the actual bleaching is done by active oxygen. A few bleaches are reducing agents and are used to strip color from poorly dyed fabrics. Bleaches may be either acid or alkaline in nature. They are usually unstable, especially in the presence of moisture. Bleaches that are old or have been improperly stored lose their oxidizing power. In bleaching the goals are a uniform removal of hydrophobic impurities in the fabric and a high, uniform degree of whiteness of the fabric in order to get clear uniform colors when dyeing.

Any bleach will damage fibers. Since damage occurs more rapidly at higher temperatures and concentrations, these two factors must be carefully controlled.

The same bleach is not suitable for all kinds of fibers. Because fibers vary in their chemical reaction, bleaches must be chosen with regard to fiber content. In addition, environmental regulations are restricting use of bleaches containing chlorine.

The finisher uses bleaches to clean and whiten gray goods. The natural fibers are an off-white color because of the impurities they contain. Because these impurities are easily removed from cotton, most cotton gray goods are bleached without damage. The bleaching step may be omitted with wool because it has good affinity for dyes and other finishes even if not bleached.

*Peroxide bleaches* are common factory bleaches for cellulose and protein fibers and fabrics. *Hydrogen peroxide* is an oxidizing bleach. Peroxide bleaches best at a temperature of 180–200°F in an alkaline solution. These bleaching conditions make it possible to do peroxide bleaching of cellulose gray goods as the final step in the kier boil.

In the peroxide cold bleach procedure, the fabric is soaked overnight or for a period of 8 hours. This procedure often is used on cotton-knit goods and wool to preserve a soft hand.

**OPTICAL BRIGHTENERS** **Optical brighteners** are also used to whiten off-white fabrics. They are fluorescent whitening compounds, not bleaches. These compounds are absorbed by the fiber and emit a bluish fluorescence that masks yellow. At the mill, optical brighteners give best results when used in combination with bleach rather than as a substitute for it. They are also added to the spinning solution of some manufactured fibers to optically brighten them, since bleach may not be effective on these fibers. Optical brighteners can be used with delustered and nondelustered fibers without affecting fiber luster.

## Further Preparation Steps

**MERCERIZATION** **Mercerization** is the process of treating a cellulosic fabric or yarn with an alkali (caustic soda). Although Native Americans used wood ash (lye) to strengthen plant fibers, modern mercerizing was discovered in 1853 by John Mercer, a calico printer. He noticed that his cotton-filter cloth shrank and became stronger, more lustrous, and more absorbent after filtering caustic soda used in the dye process. Mercerization was little used until H. Lowe discovered in 1897 that fabrics under tension became lustrous and silky.

Mercerization is used on cotton, linen, and some rayon fabrics. It increases the luster and softness, gives greater strength, and improves the fabric's affinity for dyes and waterborne finishes. Plissé effects can be achieved in cotton fabrics (see Chapter 17). Cotton is mercerized for luster in both yarn and fabric form.

*Yarn mercerization* is a continuous process in which the yarn under tension passes from a warp beam through a series of boxes with guide rolls and squeeze rolls, a boil-out wash, and a final wash (Figure 16–3). Cotton sewing thread is also mercerized for greater strength.

*Fabric mercerization* is done on a frame that contains mangles for saturating the cloth; a tenter frame for tensioning the fabric both crosswise and lengthwise while wet; and boxes for washing, neutralizing the caustic soda with dilute sulfuric acid, scouring, and rinsing. In *tension mercerization* the fabric or yarn being mercerized is held under tension. The concentration of the sodium hydroxide solution is high, generally around 20 percent. The sodium hydroxide causes the fiber to swell. Because of the tension during the swelling, the fibers become more rodlike and rounder in cross section, and the number of convolutions decreases (Figure 16–4). Because the fiber is smoother, it reflects more light. Mercerization to increase luster is done to a small percentage of cotton, primarily long-staple cotton yarns and fabrics.

**FIGURE 16–3** ❖ Mercerization of warp yarn. (COURTESY OF COATS & CLARK INC.)

**FIGURE 16–4** ❖ Photomicrographs of mercerized cotton: cross-sectional view (left); longitudinal view (right). (COURTESY OF THE BRITISH TEXTILE TECHNOLOGY GROUP.)

Greater absorbency results from mercerization because the caustic soda causes a rearrangement of the molecules, making more of the hydroxyl groups available to absorb more water and waterborne substances. Moisture regain improves to approximately 11 percent. Dyes enter the fiber more readily. When they are fixed inside the fiber, they have better colorfastness characteristics. Mercerized fabrics take resin finishes better for the same reason.

Mercerized cotton fibers are stronger because, in the swollen fiber, the molecules are more nearly parallel to the fiber axis. When stress is applied, the end-to-end molecular attraction is harder to rupture than in the more spiral fibril arrangement. Fiber strength increase is approximately 30 percent.

**Slack mercerization** consists of dipping cotton fabric in a weaker caustic soda solution for a shorter time before neutralizing and washing. The cloth shrinks and the yarn crimp increases. The straightening of the crimp when stress is applied produces stretch. Slack mercerization increases the absorbency and improves the dyeability of cotton yarns and fabrics.

**AMMONIATING FINISHES** An **ammoniating finish** is an alternate finish to mercerization used on cotton and rayon yarns and fabrics. Yarns or fabrics are treated with a weak ammonium solution at −33°C and are then passed through hot water, stretched, and dried in hot air. The finish is similar to mercerization but is less expensive and less polluting. The ammonia swells the fiber, but not to the degree that sodium hydroxide does. Fabrics that have had the ammonia treatment have good luster and dyeability. These fabrics do not dye to the same depth as mercerized fabrics, however. Because the amount of resin needed is less than with mercerized fabrics, ammonia-treated fabrics have better crease recovery and less loss of strength and abrasion resistance following wrinkle-resistant finishes than mercerized fabrics. Ammonia-treated fabrics are also less stiff and harsh than mercerized fabrics. Ammonia-treated fabrics have an increase in tensile strength of 40 percent and an increase in elongation of two to three times that of untreated cotton. These fabrics also are less sensitive to thermal degradation. Duralized and Sanforset are trade names that refer to improving the easy-care properties of heavy cotton fabrics like denim. Liquid ammonia treatments frequently are used as a substitute for mercerization on cotton sewing threads.

## Coloration

Color is normally added to the fabric at this stage in the sequence. Properly prepared goods are critical to the quality of the dye or print. Dyeing and printing are discussed in detail in Chapter 19.

## Finishing

**SPECIAL-PURPOSE FINISHES** **Special-purpose finishes** that would be appropriate for the cotton/polyester-blend fabric might include wrinkle resistance, soil-release, and a fabric-softening finish. These finishes usually follow dyeing to avoid interfering with the absorption of the dye by the fibers. These finishes are discussed in Chapter 18.

**TENTERING** **Tentering,** one of the final finishing operations, performs the double process of straightening and drying fabrics. In tentering, the fabric can be fed to the pins or clips at a speed slightly greater than that of the chains of the tentering frame. The result is that the amount of lengthwise shrinkage can be reduced to a degree.

Tentering is an important finishing step in terms of the fabric's quality. If the filling yarns are not perfectly perpendicular to the warp yarns, the fabric is off-grain. If the filling yarn does not cross each warp yarn at a 90° angle, the fabric will exhibit *skew.* If the center of the fabric moves at a slower speed than the two edges, the fabric will exhibit *bow* (see Chapter 12). Both of these off-grain problems can be eliminated by proper tentering. However, if a fabric was tentered off-grain, it will be printed off-grain as well. Some tentering frames have electronic sensors that help control the grain. The fabric may go through the tentering frame several times during finishing.

Tenter machines are of two types: the pin tenter and the clip tenter (Figure 16–5). The mechanism on the two sides moves around like a caterpillar tractor wheel, holding the fabric by a series of pins. More tension can be exerted by the clip tenter, but in cases where its use may damage the fabric, the pin tenter is used. The marks of the pins or the clips are often evident along the selvage (Figure 16–6).

## Drying

Because of the frequent wetting of textiles in finishing, drying also is frequent, especially with cellulosics to minimize mildew and weight. The drying process usually uses hot air blowing past the textiles in a large convection oven at a temperature above the boiling point of water to remove the water quickly by evaporation. Fabrics in convection ovens are usually tentered as discussed in the previous section. Other, less efficient means of drying fabrics include contact with hot metal rollers (conduction drying) and use of an infrared lamp, radio waves, or microwaves (irradiation). In drying, it is important not to create wrinkles or creases. Overdrying of cotton can create problems in dyeing.

**LOOP DRYING** Fabrics with a soft finish, towels, and stretchy fabrics such as knits are not dried on the tenter frame but on a *loop dryer,* where the drying can be done without tension. Many rayon fabrics are dried on loop dryers because of rayon's lower wet strength and soft hand.

**HEAT SETTING** In **heat setting** the fabric is usually placed on a tenter frame and passed through an oven where the time of exposure and the temperature are carefully controlled based on the fiber content and resins added to the fabric. The cotton/polyester fabric would require heat curing if it had been given a wrinkle-resistant or soil-release finish or if the percentage of polyester was high enough, generally 50 percent or more, to achieve a degree of shrinkage control. Heat setting needs to be carefully controlled because the heat history of polyester and other synthetic fibers can affect their dyeability. Heat setting of synthetics can also set yarn twist, weave crimp, and wrinkle resistance.

(a)

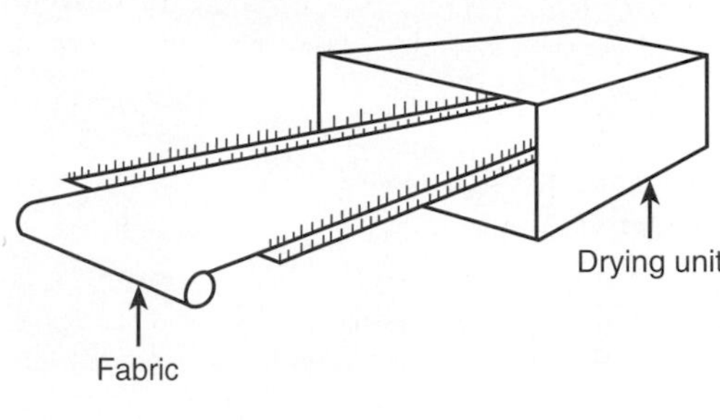


(b)

(c)

**FIGURE 16–5** ❖ Tenter frames: (a) clip tenter; (b) drawing of pin-tenter frame, (c) modern tentering line. (COURTESY OF MARSHALL & WILLIAMS CO.)

**CALENDERING** **Calendering** is a mechanical finishing operation performed by a series or stack of rollers through which the fabric passes. There are several types: the simple calender, the friction calender, the moiré calender, the schreiner calender, and the embossing calender. Each type produces a different finish; since most of these calenders are used to modify the fabric's appearance, they will be discussed in Chapter 17.

Most calender machines have three rollers, but others may have two, five, or seven rollers. Hard-metal rollers alternate with softer rollers of foam, solid paper, or cloth-covered metal. Two metal rollers never run against each other.

The *simple calender* gives a smooth, flat, ironed finish to the fabric. The cloth is slightly damp before it enters the calender. The metal roll is heated. The cloth travels through the calender at the same speed the rollers rotate, so they simply exert pressure to smooth out the wrinkles and give a slight sheen (Figure 16–7).

## Reworking

**INSPECTING** Fabrics are **inspected** by pulling or running them over an inverted frame in good light. Fabric inspectors mark flaws in the fabric and record its quality at the same time. Flaws may be marked on the fabric, usually on the selvage, so that subsequent cutting and sewing operators can avoid working with and adding value to product parts that incorporate flaws. Computers and electronic sensors are also used to assess fabric quality automatically. Fabric quality is a complex

FIGURE 16–6 ❖ Fabric selvages of clip tentering (top fabric) and pin tentering (two bottom fabrics). Clip tentering rarely leaves easily visible marks. Pin tentering almost always leaves telltale holes along the edge.

area related to the number of flaws, the severity of the flaws, and the length or size of the flaws. Mills and buyers must work together to define quality levels acceptable to both parties.

**REPAIRING** Flaws marked by the inspectors are **repaired,** if economically feasible or possible. Broken yarns are clipped, snagged yarns are worked back into the fabric, and defects are marked so that adjustments can be made when fabrics are sold. The fabric is then wound on bolts or cylinders ready for shipment.

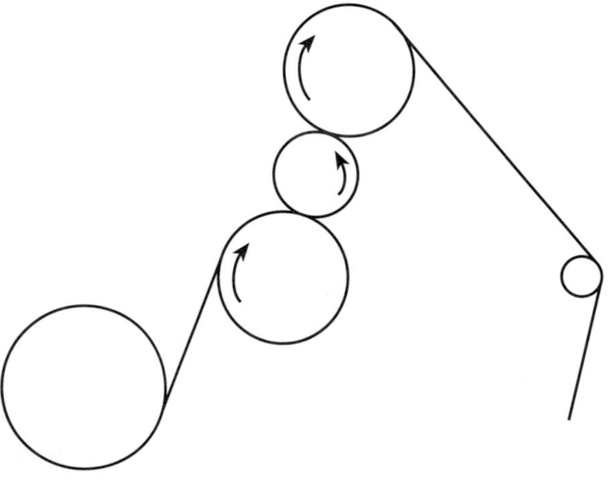

FIGURE 16–7 ❖ Calender machine.

# ROUTINE FINISHING STEPS FOR WOOL FABRICS

## Carbonizing

**Carbonizing,** the treatment of wool yarns or fabrics with sulfuric acid, destroys plant matter in the fabric and allows for more level dyeing. Carbonizing also is done on recycled wool to remove any cellulose that may have been used in the original fabric. Carbonizing gives better texture to all-wool fabrics, but the acid must be neutralized to avoid problems in dyeing or in consumer use.

## Crabbing

**Crabbing** is a wool-finishing process used to set wool fabrics. Fabrics are immersed in hot water, then in cold water, and passed between rollers.

## Decating

**Decating** produces a smooth, wrinkle-free finish and lofty hand on woolen and worsted fabrics and on blends of wool and manufactured fibers. The process is comparable to steam ironing. A high degree of luster can be developed by the decating process because of the smoothness of the surface. The dry cloth is wound under tension on a perforated cylinder. Steam is forced through the fabric. Moisture and heat relax tensions and remove wrinkles. The yarns become set and are fixed in this position by cooling in cold air. For a more permanent set, dry decating is done in a pressure boiler. Wet decating often precedes napping or other face finishes to remove wrinkles that have been acquired in scouring. Wet decating as a final finish gives a more permanent set to the yarns than does dry decating. Decating may also be used with rayon and other manufactured fiber or blend fabrics or with knits.

## Pressing

**Pressing** is the term used with wool or wool blends. In pressing the fabric is placed between metal plates that steam and press the fabric.

## Environmental Impact of Finishing

Finishing transforms a harsh and unattractive fabric into an attractive one. Unfortunately, the environmental impact of this transformation can be significant. Almost every step in finishing a fabric has a potential for creating environmental damage. The textile industry is acutely aware of the situation and recognizes that it must become more proactive in terms of safeguarding the environment. Finishing facilities incorporate systems for air pollution control, pollution prevention, and hazardous waste disposal. These systems are designed to minimize discharge into any part of the environment (air, land, or water).

Finishing makes use of significant quantities of water and energy. In the 1970s, it was not unusual for a large finishing facility to use more than two million gallons of water daily! Water use has decreased, but water continues to be used to dissolve chemicals and to remove waste and soil from the system. Quality of the water supply is a growing concern. Foam finishing and other less water-intensive processes are increasing in importance. Better and more efficient means of extracting water from fabrics prior to drying and heat-recovery systems minimize energy use.

Finishing uses quantities of potentially hazardous chemicals. There are restrictions on the discharge of waste with high biological oxygen demand (BOD), such as sizing agents, and high chemical oxygen demand (COD), such as chlorine-containing compounds. Hazardous, toxic, and carcinogenic finishing chemicals are being replaced with less hazardous, nontoxic, and noncarcinogenic chemicals. Biodegradable finishes are becoming more common.

In addition, changes in technology and good operating practices that ensure that fabrics are finished correctly limit excessive use of chemicals, water, and energy and minimize environmental impact. Many finishers have added preliminary treatment facilities on site before discharging waste to municipal facility so that they can reclaim and reuse chemicals and remove contaminants. Membrane technology and reverse osmosis provide effective means of producing high-quality discharge by separating salts, metals, organic compounds, and other contaminants before water leaves the finishing plant's treatment facility.

## Key Terms

Finish
Converters
Permanent finish
Durable finish
Temporary finish
Renewable finish
Gray goods
Converted goods
Mill-finished fabrics
Water-bath finishing
Foam finishing
Solvent finishing
Preparation
Slashing
Fabrication
Handling
Minimums
Run
Open-width finishing
Rope or tubular finishing
Batch processing
Continuous processing
Desizing
Cleaning
Singeing
Bio-polishing
Scouring
Bleaching
Optical brighteners
Mercerization
Slack mercerization
Ammoniating finish
Special-purpose finish
Tentering
Heat setting
Calendering
Reworking
Inspecting
Repairing
Carbonizing
Crabbing
Decating
Pressing

## Questions

1. Differentiate among these terms: permanent finish, durable finish, temporary finish, renewable finish.
2. Why do yarns need to be finished before fabrication? What finishes are used?
3. At what stage is bleaching normally done? Why is it done at that time?
4. What problems can occur if tentering is improperly done? How does this affect fabric quality?
5. What terms are used to refer to cleaning the following fibers?
   cotton
   silk
   wool
6. What differences may occur in finished fabrics between open-width and tubal or rope finishing?

## Suggested Readings

Buschle-Diller, G., Zeronian, S. H., Pan, N., and Yoon, M. Y. (1994). "Enzymatic Hyrolysis of Cotton, Linen, Ramie, and Viscose Rayon Fabrics." *Textile Research Journal, 64,* pp. 270–279.

Cook, Fred L. (1994, March). "Less Is More in Applying Chemicals to Textiles." *Textile World,* pp. 59–60, 62, 65.

Cook, Fred L. (1993, May). "Prep, Finishing Chemicals Turn Green Nature Friendly." *Textile World,* pp. 37, 39, 41, 43, 45.

Fulmer, T. D. (1992, November). "Cotton Preparation Is Crucial." *America's Textiles International,* pp. 52, 53, 55.

Needles, Howard (1986). *Textile Fibers, Dyes, Finishes, and Processes.* Park Ridge, NJ: Noyes Publications.

Powderly, Daniel (1987). *Fabric Inspection and Grading.* Columbia, SC: Bobbin International.

Thomas, Howard (1994, April). "The Current State of Weaving Preparation." *America's Textiles International,* pp. 71–73.

Trotman, E. R. (1984). *Dyeing and Chemical Technology of Textile Fibers.* New York: John Wiley & Sons.

Woerner, Douglas I., and Wheeler, Nancy E. (1993, May). "How Mills Can Save Money While Treating Wastewater." *Textile World,* p. 65.

Zein, Karim (1994, July). "Teamwork Needed to Combat Industry's Environmental Problems." *Textile Month,* pp. 9–13.

Chapter 17

# Aesthetic Finishes

OBJECTIVES

- To understand how finishes can alter aesthetic aspects of fabrics.
- To know the ways the aesthetic finishes can be applied to fabrics.
- To predict the performance of textiles with aesthetic finishes.
- To differentiate between applied designs and structural designs and the implications for quality and performance.

**A**esthetic finishes change the appearance and/or hand of fabrics. The finished fabric's name often reflects the change in appearance or the technique. For example, eyelet embroidery, ciré satin, and organdy are made by special finishes. Figure 17–1 shows several fabrics that were converted from print cloth: percale (printed), chintz (waxed and friction calendered), plissé (caustic soda print), and embossed cotton (embossed). This fabric also could be flocked, embroidered, or surface coated.

Aesthetic finishes create an **applied design.** They are quicker and less expensive than incorporating the design as the fabric is produced (structural design). Table 17–1 compares applied and structural design.

Aesthetic finishes can be grouped according to the change they produce in the fabrics: luster, drape, texture, and hand. The process, its effect, and the relationship of the finish to the fabric name will be explained for each group.

Many of these finishes are additive finishes that produce texture (body, stiffness, softness), luster, embossed designs, and abrasion resistance in the fabric. Some are subtractive finishes: something is removed from the fabric during finishing. Some finishes mechanically distort or alter the fabric with heat or pressure; others chemically change the fabric. Finish permanence depends on the process, the fiber content, and the type of finish itself.

The **padding machine,** often called the "workhorse" of the textile industry, is used to apply dyes and finishing chemicals. These special chemicals are applied in either liquid or paste form to one or both sides of a fabric (Figure 17–2).

*Padding* is done by passing the fabric through the solution, under a guide roll, and between two padding rolls. The type of roll depends on the finish to be applied. The rolls exert tons of pressure on the fabric, forcing the finish into the fiber or yarn to assure good penetration. Excess liquid is squeezed off. The fabric is then steamed, cleaned, and dried.

The **backfilling machine** is a variation of the padding machine. It applies the finish to one side only, usually to the back of the fabric (Figure 17–3).

# LUSTER

**Luster finishes** result in a change in the light reflectance of a fabric. Most finishes in this group increase light reflectance and improve the luster or shine

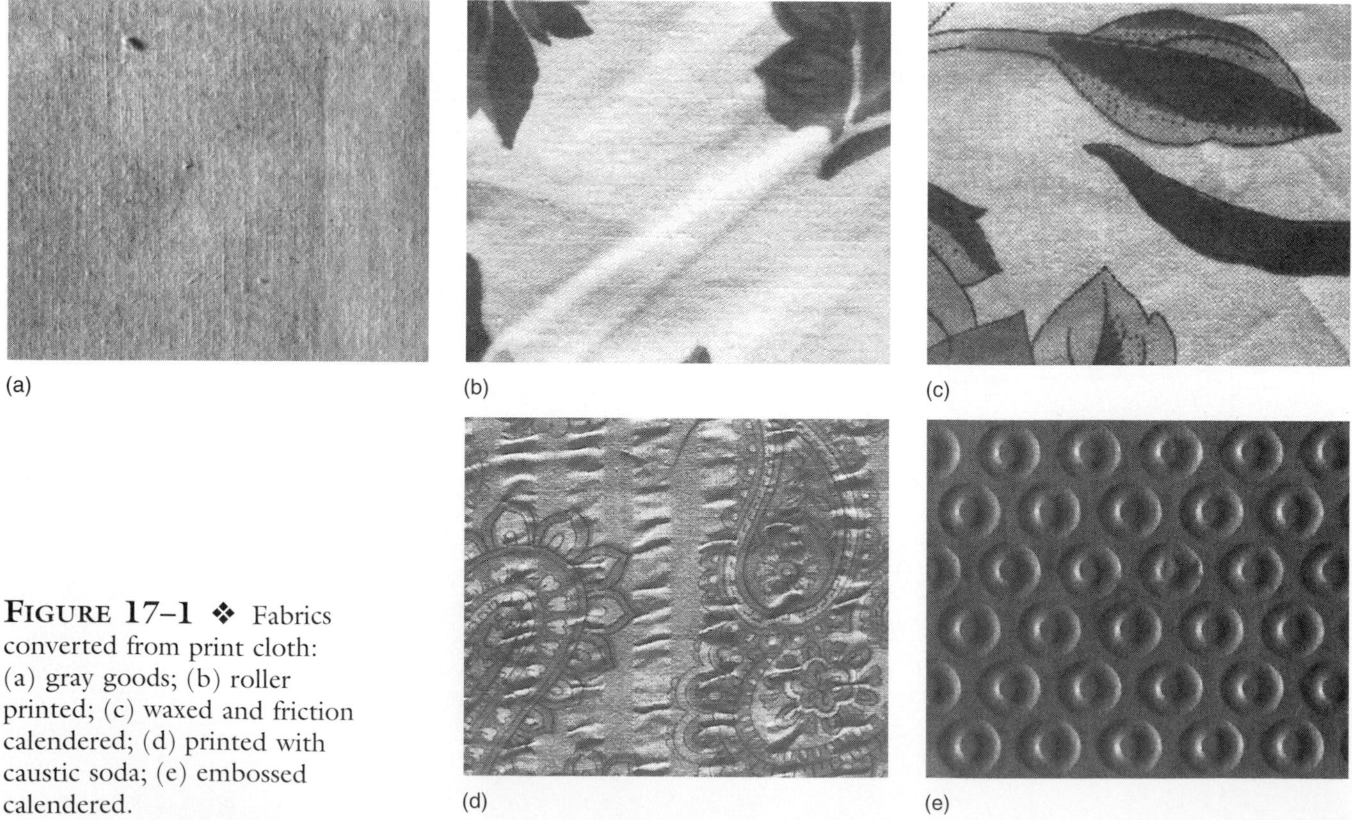

**FIGURE 17–1** ❖ Fabrics converted from print cloth: (a) gray goods; (b) roller printed; (c) waxed and friction calendered; (d) printed with caustic soda; (e) embossed calendered.

**TABLE 17–1** ❖ Comparison of structural and applied designs.

| STRUCTURAL DESIGNS | APPLIED DESIGNS |
|---|---|
| Usually more expensive because decisions must be made farther in advance of market and process is more time consuming | Usually less expensive |
| Permanent design | Permanent, durable, or temporary |
| Woven figures are always on-grain (circular-knit jacquards may be skewed) | Figures may be off-grain<br>May tender or weaken fabric |
| Process does not weaken or tender fabrics | |
| **Kinds and Types** | |
| Woven—jacquard, dobby, extra yarns, swivel dots, lappet designs, piqué, double cloth | Printed<br>Flocked<br>Tufted<br>Embroidered<br>Burned out |
| Knitted—jacquard single knits, jacquard double knits | Embossed<br>Plissé<br>Napped |
| Lace | Emerized<br>Abrasive or chemical wash |
| **Typical Fabrics** | |
| Huck, damask, brocade, tapestry, shirting madras, piqué, dotted swiss, matelassé | Flock dotted swiss, embroidered linen, burned out, glazed chintz, moiré taffeta, embossed, frosted denim, sueded silk |

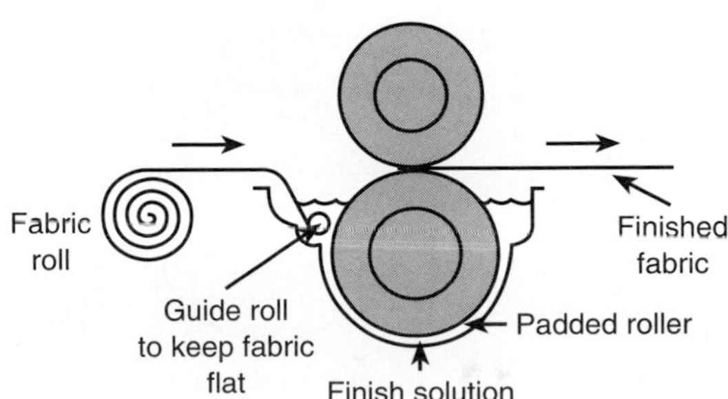


**FIGURE 17–2** ❖ Padding machine.

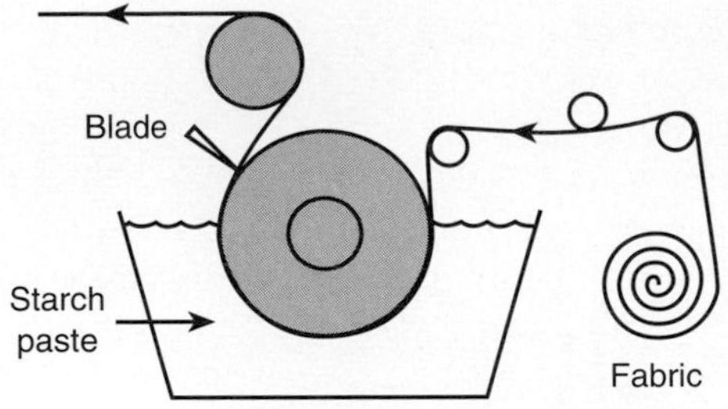


**FIGURE 17–3** ❖ Backfilling machine.

of the fabric. The increase in luster may be over the entire fabric—as in the glazed, ciré, and schreiner finishes—or it may be a localized increase in luster—as in the moiré and embossed finishes. These finishes are done by calendering—passing the fabric between two cylinders. The cylinders exert pressure on the fabric. Different calenders produce a different effect on the fabric and include glazed, ciré, moiré, schreiner, and embossed.

## Glazed

**Glazed** chintz and polished cotton are two fabrics that have received this surface glazing. A **friction calender** produces a highly glazed surface. If the fabric is first saturated with starch and waxes, the finish is temporary. If resin finishes are used, the glaze is durable. The fabric is passed through the finishing solution and partially dried. It is then calendered. The speed of the metal roller is greater than the speed of the fabric, and the roller polishes the surface. (See Figure 17–1c.)

## Ciré

A **ciré finish** is similar to a glazed finish, except that the metal roll is hot. The hot roller produces greater luster on the fabric's surface. These fabrics often are made of thermoplastic fibers. Because thermoplastic fibers are heat sensitive, the fiber surface that comes in contact with the metal roll melts and flatten slightly and produces the highly polished fabric. Ciré is a taffeta or satin fabric hot-friction calendered to give a high gloss, or "wet" look.

## Moiré

These fabrics have a wood grain or watermarked appearance. Two techniques are used to produce a **moiré pattern** on a fabric. In *true moiré,* unbalanced plain weave rib fabrics such as taffeta or faille are used. True moiré is made by placing two layers of ribbed fabric face to

**FIGURE 17–4** ❖ Moiré taffeta.

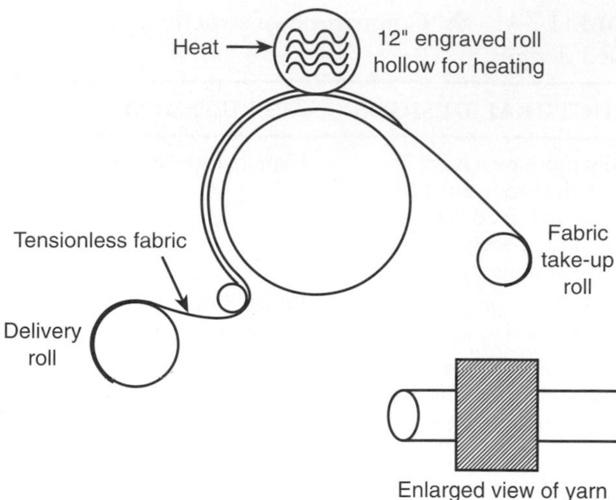


**FIGURE 17–5** ❖ Schreiner calender machine for tricot.

face, so that the ribs of the top layer are slightly off-grain in relation to the under layer. The two layers are stitched or held together along the selvage and are then fed into the smooth, heated-metal roll calender. Pressure of 8 to 10 tons causes the rib pattern of the top layer to be pressed into the bottom layer and vice versa. Flattened areas in the ribs reflect more light and contrast with unflattened areas. This procedure can be modified to produce patterned moiré designs other than the traditional watermarked one.

In the second procedure an embossed-metal roll is used. The embossed roll has a moiré pattern engraved on it. When the roll passes over a ribbed fabric, the ribs are flattened in areas and a moiré pattern is created. If the fabric is thermoplastic and the roll is heated, the finish is permanent (see Figure 17–4).

## Schreiner

Fabrics with a schreiner finish have a softer luster than most of the other luster finishes. The **schreiner calender** (Figure 17–5) has a metal roller engraved with 200–300 fine diagonal lines that are visible only under a magnifying glass. (The lines should not be confused with yarn twist.) Unless resins and thermoplastic fibers are used, this finish is temporary and removed by the first washing. This finish produces a deep-seated luster, rather than a shine, by scattering the light rays. It also flattens the yarns to reduce the openness between them and give smoothness and cover. It can be used to upgrade a sleazy or lower quality fabric. A schreiner finish is used on cotton sateen and table damask to make them more lustrous and on nylon tricot to increase its cover.

## Embossed

**Embossed designs** are created using an embossing calender that produces either flat or raised designs on the fabric. Embossing became a much more important finish with the development of the heat-sensitive fibers because it was possible to produce a durable, washable, embossed pattern. If the fabrics are made of solution-dyed fibers, they can be embossed directly off the loom and sold.

The embossing calender consists of two rolls, one of which is a heated hollow, engraved-metal roll. The other is a solid paper roll exactly twice the size of the engraved roll (Figure 17–6). The fabric is drawn between the two

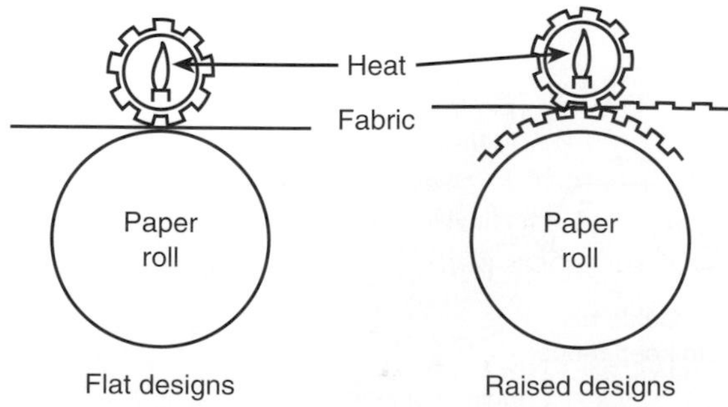


**FIGURE 17–6** ❖ Embossing process.

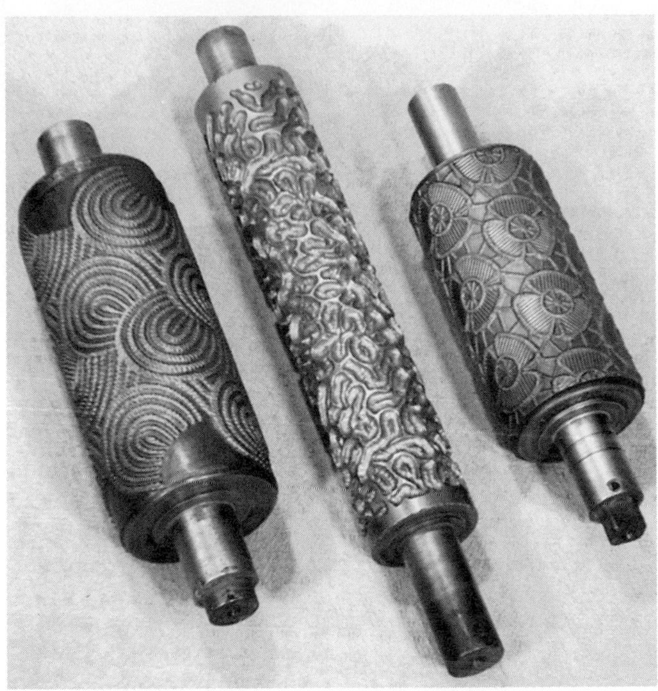

**FIGURE 17–7** ❖ Embossing rolls. (COURTESY OF CONSOLIDATED ENGRAVERS CORP.)

rollers and is embossed with the design. Embossing can be done to both flat and pile fabrics.

The process differs for the production of flat and raised designs. Raised embossed designs will be discussed later in this chapter under the section on texture. Flat embossed designs are the simplest to produce. A metal, foam, or plastic roll engraved in deep relief (Figure 17–7) revolves against a smooth paper roll. The hot, engraved areas of the roll produce a glazed pattern on the fabric. Embossed brocades are an example of this type of design. The effect can be seen as a difference in luster, but the design cannot be detected by touch.

❖

# DRAPE

Drape finishes change the way a fabric falls or hangs over a three-dimensional shape. These finishes make the fabric stiffer or more flexible. They usually add a chemical compound to the fabric (additive finish) or dissolve a portion of the fibers present (subtractive finish).

## Crisp and Transparent

Transparent or parchment effects in cotton fabrics are produced by treatment with sulfuric acid. This fabric may be referred to as **parchmentized.** Since acid dissolves or damages cotton, this subtractive process must be very carefully controlled. Split-second timing is necessary to prevent **tendering,** or weakening of the fabric. Several effects are possible: allover, localized, or a plissé effect.

Because *allover parchmentizing* produces a transparent effect, a sheer fabric of combed lawn is used. The goods are singed, desized, bleached, and mercerized. Mercerization may be repeated after the acid treatment to improve the transparency. The fabric is then dyed or printed with colors that resist acid damage. The cloth is immersed in the acid solution and partial dissolution of the fiber surface takes place. On drying, this surface rehardens as a cellulosic film and gives permanent crispness and transparency. After the acid treatment, the cloth is neutralized in weak alkali, washed, and calendered to give more gloss to the surface. This allover treatment produces *organdy* fabric.

In *localized parchmentizing,* if the design is a small figure with a large transparent area, an acid-resist substance is printed on the figures and the fabric is run through the acid bath. The acid-resistant areas retain their original opacity and contrast sharply with the transparent background (Figure 17–8). If a small transparent design is desired, the acid is printed on in a paste form and then quickly washed off.

## Burned Out

**Burned-out effects** are produced by printing a chemical on a blend fabric made of fibers from different groups,

**FIGURE 17–8** ❖ Localized parchmentizing (acid finish) gives transparent background to some parts of the design while untreated areas remain opaque. Note coin in center under fabric.

**FIGURE 17–9** ❖ Burned-out design

such as rayon and polyester. One fiber, usually the less expensive or more easily dissolved fiber, is dissolved, leaving sheer areas. Figure 17–9 shows an **etched** rayon/polyester fabric. The rayon has been dissolved by acid. This finish is also known as etched or devoré because part of the fibers are removed by this subtractive finish.

## Sizing

In **sizing,** or **starching,** the fabric is immersed in a mixture containing waxes, oils, glycerine, and softeners. For added weight, talc, clay, or chalk may be used, but their use is not necessarily an indication of high-quality fabric. Gelatin is used on rayons because it is a clear substance that enhances the natural luster of the fibers. Sizing adds stiffness, weight, and body to the fabric. Its permanence is related to the type of sizing and method of application. If the sizing is water soluble, it will be removed during washing. If the sizing is resin based and heat set, it will be permanent.

## Weighting

Weighting is another technique used to add weight and body to a fabric. A metallic salt like stannic chloride is used. Salts that bond with the fiber are durable; others produce temporary surface coating. Silk may be weighted; however, weighted silks are not common today. Weighted silks are more sensitive to light damage and do not age well.

# Texture

Texture finishes modify fabric texture or add components that produce a completely different texture compared to that of the original fabric.

## Sheared

A **sheared fabric** is a pile or napped fabric in which the pile or nap has been cut to remove loose fiber or yarn ends, knots, and similar irregularities or surface flaws. Shearing is a finishing process done by a machine similar to a lawn mower. Shearing controls the length of the pile or nap and may create a patterned or a smooth surface. Sculptured effects are made by flattening portions of the pile with an engraved roller and then shearing off the areas that are still erect. Steaming the fabric raises the flattened and now taller portions. Most pile fabrics and many napped fabrics, including cut pile carpet, are sheared.

## Brushed

On a **brushed fabric** the surface of the fabric has been cleaned of fiber ends. Brushing follows shearing to clean the surface of clear-face fabrics. When brushing is combined with steaming, the nap or pile slants and is set in one direction, thus giving the up-and-down direction of pile and nap fabrics. This can be seen in corduroy and many other pile fabrics. (See Figure 17–10.)

## Embossed

Some *embossed fabrics* have a raised design or pattern. The embossed design may be permanent if the fabric

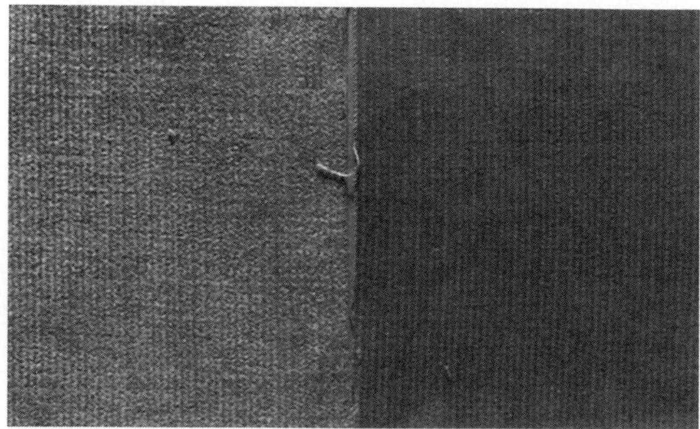

**FIGURE 17–10** ❖ When the nap in corduroy does not match, two pieces may look as if they are different colors.

has a thermoplastic-fiber content or if a resin is used and heat set. Raised, or relief, designs require a more complicated routine than flat embossed fabrics. The paper roll is soaked in water and then revolved against the engraved roll (without fabric) until the pattern of engraving is pressed into the paper roll. The temperature is adjusted to suit the fabric, which is then passed between the rolls. Three-dimensional designs are created that can be seen and felt.

## Pleated

A **pleated fabric** is made by a special variation of embossing. Pleating methods are highly specialized operations done by either the paper-pattern technique or by the machine process.

The paper-pattern technique is a more costly hand process, but it is used to produce a wider variety of pleated designs. Garments in partly completed condition, such as hemmed skirt panels, are placed in a pattern mold by hand. Another pattern mold is placed on top so that the fabric is pleated between two pleating papers. The three layers are rolled into a cone shape, sealed, and heat set in a large curing oven.

The machine-pleating process is less expensive. The machine has two heated rolls. The fabric is inserted between the rolls as high-precision blades pleat the fabric. A paper backing is used under the pleated fabric and the pleats are held in place by paper tape. After leaving the heated roll machine, the pleats are set in an aging unit. The pleats may be stitched in place for permanent three-dimensional effects in apparel, upholstery, wall coverings, window treatments, and lampshades. Pleated fabric without stitching is used in similar products, but the pleats may soften with use.

## Puckered Surface

**Puckered surfaces** are created by partially dissolving the surface of a nylon or polyester fabric. Sculptured and "damasque" effects are made by printing phenol on the fabric to partially dissolve or swell it. Shrinkage occurs as the fabric dries, thus creating a puckered surface.

## Plissé

**Plissé** is converted from either lawn or print-cloth gray goods by printing sodium hydroxide (caustic soda) on the cloth in the form of stripes or designs. The alkali causes the fabric to shrink in the treated areas. As the treated stripe shrinks, the untreated stripes pucker. Shrinkage causes a slight difference in count between the two stripes. The treated or flat stripe increases in count as it shrinks. The upper portion of the fabric in Figure 17–11 shows how it looked before finishing, and the lower portion shows the crinkle produced by the caustic-soda treatment. This piece of goods is defective because the roller failed to print the chemical in the unpuckered area.

The crinkle stripes can be narrow, as shown in Figure 17–11, or wide. In piece-dyed fabrics, the flat treated area may be a deeper color than the puckered area. The texture change is permanent but can be flattened somewhat by steam and pressure.

Seersucker, plissé, and embossed fabrics can be very similar in appearance. These fabrics are frequently found in the same price range. Table 17–2 compares these and other similar fabrics.

## Flocked

**Flocked fabrics** imitate pile fabrics. In a flocked fabric a surface fiber is applied to the fabric after the base fabric has been produced. Flocking can be localized to imitate extra yarn weaves or all over to imitate pile fabrics.

*Flock fibers* are very short fibers attached to a fabric surface by an adhesive to create an inexpensive pile. Flocking was used as a technique for wall decoration as early as the 14th century when short silk fibers were applied to freshly painted walls. Flock can be applied to many base materials—cloth, foam, wood, metal, and concrete—or it can be applied to an adhesive film and laminated to a base fabric. Current aqueous-based

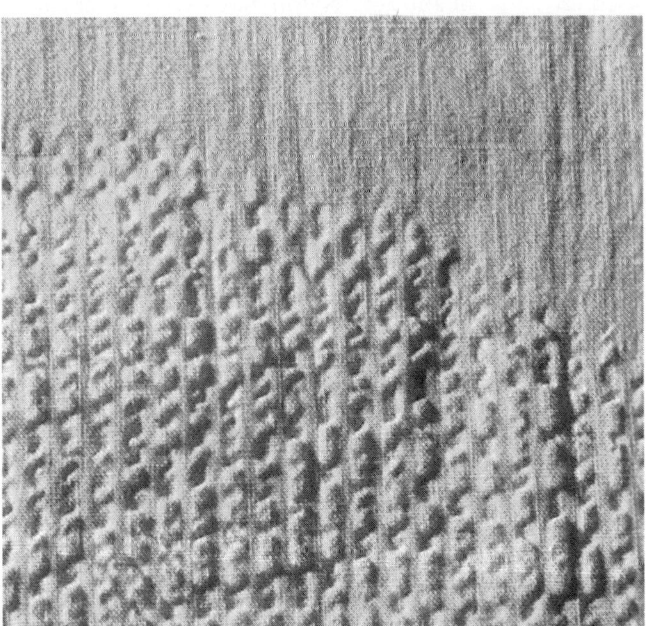

**FIGURE 17–11** ❖ Plissé, showing treated (bottom portion) and untreated (upper portion) areas.

TABLE 17–2 ❖ Comparison of crepelike fabrics.

| HIGH-TWIST NATURAL OR MANUFACTURED YARNS (40–80 tpi) | HIGH-TWIST THERMOPLASTIC YARNS | BULKY YARN | WEAVE | FINISH |
|---|---|---|---|---|
| Permanent crinkle<br>Flattens during use<br>Moisture will restore | Permanent crinkle<br>Retains appearance during use and care | Permanent crinkle<br>Does not flatten or need ironing | Crinkle does not flatten in use | Crinkle may flatten or be less prominent after washing |
| High potential shrinkage | Low potential shrinkage | Low potential shrinkage | Lower potential shrinkage | Lower potential shrinkage |
| Good drapeability | Good drapeability | Less drapeable | Less drapeable | Less drapeable |
| Stretches | Moderate stretch | Low stretch | Low stretch | Low stretch |
| Resilient, recovers from wrinkles | Resilient | Does not wrinkle | Wrinkles do not show because of rough surface | Wrinkles do not show because of rough surface |
| Dry cleaning preferable | Easy care | Easy care | Washable unless fiber content requires dry cleaning | Washable unless fiber content requires dry cleaning |
| Typical fabrics:<br>Wool crepe<br>Crepe de chine<br>Matelassé<br>Chiffon<br>Georgette<br>Silk crepe | Typical fabrics:<br>Chiffon<br>Georgette | Typical fabrics:<br>Silky synthetics | Typical fabric:<br>Sand crepe<br>Granite cloth<br>Seersucker | Typical fabrics:<br>Plissé<br>Embossed |

acrylic, nylon, or polyester adhesives have good flexibility, durability, drape, and hand and are colorless and free of undesirable odor.

Rayon fibers are inexpensive and easy to cut, and are used in large quantities. Nylon has excellent abrasion resistance and durability. Acrylics, polyesters, and olefins also are used. Fibers for flocking must be straight, not crimped. As the fiber length increases, the denier also must increase so that the fiber will remain erect in the fabric. Fibers that are cut square at the ends anchor more firmly in the adhesive (Figure 17–12).

Some of the major end uses of flocking include velvet upholstery fabrics, draperies, bedspreads, blankets, designs on apparel fabrics, carpets, wall coverings for aesthetics and noise reduction, automotive fabrics, toys, books, shoes, hats, and industrial uses such as conveyor

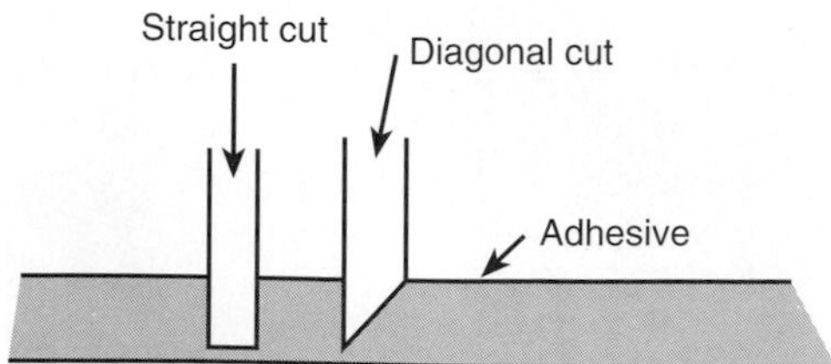


FIGURE 17–12 ❖ Flock with square-cut ends is attached more firmly.

belts and air filters. Examine Tables 15–6 and 15–7 to compare flocking with other methods used to produce fabrics with a pile or imitation pile surface.

The two basic methods of applying the flock fibers are mechanical and electrostatic. In both processes the flock is placed in an erect position and, after flocking, the adhesive is oven dried. A comparison of the two methods is given in Table 17–3. Overall flocking, or area flocking, can be done by either method. A rotating screen is used to deposit the flock.

## Tufted

**Tufted fabrics** also imitate more expensive pile fabrics. In tufting, a surface yarn is stitched to the fabric to create a pile or three-dimensional effect. Tufting can be all over the fabric, as in carpeting and upholstery, or in localized areas to create an imitation extra yarn weave or a fabric like that used in chenille bedspreads. See Chapter 15 for details of the process.

## Embroidered

**Embroidered fabrics** can be produced either by hand or by machine. These fabrics are decorated with a surface-applied thread. The machine-embroidery operation uses zigzag stitches of various lengths very close

**TABLE 17–3** ❖ Flocking process.

| MECHANICAL FLOCKING | ELECTROSTATIC FLOCKING |
|---|---|
| 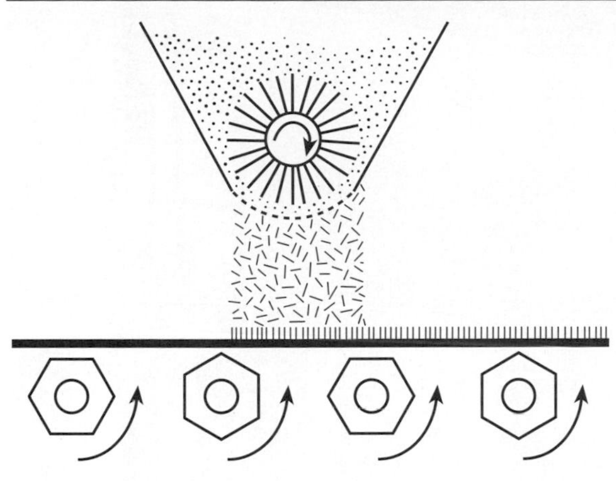 | 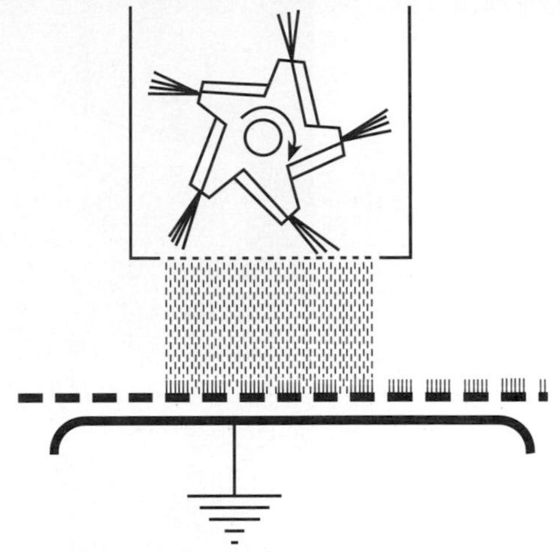 |
| 1. Short fibers are sifted onto the adhesive-coated fabric. Vibration of beater bars causes fibers that do not fall flat against the adhesive to stand erect. Once erect, the fibers penetrate fully into the adhesive. The erect fibers help the free fibers to align themselves and to work down to the adhesive.<br>2. Most units consist of 6 to 20 beater bars and one or more sifting hoppers and run as high as 10 or more yards per minute.<br>3. Simpler in design, usually less expensive, and most widely used in the United States. | 1. Flock passes through an electrostatic field that orients the fibers. In coating irregular surfaces, the lines of force are always perpendicular to the substrate, so this method is best for three-dimensional surfaces.<br>2. Most units operate at speeds of 3–5 yards per minute.<br>3. Can apply fiber to both sides of a fabric.<br>4. Requires generators, proper insulation. Gives better end-on-end fiber orientation. Higher densities are possibilities. |

*Source:* Courtesy of the Fibers Division of Monsanto Chemical Co., a unit of Monsanto Co.

together. There are two machines available for embroidery: the shuttle and the multihead. The shuttle embroidery machine produces allover embroidered fabrics such as eyelet. (See Figures 17 13 and 17–14.) **Schiffli embroidery** is a term sometimes used to describe earlier types of machines used to produce allover embroidered fabrics. Shuttle embroidery machines use computers to control the pattern. Earlier Schiffli machines used punched cardboard rolls.

**Multihead embroidery** can be used to create flat embroidery or pile embroidery. These machines are extremely versatile and can work with a variety of threads, ribbons, or bead/sequin strands. They can incorporate one or more colors of threads to create elaborate or simple designs in small or large scale. These machines are referred to as multihead because several machines are operated by the same computer system simultaneously (see Figure 17–15). Multihead machines create designs and emblems that are sewn to other products like letter jackets, hats, and shirts. The machines are also used to stitch crests, logos, and other designs on finished items. (See Figure 17–16.)

Embroidered figures are very durable, often outlasting the ground fabric. The fabric is more expensive than the same fabric unembroidered. Like other applied designs, the figure may or may not be on-grain.

**Eyelet** is an embroidery fabric with small, round holes cut in the fabric with stitching completely around the holes. The closeness and amount of stitching, as well as the quality of the background fabric, vary tremendously.

## Expanded Foam

Another technique to create surface texture uses **expanded foam.** A colored compound is printed on the fabric. The compound expands during processing to give a three-dimensional effect. Expanded foam patterns add three-dimensional texture to the fabric. These foams are durable but create problems with pressing.

## Napped

**Nap** is a layer of fiber ends on the surface of the fabric that are raised from the ground weave by a mechanical

**FIGURE 17–13** ❖ Shuttle embroidery machine. (COURTESY OF SAUER TEXTILE SYSTEMS CHARLOTTE.)

brushing action. Thus napped fabrics are literally "made" by a finishing process. Figure 17–17 shows a fabric before and after napping.

Napping was originally a hand operation using several teasels (dried plant burrs) to gently brush up fiber ends. Napping is less expensive than many other ways of producing a three-dimensional fabric.

Napping is now done by rollers covered by a heavy fabric in which bent wires are embedded (Figure 17–18). Napping machines may be single action or double action. Fewer rollers are used in the single-action machine. Called pile rolls, they are all alike and travel at the same speed. The bent ends of the wires point in the direction in which the fabric travels, but the rollers are

**FIGURE 17–14** ❖ Embroidered linen (right); printed to look like embroidery (left).

**FIGURE 17–15** ❖ Multihead embroidery machine. (COURTESY OF BARUDAN CO., LTD. DISTRIBUTED BY MACPHERSON MEISTERGRAM.)

FIGURE 17–16 ❖ Multihead embroidered design.

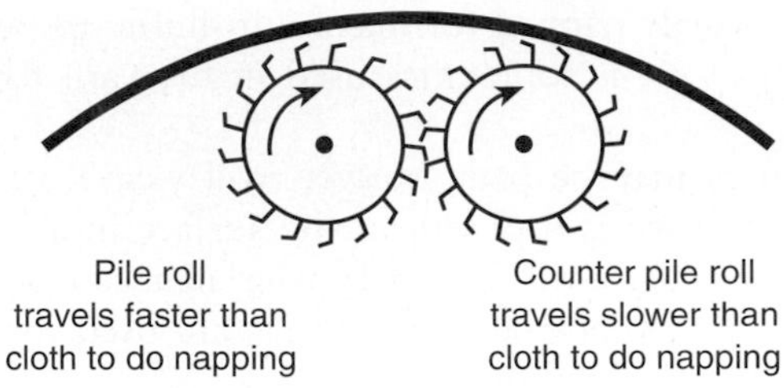


FIGURE 17–18 ❖ Napping rolls.

all mounted on a large drum or cylinder that rotates in the same direction as the fabric. The pile rolls must travel faster than the fabric to do any napping.

In the double-action napping machine, every other roll is a counterpile roll with wires that point in the direction opposite to those of the pile roll. The counterpile roll must travel slower than the fabric to produce a nap. When the speed of the rolls is reversed (pile rolls at slower speed and counterpile rolls at faster speed), a "tucking" action occurs. Tucking pushes the raised fibers back into the fabric and makes a smooth surface.

Napping produces a fabric with appealing characteristics. A napped surface and the soft twist of the filling yarns increase the air volume, providing good insulation. The fabric is soft and attractive. A dense mat of fiber ends on the surface imparts a degree of water repellency.

The amount of nap does not indicate the quality of the fabric. The amount may vary from the slight fuzz of flannel to the thick nap of imitation fur. Short compact nap on a fabric with firm yarns and a closely woven ground wears best. Stick a pin in the nap and lift the fabric. A good, durable nap will hold the weight of the fabric. Hold the fabric up to the light and examine it. Press the nap aside and examine the ground weave. A napped surface may be used to cover defects or a sleazy construction. Rub the fabric between your fingers and then shake it to see if short fibers drop out. Thick nap may contain flock (very short wool fibers). Rub the surface of the nap to see if it is loose or likely to pill.

Napped fabrics must be made from specially constructed gray goods in which the filling yarns are made of low-twist staple (not filament) fibers (see Chapter 11 for information about yarn twist). The difference in yarn structure makes it easy to identify the lengthwise and crosswise grain of the fabric. Figure 17–19 shows warp and filling yarns from a fabric before and after napping.

Fabrics can be napped on either or both sides. The nap may have an upright position or it may be "laid down" or "brushed." When a heavy nap is raised on the surface, however, the yarns are sometimes weakened.

Yarns of either long- or short-staple fibers may be used in napped fabrics. Worsted flannels, for example, are made of long-staple wool. The short-staple yarns used in woolen flannels have more fiber ends per inch and thus can have a heavier nap. In wool blankets,

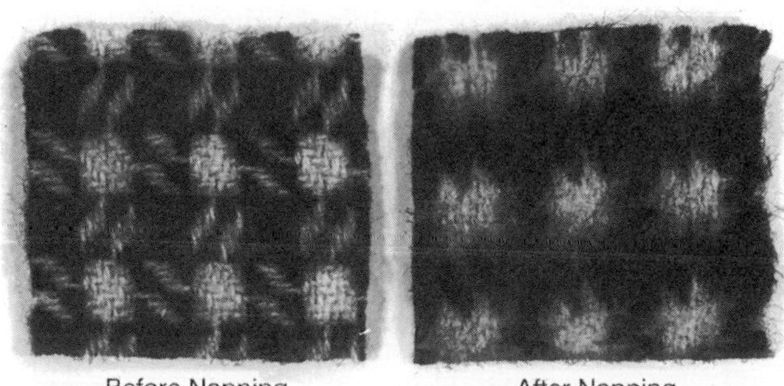


FIGURE 17–17 ❖ Fabric before and after napping.

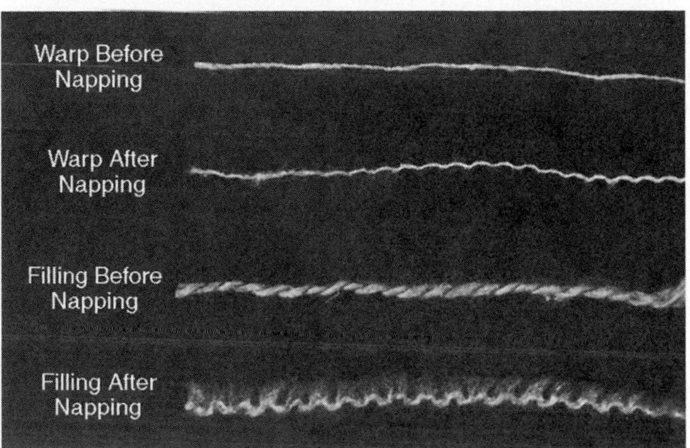


FIGURE 17–19 ❖ Yarns before and after napping.

which may be heavily napped for maximum fluffiness, a fine-cotton (core) ply is sometimes used in the yarn to give strength.

Napped fabrics may be plain weave, twill weave, or knit. More filling yarn is exposed on the surface in a $\frac{2}{2}$ twill or a filling-faced twill, and a heavier nap can be raised on twill fabrics. Napped knit fabrics are used for extremely soft and flexible items.

*Flannel* is an all-wool napped fabric made in dress, suit, or coat weights. It may be made with either worsted or woolen yarns, which may be yarn dyed. Worsted flannels are important in men's suits and coats and are used to a lesser extent in women's suits and coats. They are firmly woven with a very short nap. They wear well, are easy to press, and hold a press well. Woolen flannels are fuzzier, less firmly woven fabrics. Because napping causes some weakening of the fabric, 15–20 percent nylon or polyester may be blended with the wool to improve the strength. *Fleece* is a coatweight fabric with a long brushed nap or a short clipped nap.

*Cotton flannels* flatten under pressure and give less insulating value than wool because cotton fibers are less resilient. The fibers are also shorter; thus there is more shedding of lint from cotton flannels. These fabrics are used in robes, nightwear, baby clothes, and sweatshirts. *Flannelette* is a plain-weave fabric that is converted from a gray goods fabric called soft-filled sheeting. It is napped on one side only, has a short nap, and often has a printed design. The nap will form small pills and is subject to abrasion. *Suede* and *duvetyn* also are converted from the same gray goods but are sheared close to the ground to make a smooth, flat surface. Of the two, duvetyn is lighter weight. *Outing flannel* is a yarn-dyed, white, or printed fabric that is similar in fabric weight and nap length to flannelette but is napped on both sides.

Since the warp yarns in both flannelette and outing flannel are standard yarns, it is easy to identify fabric grain. Napped, knitted fabrics may be given pile-fabric names such as velvet or velour.

## Fulled

**Fulling** is done on wool fabrics to improve the appearance, hand, body, and cover. Fabrics are fulled by moisture, heat, and friction—a very mild, carefully controlled felting process. Fabric that has been fulled is denser and more compact (see Figure 17–20).

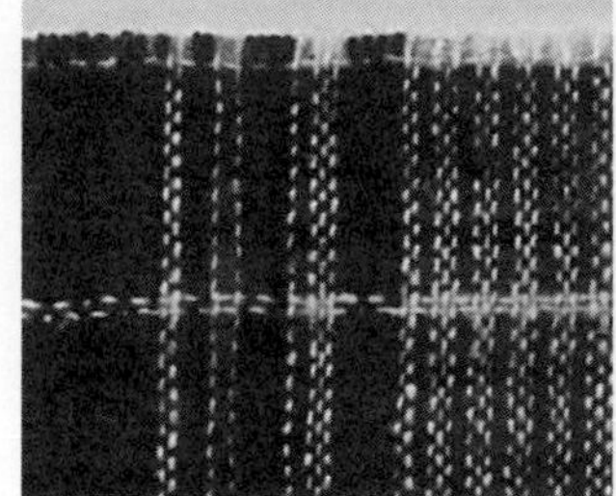
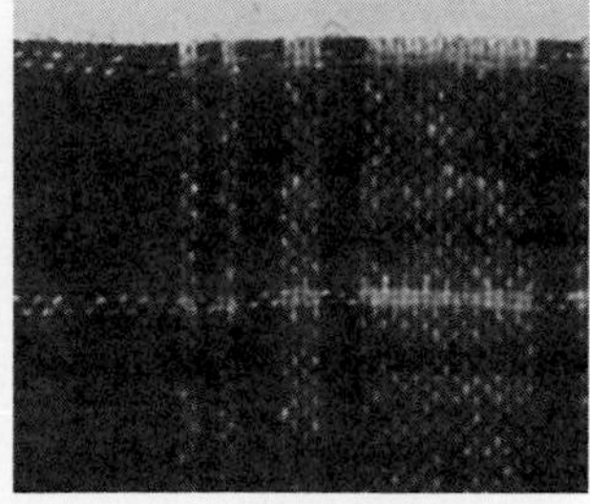

**FIGURE 17–20** ❖ Wool cloth before (left) and after (right) fulling.

## Beetled

**Beetling** is a finish originally used on linen and fabrics resembling linen. As the cloth revolved slowly over a huge wooden drum, it was pounded with wooden-block hammers. This pounding continued until it flattened the yarns into an oval, not round, cross section. The weave appeared tighter than it really was. The increased surface area gave more luster, greater absorbency, and smoothness to the fabric.

A contemporary method of producing a beetled fabric uses extreme pressure, resin, and thermoplastic fibers. In this case, the pressure flattens the yarns into the oval shape associated with beetled fabrics. The heat and resin result in a permanent flattening of the yarns. This finish is used on damask, crash, and other linenlike fabrics.

## Coronized

**Coronizing** is a process for heat setting, dyeing, and finishing glass fiber in one continuous operation. Since glass is low in flexibility, the yarns resist bending around one another in the woven fabric. Heat setting at a temperature of 1,100°F softens the yarns so that they will bend and assume yarn crimp. Coronized fabrics have greater wrinkle resistance and softer draping qualities.

After heat setting, the glass fabric is treated with a lubricating oil; then color and a water-repellent finish are added. For this treatment, the Hycar-Quilon process is used. Hycar is an acrylic latex resin which, with the colored pigment, is padded on the fabric and then cured at a temperature of 320°F. This is followed by a treatment with Quilon, a water-repellent substance, and the fabric is again cured. The resin used in the color treatment increases the flexibility of the fiber. Screen printing as well as roller printing can be done by this process, since the color paste dries fast enough to allow one screen to follow another rapidly. It gives good resistance to rubbing off (crocking), a disadvantage of other coloring methods.

# HAND

Hand finishes are used to alter the hand or touch of a fabric.

## Emerizing, Sueding, or Sanding

**Emerizing, sueding, sanding,** or *peach skin* is a process used on fine silky fabrics of natural or manufactured fibers. The different terms describe different starting plain or twill-weave fabrics and different surface effects produced by the process. It may be applied to polyester microfiber fabrics to improve their hand and comfort. The finish is usually applied to washed fabrics before they are heat set or dyed. The fabric moves at a speed of 15–20 meters per minute under two or more rollers. Each roller is coated with a different grade of emery or abrasive paper, from fine papers on the first roller to more abrasive paper on each additional roller. The process abrades the surface fibers and causes fibrils to split from the fibers. These fibrils give the fabric its soft hand and unusual appearance. Too much abrasion or too coarse an abrasive will rip or tear the fabric. Too little abrasion may generate sufficient heat to produce a harsh hand with thermoplastic fibers. The process damages the fabric and can decrease its tensile strength by as much as 60 percent. After treatment, the fabrics are heat set and washed to remove the dust. Dyeing follows. These fabrics need to be handled carefully. Machine washing may abrade the fibrils and destroy the look of the fabric.

## Abrasive, Chemical, or Enzyme Washes

**Abrasive, chemical,** or **enzyme washes** are processes that were used originally on denim garments and have been popular in that application for years under a variety of names, including acid wash, frosted, pepper, and enzyme wash. These finishes are modified for application to other fabrications of cotton as well as a variety of fabrications of other fibers, like silk, polyester, and cotton/polyester blends. The washing process alters the surface of the fabric and damages it to some degree.

Many manufacturers use these finishes on their products. The washing can be done by the sewing facility in an area of the plant referred to as the laundry. These processes require special equipment and knowledge and cannot be duplicated in the home. Some consumers have attempted stone washing at home with real stones. This usually results in an expensive repair or replacement of the washing machine.

**CHEMICAL WASHES** In this process a special chemical is added to the wash solution to alter the fiber's surface. Chemicals include alkalis, oxidizing agents, and others that are specific to the fiber being treated. These chemicals may partially destroy the fiber and create irregularities, pits, pores, or other surface aberrations. Note that even though the term "acid wash" may be used, acid is not used in the process. This technique is used to produce fashion denims, comfort polyesters, and washed silks.

**ABRASIVE WASHES** With the abrasive washes, pumice or some other abrasive material is saturated with a chemical like potassium permanganate and tumbled with the fabric or garment for several hours. The abrasive material is removed and the chemical is neutralized in a bath. With fabrics like cotton, the abrasion is controlled by the length of time the fabric is treated and the style and type of pumice or stone used. With fabrics like silk that are lighter weight, the abrasion may result from tumbling against other fabrics in the chamber. Fabrics finished in this manner are referred to by a variety of fashion terms including stonewashed denim, sanded silk, and mudwashed silk.

**ENZYME WASHES** These washes are similar to chemical washes except that they use cellulase, an enzyme that dissolves part of the cellulose molecule. The permanent effect occurs on the surface of the fabric and the hand becomes softer. The enzyme removes surface fuzz, reduces the likelihood of pilling with use or care, and decreases fabric weight, with a slight loss in fabric strength of less than 10 percent. (See Figure 17–21.) Cellulase, usually produced by the fermentation of molds, is a naturally occurring protein. It requires an incubation time in order for the degradation to take place. Relatively small concentrations of these biodegradable enzymes are used with little negative environmental effect compared to that of chemical washes. After treatment with the enzyme, mechanical action removes the weakened fiber ends. In some instances,

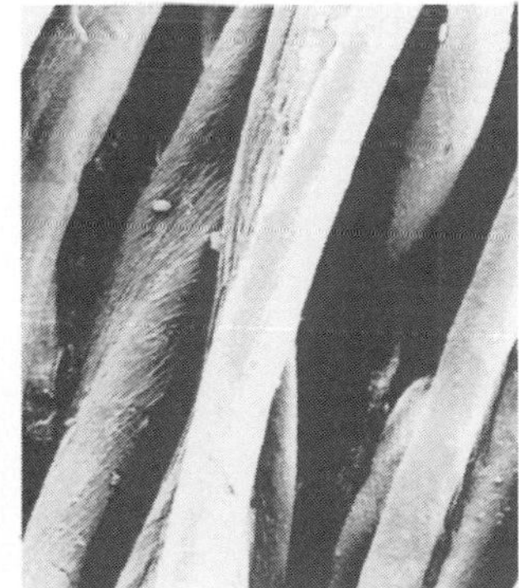

**FIGURE 17–21** ❖ Enzyme-polished cotton fibers: original fibers (left) and bio-polished fibers (right). (REPRINTED WITH PERMISSION FROM THE CANADIAN TEXTILE JOURNAL, VOL. 109, NO. 10, DECEMBER, 1992.)

abrasive stones are combined with the enzyme to produce the mechanical abrasion. Enzyme washes have resulted in greater productivity with fewer seconds in finishing facilities.

## Crepeing

**Crepeing** is a special compacting process to produce a fabric with a soft hand. Additional benefits include comfort stretch and soft drape. In crepeing the fabric is fed into the machine by a special blade at a faster rate than it is removed from the machine. Crepeing can create an allover texture or a localized plissé effect.

## Silk Boil-Off

In silk fabric sericin makes up about 30 percent of the weight. The boil-off process removes the sericin and creates a looser, more mobile fabric structure. If the fabric is in a relaxed state while the sericin is being removed, the warp yarns take on a high degree of fabric crimp. This crimp and the looser fabric structure together create the liveliness and suppleness of silk, a suppleness that has been compared to the action of the coil-spring "Slinky" toy.

The properties are quite different when the boil-off is done under tension. The fabric crimp is much less, and the response of the fabric is more like that of a flat spring; thus the supple nature is lost. This helps to explain the difference between qualities of silk fabric.

## Caustic Treatment

With the microfibers, caustic treatment is less important. However, because microfibers are so expensive, **caustic treatment** is a more economical alternative.

Manufactured fibers are normally processed under tension by a continuous method rather than by a batch method. Trilobal fabrics are processed in a completely relaxed condition. Finishing starts with a heat-setting treatment to stabilize the fabric to a controlled width, remove any wrinkles, and impart resistance to wrinkling. The next step is a caustic-soda (alkali) treatment to dissolve a controlled amount of the fiber, usually 5 to 18 percent. Similar to the degumming of silk, this step gives the fabric structure greater mobility with a slight loss in tensile strength and abrasion resistance. The fabric is more hydrophilic and more comfortable. All remaining finishes are done with the fabric completely relaxed to get maximum fabric crimp. Figure 17–22 shows the effect of the alkali treatment on a fabric made of a circular-cross-sectional polyester.

## Hand Builders

**Hand builders** are compounds that soften fabric hand. They include silicone softeners and cellulase enzyme. These compounds produce a dryer hand compared to compounds previously used. Better performance properties of the fabrics in terms of wrinkle resistance and improved durability occur with some of the silicone softeners.

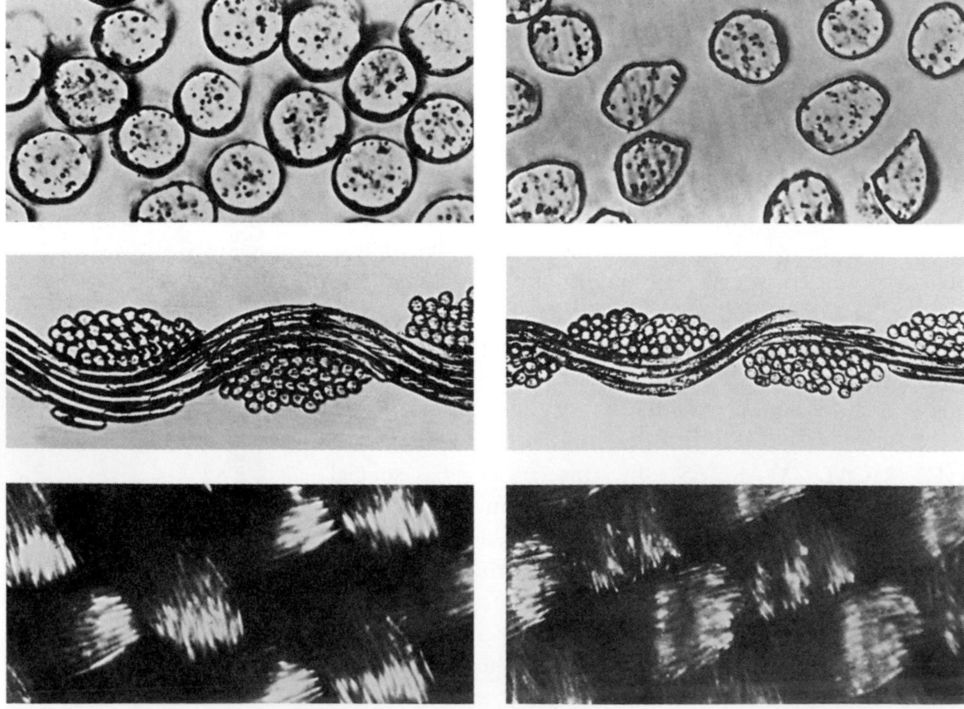

**FIGURE 17–22 ❖** Photomicrographs showing effect of heat-caustic treatment. Original fabric on left; fabric after treatment on right. Dacron polyester fiber cross-section 1000× (top); fabric cross-section 200× (center); fabric surface 50× (bottom). (COURTESY OF E. I. DU PONT DE NEMOURS & COMPANY.)

## Key Terms

Aesthetic finishes
Applied design
Padding machine
Backfilling machine
Luster finish
Glazed
Friction calender
Ciré finish
Moiré pattern
Schreiner calender
Embossed design
Parchmentized
Tendering
Burned-out
Etched
Sizing
Starching
Sheared fabric
Brushed fabric
Pleated fabric
Puckered surface
Plissé
Flocked fabric
Tufted fabric
Embroidered fabric
Schiffli embroidery
Multihead embroidery
Eyelet embroidery
Expanded foam
Nap
Fulling
Beetling
Coronizing
Emerizing, sueding, or sanding
Abrasive, chemical, or enzyme wash
Crepeing
Caustic treatment
Hand builders

## Questions

1. Explain the differences between embossed and plissé in terms of process and fabric.
2. Explain the changes in serviceability of a fabric after it has been napped.
3. What kinds of fabrics are generally sheared? What is the purpose of shearing?
4. Describe the manner in which each fabric of these pairs was produced. Which are applied designs and which are structural?
   - swivel dotted swiss and flocked dotted swiss
   - extra yarn eyelash fabric and burned out
   - plissé and seersucker
   - tufted velvet and true velvet
   - flocked corduroy and napped flannel
5. Predict the serviceability of each fabric listed in question 4.
6. Which of the finishes listed below would be permanent (last for the life of the fabric) and which would diminish with time or use? Why?
   - heat-embossed nylon tricot
   - pressure-embossed cotton
   - burned-out rayon/polyester sheer drapery
   - fulled wool gabardine
   - water-soluble sizing on 100 percent cotton printcloth
   - 65 percent polyester/35 percent cotton glazed chintz upholstery (resin compound)
   - 100 percent polyester crepe de chine with caustic treatment

## Suggested Readings

Creswell, Frank (1994, October/November). "Finishing Fabrics in the Nineties." *Canadian Textile Journal*, pp. 28–29.

Goldstein, Herman G. (1993). "Mechanical and Chemical Finishing of Microfabrics." *Textile Chemist and Colorist, 25*(2), pp. 16–21.

Jerg, Gunter, and Baumann, Josef (1990). "Polyester Microfibers: A New Generation of Fabrics." *Textile Chemist and Colorist, 22*(12), pp. 12–14.

Kumar, Akhil, Purtell, Charles, and Lepola, Marja (1994). "Enzymatic Treatment of Man-Made Cellulosic Fabrics." *Textile Chemist and Colorist, 26*(10), pp. 25–28.

Needles, Howard (1986). *Textile Fibers, Dyes, Finishes, and Processes.* Park Ridge, NJ: Noyes Publications.

Scott, Ken (April, 1990). "A Look at the Denim Processing Scene." *Laundry and Cleaning News International*, pp. 4–7.

Taylor, Marjorie (1993). "What Is Moiré?" *Textiles*, no. 1, p. 14.

Trotman, E. R. (1984). *Dyeing and Chemical Technology of Textile Fibers.* New York: John Wiley & Sons.

Tyndall, R. Michael (1992). "Improving the Softness and Surface Appearance of Cotton Fabrics and Garments by Treatment with Cellulase Enzymes." *Textile Chemist and Colorist, 25*(6), pp. 23–26.

## Chapter 18

# Special-Purpose Finishes

## OBJECTIVES

- To recognize the effects (both positive and negative) of special-purpose finishes.
- To relate special-purpose finishes to fabric, yarn, fiber, and end-use aspects.
- To understand the processes used to apply special-purpose finishes.
- To recognize the problems special-purpose finishes are designed to eliminate or minimize.

**Special-purpose finishes** are also known as **functional finishes.** These are treatments that are applied to fabrics to make them better suited for a specific end use. Although they usually do not alter the appearance of fabrics, they improve performance. They help solve some consumer problems or performance deficiencies with textile products or make the fabric more suitable for a specific purpose. This chapter is organized by the performance aspect the finish addresses.

Special-purpose finishes add to the cost of the product, but their impact on performance may be difficult for consumers to recognize. This is especially true since the effect of the finish may be invisible or beyond consumer perception, especially at point of purchase. Even during use, assessment is difficult—how does one measure the effectiveness of a soil-resistant finish if the fabric stays cleaner longer? Another important fact to remember is that improved performance in one area usually means a loss of performance in another area. When finishes fail to perform at the expected or guaranteed level, consumers may complain. If the cost of the item is high or the yardage is great, civil lawsuits may be filed. For example, there may be lawsuits about carpeting in shopping malls if the carpet soils quickly or if the soil cannot be removed with appropriate treatment. This is especially common when guarantees have been made (see Chapter 21 for more information).

Many functional finishes are topical finishes. A chemical compound is added to the surface of the fabric. Penetration to the interior may not occur.

# Stabilization: Shrinkage Control

A fabric is **stabilized** when it retains its original size and shape during use and care. Unstable fabrics shrink or stretch, usually as a result of care. **Shrinkage,** the reduction in size of a product, is the more serious and more frequent problem. Shrinkage is most often measured as a percentage of the original dimension. It is generally reported separately for length and width, for example, 2.5 percent warp and 1.5 percent filling.

The shrinkage problem begins in spinning, weaving, and finishing. Yarns are under tension during spinning and slashing. Fabrics are under tension during fabrication. In wet finishing, fabrics may be pulled through machines in long continuous pieces and finally set under excessive tension that leaves the fabric with high residual shrinkage. Shrinkage occurs when tensions are released by moisture and heat, as in laundering or steam pressing. It is difficult to predict how much shrinkage will occur in lengthwise and crosswise directions since so many factors contribute to shrinkage: fiber type, blend level, yarn process, fabrication type, and number and type of finishing processes used. Some manufacturers of sewn products try to address this problem at the pattern-making step by oversizing the pattern, but these efforts are inaccurate at best.

Shrinkage is used to advantage in the manufacture of some fabrics, as in fulling or shrinkage of crepe yarn in matelassé. Shrinkage is a disadvantage to the manufacturer and the consumer when it changes a product's dimensions.

There are two major types of shrinkage of interest here: relaxation shrinkage and progressive shrinkage. **Relaxation shrinkage** occurs during washing or dry cleaning. Most relaxation shrinkage occurs during the first care cycle. However, many manufacturers and retailers test for shrinkage through three or more cleaning cycles because shrinkage may continue to occur at smaller rates for several additional care cycles; this is **progressive shrinkage.** If the care is mild in the first cycle and more severe in later cycles, more shrinkage may occur during these later cycles than in the first cycle. For example, if the item was dried flat in the first cycle and machine dried in later cycles, shrinkage will be more severe with machine drying. The following list groups fibers by the kind of shrinkage they normally exhibit:

1. *Cotton, linen, and high-wet-modulus rayon:* Exhibit relaxation shrinkage. Little progressive shrinkage.
2. *Regular rayon:* Exhibits high relaxation shrinkage. Moderate progressive shrinkage.
3. *Wool:* Exhibits moderate relaxation shrinkage. High progressive shrinkage.
4. *Other properly heat-set manufactured fibers:* Exhibit relaxation shrinkage. No progressive shrinkage.

Mechanical-control methods or heat are used to eliminate relaxation shrinkage. Chemical-control methods are used to prevent progressive shrinkage.

## Relaxation Shrinkage and Methods of Control

**Knit Fabrics** Knit fabrics shrink because the loops may be elongated 10–35 percent lengthwise in knitting and wet finishing (Figure 18–1). During laundering, the stitches reorient themselves to their normal shape and the item becomes shorter and wider.

Shrinkage of knits can be minimized by overfeeding the fabric between sets of rollers to induce lengthwise shrinkage. The use of polyester in blends with cotton permits the knit fabric to be stabilized by heat setting.

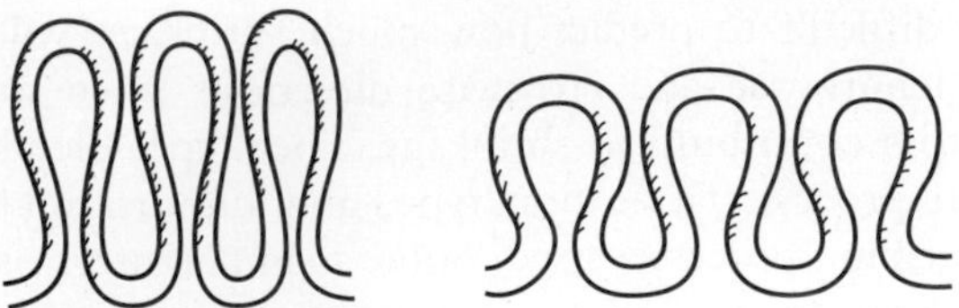

**FIGURE 18–1** ❖ Knit stitches: (a) under stress; (b) in normal state.

**WOVEN FABRICS** All woven fabrics shrink when wetting relaxes the strains of yarn production, weaving, preparation finishes, and wet finishing. The warp yarns are under tension while they are on the loom, and the filling is inserted in a straight line. The filling takes on crimp as it is beaten back into the fabric, but the warp stays straight (Figure 18–2). When the fabric is thoroughly wet and allowed to relax, the yarns readjust themselves and the warp yarns also become crimped, but to a lesser degree (Figure 18–2). This crimp shortens the fabric in the warp direction. With the exception of crepe fabrics, less change occurs in the filling direction.

**Compressive shrinkage processes** are used on woven fabrics of cotton, linen, and high-wet-modulus rayon. Regular rayons will not hold a compressive shrinkage treatment because of their high swelling and wet elongation.

In this process, a thick felt blanket is used since a thick blanket will shrink the fabric more than a thin one. The blanket, with the moist cloth adhering to its surface, is passed around a feed-in roll. In this curved position, the outer surface stretches and the inner surface contracts. The blanket then reverses its direction around a heated drum. The outer curve becomes the shorter, inner surface, and the fabric adhering to it is compressed. The fabric against the drum is dried and set with a smooth finish. The count will increase, and the fabric will actually be improved after compressing (Figures 18–3 and 18–4).

**FIGURE 18–2** ❖ Position of the warp on the loom (left); after the fabric relaxes when it becomes wet (right).

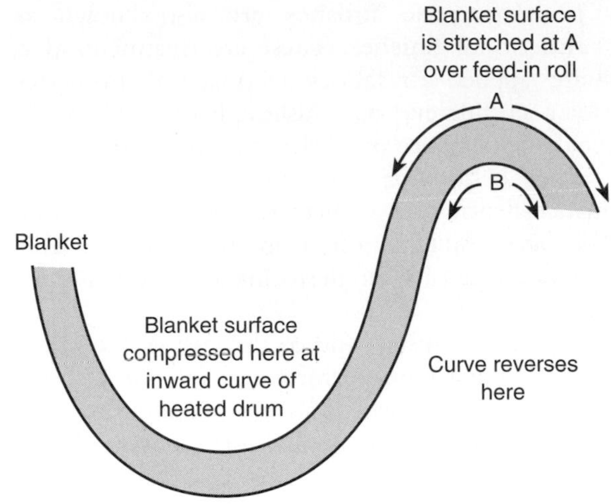


**FIGURE 18–3** ❖ Reversal of curve causes change in size to compress fabric.

However, improper laundering may cause these fabrics to shrink as much as 6 percent. Tumble drying also may compress the yarns beyond their normal shrinkage.

**London shrunk** is an 18th-century relaxation finish for wool fabrics that removes production strains. A wet blanket—wool or cotton—is placed on a long platform, a layer of fabric is spread on it, and alternate layers of

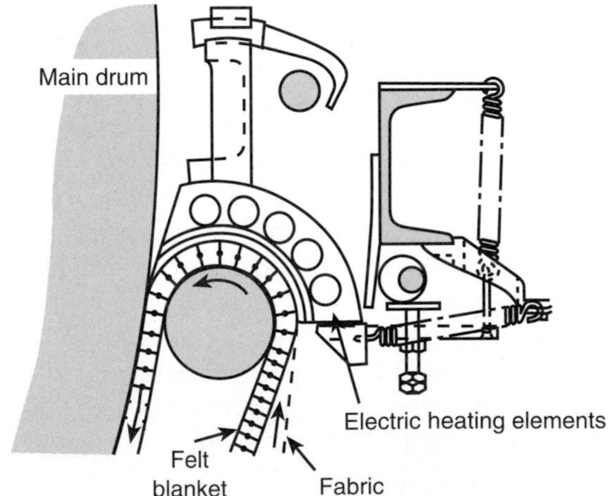


**FIGURE 18–4** ❖ Closeup of compressive shrinkage process. The electrically heated shoe holds the fabric firmly on the outside of the blanket so that when the blanket collapses in straightening out, the fabric is shrunk accordingly. (COURTESY OF THE SANFORIZED COMPANY.)

blanket and fabric are built up. Sufficient weight is placed on top for about 12 hours to force the moisture from the blankets into the wool. The fabric is hung to dry naturally. When dry, the fabric is pressed by building up layers of fabric and special press boards with a preheated metal plate inserted at intervals and on the top and bottom of the stack. This setup of fabric, boards, and plates is kept under 3,000 pounds of pressure for 10–12 hours. London shrunk is used for fine worsteds, but not for woolens.

The label "Genuine London Process" or similar wording is licensed by the Parrot Group of companies to garment makers all over the world. The permanent-set finish Si-Ro-Set for washable, wrinkle-free wool fabrics is applied to some London-shrunk fabrics during processing.

## Progressive Shrinkage and Methods of Control

**THERMOPLASTIC FIBERS** Thermoplastic fibers are stabilized by **heat setting,** a process in which fabrics are heated at temperatures at or above the **glass transition temperature ($T_g$)** and then cooled. At this temperature the amorphous regions of the fiber are easy to distort. It is lower than the melting point of a fiber and differs for each fiber type. When properly heat set, fabrics will exhibit no progressive shrinkage and relaxation shrinkage will be controlled (Figure 18–5).

**WOOL FIBERS** Washable wool is important in apparel and some furnishings and in blends with washable fibers. If wool is to improve its position in the competitive market with wool-like fibers that have easy-care characteristics, wool fabrics must be finished to keep their original size and surface texture during laundering. Controlling felting shrinkage remains an important issue, judging by the fact that patents for feltproofing wool continue to be issued. Figure 18–6 illustrates the shrinkage of wool.

To prevent felting shrinkage, the finish alters the scale structure by "smoothing off" the free edges and thus reduces the differential-friction effect that prevents wool fibers from returning to their original position in the fabric. The effectiveness of felting shrinkage treatments depends on the kind and amount of finish used and on the yarn and fabric construction. Worsteds need less finish than woolens. Low-count fabrics and low-twist yarns need more finish to give good washability. Treated-wool fabrics are usually considered machine washable, but care should be taken to use warm, not hot, water and a short agitation period. Handwashing is preferable, because soil is easy to remove from the fiber and handwashing ensures a lower temperature and less agitation. Machine washing may loosen fibers, resulting in a fuzzy or slightly pilled surface.

Two methods are used to smooth off the free edges of the scales: surface coatings and halogenation treatments. **Surface coatings** of a polyamide solution coat the scales. This is a very thin, microscopic film on the

FIGURE 18–5 ❖ Comparison of thermoplastic fiber fabrics. Bottom fabric has been heat set. Note wrinkling and shrinkage of upper fabric (not heat set).

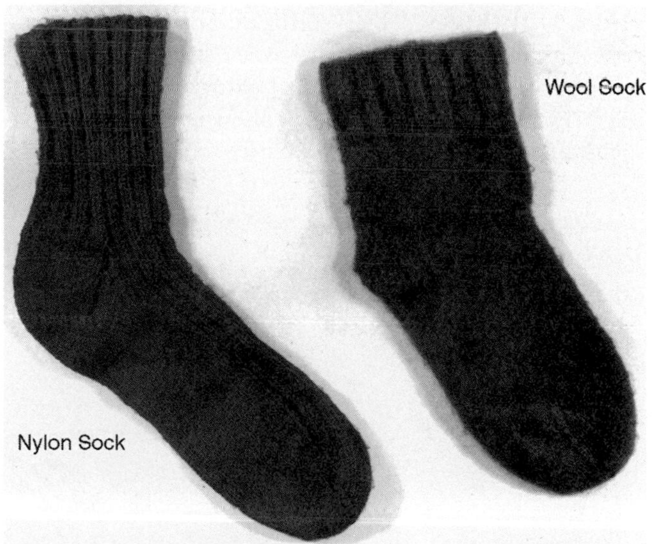


FIGURE 18–6 ❖ These socks were the same size when purchased. Nylon (left); wool (right).

fiber. In addition to controlling shrinkage, the coating tends to minimize pilling and fuzzing (one of the greatest problems in wash-and-wear wools), gives the fabrics better wash-and-wear properties, and increases resistance to abrasion. This process carries the trade name Wurlan.

**Halogenation** treatments, primarily with chlorine, also are used. They are low cost, can be applied to large batches of small items such as wool socks, do not require padding or curing equipment, and are fairly effective. Since the scales are partially dissolved, felting shrinkage is lessened. The process damages the fibers and must be carefully monitored to minimize damage. The scales are more resistant to damage than the interior of the fiber and should not be completely removed or there will be considerable reduction in wearing properties, weight, and hand. The fabric will feel harsh and rough. To maintain the strength of the fabric, nylon fiber often is blended with the wool. Halogenation is especially good for handwashable items. A process combining chlorination and resin makes wool knits machine washable and dryer dryable. Shrinkage is less than 3 percent in length and 1 percent in width, and goods retain their loft and resiliency. Superwash® is a trade name.

Both processes result in a wool that is washable, but hand washing is generally preferred to machine washing. Both processes also significantly alter the hand of wool and affect moisture absorbancy.

Environmental pressures are restricting use of chlorine. Hence, alternate methods that use other oxidizing agents and enzymes are being investigated.

**RAYON FIBERS** The shrinkage of regular rayon varies with the handling of the wet fabric during finishing. Wet fabric can be stretched easily and overstretching may occur. If it is dried in this stretched condition, the fabric will have high potential shrinkage. It will shrink when wet again and dried without tension. It is almost impossible to determine this without laboratory or home testing.

Shrinkage-control treatments for rayon reduce the swelling property of the fiber and make it resistant to distortion. Resins form cross-links that prevent swelling and keep the fiber from stretching. The resin also fills up spaces in the amorphous areas of the fiber, making it less absorbent. Aldehyde resins are superior to other resins because they do not weaken the fabric, are nonchlorine retentive, and have excellent washfastness. Treated rayons are machine washable, but the wash cycle should be short. High-wet-modulus rayon is also resin treated, mainly for durable-press purposes, because its shrinkage can be controlled by relaxation shrinkage–control methods.

# SHAPE-RETENTION FINISHES

Even though care of contemporary textiles is a time-consuming task, it is hard to imagine the time and physical effort that it used to require! Imagine having to iron almost every item of apparel and bedding! With thermoplastic fibers, special shape-retention finishes, and modern washers and dryers, easy-care textiles are the norm. It is only the occasional object that requires the extra effort of ironing.

## Theory of Wrinkle Recovery

Wrinkles occur when fabrics are crushed during use and care (creases and pleats made by pressing are desirable style features, however). Wrinkle recovery is dependent on **cross-links** that hold adjacent molecular chains

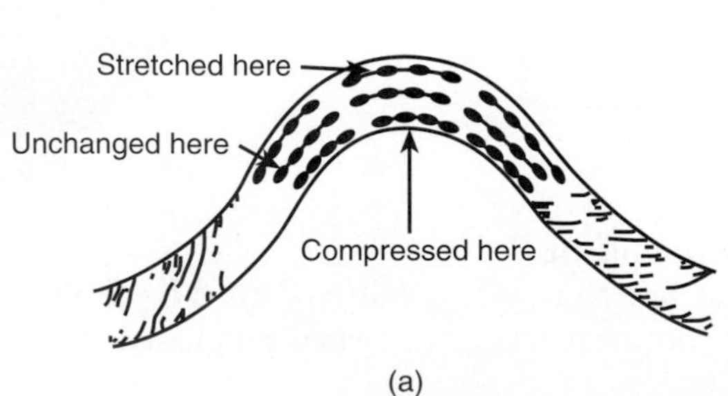


FIGURE 18–7 ❖ (a) Effect of internal structure when fiber is bent; (b) resin cross-link.

together and pull them back into position after the fiber is bent, thus preventing the formation of a wrinkle. Fibers that have strong intermolecular bonds have good molecular memory. These fibers resist wrinkling and creasing, whereas fibers with weak bonds wrinkle and crease readily.

The cellulosic fibers do not have natural strong cross-links. Molecular chains are held together by weak hydrogen bonds that break with the stress of bending. New bonds form to hold the fiber in this bent position, thus forming a wrinkle. Resin cross-links give fibers a "memory" and good wrinkle recovery (Figure 18–7).

Resin finishes were first used in England in 1920 and in the United States in 1940 on rayon, cotton, and linen fabrics. Urea formaldehyde was the first resin used to prevent wrinkles; other resins and improved resin combinations were developed later. Although fabrics treated with these resins were smooth, flat, and **wrinkle resistant,** they had poor abrasion resistance, lower tear strength, a tendency to yellow and retain chlorine from bleach, a poor hand, affinity for oily soils, static, pilling, and a fishy odor. Color problems included frosting and migration of color from the thermoplastic fibers to the cellulosic fibers because of the high curing temperatures. In addition, construction problems with seam pucker or alterations occurred. Finally, formaldehyde has been identified as a possible carcinogen.

Alternatives to the formaldehyde-based durable-press finishes are becoming more important with increasing limits on formaldehyde use. New finishes include modified glyoxal-based reactants that decrease the formaldehyde release to a tiny fraction or reactants based on polycarboxylic acid derivatives. The polycarboxylic acid derivatives produce fabrics with better abrasion resistance, good durable press performance, and low shrinkage. These problems continue to exist; they are less pronounced with the new finishing agents. However, colorfastness may be decreased. Unfortunately, both alternatives result in significantly higher costs of finished goods.

## Durable Press

**Durable press** applies to items that retain their shape and their pressed appearance even after many uses, washings, and tumble dryings. The terms *durable press, wrinkle free,* and *permanent press* are used interchangeably, but durable is a more realistic description because the effectiveness of the finish decreases with age. Older items may require some touch-up ironing to meet appearance standards. Wrinkle free is misleading because many almost new products may require some touch-up ironing to meet consumer standards. Other terms for durable press are wrinkle resistant, anticreasing, and crease retention.

Several processes for durable-press items and fabrics are outlined here. Major differences in these processes are when the chemical is applied and the stage at which cutting, sewing, and pressing take place. In the first two processes, **precured** and **postcured,** the finish is applied to the fabric (Figures 18–8 and 18–9). In the final two processes, **immersion** and **metered addition,** the finish is applied to the garment or product (Figures 18–10 and 18–11).

### The Precured Process

1. Saturate the fabric with the resin cross-linking solution and dry.
2. Cure in a curing oven to form cross-links between molecular chains.
3. Cut and sew item. Press.
4. Used for shirting, draperies, and other items that do not require set-in creases or pleats.
5. Often used with cotton/polyester blends.

### The Postcured Process

1. Saturate the fabric with a resin cross-linking solution and dry.
2. Cut and sew the item and press shape with hothead press.
3. Cure by putting pressed item into a curing oven at 300°–400°F.
4. Curing gives shape to the cellulosic fibers. The thermoplastic fibers were *set* by the hothead pressing.
5. Used for skirts, slacks, and other products with set-in creases or pleats.
6. Often used with cotton/polyester blends.

### The Immersion Process

1. Dye and finish the product for a specific fashion look.

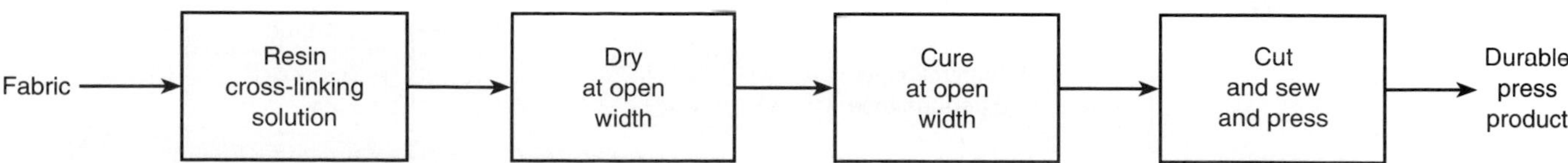


**FIGURE 18–8** ❖ Precured process.

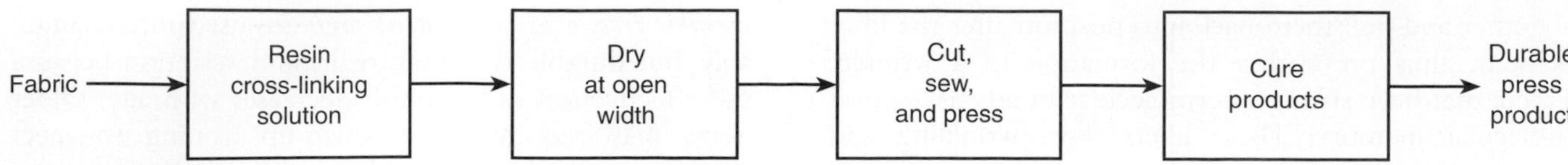


**FIGURE 18–9** ❖ Postcured process.

2. Immerse finished garment or product in the finishing agent and extract excess finish. Dry the product.
3. Hand and performance can be adjusted with fabric softeners and other compounds so that the finished product will be appealing to consumers.
4. Press desired features (creases, pleats, etc.) into garment with special hothead press.
5. Cure by putting product in curing oven at 300°F for 5–15 minutes.
6. Used for fashion apparel of 100 percent cotton.
7. Also known as the garment or product dip process.

### THE METERED ADDITION PROCESS

1. Dye and finish the product for a specific fashion look.
2. Spray finished garment or product with the finishing agent in a chamber as it rotates. Tumbling continues until product is uniformly processed.
3. Hand and performance can be adjusted with fabric softeners and other compounds so that the finished product will be appealing to consumers.
4. Press desired features (creases, pleats, etc.) into garment with special hothead press.
5. Cure by putting product in curing oven at 300°F for 5–15 minutes.
6. Used for fashion apparel and furnishings (bed linens and toweling) of 100 percent cotton.

Many problems continue to be associated with resin finishes. Table 18–1 summarizes these processes.

By using blends of cotton/polyester instead of 100 percent cotton, less resin is needed. The high strength and abrasion resistance of polyester make these fabrics much more durable. Pretreating cotton with liquid ammonia or mercerizing cotton under tension adds strength to fabrics so they are not weakened so much from the finish. Polymer sizing added to the yarns before curing gives the fabric greater abrasion resistance. Although most curing is done using forced air convection ovens, microwave ovens are being developed. These ovens produce a more uniform cure for lighter-weight fabrics such as shirtings.

Conepress, by Cone Mills, is a process in which precured fabrics are made into garments. Where creases are desired the garment is sprayed with a substance that temporarily inactivates the wrinkle-resistant finish. The garments are then pressed under pressure to recur the finish.

Creaset is a silicone-based finish by the company of the same name, Creaset, for all-wool and all-cotton fabrics.

Other trade names include PressFree cotton by McGregor, Presset by Cotton, Inc., and Process 2000 by Farah U.S.A.

**DURABLE-PRESS WOOL** Wool has good resiliency when it is dry, but it does not have durable-press characteristics when it is wet. *Durable-press wool* is achieved with resin treatments, but this must be accompanied by a treatment with shrink-resist resins in order to control wool's tendency to excessive shrinkage. Several procedures are used, but the one described here is typical. Si-Ro-Set is a trade name.

1. Flat fabric is treated with 1–2 percent of the durable-press resin and steamed (semidecated) for 3–5 minutes.
2. The item is made up, sprayed with more durable-press resin, and pressed. This gives the permanent-crease effect.

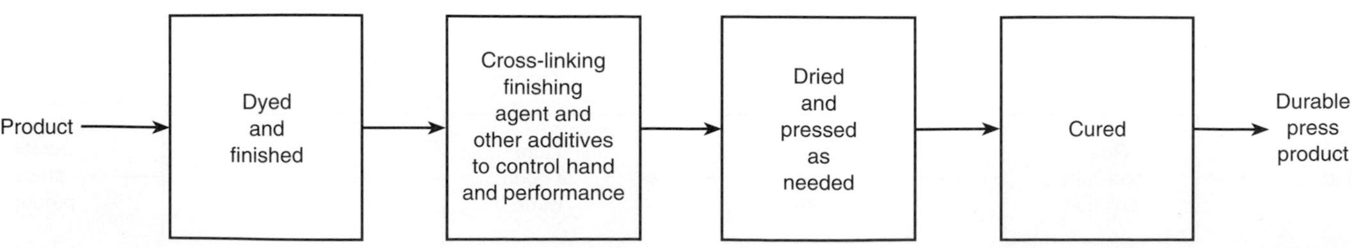


**FIGURE 18–10** ❖ Immersion process.

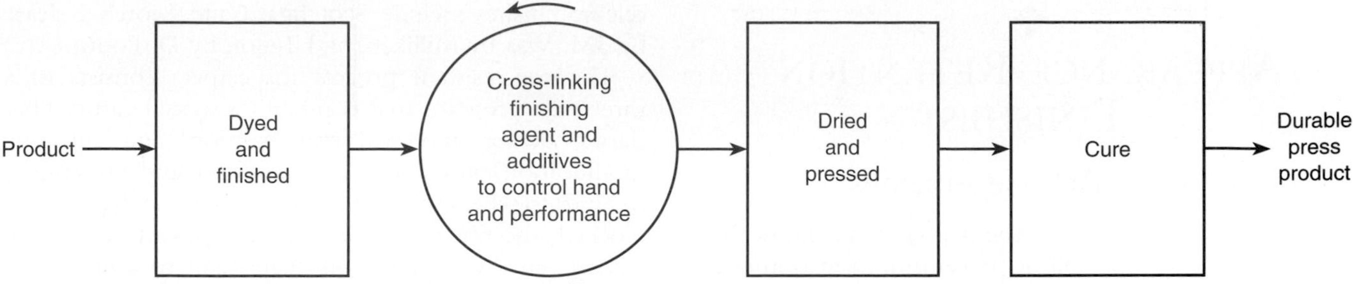


**FIGURE 18–11** ❖ Metered addition process.

3. Shrink-resist resin is mixed with a dry cleaning solvent and the item is dry cleaned. The resin is then allowed to cure in the item for 3–7 days before it can be laundered.

**DURABLE-PRESS SILK** Silk wrinkles easily when wet. Polycarboxylic acid has been found to be an effective durable-press or wrinkle-resistant agent for silk. The finish is durable to laundering but produces a 20 percent loss in strength, increase in stiffness, and decrease in whiteness.

## Quality Standards and Care

**Quality-control standards** had not been developed during the wash-and-wear era and there was wide variation in fabric performance. To avoid problems, the industry developed standards for durable press and quality has been much more dependable. Registered trade names indicate to the consumer that the product has met certain performance tests. The consumer also can check the fabric for objectionable odor or excessive stiffness that indicate poor processing. If the fabric is a blend, there should be an adequate amount of thermoplastic fiber to meet performance standards.

General care guidelines for durable-press items include the following:

- Wash these items frequently. Do not allow soil to build up. Resins have a special affinity for oil and grease, which should be removed quickly before they can penetrate.
- Pretreat stains, collars, and cuffs. Use a spot-removal agent on grease spots.
- Keep wash loads small. Crowding contributes to wrinkling.
- Heat sets wrinkles, so avoid heat as much as possible in the laundering process. Avoid wringing and squeezing. Use an automatic dryer, but remove items promptly.

**TABLE 18–1** ❖ Durable-press finishes.

| | PRECURE | POSTCURE | IMMERSION | METERED ADDITION |
|---|---|---|---|---|
| **Applied to** | Fabric | Fabric | Product | Product |
| **Stage of curing** | Fabric | Product | Product | Product |
| **Advantages** | Smooth fabric<br>Dimensionally stable<br>Lowest cost process | Smooth fabric<br>Dimensionally stable<br>Crease retention<br>Minimal seam puckering | Untreated fabric in sewing plant<br>No premature setting<br>Used with wet-finished goods<br>Control performance, hand, aesthetics<br>Greater flexibility | Untreated fabric in sewing plant<br>No premature setting<br>Used with wet-finished goods<br>Control performance, hand, aesthetics<br>Greater flexibility<br>Wet on wet processing possible |
| **Disadvantages** | No permanent creases<br>Puckered seams<br>Difficult to alter<br>Strength loss<br>Abrasion sensitive | Higher costs<br>May set prematurely<br>Overfinished areas | Higher costs<br>Process control difficult<br>Fabric preparation critical | Higher costs<br>Process control difficult<br>Fabric preparation critical |

# Appearance-Retention Finishes

## Soil- and Stain-Release Finishes

**Soil-release finishes** reduce the degree of soiling of the fabric by repelling the soil or preventing formation of a bond between the soil and the fabric. Thus these fabrics are easier to clean than those without soil-release finishes. Fluorochemicals are common, durable, and effective soil-resistant finishes.

Soil-release finishes improve the fabric's performance in resisting soil, releasing soil, and retaining whiteness by resisting redeposition of soil from the wash water. Unfortunately, these finishes may not last the life of the item. Some are durable enough to last through 20–30 washings. Lack of permanence results from the surface application of the finish.

There are several companies that can be hired by design firms or consumers to add a chemically protective finish to fabrics on site, including products such as carpeting, upholstery, or wall coverings. These finishes impart soil and stain resistance. The firms provide a follow-up service as needed, a cleaning kit, and care instructions. There are also soil-resistant finishes the consumer can apply on site. However, research has shown that some of these finishes may actually increase soiling (Reagan, et al., 1990).

Soil-release finishes were developed because of the tendency of durable-press items to pick up and hold oily stains and spots. Oil affinity means that oil is absorbed into the resin or the fiber. Soil-release finishes either attract water and permit the soil to be lifted off the fabric or coat the fibers and prevent the soil from penetrating the coating.

Many cotton/polyester blends have been treated to be durable press. Untreated cotton is hydrophilic with excellent oily soil-release performance. Cotton releases oily soil when it is laundered. The resin finish, however, is hydrophobic and does not release the oily soil. Polyester is hydrophobic and oleophilic. It must be spot treated to remove oily soil from contact areas, such as a shirt collar. When the polyester is coated with resin as it is in durable press, its oil affinity is increased. Finer fibers soil more readily than coarse fibers, and soil can penetrate low-twist yarns more easily than high-twist yarns.

Soil-release finishes make the surface less attractive to oil and more easily wetted—more hydrophilic. Many finishing materials fall into two general classes: They are mechanically or chemically bonded to the surface. Many soil-release finishes are organosilicon substances. Soil-release finishes include Scotchgard and Scotch Release by 3M, Visa by Milliken, and Teflon by DuPont.

The soil-resistant process for carpets consists of a three-part program that combines a special carpet fiber (larger denier, modified cross section, and antistatic modification) with a stain-resistant finish and a treatment to block the dye sites on the fibers. When the dye sites are blocked, the fibers are no longer receptive to accepting color from stains. These blockers tend to concentrate near the surface of the fiber since that is the area most susceptible to staining. These finishes are most effective against the coloring agents found in food and beverages (acid dyes) and are not effective against coloring agents of other types like cationic or disperse dyes. The stain-resistant treatments are fluorochemicals or silicon based, which are not easily wetted by oil or water. These finishes may yellow with exposure to heat, ultraviolet light, or high relative humidity. Ultraviolet light may also destroy the stain blocker part of this program. A side benefit is that these carpets are more resistant to ozone fading.

## Abrasion-Resistant Finishes

**Abrasion-resistant finishes** are used on lining fabrics, especially for pockets, waistbands, and other areas that receive significant abrasion. Thermoplastic resins, often an acrylic type, fix fibers more firmly into the yarns so they do not break off as readily. The resin may increase the wet soiling of the fabric. Blending nylon or polyester with cotton or rayon gives better resistance to abrasion than using finishes, but blend fabrics may cost more than finished fabric.

## Antislip Finishes

**Antislip finishes** are used on low-count, smooth-surfaced fabrics. Fabrics are treated with resins, stretched, and dried under tension, causing the yarns to be bonded at their interlacing points. Antislip finishes are used to reduce seam slippage and fraying. Seam slippage occurs when the yarns within the seam slide toward the seam allowance. This results in an area next to the seam where only one set of yarns can be seen. Slippage is especially noticeable where warp and filling yarns differ in color. Areas that have exhibited seam slippage have poor abrasion resistance and an unacceptable appearance. In some cases the seam can ravel completely. Antislip finishes are also called *slip-resistant,* or *nonslip, finishes.* The most effective and durable finishes are resins of urea or melamine formaldehyde.

## Fume Fading–Resistant Finishes

**Fume fading–resistant finishes** are available for use on those fibers dyed with dyes susceptible to fading when exposed to atmospheric fumes or pollutants. The most common are acetate fibers dyed with disperse dyes. Of course, this problem was decreased significantly with the use of mass pigmentation. However, there are some cases where mass pigmentation is not economically practical. In these cases, fume fading–resistant finishes of tertiary amines and borax are used. These finishes are also known as antifume and atmospheric fading protective finishes. They are used primarily for furnishing fabrics, especially draperies.

## Surface or Back Coatings

**Metallic, plastic,** or **foam coatings** are used on the back of fabrics to reduce heat transfer through the fabric, alter the appearance of the fabric, lock yarns in place, and minimize air and water permeability. Metallic or aluminum coatings are used on apparel and window treatment fabrics. A very thin layer of aluminum is bonded to the back of a drapery fabric for greater heat retention or to block heat transfer. In apparel, these coatings are found in winter coats for cold climates and specialized protective apparel for extreme temperature conditions such as fire fighting and spacesuits. In spacesuits the coating is on the exterior of the fabric to reflect heat from the sun when the wearer is in direct sunlight.

Plastic coatings reduce fabric soiling and give a smooth, leatherlike look to fabrics. (See "Coated Fabrics," Chapter 15.) Problems of metallic and plastic coatings include cracking and peeling of the finish. In order to increase the life of these fabrics, care label instructions must be followed.

Acrylic-foam coatings are common on drapery fabrics. These back coatings are used to minimize air movement through the draperies, give a greater comfort factor by increasing the thickness of the fabric, and minimize the need to have a separate lining fabric. Draperies with the foam-back coating often are sold as self-lined draperies (Figure 18–12).

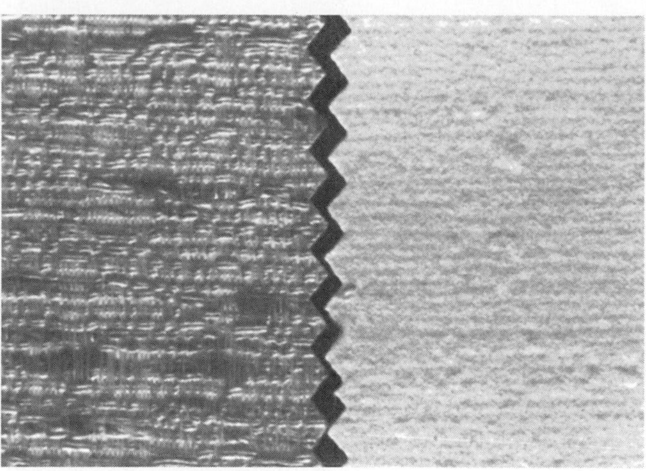

**FIGURE 18–12** ❖ Window treatment fabric with acrylic-foam coating: face (left) and back (right).

Latex back coatings are almost always used on tufted fabrics for furnishing uses. Tufted carpet and tufted upholstery use latex to lock the tufted yarns in place and to add dimensional stability to the fabric. Latex back coatings can be used to add durability to low-count upholstery fabrics. Latex back coatings create problems with comfort because of their low permeability of air and moisture. Outgassing of fumes from the latex can also create environmental problems.

These coatings may have poor aging resistance. They may separate, peel, flake off, or experience a change in hand with age or exposure to degrading aspects in the environment, like heat or light. For example, acrylic-foam backings may become tacky or sticky. When used on draperies, these finishes may cause the drapery to stick together when it comes in contact with another portion of the fabric.

## Light-Stabilizing Finishes

Light-stabilizing finishes incorporate light stabilizers or ultraviolet absorbers to minimize damage from light exposure. This is especially important in some furnishings, apparel, and many industrial products. Products that are exposed to sunlight on a regular basis or to interior lighting that has a high percentage of ultraviolet light may require this finish. Artificial light sources that may contribute to fading include fluorescent lights found in many office buildings and retail establishments. Products that require light stabilizers include tarpaulin and awning fabrics, tents, sewing thread for outdoor products, outdoor furniture, car interiors, and some carpeting.

❖

# COMFORT-RELATED FINISHES

## Water-Repellent Finishes

A **water-repellent** fabric is resistant to wetting, but if the water strikes with enough force, it will penetrate the fabric. A **waterproof fabric** is a fabric that will not wet regardless of the water exposure time or the force with which the water strikes the fabric. Waterproof fabrics are almost always films or coated fabrics. Waterproof fabrics are compared with water-repellent and microporous fabrics in Table 18–2. (The Federal Trade Commission has

**Table 18–2** ❖
Comparison of waterproof and water-repellent fabrics.

| WATERPROOF FABRICS | WATER-REPELLENT FABRICS | WATER-REPELLENT MICROPOROUS FABRICS |
|---|---|---|
| Fabrics are films or low-count fabrics with a film coating. | High-count fabrics with a finish that coats the yarn but does not fill up the interstices of the fabric. | Fabric is a composite. |
| | **Characteristics** | |
| No water can penetrate. | Heavy rain will penetrate. | Liquid water and wind will not penetrate. |
| Most plastic fabrics stiffen in cold weather. | Fabric is pliable and little different from untreated fabric. | Fabric is pliable |
| Cheaper to produce. | | Expensive to produce. |
| | Fabric "breathes" and is comfortable for rainwear. | "Breathes" but pores may stretch or fill with soil. |
| Permanent. | Durable or renewable finish. | Permanent. |

suggested the use of the terms *durable* and *renewable* in describing water-repellent fabrics.) Many fabrics are water repellent because they incorporate a membrane. These fabrics were discussed in Chapter 15.

Water repellency is dependent on surface tension and fabric penetrability and is achieved by a combination of finish and fabric construction. Finishes that can be applied to fabric to make it repellent are fluorocarbons, wax emulsions, metallic soaps, and surface-active agents. They are applied to fabrics that have a very high warp count and are made with small regular yarns.

Fluorocarbons are a popular chemical for improving both water and oil repellency. Water repellency decreases significantly with washing but recovers with heat treatment. Fluorocarbons were discussed in more detail with soil- and stain-resistant finishes.

*Wax emulsions* and *metallic soaps* coat the yarns but do not fill the interstices or spaces between the yarns. These finishes are not permanent and are removed in care. They can be renewed.

*Surface-active agents* have molecules with one end that is water repellent and one end that reacts with the hydroxyl (OH) groups of cellulose. After these agents are applied, heat is used to bond the finish to the fabric. This finish is permanent to washing and dry cleaning.

Silicone finishes are the most common type of water-repellent chemical. When combined with durable press chemicals, they are durable. Silicone also gives a fabric good drape, soft hand, and stain resistance.

Although not achieved by use of a finish, microporous composite fabrics also produce a water-repellent effect. See Chapter 15 for more detail.

Water-repellent finishes render fabrics stain resistant to waterborne stains, oil-borne stains, or both. Durable water-repellent finishes often hold greasy stains more tenaciously than untreated fabrics. Unisec, Scotchgard, and Teflon are trade names for finishes that give resistance to both oil- and waterborne stains. Hydro-Pruf and Syl-mer are silicone finishes that resist waterborne stains. Teflon, Scotchgard, and Fybrite are trade names for fluorocarbon finishes.

## Absorbent Finishes

**Absorbent finishes** are designed to increase the moisture absorbency of the fabric. These finishes also increase the time needed to dry the fabric. They may aid in the dyeing process. Absorbent finishes are fair in durability. They are used on towels, diapers, underwear, and sportswear. They are applied as surface coatings for fibers and yarns. On nylon a solution of nylon 8 is used; on polyesters the finish changes the molecular structure of the fiber surface so that moisture is broken up into smaller particles that wick more readily; on cellulosics the finish makes them absorb more moisture. Fiber modifications and different fabric structures are more effective than finishes. Fantessa, Visa, and Zelcon are trade names.

## Antistatic Finishes

**Antistatic finishes** are important in both the production and use of fabrics. Static charges that develop on fabrics cause them to cling to machinery in the factory and to people, attract dust and lint, and produce sparks and shocks.

Control of static buildup on natural-fiber fabrics is done by increasing humidity and using lubricants, but these controls were not adequate with the thermoplastic fibers. Antistatic finishes were developed that (1) improve the surface conductivity so that excess electrons move to the atmosphere or ground; (2) attract water molecules, thus increasing the conductivity of the fiber; or (3) develop a charge opposite to that on the fiber, thus neutralizing the electrostatic charge. The most effective finishes combine all three effects. Most antistatic finishes are not durable and must be replaced during care. Most finishes use quaternary ammonium compounds. Washing aids such as fabric softeners also help to control static.

Incorporating antistatic substances into the fibers gives the best static control. Most manufactured fibers are produced in antistatic form especially for rugs, carpets, lingerie, and uniforms (see Chapter 6). Some trade names of antistatic nylon variants are Ultron, Antron, Staticgard, and Anso.

## Fabric Softeners

**Fabric softeners** or hand builders were developed to improve the hand of harsh textiles, which may develop as a result of resin finishes or heat setting of synthetics. Types of softeners include anionic, cationic, and nonionic. *Anionic softeners* are usually sulfonated, negatively charged fatty acids and oils. These softeners are padded onto the fibers because of a lack of affinity for the fiber. Anionic softeners often are used commercially on cellulosic fibers and silk. *Cationic softeners* are most often used in domestic washing. These softeners have an affinity for the fiber. They tend to yellow with age and may build up on the fiber if used frequently, reducing the absorbency of the fabric. Cationic softeners may contain quaternary ammonium compounds, and these compounds may confer some incidental antibacterial properties. *Nonionic softeners* must be padded onto the fabric. These commercial softeners are usually a fatty acid.

Silicone softeners produce a dryer hand compared to that of the other compounds listed here. Better wrinkle resistance and durability occur when these softeners are combined with durable-press finishes.

## Thermal Finishes

**Thermal finishes** are used to minimize heat flow through a fabric. They insulate from temperature extremes: very hot or cold conditions.

Polyethylene glycol (PEG) can be used as a thermal finish because of its ability to absorb or release heat in appropriate environmental conditions as it undergoes a phase change. The chemical can change phase several times: from solid to liquid (absorb heat) or liquid to solid (release heat). Thus, the wearer is warmed or cooled depending on the phase change that is occurring. The time span of these phase changes is generally

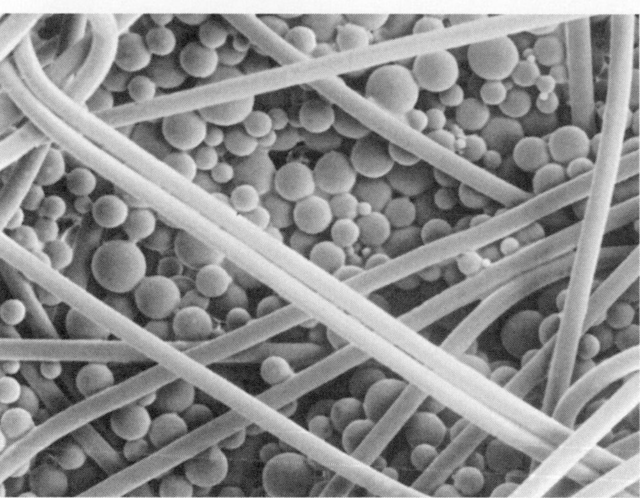

**FIGURE 18–13** ❖ Microencapsulated phase-change thermal finish. (COURTESY OF GATEWAY TECHNOLOGIES, INC.)

in the range of 20 minutes. The finish is applied by Neutratherm as Polytherm. It is used on active sportswear. Besides the heat aspects, the finish also contributes antistatic characteristics, water absorbency, resiliency, soil release, and pilling resistance. Polytherm has also been investigated as an effective shrink-resist finish for machine-washable wools.

Another phase-change thermal finish is Outlast® by Gateway Technologies, Inc. The phase-change chemical is microencapsulated and applied in a thin coat onto a hydroentangled nonwoven fabric (see Figure 18–13). The coating adds only 0.002 inch to the thickness of the nonwoven fabric. The insulation properties are not affected by compression, washing, or moisture. The chemicals change phase at temperatures very close to skin temperature. This finish is used in gloves, boots, socks, garment liners, sleeping bags, ski and winter wear, wetsuits, jackets, blankets, and hats.

# BIOLOGICAL CONTROL FINISHES

## Insect and Moth Control Finishes

Moths and carpet beetles are likely to damage fibers containing protein, such as wool. In addition, insects are likely to cause damage to other fibers if soil is present. More than 100 species of insects and spiders have been known to damage textiles, including silverfish, crickets, and cockroaches. In most cases, a combination of soil as a food source and environmental conditions are necessary for a problem to develop. Manufactured fibers are not immune, but natural fibers are far more likely to fall victim to insect damage.

**Insect and moth control finishes** are also known as fumigants, insecticides, insect-repellent finishes, and other terms implying resistance to a specific insect pest, like silverfish or moths. Both moths and carpet beetles attack not only 100 percent wool but also blends of wool and other fibers. Although they can digest only the wool, the insects eat through the other fibers. The damage is done by the larvae, not the adult moth. Clothes moths are small, about ¼ inch long. Their larvae shun bright sunlight and live in the dark. For this reason, it is necessary to clean often under sofas, under furniture cushions, in the creases of chairs and garments, and in dark closets.

Most furnishing fabrics of wool are treated with a moth control or mothproofing agent. Approximately 70 percent of mothproofing agents are used by the carpet industry so that wool and wool blend carpets obtain the "Wool Mark" standard of quality. If information to that effect is not on the label, check into it.

Traditionally, mothproofing used a chemical, often Permethrin, at the scouring or dyeing stage. Because excess chemical would be flushed into nearby water systems, killing invertebrates, methods of applying Permethrin via foam processes are being developed.

Permethrin repels and kills spiders, ticks, mosquitoes, and other crawling and flying insects. It is being applied to tents of all kinds and canvas used in fold-down camping trailers and hunting blinds. Expel® by Graniteville is odorless and resistant to washing, heat, and ultraviolet light.

Means of controlling insect damage include:

1. Cold storage. It decreases insect activity so damage is much less likely to occur. Museums use freezing to control insect problems in storage areas because the extreme conditions kill the insects. This technique is generally not practical for consumer use.
2. Odors that repel. Paradichlorobenzene and naphthalene (mothballs) can be used during storage, but use should be carefully monitored and only when absolutely necessary. These insecticides are poisons and should be used with caution.
3. Stomach poisons. Fluorides and silicofluorides are finishes for dry-cleanable wool.
4. Contact poisons. DDT is very effective but has been banned in the United States and elsewhere.
5. Chemical additives in the dye bath. These permanently change the fiber, making it unpalatable to the larvae. Surface and on-site applications may result in color loss or yellowing of carpet fibers.

## Mold and Mildew Control Finishes

**Molds** and **mildew** will grow on and damage both cellulosic and protein textiles, although the problem is far more common on cellulosics. They will grow on, but not damage, thermoplastic fibers. Finishes to prevent this growth are also known as fungicides or mildew-preventative finishes.

Prevention is the best solution to the problem because cures are often impossible. Mildew is an attack in which the microorganism feeds on the fiber surface, creating tiny pits and craters. The color associated with mildew is due to shadows from the pits. To prevent mold or mildew, keep textiles clean and dry. Soiled items should be kept dry and washed as soon as possible. Sunning and airing should be done frequently during periods of high humidity. An electric light and dehumidifiers can be used in dark, humid storage places.

If mildew occurs, wash the article immediately. Mild stains can be removed by bleaching. Mold and mildew growth is prevented by many compounds. Salicylanilide is often used on cellulosic fibers and wool under the trade names of Shirlan and Shirlan NA.

## Rot-Proof Finishes

**Rot-proof finishes** are used primarily on industrial products used outdoors to improve their durability and longevity. Textiles rot when they are exposed to moist, warm conditions for several days or more. Microbes present in the soil secrete an enzyme that disintegrates the textile. Cellulosic textiles are most susceptible to rotting, but protein fibers will rot under the right conditions. N-methylol and glyoxal are finishing agents that impart rot resistance to textiles. These finishes are most often used on cotton canvas for tents, tarpaulins, awnings, lawn and deck furniture, and other outdoor applications.

## Antimicrobial Finishes

**Antimicrobial finishes** are used to inhibit the growth of bacteria and other odor-causing germs, prevent decay and damage from perspiration, control the spread of disease, and reduce the risk of infection following injury. Antimicrobial finishes are also known as *antibacterial, bacteriostatic, germicidal, antiodor,* or *antiseptic finishes.*

These finishes are important in skin-contact clothing, shoe linings, hospital linens, and contract carpeting. The chemicals used are surface reactants, mostly quaternary ammonium compounds. Zirconium peroxides can be formed on the surface of cotton fabrics to give antimicrobial properties. Those substances can be added to the spinning solution of manufactured fibers for use in wall coverings and upholstery. Most diaper-services add the finish during each laundering. Eversan and Sanitized are two trade names.

These finishes include chemical treatment, gas treatment, and irradiation treatment. Chemical antimicrobial finishes may cause yellowing and fading on nylon; this can be a major problem for carpet. The gas treatment involves exposure to ethylene oxide gas. Since the gas is a hazardous material, it is being replaced with irradiation sterilization, also known as electron beam sterilization. This treatment is cheaper, simpler, safer, and ideal for medical products like bandages, sutures, and surgical gloves. Since the beam can penetrate thermoplastic and foil packaging, items can be packaged and then treated. This process maintains the sterile environment until the package is opened.

## Microencapsulated Finishes

**Microencapsulated finishes** incorporate a water-soluble material in a tiny capsule form. The capsules are between 5 and 50 microns in size and may contain fragrance, insect repellents, disinfectants, cleaning agents, or other materials (Figure 18–14). The microcapsules are sprayed onto a nonwoven material and held in place with a polyvinyl alcohol or acrylic binder. The finished fabric may be durable for up to ten washings for some products. Toxicological tests show no skin irritation. End uses for microcapsules with fragrance include ribbons, handkerchiefs, scarves, curtains, furnishings, women's hosiery, sweaters, ties, and T-shirts. Normal physical forces during wear rupture the capsules and release the fragrance. Insect-repellent microcapsules have been used in underwear. Extra repellent can be released by squeezing the fabric. Mothproofing agents have been microencapsulated for application to wool carpet. Microcapsules containing bactericidal agents are applied to hospital gowns and bed linens, protective clothing worn in the pharmaceutical and food industries, socks, underwear, and active wear.

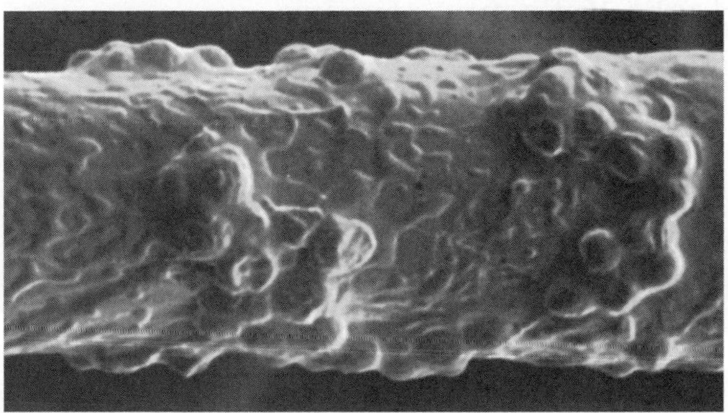

**FIGURE 18–14** ❖ Microencapsulated insect repellent finish. (COURTESY OF *REVIEW OF PROGRESS IN COLORATION*.)

# SAFETY-RELATED FINISHES

## Flame-Retardant Finishes

Each year a large number of fatalities and injuries result from fires associated with flammable fabrics. Financial loss from such fires is estimated in the millions of dollars. Five common causes of these fires are smoking in bed, starting fires with flammable liquids, children playing with matches and lighters, burning trash, and being trapped in a burning structure.

Fabrics that burn quickly are sheer or lightweight fabrics and napped, pile, or tufted surfaces. Some items made from these constructions ignite quickly, burn with great intensity, and are difficult to extinguish. "Torch" sweaters, fringed cowboy chaps, and chenille berets are examples of some apparel items that caused tragic accidents. Some style features also present a fire hazard. Long, full sleeves, flared skirts, ruffles, frills, and flowing robes are examples in apparel.

Many terms are used when discussing the ability of a fabric to resist ignition, burn more slowly than normal, or self-extinguish once the source of ignition has been removed from the fabric. The following is a list of definitions from the American Society for Testing and Materials:

- **Fire retardance:** The resistance to combustion of a material when tested under specified conditions.
- **Flame resistance:** The property of a material whereby flaming combustion is prevented, terminated, or inhibited following application of a flaming or nonflaming source of ignition, with or without subsequent removal of the ignition source.
- **Flammability:** Those characteristics of a material that pertain to its relative ease of ignition and relative ability to sustain combustion.

Fabrics may be made flame resistant by using inherently flame-resistant fibers or fiber variants that have been made flame resistant by adding flame retardants to the spinning solution, or by applying flame-retardant finishes to the fabrics.

The burning characteristics of fibers are listed in Table 3–15. Fibers that are inherently flame resistant are aramid, modacrylic, novoloid, saran, PBI, sulfar, and vinal/vinyon matrix fibers. Fibers in which flame-retardant chemicals have been added to the spinning solution are some acetates, nylons, polyesters, and rayons.

**Flame-retardant finishes** function in a variety of ways. The finish may block the flame's access to fuel and hinder further flame propagation. A foam-containing, flame-extinguishing gas may be produced. The solid may be modified so that the products of combustion are not volatile or require excess heat to continue the fire.

Flame-retardant finishes are used on cotton, rayon, nylon, and polyester fabrics. Flame-retardant finishes must be durable (able to withstand 50 washings), nontoxic, and noncarcinogenic. Ideally, they should not change the hand and texture of fabrics or have unpleasant odors. Most of these finishes are not visible and they add significantly to the cost of the item, so the consumer is asked to pay for something that cannot be seen.

Flame-retardant finishes can be classified as durable and nondurable. These durable finishes are specific to fiber type and are usually phosphate compounds or salts, halogenated organic compounds, or inorganic salts. Examples of durable finishes for polyester and cellulosics include the trade names of Antiblaze and Pyroset. Many other flame-retardant finishes are sold by trade names in addition to these mentioned here, but few consumer products are sold with the finish identified by trade name.

Flame-retardant finishes are less expensive than flame-resistant fibers or fiber variants. Knitting or weaving gray goods that can be given a topical flame-retardant finish when necessary is a more economical procedure for fabric producers.

Flame-retardant finishes generally require that a fairly high amount of finish be added to the fabric. **Add-on** describes the percentage by weight of solids left on a fabric after finishing and drying. Normal rates for cellulosics range from 5 to 30 percent of the weight of the fabric. For polyester, the normal rates are 1 to 10 percent of the weight of the fabric. The range of add-on is related to the specific chemical used, the performance expectations for the product, and the cost of the finish. The finishes for cotton are of two general types. The first is referred to as the ammonium cure and provides excellent flame-retardant protection with minimal strength loss. However, it requires the use of special equipment, so the investment in capital is great. The ammonium cure finish is more commonly used on apparel. The second type is the pyrovatex process by Ciba-Geigy, which uses conventional finishing equipment and a resin. The resin results in greater strength loss. This finish is more commonly used in furnishings.

**CONCERNS AND LIMITATIONS** Cost, durability, and care of these finishes are the greatest problems for the consumer. The higher cost of research and development of fibers and finishes, testing of fabrics and products, and liability insurance result in a high cost of apparel and furnishing items. Because the items look no different, the consumer often thinks the item is overpriced. Because of government standards, the consumer has limited choice; for example, people who do not smoke in bed must pay a higher price for mattresses, because only those mattresses that pass flammability standards can be sold in interstate commerce. However, the safety component is present regardless of the consumer's preference.

Most of the topical finishes require special care in laundering to preserve the flame resistance. Labels should be followed carefully. Labels may include these statements: Do not bleach, do not use soap, do not use hot water. Excess soil can block the effectiveness of these finishes, so frequent care may be required.

Flame-retardant-treated fabrics may exhibit some problems for consumers. Cost is greater. The hand may be harsh. The fabric may be weaker and less abrasion resistant than it would be without the finish. The finish may give the wearer a false sense of security. Remember, the finish is designed to make the fabric flame retardant. It will not prevent the fabric from igniting or burning, although ignition and rate of burning will be slower with the finish.

## Liquid Barrier Finishes

**Liquid barrier finishes** protect the wearer from liquids penetrating through a fabric. These finishes are important to health care professionals because of the presence of viral and bacterial pathogens in body fluids. Agricultural and chemical workers also require liquid barrier protection because of the toxic and hazardous liquids with which they work. It is difficult to develop finishes that provide the degree of protection and comfort required. Researchers continue to work with materials, including polyethylene glycol, that look promising.

*Antipesticide protective finishes* protect the wearer of protective clothing from pesticides penetrating through the fabric and aid in pesticide removal during washing. Research in this area continues.

## Light-Reflecting Finishes

**Light-reflecting finishes** are used on fabrics to produce increased visibility of wearers at night. There are two types: fluorescent dyes and small glass spheres. Fluorescent dyes will be discussed in more detail in Chapters 19 and 20. The small glass spheres are used in retroreflective tape that is used on apparel. The spheres alter the angle of reflected light and make objects more visible. Both types of finishes are painted or printed on the fabric's surface. Bonding agents are used with the retroreflective finish. These finishes are expensive and durable to a limited number of washings and are used most often on trim for footwear and action wear. Occasionally, these finishes are used on fabric for social events because of the effect with black light.

## KEY TERMS

Special-purpose finish
Functional finish
Stabilization
Shrinkage control
Relaxation shrinkage
Progressive shrinkage
Compressive shrinkage process
London shrunk
Heat setting
Glass transition temperature ($T_g$)
Surface coating
Halogenation
Shape-retention finish
Cross-links
Wrinkle-resistant finish
Durable press
Precured process
Postcured process
Immersion
Metered addition
Quality-control standards
Soil-release finish
Stain-release finish
Abrasion-resistant finish
Antislip finish
Fume fading–resistant finish
Metallic coating
Plastic coating
Water-repellent finish
Waterproof
Absorbent finish
Antistatic finish
Fabric softener
Thermal finish
Insect and moth control finish
Mold and mildew control finish
Rot-proof finish
Antimicrobial finish
Microencapsulated finish
Add-on
Fire retardance
Flame resistance
Flammability
Flame-retardant finish
Liquid barrier finish
Light-reflecting finish

## QUESTIONS

1. In what manner do the stabilization finishes work for the following products?
   100 percent wool sweater
   100 percent cotton upholstery of polished cotton
   100 percent acetate antique satin draperies
   65 percent cotton/35 percent polyester flannelette bedsheet
2. Differentiate between postcured and precured durable-press fabrics and garments in both the process and product performance.
3. Compare and contrast water-repellent and stain-repellent/soil-release finishes.
4. For what end uses are metallic, plastic, and foam coatings used? What purpose do these coatings serve?
5. Explain how these finishes enhance comfort:
   water-repellent — fabric softener
   antistatic — thermal finish
6. For what fibers and products are moth control finishes likely to be used? How do they function?
7. How can flame retardancy be achieved with fabrics?
8. Explain how these finishes affect other fabric or product properties such as comfort, care, durability, and appearance.
   halogenated wool — antistatic nylon
   durable-press cotton — flame-retardant rayon

## SUGGESTED READINGS


"Carpets: Mothproofing the Ecology-Safe Way." (1994/1995, December/January). *Canadian Textile Journal,* p. 28.

Bain, P. J. (1995, March). "The Post-Sew Phenomenon." *Bobbin,* pp. 82, 84–88.

Blanch, Robert M. (1995, May). "Optimization of Properties for Wrinkle-Free Fabrics." *American Dyestuff Reporter,* pp. 26, 28, 30.

Cotton, Inc. (1995, April). "Cotton Incorporated: Controlled Chemical Metering for Wrinkle-Resistant Garment Finishing." *Textile World,* p. 72.

Dunn, Kenneth L. (1995, May). "The Evolution of Durable Press Products." *American Dyestuff Reporter,* pp. 1, 53.

Harris, Paul W., and Hangey, Dale A. (1989). "Stain Resist Chemistry for Nylon 6 Carpet." *Textile Chemist and Colorist, 21*(11), pp. 25–30.

Jackson, Doug, and Shinall, Keith (September, 1988). "Taking the Heat." *Industrial Fabric Products Review,* pp. 63–65.

Johnson, Ann S., Gupta, Bhupendar S., and Tomasino, Charles (1994, June). "Topical Treatments of Nylon Carpets: Fluorochemicals and Stainblockers." *American Dyestuff Reporter,* pp. 17–21, 39.

Needles, Howard (1986). *Textile Fibers, Dyes, Finishes, and Processes.* Park Ridge, NJ: Noyes Publications.

Nelson, G. (1991). "Microencapsulates in Textile Coloration and Finishing." *Review in the Progress of Coloration, 21,* pp. 72–85.

North, Bernard F. (1991). "Reactants for Durable Press Textiles: The Formaldehyde Dilemma." *Textile Chemist and Colorist, 23*(10), pp. 21–22.

Payne, John D. (1996, May). "A Durable Antiodor Finish for Cotton Textiles." *Textile Chemist and Colorist, 28*(5), pp. 28–30.

Reagan, Barbara M., Dusaj, Shailendra, Johnson, Diana G., and Hodges, Diane M. (1990). "Influence of Aftermarket Carpet Protectors on the Soiling, Flammability, and Electrical Resistivity of Nylon 6." *Textile Chemist and Colorist, 22*(4), pp. 16–20.

Refal, R. (1992, May). "Rot Proofing and Easy Care Properties of Cotton and Modified Cotton Fabrics Through Treatment with Glyoxal." *American Dyestuff Reporter,* pp. 40, 42, 44, 46, 47, 49, 50.

Trotman, E. R. (1984). *Dyeing and Chemical Technology of Textile Fibers.* New York: John Wiley & Sons.

Zeronian, S. Haig, and Collins, Martha J. (1988). "Improving the Comfort of Polyester Fabrics." *Textile Chemist and Colorist, 20*(4), pp. 25–28

*Chapter 19*

# DYEING AND PRINTING

OBJECTIVES

- To understand the theory, techniques, and processes of dyeing and printing textiles.
- To relate quality and performance to the materials and processes used in dyeing or printing.
- To differentiate among the stages of dyeing and types of printing.
- To relate dyeing or printing to the marketability and serviceability of textile products.
- To identify problems related to dyed and printed textiles and textile products.
- To understand the basics of color matching.

Color is one of the most important characteristics of apparel and furnishing items. It is a significant factor in the appeal and marketability of textile products. This chapter discusses the characteristics of color from an identification perspective (when color was added to the product), a process perspective (how color was added to the product), a serviceability perspective (how color affects the serviceability of the product), and a problem-solving perspective (what kind of problems can develop because of color).

Although home dyeing has been a common practice, most consumers are not happy with the process because it is difficult to predict the final color, the color may not be fast, uniform and level colors are hard to achieve, and the mess and clean-up can be a problem. Commercial dyeing uses specialized equipment and dyes or pigments not available to the consumer. In addition, dyers and printers have a great deal of training and experience that minimize problems with the process or finished product.

The goal of adding color to textiles is to produce an appealing, level, fast color on a product at a reasonable price with good performance and minimal environmental impact. **Level** describes a color that is uniform and looks the same throughout the product. Fast colors are those that do not shift hue or fade when exposed to light and other environmental factors. Fast colors do not move onto other fabrics or material during storage, processing, use, or care. Evaluating **colorfastness** is crucial to understanding factors that may create problems in production or in consumer use. Evaluating colorfastness includes procedures related to finishing in textile mills, heating and pressing in production facilities, and use and care by consumers.

Color has always been important in textiles. Until 1856, natural dyes and pigments obtained from plants, insects, and minerals were used as coloring agents. When William Henry Perkin discovered mauve, the first synthetic dye, the synthetic dye industry came into being. Europe was the center for synthetic dyes until World War I interrupted trade with Germany and a dye industry developed in the United States. Today there are hundreds of colorants or coloring agents from which to choose.

Consumers are not aware of the complex problems involved in achieving a particular color in a uniform manner on a textile product. They expect that the color will remain vivid and uniform throughout the life of the product, and that it will not create problems in use, care, or storage. It is remarkable that color creates as few complaints from consumers as it does, since achieving a uniform or level dyeing is a difficult process. Slight differences in fabric due to minor irregularities in fiber, yarn, fabric, or finishing can result in subtle color variations that can be very obvious in finished products when seams join parts cut from different bolts.

Adding color to a textile product is a complex process. Fiber chemistry plays an important role. Differences in chemical composition of fibers were discussed in Chapters 3 through 9. These differences can be seen in various properties and performance characteristics. A match between the chemistry of the dye and that of the fiber is needed in order for the color to be permanent. Any colored textile product may be exposed to a wide variety of potential color degradants, such as detergent, perspiration, dry cleaning solvents, sunlight, and makeup. To achieve a permanent or fast color, the dye must be permanently attached to or trapped within the fiber by using a combination of heat, pressure, and chemical assistants. Since access to the fiber's internal regions is critical, crystallinity, chemical finishes, and fabric and yarn structure are factors that influence the success of dyeing.

## Color Theory

Color theory describes a complex phenomenon that requires studying the physics of light, the chemistry of colored objects, the biology of the eye, the behavioral sciences in terms of what colors mean to society or the individual, and the aesthetics of how one appreciates what one sees. These elements interact to determine what is seen and how it is perceived. Understanding these interactions helps us understand why colors are hard to perceive in low light, why items that match in the store don't match at home, and why some colors are used in certain settings.

The color we see depends on the light source, the colorant used, and the human eye. Color vision or color blindness may restrict the perception of colors. When we work with different textiles, the colors may not always match. Even though both textiles may be 100 percent cotton, the colorant may differ. **Metamerism** describes a color matching under one light source, but not under any other light source. The **Bezold effect** describes two or more colors merged into one new color. This effect is seen when small-scale prints or yarn-dyed fabrics are viewed from a distance. One does not see each color, but rather a new color that blends the individual colors together. This effect was used by Impressionist painters and is used in color printers such as ink-jet printers.

Color measurement, the process of assigning numerical values to a color, is done to assist in color matching and shade sorting. Color measurement can be done with the trained human eye or with instruments that assess color in three or more dimensions. Many different instruments and systems are used in this complex process. **Color matching** describes the process of developing a formula to reproduce a color. Color matching is important when designers submit a color swatch or when coordinating fabrics are desired. **Shade sorting,** grouping fabrics by color, is done so that all fabric of one color purchased by a manufacturer match. Thus, when fabric is layered prior to cutting out product parts, there is less concern that parts from different layers will not match when sewn into a completed product.

❖

# Colorants

Color can be added to textile objects by either dyes or pigments. Because there are major differences between these coloring substances and the ways they are added to fabrics, this section will differentiate between pigments and dyes.

## Pigments

Pigments have become very important in coloring fabrics. More than 80 percent of the printed fabrics on the U.S. market are colored with pigments. Although previously pigment prints were considered low quality and cheap, that is no longer the situation. Pigments are used on all kinds of goods at various quality levels and price points for a variety of reasons. Pigmented fabrics do not require a *wash-off* step to rinse excess colorant from the fabric. However, *washdown* with fabrics laundered by consumers can be a problem if the binder has poor resistance to water or abrasion. Pigments' popularity is due to their relatively simple procedures for application, ability to be applied to almost all fibers and fabrics, extensive color range, excellent light fastness, potential to combine some finishing with pigment coloration, and low cost. *Ink* is another term for pigments when they are combined with other ingredients in a paste form. Besides being used in printing, pigments are used to color some solid-colored garments during garment "dyeing."

**Pigments** are insoluble color particles that are held on the surface of a fabric by a binding agent. Their application is quick, simple, and economical. Any color can be used on any fiber, because the pigments are held on mechanically. Fabric problems such as stiffening, crocking, and fading may be encountered.

Pigments need to be bonded to the fiber surface. The binder works like a glue and binds the pigment to the fiber. The type of binder is determined by the fiber content of the fabric and the performance expectations for the product. Binders can be used to produce soft and flexible fabrics. Ideally, binders should not interfere with the color of the pigment, nor with the hand and function of the fabric. Binders are heat activated or catalyst activated.

Pigments combine several ingredients to produce the desired appearance. Catalysts help bond the pigment to the fiber. Opacifiers produce a pigment with good covering power. some opacifiers produce a matte luster, others a full gloss luster, and still others a pearlescent or metallic luster. Thickeners produce dark shades and a paste that does not migrate or spread from the area applied. Thinners or reducers are used with pastes that are too thick for one reason or another. Antibleeding agents eliminate the halo effect and keep the edges of a print sharp and clear. Softeners maintain a soft hand after printing. Retarders slow the drying rate. This is especially important in screen printing to keep the screens working. Dryers speed the drying of slow-drying inks.

Pigments produce the color of the paste, although some other ingredients may alter the color. Pigment colors are easier to match than dye colors because the color is held on the surface. Dyes are more difficult to match because the chemical reactions of dyeing may cause the dye to shift color. The hue shift is more difficult to control in dyeing compared to pigment printing. Some of the biggest problem areas with pigments are the change in hand with some inks, washdown problems, and poor dry cleaning fastness of some binders.

Pigments also may be mixed in the spinning solution of manufactured fibers. Mass pigmentation of manufactured fibers will be discussed with the stages of dyeing.

## Dyes

A **dye** is an organic compound composed of a chromophore, the colored portion of the dye molecule, and an auxochrome, which slightly alters the color. The auxochrome makes the dye soluble and is a site for bonding to the fiber. Figure 19–1 shows examples of dye molecules.

Dye must be molecules that can be thoroughly dissolved in water or some other carrier in order to penetrate the fiber. Undissolved particles of dye stay on the outside of the fiber and have poor fastness to surface abrasion and bleeding. Dyes have great color strength; a small amount of dye is able to color large quantities of fabric. Pigments have much lower color strength; much more pigment is needed to color an equal amount of fabric. Most dyes bond chemically with the fiber and are found in the interior of the fiber, rather than on the surface where pigments are found. Most colors on textiles are achieved by dye or pigment mixtures rather than a single dye or pigment.

A *fluorescent dye* absorbs light at one wavelength and re-emits that energy at another wavelength. Fluorescent dyes are used for many applications. In detergents, they make whites appear whiter and mask yellowing of fibers.

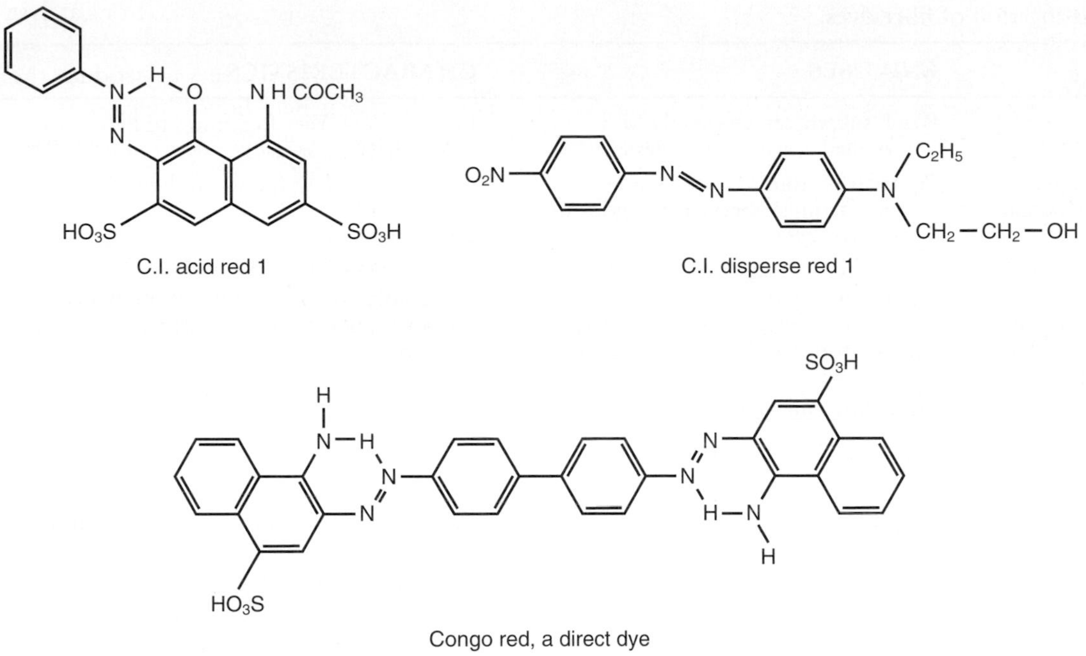

C.I. acid red 1

C.I. disperse red 1

Congo red, a direct dye

**FIGURE 19–1** ❖ Dye molecules: (a) C. I. Acid Red 1; (b) C. I. Disperse Red 1; (c) Direct Dye Congo Red. (COURTESY OF COLOUR INDEX.)

Fluorescent dyes are used in safety clothing to increase the wearer's visibility at night, to give a bright, intense glow to the color, and in some medical procedures. These dyes also are used in costumes for their safety and glow-in-the-dark effects and in fashion apparel for bright, neonlike colors.

A **dye process** describes the environment created for the introduction of dye by hot water, steam, or dry heat. Chemical additives like salt or acid are used to regulate penetration of the dye. A knowledge of fiber-dye interactions, methods of dyeing, and equipment results in a better understanding of color behavior.

The stage at which color is applied has little to do with fastness but has a great deal to do with dye penetration. It is governed by fabric design, quality level, and cost. In order for a fabric to be colored, the dye must penetrate the fiber and either be combined chemically with it or be locked inside it. Fibers that dye easily are those that are absorbent and have sites within their molecules that react with the dye molecules. The dye reacts with the surface molecules first. Moisture and heat swell the fibers, causing their polymer chains to move farther apart so that sites in the internal regions of the fiber are exposed to react with the dye. During cooling and drying the chains move back together, trapping the dye in the fiber. Wool dyed with an acid dye is a good example of a fiber that is absorbent and has many sites that chemically react with the dye to color the fiber.

The thermoplastic fibers can be difficult to dye because their absorbency is low. However, most of these fibers are modified to accept different classes of dyes. This makes it possible to achieve different color effects or a good solid color in blends of unlike fibers by piece dyeing.

No one dye is fast to everything, and the dyes within a class, a grouping of similar dyes, are not equally fast. A complete range of shades is not available in each of the dye classes; for example, some dye classes are weak in greens. The dyer chooses a dye or mixes several dyes suited to the color desired, the fiber content, the end use of the fabric, the performance expectations of the product, and the cost of the process. The dyer must apply the color so that it penetrates and is held in the fiber. Occasionally the manufacturer or the consumer selects fabrics for uses for which they were not intended. For example, an apparel fabric used for draperies may not be fast to sunlight. Suppliers or retailers should be notified when products or fabrics do not give satisfactory performance.

Dyes are classified by chemical composition or method of application. Table 19–1 lists major dye classes along with some of their characteristics and end uses.

❖

## STAGES OF DYEING

Color may be added to textiles during the fiber, yarn, fabric, or product stage, depending on the color effects

**TABLE 19–1** ❖ Classification of fiber dyes.

| DYES | END USES | CHARACTERISTICS |
|---|---|---|
| **Acid** (anionic). Complete color range. | Wool, silk, nylon, modified rayon. Modified acrylic and polyester. | Bright colors. Vary in fastness to light. May have poor fastness to washing. |
| **Azoic** (naphthol and rapidogens). Complete color range. Moderate cost. | Primarily cotton. May be used on manufactured fibers such as polyester. | Good to excellent fastness to light and washing. Bright shades. Poor resistance to crocking. |
| **Cationic** (basic). Used with mordant on fibers other than silk and wool and acrylic. Complete color range. | Used primarily on acrylics. Direct prints on acetate. Discharge prints on cotton. Used on modified polyester and nylon. | Fast colors on acrylics. On natural fibers, poor fastness to light, washing, perspiration. Tend to bleed and crock. |
| **Developed,** direct. Dyes developed in the fiber. Complete color range. Duller colors than acid or basic. | Primarily cellulose fibers. Discharge prints. | Good to excellent lightfastness. Fair washfastness. |
| **Direct** (substantive). Largest and most commercially significant dye class. Complete color range. | Used on cellulosic fibers. | Good colorfastness to light. May have poor washfastness. |
| **Disperse.** Dye particles disperse in water. Good color range. | Developed for acetate, used on most synthetic fibers. | Fair to excellent light and wash fastness. Blues and violets on acetate fume fade. |
| **Fluorescent** brighteners. Specific types for most common fibers. | Used on textiles and in detergents. | Mask yellowing and off-white aspects that occur naturally or develop with age and soil. |
| **Mordant** (chrome). Fair color range. Duller than acid dyes. | Used on same fibers as listed for acid dyes. | Good to excellent light and wash fastness. Dull colors. |
| **Natural** or vegetable. Derived from plant, animal or mineral sources. Earliest dyes used. | Minor dye class; used to dye some apparel and furnishings. | Fastness varies. Limited colors and availability. |
| **Reactive** or fiber-reactive. Combines chemically with fiber. Produces brights shades. | Primarily used on cotton. Some are used on other cellulosics and wool, silk, or nylon. | Good light and wash fastness. Sensitive to chlorine bleach. |
| **Sulfur.** Insoluble in water. Complete color range except for red. Dull colors. | Primarily for cotton. Heavy work clothes. Most widely used black dye. | Poor to excellent light and wash fastness. Sensitive to chlorine bleach. Stored goods may become tender. |
| **Vat.** Insoluble in water. Incomplete color range. | Primarily for cotton work clothes, sportswear, prints, drapery fabrics. Some use on cotton/polyester blends. | Good to excellent light and wash fastness. |

desired and on the quality or end use of the fabric. Better dye penetration is achieved with fiber dyeing than with yarn dyeing, with yarn dyeing than with piece dyeing, and with piece dyeing than with product dyeing. Good dye penetration is easier to achieve in products where the dyeing liquid or liquor is free to move between adjacent fibers. This freedom of movement is easiest to achieve in loose fibers. It is more difficult to achieve in products where yarn twist, fabric structure, and seams or other product features minimize liquor movement.

As manufacturers and producers attempt to produce specific colors as needed, they try to add color to products as late in processing as possible. But this puts tremendous demands on dyeing. The earlier in processing color is added, the less critical is the uniformity or *levelness* of the dyeing. For example, in fiber dyeing, two adjacent fibers need not be exactly the same color since minor color differences in the yarn will be masked because of the small amount of each fiber that is visible. However, the color must be level in products that are

**TABLE 19–2** ❖ Stages of dyeing.

| STAGE | INDUSTRY TERM | ADVANTAGES | DISADVANTAGES | IDENTIFYING FEATURES |
|---|---|---|---|---|
| Prefiber | Mass pigmentation or solution dyeing.<br>Gel dyeing. | Excellent fastness.<br>Good for hard-to-dye fibers or products or uses that require exceptional fastness. | Cannot respond to rapid fashion change.<br>High cost.<br>Limited to manufactured fibers. | Solid uniform color throughout fiber; used for hard-to-dye fibers. |
| Fiber | Stock or top* dyeing. | Heather and tone-on-tone fashions possible.<br>Good dye penetration.<br>Considered high quality. | Slower response to rapid fashion change.<br>High cost. | Color may vary from fiber to fiber. |
| Yarn | Skein, package, or beam dyeing*. | Used for structural design plaids, stripes, and other patterns.<br>Good dye penetration.<br>Considered high quality. | Slow response to rapid fashion change.<br>High cost.<br>Used to produce patterned fabric. | Can trace yarn path in fabric.<br>Rare with solid colors.<br>Yarn color forms pattern. |
| Fabric | Piece dyeing.<br>Flat or rope dyeing*.<br>Cross or union dyeing**. | Inexpensive process.<br>Quick response to fashion changes.<br>Low cost. | Rope form may cause irregular color.<br>Continuous process may contribute to ending problems. | Solid-color fabric of single fibers and union-dyed blends; patterns or heather effect with cross-dyed blends. |
| Sewn product | Garment (for apparel).<br>Product (for other items). | Least expensive process.<br>Quickest response to fashion change.<br>Low cost.<br>Distressed looks and other product finishes possible. | Requires well-prepared materials.<br>Layered areas may have poor penetration.<br>Matching of all parts, thread, trim, and fasteners difficult. | Solid color fabric (trims and other materials may not match).<br>Labels may be tinted. |

* Describes the form of the textile or the manner in which it is handled.

** Refers to presence of two or more generic fiber types.

sewn before the color is added. Areas where the color is slightly irregular will be apparent to the casual observer and will result in the item being labeled a second. Level commercial dyeing is not easy, as anyone who has attempted dyeing on a small scale can attest.

This section discusses the stage at which the dye or pigment is added to the textile. (See Table 19–2.) Dyeing can be done at any stage; printing is usually done at the fabric stage. However, some yarns are printed and some finished products are printed. Current product printing is usually in the form of a design applied to one area of the product, such as the designs on fronts or sleeves of active sportswear. This section does not address color-grown fibers such as wool from a black sheep or naturally colored cotton. For information regarding color grown fibers, see Chapters 4 and 5.

## Fiber Stage

In the **fiber-dyeing process,** color is added before yarn spinning. Fiber-dyed items usually have a slightly irregular color like a heather or tone-on-tone gray.

1. **Mass pigmentation** is also known as **solution dyed,** *spun dyed, dope dyeing, mass coloration,* or **producer colored.** It consists of adding colored pigments or dyes to the spinning solution before the fiber is formed. Thus each fiber is colored as it is spun. The color is an integral part of the fiber and fast to most color degradants. This method is preferred for fibers that are difficult to dye by other methods, for certain products, or where it is difficult to get a certain depth of shade. Colors are generally few because of inventory limitations. Examples of mass pigmented fibers include many olefins, black polyester, and acrylics for awnings and tarpaulins.

   Another type of dyeing similar to mass pigmentation is *gel dyeing.* The color is incorporated in the fiber, usually acrylic, while it is in the soft gel stage. This occurs in the narrow time frame between fiber extrusion and fiber coagulation.
2. *Stock,* or *fiber, dyeing* is used when mottled or heather effects are desired. Dye is added to loose fibers before yarn spinning. Good dye penetration is

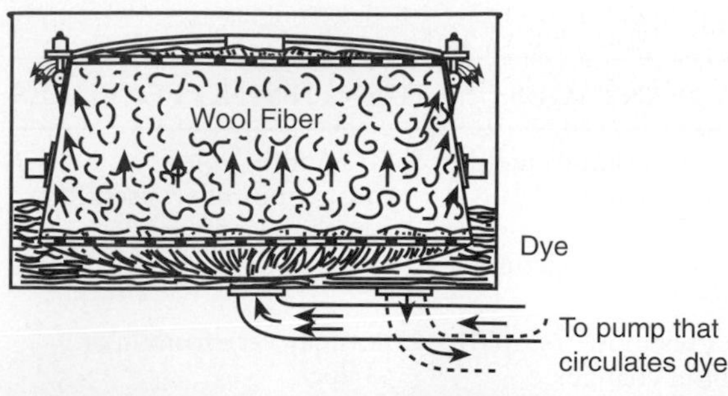


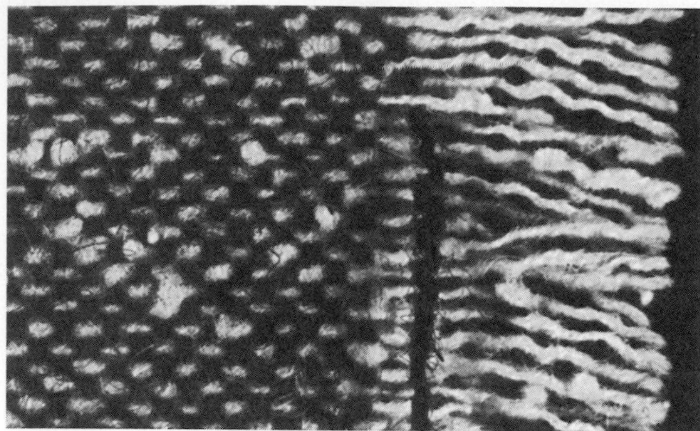

**FIGURE 19–2** ❖ Stock or fiber dye: process and tweed fabric example (cross dyeing).

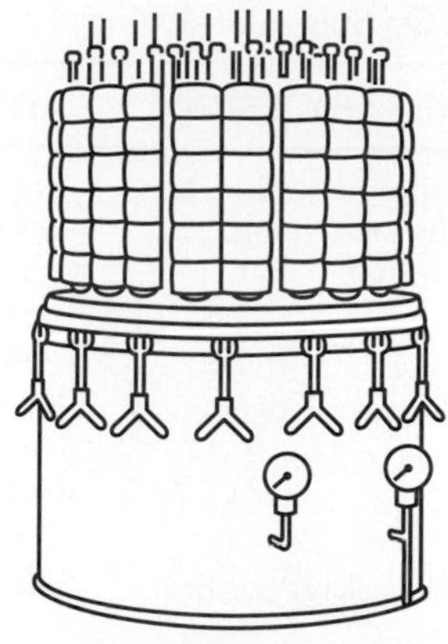

**FIGURE 19–3** ❖ Yarn dyeing: process and fabric.

obtained, but the process is fairly expensive (Figure 19–2).

3. *Top dyeing* gives results similar to stock dyeing and is more commonly used. Tops, the loose ropes of wool from combing, are wound into balls, placed on perforated spindles, and enclosed in a tank. The dye is pumped back and forth through the wool. Continuous processes on loose fiber and wool tops use a pad-stream technique.

## Yarn Stage

**Yarn dyeing** can be done with the yarn in skeins, called *skein dyeing;* with the yarns wrapped on cones or packages, called *package dyeing;* or with the yarn wound on warp beams, called *beam dyeing.* Yarn dyeing is less costly than fiber dyeing but more costly than piece dyeing and printing. Yarn-dyed designs are more limited and larger inventories are involved (Figure 19–3).

Yarn dyeing is less expensive than fiber dyeing, but significantly more expensive than fabric or product types. Yarn-dyed fabrics are more expensive to produce because larger inventories of yarns in a variety of colors are required and more time is needed to thread the loom or set up the knitting machine correctly. In addition, whenever the pattern of color is changed, time is needed to rethread the loom or change the setup for the knitting machine. Yarn-dyed fabrics are considered to be better quality fabrics, but it is rare to find solid-color yarn-dyed fabrics. It is much cheaper to produce solid-color fabrics by other processes. Yarn-dyed fabrics have stripes, plaids, checks, or other patterns due to the presence of yarns of different colors in different areas within the fabric. Examples of yarn-dyed fabrics include gingham, chambray, and many fancy or patterned fabrics, both woven and knit.

## Piece or Fabric Stage

When the bolt or roll of fabric is dyed, the process is referred to as **piece dyeing.** Piece dyeing usually produces solid-color fabrics. It generally costs less to dye fabric to a single color than to dye loose fiber or yarns. With piece dyeing decisions on color can be delayed so that quick adjustments to fashion trends can be made.

**CROSS DYEING** **Cross dyeing** is piece dyeing of fabrics (Figure 19–4) made of fibers from different generic groups—such as protein and cellulose—or by combining acid-dyeable and basic-dyeable fibers of the

**FIGURE 19–4** ❖ Cross-dyed fabric: dark yarns are 100 percent cotton; light yarns are 100 percent polyester.

same generic group. Each fiber type or modification reacts with a different dye class. When different colors are used for each dye class, the dyed fabric has a yarn-dyed appearance. An example is a fabric made of wool yarns and cotton yarns dyed with a red acid dye and a blue direct dye, respectively. If the fabric was made with wool warp and cotton filling, the warp would be red and the filling blue.

**UNION DYEING** **Union dyeing** is also piece dyeing of fabrics made of fibers from different groups. Unlike cross dyeing, union dyeing gives the finished fabric a solid color. Dyes of the same hue, but of a type suited to the fibers to be dyed, are mixed together in the same dye bath. Union dyeing is common; witness all the solid-color blend fabrics on the market. A frequent problem with these fabrics involves the different fastness characteristics of each dye class used. Aged, union-dyed fabrics may take on a heather look, due to the differences in colorfastness of the dyes. Piece dyeing is done with various kinds of equipment.

## Product Stage

Before **product dyeing,** the fabric is cut and sewn into the finished product. Once the color need has been determined, the product is dyed. Properly prepared gray goods are critical to good product dyeing. Great care must be taken in handling the materials and in dyeing to get a level, uniform color throughout the product. Careful selection of components is required, or buttons, thread, and trim may be a different color because of differences in dye absorption between the various product parts. Product dyeing is important in the apparel and furnishing industries with an emphasis on quick response to retail and consumer demands (see Figure 19–5).

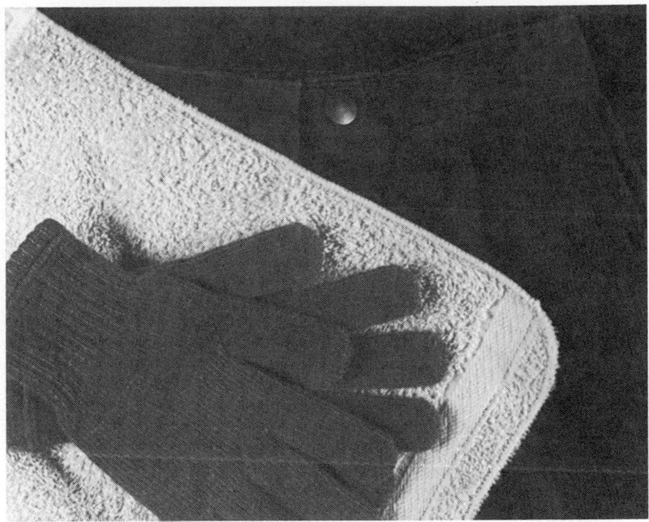

**FIGURE 19–5** ❖ Product-dyed items: corduroy slacks, washcloth, and gloves.

# METHODS OF DYEING

The method chosen for dyeing depends on fiber content, fabric weight, dye, and degree of penetration required in the finished product. Time is money in mass production so that processes in which the goods travel quickly through a machine are used whenever possible. Dyeing and afterwashing require a great deal of water, and waste water contributes to stream pollution. Minimizing the environmental impact of dyeing and finishing continues to be a major industry goal and current efforts are discussed at the end of this chapter.

Many methods and processes are used in dyeing. The methods tend to involve one of three procedures for combining the dye with the textile: textile is circulated in a dye bath; dye bath is circulated around the textile; or both textile and dye bath are circulated together.

## Batch Dyeing

Batch dyeing is also referred to as exhaust dyeing. In this process the textile is circulated through the dyebath. Batch dyeing can be used for textiles in any stage of production from fiber to product but tends to be used for smaller lots or shorter yardages. The process has good flexibility in terms of color selection and cost is low, especially if done close to the product stage. Temperature can be controlled depending on the dye-fiber combination. Equipment used includes the beck, pad, and jig.

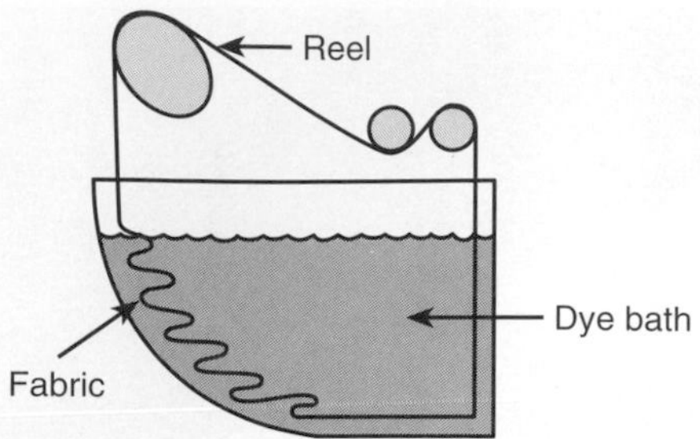


FIGURE 19–6 ❖ Winch dyeing.

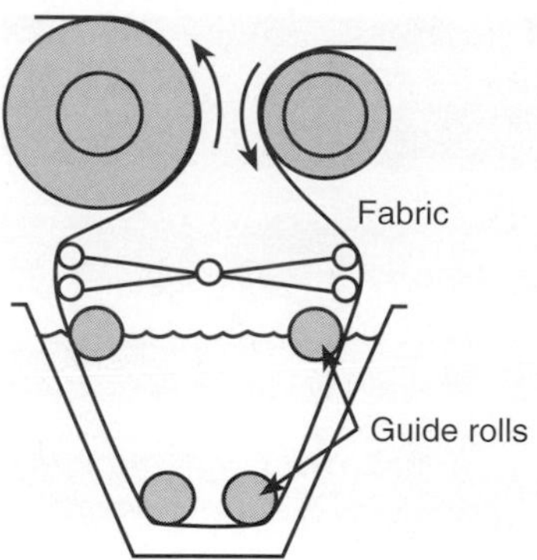


FIGURE 19–7 ❖ Jig dyeing.

**BECK, REEL, OR WINCH DYEING** The oldest type of piece dyeing is *beck, reel,* or **winch dyeing** (Figure 19–6). The fabric, in a loose rope sewed together at the ends, is lifted in and out of the dye bath by a reel. Most of the fabric is immersed in the dye bath except for the few yards around the reel. Penetration of dye into the fiber is obtained by continued immersion of slack fiber or goods rather than by pressure on the wet goods under tension, as is done in some other processes. This method is used on lightweight fabrics that cannot withstand the tension of the other methods and on heavy goods, especially woolens.

In beck dyeing, a pressurized liquor ratio of 5:1 or 4:1 is used. Liquor ratio refers to the weight of solution compared to the weight of textile to be dyed. Thus, liquor ratios of 5:1 have five times as much liquid as textile by weight in the process. Beck dyeing is generally used for fabric lengths ranging from 50 to 100 meters in rope or full width forms. It is simple, versatile, and low cost. Fabrics are subjected to low warp tension and bulking of yarns occurs. Beck dyeing uses large amounts of water, chemicals, and energy. It also causes abrasion, creasing, and distortion of some fabrics when dyed in rope form.

**JIG DYEING** **Jig dyeing** uses a stationary dye bath with two rolls above the bath. The fabric is carried around the rolls in open width and rolled back and forth through the dye bath every 20 minutes or so. It is on rollers for the remaining time. This process has some problems with level dyeing. Acetate, rayon, and nylon are usually jig dyed (Figure 19–7).

In jig dyeing, much larger runs of fabric at open width are used; several thousand meters are common. Warp tension can be great because of the way the fabric is moved in the process. Fabrics that may crease in rope form are dyed in this manner, such as carpet, some twills, and some satins.

**PAD DYEING** In **pad dyeing,** the fabric is run through the dye bath in open width and then between squeeze or nip rollers that force the dye into the fabric with pressure. Notice in Figure 19–8 that the pad box holds a very small amount of dye bath or dye liquor, making this an economical method of piece dyeing. The cloth runs through the machine at a rapid rate, 30–300 yards a minute. Pad-steam processes are one of the most widely used methods of dyeing fabric.

## Package Dyeing

In **package dyeing,** the dye bath is forced through the textile Normally, the textile is in the yarn stage and the yarn is wound on a perforated core of stainless steel, plastic, or paper and placed on a perforated spindle in a pressurized machine. This technique is also used for some fiber and fabric dyeing. In beam dyeing, the yarn or fabric is wound on perforated beams. This technique is especially practical for fabrics whose warp is one color and filling another. In skein dyeing, the yarn skeins are hung in the machine and the dye circulates around the hanging skeins. Package dyeing is used primarily for bulky yarns like acrylic and wool for knits and carpet. Liquor ratios for all types are high to ensure uniformity of the dyeing,

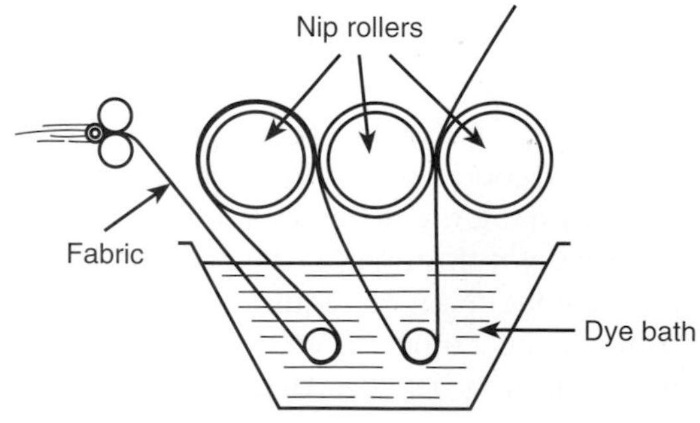


FIGURE 19–8 ❖ Pad dyeing.

usually ranging from 10:1 to 4:1 depending on the process, dye-fiber combination, and quality desired.

## Combination Dyeing

In combination dyeing both the textile and the dye bath are circulated. Several techniques are used here: jet dyeing, paddle machines, rotary drums, tumblers, and continuous dyeing.

**JET DYEING** **Jet dyeing** is similar to beck dyeing. Here the fabric is processed as a continuous loop. The technique is especially useful for delicate fabrics of polyester; but, depending on the machine, almost any weight, structure, or fiber type can be used. It involves vigorous agitation of the dye bath and the textile. Because of the rapid speed of the process (200–800 meters per minute), wrinkling of fabric is minimal. Low warp tension helps develop bulk and fullness. High temperatures result in rapid dyeing, increased efficiency of dyes and chemicals, good fastness characteristics, and lower use of energy. However, equipment and maintenance costs are high, foaming can be a problem, and certain fabrics may be abraded in the process.

**PADDLE MACHINES, ROTARY DRUMS, OR TUMBLERS** Paddle machines and rotary drums are used primarily for product dyeing (see Figure 19–9). Both the dye bath and the product are circulated by a paddle or rotation of the drum. Tumblers are similar to rotary drums except that they tilt forward for easier loading and unloading. Tumblers are used in product dyeing and in abrasive or chemical washes.

**CONTINUOUS MACHINES** *Continuous machines,* called *ranges,* are used for large fabric lots. Ranges include compartments for wetting-out, dyeing, aftertreatment, washing, and rinsing.

In continuous dyeing, fabrics or yarns are used. The fabrics are often cotton/polyester blends; the yarns are usually warp yarns for denim. Another fabric often dyed with the continuous method is carpet. About 25 percent of all carpet is colored in this way. **Continuous dyeing** is efficient for long runs, but color tolerances generally are relaxed for this method because of the variables involved. This technique is most commonly used in union dyeing of blends, but it can be used in cross dyeing, too. In one-bath dyeing, both dyes are present in one bath. One-bath processes are used for disperse/direct dye combinations in many medium dark shades. The two-bath process is used for heavier weight goods, darker shades, or dyes that cannot be combined in one bath. In this process, the dye is added from two separate dye baths, one for each dye type.

The long-chain method is continuous dyeing of yarns. It usually involves indigo or a sulfur dye. Yarn is immersed in the dye, squeezed to remove excess dye, and skyed or exposed to air to oxidize and develop the color and fix the dye inside the fiber. Consecutive dips and skying progressively darken the shade until the desired color is reached. Indigo yarns may experience as many as

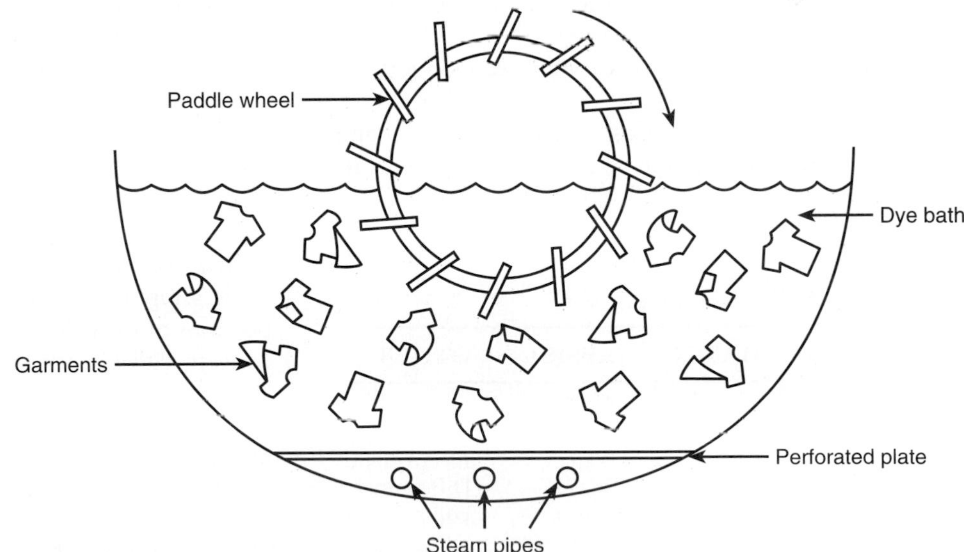


**FIGURE 19–9** ❖ Paddle dyeing.

sixteen separate dips to achieve a very dark navy blue. The ranges normally run at 30 to 35 yards per minute.

# PRINTING

Color designs are produced on fabrics by **printing** with pigments or dyes in paste form or by positioning pigments or dyes on the fabric with specially designed machines. Printing is used to add color in localized areas only. Wet prints use a thick liquid paste; dry prints use a powder. Printed fabrics usually have clear-cut edges in the design portion on the face and the color seldom penetrates completely to the back of the fabric. Yarns raveled from printed fabrics show the color unevenly positioned on them.

Printing allows for great design flexibility and relatively inexpensive patterned fabric. Patterns can be achieved with printing that are not possible from any other method. Some firms such as Brunswig and Fils allow custom coloring of their prints.

The use of foam prints is another option. In **foam printing** the color is dispersed in the foam. The foam is applied to the fabric and then collapses. The small amount of liquid limits color migration. Foam printing has less environmental impact than some other printing methods.

Table 19–3 lists the various methods of creating printed designs. Table 19–4 summarizes the characteristics of printing.

## Direct Printing

In **direct printing,** color is applied directly to the fabric in the pattern and location desired in the finished fabric. Direct printing is a common method of printing a design on a fabric because it is easy and economical.

**BLOCK PRINTING** **Block printing** is a hand process and probably the oldest technique for decorating textiles. It is seldom done commercially because it is expensive and slow. A pattern is carved on a block. The block is dipped in a shallow pan of dye paste and stamped on the fabric (Figure 19–10). More than one color print are possible, but a separate block is needed for each color. Extra time and attention are needed to align blocks correctly. Slight irregularities in color register or positioning are clues to block prints, but these can be duplicated by other techniques.

**TABLE 19–3** ❖ Printing process.

| DIRECT | DISCHARGE | RESIST | OTHER |
|---|---|---|---|
| Block<br>Direct roller<br>Warp | Discharge | Batik<br>Tie-dye<br>Ikat<br>Screen<br>Flat<br>Rotary<br>Stencil | Jet<br>Heat transfer<br>Electrostatic<br>Differential<br>Foil printing |

**FIGURE 19–10** ❖ Carved wooden block and the print made using it.

**DIRECT-ROLLER PRINTING** **Direct-roller printing** was developed in 1783, about the time all textile operations were becoming mechanized. Figure 19–11 shows the essential parts of the printing machine. The fabric is drawn around a metal or high-density foam cylinder during printing. A different printing roller applies each color. The engraved printing roller is etched with the design. There are as many different rollers as there are colors in the fabric. Furnisher rollers are covered with hard rubber or brushes made of nylon or hard-rubber bristles. They revolve in a small color trough, pick up the dye paste, and deposit it on the rollers. A doctor blade scrapes off excess color so that only the engraved portions of the roller are filled with dye when it comes in contact with the fabric. The fabric to be printed, a rubberized blanket, and a back unfinished fabric pass between the cylinder and the engraved rollers. The blanket gives a good surface for sharp printing; the gray goods protects the blanket and absorbs excess dye.

Rayon and knitted fabrics are usually lightly coated with a gum sizing on the back to keep them from stretching or swelling as they go through the printing

**TABLE 19–4** ❖ Methods of printing.

| STAGE | INDUSTRY TERM | ADVANTAGES | DISADVANTAGES | IDENTIFYING FEATURES |
|---|---|---|---|---|
| Direct print on fabric | Block print | Handmade craft.<br>Used to produce unique, one-of-a-kind items. | Expensive process.<br>Slow.<br>Pattern alignment difficult. | Irregular depth of color.<br>Repeat blocks may be out of alignment.<br>One to several colors in pattern. |
| Direct print on fabric | Roller print | Multiple colors.<br>Less expensive method.<br>Versatile in colors, pattern, and scale.<br>Duplex prints possible. | Number of colors limited by equipment.<br>Creating engraved rollers expensive.<br>Out-of-register prints.<br>Scale limited by size of roller. | From 1 to 16 colors in pattern.<br>Scale of repeat can vary. |
| Direct print on yarn | Warp print | Soft edge to pattern.<br>Unique look. | Expensive process.<br>No quick response. | Hazy, irregular edge to pattern in fabric, becomes more distinct when filling removed. |
| Dyed fabric printed with discharge paste | Discharge print | May be less expensive than other methods, depending on design. | Discharge paste may tender fabric.<br>Limited to patterns with few colors and dark ground. | Patterned areas tend to show ground color on back; usually white or 1–2 colors with dark ground. |
| Wax resist on fabric, then dyed | Batik | Hand process.<br>Multiple color patterns.<br>Unique look. | Expensive.<br>Wax removal difficult.<br>Slow, labor-intensive process. | Fabric may have wax cracks or drips.<br>Patterns vary from simple to elaborate. |
| Fabric tied, then dyed | Tie-dye | Hand process.<br>Unique look.<br>May use many colors. | Hand process.<br>Expensive.<br>Labor intensive. | Sunburst ray effect and undyed ground in tied areas.<br>Patterns vary from simple to elaborate. |
| Yarn tied, dyed, and woven | Ikat | Warp, filling, or double ikat possible.<br>Hand process.<br>Unique look.<br>May combine many colors and bands of ikat with solid color. | Labor intensive.<br>Hand process.<br>Requires careful planning.<br>Expensive. | Woven-in pattern due to planned variations in yarn color in warp, filling, or both.<br>Simple to elaborate patterns possible. |
| Print fabric or product with resist screens | Screen print | Fine detail possible.<br>Many colors possible with overprinting.<br>Inexpensive process.<br>Quick response.<br>Applicable to fabric and product.<br>Minimal down time.<br>Quick change of colorways.<br>Hand or commercial process.<br>Can imitate many other hand and commercial techniques. | Registration of screens critical to process.<br>Pigment pastes can change hand of fabric.<br>Separate screen for each color of print.<br>Quality of screen related to quality of fabric. | Most common method of printing. |
| Resist stencil on fabric, then painted | Stencil print | Hand process.<br>Unique look. | Expensive.<br>Easily duplicated with other processes.<br>Color may be irregular. | Most often simple patterns. |

TABLE 19–4 ❖ *(continued)*

| STAGE | INDUSTRY TERM | ADVANTAGES | DISADVANTAGES | IDENTIFYING FEATURES |
|---|---|---|---|---|
| Fabric (carpet) | Jet print | Inexpensive. Quick response. Minimal down time. Quick change of colorways. | Currently commercially limited to carpet. Fineness of detail limited. | Most common method of printing carpet. Simple to elaborate patterns. |
| Print paper, transfer pattern to fabric or product with heat and pressure | Heat transfer print or sublimation transfer print | Quick response. Minimal down time. Detailed prints possible. Minimal environmental impact from dyes. Inexpensive. Low capital and space needs. | Disposal of waste paper. Most often limited to sublimable disperse dyes and synthetic fibers. Storage conditions may cause dye transfer. | Sharp print on face; little if any transfer to fabric back. |
| Powered dye applied to fabric | Electrostatic print | No washdown needed. Minimal environmental impact from dyes. Inexpensive. | Powder difficult to control. Minor technique limited to synthetic fibers and disperse dyes. | Printed face, unprinted back. |
| Dye applied to carpet with fibers of different dye affinities | Differential print | Unique looks possible. Quick response. | Limited to carpet. Difficult to control design. | Carpet with less precise patterns. |
| Adhesive applied to fabric or product, then heat transfer printed | Foil print | Metallic film designs possible. Can combine with screen or heat transfer printing for multicolor patterns. | Detailed and time-consuming process. Expensive. | Metallic film design. |

machine. After printing, the fabric is dried, steamed, or treated to set the dye. The sizing may cause water spotting during use or care.

**Duplex printing** is roller printing that prints on both sides of the fabric with the same or different patterns. In duplex prints, both sides of the fabric may be printed at the same time. However, the more common method prints the face and back in two steps.

**WARP PRINTING** **Warp printing** is a type of yarn printing done on the warp yarns prior to weaving. This technique gives an interesting, rather hazy pattern, softer than other prints. To identify it, ravel adjacent sides. Color in the form of the design is on the warp yarns. Filling yarns are white or solid color. Imitations have splotchy color on both warp and filling yarns. Warp printing is usually done on taffeta, satin ribbons, or cotton fabric, and on upholstery or drapery fabric (Figure 19–12). Since the practice is time consuming and expensive, it is not common.

## Discharge Printing

**Discharge prints** are piece-dyed fabrics in which the design is made by removing color from selected areas of the fabric (Figure 19–13). Discharge printing is usually done on dark backgrounds. The fabric is first piece dyed in any of the usual methods. A discharge paste containing chemicals to remove the color is printed on the fabric using roller or screen techniques. Dyes that are not harmed by the discharging chemicals can be mixed with printing solution if color is desired in the discharge areas. The fabric is then steamed to develop the design, as either a white or a colored area. Discharge printing is done because better dye penetration is obtained with

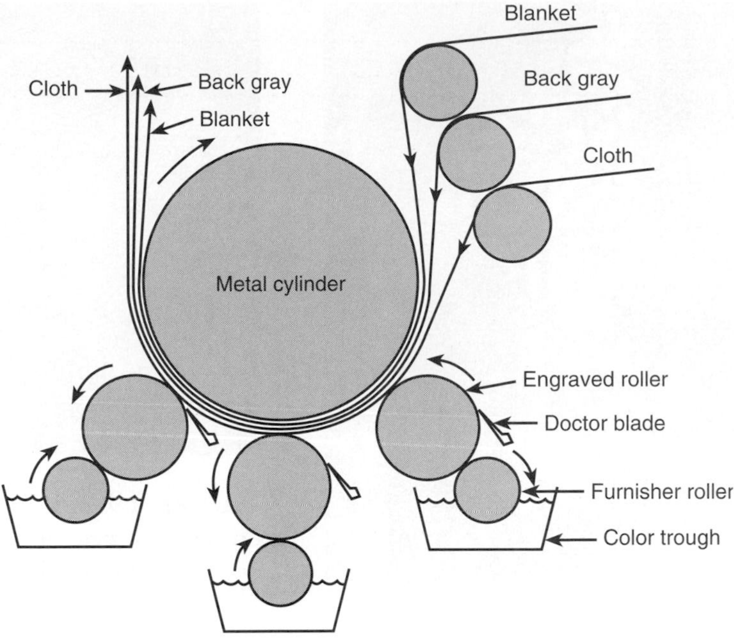


**FIGURE 19–11** ❖ Direct-roller printing. This diagram shows the set up for a three-color print.

piece dyeing than with printing, and it is difficult to get good dark colors except by piece dyeing.

Discharge prints can be detected by examining the back of the fabric. In the design area the background color may not be completely removed, especially around the edges of the design. Background colors must be from dyes that can be removed by strong alkali. However, the discharge chemical or bleach may cause tendering or weakening of the fabric in the areas where the color was discharged.

## Resist Printing

**Resist prints** are fabrics in which color absorption is blocked during yarn or fabric dyeing.

**BATIK** **Batik** is generally a hand process in which hot wax is applied to a fabric in the form of a design. When the wax has set or hardened, the fabric is piece dyed. The wax prevents penetration of dye into the wax-

**FIGURE 19–12** ❖ Warp printed fabric. Note the difference in yarn appearance and clarity of design between woven and raveled areas.

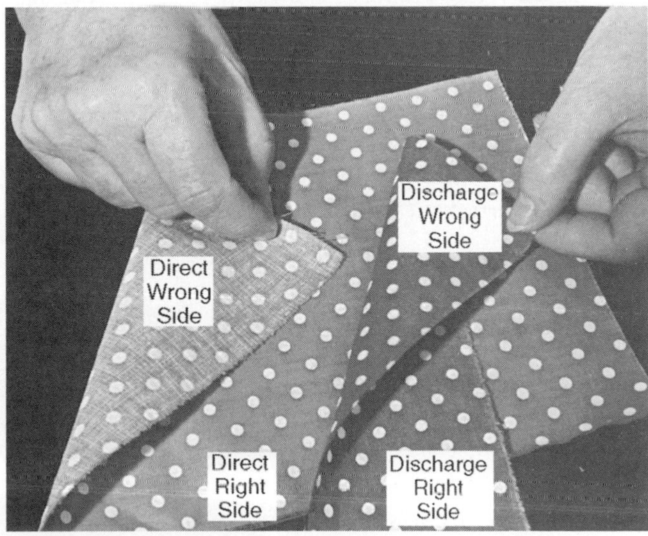


**FIGURE 19–13** ❖ Discharge print versus direct print.

**FIGURE 19–14** ❖ Hand-produced batik.

**FIGURE 19–16** ❖ Tie-dye. This fabric was rolled on the bias, tied, and piece dyed. A second dyeing was done with the fabric rolled in the opposite direction.

covered portions. Colors are built up by piece dyeing light colors first, waxing new portions, and redyeing until the design is complete. The wax is later removed by a solvent. Figure 19–14 shows a hand-produced batik from Indonesia. Figure 19–15 shows mass-produced yarn-dyed batiks from India.

**TIE-DYE** **Tie-dye** is a hand process in which yarn or fabric is wrapped in certain areas with thread or string. The yarn or fabric is dyed and the string removed, leaving undyed areas (Figures 19–16 and 19–17). Manufacturing techniques using fabric in rope form have been developed to imitate tie-dyed fabric.

**IKAT** **Ikat** is an ancient form of resist printing. In ikat, the yarn is tied, dyed, then woven. The technique can be applied to only the warp yarns (warp ikat), only the filling yarns (filling ikat), or to both sets of yarns (double ikat). Ikat designs do not have precise edges. Ikat requires great skill in determining the placement of the design in the finished fabric (see Figure 19–18).

**SCREEN PRINTING** Screen printing is an incredibly versatile process. The concept is simple. The design is applied to a mesh screen so that all but the part of the design to be printed with this screen is coated with a compound that seals the openings in the screen, preventing the dye paste from moving through the screen.

**FIGURE 19–15** ❖ Mass-produced, yarn-dyed batiks.

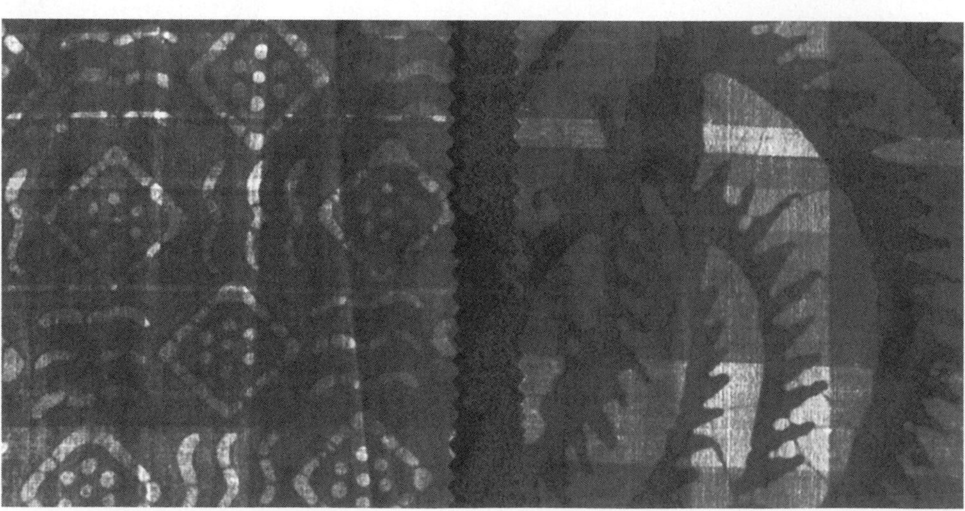

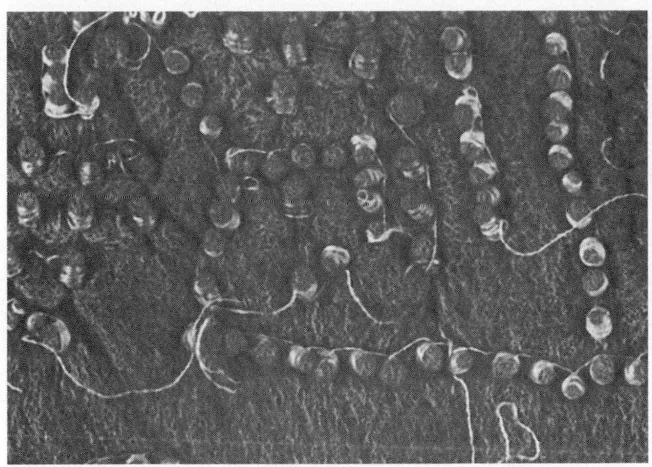

FIGURE 19–17 ❖ Tie-dye fabric showing thread used to make the design.

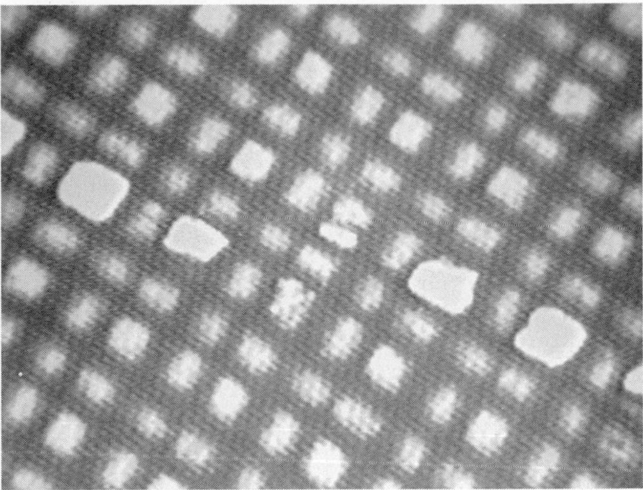

FIGURE 19–19 ❖ Close-up of a screen used in screen printing. Note the larger clear areas where the paste is forced through the screen.

One screen is used for each color. The paste is forced through the openings within the screen by a squeegee. Fabrics with up to 24 colors, in widths up to 10 feet, can be printed at speeds of 40–85 yards per minute. Figures 19–19 and 19–20 show a close-up and a screen used in screen printing.

**Flat-screen printing** is done commercially for yardages from 50 to 5,000 yards and often is used for designs larger than the circumference of the rolls used for roller printing. Approximately 18 percent of print fabrics worldwide are flatbed screen prints.

In the hand process, the fabric to be printed is placed on a long table. Two people position the screen on the fabric, apply the color, move the screen to a new position, and repeat the process until all the fabric is printed with that color. Then they repeat the process until all the colors have been applied. For screen printing

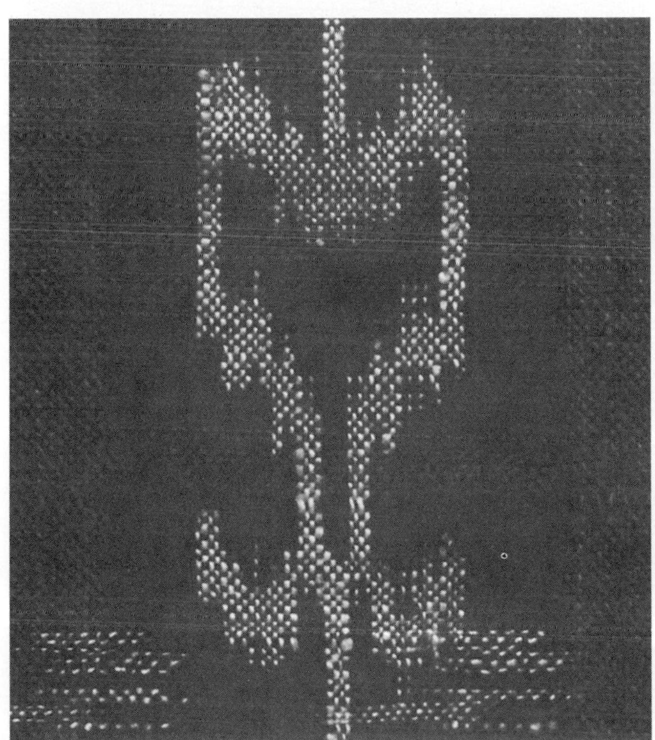

FIGURE 19–18 ❖ Double ikat from Guatemala.

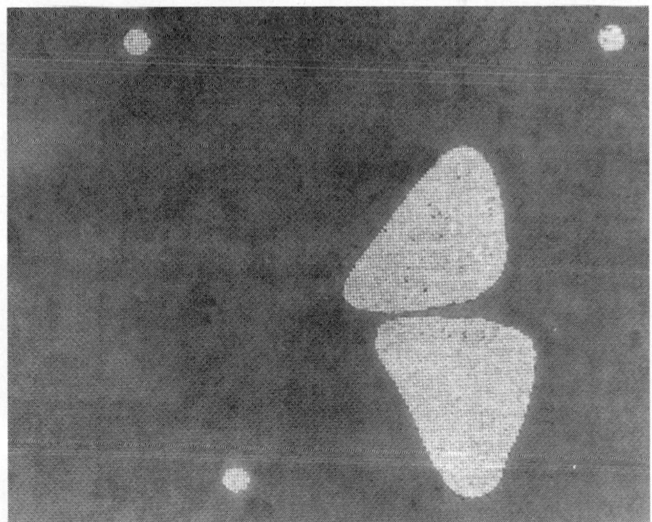

FIGURE 19–20 ❖ Screen used in flatbed screen printing.

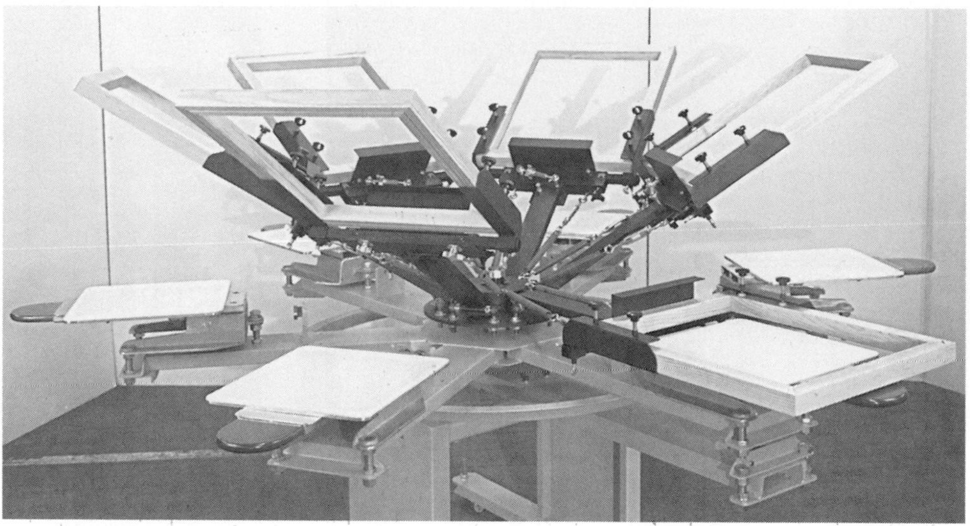

**FIGURE 19–21** ❖ Printing machine used to print items after sewing. (COURTESY OF ADVANCE PROCESS SUPPLY)

products, a similar process is used, but the equipment is specifically adapted to the type of product. Figure 19–21 shows a screen printer for T-shirts.

In the automatic-screen process the fabric to be printed is placed on a conveyor belt. A series of flat screens are positioned above the belt and are lowered automatically. Positioning of the screen is carefully done to be sure print edges match. On screen-printed yardage, small color squares or blocks along the selvage are used to align the print and help identify a screen print. Color is applied automatically, and the fabric is moved automatically and fed continuously into ovens to be dried.

**Rotary-screen printing** is done with cylindrical metal screens that operate in much the same way as the flat screens, except that the operation is continuous rather than the discontinuous starting and stopping of the flat process (Figure 19–22). The rotary screens are cheaper than the copper rollers used in roller printing

**FIGURE 19–22** ❖ Rotary-screen printing. (COURTESY OF STORK BRABANT, B. V.)

**FIGURE 19–23** ❖ Screen used in rotary screen printing. (COURTESY OF STORK SCREENS B. V.)

(Figure 19–23). Rotary screen printing is more common than flatbed screen printing.

Screen printing is useful for printing almost any size design on fabrics. Approximately 80 percent of the printed fabrics in the U.S. market are screen prints.

**STENCIL PRINTING** **Stencil printing** was the precursor of screen printing. The pattern is cut from a special wax paper or thin metal sheet. As in screen printing, a separate stencil is cut for each color. Color in a thick solution or paste is applied by hand with a brush or sprayed with an air gun. Stencilling is done on limited yardage.

## Other Printing Methods

**JET PRINTING** **Jet printing** uses continuous streams of dye forced from jets. The process is very much the same as that used in ink-jet printers for computers. The ink-jet system is used primarily to print carpets. In this system, small jets inject color onto the fabric. The size of the nozzle, number of jets, and bleeding characteristics of the dye or pigment paste used determine the intricacy of the pattern, its size, and clarity. Pattern ink-jet systems are available with 172 jets per inch. Figure 19–24 shows a jet printing machine.

At present, there are no commercial continuous ink-jet printers for fabric. Ink-jet printers for continuous printing of full fabric widths in fine detail comparable to 600 dpi paper ink-jet printers are in the developmental stages. These printers have the potential for using four basic colors to create any color and many unique looks (see Figure 19–25).

The ink-jet machine holds a series of horizontal bars containing the dye, which is fed through small dye jets. The prepared carpet passes under the bars. By use of an electronically controlled tape, the jets spray the dye in

**FIGURE 19–24** ❖ Jet printing machine. (COURTESY OF MILLIKEN & COMPANY.)

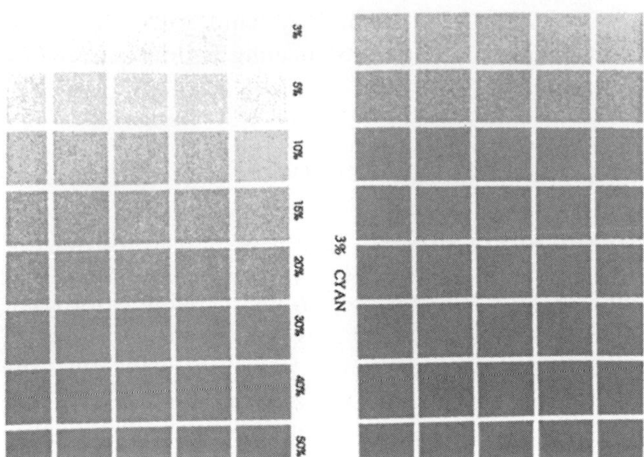


**FIGURE 19–25** ❖ Batch process printed fabric sample from ink-jet printer. This piece of fabric required 23 minutes to print.

the location designated. With this process, patterns can be easily changed (see Figure 19–26).

Jet printing is economical for use with other pile or thick fabrics whose designs range from specific patterns to multicolored stripes, abstract splashes, or tie-dye effects. Several colors are applied in one operation from jets set in bars. The fabric moves over an inclined plane, dye is sprayed from jets onto the fabric, and the cloth then goes through heavy rollers that press the dye completely through the fabric.

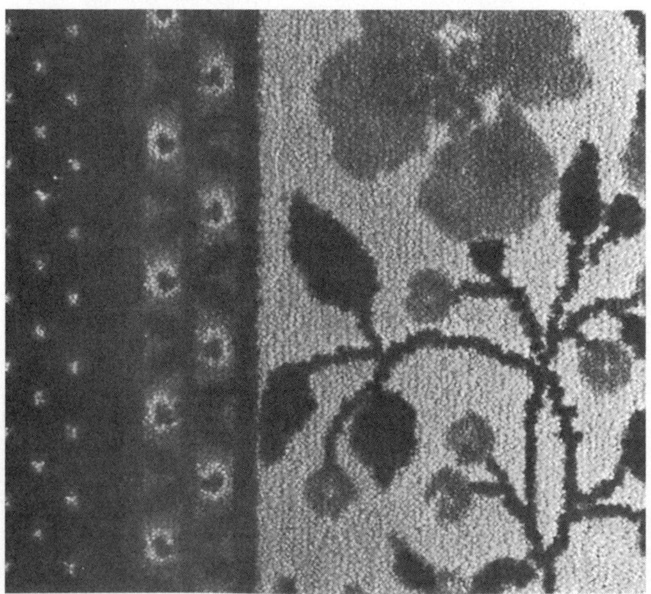

**FIGURE 19–26** ❖ Jet-dyed carpet.

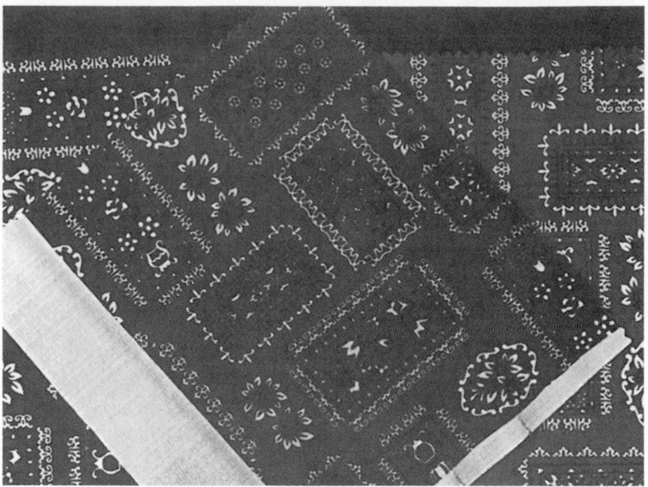

**FIGURE 19–27** ❖ Heat-transfer printing: design on paper (left) is transferred by heat to fabric (center). Design on paper is lighter after printing (right).

**HEAT-TRANSFER PRINTING** In **heat-transfer printing** designs are transferred to fabric from specially printed paper by heat and pressure (see Figure 19–27). The paper is printed by one of several paper-printing techniques: gravure, flexograph, offset, or converted rotary-screen. The fabric, yarn, or item is placed on a plastic frame and padded with a special solution. Paper is placed over the fabric and then covered with a silicone-rubber sheet. These layers are compressed under high pressure at a temperature of 200°C for a few seconds so that the print sublimes and migrates from the paper to the fabric. In sublimation, a solid evaporates and recondenses as a solid in a new location. Pressure ensures that the edges of the print are sharp and clear.

The advantages of heat-transfer printing are better penetration and clarity of design, lower production costs, and elimination of pollution problems. (However, dealing with waste paper can be a problem.) Clear, photographic prints are possible with this technique. Transfer printing can be done on three-dimensional fabrics like circular knits without splitting them first and on three-dimensional products like garments.

Print papers using disperse dyes are successful on high-polyester/cotton blends and on nylon. Cotton fabrics and 50/50 blends of cotton/polyester are treated with a resin that has an affinity for disperse dyes. Print papers with acid dyes for nylon, silk, and wool and with cationic dyes for acrylics are available. Although these other options exist, synthetic fibers and disperse dyes are the most common combination on the market. Transfer printing is used for apparel, drapery fabrics, upholstery, shower curtains, and floor coverings.

**Electrostatic Printing** **Electrostatic printing** is similar to electrostatic flocking. A prepared screen is covered with powdered dye mixed with a carrier that has dielectric properties. The screen is positioned about ½ inch above the fabric. When passed through an electric field, the dye mixture is pulled onto the material, where it is fixed by heat.

**Differential Printing** **Differential printing** describes screen printing on carpets tufted with yarns that have different dye affinities.

### Foil Printing

In **foil printing,** a special adhesive is applied to the fabric by a flatbed or rotary screen. The fabric is dyed and partially cured. The foil combines a thin polyester film with a heat-sensitive release coating, a very thin layer of aluminum, and a clear or tinted lacquer. The metallic foil is transferred by a heat transfer press. The foil bonds only where the adhesive pattern exists on the fabric.

## Recent Developments in Dyeing and Printing

Recent advances in commercial coloration include a photosensitive dye in some portion of a design that changes hue when exposed to ultraviolet light or sunlight. Other combinations that have been marketed are heat-sensitive dyes combined with another dye. With body heat, dramatic color changes, such as purple to bright blue, occur.

A system by Kanebo of Japan incorporates tiny liquid crystals in a surface coating. The crystals change color depending on temperature. The coating is used on swimwear and trim; the high cost of the system limits its application to other products.

Holographic prints used for swim, rain, and ski wear combine a urethane coating, holographic image, and a poplin backing.

Some techniques combine dyeing and printing, such as ginghams from India that have a batik top dye. Another example is yarn-dyed denim that is printed or overdyed. In overdyed denims, the yarn-dyed fabric is dyed another color. Often the overdyeing follows an abrasive or chemical wash. (See Chapter 17.)

Other developments in coloration relate to changes in the textiles industry, including technological advances and computer applications in dyeing and printing. The shift away from large runs of the same color or print continues. Speeds of 100 meters per minute do not contribute to extremely high quality or intricate prints. As quality increases in importance, production speeds and length of standard runs decrease. For example, in the 1950s and 1960s standard runs were 100,000 yards. By the 1980s, standard runs were less than 10,000 yards. In the 1990s, standard runs as short as 250 yards are becoming more common. Even with this decrease in standard run size, costs are higher for shorter runs. The processing cost for runs of 10,000 yards is approximately \$120 per 1,000 yards; for 5,000 yards, it is \$130; and for 1,000 yards, it is \$240. Thus, shorter runs will cost more.

Specialization of fabric or design continues. The industry is strongly committed to minimal seconds, strict color control, and decreased dead time. Dead time refers to the time the equipment is not operating because of the need to change equipment components, like screens, or to change colors for different patterns. Dead time in screen printing has decreased to less than 30 minutes for most systems and patterns.

Efficient use of dyes, chemicals, and water or other solvents is another concern of the industry. For example, with reactive dyes, standard utilization rates were 60–80 percent. New reactive dyes with utilization rates of 80 percent or more are available. Solvent dyeing systems, which are standard for some fibers like aramid, require high recovery rates, such as 98 percent, to be economically feasible. Solvent dyeing has great potential, especially as water costs and water quality standards become greater. With solvent dyeing, dyeing could expand into regions where dyeing has not been feasible due to the limited availability of water.

Computer use increases automation of the process and decreases costs associated with labor, raw materials, and inventory. Computer-aided design systems (CAD), computer-aided engraving systems (CAE), and computer-aided manufacturing systems (CAM) make it possible to create designs and convert them into fabrics in a matter of hours or days rather than months. Using CAD, the textile designer can experiment with changes in scale and color.

Different colorways, variations in scale, or changes in pattern detail can be examined in seconds with a few simple commands. **Colorways** describes changing one or more colors in a fabric. Some fabrics are produced in one color combination only, but most are available in several colorways. In this fashion, fabric designers keep product development costs down.

CAD allows designers to quickly create coordinating prints for apparel and furnishing uses by selecting a portion of the original design and copying it. CAD systems are so versatile, they can simulate how a print will look in a completed product. Computers automatically register each color in a print so edges match.

Computer monitoring of dyeing and printing processes decreases the environmental impact as manufacturers recognize the direct costs of inefficient use of materials and energy and incorporate closed-loop recycling of chemicals, solvents, water, and energy. Dye chemists use computers to calculate formulas to match swatches submitted by designers and monitor dyeing or printing processes so color is consistent.

The progress in printing techniques has been so great that predictions for capabilities by the year 2000 include making direct imaging techniques available in retail stores. Consumers will be able to select the product in an acceptable ground or base color, select a pattern to be applied to the product, or design their own pattern and have it applied as they wait. Research on techniques currently used in color xerography on paper show that this technique can be modified for use on textiles. Fabric width, chemicals used in the process, and the relatively slow printing rate are some of the concerns limiting adaptation of this technique to textiles.

**FIGURE 19–28** ❖ Bleeding of embroidery on shirt pocket. Note the halo of dye around the embroidered emblem.

❖

# COLOR PROBLEMS

Good colorfastness is expected, but it is not always achieved. When one considers all the variables connected with dyeing and printing and the hostile environment in which fabrics are used, one can appreciate how good most colored fabrics are.

The factors that influence colorfastness are:

1. Chemical nature of fibers
2. Chemical nature of dyes and pigments
3. Penetration of dyes into the fabric
4. Fixation of dyes or pigments on or in the fabrics

The coloring agents must resist washing, dry cleaning, bleaching, and spot and stain removal with all of the variables of time, temperature, and substances used. Colorants must be resistant to light, perspiration, abrasion, fumes, and other factors. Dyes for certain products, like car interiors and outdoor furniture, must be ultraviolet-light-stabilized. Textiles used in furnishings may experience color problems from exposure to acne medication, bleaches, acids, and alkalis. These color-damaging agents are found in a host of materials with which furnishing textiles are likely to come in contact, such as vomit, drain and toilet cleaners, urine, plant food or fertilizers, insecticides, furniture polish, and disinfectants and germicides found in bathroom cleaners.

If the color is not fast in the fabric as purchased, it is not possible to make it fast. Salt and vinegar are used as exhausting agents for household dyes, but research does not support the theory that they will "set" color. If the dye could not be set using the knowledge of the dye chemist, the specialized equipment available in the dyehouse, and selected dyeing chemicals, the consumer will not be able to accomplish this task at home with salt, vinegar, or any other common household ingredient identified on some improper care labels.

Color loss occurs through bleeding, crocking, and migration or through chemical changes in the dye. **Bleeding** is color loss in water. In bleeding, other fibers present in the wash load may pick up the color. **Crocking** is color loss from rubbing or abrasion. In crocking, some color may be transferred to the abradant. For example, some tight-fitting denim jeans may color the front of the thighs during wear. **Migration** is shifting of color to the surrounding area or to an adjacent surface. An example of migration occurs with some red and white striped fabrics when the white closest to the red takes on a pinkish cast. Figure 19–28 shows a shirt whose embroidery was not fast to washing. Atmospheric gases (fume fading), perspiration, and sunlight may cause fading as a result of a chemical change in the dye.

Certain vat and sulfur dyes **tender,** or destroy, cotton cloth. Green, red, blue, and yellow vat dyes and black, yellow, and orange sulfur dyes are the chief offenders. Manufacturers know which dyes cause the trouble and can correct it by thoroughly oxidizing the dye within the fiber or aftertreating the fabric to neutralize the chemical causing tendering. The damage is increased by

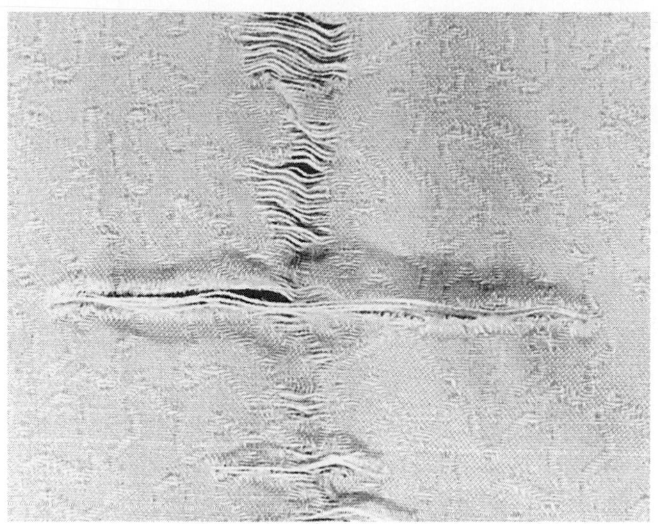

**FIGURE 19–29** ❖ Cotton-and-rayon drapery fabric. After dry cleaning, yellowish streaks indicating fiber photo-degradation were obvious; after washing, slits had occurred in the fabric, resulting from fiber swelling in water and abrasion in the washer.

moisture and sunlight, a problem that is sometimes critical in draperies. Damage may not be evident until the draperies are cleaned and then slits or holes occur (Figures 19–29 and 19–30). Sunlight, smog, and acidic atmospheric gases, as well as dyes, cause fabric damage. **Frosting** occurs when wear removes the colored portion of fibers or yarns (Figure 19–31).

**FIGURE 19–30** ❖ Tendering of cotton draperies caused by sulfur dye, atmospheric moisture, and heat.

**FIGURE 19–31** ❖ Denim jeans: loss of surface color.

Frosting also occurs with blends and with durable-press garments that have been dyed with two different but color-matched dyes (union dyed). During wear, the surface is abraded and becomes lighter in color, while the unabraded or more durable area keeps its color.

The movement of yarns during use may cause undyed fibers to work their way to the surface. Color streaks may result from uneven removal of sizing before the dye is applied. Some resin-treated fabrics show this sort of color problem because either the dye was applied with the resin and did not penetrate sufficiently or the fabric was dyed after being resin treated, in which case there were not enough available dye sites for the dye to be anchored. The best way to check the dye penetration in heavy fabrics is to examine the fabric. With fabric, ravel a yarn to see if it is the same color throughout. With finished products, look at the edge of seams. In heavy prints, look at the reverse side. The more color on the back, the better the dye penetration.

A defect in printed fabrics occurs when two colors of a print overlap each other or do not meet. This defect is referred to as **out of register** (see Figure 19–32).

Printed fabrics may be printed off-grain. **Off-grain prints** create problems because the fabric cannot be both straight with the print and cut on-grain. If cut off-grain, the fabric tends to assume its normal position when washed, causing twisted seams and uneven hemlines. If cut on-grain, the print will not be straight. In an allover design this may not be important, but in large checks and plaids or designs with crosswise lines, matching at seams becomes impossible and slanting lines across the fabric are seldom desirable. Off-grain prints

**FIGURE 19–32** ❖ Printed fabric: out of register (left); in register (right).

are created by incorrect finishing of the fabric. The gray goods are started into the tentering machine crooked or the mechanism for moving the fabric does not work properly so that the two selvages move at slightly different speeds, or the fabric is not properly supported in the center of its width. The off-grain problem can be corrected at the mill before printing.

Other problems related to dyeing and printing are concerns of the producer and manufacturer. These are problems related to the consistency of the color throughout the width and length of the fabric or from dye lot to dye lot. Manufacturers of apparel and furnishing items need to have a fabric that is consistent in color. The color needs to be the same from side to side (selvage to selvage); side to center (selvage to center), and end to end (from one end of the roll of fabric to the other). If the color is not consistent, the producer will have problems with *off-shade* or with product parts not matching in color. When several rolls of the same color fabric are required, it is important that all the rolls are consistent in color. Color matching equipment, like a

**TABLE 19–5** ❖ Color problems.

| PROBLEM | COMPONENT | DESCRIPTION | CAUSE |
|---|---|---|---|
| Bleeding | Fiber | Dye loss in water. May color other items in water. | Poor fiber-dye bond, poor wash fastness. Poor washdown (excess dye on fabric). |
| Crocking | Fiber | Color transfers to abradant (other fabrics, skin, etc.). | Dye sits on fiber surface. |
| Migration | Fiber | Color transfers to other portions or materials. | Poor fiber-dye bond; dye migrates readily. |
| Fume fading | Disperse dye (most common) | Fading or hue shift when exposed to some atmospheric pollutant. | Dye sensitive to pollutants. |
| Poor fastness to sunlight, perspiration, etc. | Dye | Fading or hue shift when exposed to the degrading factor. | Energy in sunlight degrades dye. Chemical reaction of dye with perspiration or ingredients in deodorant or antiperspirant or reaction with bacterial enzymes. |
| Tendering | Fiber | Fabric becomes weak or sensitive to abrasion. | Dye-fiber interaction. |
| Frosting | Fiber | With abrasion, white areas appear on fabric. Often seen at seams or hems. | Poor dye penetration into fiber. As colored portion of fiber is abraded away, uncolored portion shows through. Also seen in blends where one fiber is more abrasion resistant. |
| Out of register | Fabric | Edges of print do not match. | Poor alignment of screens or rollers in printing. |
| Off-grain | Fabric | Fabric printed off-grain. | Fabric not tentered properly and defect not detected before printing. |
| Off-shade | Fabric | Products, product parts, thread, other materials, or coordinating fabrics don't match in color or don't meet color specifications. | Many factors contribute to this: evaluation of color match under differing light sources, chemical composition of materials requiring dyes from different classes, poor control of bath or paste. |

colorimeter, is commonly used to assess color uniformity within or among fabric rolls.

The fastness of the dye often determines the method of care that should be used. The consumer must depend on the label, but some knowledge of color problems that occur in use and care will allow for more intelligent choices. Table 19–5 summarizes these basic color problems.

## Environmental Impact of Dyeing and Printing

Dyeing and printing textiles can have a significant environmental impact from discharge of dyes, pigments, and other chemicals into water systems. Components that contribute to pollution include color, salt, acids, and heavy metals. Some of the materials create problems because of high biological oxygen demand (BOD); others have high chemical oxygen demand (COD). High BOD and COD materials create environments that are hostile to aquatic plants and animals and may create problems with future use of the water. Color in water creates problems with photosynthesis of aquatic plant life.

Most textiles are colored in one manner or another because consumers demand color. One option to decrease environmental impact is to use fewer dyed or printed textiles. White textiles create problems with the use and disposal of chemical bleaches. Even though consumers purchase beige and off-white goods, they will probably continue to demand a broader range of colors. Another option is to use color-grown textiles like the naturally colored cottons and wools. However, a full color spectrum is not available and these natural colors tend to be low in intensity.

Another alternate is using natural dyes. Although natural dyes are not available in a complete palette, some natural dyes are used commercially (see Figure 19–33). In order to be competitive with synthetic dyes and pigments, natural dyes must be economical, consistent in quality, and available in quantity. Mordants used with natural dyes will be restricted to those that have little, if any, environmental impact. Examples of commercially important natural dyes from Caracol and Allegro Natural Dyes include indigo, madder, cochineal, cutch, and osage. Natural dyes are used on cotton, wool, and silk fabrics for apparel and furnishing uses.

Color in water systems in very dilute concentrations can be detected by the unaided eye. Unfortunately color is very difficult to remove by traditional sludge treatment facilities. Alternatives for treating color in water systems include use of hyperfiltration, electrochemical methods, ozonation, and chemical coagulation. Reconstitution and reuse of textile dyeing water is another possibility being investigated.

Efforts to limit use of salt and other chemicals are being made. For example, current reactive dyes use large amounts of salt, but new Remazol EF reactive dyes use significantly less salt and have higher fixation rates. New lower sulfide sulfur dyes are replacing older higher sulfide sulfur dyes. Use of heavy metals in dyes, catalysts, or after treatments is restricted. Dye producers are developing dyes that incorporate iron rather than chromium because iron is much safer than chromium. Dyes and pigments with low environmental impact will continue to be a major thrust in preparing goods with consumer appeal.

Using liquid carbon dioxide or supercritical carbon dioxide as the carrier rather than water for dyeing polyester and other synthetics is another research focus. Liquid carbon dioxide dyeing increases dye fixation rates, decreases energy use, and decreases treatment of waste. In addition, this process does not require use of salt or other dye bath chemicals and drying is not needed. The process is quick and efficient with good leveling. Carbon dioxide can be recycled and is readily available, nontoxic, and economical.

**FIGURE 19–33** ❖ Wool rug dyed with natural indigo, cochineal, and pecan.

# Key Terms

Level
Colorfastness
Metamerism
Bezold effect
Matching
Shade sorting
Pigment
Dye
Fluorescent dyes
Dye process
Acid dyes
Azioc dyes
Cationic dyes
Developed dyes
Direct dyes
Disperse dyes
Mordant dyes
Natural dyes
Reactive dyes
Sulfur dyes
Vat dyes
Fiber dyeing
Mass pigmentation
Solution dyed
Producer colored
Yarn dyeing
Piece dyeing
Cross dyeing
Union dyeing
Product dyeing
Winch dyeing
Jig dyeing
Pad dyeing
Package dyeing
Jet dyeing
Continuous dyeing
Printing
Foam printing
Direct printing
Block printing
Direct-roller printing
Duplex printing
Warp printing
Discharge printing
Resist printing
Batik
Tie-dye
Ikat
Flat-screen printing
Rotary-screen printing
Stencil printing
Jet printing
Heat-transfer printing
Electrostatic printing
Differential printing
Foil printing
Colorways
Bleeding
Crocking
Migration
Tendering
Frosting
Out of register
Off-grain print

# Questions

1. What are the factors that influence the color seen and how do these factors interact?
2. What are the visual clues to determine if a fabric has been dyed or printed? How can the product stage or the technique used in printing be determined?
3. Identify the coloration process (stage of dyeing or type of print) that was probably used for these products:
   solid blue cotton and nylon upholstery velvet
   patterned carpet of nylon for hotel lobby
   100 percent cotton chambray work shirt
   irregular or fuzzy plaid gingham
   floral pattern 100 percent rayon faille dress
   100 percent cotton T-shirt with local ski club name on front
   cartoon print on 100 percent polyester quilt for child's bed
   100 percent wool tweed upholstery
4. Describe the appearance and problems created by these color defects:
   poor leveling
   migration
   frosting
   bleeding
5. What factors influence colorfastness? How can colorfastness be determined?
6. What dye class or classes are commonly used to color these fibers?
   cotton, rayon, flax, or ramie
   wool, nylon, or silk
   leather
   acetate, polyester
   olefin
   acrylic

# Suggested Readings

Aspland, J. R. (1993). "Pigments as Textile Colorants: Pigmenting or Pigmentation." *Textile Chemist and Colorist, 25*(10), pp. 31–37.

Broadbent, Arthur D. (1994, March, May, June, October/November, and 1995, April/May). "Colorimetry." Parts 1–5. *Canadian Textile Journal,* pp. 15–18, 16–19, 18–21, 19–22, 14–18.

Cook, Fred L. (1995, March). "Textile Printing Enters the Technological Revolution." *Textile World,* pp. 73–74, 77–79.

Crews, Patricia Cox (1989). "Effectiveness of Dye Setting Treatments on Cotton Fabrics Dyed with Direct, Reactive, and Vat Dyes." *Clothing and Textile Research Journal, 7*(4), pp. 1–7.

Fulmer, T. D. (1991, December). "The How-To of Pigment Dyeing." *America's Textiles International,* pp. 105–107.

Fulmer, T. D. (1995, January). "Where Is Garment Dyeing Today?" *America's Textiles International,* pp. 94, 96.

Glover, Brian (1995). "Are Natural Colorants Good for Your Health? Are Synthetic Ones Better?" *Textile Chemist and Colorist, 27*(4), pp. 17–20.

Glyn-Woods, Sarah (1992, March). "Developments in Transfer Printing." *America's Textiles International,* pp. 89–91.

Liles, J. N. (1990). *The Art and Craft of Natural Dyeing: Traditional Recipes for Modern Use.* Knoxville, TN: University of Tennessee Press.

Needles, Howard (1986). *Textile Fibers, Dyes, Finishes, and Processes.* Park Ridge, NJ: Noyes Publications.

Perkins, Warren S. (1995, June). "The Principles of Textile Dyeing." *America's Textiles International,* pp. 86, 88–89.

Perkins, Warren S. (1995, September). "The Fundamentals of Textile Printing." *America's Textiles International,* pp. 246, 248.

Saus, Wolfgang, Knittel, Dierk, and Schollmeyer, Eckhard. (1993). "Dyeing of Textiles in Supercritical Carbon Dioxide." *Textile Research Journal, 63,* pp. 135–141.

"Screen Printing." *Textiles Magazine,* pp. 18–21.

Trotman, E. R. (1984). *Dyeing and Chemical Technology of Textile Fibers.* New York: John Wiley & Sons.

*Section Six*

# Other Issues Related to Textiles

# Chapter 20

# CARE OF TEXTILE PRODUCTS

OBJECTIVES

- To understand the theory of detergency.
- To relate care requirements to fiber, yarn, fabrication, finish, dye, and construction of the textile product.
- To recognize the differences and similarities among the common cleaning procedures available to consumers.
- To know the function of the various compounds used in cleaning textile products.
- To relate proper cleaning and storage to product serviceability.

**Care** refers to how textile products are stored and the cleaning procedures or techniques necessary to remove soil from them and return them to their new or nearly new condition. Table 20–1 summarizes standard care terminology.

# Factors Related to Cleaning

In discussing care, it is important to understand the nature of soil and soiling, the manner in which a detergent and solvent interact, and the additives that are used to improve the removal of soil or the appearance of the cleaned item.

## Soil and Soil Removal

**Soil** can be classified into several categories based on the soil type and how it is held on the fabric. Soil such as gum, mud, or wax are held on the fabric mechanically. These soils can be removed mechanically by scraping or agitation. However, excessive agitation can abrade fabrics. Figure 20–1 shows the effect that mechanical agitation can have over time. Soil such as lint and dust are held on the fabric by electrostatic forces. If the electrostatic force is neutralized, the soil can be removed. Because water is such an excellent conductor of electricity, immersing the fabric in water, as is done in laundering, neutralizes any static charge on the surface of the fabric. Water-soluble soils such as coffee, sodas, and sugar water are absorbed into hydrophilic fibers. When the fabric is immersed in water, the water dissolves the soil. Organic soils such as grease, oil, and gravy can be

**TABLE 20–1** ❖ Standard care terminology.

1. **Washing, Machine Methods**
   - a. *Machine wash*—A process by which soil may be removed from products through the use of water, detergent or soap, agitation, and a machine designed for this purpose. When no temperature is given, e.g., "warm" or "cold," hot water up to 150°F (66°C) can be regularly used.
   - b. *Warm*—Initial water temperature setting 90°–110°F (32°–43°C) (hand comfortable).
   - c. *Cold*—Initial water temperature setting same as cold water tap up to 85°F (29°C).
   - d. *Do not have commercially laundered*—Do not employ a laundry that uses special formulations, sour rinses, extremely large loads, or extremely high temperatures or that otherwise is employed for commercial, industrial, or institutional use. Employ laundering methods designed for residential use or use in a self-service establishment.
   - e. *Small load*—Smaller than normal washing load.
   - f. *Delicate cycle or gentle cycle*—Slow agitation and reduced time.
   - g. *Durable press cycle* or *permanent press cycle*—Cool-down rinse or cold rinse before reduced spinning.
   - h. *Separately*—Alone.
   - i. *With like colors*—With colors of similar hue and intensity.
   - j. *Wash inside out*—Turn product inside out to protect face of fabric.
   - k. *Warm rinse*—Initial water temperature setting 90°–110°F (32°–43°C).
   - l. *Cold rinse*—Initial water temperature setting same as cold water tap up to 85°F (29°C).
   - m. *Rinse thoroughly*—Rinse several times to remove detergent, soap, and bleach.
   - n. *No spin* or *Do not spin*—Remove material at start of final spin cycle.
   - o. *No wring* or *Do not wring*—Do not use roller wringer, nor wring by hand.
2. **Washing, Hand Methods**
   - a. *Hand wash*—A process by which soil may be manually removed from products through the use of water, detergent or soap, and gentle squeezing action. When no temperature is given, e.g., "warm" or "cold," hot water up to 150°F (66°C) can be regularly used.
   - b. *Warm*—Initial water temperature 90°–110°F (32°–43°C) (hand comfortable).
   - c. *Cold*—Initial water temperature same as cold water tap up to 85°F (29°C).
   - d. *Separately*—Alone.
   - e. *With like colors*—With colors of similar hue and intensity.
   - f. *No wring or twist*—Handle to avoid wrinkles and distortion.
   - g. *Rinse thoroughly*—Rinse several times to remove detergent, soap, and bleach.
   - h. *Damp wipe only*—Surface clean with damp cloth or sponge.
3. **Drying, All Methods**
   - a. *Tumble dry*—Use machine dryer. When no temperature setting is given, machine drying at a hot setting may be regularly used.
   - b. *Medium*—Set dryer at medium heat.
   - c. *Low*—Set dryer at low heat.
   - d. *Durable press* or *permanent press*—Set dryer at permanent-press setting.
   - e. *No heat*—Set dryer to operate without heat.
   - f. *Remove promptly*—When items are dry, remove immediately to prevent wrinkling.
   - g. *Drip-dry*—Hang dripping wet with or without hand shaping and smoothing.
   - h. *Line dry*—Hang damp from line or bar in or out of doors.
   - i. *Line dry in shade*—Dry away from sun.
   - j. *Line dry away from heat*—Dry away from heat.

absorbed by oleophilic fibers and require the assistance of the chemical action of a detergent or solvent other than water, as in dry cleaning, and heat or thermal energy to be removed. Of course, many soils are mixtures and are removed by a combination of thermal, mechanical, and chemical actions. If one aspect of removal is decreased, another aspect must be increased in order to maintain the degree of soil removal. For example, if the water temperature is decreased, either more detergent or more agitation will be required for the cleaning process to be as effective. As temperature decreases, cleaning power, even when cycles are repeated, decreases. (See Figure 20–2.)

## Detergency

**Detergency** refers to the manner in which the soap or detergent removes soil. Adding soap or synthetic detergent to solvent lowers the surface tension of the solvent; thus the solvent wets things faster. The solvent does not bead up but spreads over and wets the surface. A **soap** or **detergent** molecule consists of an organic "tail" that has an affinity for organic soils and a polar "head" that has an affinity for the solvent. Thus the two parts of the soap or detergent molecule literally dislodge the soil. Agitation breaks the soil into very tiny globules that are held in suspension until they are rinsed away (Figure 20–3). If hot solvent is used, the oily soils soften and are more likely to break into small globules. Because of the many functions of the ingredients in detergents, the amount of detergent needs to be sufficient to clean. Instructions for the proper amount to use are included on labels. Research has determined the correct amount. Consumers should use a measuring cup to be sure they have added the correct amount. If too much detergent is used, detergent will build up on textiles. If too little detergent is used, soil will remain on the textiles.

**TABLE 20–1** ❖ *(continued)*

- k. *Dry flat*—Lay out horizontally for drying.
- l. *Block to dry*—Reshape to original dimensions while drying.
- m. *Smooth by hand* By hand, while wet, remove wrinkles, straighten seams and facings.

**4. Ironing and Pressing**
- a. *Iron*—Ironing is needed. When no temperature is given, iron at the highest temperature setting may be regularly used.
- b. *Warm iron*—Medium temperature setting.
- c. *Cool iron*—Lowest temperature setting.
- d. *Do not iron*—Item not to be smoothed or finished with an iron.
- e. *Iron wrong side only*—Article turned inside out for ironing or pressing.
- f. *No steam* or *Do not steam*—Steam in any form not to be used.
- g. *Steam only*—Steaming without contact pressure.
- h. *Steam press* or *Steam iron*—Use iron at steam setting.
- i. *Iron damp*—Articles to be ironed should feel moist.
- j. *Use press cloth*—Use a dry or a damp cloth between iron and fabric.

**5. Bleaching**
- a. *Bleach when needed*—All bleaches may be used when necessary.
- b. *No bleach* or *Do not bleach*—No bleaches may be used.
- c. *Only nonchlorine bleach, when needed*—Only the bleach specified may be used when necessary. Chlorine bleach may not be used.

**6. Washing or Dry Cleaning**
- a. *Wash or dry clean, any normal method*—Can be machine washed in hot water, can be machine dried at a high setting, can be ironed at a hot setting, can be bleached with all commercially available bleaches and can be dry cleaned with all commercially available solvents.

**7. Dry Cleaning, All Procedures**
- a. *Dry clean*—A process by which soil may be removed from products or specimens in a machine that uses any common organic solvent (for example, petroleum, perchlorethylene, fluorocarbon) located in any commercial establishment. The process may include moisture addition to solvent up to 75 percent relative humidity, hot tumble drying up to 160°F (71°C) and restoration by steam-press or steam-air finishing.
- b. *Professionally dry clean*—Use the dry cleaning process, but modified to ensure optimum results either by a dry cleaning attendant or through the use of a dry cleaning machine that permits such modifications or both. Such modifications or special warnings must be included in the care instruction.
- c. *Petroleum, fluorocarbon* or *perchlorethylene*—Employ solvent(s) specified to dry clean the item.
- d. *Short cycle*—Reduced or minimum cleaning time, depending on solvent used.
- e. *Minimum extraction*—Least possible extraction time.
- f. *Reduced moisture* or *Low moisture*—Decreased relative humidity.
- g. *No tumble* or *Do not tumble*—Do not tumble dry.
- h. *Tumble warm*—Tumble dry up to 120°F (49°C).
- i. *Tumble cool*—Tumble dry at room temperature.
- j. *Cabinet dry warm*—Cabinet dry up to 120°F (49°C).
- k. *Cabinet dry cool*—Cabinet dry at room temperature.
- l. *Steam only*—Employ no contact pressure when steaming.
- m. *No steam* or *Do not steam*—Do not steam in pressing, finishing, steam cabinets, or wands.

**8. Leather and Suede Cleaning**
- a. *Leather clean*—Have cleaned only by a professional cleaner who uses special leather- or suede-care methods.

*Source:* Federal Trade Commission (1984). *Writing a Care Label.* Washington, D.C.: U.S. Government Printing Office.

**FIGURE 20–1** ❖ Effect of cumulative mechanical agitation on fabrics: original fabric (top left); fabric after 5 washings (top right); fabric after 8 washings (bottom) (COURTESY OF MAYTAG CORP.).

## Solvents

A **solvent** is a liquid that dissolves other materials. The most common and widely used solvent is water. Other solvents used in cleaning include organic liquids such as perchlorethylene. Solvents dissolve common soils like salt from perspiration or body oils. The choice of a particular solvent is based on the type of soil present, the cost and availability of the solvent, and the characteristics of the textile product. The care methods, washing and dry cleaning, are differentiated by the solvents used and the equipment in which cleaning occurs.

**WATER** **Water** is used as the solvent in washing because it is cheap, readily available, nontoxic, and does not require special equipment for use. Water has several aspects of importance in care: hardness, temperature, and volume. *Water hardness* refers to the type and

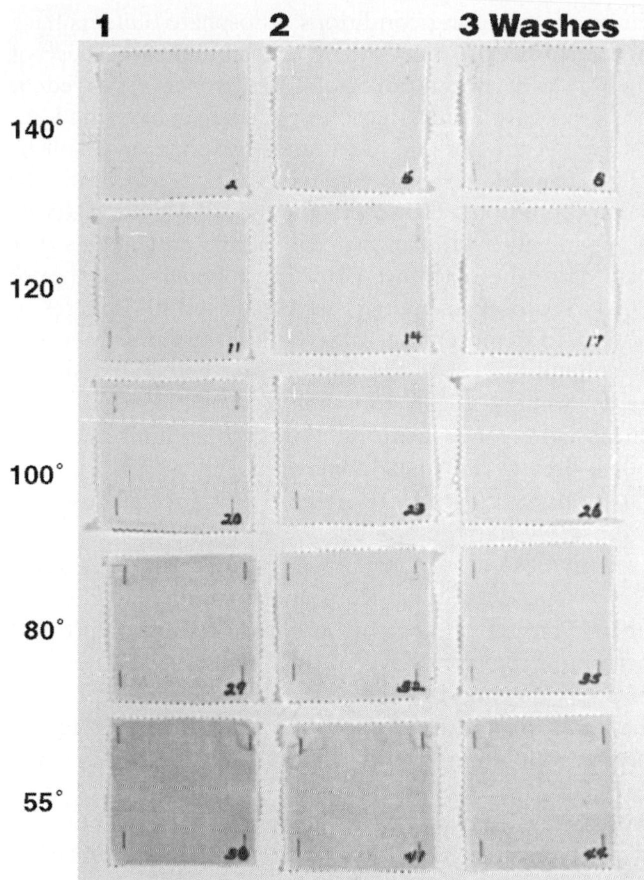


**FIGURE 20–2** ❖ Effect of water temperature on cleaning. (COURTESY OF MAYTAG CORP.)

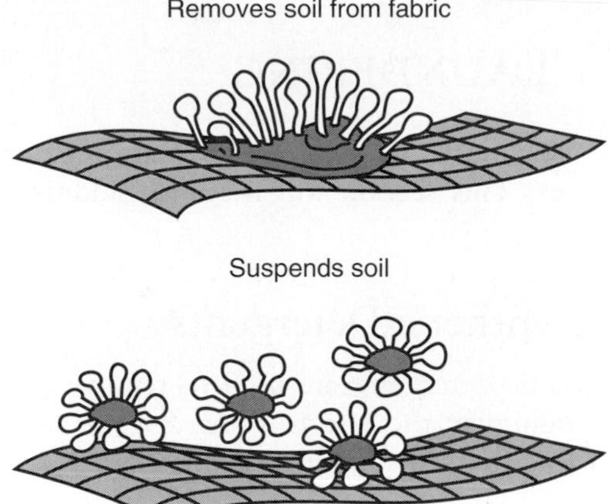


**FIGURE 20–3** ❖ Mechanism of soil removal: detergent surrounds soil and lifts it off the fabric.

amount of mineral contaminants present. Water that contains mineral salts is referred to as *hard water*. The more mineral salts dissolved in the water, the harder it is. Hard water makes cleaning more difficult. In order to soften the water, the minerals must be removed, or *sequestered* (bonded to another molecule). Common procedures for softening water include adding a water-softening agent, such as sodium hexametaphosphate, to the water or using an ion-exchange resin in a water softener.

*Water temperature* is important in determining the effectiveness of the cleaning additives used. Some additives are more effective at certain temperatures. Water temperature is also important in removing some soils. The following are water-temperature ranges as identified by the Federal Trade Commission in the Care Labeling Rule: cold water is 85°F, or the initial water temperature from a cold water tap; warm water is 90°F–110°F, or hand comfortable; and hot water is up to 150°F. Note that these temperatures may not correspond to water temperatures in the home.

*Water volume* is important in order to allow for agitation, remove soil and keep soil suspended, and avoid wrinkling items in the load. Water volume should be considered in relation to the amount of fabric present in the machine.

**OTHER SOLVENTS** This section focuses on solvents that are used in dry cleaning, spot removal or spotting agents, and carriers for other spotting materials. The solvent of greatest interest is perchloroethylene because it is the solvent most often used in dry cleaning. Perchloroethylene, also known as perc or PCE, is used by approximately 90 percent of dry cleaners. Another common solvent is trichloro-trifluoroethane, also known as CFC 113. Both solvents dissolve oils, greases, and other stubborn stains that are difficult to remove in water-based systems. These solvents have been popular for dry cleaning because they create fewer problems with fabric shrinkage, do not affect water-soluble dyes, and are nonflammable. Petroleum distillates are used as solvents in some stain removal compounds and by a few dry cleaners as their prime solvent in cleaning.

Both solvents are hazardous to the environment. CFC 113 is being phased out of use because of its detrimental effect on the ozone layer. Perc has been labeled a possible carcinogen and identified as contributing to forest decline. Its use is carefully regulated. Research with other solvents has identified some that equal or exceed perc's effectiveness in some areas of cleaning, but no one solvent is consistently equal to perc in all areas. These other solvents include petroleum distillates, dibasic esters, isooctane, isopropyl lactate, and limonene.

❖

# LAUNDERING

Laundering is the most common means of caring for consumer textiles. This section will focus on additives and methods.

## Soaps and Synthetic Detergents

Soaps and synthetic detergents are used to remove and suspend soils, minimize the effects of hard water, and alter the surface tension of solvents, including water.

**SOAPS** Soaps are salts of long, linear-chain fatty acids produced from naturally occurring animal or vegetable oils or fats. Soaps react with hard water minerals and produce insoluble curds that form a greasy, gray film on textiles and a ring on tubs or sinks. Soaps are effective in removing oily or greasy stains, but they are not vigorous soil-removal agents.

**SYNTHETIC DETERGENTS** Synthetic detergents are really mixtures of several ingredients. The recipe depends on the type of detergent. Detergent formulas are different in different parts of the country. The differences are related to the type of soil, water conditions, and laws. In this text the term *detergent* will be used to refer to the box or bottle of cleaning compound called a detergent.

**Surfactants** are sulfonated organic compounds that are soluble in hard water and do not form an insoluble curd. Surfactants are vigorous soil-removal agents and are frequently sulfonated, long, linear-chain fatty acids. There are several types of surfactants: nonionic, anionic, and cationic. *Nonionic surfactants,* such as ethers of ethylene oxide, are used in liquids and recommended for use in cold or warm water because they become less soluble at high temperatures. *Anionic surfactants* are good for oily soils and clay-soil suspension. These surfactants are usually linear alkyl sulfonates (LAS) and are biodegradable. Powder anionic surfactants are most effective in warm and hot water. Liquid anionic surfactants are used in liquid detergents. *Cationic surfactants* are used primarily in disinfectants and fabric softeners.

**Builders** may not be present in large quantities in ultra or concentrated formulations. Builders soften the water, add alkalinity to the solution since a pH of 8–10 is best for maximum cleaning efficiency, emulsify oils and greases, and minimize soil redeposition. Builders include phosphates (usually sodium tripolyphosphate), carbonates (sodium carbonate), citrates (sodium citrate), and silicates (sodium silicate). Of these, phosphate builders offer the best performance over the widest range of laundering conditions. Phosphate builders have been replaced in the U.S. by other builders because of their role in water pollution. Researchers in Sweden, however, have found that phosphates may have the lowest life cycle costs and are urging reevaluation of phosphate bans. Carbonate builders do not contribute to water pollution. However, they combine with hard-water minerals to form water-insoluble precipitates that may harm the machine, fabric, and zippers (see Figure 20–4). Carbonate builders have replaced phosphates in powdered detergents. Citrate builders are much weaker at softening hard water and are used in liquid detergents. Sodium silicate functions as a builder when present in large concentrations. However, sodium silicate is often present in small concentrations because it also functions as a corrosion inhibitor. Zeolites are used in most heavy-duty detergents.

**Enzymes,** an important ingredient in detergents, remove fuzz resulting from the abrasion of cellulosic fibers. Since cotton or cotton blends comprise up to 80 percent of the fabrics in a normal load, this ingredient is having a profound effect on the home laundry process. Enzymes prevent the formation of pills and keep textile products looking newer longer. By removing fuzz, enzymes also minimize physical entrapment of soil in worn areas of fibers. Use of biodegradable enzymes may slightly decrease the product's life because a tiny portion of the fibers are destroyed with each laundering.

Other ingredients enhancing product appearance are **antifading agents** and **color transfer inhibitors.**

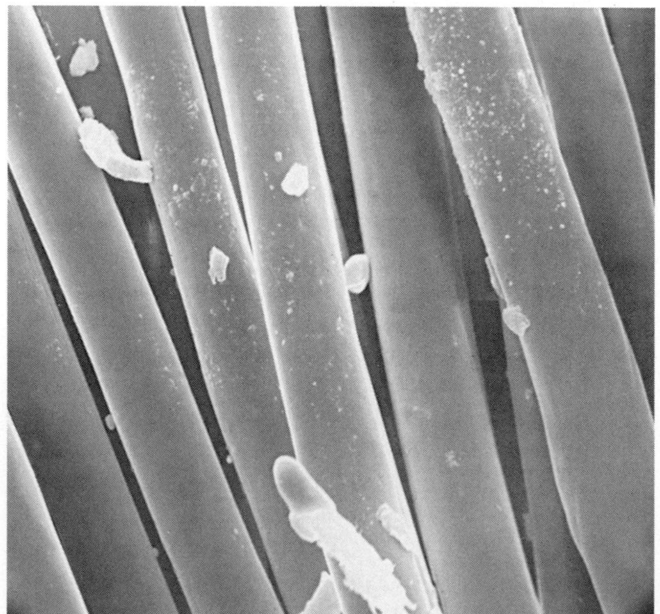

**FIGURE 20–4** ❖ Residue forms on fabrics laundered with carbonate builders in hard water.

Antifading agents keep colors at their original intensity longer by minimizing color bleed in the wash. Color transfer inhibitors usually contain borax compounds to prevent any dye that bled in the wash from redepositing on lighter colored products. (See Figure 20–5.)

**Fillers,** such as sodium sulfate in powder detergents and water and alcohol in liquid detergents, are used to add bulk to the detergent, allow for a uniform mix of the ingredients, increase the size of the micelle (the grouping of soap or detergent molecules that remove soil from fabric), protect washer parts, and minimize caking in powders. Fillers are used in very small amounts in ultra or concentrated formulations. **Antiredeposition agents,** such as sodium carboxymethylcellulose, are used to minimize the soil redepositing from the wash water on the fabric. **Perfumes** are designed to mask the chemical smell of detergents and to add a "clean" smell to the wash. *Dyes* make the detergent look better and function as bluing. Perfume-free and dye-free formulations are available.

**Fluorescent-whitening agents** are also known as *fluorescent-brightening agents, optical-whitening agents,* and *optical-brightening agents.* These compounds are low-grade or weak dyes that fluoresce, or absorb, light at one wavelength and reemit the energy at another wavelength. Thus it is possible to have whites that are "whiter than white." These ingredients do not contribute to soil removal; they mask soil and make yellow or dingy fabrics look white.

**FIGURE 20–5** ❖ Color transfer inhibitors would minimize the stains on this multifiber test fabric laundered with a fabric sample that bled. Darker stripes in the multifiber test fabric indicate greater color transfer during washing.

Other ingredients that may be found in detergents include fabric softeners and bleaches (which will be discussed later in this chapter), processing aids that keep powders from caking and liquids from separating, suds-control agents, and foam-control agents. Processing aids include sodium sulfate in powders and water, alcohol, and propylene glycol in liquids. Alcohol dissolves some ingredients of the detergent, assists in stain removal, and acts as an antifreeze during shipping. Opacifiers give a rich, creamy appearance to some liquid detergents.

## Other Additives

Other additives include bleaches, fabric softeners, water softeners, disinfectants, presoaks, pretreatments, starches or sizing, and bluing. Some additives are seldom used today.

**BLEACH** Most **bleaches** are oxidizing agents. The actual bleaching is done by active oxygen. A few bleaches are reducing agents that are used to strip color from dyed fabrics. Bleaches may be either acid or alkaline in nature. They are usually unstable, especially in the presence of moisture. Bleaches that are old or have been improperly stored lose their oxidizing power.

Any bleach will cause damage, and because damage occurs more rapidly at higher temperatures and concentrations, these factors should be carefully controlled.

No bleach is suitable to every kind of fiber. Because fibers vary in their chemical composition, bleaches must be chosen with regard to fiber content. The sock in Figure 20–6 had been white, but when bleached with a chlorine bleach, the wool-ribbed cuff section became discolored while the cotton foot remained white.

Liquid chlorine bleaches are a common household bleach. They are effective bactericidal agents (disinfectants) and, as such, can be used for sterilizing fabrics. They are cheap and efficient bleaches for cellulosic fibers. The bleaching is done by hypochlorous acid liberated during the bleaching process. Because this tenders cellulosic fibers, the bleach must be thoroughly rinsed out. Chlorine bleaches will cause yellowing on protein and thermoplastic fibers.

Powdered-oxygen bleaches, also called all-fabric bleaches, may be used safely on all fibers and colored fabrics. Their bleaching effect is much milder than chlorine bleaches. These bleaches include sodium perborate and sodium percarbonate.

Sodium perborate is a powder bleach that becomes hydrogen peroxide when it combines with water. It is a safe bleach for home use with all fibers. Powder bleaches

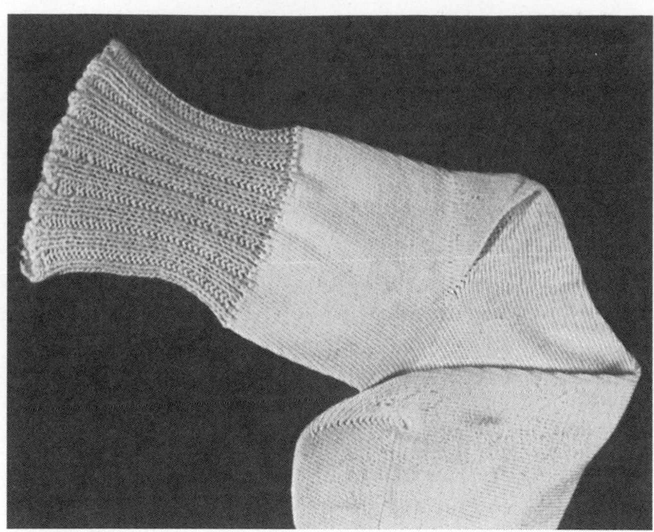

**FIGURE 20–6** ❖ Cotton-and-wool sock after bleaching. Chlorine bleach caused wool in ribbed top to yellow and stiffen.

are recommended for regular use in the wash water to maintain the original whiteness of the fabric rather than as a whitener for discolored fabrics. Liquid hydrogen peroxide bleaches are available.

Acid bleaches, such as oxalic acid and potassium permanganate, have limited use. Citric acid and lemon juice are also acid bleaches that may be used as rust-spot removers.

**FABRIC SOFTENER** **Fabric softeners** coat the fabric to increase the electrical conductivity of the fabric, minimize static charges, and decrease fabric stiffness. The types of fabric softeners include those added in the final rinse, those present in detergent, and those added in the dryer. The instructions for use of any fabric softener need to be followed or problems may result. For example, dryer fabric softener sheets should be added to a cold dryer. If they are added to a warm or hot dryer, oil from the fabric softener may spot synthetic items. Fabric softeners have a tendency to build up on fabrics in a greasy layer, resulting in less absorbent fabrics. Hence it is not recommended that a fabric softener be used every time a product is laundered. Every other time or every third time may be sufficient.

**WATER SOFTENER** **Water-softening agents** are found as builders in detergent or as separate ingredients that can be added to increase the efficiency of the detergent if the water is especially hard. If a water-softening additive is used, a nonprecipitating type is recommended to avoid buildup of precipitates on washer parts and items in the wash.

**DISINFECTANT** **Disinfectants** include pine oil, phenolics, chlorine bleach, and coal-tar derivatives. These items are used occasionally to disinfect sickroom garments and bed and bath linens. Any product with an EPA registration number on the label has met EPA requirements for disinfectants. Not all compounds with these ingredients will meet EPA requirements, so be sure to check the label.

**PRESOAK** Enzymatic presoaks are used to remove tough stains. These additives contain enzymes—such as protease (for protein stains), lipase (for fat stains), and amylase (for carbohydrate stains)—that aid in removal of these soils. Enzymatic presoaks need more time to work than most other additives so a long presoak of one-half hour or more, even overnight, is recommended. Presoaks often include a builder and a surfactant to improve the efficiency of the presoak. These additives are not safe for use with protein fibers, such as silk and wool, and other specialty wool fibers.

**PRETREATMENT** **Pretreatments** are another means of removing difficult stains. They are usually added directly to the stain shortly before the item is laundered. Pretreatment products often contain a solvent, surfactant, and builder.

**STARCH OR SIZING** **Starch** or sizing is used after washing to add body and stiffness to fabrics. Starch as a laundry additive is seldom used today, but spray starches and sizings to be applied during ironing are widely available.

**BLUING** Bluing is a weak blue dye that masks yellowing in fabrics. Bluing is seldom used by itself because it may be incorporated in detergents as a dye. Use of fluorescent-whitening agents in detergents may make it unnecessary to add bluing.

**SPECIAL PRODUCTS** There are many specialized products for cleaning or caring for a variety of textile items. Many products available in the fabric care section of grocery and discount stores are designed for home use.

Compounds for cleaning items containing down minimize clumping of down and damage by alkaline detergents. Sometimes manufacturers' care labels suggest placing tennis balls or other objects in the dryer with down-filled items to minimize clumping. These items may cause problems: the rubber in the ball may not be sufficiently resistant to heat; dye may transfer; and balls may become wedged between the baffles and the bulkhead, creating expensive repair problems. Stopping the dryer periodically and shaking the item vigorously reduces clumping.

Special soaps and detergents for hand washing of wool and other items work in cooler water and remove body and light soils and perspiration. Some detergents are formulated to remove baby formula and diaper accident soils.

Compounds in powder or spray form are used to remove stains from carpet and home or car upholstery and to mask or neutralize odor from carpets. Other products retard soiling for leather, upholstery, carpet, and outdoor textiles. Antistatic sprays minimize problems with static soiling from dust and lint.

Specific laundry aids for removing grease and rust stains should be used with caution because they may change the color of dyes or pigments or damage fibers. With skin contact, these products may cause minor chemical burns.

With the increasing concern for health and environmental protection, consumers can find laundry compounds that include all natural ingredients or that minimize health problems associated with chemical sensitivities, such as perfume- and color-free detergents.

## Sorting

Before laundering, it is important to **sort** the items to be washed in order to minimize problems and remove soil as efficiently as possible. Sort by color, type of garment (for example, work garments separate from delicate items), type of soil, recommended care method, and propensity of fabrics to lint. Consumers should close zippers and buttons so they do not snag other items in the wash. It is also a good idea to check pockets for pens, tissues, and other items that may create problems during washing. Sorting is a good time to check items for stains, holes, or tears and treat or repair as needed.

Table 20–2 summarizes the care required, based on fiber content. It is important to remember that care is dependent not only on fiber content, but also on dye, fabrication, finish, product construction, other materials present in the product, type of soil, and extent of soiling.

**TABLE 20–2** ❖ Suggested care of textile products by fiber group.

| FIBER GROUP | CLEANING METHOD | WATER TEMPERATURE | SAFE TO USE CHLORINE BLEACH | DRYER TEMPERATURE | IRON TEMPERATURE | SPECIAL STORAGE CONSIDERATIONS |
|---|---|---|---|---|---|---|
| Acetate | Dry clean* | Warm (100°–110°F) | Yes | Low | Very low | Avoid contact with nail polish remover |
| Acrylic | Launder | Warm | Yes | Warm | Medium | — |
| Cotton | Launder | Hot (120°–140°F) | Yes | Hot | High | Store dry to prevent mildew |
| Polyester/ cotton DP | Launder | Hot | Yes | Warm | Medium | — |
| Flax | Launder | Hot | Yes | Hot For longest wear, do not press in sharp creases | High | — |
| Glass | Hand wash only | Hot | Yes | Line dry | Do not iron | Prevent fiber breakage by storing as flat as possible |
| Lyocell | Dry clean or launder | Warm | Yes | Warm | Hot | Minimize agitation |
| Modacrylic | Launder | Warm | Yes | Low | Very low | — |
| Nylon | Launder | Hot | Yes | Warm | Low | — |
| Olefin | Launder | Warm | Yes | Warm | Very low | — |
| Polyester | Launder | Hot | Yes | Warm | Low | — |
| Rayon | Launder | Hot | Yes | Hot | High | Store dry to prevent mildew |
| Silk | Dry clean* | Warm | No | Warm | Medium | — |
| Spandex | Launder | Warm | No | Warm | Very low | — |
| Wool | Dry clean* | Warm | No | Warm | Medium, with steam | Protect from moths; do not store in plastic bags |

* Or hand wash, avoiding excessive agitation and stretching.

## Washing

Most contemporary washing machines allow for easy use by providing predetermined wash cycles for today's textiles. Consumers can select wash and rinse water temperatures, agitation speeds, and time. But, spin speed, type of agitation, number of deep rinses, and other factors are determined by the washing machine producer. Instruction booklets for each machine help the consumer understand more of the science of laundering so that the machine's performance will be enhanced if these instructions are followed. Wash cycle information for textiles is provided on care labels and should be followed.

## Drying

The **drying** procedure is usually specified on the care label. Machine drying is considered the most severe method because of the abrasion and agitation. Line drying also may be too severe for some items because wet fabrics are extremely heavy. Fibers that are weaker when wet, such as wool and rayon, may be under too much stress if the item is hung to dry. Drying flat is the least severe method because the fabric is under little stress. Prototype microwave dryers are being consumer tested for home use. These dryers may be available in the next few years and should cut drying time in half.

## Dry Cleaning

In **dry cleaning,** the solvents include the following: perchloroethylene (perc), a petroleum solvent (Stoddard's solvent), or a fluorocarbon solvent (Valclene or CFC 113). Of these, perc is most common. However, concerns regarding the toxicity and environmental impact of perc and Valclene have resulted in new efforts to find replacement solvents and replacements are expected over the next several years. You may need to check with your dry cleaner to determine the solvent used. Along with items labeled for dry cleaning, many machine-washable items may be dry cleaned.

A professional organization, the International Fabricare Institute (IFI), trains and educates dry cleaners, establishes a fair-claims adjustment guide for use in consumer complaints, and provides an evaluation service to members when problems develop. Members of IFI display an IFI plaque in their business.

In dry cleaning, the items are brought to the cleaners and identified with a tag that includes special instructions, the owner's identification number, and the number of pieces in the group. Items are inspected. Because a solvent is used, stains that are water soluble and other hard-to-remove spots must be treated before cleaning at the spot board. Customers who identify stains for the dry cleaner make the cleaning task easier and ultimately improve their satisfaction with the cleaned product.

After treatment at the spotting board, items are placed in the dry cleaning unit to be tumbled with a charged solvent (solvent plus detergent plus a small percentage of water) (Figure 20–7). After tumbling, the solvent may be reclaimed in the same unit, called dry-to-dry, or a separate unit called a reclaimer. The reclaimer serves the same function as a dryer in laundering, except that the solvent is condensed and filtered to be used again. Reclaimers are being replaced with dry-to-dry units because reclaimers allow for too much solvent loss during transfer. Solvents are reclaimed to minimize environmental impact and because of their high cost. Filtering and distilling remove soil, color, odor, and other residue and allow the solvent to be reused many times.

After the items are dry, they go to the pressing area, where steam and special steam-air forms are used to give a finished appearance to the item. For example, pants are pressed with a topper that finishes the top part of the pants. Each leg is pressed separately with a press. Jackets, shirts, and blouses are finished with a suzie, a steam-body torso form (see Figure 20–8).

Additional treatments that many dry cleaners are equipped to provide include replacing buttons; doing minor repairs to items; replacing sizing, water repel-

**FIGURE 20–7** ❖ Dry cleaning unit.

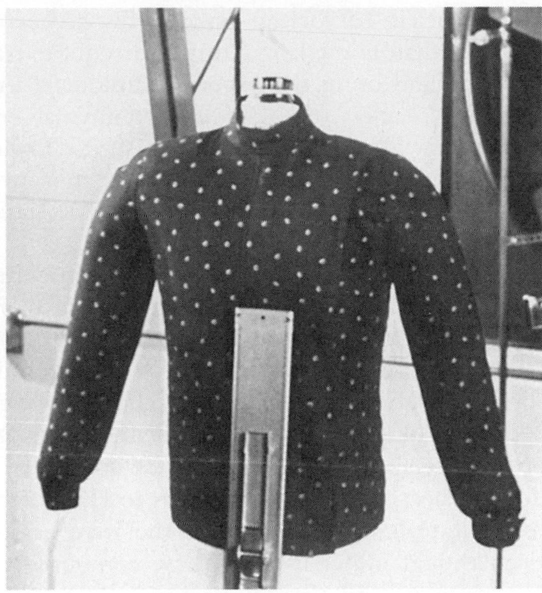

**FIGURE 20–8** ❖ Pressing equipment: pants press (left); inflatable "suzie" for steaming blouses and shirts (right).

lency, and other finishes; adding permanent creases to pants; and cleaning fur and leather. Some dry cleaners can also clean and sanitize feather pillows and clean and press draperies.

Many dry cleaners offer a combination service for wedding dresses that includes cleaning the gown, preparing it for storage, and providing a special box for storage. Although this service is appealing, it may not completely protect the gown from aging and the dry cleaner may not use archival materials in the box or packing materials. Some specialty gowns with lots of bead and sequin trim may require a special cleaning process that was developed specifically for them. The process is expensive and time consuming because most gowns must be sent away to undergo this special process.

Other unique items like quilts, old laces, and embroideries also require special care. In some cases, dry cleaners may refuse to work with these items if the dyes are not fast (a problem that may occur with pieced quilts and embroideries) or if the fabric is fragile, as it is with some old laces. Dry cleaners that work with items of this nature may require customers to sign disclaimer forms. These unique textiles are very difficult to care for since they often incorporate incompatible materials.

## Dry Cleaning of Leather and Fur

Because of the complex nature of leather and fur, products made of these materials or products that contain these materials should be cleaned by specialists. **Leather** and **fur** (furrier) **dry cleaning** involves removing soil without damaging the dye or finish and restoring oils that cleaning removes. This is a complex and expensive process. Wide variations in hides or skins and processing create potential problems for the consumer and dry cleaner. Frequently, the leather/fur cleaner is required to redye or refinish the item to restore it to a form that will satisfy the customer. Because of this additional processing, leather and fur cleaning is expensive. Most dry cleaners do not clean these items themselves but send them to a specialist.

Dry cleaners frequently see problems with leather dyes that are not fast to dry cleaning. This is especially common with high fashion items and items that combine leather trim with woven or knit fabrics. The problem is more common with apparel because apparel items are more likely to have leather trim. However, furnishing items made of leather or trimmed in leather may also present problems in dry cleaning.

# Multiprocess Wet Cleaning

Because of concern about using organic solvents such as perc, **multiprocess wet cleaning,** trademarked Green Clean™ by Environment Canada, is being considered as a commercial alternative to traditional dry cleaning for items labeled "dry clean only." This process is more complex than home laundering and requires training in selecting and using the proper technique. Partnerships with dry cleaners, the U.S. Environmental Protection Agency, the Ontario (Canada) Ministry of Environment and Energy, and other environmental and government groups are investigating the commercial feasibility of wet cleaning.

Almost every type of dry-cleanable fabric can be wet cleaned provided there is careful control of temperature, mechanical action, moisture levels, soap, and other cleaning additives. Before cleaning, products are sorted by fabric type, not color, checked for the presence of water-soluble dyes, and stains are treated. The process is labor intensive and uses controlled applications of heat, steam, natural soaps to clean textiles, and pressing techniques to restore the item's appearance. Even though water is used, these computer-controlled wet cleaning and drying machines differ from home washing machines and dryers. The item may not be fully immersed in water during the process. The cleaner can select from steam cleaning, spot removing, hand washing, gentle machine washing, tumble drying, and vacuuming. Microwave drying may be used to minimize shrinkage during drying. The method selected depends on the garment and fabric type, degree of soiling, and fabric condition. Research has found that perhaps as much as 80 percent of the items labeled "dry clean only" can be wet cleaned successfully.

Consumers have found that the wet cleaning process offers essentially the same cleaning potential as dry cleaning and especially appreciate the lack of solvent odor on wet-cleaned items. Consumers also are pleased with the short-term effects on general cleanliness, shrinkage or stretching, and overall appearance; however, some shrinkage, wrinkling, and color loss may occur. Long-term effects of repeated wet cleanings have not been reported. In addition, there is some concern that care label regulations regarding dry cleaning may not allow wet cleaning labels without modifications to the regulation.

Because the process uses less expensive equipment, less capital is needed to open a plant. Wet cleaning makes significant use of water and energy during the cleaning process, but there are fewer risks in terms of the flammability, health problems, and environmental contamination that are associated with traditional dry cleaning solvents. To clean 100 items, wet cleaning uses only one-fourth to one-third the electricity and approximately 1.4 times more natural gas/steam and 1.2 times more water than dry cleaning. Discharge from wet cleaning facilities has not created problems in water treatment facilities, but more research in this area is needed. Wet clean–only plants have opened in the U.S., Canada, Austria, England, and Germany.

Other alternatives to dry cleaning being investigated include using supercritical carbon dioxide, which cleans under very high pressures, but at high costs; ultrasonic cleaning, which may damage fragile items; and use of some flammable solvents with systems that minimize the risks associated with working with these solvents.

## STORAGE

**Storage** is another important aspect to consider for textile products. Most textile materials are placed in storage during one or more stages of their production. With quick response and just-in-time initiatives, the amount of storage time in the production sequence has decreased for many items. Nevertheless, storage continues to generate concerns regarding the potential for damage that may occur. The conditions under which textile materials and products are stored may influence their appearance, quality, and performance. For example, natural fibers are stored from the time they are harvested until they are cleaned and processed into yarns. If storage conditions are not good, the fibers might develop mildew problems, become infested with insects, or experience discoloration. Incorrect storage of finished fabrics or products may result in permanently set wrinkles, discoloration from contact with other materials and dye or print transfer, and damage from insects, mold, or heat. Storage concerns also relate to conditions in transportation and shipping, especially with so many items being produced offshore.

**FIGURE 20–9** ❖ Yellowed cotton tablecloth stored next to wooden drawer bottom for several years.

Most products should never be stored in direct contact with raw wood or wood finishes. Raw wood produces acid as it ages. Cellulosic fibers are degraded by acid, and brown or yellow stains may develop as a result of exposure to the wood (see Figure 20–9). Plastic bags from dry cleaners are provided as a service to avoid soiling freshly cleaned items during transport. These bags are not intended for storage and should be discarded immediately after the product is brought into the house. Items stored in dry cleaning bags may discolor because of the acids in the bag; build up static and attract dust; or trap moisture, creating an ideal environment for mildew. For more information regarding storage, see the appropriate fiber chapter.

# Other Cleaning Methods

This section discusses methods of cleaning carpets and upholstery. Table 20–3 lists upholstery cleaning codes.

## Vacuuming

**Vacuuming** is the most common and important method of cleaning carpets. Vacuuming removes soil that is not adhered to the fibers, especially particulate soil such as dust, lint, and dirt. Large particles such as small rocks and paper clips may not be removed by vacuuming and may need to be swept or picked up by hand. Vacuuming also is used to remove dust and soil from upholstered furniture and wall and window coverings. However, remember that vacuuming only removes particulate soil. Other types of soil must be removed by other means. For industrial and commercial carpets, it is critical that the vacuum cleaner be one with a heavy-duty rating that cleans deeply into the surface pile and that can withstand frequent, heavy use. Most home vacuum cleaners are not of this type.

On any carpet, localized spots and stains should be treated as soon as possible after soiling. Carpet manufacturers provide a list of recommended cleaning compounds for specific stains. If carpets have an accumulation of oily soils or airborne dust and dirt that is not removed with regular vacuuming, corrective action should be taken. A variety of procedures are discussed in this chapter. However, before any of these other methods are attempted, a thorough vacuuming should be done first to remove surface soil and separate and loosen packed pile.

**TABLE 20–3** ❖ Upholstery cleaning codes.

| | |
|---|---|
| W | Use water-based upholstery cleaner only |
| S | Use solvent-based upholstery cleaner only |
| WS | Can use either water- or solvent-based upholstery cleaner |
| X | Do not clean with either water- or solvent-based upholstery cleaner; use vacuuming or light brushing only |

## Wet Cleaning

**Wet cleaning** or **shampooing** of carpets is a method that uses water-based detergents and may require long periods of time to dry. A diluted water-detergent solution is worked into the pile with rotating brushes (thus this method also is referred to as the rotary brush method). A thorough wet vacuuming follows to remove the soil-laden solution. In some cases, several days may elapse before carpets are completely dry. It is generally recommended that the cleaning solution be tested on an inconspicuous area of the carpet before the entire surface is cleaned in this manner.

Oversaturation of carpets can cause problems with fading and shrinkage. Solutions may not be completely removed, causing brown stains to appear on the surface of the pile yarns. The action of the brushes may permanently distort pile yarns. Choose detergents that prevent dulling of the surface of the carpet, minimize rapid resoiling of the carpet, avoid creating problems with static electricity, and disinfect the carpet. After wet cleaning, problems with static electricity may develop if a water-based solution of an antistatic agent was originally applied to the carpet and not restored after wet cleaning. If compounds containing chlorine, such as bleach, are added to the shampoo, a yellow discoloration may appear on the carpet. This is a real problem in communities where chlorine is used to treat the water.

## Dry Foam Cleaning

**Dry foam cleaning** or aerosol cleaning of carpet can be done by hand with a foam sprayed onto the carpet or by employing a machine that deposits a detergent solution as a foam on the carpet just ahead of an agitating brush. The brush works the solution into the carpet, loosens soil particles, suspends them in the foam, and the vacuum removes the soil. The application of the foam, agitation, and vacuuming can be almost simultaneous. Hence, complete wetting of the carpet is avoided. Dry foam cleaning does not remove deeply embedded soil because the solution works more on the surface. Dry foam processes allow the carpet to be used soon after cleaning, often within the hour. Dry foam also may be used to clean upholstery.

## Hot Water Extraction

In the **hot water extraction** method a hot water-detergent solution is injected into the carpet. The solution is under pressure and wets the carpet quickly but is removed almost immediately by a vacuum. As the water is removed by vacuuming, so too is the soil. Overwetting of the carpet can occur if an area is not treated quickly. To minimize rapid resoiling, the detergent must be completely removed. Since no brushes are used in this process, pile distortion is kept to a minimum. This method is sometimes referred to as steam cleaning, even though no steam is used in the process.

## Powder Cleaners

**Powder cleaners** are absorbent powders combining detergents and solvents. The powder is applied in a dry form, sprinkled on the surface of the carpet or upholstery and brushed or otherwise worked into the pile. The powder combines with the soil and holds it in suspension until it is removed by vacuuming. It is recommended that the powder remain in contact with the fabric's surface for a short time before being removed by vacuuming. The method is fast, requires no time for drying, but removes surface soil only. Pile distortion is related to the vigor with which the powder is worked into the pile. This method may be referred to as dry extraction cleaning, absorbent powder cleaning, or absorbent compound cleaning.

## Ultrasonic Cleaning

**Ultrasonic cleaning** requires that the carpet be removed from the use site and taken to a special cleaning facility. High-frequency sound waves attract the soil and remove it from the carpet fibers. At present, this method is not used on carpets that cannot be removed from the location.

❖

# Conservation Practices

Vintage and collectible textiles in private and museum collections require different methods of handling, cleaning, and storage because many are one-of-a-kind, irreplaceable items. Conservators use special techniques that require training, specialized equipment, and mild chemicals.

These special textiles are analyzed in detail before cleaning to determine fiber content, type of other materials present, condition, and colorfastness of all colors and materials to water and detergent. Cleaning normally includes hand removal of particulate soil and lint, carefully controlled vacuuming, supported immersion soak in a warm water and mild detergent solution, and flat drying. The goal of cleaning in conservation is not the same as in the other processes discussed in this chapter. **Conservation** cleaning is done to remove harmful materials from the textile, but stains and soil may remain once cleaning has been completed. Harsh and potentially damaging spot-removal agents and bleach are rarely used in conservation cleaning because they threaten the integrity of the item.

Proper storage is especially important for these textiles since that is where they will spend most of their time. Techniques that protect items from light, dust, insects, abrasion, tension, environmental pollution, and changes in temperature and humidity are used. Materials that neutralize damaging by-products of aging and provide protection from the surrounding environment support and cushion each item individually.

❖

# Environmental Impact of Cleaning

The environmental impact of cleaning textile products is profound and multidimensional. Newer dry cleaning solvents that replaced highly flammable ones have been linked to cancer and environmental hazards. In addition, ground contamination by dry cleaning solvents leads to contamination of water systems. Several communities have experienced problems with perc contamination of water because of accidental or deliberate spills of perc. Therefore, dry cleaners have modified the way they handle perc. Cleaners also have changed the handling of all items cleaned with any solvent and are converting to dry-to-dry equipment to minimize the loss of solvent by evaporation in the air.

Phosphate builders in laundry detergents have been largely replaced in the U.S. and Europe because of their suspected contribution to accelerated eutrophication of ponds and lakes, yet current research from Sweden indicates that these builders may have the least impact on the environment compared to other builders when one also considers the costs and efficiency of water treatment. Phosphate builders generally have not been restricted or banned in other cleaning compounds like bathroom cleansers and dishwashing detergents. Bans on phosphates in detergents have had little effect on the problems with water systems that the bans were designed to address.

In the 1960s detergent manufacturers voluntarily switched to biodegradable surfactants. Manufacturers have changed formulations of detergents to concentrated ultra forms for liquids and powders that incorporate smaller amounts of builder and filler and require less packaging. In addition, recycled plastic and paper packaging is used. Refillable containers decrease the use of packaging materials even more. Some ingredients in the new formulations are multifunctional. This decreases the number of ingredients and reduces the environmental impact of producing many different ingredients to be combined in laundry detergents. In addition, the ultra formulations decrease transportation costs.

Each load of home laundry consumes between 35 and 50 gallons of water and a significant amount of energy in washing and drying. Few consumers hang items to air dry. Concerns with the high amounts of energy and water usage have prompted the government to require laundry equipment manufacturers to decrease water and energy use for each load. Traditional vertical-agitation washers, which are common in the U.S., may be replaced with horizontal-agitation washers to decrease water and energy use. Horizontal washers have been used for years in Asia and Europe, but U.S. consumers have never been partial to this type of washer. When horizontal washers are introduced to the U.S. market over the next few years, they will be accompanied by detergent formulations that work better with this agitation method to clean dirty textiles. In addition, new microwave dryers will decrease the energy consumed in drying textiles.

## Key Terms

Care
Soil
Detergency
Soap
Detergent
Solvent
Water
Surfactant
Builder
Enzyme
Color transfer inhibiter
Antifading agent
Filler
Antiredeposition agent
Perfume
Fluorescent-whitening agent
Bleach
Fabric softener
Water softener
Disinfectant
Pretreatments
Starch
Sorting
Drying
Dry cleaning
Leather cleaning
Fur cleaning
Multiprocess wet cleaning
Storage
Vacuuming
Wet cleaning
Shampooing
Dry foam cleaning
Hot water extraction
Powder cleaners
Ultrasonic cleaning
Conservation

## Questions

1. Define detergency and explain what happens when a soiled textile product is cleaned.
2. Explain how the function of a soap can be adversely affected by hard water.
3. Why is water used in laundering and many other methods of cleaning?
4. How does dry cleaning differ from laundering?
5. Read the label on a box or bottle of detergent and explain the function of each ingredient listed.
6. What ingredients are present to minimize the effort of the person doing the laundry (i.e., what ingredients have been incorporated in one container to minimize the consumer having to use additional other products)?
7. How does carpet or upholstery cleaning differ from laundering? How should selection of a specific method be made?
8. How has concern for the environment affected how textile products are cleaned?
9. What problems with textiles can develop during storage that affect consumer satisfaction?

## Suggested Readings

Ainsworth, Susan J. (1996, January 22). "Soaps & Detergents." *Chemical and Engineering News,* pp. 32–54. (Each January, this journal has an in-depth article on soaps and detergents.)

American Association of Textile Chemists and Colorists (1996). *Technical Manual,* 71. Research Triangle Park, NC: AATCC.

"Dry Cleaning." (1994). *Textiles Magazine,* no. 2, pp. 11–13.

Environment Canada Staff and Green Clean Project Participants (1995, October). *Final Report of the Green Clean™ Project.* Toronto, Ontario, Canada.

Novina, Trudi (1993, April). "Breakthrough in Care of Colored Cotton." *America's Textiles International,* p. 96.

Reznikoff, S. C. (1989). *Specifications of Commercial Interiors.* New York: Whitney Library of Design.

Rydberg, T. (1994). "Alternatives to Perchlorethylene as a Dry Cleaning Solvent." *Journal of the Textile Institute, 85,* pp. 402–405.

Soap and Detergent Association (1989). *Detergents: In Depth.* New York: Soap and Detergent Association. (Also consult previous editions of *Detergents: In Depth.*)

*Chapter 21*

# Legal and Environmental Concerns

## OBJECTIVES

- To understand laws and regulations related to textiles and textile products.
- To understand federal requirements for labeling textiles and textile products.
- To understand professional and consumer rights and responsibilities in terms of legal and environmental concerns.
- To recognize how textiles and textile products affect the environment.
- To realize efforts within the textile industry to minimize health, safety, and environmental problems related to the production, use, and care of textiles and textile products.

The textile industry is affected by federal regulations and laws related to fair trade practices, information labeling, worker and consumer safety, and environmental protection. It is clear that laws and regulations will continue to affect the textile industry in terms of general operations, label requirements, environmental issues, design aspects, and health/safety concerns. This chapter focuses on pertinent laws and regulations. Some areas of discussion are related more closely to certain portions of the industry. It is beneficial to understand how these issues affect the industry. It is equally important to recognize where professional responsibilities imply legal responsibility.

❖

## Laws and Regulations

This chapter discusses U.S. laws and regulations. Many countries have laws or regulations of a similar nature, but specific details often differ. In addition, this discussion encompasses only those U.S. laws and regulations that relate to producing safe products and providing the consumer with information about the product. Laws and regulations regarding import/export and other trade practices are not discussed. Professionals need to know, understand, and abide by all laws and regulations related to textiles and textile products in any country in which they work. Most regulations and laws relating to textiles and textile products focus primarily on providing the ultimate consumer with information. The justification of these **labeling requirements** is that the informed consumer is better prepared to make decisions regarding purchase, use, and care of textile products (see Figure 21–1). Generally, these laws and regulations are the responsibility of the **Federal Trade Commission** (FTC) for interpretation and enforcement. The activities of the FTC are designed to protect not only the ultimate consumer, but also legitimate segments of the industry itself. It is the responsibility of the FTC to prevent unfair or deceptive trade practices. An example of such an unfair trade practice would include the marketing of a rayon/polyester blend crash in such a way as to suggest that it was made of flax, implied by the use of the term *linen*. Trade publications such as *Women's Wear Daily, Daily News Record,* and *Home Furnishings Network* frequently carry articles describing current efforts of the FTC to prevent unfair or deceptive trade practices in the industry.

The first four laws and regulations deal with "truth-in-fabrics" aspects. For these to be beneficial, the consumer must have some knowledge about fibers and fabrics.

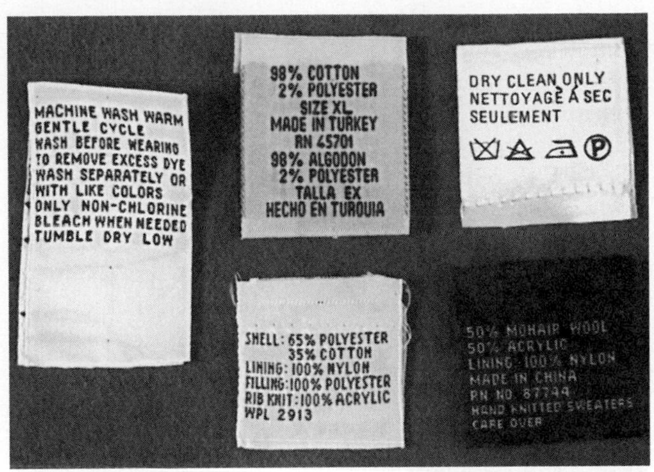


**FIGURE 21–1** ❖ Examples of garment labels. Note the type of information and the manner in which it is presented.

### Silk Regulation, 1932

Silk may be weighted (treated with a solution of metallic salts) to increase the fabric's weight and hand and improve its dyeability. However, weighted silk is not as durable as regular silk, and it wrinkles more easily. Because of these problems, the Federal Trade Commission ruled in 1932 that anything labeled pure silk or pure dye silk could contain no more than 15 percent weighting for black and no more than 10 percent for all other colors. Anything exceeding these levels is weighted silk. At present, very little silk on the market is weighted. However, museum collections have many weighted silk items that are disintegrating and shattering.

### Wool Products Labeling Act, 1939 (Amended 1986)

Wool may be blended with less expensive fibers to reduce the cost of the fabric or to extend its use. The **Wool Products Labeling Act** of 1939 (amended in 1986) was designed to protect consumers as well as producers, manufacturers, and distributors from the unrevealed presence of substitutes and mixtures and to inform the consumer of the source of the wool fiber. This act applies to any textile product containing wool, unless otherwise exempt. Major exemptions include carpets, rugs, mats, and upholstery. The law requires that the label must give the fiber content in terms of percentage and the source of the fiber. The term *fur fiber* can be used for the fiber from any animal other than sheep, lamb, angora goat, cashmere goat, camel, alpaca, llama, and vicuña. Under the act, the fiber produced from those animals can be referred to as wool. The name of the manufacturer or the registered identification number of the manufacturer also must be on the label. The registered number is designated **WPL** or **RN,** where WPL refers to the wool product label, RN refers to the registered number, and the next several digits are the actual number. Finally, the act requires that the name of the country where the product was manufactured or processed be listed on the label. These labels must be sewn in the item; their location is designated in the act. The act does not state or imply anything regarding the quality of thc fibers used in the product. Consumers must rely on their knowledge to determine the quality and suitability of the product.

The terms that appear on the labels of wool items are defined by the FTC as follows:

1. Wool—new wool or wool fibers reclaimed from knit scraps, broken thread, and noils. (Noils are short fibers combed out in the making of worsted wool.)
2. Recycled wool—scraps of new woven or felted fabrics that are garnetted or shredded back to the fibrous state and used again in the manufacture of woolens.
3. Virgin wool—wool that has never been processed in any way; thus knit clips and broken yarns cannot be labeled virgin wool.

## Fur Products Labeling Act, 1952 (Amended 1980)

The **Fur Products Labeling Act** applies to furs, those items of animal origin with the hair/fiber attached. The act requires that the true English language name of the animal be used on labels for wearing apparel and that dyed furs be so labeled. In addition, the country of origin must be identified. The presence of used, damaged, or scrap fur must also be identified. The act has been amended to identify animals by name and has expanded the list of modifications to the natural fur to include tip dyeing, pointing (coloring the tips of the guard hairs), and other means of artificially altering the color or appearance of the fur. This law does not provide for a quality designation; poor quality fur is available on the market.

The law protects the consumer from buying furs sold under names resembling expensive furs. For example, prior to the enactment of this law, rabbit was sold under many names (some highly imaginative and some blatantly false), including lapin, chinchilette, ermaline, northern seal, coney, marmink, Australian seal, Belgian beaver, and Baltic leopard. "Hudson seal" was muskrat plucked and dyed to look like seal.

## Textile Fiber Products Identification Act, 1960 (Amended 1986)

In 1958 Congress passed legislation to regulate labeling of textiles in order to protect the consumer through the enforcement of ethical practices and to protect the producer from unfair competition resulting from the unrevealed presence of substitute materials in textile products. The **Textile Fiber Products Identification Act** (TFPIA) covers *all* fibers except those already covered by the Wool Products Labeling Act, with certain other exceptions.

Although the law was passed in 1958, it did not become effective until 1960. During this interval the Federal Trade Commission held hearings to discover inequalities or injustices that the law might cause. The list of manufactured fiber generic names in Table 21–1 was established by the Federal Trade Commission in cooperation with the fiber producers. A **generic name** is the name of a family of fibers all having similar chemical composition. (Definitions of these generic names are included with the discussion of each fiber.)

TFPIA does not require that the label be sewn into the item, but that the information be available at point of sale. Hangtags or printed packaging materials like those used for some garments or bedding may list fiber content. Hangtags may combine fiber content information as required by TFPIA with suggested price, size, style number, trade name, trademark, or other promotional information. Since hangtags are removed before use and often discarded or lost, many manufacturers combine fiber content information with other required information and sew it into the item as a permanent label. Often, care instructions, manufacturer identifica-

**TABLE 21–1** ❖ Generic names for manufactured fibers.

| CELLULOSIC | NONCELLULOSIC OR SYNTHETIC | | MINERAL |
|---|---|---|---|
| Acetate | Acrylic | Olefin | Glass |
| Triacetate* | Anidex* | PBI | Metallic |
| Rayon | Aramid | Polyester | |
| Lyocell | Azlon* | Rubber | |
| | Lastrile* | Saran | |
| | Modacrylic | Spandex | |
| | Novoloid* | Sulfar | |
| | Nylon | Vinal* | |
| | Nytril* | Vinyon* | |

* Not produced in the United States.

tion information, and fiber content are combined into one label. (See Figure 21–1).

The following information, in English, is required on the label of most textile items, including apparel, outer coverings of furniture and mattresses/box springs, bedding, and toweling.

1. The percentage of each natural or manufactured fiber present must be listed in the order of predominance by weight. The percentage listed must be correct within a tolerance of 3 percent. This means that if the label states a fiber content of 50 percent cotton, the minimum can be no less than 47 percent and the maximum can be no more than 53 percent.

   If a fiber or fibers represent less than 5 percent by weight of the item, the fiber cannot be named unless it has a clearly established and definite functional significance. Where the fiber has a definite function, the generic name, percentage by weight, and functional significance must be listed. For example, a garment that has a small amount of spandex may have a label that reads "96% Nylon, 4% Spandex for elasticity."
2. The name of the manufacturer or the company's registered number such as WPL or RN must be stated. In many cases the company's registered number is listed with the letters and the number. (Trademarks may serve as identification, but they are not required information. Often a trademark is listed with the generic fiber name.)
3. The first time a trademark appears in the required information, it must appear in immediate conjunction with the generic name and in type or lettering of equal size and conspicuousness. When the trademark is used elsewhere on the label, the generic name must accompany it in legible and conspicuous type the first time it appears.
4. The name of the country where the product was processed or manufactured must be stated, such as "Made in USA." Country of origin is identified as the country where the item was assembled. That can be very confusing since the law allows labels to identify when products have been made of components assembled elsewhere. For example, a pair of jeans may be labeled "Made in USA" if it was completely assembled in the United States of domestic fabric. If the most labor-intensive parts were assembled in Jamaica, the jeans would be labeled "Made in USA of imported components" or "Made in USA of components made in Jamaica." For fabrics, country of origin refers specifically to the country where the fabric was finished. A pair of jeans made in the U.S. of imported fabric would be labeled "Made in USA of imported fabric."

## Permanent Care Labeling Regulation, 1972 (Amended 1984)

In 1971 the Federal Trade Commission issued the **Care Labeling Regulation.** Because of some problems with the regulation, an amended version became effective in 1984. Further revisions are expected because of changes brought about by problems with current labels, environmental issues, NAFTA (North American Free Trade Agreement), detergent formulations, and equipment design. The rule requires manufacturers or importers of textile wearing apparel and certain piece goods to provide an accurate, permanent label or tag that contains regular-care information and instructions (relative to washing, drying, ironing, bleaching, warnings, and dry cleaning) and that is permanently attached and legible. The regulation specifies the location of the label by product type. For example, most shirts and blouses should have the label attached at the center back neckline. Pants and trouser labels should be at the center back waistband.

The regulation was developed because of consumer complaints regarding care instructions. The 1984 revision of the rule requires more specific, detailed information concerning only one care method for a product. The label should use common terms that have a standard meaning (see Table 20–1). The instructions must be described in carefully defined words or in standard symbols. (See Figure 21–1.) A care labeling symbol system is being developed for use in NAFTA countries. When products are produced offshore and sold in the United States, they must meet U.S. care-labeling requirements. When a label identifies washing, it must state the washing method, water temperature, drying method, drying temperature, and ironing temperature when ironing is necessary. Procedures to be avoided must be identified, such as "Only nonchlorine bleach, when necessary." If multiple care methods are appropriate for that product, the manufacturer is not required to list them on the label. If the care-label instructions are followed and some problem develops during care, the manufacturer is liable. However, if the care-label instructions are not followed, the manufacturer is not liable for any problems caused by improper care.

The rule applies to most apparel. It does not apply to leather, suede, fur garments, ties, belts, and other apparel not used to cover or protect a part of the body. Certain other apparel items such as reversible garments are only required to have removable, not permanent, care labels. For piece goods, the information must be supplied on the end of the bolt, but neither the manufacturer nor the retailer is required to provide a label to be sewn to the finished product. The rule does not apply to remnants. Although furnishing textiles are not required to have care labels, voluntary care labels appear on most sheets, towels, and other items.

The Federal Trade Commission and the International Fabricare Institute are working together to identify problems with compliance with the labeling regulation and to minimize future problems with inadequate and incorrect care labels. Yearly reports by the IFI indicate that many problems encountered in cleaning are due to faulty or misleading care labels.

## Laws and Regulations Related to Safety

Laws and regulations dealing with textile products and safety issues generally require that selected textile products meet a predetermined level of performance in terms of flammability. The procedure for flammability testing and a pass/fail scale identifying acceptable performance are included in these laws and regulations. Federal regulations often are referred to by the designation CFR **(Code of Federal Regulations)** with the identifying numbers indicating the product category into which they fall (see Table 21–2). Various governmental agencies are responsible for the enforcement of these safety standards, including the **Consumer Product Safety Commission** (CPSC, a subdivision of the FTC) and the Department of Transportation. These performance requirements may be identified as part of federal, state, or local building codes for interior furnishings for public-use areas. However, when more stringent requirements are identified, these must be met by any textile product used in a structure.

## Flammable Fabrics Act, 1953, and Its Amendment

Congress enacted the first national law dealing with flammable fabrics in 1953, following several apparel-fire deaths. The **Flammable Fabrics Act** prohibits the marketing of dangerously flammable material, including all wearing apparel, regardless of fiber content or construction. The act covers imported items or those in interstate commerce. One purpose of the law was to develop standards and tests to separate dangerously flammable fabrics from normally combustible ones.

The act was amended in 1967 to cover a broader range of apparel and furnishings. In 1972 the Consumer Product Safety Act was passed establishing the Consumer Product Safety Commission (CPSC) with broad jurisdiction over consumer safety. The responsibilities and functions, as stipulated in the Flammable Fabrics Act, were transferred to the CPSC. Federal standards were established under the direction of the Department of Commerce and later under the CPSC as shown in Table 21–3. These standards and/or test methods may be modified in the future depending on further research and evaluation.

It takes considerable time to develop a standard. First, facts must be collected to indicate a need. Then a notice is published in the Federal Register that there is a need for a standard. Interested persons are requested to respond. Test methods are developed and published in a second notice. A final notice, which includes details of the standard and test method, is published with the effective date of compliance. One year is usually allowed so that merchandise that does not meet the standard can be sold or otherwise disposed of, and new merchandise can be altered as necessary to meet the standard.

Over the past several years, the CPSC has recalled several dangerously flammable garments that did not meet performance requirement. Sweatshirts, skirts, and jackets made from a fleece-type fabric and lined rayon and imported rayon/cotton chiffon skirts are some of the items recalled.

Mandatory standards have been issued for children's sleepwear, sizes 0–6X and 7–14, large and small carpets and rugs, and mattresses and mattress pads. The **Upholstered Furniture Action Council** (UFAC) has issued voluntary standards for upholstered furniture. Figure 21–2 shows a UFAC label.

Some cities and states have established standards for additional textile items. Various sectors of the industry have adopted voluntary standards for such items as tents, blankets, and career clothing for people who work near fire.

**TABLE 21–2** ❖ Flammability categories of product.

| DESIGNATION | PRODUCT CATEGORY |
|---|---|
| 16 CFR 1610 | Clothing textiles |
| 16 CFR 1611 | Vinyl plastic films used in apparel |
| 16 CFR 1615 | Children's sleepwear, sizes 0–6X |
| 16 CFR 1616 | Children's sleepwear, sizes 7–14 |
| 16 CFR 1630 | Large carpets and rugs |
| 16 CFR 1631 | Small carpets and rugs |
| 16 CFR 1632 | Mattresses and mattress pads |

### ASSESSMENT OF TEXTILE FLAMMABILITY

Summaries of procedures and pass/fail scales are given here rather than full specifications due to space restrictions. The type of textile product category determines the procedure and pass/fail scale used to assess performance. These procedures are described briefly because flammability is the only performance category specifi-

**TABLE 21–3** ❖ Federal standards implementing the Flammable Fabrics Act.

| EFFECTIVE DATE | ITEM | REQUIREMENTS | TEST METHOD |
|---|---|---|---|
| 1954 | Flammability of clothing Title 16 CFR 1610 (formerly CS 191–53) | Articles of wearing apparel except interlining fabrics, certain hats, gloves, footwear. | A 2 × 6 inch fabric placed in a holder at a 45° angle exposed to flame for 1 second will not ignite and spread flame up the length of the sample in less than 3.5 seconds for smooth fabrics or 4.0 seconds for napped. |
| 1954 | Flammability of vinyl plastic film Title 16 CFR 1611 (formerly CS 192–53) | Vinyl-plastic film for wearing apparel. | A piece of film placed in a holder at an angle of 45° will not burn at a rate exceeding 1.2 inches per second. |
| 1971 | Large carpets and rugs Title CFR 1630 (formerly DOC FF1–70) | Carpets that have one dimension greater than 6 feet and a surface area greater than 24 square feet. Excludes vinyl tile, asphalt tile, and linoleum. All items must meet standards. | "Pill" test: 9 × 9 inch specimens exposed to methenamine tablet placed in center of each specimen does not char more than 3 inches in any direction. |
| 1971 | Small carpets and rugs Title 16 CFR 1631 (formerly DOC FF2–70) | Carpets that have no dimension greater than 6 feet and a surface area no greater than 24 square feet. May be sold if they do not meet standard if labeled: Flammable. (Fails U.S. Department of Commerce Standard FF 2–70.) | Same as for large carpets and rugs. |
| 1972 | Children's sleepwear, sizes 0–6X Title 16 CFR 1615 (DOC FF3–71) | Any product of wearing apparel up to and including size 6X, such as nightgowns, pajamas, or other items intended to be worn for sleeping.<br>Excludes diapers and underwear. Items must meet requirements as produced and after 50 washings and dryings. All items must meet standard. | "Vertical Forced Ignition" test. Each of five 3.5 inch × 10 inch specimens is suspended vertically in holders in a cabinet and exposed to a gas flame along the bottom edge for 3 seconds.<br>Specimens cannot have average char length of more than 7 inches. |
| 1973 | Mattresses (and mattress pads) Title 16 CFR 1632 (DOC FF4–72) | Ticking filled with a resilient material intended for sleeping upon, including mattress pads. Excludes pillows, box springs, sleeping bags, and upholstered furniture. All items must meet standard. | "Cigarette" test. A minimum of 9 cigarettes allowed to burn on smooth top, edge, and quilted locations of bare mattress. Char length must not be more than 2 inches in any direction from any cigarette. Tests are also conducted with 9 cigarettes placed between two sheets on the mattress surfaces. |
| 1975 | Children's sleepwear, sizes 7–14 Title 16 CFR 1632 (DOC FF5–74) | Same as preceding. All items must meet standard. | Same as preceding. |

cally identified by federal law because it deals with human safety.

For large and small carpets and rugs, the methenamine pill test is required by CFR 1630. In this procedure, a piece of carpet 9 inches in diameter is placed in the bottom of an enclosed cube (open on the top) and held in place by a metal template with an 8-inch diameter hole. The methenamine pill is placed in the center of the carpet sample and ignited. Samples that burn to within one inch of the metal template fail. Eight samples are tested and seven must pass for the carpet or rug to pass the test. (Figure 21–3).

The Steiner tunnel test is another procedure used to assess carpet and rug flammability. It is required by

FIGURE 21–2 ❖ UFAC label. (COURTESY OF UPHOLSTERED FURNITURE ACTION COUNCIL.)

many state codes and some federal agencies. In this procedure, a much larger sample (24 feet long, 20 inches wide) is placed on the ceiling of a tunnel. A double gas jet burns for 10 minutes while an air draft pulls the flame into the carpet tunnel for a distance of approximately 4 feet. The distance the carpet sample burns is used to assess the flame-spread rating. Flame-spread ratings are based on a 100-point rating scale where 0 represents materials that will not burn and 100 represents the flammability of red oak flooring (classification A, flame spread 1–25; B, flame spread 26–75; C, flame spread 76–200).

The flooring radiant panel test is a third procedure used to assess carpet and rug flammability. This test is used by many federal agencies. In this procedure, a sample 39 inches long by 8 inches wide is mounted horizontally, preheated, and ignited. The burn distance is measured and converted into a flame-spread index. Higher numbers indicate greater resistance to flame spread and greater safety.

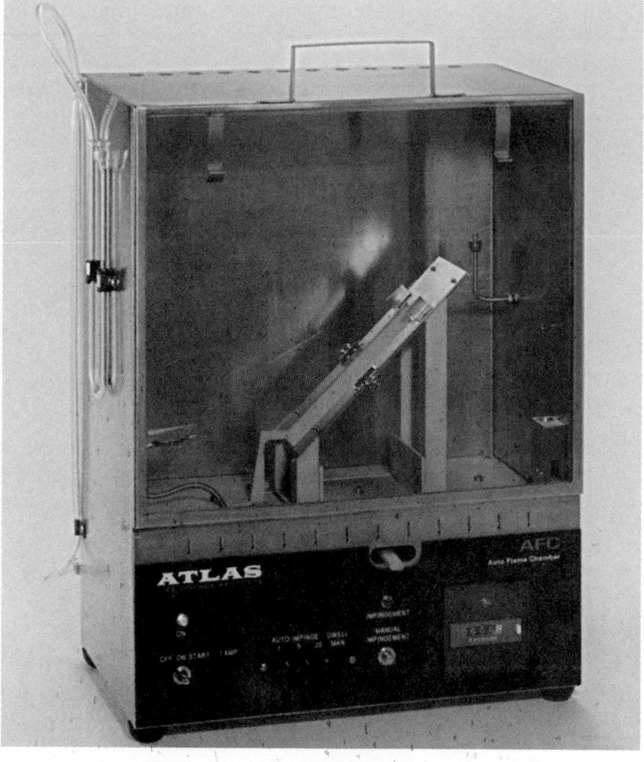


FIGURE 21–4 ❖ The 45° angle test for apparel. (COURTESY OF ATLAS ELECTRIC DEVICES CO.)

Children's sleepwear testing requires that the fabric meet minimum flammability performance standards in order for products to be sold. The fabric must meet these performance requirements after 50 care cycles. The procedures are similar for 16 CFR 1615 and 16 CFR 1616. In both cases, the fabric is suspended vertically in a draft-free cabinet and exposed to an ignition flame for 3 seconds. Pass/fail ratings are based on burn time and burn length.

Regular apparel covered by 16 CFR 1610 is tested at a 45° angle (see Figure 21–4). Ignition is not necessar-

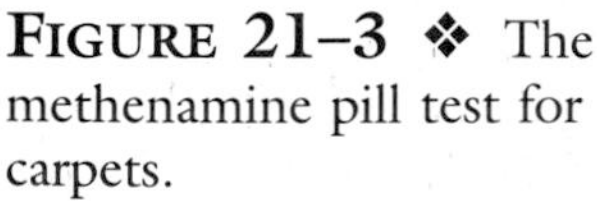
FIGURE 21–3 ❖ The methenamine pill test for carpets.

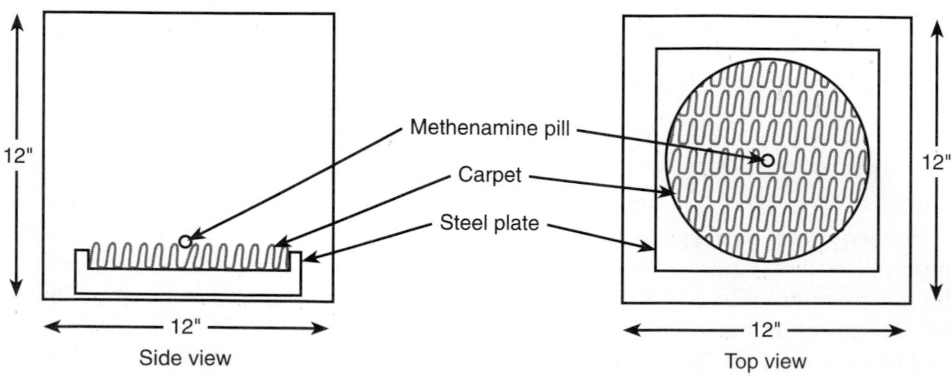

ily guaranteed since the ignition time is 1 second. Based on burning behavior, fabrics are classified as Class 1 (fabrics suitable for apparel with a flame spread time greater than 7 seconds); Class 2 (fabrics suitable for apparel with intermediate flame spread); and Class 3 (fabrics unsuitable for apparel with flame spreads of less than 3.5 seconds). There are distinctions within the class ratings for brushed surface fabrics that are not included in this discussion.

Although the Consumer Product Safety Commission has indicated an interest in developing flammability standards for upholstered furniture and certain categories of adult apparel, no new standards covering these products have appeared. However, because of concern about the flammability of upholstered furniture used by consumers, the Upholstered Furniture Action Council has developed a voluntary flame retardant upholstery standard. Two categories of ignition propensity are identified. Class 1, the safer category, indicates no ignition occurred in the fabric classification test and char lengths were less than 1.75 inches. Class II identifies those fabrics that ignited in the fabric classification test. A hangtag is used to indicate the flammability rating.

In addition to the voluntary UFAC program, interior furnishings are regulated by several federal departments and agencies. The Department of Health, Education, and Welfare sets fire safety standards for health care facilities.

The National Association of State Fire Marshals (NASFM) has petitioned the CPSC to implement a national flammability standard for upholstered furniture based on specific procedures developed and used in California to limit fires related to upholstered furniture. Although the CPSC has not acted on this petition, several states are considering including these procedures in their fire codes. One significant aspect of these procedures is the incorporation of a fire block layer in upholstered furniture and mattresses. The layer is very effective at minimizing the flammability of furnishings.

❖

# Other Label Information

## Mandatory and Voluntary Labeling Programs

Mandatory labeling describes acceptable and legal commercial practices for companies to follow. The law requires that the information be available and accurate, but requirements do not extend beyond that. Mandatory labeling includes fiber content requirements as specified in several laws and care labels.

Voluntary practices and labeling programs are often used in marketing textile products. Voluntary programs include certification and licensing programs, trademarks, trade names, and warranty programs. In many cases, a voluntary program also means an implied quality control program since products must meet company performance and quality specifications.

**Warranties** can be implied or written. Implied warranties indicate that the product is suitable for the purpose for which it was marketed. For example, an implied warranty for a raincoat says that it will not shrink significantly when wet. The written warranties offered for some apparel and furnishing items are legally binding and imply performance at a predetermined level.

**Licensing** describes the situation in which one company legally uses another company's trademarks and expertise to make, use, and/or sell a product. Licensing agreements usually are restricted to specific geographic areas. For example, Company A has a licensing agreement with Company B to produce and sell in the U.S. a print featuring one of Company B's cartoon characters. Company A cannot sell the print outside the U.S. nor can it incorporate another character in the print without negotiating another licensing agreement with Company B.

**Certification programs** describe agreements between fiber and fabric producers regarding product performance and trade names or trademarks. A fabric manufacturer must demonstrate that a fabric meets specified end use performance requirements as identified by the fiber producer before the end product can be certified. For example, pillows marketed with DuPont's Quallofil certification mark first must be tested to verify that the pillows meet DuPont's end use specifications.

A fiber may be given a **trade name (trademark),** which distinguishes the fiber from other fibers of the same generic family that are made and sold by other producers. A producer may adopt a single trade name, word, or symbol, which may be used to cover all (or a large group) of the fibers made by that company. For example, "Dacron" is no longer used to designate a single polyester fiber made by DuPont but is a broad descriptive name covering a family of related DuPont polyester fibers, each of which is sold to the manufacturer by type number. Trade names are often protected by a quality-control program.

The fiber producer assumes the responsibility for promoting the fiber. The company must sell not only to its customers, the manufacturers and retailers, but to the customer's customer—the consumer. Trademarks and trade names also are used for finishes, yarns, and fabrics for the same reason as for fibers.

## CODES

**Codes** are systematic bodies of laws or regulations. Most codes are designed to guarantee a minimum level of safety and often follow a tragedy resulting in great loss of life, such as night club or hotel fires. Federal, state, and local city or county codes for interiors often include in their purview textile products such as upholstery, wall and floor coverings, and window treatment fabrics. These codes enforce adequate standards of practice and uniformity of work. Codes generally provide minimum levels of performance and are designed to ensure safety for the people who live, work, shop, or otherwise use these buildings. Frequently codes deal with fire prevention and control the flammability of textiles used in interiors. Most fire prevention regulations are based on occupancy classification (business, apartment, industrial, mercantile, health care, educational, etc.); fuel load classification (museum, office building, retail shop, paint shop, warehouse, mobile home, underground structure, etc.); occupancy load (number of people); and type of occupancy (adults, children, elderly, or physically disabled). Unfortunately, building codes from the various agencies and government groups are not uniform. For example, federal agencies have adopted the Unified Building Code (UBC) and all standards and codes of the National Fire Protection Association (NFPA) and the American National Standards Institute (ANSI). However, county, city, and state codes often reflect situations unique to their geographic region, such as specific codes for high-rise apartment and office buildings.

The jurisdiction of codes depends on several factors, briefly discussed here. Federal codes are generally applicable to federal buildings or those built with federal funds, such as hospitals. State codes generally apply to state-owned buildings such as schools, state hospitals, and some public buildings where large crowds are common, such as exhibition halls. City and county codes often are incorporated in zoning ordinances. If two codes are applicable in a specific situation, the more stringent code generally prevails. Designers need to be sure that the textile products they select meet the specified code requirements. This may mean that products be tested following the standard procedure specified in the code and that adequate performance records be kept.

Besides knowing code requirements, designers should check with insurance company representatives early in the design process since their decisions may have a major impact on insurance rates for interiors. Designers must know that some finishes and fabrication methods may interfere with inherently flame-retardant fiber characteristics. All products, including those made from inherently flame-retardant fibers, should be tested to ensure that they meet code requirements. For example, the state of New York has a toxicity rule that requires companies to register their products with the state if they wish to sell in New York. This rule has two fire gas toxicity ratings: one for carpets and one for curtains, draperies, and wall coverings. The registration system removes the requirement of having each fabric individually tested at a cost per fabric of more than $2,000.

Codes applicable to upholstery fabrics include those listed for window treatment fabrics. The procedures identified in these codes assess flammability by a variety of methods. However, all regulate the length of time allowed for self-extinguishment of the flame and afterglow. The methods also identify the maximum allowable length or area of fabric burned or charred during the test. Samples tested include pieces of fabric, mock-ups of the upholstery and padding, and full-scale tests using a real piece of upholstered furniture that is sacrificed in the procedure.

Wall coverings are rated for flammability, durability, and stain resistance and, depending on the applicable code, may need to meet any or all of these requirements. Window treatments usually are not regulated by codes, but those that cover a large surface area (more than 10 percent of the wall area) may be considered an interior finish. Codes most often cited for window treatment fabrics are those of the city of Boston, the city of New York, the state of California, and the commonwealth of Massachusetts.

The NFPA 701 Small Scale Test and the NFPA 702 Large Scale Test are used to assess the flammability of curtains, draperies, upholstery, and wall coverings. In these procedures, the sample is ignited and afterflame and length of char for both warp and filling directions are measured. The length of afterflame cannot exceed 2 seconds. In the large-scale test, dripping also is assessed. In the small-scale test, length of permissible char is dependent on the weight of the fabric; in the large-scale test, it cannot exceed 10 inches or 35 inches if the fabric is folded.

Interior textiles used in airplanes and motor vehicles are regulated by the Federal Aviation Administration and the Department of Transportation, respectively. Flame retardancy is mandated for all textiles used in the interiors of these vehicles including seat cushions and backs, seat belts, and interior roof, side, and wall panels. In addition, the standard extends to other items to augment the crashworthiness and emergency evacuation equipment of airplanes.

## Tort

The category of **torts** includes behaviors that interfere with personal rights. Torts generally are categorized as either negligence or intentional torts. Negligence torts include substandard performance in regard to legal and regulatory requirements and contracts. Acceptable levels of performance are often referred to as professional standards of care and usually are identified in professional codes of ethics. For example, substandard performance could include a designer failing to verify that a fabric meets appropriate flame-retardant requirements for a product category.

Intentional torts are wrongful acts performed in a deliberate fashion and may include deliberate misrepresentation and strict liability. For example, deliberate misrepresentation would include deliberately labeling a rayon/polyester crash as all-linen crash. Strict liability generally applies to the physical harm caused to a user or consumer of a product if it is defective and unreasonably dangerous. Strict liability, which holds people liable even in circumstances in which they were not negligent, applies to manufacturers, suppliers, retailers, and others.

## Consumer Recourse

When consumers purchase products, they are entering into an implied contract. They expect the product to perform and to meet their needs. In most cases, textile products perform satisfactorily. However, at times products do not meet the consumer's expectations. Reasons for failure are varied, ranging from improper care labels to improper dyeing or finishing to improper use by consumers.

Problems with care labels are a great concern among consumers and within the industry. When care label instructions are followed and the result is disastrous, consumers expect to be compensated for their loss. Many stores take returns of this nature; however, some do not. In these cases, the consumer can complain to the manufacturer or the Federal Trade Commission, since incorrect care labels are prohibited by the Care Label Regulation. Other reasons for product failure include poor design, improper selection of dyes or finishes, inappropriate combination of materials in a product, improper processing of the fabric, or poor selection of the fabric for an end use. In all cases, manufacturers should be informed of the problem either by directly notifying them or by returning the item to the place where it was purchased. The address of the regional office of the Federal Trade Commission is in most telephone directories. Consumers should write to or call the Federal Trade Commission and include the manufacturer's name or RN/WPL number. The FTC can then identify the manufacturer and provide the consumer with the address for direct correspondence.

Industry professionals generally have a stronger position to take when products result in consumer complaints. Frequently, the professional is responsible for dealing directly with the unhappy consumer or for some process in the production. In either case, the professional's responsibility is to identify the source of the problem and suggest a solution that will satisfy both the consumer and the company.

## Environmental Issues

Environmental issues affect production of fiber, yarn, fabric, finishes, dyes, and pigments; distribution of components or finished goods; and disposal of waste. These are areas of concern to producers, retailers, consumers, and service workers.

Two federal agencies work to protect the environment and create safe working conditions. The **Environmental Protection Agency** (EPA) enforces and regulates air, water, and noise pollution and disposal of waste. The **Occupational Safety and Health Administration** (OSHA) develops and enforces standards for safety and educational training programs for workers. States also have environmental and worker safety departments. Many other countries are concerned with the quality of the environment. Some have adopted more severe standards, compared to those of the U.S.

Consumers greatly influence what is available in the market by their demand for **"green" or "eco" products** that claim to have minimal environmental impact. Many products are sold because of this claim regardless of its validity. At present, there are no legal restrictions or standards for these claims and no restrictions on their use in marketing or advertising. However, some producers have had their products evaluated by recognized certification organizations regarding their environmental claims. Scientific Certification Systems (SCS) is a multidisciplinary scientific organization that verifies environmental claims and provides complete environmental profiles of products and packaging based on life cycle analysis. Figure 21–5 shows the SCS Green Cross certification mark. Oeko-Tex Standard 100 is a European certification standard that identifies acceptable limits for extract pH, heavy metal content, colorfastness, carcinogenic and sensitizing dyes, pesticides, emissions

FIGURE 21–5 ❖ The Green Cross certification symbol. (COURTESY OF SCIENTIFIC CERTIFICATION SYSTEMS, INC.)

of volatile substances, and other aspects of textile products that have been found to be hazardous to the environment or the user.

Consumer practices also have a significant impact on the environment. Consider the diaper dilemma. A conservative estimate is that each baby will use 5,000 diapers in the first 30 months with an annual total of 19 billion diapers in the U.S. alone! Disposable diapers were introduced in the early 1960s. Today, at least 60 percent of all U.S. babies wear only disposables from birth through toilet training. Reusable cloth diapers may leak, require special handling, and use significant amounts of water and laundry additives in cleaning. Disposable diapers are easy to use, convenient, and readily available. But they make up at least 2 percent of landfill material and must be disposed of properly to avoid fecal contamination of ground water.

Consumers and professionals are faced with many difficult choices when it comes to textile products. Environmental correctness adds another dimension to the decisions to be made. Which of these two navy blue T-shirts is better for the environment? Polyester or cotton? The choice seems obvious until one realizes that the polyester shirt is made from recycled beverage bottles and the 100-percent cotton shirt is made from cotton produced using current large-scale farming practices.

Identifying the complete environmental ramifications of the production, distribution, use, care, and disposal of textile products is a complex and multidimensional problem. Many assumptions made by consumers are far too simplistic. For example, assuming that all natural fibers are better for the environment compared to any synthetic fiber ignores many environmental issues related to land use, current farming or harvesting practices, fiber processing needs, use and care of the product by consumers, and disposal or recycling of the product once the consumer is finished with it. A full life-cycle analysis of a product is an involved process. Unfortunately, much of the information is conflicting, misleading, or missing so that the total picture is not clear.

Apparel manufacturers who have developed corporate environmental policies require that suppliers meet their standards. Engineers visit textile facilities to ensure that wastewater treatment and recycling programs meet the expectations of the apparel firm. All environmentally conscious companies face stiff price competition from companies who operate in countries where environmental concerns and regulations are minimal.

Professionals deal with these kinds of problems on a daily basis. Although an in-depth exploration of all elements regarding environmental correctness is not possible here, several concerns and efforts within the textile industry will be addressed to provide some information to help individuals deal with these complex issues.

## Environmental Impact

The textile industry has discharged into rivers, streams, and lakes great quantities of water contaminated with dyes, finishing chemicals, cleaning compounds, and compounds removed from natural fibers (wax and lanolin) and those used to produce manufactured and synthetic fibers. Emissions into the air include excess heat, fly ash, carbon dioxide, formaldehyde, and sulfurous and nitrous compounds that contribute to acid rain. Excess packaging, discarded cardboard and paper goods, empty metal drums, and hazardous and toxic chemicals have been deposited in landfills. Other environmental problems in the textile industry have included high-intensity noise in spinning and weaving rooms and dust and airborne debris in opening and spinning areas. The processing of textiles from raw materials into finished products uses large amounts of water and energy. It is no wonder that the industry has been recognized as a major polluter. However, significant efforts have been and continue to be made to change the way textiles are processed to reduce their impact on the environment and to improve the public's perception of the industry.

Let's begin with understanding the components of **wastewater** and how it is handled in a normal water treatment facility. Several components that describe the presence and level of polluting materials in wastewater can be measured. Biological oxygen demand (BOD) describes the amount of oxygen necessary for the decomposition of organic wastes in the water. Chemical oxygen demand (COD) describes the amount of oxygen necessary to reduce a soluble organic compound to carbon dioxide and water. A high BOD or COD indicates a large amount of pollution that might kill fish and other aquatic life. Wastewater from homes, businesses, and industry is treated to speed up natural purification processes and to reduce pollutants that might interfere with these natural processes.

Treating wastewater normally consists of a series of steps. In preliminary treatment, large debris such as wood and sand is physically removed by screening the water or by slowing the water and allowing the sand and other heavy materials to settle out. In primary settling, the water spends several quiet hours in large tanks where most of the suspended solids (raw sludge) settle to the bottom. Bottom scrapers remove the sludge while surface skimmers collect oil and grease from the top of the tank. Biological oxidation uses microorganisms in oxygen-rich trickling filters or activated sludge tanks to speed up the natural decay of waste. Four to 12 hours later, in final clarification, the microorganisms are removed from the wastewater by settling or straining.

Wastewater from fiber processing, dyeing, and finishing receives additional processing to remove salts, dyes or pigments, other organic compounds, heavy metals, and finishing chemicals. These processes include activated carbon adsorption to remove organic compounds, color, and chlorine; ultrafiltration to reduce turbidity; reverse osmosis and electrodialysis to remove dissolved solids; oxidation and ozonation to remove color; and demineralization to remove salts. With membrane technology, materials such as latex used in carpet manufacturing, salt used in dyeing, and sizing materials used in weaving and finishing can be recovered and recycled.

## Environmental Laws and Regulations

At least a dozen significant laws and regulations have been passed since the establishment of the Environmental Protection Agency. This discussion focuses on those that have had the greatest impact on how the textile industry operates.

The **Pollution Prevention Act** of 1990 focuses on waste minimization (see Figure 21–6). Efforts focus on source reduction, environmentally sound recycling, treatment of toxic chemicals as necessary, and disposal of waste materials in registered toxic dump landfills. Source reduction minimizes the generation of waste materials by substituting less hazardous or harmful materials when possible, and emphasizes product reformulation, process modification, improved cleaning standards and practices, and environmentally sound, closed-loop recycling. These efforts are extremely cost effective and pay for themselves in a few years. The act also requires that companies maintain a toxic release inventory. The inventory has helped companies improve practices from both a profit and an environmental perspective.

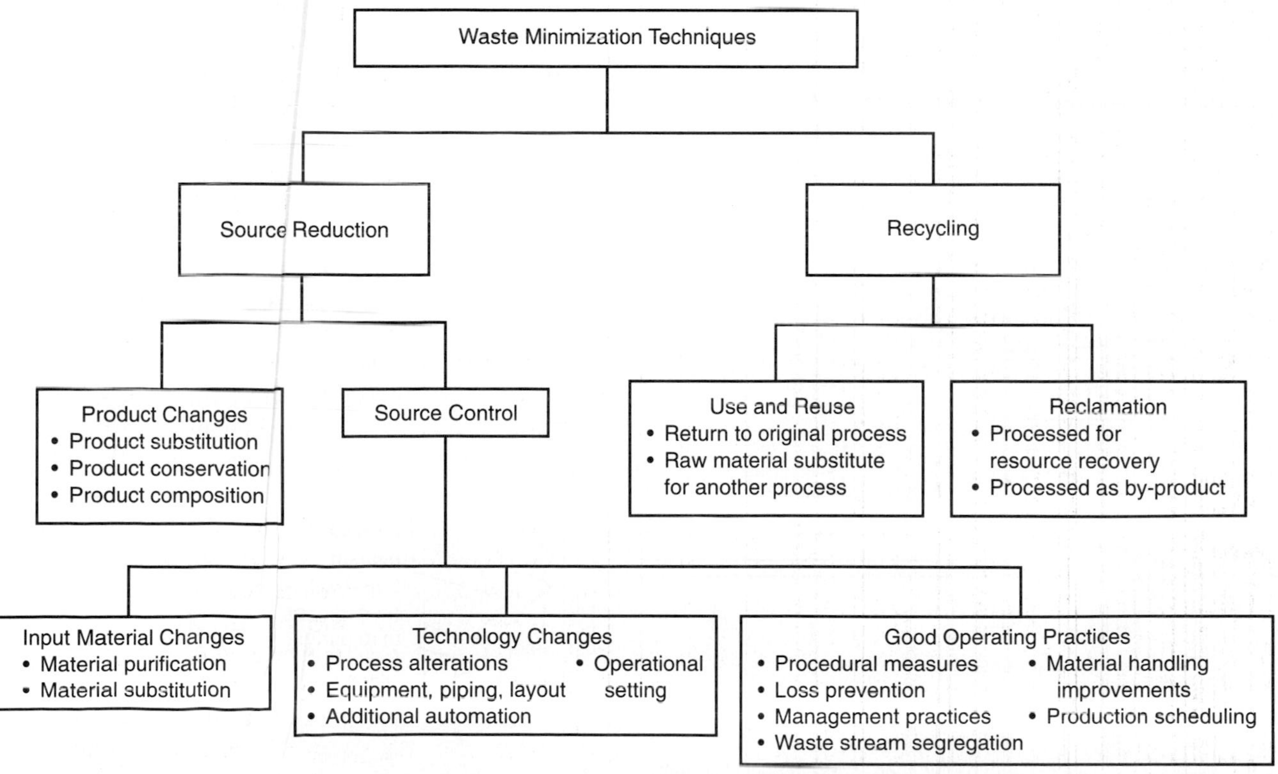


**FIGURE 21–6** ❖ Waste minimization within the textile industry. (COURTESY OF *TEXTILE WORLD*.)

The **Clean Air Act** of 1970 focuses on the quality of the air and addresses acid rain, toxic air emissions, and ozone. Acid rain is produced when water droplets in the air combine with air pollutants such as sulfur dioxide and nitrous oxides. Because the textile industry uses large quantities of hot water and steam, limiting stack emissions from steam-generating units or boilers has received much attention. Efforts include minimizing fly ash from coal-burning units, sulfur dioxide and nitrogen oxide (by-products of burning fuels that contribute to acid rain), and fume emissions from processes in the facility.

The **Clean Water Act** of 1972 is concerned with toxic pollutants and the contamination of groundwater or surface water systems. The textile industry has modified the way wastewater is handled so that discharge meets or exceeds current standards.

The **Resource Conservation and Recovery Act** of 1976 regulates solid and hazardous waste disposal from generation of a material to its final disposal. The transportation, treatment, and storage of hazardous materials are included within its purview.

## Efforts within the Textile Industry

Figure 21–7 shows a textile processing material balance model that identifies what happens to substances used to process raw materials into finished textile products. Any substance that is used in the process leaves the system as either a component of a finished product or as waste. Waste from a plant is discharged into the air or water or onto the land. The industry is working hard to minimize the negative aspects of each discharge category.

The textile industry has reduced the amount of waste generated in textile processing by 40 percent or more in many facilities by changing methods and materials so that the facility generates less waste. For example, jet-dyeing machines have traditionally used a ratio of 10 parts of water to 1 part of fiber. Newer machines are designed to use ratios of water to fiber of no more than 6 to 1. Continuous dyeing that used huge quantities of water, dyes, and chemicals has been replaced to some degree with beck dyeing that uses smaller quantities of these materials.

Dyes and pigments have changed. New sulfur dyes eliminate sulfide wastes, metal-free dyes replace metal-complex dyes, direct dyes use less salt in the process, acid and mordant dyes have replaced chromium with iron, reactive dyes with greater efficiency of use are available, and more disperse dyes work in water-based systems. More pigment inks are water based rather than solvent based; many are formaldehyde free. The metal content of pigment inks has decreased.

By focusing on improving the quality of fabrics, doing things right the first time also means less use of stripping agents to remove color and less redyeing of fabrics that were not dyed correctly the first time. Thus, a better quality of goods is produced with less waste.

Encouraging Environmental Excellence (E3) is a program of ten guidelines by the American Textile Manufacturers Institute (ATMI) that encourages and promotes environmentally sound practices within the textile

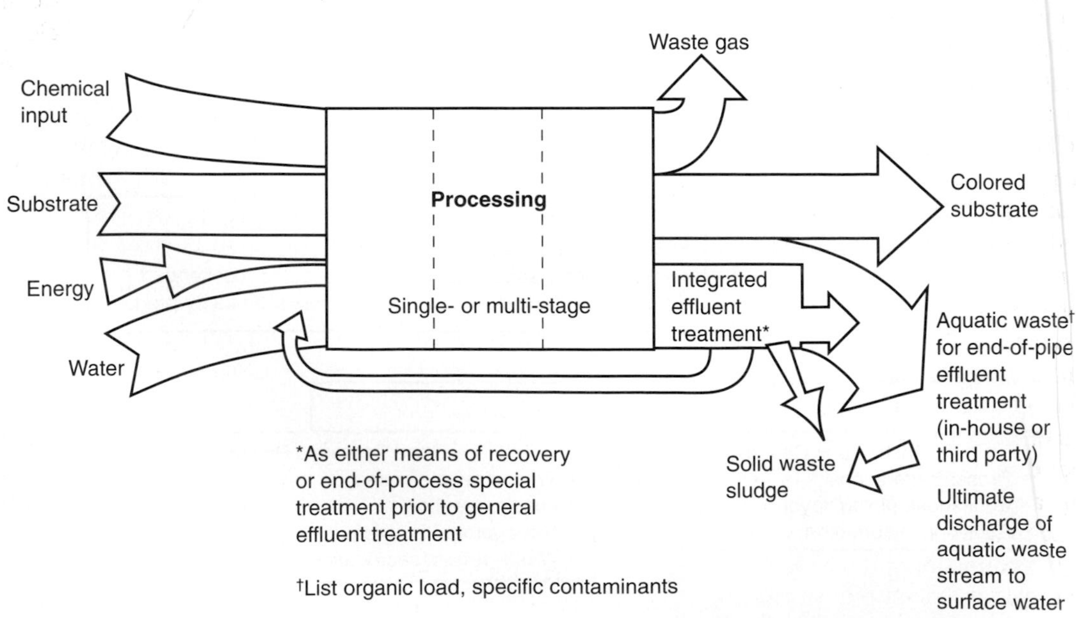


**FIGURE 21–7** ❖ Dyeing process balance sheet. (COURTESY OF *REVIEW OF PROGRESS IN COLORATION*, VOL. 21, 1991.)

industry. The E3 list of approved practices includes producing polyester fabrics from recycled beverage bottles; growing organic cotton without using any agricultural chemicals; producing lyocell (solvent spun with recycled chemicals), wool in natural sheep colors, and color-grown cotton; using low-impact, low-sulfide dyes that use little salt; using natural dyes from plants and trees and water-based dyes that replace solvent-based dyes; and producing stone-washed denim without using stones and with fewer chemicals. E3 companies, representing all segments of the textile industry from fiber and yarn producers to knitting and weaving mills to dyehouses, printing facilities, and finishing plants, have met or exceeded the guidelines of ATMI.

## Environmental Health and Safety

The EPA has issued permissible exposure levels for hundreds of chemicals that are known to be or are likely to be human carcinogens. In addition, OSHA develops standards for air quality in the workplace. OSHA's formaldehyde standard became effective in 1988. **Formaldehyde** has been identified as a carcinogen and is found in some durable-press treatments, leather finishing, and dyeing applications. Exposure limits included in the standard relate to a permissible exposure limit (PEL), a short-term exposure limit (STEL), and an action level (AL) for workers in facilities where formaldehyde is used. Off-gassing formaldehyde at levels from 0.1 ppm or more creates problems with indoor air quality and may adversely affect the health of those working or living in that environment.

Another chemical on the EPA list is perchloroethylene (perc), one of the most common solvents used in dry cleaning. Regulations at federal and state levels restrict the use and disposal of perc.

Indoor air quality has become a major concern. Indoor air pollution develops from many sources including textile products. Carpeting, carpet padding, fabrics used in furnishings and apparel, latex backcoatings, finishes, and dyes on textiles have all been identified as contributing to this problem. Buildings with poor ventilation and indoor air pollution are often referred to as having "sick building syndrome." Carpet and carpet padding manufacturers have changed production materials and methods to reduce off-gassing problems.

Health hazards that have been addressed by the textile industry relate to reducing noise and dust levels in fiber and yarn processing areas and in weaving rooms. Exposure to toxic and hazardous chemicals has been substantially reduced as procedures have been modified to use less toxic and hazardous chemicals or human exposure has been limited when the use of alternate chemicals is not feasible. Safety devices have been incorporated into equipment at the design stage or added to older equipment to minimize risk in the workplace. The dry cleaning industry is exploring options to decrease the use of perchloroethylene in cleaning textile products.

Multiple chemical sensitivity is a chronic problem for some people. Carpet and installation materials (glues, pads, etc.), fabric finishes, dyes, components in printing inks used on printed textiles, and cleaning compounds contribute to the problem. Products that incorporate no bleaches or dyes are available.

## Disposal and Recycling

Concern for the environment also extends to disposal of textiles. Currently, very few textiles are **recycled,** although the percentage is increasing with new technologies and changes in industry practices. Recycling facilities often refuse textiles because of the numbers of different fibers present, the small quantities of materials in each item, and the difficulties of shredding these items. Textiles tangle shredders and cause malfunctions or excess wear.

Studies of landfills have shown that normally easily biodegradable items such as newsprint, textiles, and grass do not degrade under landfill conditions. Many communities require recycling of newspaper, cans, clear glass bottles, plastic materials of specific types, and yard waste so that landfill space is reserved for hazardous materials. At present, textile products are not included in the list of products that must be recycled. Many consumers try to recycle apparel and furnishings by giving items to organizations that collect these products. Member firms of the Council for Textile Recycling divert 93 percent of the 2.5 billion pounds of postconsumer textile product waste from landfills to used clothing dealers, exporters, rag graders, and various parts of the textile industry for use in recycled products.

Textile products use a significant amount of packaging materials. Environmentally sound packaging includes minimizing use of materials, use of recycled materials (hangtags, plastic wraps, and cardboard), and use of quickly degradable materials. Some firms have decreased the amount and number of different types of packaging materials for consumer products. This decreases the costs of materials and labor for packaging and the weight of packaged goods. It also decreases the amount of packaging with which the consumer must deal. For example, shirts that had been packaged with six straight pins, tissue paper, a cardboard flat, a cardboard collar stand, and a plastic bag now are packaged with only the plastic bag and two straight pins.

A significant amount of the chemicals used in producing manufactured and synthetic fibers are recycled. For example, a membrane filtration system at Dan River Inc. allows the recovery and reuse of sizing from warp yarns. Not only does this process allow for reuse of a

**FIGURE 21–8** ❖ The EcoSpun label. (COURTESY OF WELLMAN, INC.)

**FIGURE 21–9** ❖ A T-shirt of recycled polyester fibers.

chemical, but it minimizes processing needed to purify water discharge from the plant. During manufacture of lyocell, a cellulose fiber, the solvent is recycled and reused numerous times.

Production methods have been revised to limit the variety of different fiber types present in some products such as carpet to facilitate its recycling once the consumer is ready to discard it. Since nylon 6 is made from a single monomer, its recycling is a simpler process than that required for recycling other polymers. The 6ix Again program for Zeftron nylon carpet fiber makes use of BASF's patented repolymerization process to produce new carpet from used carpet. Wellman, Inc. Fibers Division has developed Fortrel EcoSpun™ polyester by recycling plastic beverage bottles (see Figure 21–8). Other recycled polyesters, olefins, and nylons are also available in fiberfill, carpeting, sleeping bags, hazard fences, apparel, and other textile products (see Figure 21–9). Most fiberglass insulation used in buildings and homes is 30 to 40 percent recycled glass. Recycling synthetic fibers decreases use of landfill space, saves petroleum for other uses, uses less energy, and eliminates harmful air emissions.

Denim scrap is recycled in many forms: pencils, paper, stationery, sludge for compost to improve garden soil, and denim fabric of 50 percent reprocessed and 50 percent new fiber. (See Figure 21–10.) Textile waste fiber is used extensively in nonwoven products for furniture, wiping cloths, coating substrates, filters, geotextiles, floor coverings, car interiors, floor mats, mattresses, and shoulder pads. (See Figure 21–11.) Waste cotton fiber is recycled and used in off-white yarns for apparel, furnishings, and industrial products like mop yarns and in other materials for the absorbent trade.

**FIGURE 21–10** ❖ Two examples of recycling of denim: pencils made from shredded denim scraps and a denim rag rug.

**FIGURE 21–11** ❖ Floor mat made of recycled materials.

Materials used to protect textiles during shipping are being recycled. Mt. Vernon Mills installed new equipment to wrap cloth rolls in reusable polyethylene wrap, replacing the older method of using multiple materials that were difficult to handle and reprocess. Many firms have developed methods to decrease the use of cardboard tubes and plastic wraps while not compromising fabric condition or quality. In addition, many firms use recycled or recyclable tubes and wraps for fabric or finished products.

The Russell Corporation has an on-site recycling facility to facilitate recycling of materials such as cardboard, paper, aluminum, scrap iron, wood pallets, ink waste, and fiber waste. Arkwright Mills uses recycled dyes whenever possible. Coats American recycles returned thread packages into new cones and tubes for packaging thread. Efforts to increase recycling of textiles continues so that fewer and fewer products will be deposited in landfills.

## Key Terms

Labeling requirements
Federal Trade Commission
Wool Products Labeling Act
WPL number
RN number
Fur Products Labeling Act
Textile Fiber Products Identification Act
Generic name
Care Labeling Regulation
Code of Federal Regulations
Consumer Product Safety Commission
Flammable Fabrics Act
Upholstered Furniture Action Council
Warranties
Licensing
Certification
Trade name
Trademark
Codes
Torts
Environmental Protection Agency
Occupational Safety and Health Administration
Green or eco products
Wastewater treatment
Pollution Prevention Act
Clean Air Act
Clean Water Act
Resource Conservation and Recovery Act
Formaldehyde
Recycling

## Questions

1. What information is required by law to be on sewn-in labels? What information is required to be present to consumers at point of purchase?
2. What rights do consumers have if they are dissatisfied with the performance or serviceability of a textile product?
3. What are the legal responsibilities of manufacturers, producers, and their employees regarding textile products?
4. What law or regulation deals with issues of safety?
5. What additional requirements might furnishings be required to meet depending on building codes?
6. What are the requirements for a textile product to be marketed as a "green" product?
7. What steps has the textile industry taken to minimize environmental impact in terms of production, distribution, and disposal of textiles or related materials?
8. Describe how recycling can be beneficial to the consumer of the product and the environment.

## Suggested Readings

Damant, G. H. (1994). "Recent United States Developments in Tests and Materials for the Flammability of Furnishings." *Journal of the Textile Institute, 85*(4), pp. 505–525.

Dooms, Frans (1995, January). "Ecology from the R&D Angle." *Textile Month,* pp. 9–11.

Elliott, Edward J. (1996, February). "Recycling: Saving Money and the Environment," *Textile World,* pp. 72–74.

"Environmentally Improved Textile Products." *Canadian Textile Journal,* p. 26.

Federal Trade Commission (March, 1984). *Writing a Care Label.* Washington, D.C.: Federal Trade Commission.

Franke, D., Northeim, C., and Black, M. (1994). "Furnishings and the Indoor Environment." *Journal of the Textile Institute, 85*(4), pp. 496–504.

Glover, Brian, and Hill, Lorraine (1993). "Waste Minimization in the Dyehouse." *Textile Chemist and Colorist, 25*(6), p. 20.

Grasso, Maureen (1995). "Recycled Textile Fibers: The Challenge of the Twenty-First Century." *Textile Chemist and Colorist, 27*(4), pp. 16–20.

Huer, Charles R. (1989). *Means Legal Reference for Design and Construction.* Kingston, MA: R. S. Means Company.

Pullen, Jo Ann (1995, March). "D-13 Textile and Apparel Care Labeling Standards." *ASTM Standardization News,* pp. 42–47.

Reznikoff, S. C. (1989). *Specifications for Commercial Interiors.* New York: Watson-Guptill Publications.

Sewekow, Ulrich (1996). "How to Meet the Requirements for Eco-Textiles." *Textile Chemist and Colorist, 28*(1), pp. 21–27.

Tortora, Phyllis G., and Merkel, Robert S. (1996). *Fairchild's Dictionary of Textiles,* 7th ed. New York: Fairchild Publications.

*Chapter 22*

# Career Exploration

## OBJECTIVES

- To understand how knowledge of textiles contributes to professional roles.
- To recognize the need to communicate textiles information quickly and accurately to other professionals and consumers.
- To be aware of the diverse career options requiring a knowledge of textiles.

Now that the science of textiles has been explored in some depth, it is helpful to know how this information relates to various careers. General terms and sample job titles are used here since each company, firm, or agency is organized differently. The ability to use terms correctly when communicating with others, to apply knowledge, and to analyze products depends on both the textile product and the focus of the company, organization, or agency in which one is employed. For example, the handling and marketing of a fabric being sold to a company that will sew it into a product differs from that of a fabric being sold to the individual customer.

Each section includes a brief discussion of the general area, position types, responsibilities, and the ways in which a knowledge of textiles contributes to fulfilling the expectations and responsibilities of a position. Although this chapter explores many career possibilities, it is not designed to be a complete exploration. The goal is to help the reader understand why a knowledge of textiles will assist in obtaining and advancing in a position. In several sections, portions of conversation with professionals reflect professional roles. Whenever possible, salary information from 1995–1996 gives an idea of starting salaries in the field.

## Design

**Designers** are responsible for creating the idea or design for a product, or selecting the components for a room setting. Designers work at all levels in the industry. They may design components such as yarns, fabrics, or patterns for prints, or apparel items, furnishing items, rooms, or other settings. Their creativity is of great importance but it may need to be focused on a specific product type, price range, and target market (Figure 22–1). Designers need to know what will sell, what will satisfy the consumer, what is within the capability of the company and its equipment, and what is within the price range of the target consumer. They need to understand the performance of the textiles with which they work and select the appropriate materials to produce the serviceability desired in the finished product. When working in manufacturing, designers need to understand the sewability of materials and fabrics. For example, fabrics that are difficult to sew, heavy stiff fabrics like cotton denim and lightweight slippery fabrics like polyester ninon, demand higher piece rates because sewing machine operators cannot work as quickly with these fabrics.

**Figure 22–1** ❖ Designer Susan McKeever displays boards depicting fashions created exclusively for J.C. Penney. (Courtesy of J.C. Penney Co., Inc.)

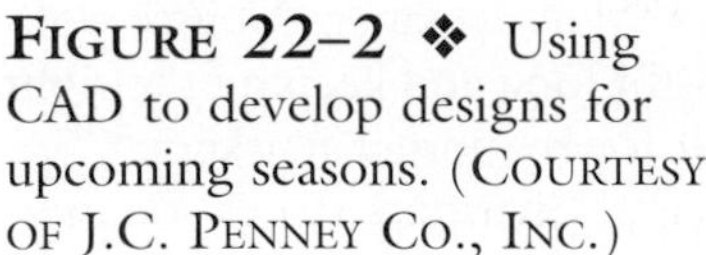

FIGURE 22–2 ❖ Using CAD to develop designs for upcoming seasons. (COURTESY OF J.C. PENNEY CO., INC.)

Designers need to be sure that their work meets the appropriate laws, regulations, and codes. Designers may need to be flexible enough to work at several quality levels and to work with knock-offs or less expensive copies of higher priced items. Most design work means problem solving and satisfying the company's target market while continuing to make a profit. Beginning positions in design include design assistant, assistant designer, or pattern maker. Design positions may be found in product development areas, especially in manufacturing firms and retail businesses. Use of computers in design is common and designers need experience working with systems and software appropriate to their specialization. CAD (computer-aided design) experience can be essential in securing a position or advancing within a firm (Figure 22–2).

Design positions are also available in the entertainment field. Designers create the set or stage and dress the cast to convey the many visual aspects of the production. Positions in the entertainment area are difficult to attain. A designer may have to spend several years as an assistant before achieving recognition as a set or costume designer. Sometimes designers sell a small portion of their work to the entertainment area, but the greatest share of their work is focused on other markets.

Design includes the **artist** or craftsperson who creates one-of-a-kind items. Most artists specialize in one medium or type of object. For example, an artist may specialize in weaving large tapestries for public buildings or office spaces. Another artist may specialize in creating wearable art, employing a variety of techniques including weaving, screen printing, and quilting. The artist must be able to select appropriate materials and be sufficiently adept to produce the piece. Becoming a self-employed artist requires a great deal of effort, talent, and discipline.

Motoku, a contract interior designer with three years' experience, describes her day as being "very busy meeting with architects, conducting on-site visits to make sure that carpet and wall coverings are being installed correctly and that everything is on schedule, visiting showrooms, and doing my design work. Good communication skills and a technical vocabulary are absolutely essential! I spend a lot of time talking to suppliers and contractors to facilitate shipping or installation. I verify that fabrics for walls, windows, or furniture are available in the quantity and colorway desired and that the various separate pieces work well together and achieve the effect my clients want. I work with clients to help them understand how various textiles will perform and why fabrics differ in look, performance, and cost. I find my job very challenging and exciting, yet very busy and demanding." She says that her work with CAD programs as a student gave her computer skills that make her job a little easier. Starting salaries in interior design range from $16,500 to $29,000 with an average of $22,100.

Dana has been a technical pattern maker for five years and has worked for three firms during that time.

Her current company "designs and produces women's sleepwear and lounge wear and is a contractor for several large retailers. I develop the patterns for production based on designers' specifications and design samples. We are given shrinkage information and have to enlarge and adjust our pattern pieces so that it still fits the customer after washing. I have to know how various fabrics hang and work together so that the pattern works out. I often work with only the name of a fabric, not a real sample, so I have to visualize how the fabric works on the body when I'm developing a pattern. When garments don't spec out, I talk to the designer to figure out how to make it (the pattern) do what Gail (the designer) wants it to do. I spend a lot of my time checking accuracy and making sure fabric use is high so waste is low and the company still makes a profit. If production has a problem with any part of the garment, they come to me so I have to know how production works, too." Starting salaries for pattern makers range from $18,000 to $24,000 with an average of $22,000. One year of experience with computerized pattern making can increase annual salary by $5,000, but often requires moving to another firm. Apparel designers generally start as assistant designers with a salary range from $19,500 to $25,750, with an average of $22,575.

## MERCHANDISING

Working in the retail setting as a merchandise buyer or manager is an exciting career goal for many students. However, many positions in **merchandising** exist beyond the retail setting There are buying positions in companies throughout the textile pipeline. For example, yarn companies buy fiber. Weaving and knitting facilities buy yarn. Converters and dyeing/finishing plants buy dyes and chemicals to finish fabrics. Sewing facilities buy fabric, wood and metal for furniture frames, padding, zippers, buttons, and a host of other materials and components to use in producing the finished item. Product coordinators keep track of all components, deadlines, and activities so that the finished product is available on schedule.

Mail order is another business category. Positions relate to buying or developing the merchandise to be presented in the catalog. Production of the catalog and presentation of the product are other important positions. Another possible option is in mall management, although this is probably not an entry-level position. These professionals manage a mall facility, see that all retail space in the mall is rented, and publicize the mall via style shows, antique shows, and other events that bring the public to the mall. Mall management is responsible for maintaining the right look and keeping the right mix of retailers in the mall for the target market.

**Managers** of departments, divisions, stores, or merchandise categories require a knowledge of textiles. Although managers may not buy the merchandise, they select products for their store and promote products to generate sales. **Visual merchandisers** deal with how the merchandise is presented to the customer. *Entrepreneurs* and *small business owners* deal with every part of running a business from identifying the target market and product mix, promoting and selling the merchandise, hiring staff, dealing with financial arrangements and budgets, to maintaining the store. In direct sales, the **nonstore retailer** sells merchandise directly to the consumer through in-home parties and telephone sales. This means of selling merchandise is used to sell cosmetics, interior decorating items, kitchen supplies, and some apparel.

Lou was promoted to merchandise manager after working for a national chain for fourteen months. "I track sales, promote merchandise within the store, keep track of inventory, and work with staff to help them know the merchandise. My product mix includes domestics and housewares and is about one-third of the store's floor space. Other merchandise managers ask me to help in selecting merchandise appropriate for a season. Since I had a knowledge of textiles, I help them out. Since my store does no merchandise training, I also work with my sales staff in educating them about the differences among the textile products we sell. With my education, I am familiar with the store's just-in-time inventory system and I understand merchandise buying." Starting salaries for merchandising positions for fashion merchandising graduates range from $20,000 to $27,750 with an average of $23,560. Compare this information to salaries for business graduates: starting salary range of $18,000 to $28,300 with an average of $23,485.

Professionals must be able to select products that will appeal to and satisfy the consumer. Often consumers assume that the employees of a retail establishment are knowledgeable about the products they carry. Consider the questions consumers ask sales associates: Will this item stain? How should it be laundered? Will it last? Will it be comfortable? These questions require textile knowledge to be answered correctly.

## WHOLESALING

Producers of textile products need someone to represent their product line to the retailer. Often this presentation takes place in a company showroom located at headquarters or in a merchandise center where similar merchandise lines are grouped together for buyers to see. Showroom managers and staff explain a company's line to retail buyers or interior designers. Sales representative positions often require someone who is willing to travel and who is self-motivated. Reps are well paid for their work. Sales reps may represent several companies, product lines, or product types that complement each other. For example, one sales rep may carry the line of one company that produces women's dresses, a line of another company that produces coordinates aimed at the same target market, and jewelry that could be worn with either of these two lines. Another rep may represent three firms: upholstered furniture, accent rugs, and household accessories. Fabric reps specialize in selling fabric to producers, interior design firms, or consumer fabric stores. Rep positions are seldom starting positions. Showroom assistant managers' starting salaries range from $20,000 to $26,500 with an average of $24,500.

❖

## Sourcing

**Sourcing** deals with identifying the firm that can supply the item needed. Sourcing agents need to understand textiles, textile products, production, marketing, performance and quality evaluation, and products or services. The ability to develop and understand specifications of products or services is critical. Sourcing agents need to have good communication skills and a global perspective. For example, if a retailer wants to carry a specific item, a sourcing agent in the retail firm would investigate companies who produce items similar to what is needed, evaluate sample products, cost the products, and analyze the ability of each company to meet production deadlines. The sourcing agent usually recommends one or more companies with whom the store should negotiate for sample runs or contract terms.

Sourcing agents are often responsible for follow-up to ensure that the contract will be met, that items are shipped on time, and that shipping is handled in the agreed-on manner. When the source of production is offshore, sourcing agents need to be familiar with import/export requirements and regulations. For example, quotas refer to specific quantities of goods allowed to be imported from one country to another. Quotas result from agreements between the importing and the exporting countries. U.S. quotas are the most elaborate and detailed of any in the world. Imports are divided by product category. For apparel, they are further divided by fiber type and gender. Sourcing agents frequently work with customs officials to minimize problems or solve problems as they develop. Sourcing positions require some industry experience.

Directors or managers of human resources deal with sourcing issues of another kind: employees within the firm. They interview potential employees and determine whom to hire based on the positions available and the knowledge and skills of the applicants. Human resource directors also may be involved with negotiating employee benefits and salaries.

❖

## Marketing

**Marketing** positions require people with an understanding of what motivates consumers to buy. Marketing positions may be in areas as diverse as advertising, journalism, and display. These professionals help the consumer become aware of the product, recognize its usefulness or desirability, and decide to purchase the product. Marketing and merchandising positions are combined in some firms. A knowledge of a product's special features or design aspects will assist in marketing it. Textile knowledge may give a firm a boost in its marketing by focusing on product quality. Other firms focus on product serviceability and highlight their product testing programs and high performance ratings. Still other firms focus on the high fashion aspects of their products. A knowledge of textiles provides an understanding of the product and an expanded vocabulary useful in marketing the product. Starting salaries in marketing range from $17,000 to $28,000 with an average of $24,390.

❖

## Product Development

**Product development** specialists work in several areas in a company. Some individuals have a background in the social sciences, others in the physical sciences, and still others in business or design. In product development, target markets and consumer expectations for products are identified. **Prototypes** of products are developed in an extremely time-consuming process that may involve large numbers of people (Figures 22–3 and 22–4). For highly innovative products, product development works with research and development, or the two may be combined in one department in a company. Prototypes (original product samples) are evaluated by combining performance testing with user, wear, or product testing. For example, in **performance testing** a

**FIGURE 22–3** ❖ Computer-aided design (CAD) used in the production of patterned textiles. (COURTESY OF STORK SCREENS, B.V.)

new product may be tested for tensile strength, abrasion resistance, washability, and comfort using standard test methods and specialized testing equipment. At the same time, in **product testing** identical products may be used by consumers to see how the product performs for them and how they react to the product. This evaluation may occur several times as the prototype is modified based on analysis of cost, consumer reaction, and performance.

Product development does not cease once the product is on the market. Follow-up studies assess how the general public accepts the product. Modifications may be necessary for the product to remain competitive. Note how often new detergents come on the market or how often detergents are labeled "new and improved." Development of a laundry detergent is just one area where textile knowledge is appropriate for a position in product development. The professional in this area needs basic textile knowledge to understand the components of the item being developed. For example, microfibers have created some unique design, production, and marketing challenges.

Product development involves developing the design, selecting the most appropriate fabrication for the

**FIGURE 22–4** ❖ Developing colorways for upcoming seasons. (COURTESY OF J.C. PENNEY CO., INC.)

design, and sourcing accessories to go with the item. For example, a firm may realize that one of its products is losing market share to a less expensive competitor. Thus, to remain competitive, the firm needs to produce the product for less. One way of remaining competitive is to use a less expensive, but equally serviceable product. A firm may work with several mills to identify fabrics that meet their requirements and test these fabrics to determine their performance. Once performance has been determined, the firm may negotiate with a mill so that the most serviceable fabric is further modified to meet the firm's performance expectations at a price level appropriate for the final product. A similar kind of sequence may occur in-house as design modifications and product groupings are evaluated. Product development is an area in the textile industry that is increasing in importance. Starting salaries range from $19,000 to $27,500 with an average of $24,275.

## Quality Assurance

**Quality assurance** (QA), **quality control** (QC), and total quality management (TQM) are important areas within the textile industry. In general, quality engineers deal with producing an item at a specified level of quality in a manner that is as safe, cost-effective, and efficient as possible. Company standards and specifications identify requirements that products must meet: fabric characteristics including weight and count, appearance aspects including matching of stripes and levelness of hems, consistency of product dimensions, functioning of zippers and other closures, or fabric performance for colorfastness and dimensional stability. QA technicians, engineers, and managers develop these standards and specifications, work with suppliers to see that components and materials meet specifications, and test to be sure that products meet specifications and perform at the predetermined level. QA staff members may develop the procedures or methods to make assessments quickly and accurately in order to identify and solve problems in purchasing, product specifications, or production in a timely manner. QA professionals need to understand textiles so that they can assess the quality of purchased items and identify possible sources of problems in production. For example, if an operator is having difficulty with seam puckering in a tightly woven fabric, the sewing thread may be too large, causing the yarns in the fabric to be distorted. Starting salaries range from $21,000 to $29,500 with an average of $26,350.

## Research, Development, and Evaluation

Many **research and development** (R&D) positions require the research and data processing skills, specialized understanding of the field, and statistical knowledge that are developed at the master's or doctoral level. R&D positions can be found throughout the

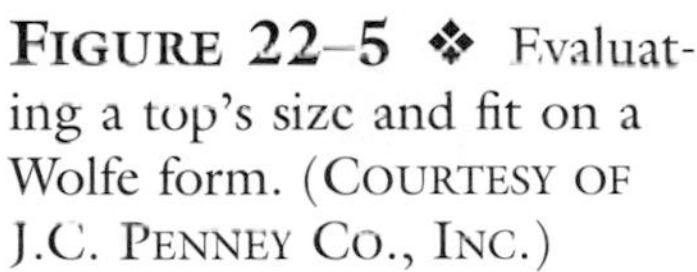

**FIGURE 22–5** ❖ Evaluating a top's size and fit on a Wolfe form. (COURTESY OF J.C. PENNEY CO., INC.)

**FIGURE 22–6** ❖ Conducting a du-pro (during production) inspection of quality. (COURTESY OF J.C. PENNEY CO., INC.)

textile industry. For example, researchers study polymer science, fiber chemistry, yarn production, fabrication efficiency and flexibility, dyeing and finishing effects on the environment, development or modification of production machinery, and application of new technology to solve problems such as meeting clean air and water requirements and dealing with competition from imports. Some researchers evaluate the appropriateness of textile products for specific end uses; others develop new end uses for existing textiles. Still others evaluate products to be sure quality and performance are consistent. (See Figures 22–5 through 22–8.) Beginning positions in research and development may be as a technician, research scientist, or assistant engineer. R&D positions in the textile industry require a general knowledge of textiles and specific knowledge in a focus area.

Kelly is a merchandise evaluation engineer with six years of experience for an international retail firm with a diverse product mix. "I evaluate product performance against our company standards and customer expectations. I need to know what our competitors are doing so that our products are reasonably competitive in both performance and price. I make sure that we know what our customer wants and I work with our buyers to make sure we offer a range of products to satisfy our target market's needs. My division provides direct support to the merchandising division, especially when we are working with fibers or fabrics with which we don't have much experience. I spend a lot of time educating our staff and our suppliers so we get the quality of merchandise we need. I help suppliers, especially new ones or experienced ones who are working with a new product, understand our dimensions of quality and suggest ways that they can check their work to make

**FIGURE 22–7** ❖ Evaluating the wear resistance of upholstery fabric. (COURTESY OF J.C. PENNEY CO., INC.)

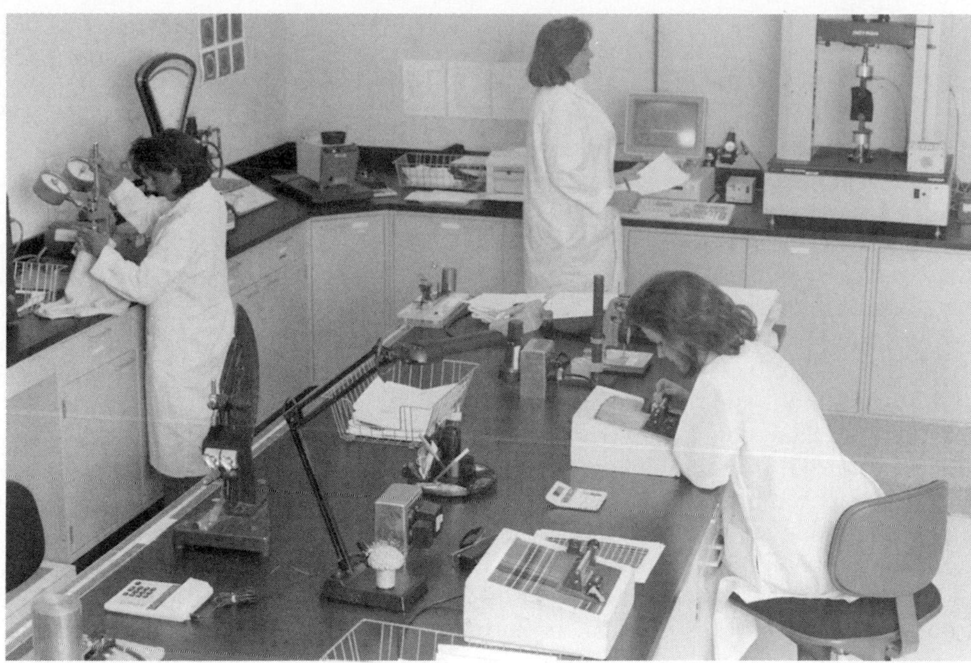

**FIGURE 22–8** ❖ Testing performance of textiles in a quality assurance lab. (COURTESY OF J.C. PENNEY CO., INC.)

sure it meets our requirements. I really like being proactive in that way rather than policing products once they have been shipped. I also work with field inspectors (people who travel to production facilities to check the production process) and fabric evaluators who work here in the evaluation center. I facilitate ways to correct problems or improve products. It's a great job that allows for a lot of creativity and gives me a lot of diversity in the things I do and the people with whom I work." Starting salaries in product or textile testing range from $20,000 to $27,500 with an average of $24,500.

❖

## PRODUCTION

**Production** deals with producing the textile or the textile product. There are positions at all levels of the industry from the raw material stage prior to fiber production, to the production of fiber, yarn, and fabric, to the dyeing and finishing of fabrics or products. Other positions are in sewn product facilities such as apparel, furnishing, and industrial production plants throughout the world. With the move of many production facilities offshore, there is a great demand for production management staff who are able to work in the international arena. These positions are exciting and often very challenging. Beginning positions are as assistant plant manager or assistant engineer. These positions require a combination of people skills and knowledge of the materials with which the facility works as well as how the equipment works with or processes the materials. Obviously, essential knowledge includes some understanding of textiles such as ease of handling, melting point of thermoplastic fibers, elongation potential of knits, and so on.

Melee works for a national firm and was promoted to senior production engineer after one year of experience. "My product mix includes luggage, tote bags, dog beds, apparel, and other miscellaneous textile products. My knowledge of textiles gives me a starting point for problem solving. When I talk with designers and product development specialists, we spend a lot of time discussing how fabrics interact, why some fabrics are traditionally used for some products and not others, and what problems, like shrinkage or pilling, might occur with these fabrics. I spend a lot of time working with sewing machine operators and helping them understand the characteristics of the different fabrics they sew. This gives them a better understanding of why some fabrics work one way and other fabrics work another way. I need quick access to basic reference material, especially when we run into problems with sourcing fabrics or fabrics create problems on the line. I spend a lot of time communicating with others on a wide variety of special issues related to the products we sew in this plant and the fabrics we work with. Even though I am an engineer, I also search for ways to expand our product mix." Starting salaries for assistant engineers range from $25,500 to $37,000 with an average of $30,300.

## Government

The U.S. government is one of the world's largest consumers of textile products and it employs many people with a knowledge of textiles. Purchasing officers locate producers of specific textile products and verify that these items meet requirements. The product or a prototype is tested and evaluated to verify that it meets the government's requirements. The performance of these items is evaluated by textile testing engineers using Federal Test Methods and Standards (FTMS). Since textile products purchased by the government must be domestically produced, **sourcing agents** are in demand. **Custom officials** and inspectors check to make sure that all imported goods meet the appropriate requirements in terms of quotas and labeling requirements, and are free of insects and disease organisms. For example, wool from certain countries is checked for anthrax, a highly contagious disease of sheep. Government employees may develop, enforce, or interpret standards, laws, and regulations. Government employees work with industry and business so that current guidelines and standards are met. Many positions are in the military, either as a member of the military or as a civilian employee. Research and development positions in government research facilities focus on textile products such as uniforms for adverse weather conditions, space suits, interiors for space vehicles and submarines, and suits that offer protection from biological and chemical warfare.

## Education

Education positions can be formal, such as university/college or secondary school **educator,** or informal, such as home economist or consumer education specialist in extension, business, or industry. In the formal setting, an advanced degree or periodic additional coursework may be necessary. Many colleges and universities require a Ph.D. College/university faculty members teach specific classes related to their area of specialization and often do research, create artistic works, or judge design competitions. A secondary teacher may be involved in several areas including family and child development, food and nutrition, and sex education. Secondary teachers may have additional responsibilities including making home visits and advising a student group or club.

In the growing informal setting, professionals have a wide variety of possible job descriptions. Some positions involve working with other employees of the company so that they better understand the consumer. For example, some **consumer education specialists** may help engineers understand problems consumers have with automatic washers and dryers. Many trade associations and businesses employ people with a background in education and textiles to write brochures describing the product, develop educational materials like the brochures handed out in class, write instructional books describing how to properly use a specific machine, or produce teaching aids such as videotapes or slide sets. Specialists may teach workshops to consumers or sales representatives and may be responsible for dealing with consumers who have questions related to the use of the product or who have a complaint with the product. It is not surprising, with this list of responsibilities, that an understanding of basic textiles is essential for these positions.

In extension positions, job titles include **extension specialist** or extension home economist. These professionals develop programs for state and regional use related to wide-ranging current concerns including cleaning clothing soiled with pesticides, disposing of leftover cleaning aids, recycling textiles in an environmentally safe manner, or storing textile heirlooms. They answer thousands of questions from consumers on an amazing array of topics, assess special needs in their geographic areas, and develop programs and materials to meet these needs. Extension professionals develop and present educational materials to diverse and specific audiences including pesticide applicators, day care workers, or 4-H members.

## Museum or Collection Work

Professionals in the museum field need an in-depth knowledge of textiles, production techniques, and evolution of design since dating an item and determining its cultural significance is often based on these specific details. **Curators** are responsible for the items in a museum's collection. This responsibility includes identifying items for display, selecting items to be added to the collection, and maintaining the collection in good condition. In museums with thousands of objects, this is a challenging position. The **conservator** performs hands-on cleaning, restoration and repair, and prepares objects for storage. Conservation requires an in-depth knowledge of the objects, how they were made, the materials and components in the objects, and how these materials age and react with environmental factors such as light, dust, and stains. Many positions require a graduate degree. Starting salaries range from $22,500 to $30,000 with an average of $28,375.

## SUMMARY

Many exciting and challenging professional positions are possible with a background in textiles. The variety and diversity of positions make it possible for anyone, regardless of individual interests, strengths, working habits, or geographic preferences, to find a position in the textile industry or a closely related area.

All professional positions require a continual updating of information. The responsibility of finding information and keeping current is one that all professionals recognize. Many of the books used in classes are excellent resources for a professional library. To keep current, make a habit of regularly reading professional journals and publications related to your area. Many professions have organizations so that members can meet others with similar interests on a regular basis and update their knowledge. In addition, workshops or short courses are offered through colleges/universities, professional organizations, or private concerns.

## KEY TERMS

Designer
Artist
Merchandising
Manager
Visual merchandiser
Nonstore retailer
Sourcing
Marketing
Product development
Prototype
Performance testing
Product testing
Quality assurance
Quality control
Research and development
Production
Sourcing agent
Customs official
Educator
Consumer education specialist
Extension specialist
Curator
Conservator

## QUESTIONS

1. Talk to a professional in your area of interest to determine the relationship of textiles knowledge to that career and to identify the responsibilities of the job.
2. Based on your current career goal, how will you use your knowledge of textiles in performing the responsibilities of your job?
3. What efforts can you take to update your textiles knowledge on a regular basis as required in your future job or career?

## SUGGESTED READINGS

Bureau of Labor Statistics. *Occupational Outlook Quarterly.* Washington, DC: U.S. Government Printing Office.

Farr, J. Michael (1994). *America's Top Jobs for College Graduates.* Indianapolis, IN: JIST Works.

Hoeflin, Ruth, Pence, Karen, Miller, Mary G., and Weber, Joe (1984). *Careers for Professionals: New Perspectives in Home Economics,* 2d ed. Dubuque, IA: Kendall/Hunt Publishing Co.

Krannick, Ronald L. (1995). *The Best Jobs for the 1990s and into the 21st Century.* Manassas Park, VA: Impact Publications.

Smith, Devon Cottrell, ed. (1990). *The Fourth of July Guide to Careers, Internships, and Volunteer Opportunities in the Nonprofit Sector.* Garett Park, MD: Garett Park Press.

U.S. Department of Labor (1990). *Occupation Outlook Handbook.* Indianapolis, IN: JIST Works.

# Appendix A

# Fiber Names in Other Languages

| ENGLISH | CHINESE | FRENCH | GERMAN | ITALIAN | KOREAN | JAPANESE* | SPANISH |
|---|---|---|---|---|---|---|---|
| **acetate** | — | acetate/acétate | Acetate faser | acetato | — | — | acetato |
| **acrylic** | — | acrylique | Acryl nachgestellf | — | — | — | acrilico |
| **cotton** | mianhua | coton/ cottonade | Baumwolle | cotone | myun | dahs-Shee-mehn | algodón |
| **linen** | mah bou | lin/linge | Leinen | tela di lino | — | ah-Sah/ Reen-neh-roo | lino/ lilo de lino |
| **nylon** | nilong | nylon | Nylon | nàilon | — | Nah-ee-rohn | nilón |
| **olefin** | — | — | — | — | — | — | olefina |
| | | — | | | — | | — |
| **polyester** | huaxian | — | Polyester | poliestere | — | poh-Ree-eh-ste-roo | poliestero |
| **ramie** | — | — | — | — | mo shi | — | rame |
| **rayon** | — | rayonne | Reyon, Kunstseide | ràion | — | — | rayón |
| **silk** | sichou | soie | Seide | seta | beton | Kee-noo/ Shee-roo-Koo | seda |
| **wool** | yangmao | laine | Wolle | lana | mo | OO-roo | lana |

* Based on pronunciation

# Appendix B

# Fibers No Longer Produced in the United States

**Anidex** a manufactured fiber in which the fiber-forming substance is any long-chain synthetic polymer composed of at least 50 percent by weight of one or more esters of a monohydric alcohol and acrylic acid ($CH_2$=CH–COOH)*

**Azlon** a manufactured fiber in which the fiber-forming substance is composed of any regenerated naturally occurring proteins*

**Lastrile** a type of rubber fiber that is made from a diene and at least 10 percent but no more than 50 percent by weight of acrylonitrile

**Nytril** a manufactured fiber containing at least 85 percent of a long-chain polymer of vinylidene dinitril (–$CH_2C(CN)_2$–) where the vinylidene dinitrile content is no less than every other unit in the polymer chain*

**Triacetate** a type of acetate where not less than 92 percent of the hydroxyl groups are acetylated

**Vinal** a manufactured fiber in which the fiber-forming substance is any long-chain synthetic polymer composed of at least 50 percent by weight of vinyl alcohol units (–$CH_2$–CHOH–) and in which the total of the vinyl alcohol units and any one or more of the various acetal units is at least 85 percent by weight of the fiber*

**Vinyon** a manufactured fiber in which the fiber-forming substance is any long-chain synthetic polymer composed of at least 85 percent by weight of vinyl chloride units (–$CH_2$–CHCl–)*

* Federal Trade Commission definition

# Appendix C

# Selected Trade Names

## FIBERS

**Cotton**
FoxFibre by Natural Cotton Colours Inc.

**Lyocell**
Tencel by Courtaulds Fibers, Inc.

**Spandex**
Lycra by DuPont
Glospan, Cleerspan by Globe Manufacturing Co.

**Aramid**
Kevlar, Nomex by DuPont

**Olefin**
Patlon, Marquessa Lana, Propex III by Amoco Fabrics & Fibers Co.
Telar by Filament Fiber Technology, Inc.
Tyvek, ComforMax IB by DuPont
Thinsulate by 3M
Fibrilawn, Fibrilon by Fibron Corp.
Herculon by Hercules, Inc.
Duraguard, Evolution, Evolution III by Kimberly-Clark
Marvess, Duon, Petromat, Alpha by Phillips Fibers
Polyloom by Polyloom Corp.
Typar, Biobarrier by Reemay, Inc.
Spectra, Spectra 900, Spectra 1000 by Allied-Signal, Inc.

**Rayon**
Bemberg by Bemberg SpA.
Fibro by Courtaulds Fibers, Inc.

**Nylon**
Antron, Cordura, Supplex, MicroSupplex by DuPont
6ix Again, Natural Touch, Silky Touch, Zeftron by BASF
Shareen by Courtaulds Fibers, Inc.
Hydrol, StayGard, Anso, Caprolan, Captiva by Allied-Signal Fibers
WearDated, Ultron by Monsanto

**Modacrylic**
S.E.F. by Monsanto Chemical Co.

**Acrylic**
Acrilan, Acrilan II, Bi-Loft, Du-Rel, Duraspun, Fi-Lana Pa-Quel, So-Lara by Monsanto Chemical
Zefran, Biokryl, Mann Acryl, Acryl Pulp by Mann Industries
Sunbrella by Glenn Raven Mills, Inc.

**Acetate**
Estron SLR by Eastman Chemical Products Inc.
MicroSafe AM, Celebrate! by Trevira

**Polyester**
Trevira, Trevira XPS, Trevira Fitness, Microfiness by Trevira
Fortrel, Fortrel Ecospun, Ecofil by Wellman, Inc.
Hollowfil, Quallofil, Dacron, CoolMax, Mylar Micromatique, Micromattique XF, Thermoloft, Thermolite, Comforel by DuPont
Primaloft by Albany International Research Co.

**Other**
Kuralon (vinal by Kuraray Co. Ltd.)
Mewlon (vinal by Unitika Kasei Co., Ltd.)
Teflon (PTFE by DuPont)
Cordelan (vinal/vinyon by Kohjin)
Ryton PPS (sulfar by Phillips Fibers Co.)
Miraflex, Beta, Fiberglas (glass by Owens-Corning Fiberglass Corp.)
Lurex (metal coating by DuPont)
Leavil (vinyon by Montefibres, SpA.)
Treviron (vinyon by Teijin Ltd.)
Basofil (melamine by BASF)
Corterra (PTTP by Shell Chemical Co.)
Rexe (polyether ester by Teijin)
Arazole (PBI by Trevira)

## YARNS

Superla by National Spinning Co., Inc.
Lanese by Trevira

## FABRICS

**Poromeric**
Goretex by W. L. Gore & Assoc.
Entrant, Entrant Hi-Resist, Entrant Thermo by Toray

**Hydroentangled**
Sontara by DuPont

**Warp Knit**
Velcro by 3M

**Imitation Leathers/Suedes**
Ultrasuede, Ultraleather by Springs Industries
Belleseime, Supersuede by Kanebo Company

**Spunbonded**
Typar by DuPont & Reemay, Inc.
Tyvek by DuPont

## FINISHES

**Enzyme Wash**
Biopolish by Novo Nordisk

**Antimicrobial**
Sanitized by Sanitized Inc.

**Insect Resistant**
Expel by Graniteville

**Shrinkage Control**
Sanfor, SanforKnit, Sanforset, Sanforized by Sanforized Co.
London Shrunk by Parrot Group

**Water Resistant**
Scotchgard, Scotch Release by 3M
Teflon by DuPont

**Absorbent**
Visa by Milliken
Zelcon by DuPont

**Durable Press**
Coneprest by Cone Mills
Press Free Cotton by MacGregor
Presset by Cotton, Inc.
Creaset by Creaset
Process 2000 by Farah U.S.A.
Si-Ro-Set

**Thermal**
Polytherm by Neutratherm
Outlast by Gateway Technologies, Inc.

**Soil Resistant**
Scotchgard, Scotch Release by 3M
Visa by Milliken
Teflon by DuPont
Zelcon by DuPont

**Cleaning Procedures**
Green Clean by Environment Canada

# Glossary

**Abaca** is a leaf fiber obtained from a member of the banana tree family.

**Abrasion resistance** is the ability of a fiber to withstand the rubbing or abrasion it gets in everyday use.

**Abrasion-resistant finish** is a process designed to improve the abrasion resistance of fabric. Commonly used in linings and pocket facings.

**Abrasive wash** is a finish designed to abrade a small portion of the fabric's surface to soften the hand and produce a slightly worn look in the finished product.

**Absorbency** is the percentage of moisture a bone-dry fiber will absorb from the air under standard conditions of temperature and moisture. Also known as moisture regain.

**Absorbent finish** improves the absorbency of the fabric; used in apparel for better comfort.

**Acetate** is a manufactured fiber in which the fiber-forming substance is cellulose acetate.

**Acetone test** is a solubility test used to identify acetate.

**Acid dyes** are a dye class used primarily with natural protein fibers and nylon.

**Acrylic** is a manufactured fiber in which the fiber-forming substance is any long-chain synthetic polymer composed of at least 85 percent by weight of acrylonitrile units.

**Additive finish** is a finish that adds a chemical compound to a fabric to improve some performance or aesthetic characteristic.

**Add on** refers to the amount of finish or dye added to a fabric based on its original dry weight, usually listed as a percentage.

**Aesthetic finishes** are finishes that alter the way a fabric looks or feels.

**Aesthetics** describes the attractiveness or appearance of a textile product.

**Air-jet loom** is a type of loom. The filling yarn is inserted in the shed with a puff or jet of air.

**Air-jet spinning** is a process of creating a spun yarn by using carefully controlled, rapidly moving jets of air.

**Alençon** (ah-lehn-sahn′) is needlepoint lace with a hexagonal mesh.

**Alpaca** is the fiber removed from the South American alpaca.

**Aluminum coating** is a very thin layer of aluminum metal designed to minimize heat flow through the fabric or add a metallic sparkle to the product.

**Ammoniating finish** increases the absorbency of cotton and some other cellulosic fabrics. Often used in conjunction with durable-press finishes to minimize their negative effects.

**Angora** is the hair fiber removed from the Angora rabbit.

**Antifading agents** are present in some detergents to help fabrics keep their original color intensity longer by minimizing color bleed in the wash.

**Antifume-fading finish** minimizes the effect of atmospheric fumes on sensitive dye-fiber combinations, such as disperse dyes on acetate.

**Antimicrobial finish** inhibits the growth of bacteria or destroys bacteria on textiles.

**Antipesticide protective finish** minimizes the wicking or absorption of pesticides by the fabric, thus protecting the user from exposure.

**Antique satin** is a reversible satin-weave fabric with satin floats on the technical face and surface slubs on the technical back created by using slub-filling yarns. It is usually used with the technical back as the fashion side for drapery fabrics and often made of a blend of fibers.

**Antiredeposition agent** is a compound used in detergents to keep soil suspended and prevent it from being deposited back on the fabric, causing a uniform grayish cast to the fabric.

**Antiseptic finish** (*See* Antimicrobial finish)

**Antislip finish** minimizes yarn slippage in fabrics; especially important in low-count, smooth filament-yarn fabrics in a satin weave.

**Antistatic finish** adds a compound to the surface of the fabric to absorb moisture, conduct electricity, or neutralize the buildup of static charges.

**Appearance retention** refers to how the product maintains its original appearance during use, care, and storage.

**Applied design** includes those appearance aspects related to luster, drape, texture, hand, or design motif that are added to the fabric after it has been produced.

**Aramid** is a manufactured fiber in which the fiber-forming substance is a long-chain synthetic polyamide in which at least 85 percent of the amide linkages are attached directly to two aromatic rings.

**Astrakhan cloth** is a fabric made with bouclé, loop, or curl yarns.

**Average twist** is the most commonly used amount of twist in the range of 20–30 tpi for yarns.

**Azoic dyes** are a solubility cycle dye class used primarily with cotton and some polyester.

**Backfilling machine** is a variation of a padding machine that adds finish to only one side of a fabric.

**Bacteriostatic** (*See* Antimicrobial finish)

**Balance** refers to the ratio of warp to filling yarns. Also used to describe twist in spun yarns when a loop will not curl or twist back on itself.

**Balanced plain weave** is a plain weave in which the ratio of warp to filling yarns is approximately 1:1.

**Basket weave** is a type of plain weave in which two or more adjacent warp yarns are controlled by the same harness and in which two or more filling yarns are inserted in the same shed.

**Bast fiber** refers to fiber removed from the stem of a plant.

**Batch processing** describes processing a relatively small amount of fabric as a unit at one time in one machine or piece of equipment.

**Batik** (buh′-tēk) is a hand process in which wax is applied to the fabric in a design to prevent dye takeup, creating a pattern on the fabric. Batik may require several steps of wax application and dyeing.

**Batiste** is an opaque, lightweight, spun-yarn, plain-weave fabric with a smooth surface. When made of cotton or cotton/polyester, the yarns are usually combed. It can be made of all wool, silk, or rayon.

**Battenberg lace** is a hand-produced lace fabric made with narrow fabric tapes connected with thin yarn stitches called brides.

**Batting** is a loose assemblage of new fibers used in textile products as lining and support layers.

**BCF** is an abbreviation used for bulk-continuous-filament yarn.

**Beating up** is the weaving step of pushing the filling yarn into place by the reed.

**Bedford cord** is a heavy, warp-faced, unbalanced pique-weave fabric with wide warp cords created by extra filling yarns floating across the back to give a raised effect.

**Bengaline** is a lustrous, durable, warp-faced fabric with heavy filling cords completely covered by the warp.

**Beetling** is a finish for linen or linenlike fabrics. The yarns are flattened to create a fabric that looks more regular and tighter.

**Bezold** (bē′zōld) **effect** describes how two or more colors seem to merge into one new color, as when small-scale prints or yarn-dyed fabrics are viewed from a distance.

**Bicomponent-bigeneric fibers** refers to bicomponent fibers whose two polymers would fall into two different generic classes.

**Bicomponent fibers** refers to fibers that consist of two polymers that are chemically different, physically different, or both.

**Binder** is the ply of a fancy yarn that holds the effect ply in place.

**Binder staple** is a semidull, crimped fiber with a very low melting point so that it bonds with other fibers when exposed to heat above its melting point.

**Biochemical oxygen demand (BOD)** describes the amount of oxygen in the water necessary for the decomposition of organic wastes.

**Bio-polishing** is a cellulase enzyme treatment of cotton and other cellulosic fabrics to produce a softer hand and fewer problems with linting and surface fuzzing.

**Bird's eye** is a type of dobby fabric with an allover small diamond-shaped filling-float design with a small dot in the center of each diamond.

**Bleach** is a compound that destroys the color compounds on fabrics. Bleach is generally used to destroy unwanted stains or yellowing on fabrics.

**Bleeding** is a problem with dyes. The dye leaves the fiber when the fiber gets wet, as in laundering. Dyes that bleed may be absorbed by other fibers, thus staining the originally uncolored fibers.

**Blend** is a fabric that consists of two or more generically different fiber types.

**Block printing** is a means of printing a fabric with a relief carved block so that only those areas protruding from the block transfer dye paste to the fabric.

**Bobbin lace** includes Cluny, a coarse, strong lace; Duchesse, which has a fine net ground with raised patterns; Maltese, with the Maltese cross in the pattern; Mechlin, with a small hexagonal mesh and very fine yarns; Torchon, a rugged lace with very simple patterns; Valenciennes, with a diamond-shaped mesh; and Chantilly, with a double ground with a filling of flowers, baskets, or vases.

**BOD** (*See* Biochemical oxygen demand)

**Bonding** produces a thick fabric from two thinner fabrics by use of an adhesive; also a means of producing a fabric from fibers with heat.

**Bottom-weight fabrics** are fabrics that weigh at least 6 oz/yd$^2$, often used for pants, trousers, skirts, and outerwear.

**Bouclé** (boo-klay′) is a woven or knit fabric with bouclé yarns. The loops of the novelty yarns create a mock-pile surface.

**Bow** is a type of off-grain fabric. The filling yarn sags in the center between the selvages.

**Braid** is a method of producing fabric by diagonal interlacing yarns; also a term describing any fabric made in such a fashion.

**Breaking elongation** describes the amount a fabric or fiber stretches at the breaking point.

**Brightener** (*See* Fluorescent whitening agent)

**Bright fiber** refers to a fiber in its original luster without the use of any delusterant.

**Broadcloth** is a close plain-weave fabric made of cotton, rayon, or a blend of either cotton or rayon with polyester. It has a fine rib in the filling direction caused by slightly larger filling yarns, filling yarns with a lower twist, or a higher warp-yarn count. High-quality broadcloth is made with plied warp and filling yarns. The fabric may be mercerized. It has a soft, firm hand. The term *broadcloth* is also used to refer to a plain- or twill-weave lustrous wool or wool-blend fabric that is highly napped and then pressed flat.

**Brocade** is a jacquard-woven fabric with a pattern that is created with different color yarns or with patterns in twill or satin weaves on a ground of plain, twill, or satin weave. It is available in a variety of fiber types and qualities.

**Brocatelle** (brohk′-uh-tel) is similar to brocade, but the pattern is raised and often padded with stuffer yarns. The pattern is warp faced and the ground is filling faced. Brocatelle is often a double cloth. It is mainly used in furnishings.

**Brushed tricot** is tricot that has been brushed to create a fibrous texture on the surface of a fabric.

**Brushing** is a finishing step that removes fiber ends from the surface of fabric. Most common with pile fabrics.

**Buckram** is a heavy, very stiff, spun-yarn fabric converted from cheesecloth gray goods with adhesives and fillers. It is used as an interlining to stiffen pinch-pleated window treatment fabrics.

**Builders** are compounds used in detergents to augment the cleaning power of the surfactant. Builders sequester hardness minerals and adjust the pH of the solution to a more alkaline level.

**Bulk-continuous-filament yarn** is made of textured or crimped filament fibers.

**Bulk yarn** is a yarn that has been processed to have greater covering power or apparent volume compared to a conventional yarn.
**Bulky yarn** is a yarn formed from inherently bulky fibers. (*See* Textured yarn)
**Bunting** (*See* Cheesecloth)
**Burlap** is a coarse, heavy, loosely woven plain-weave fabric often made of single irregular yarns of jute. It is used in its natural color for carpet backing, bagging, and furniture webbing. It is also dyed and printed for furnishing uses.
**Burned-out** is a fiber blend fabric. One fiber is dissolved in a selected area to create a pattern.
**Butcher cloth** is a coarse-rayon or rayon-blend fabric. It is made in a variety of weights. A Federal Trade Commission ruling prohibits the use of the word *linen* for this type of fabric.

**CAFE** (*See* Computer-aided fabric evaluation)
**Calendering** is a common finishing technique in which fabric is passed between cylinders to achieve a specific effect. See the specific types of calendering: embossing, friction, moiré, Schreiner, simple.
**Calico** is a printcloth of cotton or cotton blend with a small busy pattern.
**Cambric** is a fine, firm, plain-weave balanced fabric with starch, which has a slight luster on one side. It is difficult to distinguish from percale.
**Camel's hair** is the fiber from the Bactrian camel.
**Canvas** is a heavy, firm, strong fabric often made of cotton or acrylic and used for awnings, slipcovers, and covers for boats. It is produced in many grades and qualities. It may have a soft or firm hand. It is made in plain or basket weave.
**Carbon** is a fiber made of at least 96 percent pure carbon.
**Carbonizing** is a treatment for wool in which acid removes cellulosic matter and prepares the fiber for dyeing.
**Carded yarn** is a slightly irregular spun yarn with short-staple fibers and protruding fiber ends.
**Carding** is one step in yarn spinning. Staple fibers are drawn together in a somewhat parallel arrangement to form a very weak rope of fibers called a carded sliver.
**Care** refers to the treatment required to maintain a textile product's original appearance.
**Care Labeling Regulation** is a federal regulation that defines care label information, location, and terminology for textile products.
**Casement cloth** is a general term for any open-weave fabric used for drapery or curtain fabrics. It is usually sheer.
**Cashgora** is a fiber resulting from the breeding of feral cashmere goats with angora goats.
**Cashmere** is the hair fiber removed from the cashmere goat.
**Cationic dyes** are a dye class used primarily with acrylic fibers.
**Caustic treatment** is a finishing step used with some polyester fabrics to produce a more natural hand and comfortable fabric.
**Cavalry twill** is a steep, pronounced, double-wale line, smooth-surfaced twill fabric.
**Cellulose** is a polymer of glucose found in all plant fibers.
**Certification programs** describe agreements between fiber and fabric producers regarding product performance and trade names or trademarks.
**Challis** (shal′i) is a lightweight, spun-yarn, plain-weave balanced fabric with a soft finish. It can be made of any staple fiber or blend of fibers.
**Chambray** (sham′-bray) is a plain-weave fabric usually of cotton, rayon, or a blend of these with polyester. Usually chambray has white yarns in the filling direction and yarn-dyed yarns in the warp direction. Iridescent chambray is made with one color in the warp and a second color in the filling. It can also be made in striped patterns.
**Chantilly** (shan-tihl′-ē) **lace** is a bobbin lace with a double ground and a filling of flowers, baskets, or vases.
**Cheesecloth** is a lightweight, sheer, plain-woven fabric with a very soft texture. It may be natural colored, bleached, or dyed. It usually has a very low count. If dyed, it may be called *bunting* and could be used for flags or banners.
**Chemical adhesive** is a compound used to bond fibers together in fiberwebs.
**Chemical oxygen demand (COD)** describes the amount of oxygen necessary to reduce a soluble organic compound to carbon dioxide and water.
**Chemical reactivity** indicates the type of chemical reaction to which individual fibers are susceptible.
**Chemical wash** is a chemical finish in which the surface of the fiber is modified in some way by the chemical. Often used as a means of softening the fabric's hand, increasing the comfort, or modifying the appearance of the fabric.
**Chenille yarn** is fringed yarn made by producing a leno fabric, cutting it into narrow strips, and blooming open the yarn fringes to create a fuzzy yarn.
**Chiffon** (shih-fahn′) is a sheer, very lightweight, plain-weave fabric with fine crepe twist yarns of approximately the same size and twist used in warp and filling. The fabric is balanced.
**China silk** is a soft, lightweight, opaque, plain-weave fabric made from fine-filament yarns and used for apparel.
**Chino** (chī′-nō) is a steep-twill fabric with a slight sheen, often made in a bottom weight fabric of cotton or cotton/polyester. Often it is made of combed two-ply yarns in both warp and filling and vat-dyed in khaki.
**Chintz** is a medium- to heavyweight, plain weave, spun-yarn fabric finished with a glaze. Chintz may be piece dyed or printed. It is often referred to as glazed chintz.
**Circular loom** is a type of loom. The warp yarns form a full circle to weave tubular fabric.
**Circular machine** refers to a knitting machine that makes a tube of fabric.
**Ciré finish** is a process in which a thermoplastic fabric is calendered with one roll hot enough to slightly melt and flatten the surface fibers.
**Clean Air Act** is the federal law that focuses on air quality.
**Cleaned wool** (*See* Scoured wool)
**Cleaning** is the process of removing soil from fabric and a step in preparing fabrics for additional finishing steps.
**Clean Water Act** is the federal law that focuses on surface and ground water quality.
**Clipped-dot fabric** is an extra yarn weave fabric made with extra filling yarns inserted so the extra yarn interlaces with some warp yarns and floats across some filling yarns. Part of the float is cut away in finishing sometimes, leaving a fringe to add texture to the fabric.

**Clip spot** refers to a fabric in which design is created with an additional yarn that interlaces with the ground fabric in spots and floats along the technical back of the fabric. The floats are removed by shearing.

**Cloque** (klō-kay) **fabric** is a general term used to refer to any fabric with a puckered or blistered effect.

**Cluny** (klū′-nē) is a coarse, strong bobbin lace.

**Coated fabric** is a multiplex fabric with a thin plastic film combined with a woven, knit, or fiberweb fabric.

**COD** (*See* Chemical oxygen demand)

**Code of Federal Regulations** is the document published each work day in which changes in federal laws and regulations are announced.

**Codes** are systematic bodies of laws or regulations that often focus on safety or health areas.

**Cohesiveness** refers to the ability of fibers to cling together, especially important in yarn spinning.

**Coir** is the fiber obtained from the fibrous mass between the outer shell and the husk of the coconut.

**Colorfastness** refers to a colorant that does not shift hue, fade, or migrate when exposed to certain conditions.

**Color grown cotton** (*See* Naturally colored cotton)

**Color matching** describes the process of developing a formula to reproduce a color.

**Color measurement** is the process of assigning numerical values to a color to assist in color matching and shade sorting.

**Color problems** refer to any aspect that creates difficulty for consumers, producers, or manufacturers due to dyes, pigments, or technique used in coloring the fabric. See specific types of color problems: bleeding, frosting, fume fading, migration.

**Color theory** describes a complex phenomenon that requires studying the physics of light, the chemistry of colored objects, the biology of the eye, the behavioral sciences in terms of what colors mean to society or the individual, and the aesthetics of how one appreciates what one sees.

**Color transfer inhibitors** are present in some detergents to prevent any dye that bled in the wash from redepositing on lighter colored products.

**Colorway** refers to various color options available in one fabric.

**Combed yarn** is a uniform spun yarn with long-staple fibers and few protruding fiber ends.

**Combination** refers to a fabric of two or more generically different fiber types where ply yarns consist of strands of each generic type.

**Combing** is an additional step in the production of smooth, fine, uniform spun yarns made of long-staple fibers.

**Comfort** describes the way a textile product affects heat, air, and moisture transfer and the way the body interacts with the textile product.

**Comfort stretch** refers to the ability of a fabric to exhibit slight elongation as the body moves and to recover a significant portion of that elongation when the stretching force is removed.

**Composite fabric** is a fabric that combines several primary and/or secondary structures such as fiberweb and film, yarn and base fabric, and two layers of fabric.

**Composite yarn** is regular in appearance along its length, made with both staple and filament fiber components.

**Compound needle** is a type of needle used to make warp knits.

**Compressive shrinkage process** refers to finishing that removes stress from weaving and earlier finishing.

**Computer-aided fabric evaluation (CAFE)** describes the assessment of fabric quality with an instrument to identify visible irregularities, defects, or flaws.

**Conservation** refers to special handling, storage, cleaning, and display techniques used for textiles that are valued for their age, history, or type.

**Consumer Product Safety Commission** is the federal government agency responsible for ensuring the safety of products used by consumers.

**Continuous dyeing** is a process in which large pieces of fabric are run through ranges with separate compartments for wetting-out, dyeing, aftertreatment, washing, and rinsing.

**Continuous processing** describes working with long pieces of fabric that move in and out of solution.

**Conventional cotton** describes cotton grown and processed by regular mainstream practices.

**Conventional spinning** (*See* Ring spinning)

**Converted goods** is another term for finished goods.

**Converters** refers to firms that finish fabrics.

**Convolutions** are ribbonlike twists along a cotton fiber.

**Copolymer** refers to a polymer composed of more than one type of mer.

**Cord** consists of two or more ply yarns twisted or held together by some mechanism.

**Cordonnet lace** is a type of lace in which heavier yarns emphasize certain elements in the design.

**Corduroy** is a filling-yarn pile fabric. The pile is created by long-filling floats that are cut and brushed in the finishing process. The ground weave may be either a plain or twill weave.

**Core-spun yarn** is made with a central sheath of fibers completely covered by other fibers spun around it.

**Coronizing** is a finish specific to fiberglass to assist in yarn production and printing.

**Cortex** is the main part of wool fibers containing two types of cells.

**Cost** is influenced by many factors, including price of materials.

**Cotton** refers to several fibers produced by the genus *Gossypium* used to produce commercial and craft textile products.

**Count** refers to yarns per inch in warp and filling direction in woven fabrics.

**Course** refers to the path of a yarn in a filling knit fabric as it moves across the fabric.

**Cover** is the ability to occupy space for concealment or protection.

**Covered yarn** has a central yarn that is completely wrapped by another yarn.

**Covert** was first made in England, where there was a demand for a fabric that would not catch on brambles or branches during fox hunts. To make this tightly woven fabric, a two-ply yarn, one cotton and one wool, was used. Because the cotton and wool did not take the same dye, the fabric had a mottled appearance.

*Cotton covert* is always mottled. It may be made with ply yarns, one ply white and the other colored, or it may be fiber dyed white and a color. It is a $\frac{2}{1}$ twill, of the same weight as denim, and used primarily for work pants, overalls, and service coats.

*Wool covert* is made from woolen or worsted yarns. It may be mottled or solid color and may be suit or coat weight. It may be slightly napped or have a clear finish. The mottled effect is obtained by using two different-colored piles or by blending different-colored fibers.

**Crabbing** is a process used to set wool fabrics.

**Crash** is a medium- to heavyweight, plain-weave fabric made from slub or irregular yarns to create an irregular surface.

**Crease retention finish** (*See* Durable-press)

**Crepe** (krāp) refers to any fabric with a puckered, crinkled, or grainy surface. It can be made with crepe yarns, a crepe or momie weave, or a finish such as embossed or plissé. Examples of crepe fabrics include chiffon, crepe-back satin, georgette, and crepe de Chine. For more information, see these fabric names.

**Crepe-back satin** is a reversible satin-weave fabric in which the filling yarns have a crepe twist. The technical face has satin floats and the technical back looks like a crepe fabric. It is also known as *satin-back crepe*.

**Crepe de chine** (krāp-duh-sheen) is a lightweight, opaque, plain-weave, filament-yarn fabric. It has a medium luster. Silk crepe de chine usually is made with crepe yarns.

**Crepe or granite weave** are other terms for the momie weave.

**Crepeing** is a compacting process that produces a fabric with a soft hand.

**Crepe twist** refers to a yarn with extremely high twist and great liveliness.

**Crepe yarn** refers to a yarn with crepe or very high twist.

**Cretonne** (kreh′-tahn) is a plain-weave fabric similar to chintz, except that the finish is dull and the fabric is more likely to be printed with large-scale floral designs.

**Crinoline** (krihn′-uh-lihn) is a stiff, spun-yarn, plain-weave fabric similar to cheesecloth, used in book bindings, hats, and stiffening for apparel.

**Crocking** describes a color problem in which abrasion causes color to transfer to the abradant.

**Cross-dyeing** describes a special type of dyeing fiber blends. Each fiber type present in the blend is dyed a different color.

**Cross-links** are temporary or permanent bonds that connect adjacent molecular chains.

**Crushed velvet** is a warp pile fabric in which the pile yarns are crushed in a random pattern by mechanically twisting the fabric when it is wet.

**Cuprammonium rayon** is a rayon produced in Europe by the cuprammonium process.

**Cut** refers to needles per inch in knitting machines; another term for gauge.

**Cuticle** is a waxlike film covering the outermost layer of a cotton fiber.

**Damask** (dam′-ask) is a reversible, flat, jacquard-woven fabric with a satin weave in both the pattern and the ground. It can be one color or two. In two-color damasks, the color reverses on the opposite side. It is used in apparel and furnishings.

**Darned lace** has a chain stitch outlining the design on a mesh background. The needle carries another yarn around the yarns in the mesh. The mesh is square in filet lace and rectangular in antique lace.

**Deadtime** refers to time that a machine is not operating due to changing equipment settings so that another fabric can be processed.

**Decating** produces a smooth, wrinkle-free surface on wool fabrics.

**Decitex** (dec′-ĭh-teks) or dtex (d′-teks) is used to identify yarn or fiber size and is equal to 10 tex.

**Decortication** is a process used to remove ramie fiber from the plant stem.

**Defects** are flaws in fabrics that are assigned a point value based on their length or size.

**Degree of polymerization** refers to the number of small molecules or mers connected to form a polymer.

**Delustered fiber** describes a fiber with dull luster resulting from the incorporation of a white pigment within the fiber.

**Denier** (den′-yehr) describes yarn or fiber size and is defined as weight in grams for 9,000 meters of fiber or yarn.

**Denim** is a cotton or cotton/polyester blend, twill-weave, yarn dyed fabric. Usually the warp is colored and the filling is white. It is usually a left-hand twill that is commonly available with a blue (indigo) warp and white filling for use in apparel. It is available in a variety of weights.

**Density** is the weight in grams per cubic centimeter of an object.

**Dents** refers to the spaces within the reed that help establish warp yarn density in the woven fabric.

**Desizing** is the physical or biological process in which warp sizing is removed after weaving.

**Detergency** refers to the chemical action of a soap or detergent in removing soil from a textile.

**Detergent** is a chemical compound specially formulated to remove soil or other material from textiles.

**Developed dyes** are a dye class used primarily with cellulosics.

**Differential printing** is a screen printing process on carpets.

**Dimensional stability** refers to a finish that minimizes fabric shrinkage or growth in use or during care.

**Dimity** (dim′-ih-tē) is a sheer, lightweight fabric with warp cords created by using heavier-warp yarns at a regular distance, grouping warp yarns together, or using a basket variation where two or more warp yarns are woven as one. It may be printed or piece dyed. It may be made of combed-cotton yarns. *Barred dimity* has heavier or double yarns periodically in both the warp and filling.

**Direct dyes** are a dye class used primarily with cellulosics.

**Direct printing** describes a process in which the color is applied to its final location as a paste or powder.

**Direct roller printing** is a process in which a pattern is engraved on rollers. The roller picks up a colored paste and transfers the paste to the fabric as it passes under the roller. One roller is used for each color in the pattern.

**Discharge printing** describes a process in which color is removed from piece-dyed fabric in specific locations.

**Disinfectants** are compounds used in cleaning to kill bacteria.

**Disperse dyes** are a dye class used primarily with manufactured and synthetic fibers.
**Dobby loom** is a loom with a punched tape attachment or microcomputer control used to control warp yarn position and create dobby weave fabrics.
**Dobby weave** is a small-figured woven-in design in which fewer than 25 different warp yarn arrangements are required to create one design repeat.
**Dope or spinning solution** refers to the chemical solution extruded as a fiber.
**Dotted swiss** is a sheer, light- or medium-weight, plain-weave fabric with small dots created at regular intervals with extra yarns, either through a swivel weave or a clip-spot weave. Look-alike fabrics are made by flocking, printing, or using an expanded foam print.
**Double cloth** is a fabric made by weaving two fabrics with five sets of yarns: two sets of warp, two sets of filling, and one set that connects the two fabrics.
**Double-faced fabric** is made with three sets of yarns: two warp and one filling or two filling and one warp.
**Double-filling knit** is made on a machine with two sets of needles in two needle beds.
**Double knit** is a general term used to refer to any filling-knit fabric made on two needle beds.
**Double weave** is a fabric made by weaving two fabrics with four sets of yarns (two sets of warp and two sets of filling yarns) on the same loom. The two fabrics are connected by periodically reversing the positions of the two fabrics from top to bottom. Double weave is also known as *pocket cloth* or *pocket weave*.
**Doup attachment** is the device used on looms to create the leno weave in which warp yarns cross over each other to create an open, stable woven structure.
**Drape** is the manner in which a fabric falls or hangs over a three-dimensional form.
**Drawing** describes a fiber finishing step in which a manufactured fiber is elongated after spinning to alter the molecular arrangement within the fiber, increasing crystallinity and orientation and resulting in a change in specific performance properties.
**Drill** is a strong, medium- to heavyweight, warp-faced, twill-weave fabric. It is usually a $\frac{2}{1}$ left-handed twill and piece dyed.
**Dry cleaning** describes a fabric cleaning process that uses an organic solvent rather than water.
**Dry foam cleaning** is a cleaning technique for furnishings. A foam is worked into the textile and the soiled foam is removed by vacuuming.
**Drying** is the process of removing liquid water or other solvent from a textile so that it feels dry to the touch.
**Dry-laid web** is a layer of oriented or random fibers laid down by carding or air layering.
**Dry spinning** is a fiber-forming process in which a solution of polymer dissolved in solvent is extruded; the fiber coagulates as solvent evaporates.
**Duchesse** (dū-shes′) is a bobbin lace with a fine net ground and raised pattern.
**Duck** is a strong, heavy, plain- or basket-weave fabric. Duck comes in a variety of weights and qualities. It is similar to canvas.
**Duplex printing** describes a printing process in which both sides of the fabric are printed.
**Duppioni silk** is a naturally thick and thin silk resulting from two caterpillars having formed one cocoon.
**Durable finish** lasts for the life of the product, but the performance diminishes with time.
**Durable press** describes a finish designed to maintain the fabric's smooth, flat, unwrinkled appearance during use, care, and storage.
**Durability** describes how the product withstands use; the length of time the product is considered suitable for the use for which it was purchased.
**Duvetyn** (dōōv′-eh-tēn) is similar to suede but is lighter weight and more drapeable. It has a soft, velvetlike surface made by napping, shearing, and brushing.
**Dye** is an organic compound with high color strength capable of forming a bond of some type with fibers.
**Dyeing** is the process of combining a fiber with a dye and achieving a bond of some type.
**Dye process** refers to the method of applying colorant to a textile.

**Eco** (ē′-ko) **products** (*See* Green products)
**Effect ply** is the ply of a fancy yarn that creates visual or tactile interest.
**Egyptian cotton** (*See* Pima cotton)
**Elasticity** is the ability of a strained material to recover its original size and shape immediately after removal of stress.
**Elastic recovery** is the ability of fibers to recover from strain.
**Elastomer** is a natural or synthetic polymer that, at room temperature, can be stretched repeatedly to at least twice its original length and that, after removal of the tensile load, will immediately and forcibly return to approximately its original length.
**Electrical conductivity** is the ability to transfer electrical charges.
**Electrostatic printing** is a type of printing with a dye powder.
**Elongation** is the ability of a fiber to be stretched, extended, or lengthened.
**Embossed** refers to a finish in which a localized surface glazing of thermoplastic fibers is achieved or a three-dimensional effect is created to imitate a more elaborate fabric structure.
**Embossed fabrics** are created by applying a design with heated, engraved calenders. Often print cloths are embossed to imitate seersucker, crepe, or other structural-design fabrics.
**Embroidered** refers to stitching flat surface yarns to a fabric to create a pattern.
**Emerized** is a surface abrasion finish to alter the appearance, hand, and drape of the fabric.
**Environmental impact** refers to the effect on the environment of the production, use, care, and disposal of textiles and textile products.

**Environmental Protection Agency** is a federal agency that is responsible for issues related to the quality of the natural environment.

**Enzyme** (en′zīm) **wash** is a fabric finish that uses cellulase enzyme to remove surface fuzz from cellulosic fabrics.

**Etched** is another term for burned out.

**Even-sided twill** is a type of twill weave. The technical face of the fabric is formed by equal amounts of warp and filling yarns.

**Expanded film** is a film with tiny air cells incorporated in the polymer.

**Expanded foam** is a permanent surface texture or pattern created on fabric by printing.

**Extra yarn weave** is made with extra yarns of a different color or type from the ground yarns that are used to create a pattern in the fabric.

**Extrusion** is the process of forcing the dope or spinning solution through the openings in a spinneret to form a fiber.

**Eyelet embroidery** is a type of embroidered fabric with a thread pattern around and connecting small holes in the fabric.

**Fabric** is a planar substance constructed from solutions, fibers, yarns, fabrics, or any combination of these.

**Fabrication** refers to the method used to produce the fabric.

**Fabric crimp** refers to bends caused by distortion of yarns in a fabric.

**Fabric grading** refers to the process of inspecting fabrics and assigning grade or quality levels based on the number, size, and kinds of defects present.

**Fabric inspection** describes the process of examining a fabric for irregularities, defects, flaws, or other appearance problems.

**Fabric quality** refers to a fabric's freedom from defects, uniform structure and appearance related to the fabric type, and performance during production and in use by consumers. Fabric quality is graded by totaling defect points within a piece of fabric.

**Fabric softener** is a compound used in finishing and cleaning to improve the hand of harsh fabrics.

**Fabric weight** describes fabric mass or how much a fabric weighs for a given area or length of fabric; described as oz/yd$^2$ or g/m$^2$.

**Face weight** refers to the mass or weight of the tuft yarns used in a carpet.

**Faille** (file) is a medium- to heavyweight, unbalanced, plain-weave fabric with filament yarns and warp-faced, flat ribs created by using heavier filling yarns. It has a light luster.

**Fake fur** is another name for a sliver pile knit fabric.

**Fancy weave** refers to any weaving method, other than plain, twill, or satin weave, used to create a fabric with a surface texture or pattern resulting from the interlacing pattern.

**Fancy yarn** describes a yarn with an irregular or unusual appearance compared to simple, basic yarns.

**Fasciated yarn** is a yarn made with a filament grouping of fibers wrapped with staple fibers.

**Fashioning** is the process of adding or dropping stitches during knitting to shape garment parts.

**Federal Trade Commission** is the federal government agency that enforces interstate and international trade regulations.

**Felt** is a fiberweb fabric of at least 70 percent wool made by interlocking the scales of the wool fibers through the use of heat, moisture, and agitation.

**Felting** refers to a method of producing a fabric directly from wool fibers by interlocking the fibers' scales.

**Fiber** is any substance, natural or manufactured, with a high length-to-width ratio and with suitable characteristics for being processed into a fabric.

**Fiber blend** refers to an intimate mixture of two or more generic fiber types in the yarns of a fabric. Usually used to refer to the presence of more than one generic fiber in a fabric.

**Fiber crimp** refers to waves, bends, twists, coils, or curls along the length of the fiber.

**Fiber dyeing** is the addition of color, generally as dyes, to textiles while they are in fiber form. Also refers to adding pigment to fiber solutions before fibers are extruded.

**Fiberfill** is a lofty, weak structure of fibers designed to be incorporated as the center layer in a quilted fabric.

**Fiber modifications** are changes in the parent manufactured fiber to improve performance relative to a specific end use.

**Fiber spinning** is the process of producing a manufactured fiber from a solution.

**Fiberweb** refers to a fabric made directly from fibers.

**Fibrillation** refers to the longitudinal shattering of some fibers into fibrils or tiny fibers when exposed to abrasion.

**Fibroin** is the protein of silk fibers.

**Filament** refers to fibers that are extremely long (length measured in miles or kilometers); also refers to yarns made of these fibers.

**Filament tow** is an intermediate stage in the production of staple manufactured fibers; manufactured fibers produced in large bundles in filament length and crimped prior to cutting or breaking into staple fibers.

**Filament yarn** is a yarn made from filament fibers; smooth or bulky types are possible.

**Fillers** are compounds used in some detergents to add bulk and to assist in cleaning.

**Filling** refers to the yarns that interlace with warp yarns in a woven fabric; perpendicular to the selvage.

**Filling-faced twill** is a type of twill weave where the majority of the technical face of the fabric is formed by filling yarns.

**Filling pile fabric** is a pile fabric; the pile is created by extra filling yarns.

**Filling sateen** is a spun yarn satin weave fabric in which filling yarns form the technical face of the fabric.

**Filling or weft knitting** is a process in which one yarn or yarn set is carried back and forth or around and under needles to form a fabric.

**Film** is a fabric made directly from a polymer solution in a dense, firm, sheet form.

**Finish** is any process used to convert gray, unfinished goods into finished fabric.

**Fire block seating** is a layer of flame-retardant material between the upholstery and the padding of furniture to minimize flame spread.

**Fire retardance** is the resistance to combustion of a material when tested under specific conditions.

**Flame resistance** is the property of a fabric whereby burning is prevented, terminated, or inhibited following application of an ignition source.

**Flame-resistant finish** is any finish that is designed to reduce the flammability of a textile.

**Flame-retardant finish** is a finish that makes a fabric resistant to combustion when tested under specific conditions.

**Flammability** describes the characteristics of a fabric that pertain to its relative ease of ignition and ability to sustain combustion.

**Flammable Fabrics Act** is a federal act that prohibits the marketing of dangerously flammable textile products.

**Flannel** is a light- to heavyweight, plain- or twill-weave fabric with a napped surface.

**Flannelette** is a light- to medium-weight, plain-weave cotton or cotton-blend fabric lightly napped on one side.

**Flatbed machine** refers to a knitting machine that makes a flat width of fabric.

**Flat-screen printing** is a resist printing method. A flat screen is treated so that print paste passes through openings to create a design on the fabric. One screen is used for each color in the pattern.

**Flax** is the bast fiber, often called linen, produced by the flax plant.

**Fleece** is a type of weft insertion knit fabric.

**Flexibility** is the ability of a fiber to bend repeatedly without breaking.

**Float** is the portion of a yarn that is on the surface or back of fabric.

**Float or miss stitch** is a type of knit stitch in which yarn lengths float past but do not interloop with the previous stitch. It may be used to create a more stable structure or used when different yarns are used in the same course to create a pattern in the fabric.

**Floats** are formed when a yarn in one direction such as warp crosses over more than one yarn at a time in the other direction such as filling.

**Flocking** refers to the application of very short surface fibers to a fabric with an adhesive to produce an imitation pile appearance.

**Fluorescent dyes** are a dye class used primarily to create or maintain white fibers. Found in some household laundry detergents.

**Fluorescent-whitening agent** is a compound used to mask the natural color of fibers or yellowing or other colors resulting from soil or aging.

**Foam** refers to a mixture of air and liquid used in the application of finishes, dyes, or pigments; also refers to a textile product in which a polymer is extruded with a high percentage of air mixed with the polymer to form a bulky, lofty sheet.

**Foam finishing** refers to processes in which the chemical is suspended in a foam.

**Foam-flame process** uses foam partially melted by heat to adhere two layers of fabric together to create a laminate.

**Foam printing** is a type of printing; the colorant is suspended in foam prior to application.

**Foil printing** is a printing process; a special adhesive is screen printed onto fabric and an aluminum-coated polyester film is pressed onto the fabric. The foil adheres only to areas with the special adhesive.

**Formaldehyde** is a restricted hazardous chemical that has been used in finishing and dyeing textiles.

**Foulard** (fōō′-lahrd) is a soft, lightweight, filament-yarn, twill-weave fabric. It is woven in a $\frac{2}{2}$ twill weave. It can be piece dyed or printed.

**French terry** is a weft-insertion filling knit; the fabric is not further treated to develop a fleecelike hand.

**Friction calendering** is a type of calendering in which one cylinder rotates more quickly than the other, resulting in a shiny or polished appearance of the fabric; used to produce polished cotton with or without a resin.

**Friezé** (frē′uh-zay or frēz) is a strong, durable, heavy-warp-yarn pile fabric. The pile is made by the over-wire method to create a closed-loop pile.

**Frosting** is a problem with color retention due to the inability of the dye to penetrate deeply into the fiber. With abrasion, the surface components are removed, revealing the uncolored portion of the fiber. Also refers to a chemical or abrasive finish that deliberately produces this whitish cast on fabrics.

**Full fashioning** is the process of shaping knit garments during the knitting process by adding or decreasing stitches.

**Fulling** is a finish of woven or knitted wool fabrics that produces a tighter, more compact fabric by a carefully controlled felting process.

**Fume fading** is a color retention problem. Colors alter when exposed to gases, fumes, or other atmospheric pollutants.

**Fume-fading–resistant finish** refers to a finish designed to minimize the effect of atmospheric pollutants on dyes.

**Functional finish** (*See* Special-purpose finish)

**Fur** is any animal skin or hide to which the hair is attached and which has been processed to protect the hide from rotting.

**Fur cleaning** is a specialized process of removing soil from fur so that the hide does not lose its color or suppleness while not damaging the hair.

**Fur Products Labeling Act** regulates the labeling of fur products to protect the consumer from unscrupulous trade practices.

**Fusible nonwoven** is a type of fiberweb with a chemical adhesive on the technical back.

**Garbardine (gaberdine)** is a tightly woven, medium- to heavyweight, steep- or regular-angle, twill-weave fabric with a pronounced wale. The fabric can be wool, a wool blend, or a synthetic-fiber content designed to look like wool. Gabardine can also be 100 percent texturized polyester or a cotton/polyester blend.

**Gaiting** (gāt′-ing) describes the arrangement of needles in a double-knitting machine. (*See* Interlock and Rib Gaiting)

**Garment dyeing** (*See* Product dyeing)

**Garment or product dip process** (*See* Immersion process)

**Garnetted** is a term for shredding wool yarns or fabrics to produce wool fibers for recycling.

**Gauge** (gāj) refers to needles per inch in the machines used in making knits or tufted fabrics.

**Gauze** (gawz) is a sheer, lightweight, low-count, plain- or leno-weave balanced fabric made of spun yarns. It is often cotton, rayon, or a blend of these fibers. *Indian gauze* has a crinkled look and is available in a variety of fabric weights.

**Gel spinning** is a spinning method in which the dissolved polyethylene polymer forms a viscous gel in the solvent, followed by extrusion through the spinneret, solvent extraction, and fiber drawing.

**Generic group** refers to fibers with similar chemical composition.

**Generic name** refers to the family of manufactured or synthetic fibers that have similar chemical composition.

**Georgette** is a sheer, lightweight, plain-weave or momie-weave fabric made with fine-crepe yarns. It is crepier and less lustrous than chiffon.

**Gin** is a mechanical device used to separate cotton fibers from the seed.

**Gingham** is a yarn-dyed, plain-weave fabric that is available in a variety of weights and qualities. It may be balanced or unbalanced. It may be made of combed or carded yarns. If two colors of yarn are used, the fabric is called a *check* or a *checked gingham*. If three or more colors are used, the fabric is referred to as a *plaid gingham*.

**Glass** is a manufactured fiber in which the fiber-forming substance is glass.

**Glass transition temperature ($T_g$)** refers to the temperature at which amorphous regions of fibers are easily distorted. It is used in heat setting fabrics.

**Glazed** refers to a fabric that has been treated with a friction calender to polish the surface.

**Glazed chintz** (*See* Chintz)

**Glazing** is a flattening of the cross section of heat-sensitive fibers or yarns resulting from exposure to high temperatures.

**Gore-Tex** is a poromeric multiplex fabric combining a thin film of PTFE with fabric to produce a water-impermeable but comfortable fabric produced by W. L. Gore & Associates.

**Grading wool** refers to judging a wool fleece for its fineness and length.

**Graft polymer** is a type of copolymer; another type of mer is attached to the backbone polymer chain.

**Grain** refers to the natural surface characteristic of leather and is related to the species of animal.

**Grain** describes the relationship of warp to filling yarns in a woven fabric.

**Granite cloth** is a wool momie-weave fabric. The term may be used for any momie-weave fabric.

**Gray goods** (**grey goods** or **greige goods**) is a general term used to describe any unfinished woven or knitted fabric.

**Grease wool** (*See* Raw wool)

**Green cotton** describes cotton fabric that has been washed with mild natural-based soap, but it has not been bleached or treated with other chemicals, except possibly natural dyes.

**Green products** are products that are sold with claims, valid or not, that they have been produced using systems that have minimal environmental impact.

**Grin-through** occurs in elastomeric fabrics. Some elastomeric fabrics break and the broken ends or loops of broken fibers appear on the surface of the fabric. In pile fabrics, including tufted fabrics, the term describes where the base structure shows through the pile surface.

**Grosgrain** (grow′grain) is a tightly woven, firm, warp-faced fabric with heavy, round filling ribs created by a high-warp count and coarse filling yarns. Grosgrain can be woven as a narrow-ribbon or a full-width fabric.

**Ground ply** is the ply of a fancy yarn that forms the foundation for the effect ply.

**Guanaco** is the fiber removed from the South American guanaco.

**Habutai** is a soft, lightweight silk fabric. It is heavier than China silk.

**Hackling** is a process of separating bast fiber bundles into individual fibers and removing short irregular fibers.

**Hairiness** describes excessive fiber ends on the surface of a yarn that may create problems in fabrication or in consumer use because they tend to be more sensitive to abrasion and pilling.

**Halogenation** is a finish for wool that partially dissolves fiber scales in order to produce a washable fabric.

**Hand** is the way a fiber feels to the sense of touch.

**Hand builders** are compounds that soften the fabric's hand.

**Handkerchief linen** is similar in luster and count to batiste, but it is linen or linen-look with slub yarns and a little more body.

**Handling** refers to the physical form of the fabric in terms of length and width during finishing.

**Handmade lace** includes several types of lace made by individual artists or craft persons.

**Hard twist** is a high amount of yarn twist in the range of 30–40 tpi that produces a harsher hand in the fabric.

**Harness** is the part of the loom that controls the weave by controlling the up or down position of warp yarns.

**Heat conductivity** is the ability to conduct heat away from the body.

**Heat retention** is the ability of a fiber to retain heat or to insulate.

**Heat sensitivity** is the ability to soften, melt, or shrink when subjected to heat; see also thermoplastic.

**Heat setting** describes the process of producing fiber, yarn, or fabric stability through the use of heat.

**Heat-transfer printing** describes a process of adding color to fabric by using heat to cause a pattern printed on paper to transfer to the fabric.

**Heddle** is a rigid wire in the loom through which a warp yarn is threaded and which is held in place in a harness.

**Hemp** is a bast fiber produced by *Cannabis sativa*.

**Henequen** is a smooth, straight, yellow leaf fiber similar to sisal.

**Herringbone** is a broken twill-weave fabric created by changing the direction of the twill wale from right to left and back again. This creates a chevron pattern of stripes that may or may not be equally prominent. Herringbone fabrics are made in a variety of weights, patterns, and fiber types.

**High-bulk yarn** is a bulk yarn with little or no stretch.

**High-tenacity fibers** have been modified in the spinning process to increase the strength of the fiber.

**High-wet-modulus rayon** is a modification of rayon with better performance characteristics.
**Hollow fibers** are not solid and contain air spaces in their interior.
**Homespun** is a coarse, plain-weave fabric with a hand-woven look.
**Homopolymer** refers to a polymer composed of a single type of mer.
**Honan** (hō′nahn) was originally of Chinese silk. Now it is made of any filament fiber. It is similar to pongee, but it has slub yarns in both warp and filling.
**Hopsacking** is a coarse, loosely woven suiting- or bottom-weight, basket-weave fabric often made of low-grade cotton.
**Hot water extraction** is a cleaning technique for furnishings in which a hot water-detergent solution is injected into the textile and the soiled solution is removed by vacuuming.
**Houndstooth check** is a medium- to heavyweight, yarn-dyed, twill-weave fabric in which the interlacing and color pattern creates a unique pointed-check or houndstooth shape.
**Huck** or **huck-a-back toweling** is a medium- to heavyweight fabric made on a dobby loom to create a honeycomb or bird's-eye pattern. Often the filling yarns are more loosely twisted to increase the absorbency of the fabric.
**Hydroentangled web** is a layer of fibers in which jets of water are forced through the web after extrusion to entangle the fibers.
**Hydrogen bonds** are attractions between positive hydrogen atoms of one molecule and negative oxygen or nitrogen atoms in another molecule.
**Hydrophilic** describes fibers with high moisture absorbency or regain.
**Hydrophobic** describes fibers with low moisture absorbency or regain.
**Hygroscopic** describes fibers with high moisture absorbency or regain and the ability to remain dry to the touch.

**Ikat** is a resist printing method; yarns are treated to resist dye in certain areas, dyed, and woven into a fabric.
**Immersion process** is a process for creating durable-press items in which the finished item is immersed in a finishing agent mixed with appropriate additives to control for hand and performance, pressed, and cured.
**Inspection** describes the finishing step in which fabric quality is assessed.
**Intarsia** is a type of filling-knit fabric in which yarns that appear on the surface of the fabric are discontinuous; a knit counterpart to a true tapestry weave.
**Interlacing** is the point at which a yarn changes its position from one side of the fabric to the other side.
**Interlock** is a firm, double-filling knit. The two needle beds knit two interlocked 1 × 1 rib fabrics. Both sides of the fabric look like the face side of jersey.
**Interlock gaiting** refers to a double needlebed arrangement. Needles in one bed are directly opposite needles in the other bed. Used to produce interlock and other double-knits.
**Isotactic** refers to the same type of spatial arrangement of side groups attached to the backbone chain throughout the polymer.

**Jacquard double knit** is a patterned fabric made on a double knitting machine.
**Jacquard jersey** is a jersey knit with a pattern that uses a combination of knit, tuck, or miss stitches.
**Jacquard loom** is a loom with warp yarns individually controlled by punched cards or a microcomputer used to create jacquard fabrics.
**Jean** is a warp-faced twill of carded yarns. It is lighter weight than drill, and it has finer yarns but a higher warp-yarn count.
**Jersey** is a filling-knit fabric with no distinct rib. Jersey can be any fiber content and be knit flat or circular.
**Jet dyeing** is a process in which the fabric is in a continuous loop when dyed.
**Jet printing** is the application of color to fabric by spraying dye through tiny nozzles to create the pattern.
**Jig dyeing** is a process for dyeing fabric in open width form.
**Jute** is a bast fiber used to produce burlap and other industrial fabrics.

**Kapok** is fiber removed from the seed of the Java kapok or silk cotton tree.
**Kenaf** is a bast fiber removed from the kenaf plant.
**Keratin** is the protein found in animal fibers.
**Kersey** is a very heavy, thick, boardy, wool-coating fabric that has been heavily fulled and felted. In kersey, it is difficult to see the twill weave because of the fulling and the short, lustrous nap. Kersey is heavier than melton. It may be either a single or a double cloth.
**Knit stitch** is the basic stitch that forms the majority of knit fabrics.
**Knitted terrycloth** is a filling knit fabric with a loop pile.
**Knit-through fabric** includes several types of composite fabric made by knitting a fine yarn through a thin fiberweb or by knitting fibers or yarns to lock laid yarns in place.
**Knitting** refers to the production of fabric by interlooping yarns.
**Knot, spot, nub, or knop yarn** is a fancy yarn. The effect ply is twisted many times around the ground ply in the same place.

**Labeling requirements** refer to information required by law or regulation that must be available to the consumer at point of purchase.
**Lace** is an openwork fabric with yarns that are twisted around each other to form complex patterns or figures. Lace may be hand or machine made or made by a variety of fabrication methods including weaving, knitting, crocheting, and knotting.
**La coste** is a double-knit fabric made with a combination of knit and tuck stitches to create a meshlike appearance. It is often a cotton or cotton/polyester blend.
**Lamb's wool** is wool removed from young animals less than 7 months old.
**Lamé** (lah-may′) is any fabric containing metal or metallic yarns as a conspicuous feature.
**Laminated fabric** describes a composite fabric created by adhering two layers of fabrics with a thin foam.

**Laminates** are composite fabrics in which two layers of fabric are adhered by foam or adhesive.

**Lastrile** is a synthetic rubber in which the fiber-forming substance is a copolymer of acrylonitrile and a diene composed of not more than 50 percent but at least 10 percent by weight of acrylonitrile units.

**Latch needle** is a type of needle used in knitting fabrics from coarse yarns.

**Lawn** is a fine, opaque, lightweight, plain-weave fabric usually made of combed-cotton or cotton-blend yarns. The fabric may be bleached, dyed, or printed.

**Leaf fiber** refers to fiber removed from the leaves of a plant.

**Leather** is processed from the skins or hides of animals, birds, reptiles, or fish so that it does not rot.

**Leather cleaning** is a specialized process of removing soil from treated animal hides so that the hide does not lose its color or suppleness.

**Leavers lace** is a type of machine-made lace that uses bobbins that move back and forth and around warp yarns to create the open pattern in the fabric.

**Leno** (lē′-nō) refers to any leno-weave fabric in which two warp yarns are crossed over each other and held in place by a filling yarn. Leno weaves require a doup attachment on the loom.

**Level** refers to a colorant that is uniform throughout the fabric or product.

**Licensing** describes the situation in which one company legally uses another company's trademarks and expertise to make, use, and/or sell a product.

**Light-reflecting finishes** incorporate fluorescent dyes or small glass retroreflective spheres to enhance fabric visibility in low-light conditions.

**Line** refers to long, combed, and better quality flax fibers.

**Lining twill** is an opaque, lightweight, warp-faced twill of filament yarns. It may be printed.

**Lint** refers to usable cotton fibers removed in the ginning process. It also refers to fiber debris that creates pills on fabrics or accumulates in dryer lint traps.

**Linters** are very short cotton fibers that remain attached to the cotton seed after ginning.

**Liquid barrier finish** adds protection to a fabric from liquids penetrating through the fabric.

**Lisle** (lȳle) is a high-quality jersey made of fine two-ply combed cotton yarns.

**Llama** is the fiber removed from the South American llama.

**London shrunk** is a relaxation finishing process for wool fabrics.

**Loom** is the machine used to make woven fabrics.

**Loop, curl, or bouclé yarn** is a fancy yarn. The effect ply forms closed loops at regular intervals along the length of the yarn.

**Looping machine** is used to join knit garment parts in a way that is not obvious.

**Low elongation fibers** are used in blends with weaker fibers to increase the overall strength and abrasion resistance of the fabric.

**Low pilling fibers** have been engineered to have a lower flex life, thus decreasing pill formation.

**Low twist** is a very low amount of twist used in filament yarns to keep the fibers together during processing and fabrication.

**Lumen** is a hollow central canal through which nutrients travel as a cotton fiber develops.

**Luster** refers to the way light is reflected from the surface of a fiber or fabric.

**Luster finish** is a fabric treatment that changes the light reflectance characteristics of the fabric.

**Lyocel** (lī′-ō-sel) is a manufactured fiber composed of solvent-spun cellulose.

**Madras** (mad′-ras) shirting is a light- to medium-weight, dobby-weave fabric in which the pattern is usually confined to vertical stripes.

**Maltese lace** is a bobbin lace with a Maltese cross in the pattern.

**Man-made fibers** (*See* Manufactured fibers)

**Manufactured or man-made fibers** are made from chemical compounds produced in manufacturing facilities. The material's original form is not recognizable as a fiber.

**Manufactured regenerated fibers** are produced in fiber form from naturally occurring polymers.

**Marquisette** (mahr-kui-zeht) is a sheer, lightweight, leno-weave fabric usually made of filament yarns.

**Mass pigmentation** (*See* Solution dyeing)

**Matelassé** (mat-luh-sā′) is a double-cloth fabric woven to create a three-dimensional texture with a puckered or almost quilted look. Matelassés are made on jacquard or dobby looms often with crepe yarns or very coarse cotton yarns. When finished, the shrinkage of the crepe yarn or the coarse cotton yarn creates the puckered appearance. It is used in apparel as well as in furnishings.

**Mechlin** (mek′-lihn) **lace** is a bobbin lace with a small hexagonal mesh and very fine yarns.

**Medulla** is an airy, honeycombed core present in some wool fibers.

**Melt-blown fiberweb** is made by extruding the polymer into a high-velocity air stream that breaks the fiber into short pieces that are held together by thermal bonding and fiber interlacing.

**Melton** is a heavyweight, plain- or twill-weave coating fabric made from wool. It is lighter than kersey and has a smooth surface that is napped, then closely sheared. It may be either a single or double cloth.

**Melt spinning** is the process of producing fibers by melting polymer chips and extruding the molten polymer in fiber form. Coagulation occurs by cooling.

**Mercerization** is a finish in which cotton is exposed to sodium hydroxide to increase the fiber's absorbency, luster, and strength. See also slack mercerization and tension mercerization.

**Merino** is a breed of sheep that produces superior quality wool.

**Metallic coating** is a surface application of a thin layer of metal, usually aluminum, primarily to minimize heat transfer through the fabric or to add a metallic luster to the fabric.

**Metallic fibers** are manufactured fibers composed of metal, plastic-coated metal, metal-coated plastic, or a core completely covered by metal.

**Metallic yarn** is a yarn made with at least one metal monofilament fiber.

**Metamerism** (meh-tam′-uhr-izm) describes a color matching with one light source, but not with any other light source.

**Metered addition process** is a process for producing durable-press items in which finished goods are sprayed with a controlled amount of the finishing agent mixed with appropriate additives to control for hand and performance, tumbled to distribute the finish evenly, pressed, and cured.

**Microdenier** refers to a fiber of less than 1.0 denier per filament.

**Microencapsulated finishes** incorporate a water-soluble material in a tiny capsule form and may contain fragrance, insect repellents, disinfectants, cleaning agents, or other materials.

**Migration** describes a color problem in which the dye shifts from the area where it was applied to adjacent areas of the same fabric or a fabric in close proximity.

**Milanese machine** uses two sets of yarns, one needle bed, and one guide bar to knit milanese fabrics.

**Mildew control** describes a finish that inhibits the growth of mold or mildew.

**Mill-finished** describes a fabric finished by the same company that produced the fabric; a type of vertical integration within the textile industry.

**Milling** (*See* Fulling)

**Minimum or minimum yardage** refers to the shortest length of fabric a textile firm will produce or sell to another firm.

**Mixed denier filament bundling** combines fibers of several denier sizes, such as microfibers (0.5 dpf) with macro or regular denier (2.0 dpf) fibers, in one yarn.

**Mixture** is a fiber blend. Yarns of one generic type are present in one area in the fabric (i.e., the warp) and yarns of another generic type are present in another area of the fabric (i.e., the filling).

**Modacrylic** is a manufactured fiber in which the fiber-forming substance is any long-chain synthetic polymer composed of less than 85 percent but at least 35 percent by weight acrylonitrile units except when the polymer qualifies as rubber.

**Mohair** is the hair fiber removed from the Angora goat.

**Moiré calendering** (mwah-rā′) describes a finish that produces a watermarked or wood-grain texture on the fabric; most common on rib or unbalanced plain-weave fabrics like taffeta.

**Moiré pattern** is a wood grain or watermarked pattern produced on some unbalanced plain-weave fabrics by finishing.

**Moisture vapor transport rate** (MVTR) measures how quickly moisture vapor moves from the side of the fabric next to the body to the fabric's exterior side.

**Mold control** (*See* Mildew control)

**Moleskin** is a napped, heavy, strong fabric often made in a satin weave. The nap is suedelike.

**Momie weave** is a class of weaves with no wale or other distinct weave effect resulting from an irregular interlacing pattern.

**Momme,** also known as momie or mommie (mahm′mē), abbreviated mm, is a standard way to describe the weight of silk fabrics; one momme weighs 3.75 grams.

**Monk's cloth** is a heavyweight, coarse, loosely woven, basket-weave fabric usually in a 2 × 2 or 4 × 4 arrangement. Although it can be made in a 6 × 6 or 8 × 8 arrangement, it seldom is because of the low durability. It is often made of softly spun, two-ply yarns in oatmeal color.

**Moss crepe** combines a momie weave with crepe twist yarns.

**Moth resistance** describes a finish in which the wool fabric is treated to be unpalatable or harmful to insects.

**Multihead embroidery** refers to the machine that creates several identical designs or emblems simultaneously.

**Multiple-shed weaving** is a type of loom. The filling yarn is inserted in a series of sheds that form as the filling yarn moves across the fabric.

**Multiplex fabric** describes a variety of fabrics that combine fibers, yarns, fabrics, or a combination of these into one fabric.

**Multiprocess wet cleaning** is a commercial alternative to dry cleaning that uses carefully controlled wet processes to clean textiles that cannot be machine washed.

**Muslin** is a firm, medium- to heavyweight, plain-weave cotton fabric made in a variety of qualities. Muslin made with low-grade cotton fiber with small pieces from the cotton plant is often used in apparel design.

**Nap** refers to bringing fiber ends to the surface of the fabric in finishing.

**Napping** is a finish in which fiber ends are brushed to the surface to produce a softer hand.

**Napping twist** is a small amount of twist used to produce lofty spun yarns for fabrics that will be napped.

**Narrow fabric** describes any fabric up to 12 inches wide.

**Natural bicomponent fiber** contains the two types of cortex cells such as found in wool fibers.

**Natural dyes** are a dye class produced by plants used primarily with natural fibers.

**Natural fibers** are grown or developed in nature in recognizable fiber form.

**Naturally colored cotton** is cotton grown in colors of brown, tan, yellow, green, rust, etc.

**Needlepoint lace** includes Alençon, which has a hexagonal mesh; rosepoint and Venetian point, which have an irregular mesh.

**Needle punching** is a fiberweb made by passing barbed needles through a fiber web to entangle the fibers.

**Neoprene** describes a composite fabric combining a film of polychloroprene with a woven, knitted, or fiberweb fabric.

**Nep** is a small knot of entangled fibers. The fibers may be immature or dead and create problems in dyeing.

**Net** is a general term used to refer to any open-construction fabric whether it is created by weaving, knitting, knotting, or another method.

**Ninon** (nē′-nohn) is a sheer, slightly crisp, lightweight, plain-weave fabric made of filament yarns. The warp yarns are grouped in pairs, but ninon is not a basket-weave fabric.

**Nodes** are irregular crosswise markings present on many bast fibers.

**Nonreinforced film** is another term for plain film.

**Nonwoven** is a general term for fabrics directly made from fibers.

**Novelty yarn** is another term for a fancy yarn.

**Novoloid** is a manufactured fiber in which the fiber-forming substance contains at least 35 percent by weight of cross-linked novolac.

**Nylon** is a manufactured fiber in which the fiber-forming substance is any long-chain synthetic polyamide in which less than 85 percent of the amide linkages are attached directly to two aromatic rings.

**Occupational Safety and Health Administration** is a federal agency that enforces laws and regulations that ensure safety in the workplace.

**Off-grain** refers to a fabric when warp and filling yarns do not cross each other at a 90° angle.

**Off-grain print** describes a fabric defect where an off-grain fabric was printed or where the print pattern does not line up with the fabric grain.

**Off-shade** describes when one fabric or portion of a product does not precisely match the color of another fabric or portion of a product.

**Olefin** is a manufactured fiber in which the fiber-forming substance is any long-chain synthetic polymer composed of at least 85 percent by weight of ethylene, propylene, or other olefin units except amorphous (noncrystalline) polyolefins qualifying as rubber.

**Oleophilic** refers to fibers that have a high affinity for oil.

**Open-end rotor spinning** is a spun yarn process that eliminates roving and twisting.

**Opening,** an initial step in the production of spun yarns, loosens fibers from bale form and cleans and blends the fibers.

**Open-width finishing** refers to holding the fabric out to its full width during finishing.

**Optical brighteners** are chemical compounds used to produce a white appearance.

**Organdy** is a transparent, crisp, lightweight, plain-weave fabric made of cotton-spun yarns. The fabric has been parchmentized or treated with acid to create the crisp, wiry hand.

**Organic cotton** describes cotton produced following state fiber certification standards on land where organic farming practices have been used for at least three years.

**Organza** is a transparent, crisp, lightweight, plain-weave fabric made of filament yarns.

**Orientation** refers to the alignment of the fiber's polymers with its longitudinal axis.

**Osnaburg (osnaberg)** is a coarse, bottom-weight, low-count cotton fabric characterized by uneven yarns that have bits of cellulosic waste.

**Ottoman** is a firm, plain-weave, unbalanced fabric with large and small ribs made by adjacent filling yarns of different size that are completely covered by the warp.

**Outing flannel** is a medium-weight, napped, plain- or twill-weave, spun-yarn fabric. It may be napped on one or both sides. It is heavier and stiffer than flannelette.

**Out-of-register** is a problem with printed fabrics. The edges of a print do not match as the designer intended.

**Over-wire method** is one technique used to create pile fabrics such as friezé.

**Oxford chambray** is an oxford cloth made with yarn-dyed warp yarns and white filling yarns. Sometimes a second color is used for the filling yarns.

**Oxford cloth** is a light- to medium-weight fabric with a $2 \times 1$ half-basket weave.

**Package dyeing** is a process for dyeing yarn cones or other textiles in which the dye bath is forced through the textile.

**Padding machine** passes the fabric through a solution, under a guide roll, and between two padding rolls to evenly distribute a finish across the fabric.

**Pad dyeing** is a process for dyeing fabric in open width form where dye is forced into the fiber by nip or squeeze rollers.

**Panné velvet** is a warp pile fabric in which the pile yarns are pressed flat in the same direction.

**Parchmentizing** is an acid finish to cotton fabrics that produces a thinner fabric with a crisper hand than the original fabric; used in the production of organdy.

**Parent fiber** is the simplest form of a fiber that has not been modified in any way.

**PBI** is a manufactured fiber in which the fiber-forming substance is a long-chain aromatic polymer having reoccurring imidazole groups as an integral part of the polymer chain.

**Peau de soie** (pō-deh-swah) is a very smooth, heavy, semidull, satin-weave fabric. It often has satin floats on both sides of the fabric. It can be made of silk, acetate, or other manufactured fibers.

**Percale** is a balanced plain-weave, medium-weight, piece-dyed or printed fabric finished from print cloths of better quality.

**Performance** is the manner in which a textile, textile component, or textile product responds when something is done to it or when it is exposed to some element in the environment that might adversely affect the textile.

**Performance fibers** are fiber modifications that provide comfort and improve human performance for products such as active sportswear.

**Performance testing** refers to subjecting textiles to selected procedures and determining how the textile reacts.

**Perfume** is a compound added to some detergents to mask an unattractive odor with one that is more pleasant.

**Permanent finish** describes a finish whose effectiveness will not diminish with time or use.

**Picking** is the step in weaving where the filling yarn is inserted in the shed.

**Piece dyeing** describes adding color to the textile when it is in fabric form. See also union dyeing and cross-dyeing.

**Pigment** is a colorant that is inorganic in nature; must be attached to the fiber with the use of a binding agent.

**Pile jersey** is a filling knit made with two sets of yarns where one set forms the base structure and the other set forms the pile.

**Pile weave** is a three-dimensional structure made by weaving an extra set of warp or filling yarns with the ground yarns so that loops or cut yarn ends create a pile.

**Pilling** is the formation of tiny balls of fiber ends and lint on the surface of the fabric.

**Pima cotton** is a type of extra-long-staple cotton.

**Piña** is a leaf fiber obtained from the pineapple plant.

**Pinsonic quilting** is the production of a composite fabric by using ultra-high frequency sound to heat-seal face fabric, fiberfill, and backing fabric together in localized areas.

**Piqué** (pē-kay′) is a fabric made in a variety of patterns. It can be made on a dobby or jacquard loom with carded or combed yarns. Some piqués have filling cords. Most piqués have three or more sets of yarns.

**Plain film** consists of the polymer solution in sheet form with no supporting layer.

**Plain weave** is the simplest weave structure in which two sets of yarns at right angles to each other pass alternately over and under each other to form the maximum number of interlacings.

**Plastic coating** is the surface application of a thin film to a fabric for increased luster and water repellency, or to minimize yarn slippage.

**Pleating calender** is a special type of embossing calendering that produces three-dimensional pleats in the fabric.

**Plissé** (plih-sā′) is a fabric usually finished from cotton-print cloth by printing with a caustic-soda (sodium hydroxide) paste. The paste causes the fabric to shrink, thus creating a three-dimensional effect. The stripe that wax printed usually is darker in piece-dyed goods because the sodium hydroxide increases the dye absorbancy.

**Plush** is a woven warp pile fabric with a deep pile.

**Ply yarn** consists of two or more strands of fibers held together by twist or some other mechanism.

**Pocket weave** is another term for a double weave.

**Point paper** is a type of paper used to diagram warp knits.

**Polished cotton** is a balanced, medium-weight, plain-weave fabric that has been given a glazed-calender finish.

**Pollution Prevention Act** is the federal law that focuses on waste minimization.

**Polyamide** is a generic term for polymers containing an amide group and a term used for nylon in some countries.

**Polyester** is a manufactured fiber in which the fiber-forming substance is any long-chain synthetic polymer composed of at least 85 percent by weight of an ester of a substituted aromatic carboxylic acid, including but not restricted to substituted terephthalate units or substituted hydroxybenzoate units.

**Polyethylene** is a type of olefin made from polymerizing ethylene.

**Polymer** is a very large molecule made by connecting many small molecules or mers together.

**Polymerization** is the process of connecting many small molecules (mers) to produce one very large molecule called a polymer.

**Polypropylene** is a type of olefin made from polymerizing propylene.

**Polytetrafluoroethylene** is a fiber made of tetrafluoroethylene units.

**Pongee** (pahn-jē′) is a medium-weight, balanced, plain-weave fabric with a fine regular warp and an irregular filling. It was originally a tussah or wild-silk fabric, but now pongee is used to describe a fabric that has the general appearance of fine warp yarns and irregular filling yarns.

**Poplin** is a medium- to heavyweight, unbalanced, plain-weave, spun-yarn fabric that is usually piece dyed. The filling yarns are coarser than the warp yarns. Poplin has a more pronounced rib than broadcloth.

**Poromeric fabric** incorporates a thin film that is microporous in nature.

**Postcured process** is a durable-press process in which the fabric is saturated with the cross-linking solution, cut and sewn into a product, and cured.

**Powder cleaners** are dry absorbent powders combining detergent and solvent that are applied to the textile in dry form, worked in, and removed by vacuuming.

**Power net** is a raschel-warp knit in which an inlaid spandex fiber or yarn is used to give high elongation and elasticity.

**Power stretch** refers to the ability of a fabric to exhibit high retractive forces that mold, support, or shape the body.

**Precured process** is a durable-press process in which the fabric is saturated with the cross-linking solution, cured, cut and sewn into a product.

**Preparation** refers to a series of steps to get yarns ready for weaving or dyeing or fabrics ready for dyeing, printing, or finishing.

**Pressing** is a finishing process used with wool or wool blends in which the fabric is placed between metal plates that steam and press the fabric.

**Pretreatment** includes a variety of chemicals that make it easier to remove stains during cleaning.

**Primary fiber bundle** refers to naturally occurring groupings of individual bast fibers that are difficult to separate completely and that contribute to the natural thick and thin appearance of yarns made from bast fibers.

**Print cloth** is a general term used to describe unfinished, medium-weight, balanced plain-weave, cotton or cotton-blend fabrics. These fabrics can be finished as percale, embossed, plissé, chintz, cretonne, or polished cotton.

**Printing** is the localized application of color to the surface of the fabric or yarn. See also resist printing, screen printing, direct printing, and roller printing.

**Producer colored** is another term for solution dyed.

**Product development** is the design and engineering of a product so that it has the desired serviceability characteristics, appeals to the target market, can be made within an acceptable time frame for a reasonable cost, and sold at a profit.

**Product dyeing** refers to the process of adding color to the textile after it has been cut and sewn into the final product.

**Product testing** refers to consumers using textile products and evaluating how the products perform.

**Progressive shrinkage** is shrinkage that occurs through several care cycles.

**Projectile loom** or gripper loom is a type of loom where the filling yarn is inserted in the shed with a small metal projectile or gripper.

**Puckered surface** is created on nylon and polyester fabrics by printing them with a chemical that causes the fibers to shrink slightly when dry.

**Pure silk** and **pure dye silk** describe 100 percent silk fabrics that do not contain any metallic weighting compounds or where the metallic weighting compounds are within the minimums set by the 1932 federal silk regulation.

**Purl knit** is made on a special type of double knitting machine that can produce plain jersey knits, rib knits, and purl knits.

**Purl or reverse stitch** forms a stitch that looks the same on both sides of the fabric.

**Qiviut** is the fine underwool fiber removed from the musk ox.

**QSC** (*See* Quick Style Change)

**Quality** refers to the sum total of product characteristics, including appearance, appropriateness for the end use, performance and interactions of materials in the product, consistency among identical products, and freedom from defects in construction or materials.

**Quality assurance** refers to the broad area of incorporating quality into and evaluating the quality of textile materials and products.

**Quality control** refers to inspecting textile and materials to determine if they meet quality requirements.

**Quality control standards** refer to expected fabric performance.

**Quick Style Change (QSC)** describes changes in looms and loom control mechanisms to facilitate a rapid change for a loom from one structural design fabric to another.

**Quilted fabric** is a composite fabric consisting of a face or fashion fabric, a layer of fiberfill or batting, and a backing fabric. The three layers may be connected with heat (pinsonic quilting) or thread (regular quilting).

**Ramie** is a fiber removed from a perennial shrub grown in hot, humid climates.

**Rapier loom** is a type of loom. The filling yarn is inserted in the shed using a rigid or flexible rod or steel tape.

**Raschel** (rah-shel′) **knit** is a general term for patterned, warp-knit fabric made with coarser yarns than other warp-knit fabrics.

**Raschel lace** is a type of lace made using warp knitting.

**Ratiné yarn** is a fancy yarn. The effect ply is twisted in a spiral arrangement around the ground ply with an occasional longer loop.

**Raw or grease wool** is wool as it is removed from the animal with soil, suint, and other impurities present.

**Raw silk** or silk-in-the-gum is silk that has not been processed to remove the sericin.

**Rayon** is a manufactured fiber composed of regenerated cellulose in which substituents have replaced not more than 15 percent of the hydrogens of the hydroxyl groups.

**Reactive dyes** are a dye class used primarily with natural fibers and rayon.

**Recycled wool** is wool that has been processed into fabrics, garnetted, and processed into another fabric.

**Recycling** is the process of using materials more than one time before they are disposed of in such a way that they cannot be reused in any form.

**Reed** is the part of the loom through which warp yarns are threaded and which is used to push filling yarns in place after they have been inserted in the shed.

**Reeling** refers to the process of removing silk fibers from several cocoons and winding them onto a reel.

**Reembroidered lace** is another term for cordonnet lace.

**Regular twill** is a twill with a wale angle of approximately 45°.

**Relaxation shrinkage** refers to loss of dimensions resulting from tensions introduced during fabric production or finishing.

**Renewable finish** is a finish that, when its effectiveness has been decreased or destroyed, can be replaced by consumers, dry cleaners, or other firms.

**Rep** is another term for an unbalanced plain weave.

**Repairing** is a finishing step in which minor flaws in fabrics are corrected.

**Resiliency** is the ability to return to original shape after bending, twisting compressing, or a combination of these deformations.

**Resistance to shifting** describes a characteristic of fiberfill, batting, and wadding where the fibers do not move or shift with use.

**Resist printing** refers to a coloration process in which a portion of the yarn or fabric is treated so dyes will not be absorbed during dyeing; includes screen printing, ikat and batik.

**Resource Conservation and Recovery Act** is the federal law that regulates solid and hazardous materials from their generation to final disposal.

**Retting** is the process of bacterial rotting or decomposing the pectin in plant stems in order to remove bast fibers.

**Reworking** refers to repeating steps in finishing that were done incorrectly to achieve appropriate performance.

**Rib** is a ridge formed in tle fabric when the balance is something other than 1:1 or when the size of one set of yarns is significantly greater than the size of the other set of yarns in the fabric. Also refers to double knit structure when one stitch is made on one bed and the next stitch is made on the other bed.

**Rib gaiting** refers to the double needle bed arrangement. Needles in one bed are directly opposite spaces in the other bed. Used to produce rib knits and other double knits.

**Ring spinning** is a process for producing spun yarns. A series of operations removes fibers from a bale, removes debris, makes the fibers parallel, draws them into a fine strand, and adds twist to hold them together.

**Rippling** is the process of removing seeds by pulling a plant through a machine in order to obtain a bast fiber.

**RN number** refers to the manufacturer's identification number assigned to the firm as a result of the Textile Fiber Products Identification Act.

**Roller printing** is the application of color in localized areas through the use of rollers.

**Rope finishing** refers to allowing the fabric to roll and fold in on itself and form a tube or rope during finishing.

**Rotary-screen printing** is a resist printing method. A cylindrical screen is treated so that print paste passes through openings to create a design on the fabric. One screen is used for each color in the pattern.

**Rot-proof finish** is a finish that improves the longevity of fabrics used outdoors.

**Roving** is a step in the production of some spun yarns. The drawn sliver is reduced in size, fibers are made more parallel, and a small amount of twist is inserted.

**Rubber** is a manufactured fiber in which the fiber-forming substance is comprised of natural or synthetic rubber.

**Run** describes a quantity of fabric receiving the same processing at the same time. For knits, it may refer to the collapse of a wale.

**Safety** describes the ability of a textile or textile product to protect the body from harm.

**Sailcloth** is a bottom-weight half-basket-weave (2 × 1), unbalanced fabric. It may be made of spun- or textured-filament yarns. It can be piece dyed or printed.

**Sand crepe** is a momie weave fabric with a repeat pattern of 16 warp and 16 filling yarns that produce a sanded or frosted appearance.

**Saran** is a manufactured fiber in which the fiber-forming substance is any long-chain synthetic polymer composed of at least 80 percent by weight of vinylidene chloride units.

**Sateen** is a strong, lustrous medium- to heavyweight, spun-yarn, satin-weave fabric that is either warp faced or filling faced. A warp faced, spun yarn fabric with a satin weave may be called cotton satin.

**Satin** is a strong, lustrous medium- to heavyweight, filament-yarn, satin-weave fabric.

**Satin weave** is a weave in which each warp or filling yarn floats across four or more filling or warp yarns with a progression of interlacings by two to the right or to the left.

**Scales** are a horny, nonfibrous layer on the exterior of wool fibers.

**Schiffli embroidery** is the application of decorative thread to the surface of a fabric to achieve a pattern, as in eyelet embroidery.

**Schreiner calender** etches hundred of fine lines on the surface of a fabric to increase cover, as in tricot, or add a subtle luster, as in sateen.

**Scoured or cleaned wool** is wool that has been cleaned to remove soil, suint, and other impurities.

**Scouring** refers to a finishing step in which soil, excess chemicals, or fiber coatings such as natural waxes or oils are removed.

**Screen printing** is a process during which application of color to the surface of a fabric is controlled by a specially prepared screen so that dye or pigment paste penetrates the screen in selected areas only. Includes rotary and flatbed screen printing.

**Scroop** refers to the natural rustle made when two layers of silk fabric are rubbed together.

**Scutching** is a process in which bast fiber plant stems are passed through fluted metal rollers to break up and remove the woody outer layers.

**Sea Island cotton** (*See* Pima cotton)

**Seed fiber** refers to fiber removed from the seed pod of a plant.

**Seersucker** is a light- to heavyweight, slack-tension weave fabric. It can be made with a variety of interlacing patterns. Seersucker always has vertical crinkled or puckered stripes made by two sets of warp yarns. One set is under normal tension for weaving. The other set has a much looser, slack tension.

**Selvage** is the self-edge of the fabric where filling yarns end or turn to go through another shed.

**Serge** is a general term used to refer to twill-weave fabrics with a flat right-hand wale. The interlacing pattern is $\frac{2}{2}$. The fabric is often wool or wool-like.

**Sericin** is the water-soluble protective gum that surrounds silk when extruded by a caterpillar.

**Sericulture** is the production of cultivated silk.

**Serviceability** is the measure of a textile product's ability to meet consumers' needs.

**Shade sorting** describes manufacturers grouping fabrics by color so that all fabrics of one color match.

**Shagbark** is usually a gingham with an occasional warp yarn under slack tension. During weaving, the slack-tension yarns create a loop at intervals giving the fabric a unique surface appearance.

**Shampooing** is another term for wet cleaning of furnishings.

**Shantung** is a rough-texture, plain-weave, filament-warp yarn and irregular-spun filling-yarn fabric. Shantung is heavier than pongee.

**Shape-retention finish** refers to any finish that controls wrinkling or creasing with heat or resin; includes crease-retention and durable-press finishes.

**Sharkskin** is a wool or wool-like $\frac{2}{2}$ twill made with alternating warp and filling yarns of two different colors and having a smooth, flat appearance. The twill line, unlike most of the wool-twill fabrics, is left-handed. Occasionally a plain-weave or basket-weave fabric is called sharkskin.

**Shearing** cuts away protruding fiber or yarn ends to achieve a level pile or surface nap; also can be done to achieve a sculptured effect.

**Shed** is the space that is formed between warp yarns when at least one harness is raised and at least one harness is lowered during weaving.

**Shedding** is the step in weaving during which the harnesses are raised or lowered.

**Shin-gosen** (shin′-gō-sen) is an ultrafine fiber, often polyester, with modified cross sections and occasional fiber irregularities, produced in Japan.

**Shrinkage control** refers to finishes that minimize tension on fabrics during finishing to reduce shrinkage in consumers' hands.

**Shrinkage resistance** is the ability of a textile to retain its original size during cleaning.

**Shuttle** is the part of some looms that is used to carry filling yarns through the shed.

**Shuttle embroidery** is a technique that produces an allover embroidered pattern on a fabric; similar to Schiffli embroidery but a more advanced process.

**Silence cloth** is a white double-faced fabric used under table linens to minimize noise during dining.

**Silk** is the fiber produced by several varieties of caterpillars, including *Bombyx mori, Antheraea mylitta,* and *Antheraea pernyi.*

**Silk-in-the-gum** (*See* Raw silk)

**Silk noils** refers to staple silk from broken filaments and inner portions of cocoons or waste silk from cocoons where the caterpillar matured into a moth.

**Simple calendering** is a mechanical finish. The fabric is passed between two rollers or calenders to remove wrinkles; the simplest calendering process, often precedes printing.

**Simplex machine** is similar to the tricot machine but uses two needle bars and two guide bars to create a simplex knit.
**Simple yarn** is a yarn alike in all its parts.
**Singeing** burns fiber ends from the fabric to produce a smooth surface.
**Single-figured jersey** is a type of jacquard jersey.
**Single-filling knit** is the simplest filling knit made using one set of needles.
**Single yarn** consists of one strand of fibers held together by some mechanism.
**Sisal** is a leaf fiber produced in Africa, Central America, and the West Indies.
**Sizing** is a starch, resin, or gelatinous substance added to fabrics to increase body and abrasion resistance; especially important in preparing warp yarns for weaving.
**Skew** describes an off-grain problem. Filling yarns interlace with warp yarns at an angle less than or greater than 90°.
**Skye** (sky) is the process of exposing fabric or yarn to air to oxidize the leuco or soluble form of a solubility cycle dye to the pigment or nonsoluble colored form.
**Slack mercerization** is a treatment of cotton fabric with sodium hydroxide to increase absorbency; especially important as a preparation step in dyeing.
**Slack tension weave** is a weave in which two warp beams are used with one beam at regular loom tension and the other beam at a lower tension. Used to create seersucker and terrycloth.
**Slashing** is the process of adding sizing to warp yarns prior to weaving.
**Sliver** is a very weak rope of fibers produced in intermediate steps in the production of spun yarns.
**Sliver-pile knit** is a filling knit fabric in which the pile is created by using fibers from a sliver.
**Slub effects** refer to true slub yarns and to yarns that incorporate small tufts of fiber to create an appearance similar to a true slub yarn.
**Slub yarn** is a single thick-and-thin fancy yarn.
**Smooth filament yarn** is a yarn of filament fibers that have not been crimped or textured.
**Soap** is a cleaning compound made from sodium or potassium salts of fatty acids.
**Softener** refers to a compound used to remove hardness ions from water (water softener); also a compound to improve the hand of fabric (fabric softener).
**Soil** describes contaminants on fabric.
**Soil-release finish** is a chemical surface coating on fabrics to improve the removal of soil during laundering or other cleaning procedure.
**Solution dyeing** describes the addition of colored pigments to polymer solutions prior to fiber extrusion; also called mass pigmentation.
**Solvent** is a liquid that dissolves other materials; includes water and dry cleaning solvents.
**Solvent finishing** refers to processes in which the chemical is dissolved in some liquid other than water.
**Solvent spinning** is a fiber-forming method in which the raw material is dissolved in amine oxide, spun into weak amine oxide solution, and precipitated out of the solution. The amine oxide is recycled.
**Sorting** is the process of grouping textiles of similar characteristics to avoid creating problems in cleaning or to allow similar treatments.
**Sorting wool** refers to dividing a fleece into different quality fibers.
**Spandex** is a manufactured fiber in which the fiber-forming substance is a long-chain synthetic polymer consisting of at least 85 percent of a segmented polyurethane.
**Special-purpose finish** includes all finishes designed to improve the performance of a fabric or minimize a problem with the fabric.
**Specific gravity** is the ratio of the mass of the fiber to an equal volume of water at 4°C.
**Spike or snarl yarn** is a fancy yarn where the effect ply forms alternating unclosed loops along both sides of the yarn.
**Spinneret** is the thimblelike nozzle through which the solution is extruded to form a fiber.
**Spinning** refers to the process of producing a yarn from staple fibers; also refers to the production of a fiber by extruding a solution through tiny holes in a spinneret.
**Spiral or corkscrew yarn** is a fancy yarn. Two plies that differ in size, texture, type, or color are twisted together.
**Split leather** is one of the inner layers of leather removed from a thick hide.
**Spring-beard needle** is a type of needle used in knitting fabrics from fine yarns.
**Spun-bonded** describes a process of producing a fabric directly from fibers by adhering melt-spun fibers together before cooling.
**Spun-laced** describes a process of producing a fabric directly from fibers by entangling staple fibers with water to create a pattern in the fabric.
**Spun yarn** is a continuous strand of staple fibers held together by some mechanism.
**Stabilization** refers to any finish that is designed to minimize shrinkage or expansion of fabric during care.
**Stainless steel** is a type of metallic fiber.
**Stain-release finish** (*See* Soil-release finish)
**Staple fiber** is any natural or manufactured fiber produced in or cut to a short length measured in inches or centimeters.
**Starching** is a process of adding a sizing material to a fabric to give weight or body.
**Steep twill** is a twill with a wale angle of approximately 63°.
**Stencil printing** describes a process of adding color to a fabric by using a form to control where the color strikes the fabric; essentially a hand process.
**Stiffness** is the resistance to bending or creasing of a fabric.
**Stitch or loop** is the basic unit of construction in a knitted fabric.
**Stitch-bonded fabric** is a multiplex fabric in which fine lengthwise yarns in a warp knit are chain stitched to interlock the fiberweb base structure or inlaid yarns.
**Stock dyeing** refers to a fiber dyeing process in which loose fibers are colored.
**Stockinette or stockinet** is a coarse yarn, single-filling, heavy-knit jersey fabric.
**Storage** refers to conditions when the textile or textile product is not being used, worn, or cleaned.
**Stretching** is the process of pulling a fiber until the molecular

chains rotate and slide until they become oriented and form crystals within the fiber to enhance certain fiber properties.

**Stretch yarn** is a yarn that has a high degree of potential elastic stretch, rapid recovery, and a high degree of yarn curl.

**Striations** are the lengthwise lines present on several fibers such as rayon.

**S-twist** refers to a direction of yarn twist that conforms to the direction of the slope of the central portion of the letter S.

**Subtractive finish** is a finish that removes some portion of the fabric through either a mechanical or chemical process to enhance the fabric's appearance.

**Suede** (swād) is a leather that has been brushed or napped to pull fibrils to the surface and create a softer surface and a more matte luster.

**Suede cloth** is a plain-weave, twill-weave, or knitted fabric that is napped and sheared to resemble suede leather. Suede cloth can be napped on both sides. Any suitable fiber can be used. Also refers to brushed leather.

**Suiting** is a general term for heavyweight fabrics. Suiting can be any fiber type or fabric construction.

**Sulfar** is a manufactured fiber in which the fiber-forming substance is a long-chain synthetic polysulfide in which at least 85 percent of the sulfide linkages are attached directly to two aromatic rings.

**Sulfur dyes** are a solubility cycle dye class used primarily with cotton.

**Sunlight resistance** is a finish or fiber modification to minimize the degradative effects of sunlight on fiber or dye.

**Supported film** is a composite fabric that combines a fiberweb, woven, or knitted fabric with a film for greater durability.

**Supported-scrim structure** is a composite fabric consisting of foam bonded to a yarn structure scrim; fibers may be flocked on the surface to simulate a pile or suede fabric.

**Surah** (sōōr′-ah) (*See* Foulard)

**Surface coating** is a finish, usually metallic or plastic in nature, applied to the face of the fabric. Also refers to a polyamide solution applied to wool fabrics to minimize felting shrinkage.

**Surfactants** are sulfonate organic compounds used in detergents to assist in soil removal.

**Swivel-dot fabric** is an extra yarn weave fabric made with a tiny shuttle that wraps extra yarns around some ground warp yarns to create a spot in the fabric.

**Synthetic fibers** are produced from synthetic polymers made from basic raw materials.

**Synthetic leather** refers to a variety of fabrications or finishes that produce a surface that resembles leather in appearance or texture; some may be brushed to resemble suede.

**Taffeta** (taf′-et-uh) is a general term that refers to any plain-weave fabric with a fine, smooth, crisp hand made with filament yarns. The unbalanced taffetas have a fine rib made by heavier filling yarns and more warp yarns. Faille taffeta has a crosswise rib made by using many more warp yarns than filling yarns. Moiré taffetas have an embossed watermark design. Balanced taffetas have warp and filling yarns the same size.

**Take-up** is the step in weaving when the woven fabric is wound on the cloth beam and warp yarn is let off the warp beam so that more fabric can be woven.

**Tanning** is a finishing step in the production of leather to prevent rotting of the hide or skin.

**Tapa cloth** refers to a hand-produced fiberweb fabric made from the inner bark of selected trees.

**Tapestry** (tap′-ehs-trē) is a firm, heavy, stiff, jacquard-weave fabric made with several warp and filling yarn sets. Tapestry is also the term used for fabric made by hand in which the filling yarns are discontinuous. In handmade tapestries, the filling yarn is used only in those areas where that color is desired.

**Tape yarn** is an inexpensive yarn produced from extruded polymer film by extrusion or the split fiber method.

**Technical face** refers to the outer or upper side of the fabric as it is made.

**Technical back** refers to the inner or under side of the fabric as it is made.

**Temporary finish** describes a finish that is removed during the first care cycle or that has a very short life span.

**Tenacity** describes the strength of a fiber; usually referred to as breaking tenacity, which describes the force at which the fiber ruptures or breaks.

**Tender goods** describes fabrics that are very weak because of exposure to some environmental factor or incorrect processing.

**Tendering** describes the weakening of fibers due to exposure to degradants or due to a deleterious interaction between fiber and dye or finish.

**Tension mercerization** is the process of treating cotton yarn, thread, or fabric with sodium hydroxide while under tension.

**Tentering** is a finishing step in which the fabric is stretched out to full width; often combined with other finishing steps like heat setting. If done incorrectly, contributes to bow and skew.

**Terrycloth (terry)** is a slack-tension, warp-yarn pile fabric. Terrycloth may have loops on one or both sides of the fabric. Terrycloth may have a jacquard pattern and may be made with plied yarns for durability. There are also weft- or filling-knit terrycloths.

**Tex** is a direct yarn numbering system. The yarn size is the weight in grams of 1,000 meters of yarn.

**Textile** is a general term used to refer to fiber, yarn, fabric, or anything made from fibers, yarns, or fabrics.

**Textile Fiber Products Identification Act** regulates use of fiber names in labeling textile products to protect consumers from unscrupulous trade practices.

**Texture** describes the nature of a fabric's surface as perceived by sight or touch.

**Textured-bulk-filament yarn** is a uniformly bulky filament yarn where the bulk is added by crimping or texturizing the filament fibers.

**Textured-bulk yarn** is another term for a textured-bulk-filament yarn.

**Textured yarn** is a yarn with notably greater apparent volume than a similar conventional yarn.

**Texturing** refers to the process of adding bulk to yarns or modifying fabric surfaces.

**Thermal finish** describes a finish designed to minimize heat transfer through the fabric.

**Thermoplastic** describes a fiber's sensitivity to heat; fibers that melt or glaze at relatively low temperature.

**Thick-and-thin fibers** vary in diameter throughout their length so that in some areas they are thinner and in other areas they are thicker.

**Throwing** refers to the process of twisting silk filaments into a yarn; also refers to the process of twisting and texturing synthetic fiber filament yarns.

**Ticking** is a general term used for fabrics of any weave used for mattress covers, slipcovers, and upholstery. It may also be used in apparel.

**Tie-dye** is a resist dyeing process. Portions of the fabric or yarn are tied to prevent dye absorption in the tied areas.

**Tigaring** is a surface napping of knit fabrics to produce a suedelike texture.

**Tissue gingham** is a lightweight type of yarn-dyed plain-weave fabric.

**Top** is a precursor of a worsted yarn.

**Top grain** refers to the outermost layer of leather and includes the grain features of the hide or skin. It is the highest quality of leather removed from a thick hide.

**Topical finish** (*See* Additive finish)

**Torchon** (tor′-shohn) **lace** is a rugged bobbin lace with very simple patterns.

**Torts** include behaviors that interfere with personal rights, such as substandard professional performance or deliberate wrongful acts.

**Tow** refers to short flax fibers; also refers to a large assembly of filament fibers to facilitate handling and processing during the production of manufactured staple fibers.

**Tow-to-top system** refers to a process of converting filament fibers to staple fibers by cutting or break stretching.

**Tow-to-yarn system** refers to a process of converting filament fibers to staple fibers by break stretching, drawing out the fibers, adding twist to them, and winding the yarn on a bobbin.

**Trade name** is a term used to identify a company's products.

**Trademark** is a word, symbol, device, or combination used to designate the product of a particular company.

**Transition cotton** refers to cotton produced on land where organic farming is practiced, but the three-year minimum for certified organic cotton has not been met.

**Triacetate** is a manufactured fiber in which the fiber-forming substance is cellulose acetate in which not less than 92 percent of the hydroxyl groups are acetylated.

**Triaxial** refers to a fabric made with three sets of yarns interlaced at 60° angles to each other.

**Tricot** is a warp-knit fabric made with filament yarns with one or more bars. Tricot has fine, vertical wales on the technical face and horizontal ribs on the technical back.

**Tricot machine** is a warp knitting machine used to produce tricot warp knits.

**Trilobal shape** refers to a three-sided fiber cross-sectional shape that is designed to imitate silk.

**True crepe** is a fabric made with at least one set of crepe twist yarns.

**Tubular finishing** (*See* Rope finishing)

**Tuck stitch** is a type of knit stitch in which the previous stitch is not cleared from the needle. It creates a pucker in the fabric and is used in creating patterns.

**Tuft density** describes the number of yarn tufts per inch.

**Tufting** is a method of producing an imitation pile surface by stitching yarns to the surface of an existing fabric; used to produce carpeting and upholstery.

**Tulle** (tool) is a mesh tricot fabric used as a support fabric or as an overlay in apparel.

**Turns per inch** (tpi) is a measure of yarn twist.

**Tussah silk** is a type of wild silk.

**Tweed** is a general term used to refer to wool or wool-like fabrics made of flock or flake novelty yarns. Tweeds are most often made in plain, twill, or twill-variation weaves.

**Twill flannel** is one of several wool or wool-like fabrics made in a twill weave.

**Twill weave** is a weave in which each warp or filling yarn floats across two or more filling or warp yarns with a progression of interlacings by one to the right or to the left forming a distinct wale.

**Twist** is the spiral arrangement of fibers around the axis of the yarn.

**Twist-on-twist** refers to using the same direction of twist in plying two yarns into one yarn as in the production of each individual ply.

**Twist setting** is a yarn finishing process used to help make permanent the very high twist in crepe yarns.

**Ultrafine** denier refers to a fiber of less than 0.3 denier per filament.

**Ultrasonic cleaning** is a cleaning technique for furnishings in which high-frequency sound waves are used to clean the textile.

**Unbalanced plain weave** is a plain weave in which the ratio of warp to filling yarns is significantly greater than 1:1; common types are 2:1, 3:1, and 1:2.

**Union dyeing** is dyeing a fabric made of two or more fibers to one solid color.

**Upholstered Furniture Action Council** is an industry group that issues voluntary standards for upholstered furniture.

**Vacuuming** is a cleaning technique for furnishings in which particulate soil is removed from the textile by suction.

**Valenciennes** (val-en-sehnz′) is a bobbin lace with a diamond-shaped mesh.

**van der Waals forces** are weak attractive forces between adjacent molecules that increase in strength as the molecules move closer together.

**Vat dyes** are a solubility cycle dye class used primarily with cotton and some polyester.

**V-bed machine** is a type of knitting machine used to produce double knits.

**Velour** is a general term used to describe pile fabrics. Velours tend to have dense, long, or deep pile. Velours can be woven or knitted.

**Velvet** is a warp-pile fabric most often made as a double cloth with five sets of yarns. One pair of ground warp and filling create one side of the fabric and a second pair of ground warp and filling create the other side. A fifth set of yarns (pile warp) interlace between the two sets of ground fabrics. The woven fabric is separated into two complete fabrics when the pile warp is cut. Velvet is usually a filament-yarn fabric.

**Velveteen** is a filling-pile fabric made with long gloats that are cut in the finishing process. The ground fabric can have a plain or twill weave. The pile in velveteen is short. Velveteen is usually a spun-yarn fabric.

**Venetian** (veh-nē′-shuhn) **point lace** is a needlepoint lace with an irregular mesh.

**Vicuña** is the fiber removed from the South American vicuña.

**Vinal** is a manufactured fiber in which the fiber-forming substance is any long-chain synthetic polymer composed of at least 50 percent by weight of vinyl alcohol units and in which the total of the vinyl alcohol units and any one or more of the various acetal units is at least 85 percent by weight of the fiber.

**Vinyon** is a manufactured fiber in which the fiber-forming substance is any long-chain synthetic polymer composed of at least 85 percent by weight of vinyl chloride units.

**Virgin wool** is wool that has never been processed into a fabric before.

**Viscose rayon** is the most common type of rayon.

**Viyella™** (vī-el′-uh) is a medium-weight, twill-weave fabric made of an intimate blend of 55 percent wool and 45 percent cotton.

**Voile** (voyl) is a sheer, lightweight, low-count, plain-weave, spun-yarn fabric in which the yarns have a high, hard, or voile twist to give the fabric a crisp hand. It has a lower count than lawn.

**Voile twist** is another term for hard twist.

**Wadding** is a loose assemblage of waste fibers used in textile products as lining and support layers.

**Waffle cloth** is a dobby-weave fabric in which the interlacing pattern creates a three-dimensional honeycomb.

**Wale** refers to the diagonal line related to the interlacing pattern of twills; or the column of stitches made by one needle in a knit fabric.

**Warp** is the group of yarns threaded through the loom in a woven fabric; parallel to the selvage.

**Warp-faced twill** is a type of twill weave where the majority of the technical face of the fabric is formed by warp yarns.

**Warp insertion warp knit** is a warp knit in which a yarn has been laid in the lengthwise direction as the fabric was being knit.

**Warp knitting** is a process in which yarn sets are interlooped in essentially a lengthwise direction to form a fabric.

**Warp pile fabric** is a pile fabric. The pile is created by extra warp yarns.

**Warp printing** is a process of printing a pattern on warp yarns before weaving.

**Warp sateen** is a spun yarn satin-weave fabric in which warp yarns form the technical face of the fabric.

**Warranty** is an implied or written indication that the product is suitable for the purpose for which it was marketed.

**Wash-down** describes color loss that occurs over time as a fabric is laundered or cleaned.

**Wash-off** refers to rinsing soil, excess chemicals, contaminants, or unused dye off the fabric; usually done with water.

**Wastewater treatment** describes the procedures necessary to return water to a potable and usable condition.

**Water** is a common solvent used in fiber processing, finishing, dyeing, and cleaning textiles.

**Water-bath finishing** refers to processes in which the chemical is dissolved in water.

**Water-jet loom** is a type of loom. The filling yarn is inserted in the shed with a stream or jet of water.

**Waterproof** refers to a coated or composite fabric that water will not penetrate regardless of the time water is in contact with the fabric or the force with which the water hits the fabric.

**Water-repellent finish** minimizes the wettability of a fabric; may result in stain resistance as well.

**Water softeners** are compounds used to sequester minerals present in hard water.

**Weaver's cloth** is a general term for balanced plain-weave cotton suitings.

**Weaving** is the process of producing a fabric by interlacing two or more yarns at right angles.

**Weft insertion** is a single filling knit jersey in which a second yarn is laid in a course or knit into the fabric to add stability. Some weft insertions are napped to create a fuzzy surface on the technical back of the fabric.

**Weft insertion warp knit** is a warp knit in which a yarn has been laid in the crosswise direction as the fabric was being knit.

**Weighted silk** designates a silk fabric to which a metallic salt has been added (at an amount specified by federal law) to improve hand, dye affinity, or drape.

**Weighting** is the treatment of silk with metallic salts to increase the weight, hand, and dye affinity of the fabric; may result in accelerated degradation of the silk.

**Wet-adhesive method** uses a chemical adhesive to make laminates.

**Wet cleaning** is a cleaning technique for furnishings in which a water-based detergent is worked into the textile and the soiled solution is removed by vacuuming.

**Wet-laid web** is a layer of fibers made from a slurry of fiber and water.

**Wet spinning** is a fiber-forming process in which the polymer is dissolved in a solvent and the solution is extruded into a chemical bath.

**Whiteners** (*See* Brighteners)

**Wicking** is the ability of a fiber to transfer moisture along its surface.

**Wild silk** refers to naturally grown staple silk that is more irregular in texture and color compared to cultivated silk.

**Winch dyeing** is a process for dyeing a loose rope of fabric.

**Wool** refers to fiber from various animals including sheep, Angora and cashmere goats, camel, alpaca, and llama.

**Woolen yarn** is a slightly irregular bulky wool or wool-like yarn that has not been combed.

**Wool Products Labeling Act** is the federal law that protects the textile industry and consumers from the undisclosed presence of fibers other than wool and that informs the consumer of the source of the wool fiber.

**Worsted yarn** is a smooth, straight, and uniform wool or wool-like yarn that has received additional treatment to remove short fibers and make the remaining fibers more parallel.

**WPL number** refers to the manufacturer's identification number assigned to the firm as a result of the Wool Products Labeling Act.

**Wrap-spun yarn** is a yarn with a core of staple fibers wrapped with filament fibers.

**Wrinkle resistance** is the ability of a fiber to recover from deformations such as bending, twisting, or compressing.

**Wrinkle-resistant finish** keeps wrinkling to a minimum.

**Yarn** is an assemblage of fibers twisted or laid together so as to form a continuous strand that can be made into a textile fabric.

**Yarn dyeing** is a process of adding color, usually a dye, to yarns.

**Yarn number** describes the size of a yarn.

**Z-twist** refers to a direction of yarn twist that conforms to the direction of the slope of the central portion of the letter Z.

# INDEX